ORACLE® *Oracle Press*™

Oracle 8*i*
A Beginner's Guide

Michael Abbey
Ian Abramson
Michael Corey

Tata McGraw-Hill Publishing Company Limited

NEW DELHI

McGraw-Hill Offices

New Delhi New York St Louis San Francisco Auckland Bogotá
Caracas Lisbon London Madrid Mexico City Milan Montreal
San Juan Singapore Sydney Tokyo Toronto

Tata McGraw-Hill
A Division of The McGraw·Hill Companies

Oracle8i A Beginner's Guide

Tata McGraw-Hill Edition 2000

Reprinted in India by arrangement with The McGraw-Hill Companies, Inc., New York

For Sale in India Only

ISBN 0-07-463674-X

Published by Tata McGraw-Hill Publishing Company Limited, 7 West Patel Nagar, New Delhi 110 008, and printed at S P Printers, Noida 201 301

About the Authors...

MICHAEL ABBEY   Michael Abbey has been living and breathing the Oracle Server technology since 1986, having first seen version 3. Michael is a popular presenter at many Oracle user group events in North American and Europe, and has accumulated an avid following. Michael's other passions, Fender Precision bass guitars and grinding rock music, work well alongside his technical skills—frequent and heavy. He can be reached via e-mail at *masii@ottawa.com*. Michael entertains engagements mainly in the National Capital region around Ottawa, but supports an increasing number of Internet-based clients all over the U.S.A. and Canada remotely.

IAN ABRAMSON   Ian Abramson, the principal at IAS Inc., in Toronto, Canada, has gained his experience in the Oracle arena in a number of areas over the past fourteen years. His experience designing and delivering Oracle-based applications to numerous clients around the globe has helped him to learn how to get the most from Oracle. Ian currently is the Director of Education Programming for the International Oracle User Group of Americas. While Ian is busy during the day building Oracle applications and Data Warehouses, by night he continues to pursue his dream of being a professional hockey goalie. He can be reached via e-mail at *ias@magi.com* for Oracle or goaltending services.

MICHAEL COREY   Mike Corey, co-owner of Database Technologies, Inc., in Newton, MA, has collected quite a following in the Oracle community. He has dedicated numerous hours, months, and years to helping ensure the user community has the active ear of Oracle Corporation. Mike possesses a well-rounded knowledge of Oracle the company and Oracle the software. He offers over 11 years of experience to the Corey/Abbey team. Mike can be reached via e-mail at *mcorey@dbtink.com*.

Contents At A Glance

Contents

Foreword

As we approach the new millennium, it is becoming apparent that more and more companies and organizations require higher levels of efficiency from their computing systems to keep up with the rapidly changing environments in which they do business. When one of the few constants you can count on is change, you have to be able to evolve and transform to thrive— and survive — in the intensely competitive global economy.

To this end, businesses must turn opportunity into competitive advantage. How a company does this will depend on the quality of its information — and its ability to manage and distribute that data to the people who need it. And that will depend on the power and flexibility of its information systems.

Oracle believes that the Internet changes everything. The Internet has changed the way people live and work, and it will continue to revolutionize the way companies run their businesses. Virtually every company —large and small — is in a great position to take advantage of e-business solutions and the secure exchange of information over the Internet.

Oracle8i, the world's first Internet-enabled database, is the engine that is powering this new computing paradigm. Oracle8i is the latest generation of the world's leading database, and the first designed specifically to be an Internet development and deployment platform. It enhances Oracle8's industry-leading technology and special features to make it easier than ever for businesses, application developers, and systems integrators to create dynamic database-driven intranet and Web applications.

Oracle believes Internet technology offers the safest, most efficient access to all your data, for all your users. With Oracle8*i* as the foundation, Internet computing enables IT experts to focus on managing important data from a centralized server which, in turn, frees them to invest their time and skills where they add the most value to your organization. And with all your data professionally managed and safely stored in centralized servers, you can be sure that employees have access to the most up-to-date information and applications to make the smartest business decisions. All they need is a computer equipped with a standard Web browser.

It's that simple.

Scaleability, reliability, and uninterrupted availability are trademarks of Oracle databases. Oracle8*i* brings more than 300 enhancements over Oracle8 — all of which are intended to provide companies and organizations with the lowest possible "total cost of ownership" for their information-management systems.

Oracle8*i* has a built-in Java Virtual Machine to allow developers to write, store, and execute Java code within the database for faster, more secure, and more reliable applications. There's Oracle WebDB, an Internet-ready development tool that enables developers to build and deploy dynamic, data-driven Web sites using a standard Web browser. Oracle8*i*'s iFS (Internet File System) allows you to simply drag-and-drop any type of file — Web pages, spreadsheets, word-processing files, images, among others — directly in the database. And Oracle interMedia makes it possible to easily manage multimedia content so your dynamic Web applications can incorporate image, audio, video, spatial, text, and relational data.

Oracle is grateful to the authors for providing IT decision-makers, systems managers, developers and end-users with an excellent starting point from which to understand the value of the Oracle8*i* database. Through my tenure as President of Oracle Canada, I have continually heard some of these gentlemen's names; they are respected across the industry. Michael, Mike, and Ian have been around for a long time, building on very successful careers centering around our technology. Thanks to all three of you.

Thank you for your interest in Oracle8*i*.

Donald Woodley
President
Oracle Corporation Canada Inc.

Acknowledgments

Michael Abbey

This book is dedicated to my late father, Sydney Abbey. I would like to thank my fellow authors, Ian and Mike, for allowing me to enjoy this rewrite so immensely. Accolades as well to Mark Kerzner and Mike Mallia, whose contributions to this work help make it a class-quality product. Jim Lapatosky sat in as a technical editor extra-ordinaire! The list is endless—Donald Woodley, Paul Stulberg, Henk Dykhuizen, Susan Cunningham, and Frank Gallagher from Oracle Canada. Thanks to the gang at Osborne, led by Jeremy Judson. Throughout my IT career I have owed much to my professional colleagues, including Mike Teske, Rob Prendin, John Richer, David Teplow, Merrilee Nohr, Warren Capps, Marlene Theriault, and Rachel Carmichael. Thanks to recent business partners Paul Vallée and Steve Pickard.

Ian Abramson

When we write books, we always want to thank all the people who have left an impression on our lives and have inspired us to greatness. We thank our family, our friends, our teachers, our mentors, our co-workers, and our pets. So, the question of who to specifically thank is a task that cannot be taken lightly.

When I started to work on this book, I had to make a decision. I needed to decide whom I should acknowledge and dedicate the work on this book to. I thought I should dedicate the book to my family: my wife Susan and my daughters Baila and Jillian. After all, they are my foundation. But I had done that before in my previous books. So I thought about my father Joe or my mother Lily, but you guessed it, been there done that too. So we move into the rest of the family: brothers, aunts, uncles, nieces, nephews, or the in-laws (Harry and Esther Pakman). When I looked at that list, it included the Abramsons, Astroffs, Weiskopfs, Orleans, Rzepas, and Pakmans. The list became so long that I worried someone would be left out because this is one big family and I do mean big. Then it was on to my friends, be it Mark and Arlene Kerzner, Jack and Lynn Chadirjian, Lorne and Nicole Knsella, Jeremy and Carolyn Fitzgerald, Evan and Aviva Ross, Dan Tosello, or Marshall Lucatch and the rest of the Re/Max Allstars. Or even other people that I may have forgotten to mention. All of you are important and deserve recognition. However, dedicating it to one friend would shortchange everyone else. Then there are my two fellow authors, Michael and Michael, the dynamic duo, who have allowed me to join them as a partner in the full series of books. Together we make a dynamite trio. You both inspire me and together we make a combination that cannot be beat. So dedicating the book to them would work, except that this is our seventh work together, and I think that I have thanked them just about every time I have had the opportunity. YATFG!

So the decision of who to honor is not simple. But the solution is simple. I dedicate this book to my family and friends. You have all inspired me in one way or another to do better each day.

Michael J. Corey

Now having co-authored two books, it is very clear to me why most acknowledgments start off with "Thanks to my wife and family...." It is true, the family suffers the most. Writing a book has the ability to drain all your time, your personal time, your friends' time, your associates' time and anyone else around you. Well, to bring this book to press required a lot of time and effort from a lot of people. This list does not begin to do it justice.

A special thanks to my wife Juliann (a woman with a lot of understanding), and my children John, Annmarie, and Michael. Special thanks to Michael Abbey, my co-author. This book would not have been possible without his many phone calls/e-mails night after night. This book is a great example of the technology highway at work. You have one author in Hingham, MA, USA, the other in Ottawa, Canada, and the publisher in Berkeley, CA, USA—each able to communicate electronically.

I would also like to thank my friend and partner (at Database Technologies Inc., Newton, MA, USA) David Teplow. I consider myself very fortunate to be associated with David both professionally and personally. David has been using Oracle since version 2.0. He is probably the best application developer in all of New England.

Another associate of mine at Database Technologies Inc., deserves special mention: Darryl Smith. He was the key source of talent for our Oracle Forms 4.5 chapter. One of the things you realize after working with Oracle as long as I have—you can't know all the answers. When I first started working with the product, there were three manuals. Now I could easily fill a book case and have. So when we decided to do this book, we looked to the best Forms developer I know to help us. Well, judge for yourself.

I would also like to extend a special thanks to all my colleagues at Database Technologies. Don Briffett has nicknamed me "Hurricane man," as I have been known to send my office into a whirlwind when I arrive. Thanks to all for their patience.

Thanks to my many friends at Oracle whose talents and capabilities never fail to amaze me. Here is a short but in no way complete list: Ray Lane (Mr. Blues), Andy Laursen (Mr. Parallel Server/Media Server), Mark Porter (Video Lad), Scott Martin (Mr. SQL*TRAX), Rama Velpuri (Mr. Backup/Recovery), Stephanie Herle (Ms. Events), Gail Peterson (Ms. Road Block Breaker), David Anderson (a True Californian), Judy Boyle, (Ms. Usergroup 93), Joe Didonato (Mr. Education).

A special thanks to a friend/associate at Oracle Corporation, Gary Damiano.

Thanks to my many friends at the Oracle Users Groups. Here is a small but incomplete list: Dave Kreines, Marty Greenfield, Geoff Girvin, Merrilee Nohr, Buff Emslie, Bert Spencer, Warren Capps, Julie Silverstein, Emily Bersin, Chris Wooldridge (WIZOP on CompuServe), Mark Farnham
(great comments on *Tuning Oracle*) and so many more.

Thanks to the people at Osborne/McGraw-Hill; without them you would never have received the finished product. A special thanks to everyone who purchased *Tuning Oracle*. Your comments and encouragement have been tremendous.

Introduction

racle8*i* and the Internet computing model—just what the doctor ordered. Take one of the world's largest software giants. Add a 21st century new-fangled computing architecture. Poof! Out of the hat pops Internet computing. How many of you closed a Web browser, then CTRL-ALT-DEL'd your workstation before proceeding to the establishment whose shelves you are now checking out that led to your picking up this book?

Through most of the 90's, we went through contortions beefing up the computing power of our personal computers. Remember when you got your first 40MB hard disk? You excitedly looked at a directory listing after moving your current software from your old machine. You said to yourself—all that I had plus a whole 22MB free! What will they think of next? How about the jump from the 8086 to the 8088 with a new toy—a switchable clock speed from 4.77Mhz all the way up to 8Mhz. As the 20th century was close to bringing itself to a close, we were convinced that we had to upgrade. As soon as we were comfortable with our new configuration, it was time to do it all over again. Our pocketbooks have had enough.

The point of all this verbiage, you say! The point is we are on the precipice of jumping feet first down a path where all (not totally but very close to it) the computing is done away from the desktop computer. The industry has been abuzz about the three-tier client server—the display layer on the client, the application and business logic layer on the middle tier, and the data server becoming the upper tier. Not too many vendors have bellied up to the bar like Oracle Corporation. This book features Oracle's solutions and products tailored to address the diverse Internet-based processing requirements of today and tomorrow.

Oracle8i is the fourth production release of the Oracle8 Server that first appeared in June 1997. With it come many solutions geared at mobile computing, hand-held personal data assistants, and the thin client Internet computing model. Many existing components of the Oracle technology have been rewritten; many have a new look and feel. You may not recognize Oracle Enterprise Manager, but it's still the same product with a new look and feel.

Perhaps the Internet computing model is the last chapter in the endless rightsizing and downsizing exercise. With the thin client, we see so many companies pushing networked this and networked that. We see it as a viable solution to help stem the gazillions of dollars being spent on client upgrades every 12 to 18 months. It is the epitome of centralizing computer operations—let the professionals do what they do best. Let them guard our corporate data; let them back it up; let them do the upgrades; let them have the headaches.

Oracle8i A Beginner's Guide is designed to serve as an entry level introduction to Oracle's technology; for those more familiar with the technology, this work will boost their understanding of what Oracle8i is all about. We cover the ever popular and omni-present Server, and touch bases with the products offered by Oracle in the mobile computing arena. We give a solid introduction to some of the more technical aspects of the Oracle8i technology catering to the database administrator. Funny thing—so may DBAs we have crossed paths with in our travels around Oracle got started when they least expected it and least wanted to do it. Having been thrust into the fire feet first, they desperately looked for a way to get up to speed in a short amount of time. Along comes *Oracle8i A Beginner's Guide*. This book can help bring the following few sentences to life:

Do I ever hate being an Oracle techie. Our Oracle person quit and I found myself knee deep in Oracle and it was really rough. Then I was told to do this and do that and you know, I found it sort of interesting. All of a sudden I started delivering this, and delivering that. I had a voracious appetite for knowledge. I'm addicted. Gees, I love being an Oracle techie!

As you read *Oracle8i A Beginner's Guide*, bookmark certain of your favorite sections—you may keep coming back to them throughout your life living and breathing Oracle's technology. This introduction will self-destruct in 20 years.

CHAPTER
1

What Is Oracle?

hy bother to learn Oracle or even read this book? Perhaps you have picked up this book because you keep seeing the big O word, **Oracle**. This is the same word you keep seeing in the help wanted section of your local newspaper. This is also the same word you keep seeing in your favorite trade journal. Seeing this word makes you think about the big C word, **Career**. Of course all this thinking links up with the big M word, **Money**.

You have your reasons—career and money, for instance, or you just want to be part of the current technology movement. You have an area of interest—be it Web-enabled computing, data warehousing, the network computer, rightsizing, network computing architecture, client/server, or even video on demand. One thing is very clear: Oracle Corporation (and its technology) is a major player in today's technology movement and promises to be an even bigger player tomorrow.

This chapter introduces Oracle Corporation, its tools, and its major initiatives, including many of the interesting areas we have mentioned. We will first discuss the basics of the relational database model Oracle has implemented and its core development tools SQL*Plus, Oracle Developer (including Oracle Forms, Oracle Reports, and Oracle Graphics), Oracle Designer, and SQL*Loader. If you understand these items, you are well on your way to understanding the technology movement of which Oracle is a major part. We will then discuss how Oracle the company has grown. We'll also explain how Oracle started to use its own tools to build applications that cater to customers' standard business requirements. We will then move on to Oracle, the company today, highlighting the advancement and various flavors of the core database. We will pay special attention to data warehousing, Oracle's Web initiatives, Oracle's move toward an object-oriented database (Oracle8/8*i*), and Oracle's move into Web-deployed this and Web-deployed that. We will then end with an overview of Oracle user groups.

VIP

Joining an Oracle user group is your best insurance policy for making the most out of your investment in Oracle and its growing lists of technologies.

So here we go—you will learn what Oracle is, how it really works, and how you can use it.

NOTE

Most of you have either heard of or worked with the Oracle Server for some time. In this chapter and throughout the rest of the book, most of the material we discuss is applicable to Oracle8i in particular, but other Oracle8 releases as well.

Terminology

The following definitions will arm you with the technical jargon you need to make it through this chapter.

- An *object-oriented database* allows object extensions to be built into classic relational database technology.

- *Client/server computing* has three components. Users work with a PC (client) and communicate with a larger central computer (server). An assortment of network software is the third component, allowing communication between the client and the server.

- *Cyberspace* is another name for the World Wide Web.

- A *data warehouse* is a collection of corporate information, derived directly or indirectly from operational systems and some external data sources. Its specific purpose is to support business decisions, not business operations. To learn more about data warehouses, we suggest you obtain a copy of *Oracle8 Data Warehousing* by Corey, Abbey, Abramson, and Taub (Oracle Press, 1998, ISBN 0-07-882511-3), where we strive to give you a practical guide to building a data warehouse.

- *Fault tolerance* refers to the capability of some computers to initiate automatic corrective activities when a component or program malfunctions. The classic example is the machine that falls back to a backup disk when an online disk fails. The fall back happens with no human intervention, and a message is sent to a central location to inform of the corrective action.

- Programs are *event driven* when portions of code initiate special activities when a certain event happens. For example, when you exit your favorite word processor, an event is mapped to the Exit command. When the event occurs, the software checks to see if your document should be saved and brings up the Save dialog box, if necessary.

- A *fat client* is your traditional PC system. If purchased today, it would have at least 64 megabytes of memory, 8GB of disk storage, a Pentium III-based chip, and an internal CD-ROM drive—in other words, your typical PC purchase. In the client/server world, a fat client would contain all the code/programs locally.

- Programs are *function key/keypad–driven* when pressing certain function keys or keys on the number keypad initiates special activities.

- A *GUI (graphical user interface)* is a drag-and-drop–type interface. This means it was written to take advantage of a mouse.

- A *Telnet session* is the capability to run a connection on a server that emulates the functionality of a dumb terminal.

- A *firewall* is another term for a router. Its primary purpose is to inspect network traffic and prevent unauthorized traffic from passing through. The router inspects requests coming from external sources and determines if they are appropriate to pass into internal systems. For example, an e-mail message sent to Beto is only allowed to enter the system if the company actually has an employee with that name. In addition, a firewall can also determine what types of services will be allowed through. For example, it might not allow access to a remote client via Telnet but would still allow e-mail to pass through its filter.

- An *intranet site* is where one or more applications reside that were built using Internet technologies. To access the application, you use one of the universal browsers like Netscape Navigator or Internet Explorer. Since it is an intranet site, although the applications reside within the firewall, they are accessed using Internet technologies, such as TCP/IP, HTML, or Java. The primary purpose of intranet sites is to service internal customers.

- An *Internet site* is where one or more applications reside that were built using Internet technologies. In addition, the sites would typically be accessed by a universal browser, just as with the intranet site. Since it is an Internet site, the applications reside outside the firewall and are accessed using the same Internet technologies. The primary purpose of Internet sites is to service external customers. A typical Internet URL, or address, is *http://www.dbtinc.com*. An average Internet site typically contains marketing information.

- A *master file* is used by computer systems to store information that is used across multiple applications. In a billing system, the name, address, and other contact information may be stored in a master file and used by accounts receivable, inventory, and accounts payable.

- *MOLAP* refers to data that is stored in a multidimensional database format. In order for the data to become multidimensional, the various dimensions/attributes of the data are identified. Then a transformation of the data happens, where it is physically stored based on the intersections of those dimensions. Each intersection represents a unique point within the data.

- A *thin client* is commonly a desktop personal computer, with as little as 4 megabytes of memory, no hard drive, and one of any range of microprocessors, from a Pentium to a 32-bit RISC chip. Such a machine will retail for under $1000. Since the average PC owner only uses his or her PC for functions like e-mail and word processing, why put an expensive

"FAT Client/PC" on the desktop when only 10 percent of its functionality is ever really being used? Instead, you can put a machine on the desktop that only has to deal with the presentation of information, which means it only needs a very small operating system, a small amount of memory, a very fast processor, and little or no disk storage. Unlike the dumb terminals of the past, this machine does have its own processor. The best analogy to this device is the telephone: it might have some limited functionality on its own, but it is useless unless it is hooked up to the phone network.

- *Oracle Cooperative Applications* are a suite of off-the-shelf programs written by Oracle that provide electronic solutions to clients' business requirements. Applications satisfy Oracle customers' needs in areas such as financial management, human resources, manufacturing, and inventory.

- *OLAP* stands for online analytical processing of data. It is a category of technology that enables users to gain insight into the data in a fast, interactive, easy-to-use manner.

- *ROLAP* is where the data is stored in the relational database format but is accessible via technology geared to online analytical processing or OLAP.

- *Rightsizing* is an exercise companies go through when they assess their existing computer hardware and software, and decide on future directions. Given the direction the industry is taking toward smaller, more powerful computers, a great deal of rightsizing exercises conclude with choosing a flavor of client/server computing.

- Applications are called *turnkey* when they can do everything the users ever wanted and then some. They are easy to learn and can be used with little or no training. The metaphor refers to turning the key in an automobile's ignition so that the car (or application in this case) springs to life. Turnkey also means the complete solution; when a project or application is turnkey, the developer has done all the work and the client only needs to start it up and use it.

- A *URL* is an Internet address. An example of a URL is *http://home.istar.ca/ ~masint/*. Think of this as your roadmap to any given Internet site. URL actually stands for *Universal Resource Locator*.

- The *World Wide Web* is the graphical portion of the Internet (see Figure 1-1). Since the creation of universal browsers like Netscape Navigator and the Internet Explorer, the Internet can now easily deal with all types of data from sound to video to text. With this newfound graphical capability, anyone can easily navigate the Internet. The Web has taken the Internet from the once-sacred realm of only the highly technical person to John and Jane Q. Public. Now that the Internet has gained massive, broad-based use, we have a very viable commercial platform from which to do business.

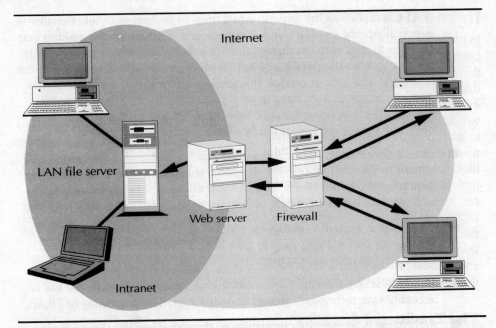

FIGURE 1-1.   *The intranet and the Internet*

What Is Oracle?

What a great question! We wish this question had been asked when we first started working with the product in version 3, when the entire documentation set for Oracle consisted of three or four books. Back then, Oracle was primarily a database company that offered few or no services. In addition, Oracle had no canned applications. Today, the picture is quite different. This multibillion-dollar company has lots of products, lots of services, and even more applications.

What makes Oracle so special is its demonstrated ability to overcome all obstacles, whether they be technological challenges or the challenges associated with rapid growth. Oracle has also demonstrated a continuous ability to build products that help us exceed the demands of the information-enabling age we live in. It's this uncanny ability to see the future of technology year after year that will help it continue to lead the charge from defining the Web computing of tomorrow to what will be the future of network computing. To help you understand Oracle the company, we will go back to its roots and its foundation—the database. From there, we will return to Oracle the company and how it is structured today.

In the Beginning

In the beginning, Oracle was just a database company—a relational database company, to be specific. At that time, relational databases were a new way of thinking about how data should be structured and stored. The key to this type of database is understanding the relationships between data, and then structuring the information base to reflect those relationships. In this way, an information base would be built that could stand the test of time. The goal in a relational database is to build a database in which only the data changes, not the underlying structures themselves. The old way of doing things is called the *traditional approach*. To illustrate the difference between these two approaches, we will start by taking a look at the traditional customer master file compared to its relational database counterpart. We will then look at characteristics of both approaches, and how changes are made using each. Finally, we will examine the differences between the two models and show why the relational approach is the preferred way to store information. In this and the next few sections, we use the terminology "approach" and "model" when discussing "traditional" and "relational." These terms can be used synonymously; they have the same meaning.

The Traditional Approach

Figure 1-2 illustrates a traditional customer master file. It contains all the normal fields you would expect to see: customer name, address, city, state, home phone, and work phone. There is a separate slot for each item of information; thus, the number of slots depends on the number of different types of data being recorded.

Customer master file
customer_name
address
city
state
home_phone
work_phone

FIGURE 1-2.   *A traditional customer master file*

This traditional design was adequate until the use of fax machines became widespread. Incorporating a fax number into the old model required an additional phone field, which in turn required a complete restructuring of the database. Also necessary was a complete redesign of the application code (that is, a rewrite of large portions, if not all, of the application) associated with the customer master file (not to mention the prohibitive cost of implementing the change). Using a traditional design, managers had to make the following decisions:

- If the application code was changed, high costs were associated with adding new functionality to applications. Installations hoped their staff could make the change rapidly; a mistake could cause an interruption in their ability to deal with customers and carry on business.

- If the application code was left as is, all the money associated with making the change was not spent. Money was saved, but there was a price to pay: you did business without access to fax machine phone numbers. Of course, if this continued to happen, your business was taking a great technological risk. In the long run, the competition (who made the change) might pass you by.

- Or you could try to replace an existing data element with the needed fax number field. The saying that best describes this is "*Robbing Peter to pay Paul.*" In the business, this is called spaghetti code, or a hack. This approach may work for a short while but always costs a lot more in the long run.

At this point, you might be sitting back and saying, "What's the big deal? Who cares if the application has to be changed every once in a while?" The reality is that we live in a changing world, and businesses that don't keep up risk dying. Fact: For over 100 years, the Swiss dominated the world's watch industry. When a new type of watch was invented using a quartz movement, the Swiss didn't react. Today, the Swiss make a very small portion of the world's watches. In today's world, businesses have to change constantly. Twenty years ago, the life expectancy of a computer line was three to five years. Today, a new line of hardware comes out every year. The business model and its computer systems must be able to keep pace. Using the traditional approach, had we altered the customer master file to include fax numbers, we would have had to reload the file (to populate the fax number field). On top of this, all the programs that used data in the customer master file would need modifying. At this point, we should also mention how data in traditional systems is stored. A traditional database might contain the customer master file, the payroll master file, the health insurance master file, and so on. Each one of these master files is separate. This is a problem when an event affects more than one of the files.

To illustrate how cumbersome the traditional approach can get (not to mention how expensive), look at the following scenario. Traditional systems keep redundant information in multiple locations. The employee benefits application stores employee names in a benefits master file. The payroll people maintain employee names in a payroll master file. On top of this, the long distance system stores employee names in the telecommunications master file. Suppose an employee changes his or her last name and needs a paycheck written with the new last name. The name might be changed in the payroll master file but may not be changed elsewhere.

VIP
Synchronizing changes to the same data in multiple locations is the single most difficult function to ensure in the traditional approach.

In the traditional database, it might take months to ensure the name is properly changed in every place it is stored, not to mention the time and effort it takes just to make the changes. Wouldn't Sally be upset if she got married and lost her health insurance benefits!

Traditional systems are *design driven*: they require design changes when one needs to capture new kinds of data. Whenever a new business need is identified (such as the need to store fax, cell phone, or car phone numbers), a high-end systems analyst or database administrator (highly technical, not to mention highly priced) is required to review the existing application design and make the necessary design modifications. The bottom line: the design changes are expensive, and worse still, many installations don't make the changes for that very reason! Now let's examine how the relational approach handles this problem.

The Relational Approach
Using this approach, system designers isolate types of information that need capturing. They then identify the relationships between those information types and implement a database structure similar to that shown in Figure 1-3. Using the relational model, what was previously referred to as *master files* are called *tables.* Notice how Figure 1-3 shows a customer table, a phone_number table, and a phone_number_types table. Each is a separate table within the database.

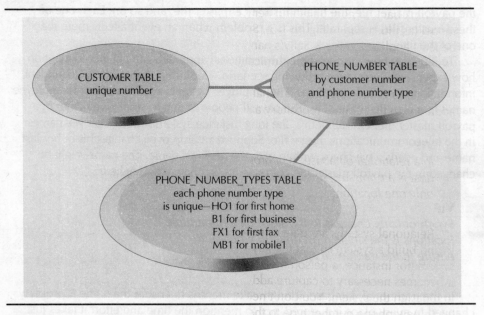

FIGURE 1-3. *Three tables (master files) using the relational model*

In Figure 1-3, the relationship between customer and phone_number is represented by the crow's feet, which show that a customer may have one or more phone numbers. We also show a relationship between phone_number_types and phone_number. This single line represents the fact that a phone_number must be associated with one type of phone. Thus, we have some rules governing the relationships between our customer and phone number data:

- Each customer may have one or more phone number(s).

- Each phone number belongs to one and only one customer.

- Each phone number must be one and only one type (for example, a home voice number, a business number, a fax number, or a mobile phone).

Now that we have designed the database to understand these relationships and to enforce our rules, all we have to do to add fax numbers is to add a row of data to the phone_number_types entity. There is no need to restructure the database; there is no need to do a complete redesign of the application programs; and there is no need to program any new functionality. Using this approach, the work required to implement the storing of fax numbers is trivial.

Think back to poor Sally and her health insurance benefits. In the relational model (as illustrated in Figure 1-3), Sally's name is stored in one location. When the benefits application reads Sally's name, it gets it from the customer table. Likewise, when the payroll and telecommunications systems need Sally's name, they get it from the customer table as well.

Systems built using the relational model store information once. Changes and additions to that central repository are reflected immediately.

VIP
In a relational database, synchronizing changes to data is a nonissue, since all data resides in one and only one location.

Relational systems are *data driven*; you pay a highly technical person to come in and build a system so that the key relationships are identified and built into the system (for instance, a person may have one or more phone numbers). Then, when it becomes necessary to capture additional phone number types, it is not necessary to redesign the system. You don't need a high-priced analyst to effect changes—you add a new phone number type to the phone_number_types table.

In the relational database model, the relationship between customer and phone number stays the same. You merely need to register a new phone number type in the phone_number_types table.

Differences Between the Two Approaches
Table 1-1 summarizes how traditional and relational systems are built, and shows how they differ, using the fax number example.

In the Beginning: Summary of Points
To summarize the features of a relational database:

■ A relational database is data driven, not design driven. It is designed once, and the data changes over time without affecting the applications.

■ The data is self-describing. For example, the phone number type is identified as phone_number_type.

■ Data is stored in one place, read from one place, and modified in one place. Data is stored once, so maintaining consistency among all applications is easier.

VIP
*In a distributed computing environment, it is
conceivable that data may be stored in more than
one place; in this case, it is the responsibility of
the relational database management system and
applications to ensure data is always in sync.*

■ Rules that control how the data will be stored are defined and enforced.

Task	Traditional	Relational
Design applications	Figure what applications need what types of information; then set up a series of master files.	Define the types of data that will be collected and define their relationships.
Implement applications	Load data into master files, placing one item of information into each slot in each master file.	Load types of data into their respective tables, ensuring each item ends up stored in one and only one location.
Modify applications (e.g., allow for capturing more types of data)	Redesign the database and modify all programs to reflect the change. Reload any master files affected by the change.	Isolate the table where the type of data affected is defined (e.g., the phone_number_types table). The data that exists in the tables remains unaffected.
Modify a subset of data	Read each master file from start to finish. If a row is part of the subset to be modified, process it; otherwise, go on to the next record.	Isolate the set of rows that are part of the subset, and implement the change in one SQL statement.

TABLE 1-1. *Differences Between Traditional and Relational Approaches*

Oracle Today

Today, Oracle Systems Corporation, based in Redwood Shores, California, manufactures software products and delivers services for the electronic management of information. Oracle is a worldwide provider of computer software, with 1999 revenues in excess of $8 billion USD. Oracle does business in over 90 countries around the world, and their software runs on upward of 100 different computers. They are a major player on the information superhighway.

Oracle is a big player in the adoption of the Internet computing model—where organizations look to the World Wide Web for the deployment of distributed applications. The Internet is an ideal infrastructure for delivering applications. Given the move toward a component-based approach, the Internet is the ideal home for the pieces that come together to make distributed applications. Coupled with three-tier client/server computing architecture, the Internet is the ideal place for these systems. The three tiers that make up this approach are

1. The client, sometimes called the presentation layer, is where information is displayed to the user, and input is accepted for processing.

2. The application layer is where all the processing is done according to the logic being implemented by the system. Business rules are enforced, data integrity is checked, and complex processing dictated by system requirements is carried out. This layer is the workhorse of the three-tier approach.

3. The data layer, often called the back end, plays a role in the storage of information to satisfy requests placed by the other two layers. In many but not all cases, this is a relational database specifically optimized to receive data from and pass information back to the application layer as users interact with the systems.

Oracle Corporation is part of the never-ending race to bring the very best technology to its customers. The ability to see the future trends in technology and the ability to embrace key technology early on not only help Oracle survive but are key reasons it continues to make giant strides ahead of the competition. The foundation of this house is the Oracle Server. Let's take a closer look at the Oracle8i Server and how it has been able to manufacture a suite of products that revolve around it.

Why Oracle Is Where It Is Today

Many significant features have catapulted Oracle to the top of the growing information management vendor community. Information technology is a moving target. Let's have a look at a few, but by no means all, of these features.

The Decision Support Arena

Decision support systems, referred to as *DSS,* are playing a large role. It seems everywhere you look, this organization is deploying an Oracle Server–based data warehouse this or that. The interest in and proliferation of data warehouses has brought the Oracle Server and associated OLAP products to the forefront of management's mind. With the acquisition of the Express product line of decision support tools, and the business view–centric Oracle Discoverer product, Oracle has itself well positioned for the present and future of this niche of the systems market.

Management of Large Volumes of Data

The hardware upon which database systems operate becomes stronger with every breath we take. At the start of this book, if we were to have researched the processor or disk storage market looking for the fastest and most powerful CPU, by the time we were finished, the technology would have advanced already. Oracle has been paying significant attention to the management of large volumes of data all along; they have paid special attention to this since release 7.3 (circa 1997) with mechanisms addressing such questions as data partitioning. With *data partitioning,* large volumes of data can be split into more manageable chunks and brought together transparently as systems operate and user sessions process queries.

Security Mechanisms

Oracle's sophisticated security mechanisms control access to sensitive data through use of an assortment of privileges. Users are given rights to view, modify, and create data according to the names they use to connect to the database. Customers use these mechanisms to ensure that specified users get to see sensitive data, while others are forbidden.

Backup and Recovery

Oracle provides sophisticated backup and recovery routines. Backup creates a secondary copy of Oracle data; recovery restores a copy of data from that backup. Oracle's backup and recovery strategy minimizes data loss and downtime when and if problems arise. Oracle Server also provides backup and recovery schemes that can allow uninterrupted access to the data 7 days a week, 24 hours a day, and 365 days a year.

Space Management

Oracle offers flexible space management. You can allocate disk space for storage of data and control subsequent allocations by instructing Oracle how much space to set aside for future requirements. It also has a series of special abilities that were designed with very large databases in mind. In fact, many of the latest features in Oracle8 and 7.3 were designed with data warehouses in mind. By design, these are typically very large databases.

Open Connectivity

Oracle provides open connectivity to and from other vendors' software. Using the Oracle Access Manager, installations can easily integrate their diverse corporate systems running on a range of different vendors' products. For example, using the manager for IBM's AS/400 platform, installations can access Oracle data transparently from applications written in third and fourth generation languages such as COBOL and C. PL/SQL is also supported, allowing you to call remote Oracle stored procedures from your AS/400 applications. Using Access Managers coupled with the Oracle Transparent Gateways, organizations can protect the investments made in their IBM hardware and software solutions.

Access Managers reside on the non-Oracle database machine, and the number of users is only limited by the underlying operating system or, in the case of the AS/400 Access Manager, the DB2/400 database. Industry standard SQL against the Oracle database is supported for these purposes:

- DDL, or data definition language, syntax is used against the Oracle database for defining objects (for example, **create table** or **create index**), changing the privileges of one or more recipients (for example, **grant select on**), or manipulating the infrastructure that supports the Oracle8*i* database (for example, **alter tablespace**).

- DML, or data manipulation language, is used for creating new data (for example, **insert into**), working with existing data (for example, **update**), removing existing rows (for example, **delete from**), or simply looking at data with the ever familiar **select** keyword.

Access Managers can be obtained for quick and easy access to Oracle data from the likes of Computer Associates' IDMS, Datacom, and Ingres, as well as Microsoft's SQL Server, Informix, Teradata's EDA/SQL, Sybase, and CICS from IBM, to mention a few.

Development Tools

The Oracle Server, commonly referred to as the database engine, supports a wide range of development tools, end-user query tools, off-the-shelf applications, and office-wide information management tools. Oracle Forms and Oracle Reports are the heart of Oracle's development offerings, with hooks into deployment on the Web and the three-tier architecture of Internet computing.

The Oracle Enterprise Developer Suite bundles a handful of components together, delivering flexible, high-performance, easily maintainable, and scalable applications with little or no effort to get started. The four major components of this suite are these:

■ Oracle Designer is a set of tools designed for definition of system components (that is, data sources and their relationships) and generation of applications and database definitions.

■ Oracle Developer is a rapid application development environment for building interactive applications and transaction or *OLTP*-based systems.

■ Oracle Developer Server is a robust deployment environment for multitier applications.

■ Oracle Application Server is an open solution designed to facilitate the deployment of transactional distributed applications.

Let's move on to the ever favorite Oracle8*i* Server.

Oracle8*i* Server

The Oracle8*i* Server is a state-of-the-art information management environment. It is a repository for very large amounts of data, and it gives users rapid access to that data. The Oracle8 Server allows for the sharing of data between applications; the information is stored in one place and used by many systems. At first, the Oracle8*i* Server was available on Sun Solaris and Windows NT. The Oracle8*i* Server now runs on dozens of different computers, supporting the following configurations:

■ **Host-based** Users are connected directly to the same computer on which the database resides.

■ **Client/server** Users access the database from their personal computers (client) via a network, and the database sits on a separate computer (server).

■ **Distributed processing** Users access a database that resides on more than one computer. The database is spread across more than one machine, and the users are unaware of the physical location of the data they work with.

■ **Web-enabled computing** Data can be accessed from an Internet-based application.

We believe Oracle's Server product over the years has helped position Oracle the company at the top of the list of successful information vendors, and Oracle8/8*i* has continued the tradition.

Oracle sells its server technology with a number of add-on options that enhance the server capabilities. The base product provides all the functionality to support the requirements of most of Oracle's customers. When customers require additional functionality, Oracle has a series of options they can purchase. The next few sections delve into the details of some of these features and options. In a nutshell, a *feature* is something that is built into the Oracle8*i* Server base product; an *option* is something that can be added on to the base server product for an additional fee.

Oracle8*i* Server Features

Reliability, availability, and serviceability—these three words are heard in the open systems arena. Oracle vends the most popular and widely adopted relational database software, with significant market share on most hardware platforms. Oracle is not there by mistake; features built into the server technology have helped them get there and stay the leader in the industry. Let's have a look at features that have helped catapult Oracle to the top of the heap.

Data Accessibility

When you purchase the Oracle Server, you get a whole host of core functionality to help you store and keep your data accessible. It provides utilities for backing up the data. These include the capability to back up the information while the user community is still using it. The term we like to use to explain this concept is "hot backup." The official Oracle term for this capability to back up live data is "archive mode backups." No longer does an organization have to shut down access to the applications while a backup is being made of the database. The bottom line is that you can keep your Oracle database up 7 days a week, 24 hours a day.

The Oracle Server also provides for data integrity. If, while a user is changing data within an Oracle database, a failure of any sort happens, the database has the capability to undo or roll back any suspect transaction. With Oracle Server, you are never in doubt as to the status of any transaction. It also includes a full, row-level, locking of all data that resides within it.

For example, if you were working on a stock purchase application built on an Oracle repository and two users wanted to buy lot #5, which is 100 shares of a Database Technologies stock, the database would not allow that to happen. Since there is only one lot left to purchase, the database would allow one user to have access to purchasing; the other user would have to wait. When the second user received the go-ahead to proceed, he or she would see the new status of the lot as sold. The Oracle Server transparently handles these situations, maintaining the integrity of the data.

Procedural Capabilities

All of the procedural features you can ever dream of are in the Oracle8*i* Server product and then some. The foundation of this option is Oracle's programming language, PL/SQL, which is discussed in Chapter 8. With PL/SQL and this component, you can implement the following features:

- **Stored procedures** Programs (or code segments) are stored in the Oracle database and perform central functions for your installation. For example, in a cable television billing application, you may use a stored procedure to create a reminder letter to customers with delinquent accounts. The execution of that procedure is triggered by the creation of a customer's monthly statement when unpaid charges are due for over 60 days.

- **Database triggers** These are code stored in the database triggered by events that occur in your applications. In a human resources application, for example, when a new employee is hired, the creation of a new set of personnel information could use a database trigger to create messages to be sent to other parts of the company. These messages, triggered by the new employee being added to the database, could alert the operators of the message center to the existence of the new individual.

- **Packages** Procedures are grouped together and store the code as a single program unit in the database. For example, a central warehouse for a chain of bookstores could design a package that takes care of the routing of special orders to the appropriate retail location. There would be procedures within this package to initiate the transfer of goods, process notifications of short orders, process reorders, and so on.

Distributed Processing

In many installations, portions of corporate data reside on different computers in different cities. Accounts receivable may be based in Dallas; procurement, in Toronto; research and development, in Jakarta; and the head office might be in Lisbon. Each location has a segment of the corporate data, yet users need to access that information as if it all resided on the same central computer. The Oracle Server's distributed capability permits this scenario to become a reality. There is *location transparency,* such that a user in Yokohama working with the information stored in Toronto is unaware of the physical location of the data. The physical location of the procurement data is unknown to all users. Oracle's distributed option permits this to work.

Parallel Query

The parallel query feature allows customers to take advantage of processing queries on computers with more than one central processing unit (commonly referred to as a CPU). On single CPU machines (or multi-CPU machines without parallel query), a single process accesses the database and displays the data that qualifies based on the selection criteria. The processing is handled as shown in Figure 1-4.

When using parallel query on multi-CPU machines, Oracle dispatches a number of query processes that work alongside one another. They partition the query processing and work simultaneously; the results are merged and presented to the user when ready. Figure 1-5 shows the basics of this option. With this capability to run parallel queries, a query that used to take an hour can run in minutes by taking advantage of all the available CPU power.

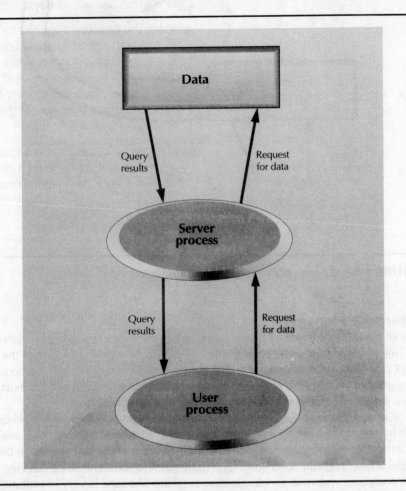

FIGURE 1-4.   *Query processing without parallel query*

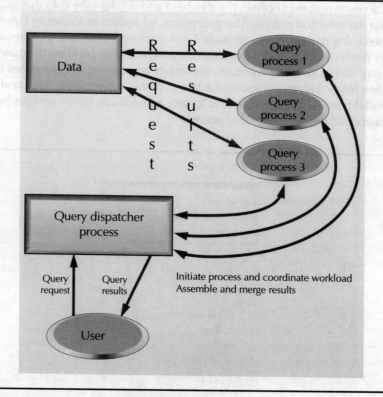

FIGURE 1-5. *Query processing with parallel query*

Enterprise Manager

One of the things we always found ironic about the move toward open systems was the lack of everyday tools. For example, we would be working on one of the fastest UNIX machines/open systems that ever existed, and yet we would have no tape management system. The reason we did not have it is that it did not yet exist. There was no vendor we could purchase the tape solutions from.

Over the past few years, this has all changed. Many a company has rebuilt itself by taking the tools it sold in the mainframe arena and making them available in UNIX. The reason these tools were built in the first place still applies in the open system arena: You still need good tape management software, since backing up your computer system to an inexpensive medium like tape is very important. Being able to find those tapes and manage those tapes is a very critical need. Platinum Corporation is a great example of a company that has rebuilt itself in the open system arena. Platinum has taken many of the tools they built for the IBM mainframe and rebuilt the equivalent for open systems/UNIX. For example, we now see transaction log analyzers being sold for the Oracle marketplace. These are crucial tools when you deploy mission-critical applications. When a need (or vacuum) arises in the marketplace, there are always companies to fill that need. This is the basic law of supply and demand at work. Overall, we think these are the good signs of a maturing marketplace, which is the type of environment you want when the application is mission critical.

It's important to recognize the fact that one of the most difficult skill sets to find in the Oracle marketplace is the knowledge that good, solid database administrators bring to their jobs. It's also important to note that without solid management tools in place, Oracle customers will not be able to deploy larger, more complex databases. Oracle has built its own answer to this problem, Oracle Enterprise Manager (or *OEM*). With this type of tool in place, your database administrator can be more productive, and a weak database administrator will have a very strong tool to help supplement his or her ability.

VIP
Solid system management tools are critical to keeping your Oracle database running smoothly. We recommend you take the time to evaluate all system management options available. The correct choice for you should be based on your budget and needs.

Oracle Enterprise Manager is a set of management tools designed to help you manage the complete Oracle environment, which includes systems, applications, networks, and databases. In addition to being able to manage different Oracle environments from one tool, you also have intelligent agents and an open interface to help you leverage third-party products.

From the Manager console, the database administrator working through a GUI interface has the ability to manage the complete Oracle environment. There are four major components to the Oracle Enterprise Manager Console:

- ■ Navigator allows the database administrator to view and manipulate all network nodes and services in a family tree–like manner.

- ■ Map Window allows the database administrator to view and map subsets of objects in a graphical manner. For example, if you worked in a major hospital, with quite a few Oracle databases, you might look at your Oracle environments in three distinct ways—admitting, emergency room, and lab results. This tool allows you to take a very complex environment and map it into more cohesive subsets.

■ Job Scheduling System allows the database administrator to automate repetitive tasks. This can be done in one location, to automate a task at a remote site. For example, you might automate the backups, freeing your time for other tasks.

■ Event Management System allows the database administrator to remotely monitor system and database events, and then, based on some preset thresholds, kick off corrective jobs working with the job scheduling system. For example, you might set up an event to monitor database free space to ensure that you never allow a database to run out of space.

Every Oracle database that is being managed has an intelligent agent process running. This process monitors the database(s) known to OEM, gathers statistics about database performance, and stores information in the Oracle8 repository to feed to OEM for perusal and corrective action by the database administrator. Through this agent, OEM can make things happen. It is also open, so that third-party products can take advantage of it. When the Oracle8i Server is installed, you end up with the Enterprise Manager base product.

Oracle8i Server Options

The Oracle8i server out of the box is the next generation of a sophisticated piece of technology used by more relational database customers than any other solution on the planet. The icing, so to say, is already on the cake with the off-the-shelf product. A number of add-ons build on the base product—let's have a look at a few of these.

Oracle Advanced Security

Oracle Advanced Security offers integrated security and directory services. More and more secure information is passing across the Internet as users begin to make purchases and pay bills on the Web. With Oracle Advanced Security, a single login can be used for multiple servers, with a centralized definition of each user and what a user may access. Oracle Advanced Security ensures that privileges given out to users to interact with Oracle data are similar across an enterprise-wide corporate database network.

Oracle Time Series

Oracle Time Series enables efficient storage of time-stamped data. Full analysis time series applications can be developed leveraging the power of the server technology.

Oracle Advanced Replication

Oracle Advanced Replication provides for the storage and distribution of data between multiple remote sites. *Replication* is a mechanism where data, stored at one or more sites, is propagated between the sites participating in the replication exercise.

Let's take a closer look at the Oracle8*i* Server itself, and then we will review some of the Oracle8*i* Server options and look at the functionality they provide for you. The Oracle Server is the foundation of the entire Oracle product and application suite. Data, in its simplest sense, is numbers and letters. As we are all learning very quickly, access to information is critical if corporations want to survive the information-enabling age we all live in. The Oracle Server is where all this data is stored. Data or information, as we all know, takes on many more forms than just letters and numbers. With the Oracle Server and its additional options, you will be able to store, manipulate, and present data in whatever form it resides. You will learn how data ranges from numbers and letters, to video and sound, to structured and unstructured forms. The Oracle Server is a repository for holding and manipulating data very quickly.

Oracle Parallel Server

Some manufacturers make clustered computers: each machine in the cluster has its own memory, yet they have common disk storage devices. The parallel server option allows Oracle to operate with this configuration. Each machine is referred to as a node in the cluster, and the term "loosely coupled" is used to refer to the nodes. Figure 1-6 shows how this works.

The bottom line of this option is that you can have two or more computers talking to the same database at the same time. This provides you with near-zero fault tolerance performance at a fraction of the cost. Downtime due to planned maintenance or outages can be minimized when work usually done by one server can transparently be picked up by another. If one machine fails for any reason, just reroute your users onto the other machine. It is near-zero fault tolerance in that it approaches 99.9 percent availability. The only time the Oracle8 Server won't be available is when both machines are experiencing hardware failure. Also, you have the power of two or more computers at your disposal. If you run out of horsepower on one machine, add another.

VIP
The Parallel Server option is not part of the base product and is purchased separately.

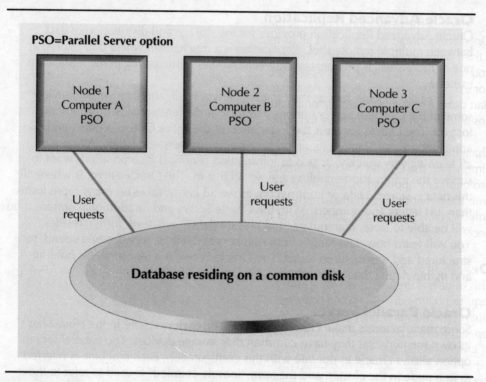

FIGURE 1-6. *Loosely coupled nodes in a cluster*

Oracle Visual Information Retrieval

Oracle8i Visual Information Retrieval (*VIR*) bundles the search capabilities of the server with the power of content-based retrieval of VIR. Users can wade through large volumes of image data stored in the Oracle8i repository using search criteria common to image data—color, texture, or pattern to name a few. With image data stored in Oracle8i, users can leverage the search capabilities of the database when looking for similarities between those images. Many popular file formats are supported using VIR, including Windows bitmap, TIFF, GIF, and PCX, as well as transcoding from one format to another.

Oracle Advanced Networking Option

The Advanced Networking Option provides a single source of integration with enterprise directory services, such as single sign-on services, network encryption, and token and user authentication. Previous releases called this option the Oracle Secure Network Services.

Think of the networking option as the peanut butter in a peanut butter sandwich. One slice of bread is Oracle and all its related software, and the other slice of bread is a third-party vendor's network software. By separating Oracle from the network layer, you never have to rewrite your applications to take advantage of a new network layer. For example, if the U.S. government mandates that all installations worldwide must start using a one-terabit encryption package, this networking option layer would help ensure that you would not have to change a line of application code.

Oracle recognizes the fact that these enterprise network services are constantly changing, and the Oracle implementation allows it to be "technology neutral." Simply put, the Oracle Advanced Network Option allows you to support any protocol, any application, and any data by integrating the connected session with the network layer transparently. With the Advanced Networking Option, you will be positioned to take advantage of new communication technologies as they become available.

Oracle *inter*Media

This option is designed to address the advanced data management services required by the diverse data types used by media-rich applications. We all see a glut of graphics and high-resolution images in online catalogs, and many corporate repositories are populated with an assortment of visual business decision aids (such as graphs, maps, and pictures of product). Oracle *inter*Media extends Oracle8*i*'s capability to manage the rich data types required for Internet business—what with lots and lots of images to support material that used to only appear in printed form (such as catalogs). The *inter*Media option is actually a number of content management services rolled into one:

- *inter*Media Text is built on a predecessor called the ConText option, where text can be searched using advanced retrieval and natural language queries.

- *inter*Media Image provides for standard image management services such as scaling and cropping.

- *inter*Media Video enables video and audio delivery to the Web browser from a variety of sources, not limited to that data stored in the Oracle8*i* database.

- *inter*Media Locator has hooks built in that locate information based on spatial variables such as distance from a specified location, or nature of the displacement from one store to another (such as north or south) in a retail application.

Oracle Spatial

Oracle Spatial offers enhanced management of spatial data. By definition, *spatial data* is data that has a location component. Oracle Spatial utilizes an integrated set of functions and procedures to store, manage, and provide spatial data to analysis exercises.

With Oracle Spatial, you are able to store and manipulate both spatial and attribute data in a single database. It allows you to include Oracle8i Spatial Data option tables in your database along with any mix of standard Oracle8i tables. You can then access both table types using the standard Oracle tool sets.

To understand what spatial data is and means to your Oracle8i Server, let's take a look at how the Oracle8i server normally accesses data stored within it. A traditional Oracle database is made up of data stored within a database object called a *table*. A table is made up of many columns of data. These columns of data are the attributes of the table.

For example, notice in Table 1-2 that we have a table called the state. It is made up of six attributes, which are columns of data.

Many of the applications that need access to state names and codes are not interested in any of the attributes associated with governor information. So in the traditional Oracle8 server, you are able to create a database object called an *index.*

An index is a database object that contains just the subset of data a typical application is interested in. When creating the index, you specify those columns you wish to be able to search upon. Those columns are called *keys.*

In Table 1-3, you see an example of an index named state_index. It is much quicker to retrieve data from the index for two reasons:

1. It is much quicker, since the data set is much smaller. Remember, you have fewer columns/attributes of data to deal with. The entries in the index are stored in such a way that it is quicker to find locations within the data set when specifying the key.

2. This method of data retrieval has worked quite well, for most applications. Your database performance was a factor of database size and index efficiency. As very large databases become more prevalent and the trend toward large data warehouses grows, the existing Oracle indexing mechanisms have not been able to keep up with a new class of users' performance needs.

To meet this new class of users' needs, Oracle engineered the spatial data option. Performance is now a function of how much data you actually retrieve, not the size of the data set. In a spatial database, the data is the index. In a spatial database table, you identify all the dimensions you are interested in. The spatial database option is able to take these various dimensions and merge them into a single value that represents the intersections of all desired dimensions. Every combination of these dimensions leads to a single unique point. Once the dimensions are identified, the data is encoded and grouped in an appropriate manner. The greater the relationship between data, the closer it is stored in the database. When a request is made to access the data, any data that is not relevant is outside the bounds of the query. Since the data is the index, data outside of your interest is ignored. A query that looks at a megabyte of data takes the same time to retrieve the data from a 10-megabyte table as it does from a 1-terabyte table. The factor that has the greatest impact on performance is the data set in which you are interested.

State_code	State_name	Gov_Lname	Gov_fname	Gov_Mi	Party_Code
MA	Massachusetts	Weld	Bill	I	R
CA	California	Steve	Tyler	E	R
ID	Idaho	Honcho	Head	A	D
WI	Wisconsin	Waters	Roger	A	D
NH	New Hampshire	Farnham	Mark	O	R
VT	Vermont	Jerry	Ben	A	D
RI	Rhode Island	Chapman	Cindy	W	D

TABLE 1-2.   *State Table Column Values*

State_code	State_name
MA	Massachusetts
CA	California
ID	Idaho
WI	Wisconsin
NH	New Hampshire
VT	Vermont
RI	Rhode Island

TABLE 1-3.   *State Codes by State_index*

Oracle ConText

The Oracle8*i* Server ConText Option is a text management solution that enables you to manage unstructured text information resources as quickly as you manage structured data. Structured data is data stored in columns, like the state_cd column. An example of your unstructured text data is a contract, or a magazine article. Figure 1-7 and Figure 1-8 illustrate the difference between structured and unstructured data. With the ConText Option, you are able to build and deploy text-based applications with an SQL-like interface.

What's ironic is that organizations for the past ten years have invested very heavily in building applications that enable us to rapidly retrieve structured data. Yet most of the data in the world is unstructured: Many studies state that 90 percent of the world's data is unstructured. Good examples of unstructured data are magazine articles, Web pages, faxes, e-mail messages, contracts, and documentation. Think of all the valuable information that is stored within these documents. What if your data warehouse application could easily have access to every contract you ever signed. What if you could store and retrieve data from every e-mail message you ever sent based on a theme search. Would this be useful? In today's information-enabled world, access to data is key. It would be foolish to ignore 90 percent of the world's textual information. The ConText Option allows your Oracle8 server to deal with unstructured data, giving your organization access to an estimated 90 percent of the world's data, today.

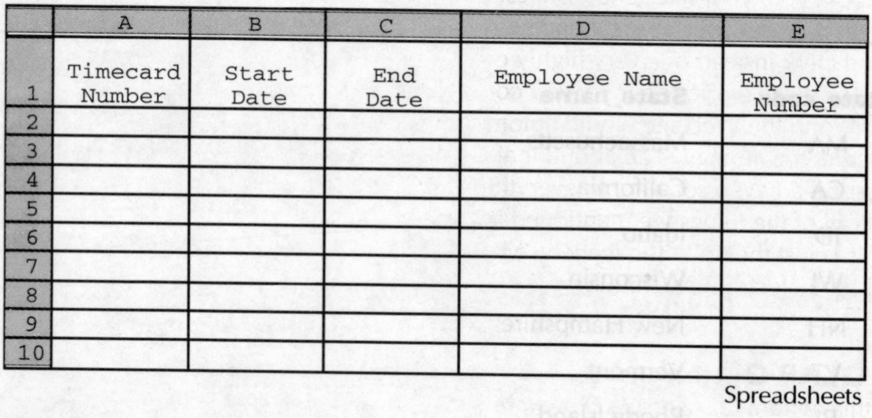

	A	B	C	D	E
1	Timecard Number	Start Date	End Date	Employee Name	Employee Number
2					
3					
4					
5					
6					
7					
8					
9					
10					

Spreadsheets

FIGURE 1-7. *Structured data*

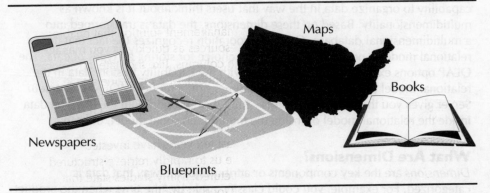

FIGURE 1-8. *Unstructured data*

WebServer

The true power of the World Wide Web does not lie in static data pages, which are the majority of Web sites today. The true power of the Web can only be realized when you can marry it to your database. When we go out and navigate the World Wide Web, what we typically see are a lot of very sophisticated billboards. Yes, they have sound and enhanced graphics, but they are still glorified billboards. The only difference? Instead of being behind the wheels of our cars, we are sitting at our desks in front of a PC.

Imagine a Web site that had access to the corporate database. It could retrieve facts about you, your likes and dislikes. It could then dynamically build a Web site on the fly to meet your needs. Imagine a Web site that could be maintained by a low-end clerk instead of a very highly compensated Web specialist. Every time you wanted to make a price change, you could make that change to your corporate database and the Web site would automatically be updated. That's what the Oracle WebServer technology is all about. It allows your Oracle8 Server to talk to current state-of-the-art Web software in everything from Java to HTML. WebServer can let you do all of the things we mentioned in this paragraph and more.

This is just the tip of the iceberg. Many works out there explain the direction of Web-based electronic technology.

The OLAP Option

With this option, OLAP users can express their data in the same way they think about it. Rather than thinking of the data in terms of flat files or spreadsheets, the OLAP option allows you to look at the data in terms of its many dimensions. This capability to organize data in the way that users think about it is known as multidimensionality. Based on these dimensions, the data is transformed into a multidimensional database. Oracle Corporation recognizes the fact that the relational model is not always the optimal choice for storing all types of data. The OLAP options extend the Oracle8 server with the capability to store data in the relational model (ROLAP) or in the multidimensional model (MOLAP). Oracle8*i* Server gives you the best of all worlds—full OLAP support with the physical data inside the relational model or inside the multidimensional model, or both.

What Are Dimensions?
Dimensions are the key components or attributes of the way that data is categorized. For example, you could classify a sale by "the time when the product was purchased"; "the particular product that was purchased"; "where the purchase occurred"; and "the price of the product." Each one of these items could be thought of as a dimension within the database. In this example, time, products, geography, and measures are the dimensions. The intersection of these dimensions produces a *cell.* A cell is defined as a single data point that occurs at the intersection defined by selecting one value from each of the dimensions in a multidimensional array. When one visualizes a multidimensional database, one might see a Rubik's cube. Rubik's cube was a game that originated in the Soviet Union, in which you had a series of blocks, and you moved the various cells of the cube to line up the colors.

Locating the value of sales in a car dealership application for Boston is quite easy. You think in terms of its position within the database as opposed to thinking about which columns you might have to join. With the OLAP option, you are given the capability of physically storing the data in the multidimensional model or storing it in the relational model.

SQL*Plus—The User-Friendly Interface

So far, we have talked about the Oracle8*i* Server. Let's move on to SQL*Plus— the way you define and manipulate data in Oracle's relational database. SQL (Structured Query Language) is the industry standard adopted by all database vendors. (Some people pronounce SQL as "sequel"; others pronounce each letter separately.) Oracle's SQL*Plus is a superset of standard SQL: it conforms to the standards of an SQL-compliant language, and it has some Oracle-specific add-ons, leading to its name (SQL and Plus). In the old days, SQL*Plus was called UFI, the user-friendly interface. Compared to writing in a typical programming language like FORTRAN, friendly it is.

SQL and Oracle

The Oracle Server only understands statements worded using SQL—when tools such as Oracle Forms interact with the database, they pass nothing other than SQL statements for processing. Oracle's implementation of SQL through SQL*Plus is compliant with ANSI (American National Standards Institute) and ISO (International Standards Organization) standards. Almost all Oracle tools support identical SQL syntax.

SQL is tailored to harness the power of the relational model. Since all your data is stored via the relationship, it is possible to work with your data in sets, as opposed to independent rows of data. With SQL*Plus, much of the work associated with retrieving data out of a traditional database goes away. For example, you no longer read a record. Instead, you write a program that deals with all the records associated with an entity. No one record is different than another. In SQL*Plus, whatever action you decide to take is done as a complete set. We demonstrate how this is done in Chapter 7 and Chapter 12.

VIP
All the vendors have gone the relational database route. The relational model is here to stay.

SQL*Plus: Summary of Points

Let's summarize what we have learned about Oracle's base programming language:

- SQL*Plus is Oracle's flavor of SQL. "Plus" refers to Oracle's addition to the SQL language.

- All work with a relational database is done with an SQL-based programming language.

- SQL*Plus is user friendly.

- When programming with SQL*Plus, you work on sets of data (that is, information is not processed one record at a time).

- Using the "Plus" component of SQL*Plus, it is easy to write useful reports (Chapters 7 and 12 highlight report writing using SQL*Plus).

Oracle Forms—The Front End

With the foundation of a strong database and complemented by a strong language for reporting (SQL*Plus), it was only natural that Oracle would expand into a screen generator, since this is the primary way most users deal with the database. Oracle Forms is part of the Developer suite of tools and is typically the front end tool of choice for mission-critical applications. It runs in a graphical user interface (GUI) environment, with the look and feel of Microsoft Windows (3.*x*, NT, or Windows 95/98).

Application developers design data entry and query screens with Oracle Forms; end users can then use these screens to manipulate data in the Oracle database. The interface with the user is event driven or function key/keypad driven. As summarized in Table 1-4, you can write three types of modules with Oracle Forms. Rolled together, they provide the developer and end user with a complete forms-based corporate data entry solution. Combining an assortment of these three types of programs into a full-blown application is part of the art of working with Oracle Forms. In Chapter 9 we discuss this tool in greater detail.

Oracle Reports—The Report Writer

With the foundation of a strong relational database and complemented by a robust suite of core development tools, Oracle continued to expand. While SQL*Plus is a great reporting tool, it was not designed with just reporting in mind. So Oracle developed various tools just for generating reports, including SQL*QMX, RPT, and Easy*SQL. Oracle Reports (and its predecessor SQL*Reportwriter) is the flagship report writer tool for the Developer suite. We discuss Oracle Reports in Chapter 9.

Program Type	Contents
forms	Allows update, creation, and deletion of data within Oracle objects
menu	Defines an assortment of main menus and an optional subset of any number of submenus
library	A repository for centralized PL/SQL code accessed by other types of Oracle Forms modules

TABLE I-4.   *Forms Module Types*

Oracle Reports is a successor to SQL*Reportwriter that appeared with Oracle version 6. SQL*Reportwriter provided a reporting environment with which the developer designs reports and the end user executes them; it evolved into Oracle Reports as users insisted they wanted a Windows-based mouse-driven interface. With Oracle Reports, you can create graphical report representations of the data in your Oracle database.

Oracle Reports (starting with version 2.0) is a true multimedia reporting environment. You can include images, sound, and charts, and you can present reports in a variety of colors using an assortment of fonts. You can easily create popular report output styles with Oracle Reports. Using its powerful default features, developers can create master/detail reports, matrix reports, and form letters with little programming.

Master/Detail Reports

When designing master/detail reports, the programmer defines a hierarchy of the data assembled for the report; you display all data for the first level, then the second level data it is related to. The following simple master/detail report uses automobile manufacturers as an example. The manufacturer is called the master; when a master is displayed, all of its associated detail information appears.

```
Manufacturer:  Nissan
Model          Style         Price Class
Quest          Minivan       D
Maxima         Sedan         G
Ultima         Sport         F

Manufacturer:  GM
Model          Style         Price Class
Safari         Minivan       D
Impala         Sedan         G
TransAm        Sport         F
```

Matrix Reports

In matrix reports, you use the values of rows and columns as labels. For example, let's consider the following set of data:

```
Salesperson        Quarter            Commission
10                 1                  500
10                 2                  400
20                 1                  600
20                 2                  900
```

20	3	350
30	2	900
30	3	235

That data would be presented in the following way in a matrix report:

	1	2	3
10	500	400	
20	600	900	350
30		900	235

Notice how the quarter column values appear as column headers and the salesperson numbers appear as row headers.

Form Letters

With form letters, you take information from the database and include it in the body of a letter. Sometimes, one simply gets name and address information from the database. Other times, the text in the body of the letter is extracted from the database. In the next example, the text in italics has been printed based on address information stored in the database; the text in bold and italics forms part of the letter's body and comes from the database too.

```
...
Dear Ms. Stroud:
This is to inform you that ...... no later than the end of May, 2004.
...
Dear Mr. Flaherty:
This is to inform you that ...... no later than the middle of July, 2004.
...
```

> **VIP**
> *Oracle Reports is a report writer. Unlike SQL*Plus, it is very graphically based. Using the power of a computer and its mouse, you are able to point and click to build very powerful reports.*

SQL*Loader

In the old days, Oracle had a special tool called ODL (Oracle Data Loader). Over time, this has evolved into SQL*Loader, a tool that very quickly allows you to load data into an Oracle database. (It should be noted you get this tool as part of the standard toolset.) Tools like this are very important to an Oracle database. In the real world, a great deal of customers' systems still use the traditional approach.

Most agree that a relational database is a great tool, but migrating traditional systems to relational systems requires conversion of your existing systems' data. Well, that's what Oracle Loader is all about. It is a tool you use to move data into an Oracle database.

VIP
*SQL*Loader is a great tool to use when you need to move data into your data warehouse.*

Like any good capitalistic company, Oracle grew its supply to meet the demands of the marketplace. A big demand exists in the industry for tools that enable you to move data from a traditional database to a relational database, just as we are seeing an even bigger demand for tools to migrate data into the data warehouse. There is also a great demand for tools that enable a relational database to talk to a traditional database.

Oracle Open Gateways bundles three product families—the Oracle Transparent Gateways; the Oracle Procedural Gateways; and, finally, the Oracle Access Managers. The functionality ranges from being able to access SQL commands to an external data source, to being able to run procedures on an external data source. The name of the game is connectivity, and the Oracle suite of products does it better than anyone else.

It's also clear that once the data is placed in an Oracle database with the Developer suite, it is very easy to generate reports and screens to manipulate the contents. It is also the reality that this migration might take years to accomplish. Oracle has developed tools to move your data into Oracle, like SQL*Loader, or tools to talk to a traditional database, like SQL*Connect.

Oracle Using Its Own Tools— The Cooperative Applications

As time went on, Oracle Corporation realized that there was a strong business opportunity available for off-the-shelf generic applications. So Oracle started to build financial applications. This had two major impacts on the rest of the Oracle environments (that is, Oracle customers using the same products Oracle the company itself was using).

For the first time, Oracle Corporation was actually using its own tools to build applications. The more they used the tools, the more the tools improved. The company started to live, eat, and breathe its own tools. The more Oracle used its own tools, the more it found ways to improve them. So very quickly, we started to see major improvements in the quality and functionality of the tools.

Second, as soon as Oracle Corporation started to build applications based on the relational database model, companies started to use the Oracle software for mission-critical business functions (such as payroll). This accelerated the proliferation of Oracle's database software, and more and more companies started to reap the benefits of the new technology Oracle had developed.

Today, Oracle has a division that puts out applications in every major product area—from accounting to manufacturing to industry-specific solutions. Administrative support of today's application customer can be done using Oracle InterOffice, which we discuss next. In addition, Oracle application has a whole list of industry solutions from education to pharmaceuticals.

Oracle Designer

Oracle Designer offers a complete solution when Oracle clients need to design, program, implement, and maintain systems. It provides for rapid application development in a client/server Windows environment. Designer's advanced functionality supports *BPR* (Business Process Reengineering) and mechanisms to take advantage of the server processing that can be done using Oracle's database engine; Designer is tightly integrated with the Oracle Server, using a common repository stored in the database. Oracle Designer has three major components:

- Business process reengineering
- Modelers
- Generators

Since Oracle Developer and Oracle Designer share the same repository of information, communication is nearly seamless. As you are gathering your requirements and recording the information, the repository is being populated. Then, based on that information, the models can be developed and the code generated. When the form is created, it utilizes the common repository.

Net8 Common GUI functionality, as embedded in Oracle's latest generation of reporting and forms development tools, provides the interface between the analyst and Oracle Designer. The development can be done in small workgroups and applications easily deployed to hundreds of users. Oracle Designer offers automatic code generation, as well as automated software distribution. PL/SQL, the language that Oracle has embedded in all its development products, offers Oracle Designer and Oracle Developer the same program development environment on client and server. Oracle Designer supports a wide range of business model functionality that enables companies to build systems ranging from the simplest to the most complex. Oracle Designer is the next generation of Oracle's suite of CASE products whose version number climbed as high as 5.1. Many readers are familiar with the obsolete line of Oracle CASE called CASE*Dictionary and CASE*Designer.

Oracle Reports Generator takes the information in the Oracle Designer repository and creates Oracle Reports. As the system evolves and changes, you go back and regenerate your reports. Changes made in the dictionary ripple through the reports as they are regenerated.

Personal Oracle8*i*

This is a full-blown version of the Oracle8*i* database, tightly integrated with the Oracle8*i* Enterprise Edition deployed on your family of servers. Some organizations have decided to offload development activities from their servers, allowing programmers and other systems personnel the luxury of working without the complexity of the network. The Oracle8*i* Navigator can be used for object management, with the standard drag-and-drop functionality users demand. Personal Oracle8*i* has a very light suggested hardware configuration of 32MB of memory and as little as 85MB of disk space. These requirements increase if you are going to use Personal Oracle8*i*'s replication services. With *replication services*, you can maintain copies of data at more than one node and propagate changes from one site to another.

Brand new (just out of the box) DBAs can come up to speed working with the technical ins and outs of database administration using Personal Oracle8*i* without interfering with what is going on in the real-life corporate database network. Especially crucial to the DBA is Oracle's distributed system capabilities, what with replication and snapshot technology. *Snapshots* are read-only copies of data from one server (in the case of Oracle8*i* Enterprise Edition) or one PC (with Personal Oracle8*i*), stored and periodically refreshed elsewhere.

Oracle Discoverer

Oracle Discoverer delivers a data analysis solution to corporate users, a key component in Oracle's decision support solutions. End users can formulate sophisticated queries without knowing anything about the underlying SQL that is passed to the Oracle8*i* database. *SQL* stands for the structured query language, the industry standard for relational databases, and the foundation of most vendors' offerings for data manipulation and definition. Oracle Discoverer output can be published to the Web at the click of a button.

An Oracle Discoverer administrator defines an End User Layer and then delivers business groups similar or different views of corporate data. The complexity of relational data definitions and their underlying relationships is hidden from the end user. Oracle has built resource control into the product, thereby alleviating, when necessary, the additional workload on the server from the ad hoc query user community. Release 3.1 is available for Windows 95/98 and NT, with access to other platforms delivered by Oracle Discoverer for the Web.

Oracle8*i* Lite

Oracle8*i* Lite is a player in the mobile computing application systems arena. It simplifies the development, deployment, and management of mobile applications. Users can access information stored in an Oracle8*i* database from anywhere using an assortment of PDAs (personal data assistants) and mobile personal computers (notebooks and laptops).

Seamless access to corporate database information anywhere eliminates the need to grab snapshots of data before leaving the office and work with out-of-date information while away. With Oracle8*i* Lite, managers can get up-to-the-minute information rather than information that may be stale. Oracle8*i* Lite is Java enabled, with support for Windows 95/98/NT as well as Windows CE and the Palm Computing Platform. The modular database kernel is only 50 to 750KB, with secure data and application synchronization mechanisms. Chapter 2 discusses the Internet-specific features of Oracle8*i*.

The Services

The services wing of Oracle Corporation is a major component of what Oracle has to offer the marketplace. These services offer the following:

- Oracle Education's skilled instructors teach about the wide range of the Oracle product set as well as some of the relational database modeling, design, and analysis theory. Oracle Education offers a wide range of courses on the full suite of products and applications. It can provide preclassroom learning via the computer-based training (CBT) electronic medium. Centers in over 50 countries provide classroom and in-house training to end users, developers, analysts, and IT (information technology) managers.

- Oracle Consulting's trained professionals are at your disposal to help facilitate corporate system solutions using Oracle's products and Oracle's partners' technology. There is a network of companies that develop and market their own products that work alongside Oracle's products; Oracle partners with these companies. Oracle Consulting helps customers realize critical solutions by providing expert guidance and technology transfer. It assists with business process reengineering exercises, the transformation to open systems, and application development, to name a few areas. Oracle Consulting offers management (including strategic planning), technical (including performance tuning), development (including custom systems), and Oracle applications implementation services. Their direction statement mentions that that they possess the "... knowledge initiative enabling the exchange of thought-provoking ideas through articles on issues that impact the world and the IT industry."

- Oracle Consulting offers many services, including the following specific areas:

  - Industry expertise is available in communications, consumer products, energy, finance, and industrials.

  - Oracle applications implementation focuses on migration issues and centralized repository-based solutions that promote reusability.

  - Core technologies/OLTP (*online transaction processing*) services people specialize in the support of the Enterprise Server technology with configuration planning, implementation services, system upgrades, performance tuning, and ongoing system audits.

  - Decision Support (a.k.a. Data Warehousing) services uses the Oracle Warehouse solution. With their intimate knowledge of state-of-the-art analysis products, Oracle Consulting is the natural choice.

  - Internet and Electronic Commerce services personnel deliver solutions that ensure Internet-modeled systems meet the client needs and provide easy access while attending to security requirements.

  - Custom Development services utilize teams of professionals with proven methods to deliver systems on time. They leverage Oracle's Web-enabled development tools to provide a system start to finish or work alongside a customer's existing professionals.

  - Business Solutions services individuals work with customers through business process reengineering and improvement activities.

  - Oracle One allows access to consultants on the Oracle team who are tops in their respective fields. These professionals have worked for many years with large multinational, global organizations in a diverse geographic and cultural community.

  - Project/Program Management Services assist the development of information technology processes to assist companies as they move with their changing business needs and expanding clientele.

  - Oracle's High Performance Scalable Solutions services implement Oracle technology specifically targeted at high-end components of the Oracle8*i* Server technology—specifically Oracle Parallel Server (*OPS*) and MPP (*massively parallel processor*) architecture. OPS allows more than one computer to share disk space and access the same database; MPP systems fall into the arena dealing with high-end computers with more than one CPU (*central processing unit*).

- Oracle Worldwide Customer Support analysts provide technical assistance to clients in the care and feeding of Oracle products. Support services are specifically geared to match customer needs, with a suite of support levels from around-the-clock personalized service (Oracle Gold) to online electronic support through the private support forum called MetaLink on the Web.

NOTE
MetaLink access is geared to your current support services contract with Oracle. It is not automatically enlivened with your contract, but membership is free for qualifying customers.

- The Oracle Partner Program works with specific pockets of industry to identify key issues, using Oracle technology to create system solutions. It works alongside industry professionals to refine business system goals and to build systems that help companies stay one step ahead of the competition. The program makes more sense than ever with the proliferation of Internet model–based solutions as we move into the twenty-first century.

An increasing portion of Oracle business is generated in the services area each year. Oracle services enable customers to implement dependable, state-of-the-art technology systems that deploy the Oracle Enterprise Server technology. Services are geared toward knowledge transfer and lasting success of system solutions realized in partnership with Oracle professionals.

Oracle User Groups— Events and Publications

A significant number of Oracle user groups and events are found around the world. Oracle Corporation, as well as the user group community, has aligned itself on a tricontinental basis: the Americas, Europe/Africa/Middle East, and Asia-Pacific. Contact information for all of these central user communities can be obtained through the headquarters of the International Oracle Users Group (IOUG)-Americas in Chicago on the Web at *http://www.ioug.org* at +1(312) 245-1579.

User groups around the world meet regularly to discuss technical issues related to using Oracle. Presentations cover a wide range of Oracle-related subjects from the user community, third-party vendors, and Oracle Corporation. The three continental user groups' central contacts are in the U.S., Austria, and Australia.

Each geographical area has one or more Oracle conferences in a year, the largest of which are the following:

- The Americas holds IOUG-A Live! in the spring of each year in North America.

- The Asia-Pacific user forum is held in Australia or New Zealand, usually in November of each year.

- Europe/Middle East/Africa holds the European Oracle User Forum (EOUF), usually in March or April of each year.

A number of Oracle user groups around the world publish newsletters and magazines with articles on Oracle products and services. As examples: *Select* magazine is published quarterly by the IOUG-Americas, *Relate* magazine is published quarterly by the UK Oracle Users Group.

Data Warehousing with Oracle

It is a fact that we live in the information-enabled age, and that information is power. We are seeing a major trend toward corporations building data warehouses and data marts. In this book, we will cover what data warehouses and data marts are, and we will also explain the two current views on the best way to implement a data warehouse strategy for your business. Then, we will talk techie and go over the new data warehousing features in Oracle. The goal of Chapter 19 is to teach you all you need to know to understand the concepts and the key features in Oracle that help you support data warehousing.

What's Next

Enough said! From reading this chapter, we trust you have a basic knowledge of what Oracle is and what they produce. You should have a clear understanding that Oracle Corporation's roots are based on the database. From this base, Oracle has branched out to become a full-service vendor that can supply a database that will run on a PC all the way up to an IBM 3090. Oracle also offers a core set of tools that will fully migrate up or down. In addition, Oracle is a full-service provider of turnkey applications, consulting, education, and new technologies, such as building Web-enabled applications to leading the industry on Internet model–based solutions. Now it's time to get your feet wet. Read on!

CHAPTER
2

The "*i*" in Oracle8*i*

his chapter addresses the "*i*" in Oracle8*i*. We will have a look at the Internet computing model, at where Oracle has positioned itself to address this architecture, and at specific products Oracle has brought and is in the midst of bringing to the marketplace. This chapter is not a hands-on look at Oracle8*i* 's Internet solution, but it is designed to give you an overview of what Oracle is up to, where the company is heading, and where you should be in terms of these things. Perhaps one can hearken back to that familiar Old McDonald and his farm—the "E" in this case stands for e-commerce, the "I," for the Internet, and the "O," for Oracle—with the familiar refrain EIEIO.

Terminology

The following definitions will arm you with the technical jargon you need to make it through this chapter:

- *WWW*, or the *World Wide Web* (simply referred to as the *Web*) is a global network of interconnected hypertext servers that allow the intermingling of text, graphics, sound, and many other forms of video.

- *TCP/IP* stands for Transmission Control Protocol/Internet Protocol. Originally designed for the UNIX operating system, TCP/IP software is now available for every major kind of computer operating system. In order to access the Internet, personal computers or other types of clients require some form of TCP/IP software supplied by most vendors in generic or proprietary offerings.

- The *Internet* is a vast network of servers all using the TCP/IP protocol, connected to and accessible easily from one another.

- An *intranet* is a private network within a company, used only by internal clients. There is no access to clients outside the organization, and the network is protected from prying eyes.

- *Java* is a network-oriented programming language invented by Sun Microsystems that is specifically designed for writing applications using small program pieces (or *applets*) that are seamlessly downloaded to the client.

- *PDA* stands for personal data assistant, which, in some cases, is a fancy name for electronic organizers. In the Internet environment, we commonly hear of Windows CE and PalmPilot as industry-standard PDAs.

- *HTML* stands for hypertext markup language, used to create documents on the World Wide Web. Text is bound by tags to turn on and turn off enhancements (such as bolding and italicizing), and links can be defined that bind text or graphics in one HTML document to locations elsewhere on the Internet.

- An *end user* is the person using a canned application on the PC. A CPA using an Excel spreadsheet is an example of an end user. These are people who use computers to accomplish day-to-day tasks but who have not been trained on the inner workings of a PC.

- A *fat client* is your traditional PC system. If purchased today, it would have at least 64 megabytes of memory, 6 gigabytes of disk storage, a Pentium III–based chip, and an internal CD-ROM drive—in other words, your typical PC purchase. In the client/server world, a fat client would contain all the code/programs locally.

- An *intranet* site is where one or more applications reside that were built using Internet technologies. To access the application, you use a universal browser like Netscape Navigator or Microsoft Internet Explorer. Since it is an intranet site, the applications reside within the company firewall, but they are accessed using Internet technologies, such as TCP/IP, HTML, or Java. The primary purpose of intranet sites is to service internal customers.

- An *Internet* site is where one or more applications reside that were built using Internet technologies. To access the application, you typically use a universal browser like Netscape Navigator or Microsoft Internet Explorer. Since it is an Internet site, the applications reside outside the firewall and are accessed using Internet technologies, such as TCP/IP, HTML, or Java. The primary purpose of Internet sites is to service external customers. A typical Internet URL is *http://www.dbtinc.com*. An average Internet site typically contains marketing information.

- A *firewall* is another term for a router. Its primary purpose is to inspect network traffic and prevent unauthorized traffic from passing through. In other words the router inspects requests coming from external sources and determines if they are appropriate to pass into internal systems. For example, an e-mail message sent to Nan Sea would only be allowed to enter into the system if you actually have an employee with that name. In addition, a firewall can determine what types of services will be allowed through. For example, it might not allow a Telnet session to run.

- A *thin client* by nature is a personal computer with as little as 4MB of RAM and no hard drive, but with any range of microprocessors from a Pentium to a 32-bit RISC chip that will retail for under $1,000.00. Since the average user of a PC only uses it for functions like e-mail and word processing, why put an expensive "FAT Client/PC" on the desktop when only 10 percent of its functionality is ever really being used? Instead, you can put a machine on the desktop that only has to deal with the presentation of information, which means that it only needs a very small operating system, a small amount of memory, a very fast processor, and little or no disk storage. The best analogy to this device is the telephone. It might have some limited functionality on its own, but it is useless unless it is hooked up to the phone network.

■ The *Internet computing model* is part of Oracle's strategy to survive the information-enabled age. It features a three-tier architecture—a thin client for the presentation layer, an application server for business rules, and a database server for data storage and manipulation. The goal is to have a common set of technologies that will allow all PCs, PDAs, and any other client devices to work with all database servers, application servers, and Web servers over any network.

■ An *open system* is one that is built on open standards, as compared to a proprietary system. The classic example of this is UNIX. You can purchase the UNIX operating system from many sources, each of which is based on a core industry standard. It is interesting to note that each vendor, as a practice, always tries to put unique enhancements on its own version of the UNIX system, in order to lock you into their "open" offering.

■ A *proprietary system* is one that is built upon a company-unique standard or capability. Systems built on the Digital Equipment Corporation's VMS operating system or the IBM MVS operating system are examples of proprietary systems. If you want to use these operating systems, you must go to either the source or one of their licensees.

■ A *URL* is an Internet address. An example of a URL is *http://www.dbtinc.com*. Think of this as your roadmap to any given Internet site. The acronym URL actually stands for *Uniform Resource Locator*.

■ A computer *virus* is a software program written to disrupt and annoy the computer systems that it "infects." Sometimes these viruses can be very harmful and initialize hard disks or even cause entire systems to crash.

■ The *World Wide Web* is the graphical portion of the Internet. Since the creation of universal browsers like Netscape Navigator and Microsoft Internet Explorer, the Internet can now easily deal with all types of data from sound to video to text. With this newfound graphical capability, anyone can easily navigate the Internet. Browsers have taken the Internet from the once-sacred realm of the highly technical person to John and Jane Q. Public. The advent of their massive embrace of Web surfing has created an extremely viable commercial platform on which to do business.

- *Zero administration for Windows* is an announcement by Microsoft to deliver software to substantially bring down the administrative costs associated with desktops. With zero administration, Microsoft hopes that the day-to-day attention many PCs and the software they run require will be reduced. With a reduction in the need for human intervention, the administrative nightmare could be reduced to zero.

- *HTTP,* or the Hypertext Transfer Protocol, is used for moving hypertext files across the Internet. Basically, a *hypertext* document is one that contains links to other documents in other locations. Readers see these links commonly underlined in blue on various HTML pages as they move around the Internet.

- *FTP* is the File Transfer Protocol, used for the exchange of text or binary documents among machines connected to the Internet.

- A *LAN* is a local area network, commonly a closed computer network whose clients reside on one floor or a local geographic network within an organization.

- *Replication* is a service that allows changes to data to be stored and subsequently forwarded from a client to a central database server. Data integrity is guaranteed through the service that supports the forwarding of these transactions.

- *XML* is the Extensible Markup Language, similar in basics to HTML, but with added functionality to create user-defined tags. Thus, the standards or tag definitions used within a document are defined in that same document before they are used.

Why the Internet Computing Model

The shot heard 'round the world is a term you heard quite often if you grew up in New England. It represents the first shot fired during the American Revolution. Fact: a tiny colony was able to make a stand against the mighty empire of England, an empire so large that, somewhere within the empire, the sun was always shining. Did anyone ever envision that great corporate giants like Microsoft, HP, and IBM would be so shaken by a concept that they would rethink and restructure their pricing, alliances, and future strategies based on Oracle CEO Larry Ellison's vision of his company's Internet computing model–based solutions? Yes, this vision is a shot heard around the world.

Electronic Business

The Internet has radically changed the way companies do business. Businesses use the Internet to attract new customers, streamline supply management and distribution of goods sold, automate business operations, and make better business decisions based on data gathered from electronic transactions. Companies can integrate, if not collapse, the ordering and inventory management wings of their workforce into one central business operation. Once the process is automated, with a series of electronic applications running cataloging, product display and information, ordering, shipping, and inventory management, companies start to realize the benefits of doing business online. Forester Research, Inc., predicts that by the year 2002, Internet-based revenue in the U.S.A. alone will exceed $350 billion, and Western European revenue will have swelled from $1.2 billion in 1998 to over $64 billion by year 2001. The following advantages are inherent when leveraging the power of the Internet-based business model:

- The Internet has no geographical boundaries—organizations do not have to wait until they are "large enough" to open that store front anywhere. By nature, once on the Internet, they reach out to all corners of the globe. There are many sophisticated players in the goods distribution and shipping arena; by using the services of the experts, the dissemination of goods can be managed effectively and with a profitable return on investment.

- The dynamic content of the Internet allows companies to make available the latest product to their customers almost immediately after it is received at the warehouse. There is no need for any delay between the time materials arrive and the time clients see them in the online catalog.

- Component-based computer architecture, the sharing of resources, and the co-management of the application and data server tiers by multiple machines means less likelihood of a complete loss of service.

- Because the whole e-commerce solution is computer based, the gathering of data regarding purchasing habits of your clientele is native to the application. Each and every transaction is recorded, stored in a database, and easily accessible with sophisticated analysis software. It's almost too good to be true.

- The opportunities to attract new clientele are endless. With a mature network of Internet search engines and directory services, companies have huge electronic solutions at their fingertips to get the word out to new potential customers.

So what makes the Internet computing model different from the client perspective? Let's see ...

Does Everyone Really Need a Fat Client?

Many users today who have fat clients on their desktops (in other words, traditional PC systems that, if purchased today, would have at least 64 megabytes of memory, 8 gigabytes of disk storage, a Pentium III-based chip, and an internal CD-ROM drive) neither need nor want to deal with all that complexity. A typical user who almost exclusively uses his or her computer for e-mail and word processing would be much happier with a lighter client and a Web browser—the simpler, the better. In today's world, these users have no choice but to purchase a fully equipped PC. How many times have we heard users talk about that big paperweight on their desk?

How many times have we heard that a critical piece of information resides only on a disk drive that just broke down? Far too many times. The reason is clear: most people who use computers are very good at their jobs but not very good at backing up or even working with PCs beyond canned software like e-mail or Microsoft Word. Perhaps the machine never breaks down. What about the complexity of upgrading the software every nine months? Does a typical end user really need to deal with all these issues? Does it make sense every time a software vendor releases a new version to force our end users to upgrade their software? Do we trust that they have the necessary skill set to upgrade the software and troubleshoot the upgrade when things go wrong? Does it make sense for support people to go out to hundreds of PCs and individually upgrade them? Is this really the best use of their time and skill set? Never mind the fact that you might be doing all of these activities for someone who only uses e-mail. How many times has a network been infected with a computer virus by someone who only needs the PC for e-mail? Even if we have software that helps automate these problems, a typical fat client is a very complex device. Can you really expect to troubleshoot these problem remotely and keep it all running?

Certainly, there is a class of users out there that need PCs, and by all means, they should have access to PCs. But if you asked most users to explain what all the icons mean on their PCs, they couldn't tell and couldn't care less. So why force them to pay for all that unused and unnecessary capability? Clearly, they don't need to have all those unused applications residing on their desktops.

When was the last time you were given (or, more than likely, demanded) a more powerful desktop at your place of work? Did the upgrade take you from a mere 386DX 66 up to a Pentium or perhaps a Pentium III? What was the cost of that upgrade? When one extrapolates the cost (let's settle on about $4,000 for a powerful Pentium III with gobs of memory and local storage) across an enterprise of 400 users, all of a sudden the most recent personal computer hardware upgrade comes to $160,000. We know this could easily happen again, thanks to the advances in computer technology that are happening as we speak.

Economics at Work

Evaluating the economics of the situation is a very reliable way to determine industry and technology trends. Everyone loves a good deal. Ever go to an auction and watch people buy things just because the opening bid is so low? Ever go to a store sale and watch people buy things they really don't need just because they are on sale? These two examples validate the point that money is a very powerful motivating tool. What caused the immense popularity of the rightsizing/downsizing movement? The answer is simple: economics. It became cheaper for corporations to migrate their legacy systems onto an open system, reengineer the applications, and have the return on investment (*ROI*) pay for itself in three to five years. This caused the corporate world to wake up and rightsize.

VIP

Economics is the source of many of our technology trends. Those technology trends with the highest ROI will typically be dominant trends.

The Internet explosion is another example of economics at work. Today, it is possible for people to create an Internet store at a very low cost and have access to over 100,000,000 people. Now that corporations see the Internet as a commercially viable platform, there is a massive trend toward the creation of corporate Internet strategies. The fact that the Internet offers the perfect client, is free, and can be deployed and maintained cheaply is the reason for this trend toward Internet/intranet-aware applications.

Every PC vendor has announced price cuts and a commitment to develop a PC for under $1,000. A while back, the Gartner Group recently did a survey to determine the yearly administrative cost of a PC, which they found to be $12,000. Intel Corporation commissioned its own study and announced the yearly administrative costs to be $8,000. Whether the costs are $8,000 or $12,000, you can see why buyers are all nervous. Imagine yourself as the CIO of a corporation defending the purchase of expensive fat clients to the budget-minded CEO. With these economics at work, things are going to change quickly.

What Is Zero Administration?

In this era, every two to three years you are forced to replace your PC, even though it works perfectly well. The Microsoft business model relies on this planned obsolescence. How do they do it? Easy: they put out a new version of the operating system, let's call it Windows 2000. They start reducing support of previous versions, let's say Windows 3.1. Due to the way the software is written, certain computers are incapable of running Windows 2000. Because Windows is the only game in town, guess what? You pay up. You are forced to upgrade to newer versions of the Microsoft family of software, which, in turn, forces you to upgrade computers if you want your desktop software to keep running.

The Microsoft solution to this problem is the "Zero Administration for Windows" initiative, which is Microsoft's promise to build a core set of tools to give information system professionals new control over the desktop by automating such tasks as updating operating systems and installing applications, profiling users, and locking down desktop systems. You are still "overpurchasing" a system for the majority of the end user community, and you still have an inherently complex configuration of technology to keep working. You still have to deal with the obsolescence of the PC every two to three years, which is something that these vendors are counting on. The majority of the potential PC users in the world are not using technology. We feel this is because we don't yet have a mature network in place; a mature network would be easy to access at very high speeds and be available virtually 24 hours a day, seven days a week.

Many people believe the model of deploying on the desktop has not changed in 20 years; perhaps it's time for a new model. Workstations that address the Internet computing model represent the next logical evolution of the desktop.

The Paradigm Must Change

As the next potential stage in desktop evolution, the success of the Internet computing model is so likely that the corporate giants are reacting very quickly to its possibilities. The world is changing due to technology, and technology is changing due to the world. The world has an insatiable hunger for information, and the desktop is the key to getting at that information. The desktop paradigm must and will change to meet this need. Larry Ellison said it best when he said that until a mature network is established, we will never see a worldwide adoption of technology that is possible. Larry Ellison is right—the model is going to change. For example, look at the explosion of the Internet. As soon as a universal browser was in existence, which made it easy to navigate the Internet, the world embraced the Internet. The browser, in many ways, hides and simplifies the complexity of the Internet for the average end user. The browser represents an open standard that makes it easy for all vendors to build and deploy software. Many of the reasons the universal browser has been so successful will be put into practice when Oracle publishes the Network Computing Architecture: the company understands the power of an open standard that vendors can embrace.

Clearly, the complexity needs to be pushed back to the network, where the end user is insulated from it. With a mature network, this will be possible; only through centralization of this network will we ever be able to support the needed infrastructure. There simply are not enough specialists to deploy at every desktop;

we need to be able to concentrate specialists in central locations, instead of trying to spread them around to every fat client. With the complexity of fat clients pushed back to the mature network, we can concentrate on building devices that everyone will be able to use.

Imagine trying to keep a telephone system working if every user had access to the internals of the phone network. With the mature network model in place, the end user would not be dealing with issues like computer viruses, backups, or upgrades. Under the mature network model, these items would be handled in central locations by trained professionals. Given the potential marketplace value, we are surprised that the mature network model has not been embraced sooner.

Recognizing that the paradigm is changing, Oracle realizes we need a new architecture. Oracle knows that the corporate world is looking for this roadmap, which will enable them to survive in the Web-enabled world. That thirst for information will never be quenched until we have an architecture that can support it. Next, we will discuss Oracle's vision of the Internet computing model, which, they believe, will enable us to build and maintain the information age.

We will now have a look at the architecture that has been given many names by the industry—the two most commonly cited being the *Internet computing model* and *network computing architecture*.

The Network Computing Architecture

The Network Computing Architecture, or *NCA*, is just what the name implies—an architecture for building and integrating applications within a networked computing environment. Remember, the World Wide Web is a network computing environment. By publishing this architecture, Oracle wants to make it as easy as possible for companies to adopt and develop solutions based upon this standard. The success of the universal browsers alone is proof that an open standard that people can build to makes sense. Oracle's early development of this much-needed architecture has placed Oracle Corporation and its technologies in the center of the network computing movement and positioned Oracle as the Internet solutions company.

VIP

The Network Computing Architecture, or NCA, is exactly what its name implies: Oracle's stated architecture for building and integrating applications within a networked computing environment. Remember, the World Wide Web is a network computing environment.

What Oracle was very quick to realize was that Web computing requires a new architecture and that the corporate world is crying out to learn "how to do it." The Network Computing Architecture provides corporations with the framework for the information age: one that is portable, scalable, and extensible (able to deal with the widest range of data types from text to video), as well as providing corporations with a clear migration path from client/server to Network-enabled computing.

Unlike the client/server model, which is based on a two-tier architecture, Oracle has developed NCA architecture, which is based on three separate tiers. The client/server architecture consists of

- A *client tier* responsible for the presentation (including user interface issues) and the application itself.

- A *server tier* in which the data resides (for example, the Oracle8*i* Enterprise Edition).

The NCA architecture has three tiers, consisting of

- A *thin client tier* responsible for the presentation of information. The Network Computing Architecture assumes that thin clients occupy this tier.

- An *application server tier,* which is the layer responsible for all the business rules. In the Network Computing Architecture, it is assumed that this is a fat client.

- A *database server tier,* which is responsible for the manipulation and storage of data. Data ranges from text to number, to video on demand.

The Network Computing Architecture is also designed to take advantage of all operating systems and all hardware platforms, which allows users to choose the operating system and hardware that gives them the best price performance.

Separating the presentation tier from the application layer allows the PC functionality to reside on a thin client. Remember our definition of a thin client—as little as 4MB of RAM and no hard drive, but with any range of microprocessors, from a Pentium to a 32-bit RISC chip, that will retail for under $1,000.

The application tier now resides on a separate server from the database server tier. Software in this tier would be put on machines with a very heavy footprint: minimally, they would be on a fat client. Remember our definition of a fat client: it would have at least 64 megabytes of memory, 8 gigabytes of disk storage, a Pentium-based chip, and an internal CD-ROM drive. The point is that the application server and the database server can be moved to a machine with many more resources, perhaps a very big UNIX machine. These machines would be placed in a central location and managed by trained specialists. The end user is shielded from all the complexity.

VIP
The Network Computing Architecture is made up of the layers—the thin client layer, the application server layer, and the database server layer. You can use different operating systems and hardware platforms with the Network Computing Architecture.

So far we have discussed the Network Computing Architecture in its most simple form. The NCA envisions a world in which the database server and the application server are networked together, as well as to thin clients. As you can see, there is a lot more to the architecture than that. At the heart of this architecture are the options that plug into the middle (application server) tier as well as the upper (data server) tier. Not long ago, Oracle coined the term *data cartridge,* which was simply another way of saying the word "software." Whatever they are called, the Internet computing model is architected to allow plugging in an assortment of software components or options. It is almost impossible to think of the out-of-the-box Oracle8i Server without additional components. Let's briefly look at the nature of these components.

Optional Software Components

As we stated before, the Network Computing Architecture envisions a world in which the database server and application server all are networked together as well as to thin clients. It also envisions a world where vendors create software cartridges that can be plugged into the client tier, the application server tier, or even the database server tier. So today, as published, the architecture envisions three types of cartridges:

- Client cartridges
- Application server cartridges
- Data cartridges

The cartridges are component-based software. Simply put, a cartridge is a program component. To use a cartridge, one must install and register it. This means an application cartridge is installed on the application server and registered. A database cartridge is installed on the database server and registered, and so forth. As we stated, cartridges are component-based software, which means that cartridges would be built with PL/SQL, SQL, C++, JAVA, or even Visual Basic. A cartridge is software.

VIP
A cartridge is software. Cartridges can be built using SQL, JAVA, or what have you. To be used, they must be installed on the appropriate server and registered.

All cartridges will be able to take advantage of all other cartridges' services. The only difference is that an application cartridge will be installed on the application server, a database cartridge will be installed on the database server, and so forth. These cartridges allow applications to become very extensible. Developers can add more features by writing additional cartridges or by taking advantage of the services of other cartridges. Because the developer has the choice of where the cartridges reside, you are given more control over the various tiers.

The backbone to this whole architecture is the intercartridge exchange. This is the bus that gives cartridges the capability to talk to other cartridges. With this backbone in place, a cartridge anywhere in the network can take advantage of the services of any other cartridge. Is this approach catching on, or has it arrived and is here to stay? Let's check it out …

Success or Failure … You Decide

Oracle has given us its version of an architecture that can meet the challenge of the information age. We are facing a new paradigm: a world with thin clients in which we have true Web-enabled computing. The network computing age is upon us. If we hope to truly realize the potential of technology, then we need to be doing a few things differently. We have no right to call this the information age when most of the world has no access to that information. The goal of this book is to give you enough information that you can make a balanced decision as to what is right for your business. After a thorough evaluation, we see the thin client playing a much stronger role in information technology. Let's round out the discussion with a look at Oracle8*i*'s Internet-centric product line.

Internet Computing Products

The Internet computing model partitions applications into three pieces. The client, or the *display layer,* is most commonly the desktop PC, running a Web browser. This layer is responsible for the presentation and display of information. The user interacts with the other pieces using this display layer. The middle tier, commonly referred to as the *application layer,* is where all the business logic is implemented. The upper tier is the *data server,* where information is stored with which the users interact as the systems operate. Oracle8*i* is positioned to position Oracle as the data-centric Internet application platform. Internet systems are playing a bigger role in corporate systems structure, especially in the electronic commerce arena. Let's conduct a high-level overview of Oracle's Internet computing solutions.

Oracle8*i* Lite

This product is a player in Oracle's solution for mobile computing. It is based on Oracle's core mobile products, allowing applications built with Oracle8*i* to be accessed by a diverse user community, be they in-house or on the road. Developers can create Java/HTML applications that run offline as well as online. Often home-based Internet users complain of the cost of maintaining a persistent connection to the network; Oracle8*i* Lite makes this constraint a thing of the past. Oracle8*i* Lite is the heart of Oracle's Internet solution when it comes to servicing the needs of the mobile corporate user. It will be discussed in more detail later in the chapter, using version 3.6 as a base point.

Oracle8*i* Appliance

The Oracle8*i* Appliance addresses customers' desire to have a dedicated database server that, in cooperation with Oracle's Internet file system, leverages the "*i*" in Oracle's Internet computing model. The Oracle8*i* Appliance permits the direct deployment of the Oracle8*i* database on Intel-based hardware. Out of the box, the Oracle8*i* Appliance is preconfigured with the Oracle8*i* database, booting just like a regular Intel-based machine. All system functions and access are provided by Oracle Enterprise Manager. With the Appliance, much of the common operating system overhead required to manage access to the database is removed. Hewlett-Packard (HP) was the first hardware vendor to support the Appliance, with a commitment to build and sell Oracle8*i*-centric hardware with only enough operating system components to support access to the database. Since its announcement, agreements have been reached with Dell Computers for their 63*xx* series of Power Edge systems, as well as Siemens AG for their Primergy line of servers based on the Intel Pentium II processor.

Internet File System (*i*FS)

The Internet File System, *i*FS, combines the power of the Oracle relational database engine with the simplicity and friendliness of the traditional file system. Virtually any file format can be dropped into the Oracle8*i* database and stored in its native format. Once there, search and query activities familiar to users of database technology solutions can be performed on that content as well as more traditional text. *i*FS documents can be accessed as files even when resident in the Oracle8*i* database by the traditional Web browser as well as the Windows Explorer interface, FTP clients, or even e-mail programs. The end user relates to the *i*FS as just another volume on the corporate network.

The following benefits are inherent when organizations use Oracle's *i*FS solution:

- Document storage directly in the database simplifies application developers' integration of different document types. Be it a spreadsheet, a word processing file, or image or sound files, centralized storage simplifies the integration of different document types into corporate applications.

- System administration of Oracle *i*FS is the same as traditional network management, since *i*FS is accessed using techniques, processes, and procedures familiar to the management personnel.

- The *i*FS can be accessed using the SMB (*server message block*) protocol for Windows 95/98 and NT; this communication mechanism enables Windows drag-and-drop functionality as well as editing documents directly on an *i*FS device. HTTP is used for browser-based access, and popular e-mail protocols (such as SMTP or POP3) are used when *i*FS is accessed from many popular e-mail clients.

- Messaging hooks in *i*FS allow users to forward and reply to files as if they were e-mail messages. Developers can use this messaging feature to trigger electronic communications between users when certain events occur. This e-mail feature can be used for auditing purposes if organizations want to track who did what to what item and when.

*i*Connect

Using *i*Connect, developers can embed replication in applications, allowing mobile computer users to receive information from and send information to corporate database servers. Wireless replication is supported, with deliberate hooks designed to compensate for the unfortunate unreliability of radio networks. This form of replication is done in conjunction with Oracle Mobile Agents. Dial-up or LAN-based replication is supported by *i*Connect accessing the Oracle8*i* database using Oracle's Net8 transport mechanism.

Project Panama

This emerging server technology is expected to revolutionize the use of mobile devices hooked up to the Internet, be they hand-held PDAs or mobile phones. Most current Internet applications expect the client to be a Windows-based personal computer running one of the assortment of Web browsers such as Netscape Navigator. The telecommunications industry has worked together to define a new *WAP* or wireless application protocol to facilitate Internet access from these small hand-held devices. At present, many applications are written with separate code segments designed to handle interaction with a variety of client types. Project Panama is designed to allow development of a set of Internet content with transparent generation of device-specific output for the assortment of wireless products on the market today and in the future. Project Panama can dynamically generate generic XML format documents, allowing more widespread sharing of data.

What's Next

Let's leave with a rhetorical question, and our comeback:

   Q.   Is Oracle doing anything especially unique and different than the host of other information technology vendors?

   A.   Yes and no. No—they have similar solutions, even though they are crafted in their unique way. Yes—they are a leader and are adding much greater impetus to the word *total* when they speak of their commitment to providing *total solutions*.

   In the next chapter, we will discuss Oracle8*i* and object-relational technology. *Object-relational technology* is a marriage of a standard relational database management solution (the Oracle Server) with *objects*—real-world collections of items of information such as purchase orders, bills of sale, inventory tickets, and the like. The object-relational technology hooks of Oracle8*i* have helped maintain the company's share of the market. Allons!

CHAPTER
3

Oracle8*i* and Object Relational Technology

I n this chapter, we will review the concepts of object-oriented databases (the foundation of Oracle8*i*), discuss the object-relational database model, and then proceed to an overview of Oracle8*i* and its new features. We relate back to examples whenever possible.

NOTE
In many places throughout this chapter, we refer to Oracle8 (the version number) rather than Oracle8i (the release number). Many of the object-related features we discuss in Oracle8i appeared in Oracle8 release 8.0.x.

Terminology

The following definitions will arm you with the technical jargon to make it through this chapter:

- An *array* in Oracle8*i* is an ordered set of built-in types or objects, called *elements*. Each array element is of the same type. Each element has an index, which is a number corresponding to the element's position in the array.

- *Encapsulation* means that each object within the database has a well-defined interface with distinct borders. This has the direct benefit of preventing illegal access to the data.

- *Inheritance* is the capability to create new classes of objects as specializations of existing classes.

- *Nested tables* are another new collection type provided with Oracle8*i*. A nested table is a table that appears as a column in another table, yet you can perform the same operations on it as on other tables.

- *Objects* are software representations of real-world entities.

- *Object views* are an extension of the traditional relational view mechanism that allows you to treat relational data as if it were object entities.

- *Object-relational database* is the term used to describe a database that is the evolution of a relational database, that now has object-oriented capabilities embedded within it. In other words, it is a database that is a hybrid between the relational model and the object-oriented model. Most analysts believe this is the future of computing.

■ *Polymorphism* is the capability of objects to react differently to an identical message.

■ Every row in an Oracle table has a unique *rowid*. This rowid uniquely identifies that row of data within the database. Before Oracle8, a rowid could be remembered using the acronym *BARF*. BARF means block, address, record, and file ID. (We learned this trick from Scott Martin, who in a previous life was an Oracle Kernel Developer.) When you put these all together, you have BARF—the unique physical location of a row within the database. In the following listing you will see the output of an SQL statement that selected rowid from an pre-Oracle8 database (see the *extended ROWID format* definition for what the Oracle8*i* rowid looks like):

```
select rowid, substr(rowid,1,8) "BLOCK",
       substr(rowid,15,4) "FILE", substr(rowid,10,4) "ROW"
  from tablex;
  ROWID               BLOCK     FILE   ROW
  ------------------  --------  ----   ----
  00000DD5.0000.0001  00000DD5  0001   0000
  00000DD5.0001.0001  00000DD5  0001   0001
```

■ The *optimizer* is a set of internal routines that come to life when Oracle processes queries. This optimizer ensures that the most efficient path is selected to access the data that needs to be assembled for a query, as well as ensuring that the execution plan selected provides the best throughput and turnaround time.

■ *VARRAY* is a new type recognized by Oracle8. Remember, an array is an ordered set of built-in types or objects, called elements. Oracle8 implementation of arrays is of variable size, which is why arrays are called VARRAYs. In Oracle8, when you create the array, you must always specify the maximum size. The statement **create type price as varray(100) of number;** is an example of a VARRAY declaration. Remember when you create a new type, the database does not actually go out and allocate any database space; it merely defines a new type and stores it in the system catalog. For example, you might use the **type** clause in a **create table** statement. You would use it as the data type of a column. **create table car (car_name varchar2(25), car_value price);** is how this user-defined type is used.

■ The Oracle8*i* Server incorporates a new *extended ROWID format,* which supports new features in Oracle8*i* such as table partitions, index partitions, and clusters. Remember, rowid uniquely identifies a row of data within an

Oracle database. The extended rowid in Oracle8*i* includes the information in the Oracle7 rowid, plus the data object number. The data object number is an identification number that the server assigns to schema objects in the database, such as nonpartitioned tables or partitions. The following listing shows the look of this extended rowid:

```
SQL*Plus 8.1.5.0.0 - Production on Fri Jun 19 07:56:01 2009
(c) Copyright 1999 Oracle Corporation. All rights reserved.
Connected to:
Oracle8i Enterprise Edition Release 8.1.5.0.0 - Production
With the Partitioning and Java Options
PL/SQL Release 8.1.5.0 - Production
SQL> create table sales
  2  (invoice_no number,
  3    sale_year      int not null,
  4    sale_month     int not null,
  5    sale_day       int not null)
  6   partition by range (sale_year,sale_month,sale_day)
  7   (partition p1 values less than (1994,04,01) tablespace p1,
  8    partition p2 values less than (1994,07,01) tablespace p2,
  9    partition p3 values less than (maxvalue,maxvalue,maxvalue)
 10                            tablespace p3);
Table created.
SQL> insert into sales values (100,1994,2,1);
1 row created.
SQL> insert into sales values (200,1994,6,1);
1 row created.
SQL>
SQL> select rowid from sales;
ROWID
------------------
AAAAfOAAFAAAAADAAA
AAAAfPAAGAAAAADAAA
```

NOTE

We like to call this new rowid OBARF—Object, Block, Address, Row, and File.

Every row in a nonclustered table of an Oracle database is assigned a unique rowid that corresponds to the physical address of a row's row piece (the initial row piece if the row is chained among multiple row pieces). In the case of clustered tables, rows in different tables that are in the same data block can have the same rowid.

What Is an Object-Oriented Database?

As we have all heard many times before, Oracle 8.0 was Oracle's first version of the database to incorporate object-oriented technology, and thus Oracle 8.0 was the corporation's first object-relational database. Notice we used the term *object-relational database* because this implementation is not a pure object-oriented database, nor is it just a relational database. It now represents a hybrid of the two, so let's call it an object-relational database.

VIP

An object-relational database is a term used to describe a database that has evolved from the relational model into a hybrid database that contains both relational technology and object technology.

For many years there have been debates as to whether the next generation of mainstream database technology would be an object-oriented database or whether it would be an SQL-based database with object-oriented extensions. We feel that there are several reasons that the object-relational approach will dominate:

- Object-relational databases such as Oracle8*i* are upward-compatible with users' current relational databases, so users can migrate their current relational databases and applications to Oracle8*i* without rewriting them, and then they can migrate their databases and applications to the object-oriented features of Oracle8*i* when they choose.

- Previous pure object-oriented databases did not support the standard ad hoc query capabilities of SQL databases; this can be a major problem when needs arise that had not been anticipated in the original design. It was also a problem in interfacing standard SQL tools to pure object-oriented databases. In fact, one of the major reasons the corporate world was so quick to embrace relational databases was this capability to create ad hoc queries.

- The integration of object-oriented and relational representations in Oracle8*i* is semantically clean and considerably more powerful than either relational or object-oriented representations alone. This makes the design of compact, efficient databases much easier.

As you can see, many compelling factors will cause the industry to adopt the evolution of the relational database into the object-relational database. One of our favorite reasons is based on the simple rule: *water will always follow the path of least resistance, and so will people.* In other words, people will go with what they feel most comfortable with. Remember the Apple computer law that Apple Corporation tried to pass in the United States? They tried to get a law passed in the United States that would give them special tax treatment, to help them donate computers into the schools. They learned as a corporation that by getting children familiar with Apple computers early on, as they moved into the corporate world, they would want to use Apple computers. This would result in future business.

Today, Oracle has won over the enterprise. People already see Oracle as a mission-critical database able to get them the results they need. People are very comfortable with the technology they bring to the corporate world. Their preference will be to go with the Oracle implementation of the relational database as long as they can bring the key features of object-oriented technologies. Well, Oracle8i represents just that. At this point, we feel they have won the battle and the war. It's also interesting to note that many industry leaders would now concur with this.

To help you appreciate and understand what Oracle8i means to the industry and why object-relational databases will become the standard, we will first discuss object-oriented technologies and then provide an overview of Oracle8i and its key changes.

VIP

An object-oriented database is one that can store data, the relationship of the data, and the behavior of the data (that is, the way it interacts with other data).

Unlike the relational database approach—which deals with data at the lowest possible level, a series of columns and rows—the object-oriented approach deals with data at a much higher level; it deals with the objects surrounding the data. In an object-oriented database, when dealing with the customer, you deal with an object called "customer." When dealing with an order, you reference an object called "order." Since an object database understands the object customer and all its relationships, it can easily deal with the object customer and all that is needed to work with it.

In the relational model, order is really a combination of many different tables, with intersection tables holding all the attributes needed to support and maintain an order. In the object model, the database has intelligence about the interrelationships. This is not the case in the relational model. When a change is made to the relational model, it usually translates into a whole new series of tables that must be developed if the model is to continue to work. These relationships must be recrafted by a database designer.

Let's take a closer look at when a customer places an order in a relational database. A number of tables are needed to support that activity. There may be a customer table, an inventory table, a price table, an inventory_price table, a line_item_table, a customer_history table, and so on. In order to manipulate these tables, the programmer must craft the needed code with the required links between tables.

As you can see, the simple act of placing an order requires a number of tables. Rows and columns in tables contain information required for the assembly of the order. A single change to the order process can have a major impact on the underlying tables that support it, requiring a database designer to come in to craft the new relationships and their associated tables to represent those relationships. In the object-oriented model, this is not the case. In fact, it assumes that these relationships will change, and that change is just a natural occurrence and progression.

What Is an Object?

Objects are software representations of real-world entities. To capture the features and capabilities of the real world, objects consist of both attributes and operational information. Remember, in an object-oriented database, the data dictionary not only stores (and allows you to understand) the relationship of one object to another, but also understands the behaviors of the object.

VIP
Objects are software representations of real-world entities.

What Is a Class?

When objects are similar to one another in behaviors and other attributes, they can be put together into a class. This concept of classes, parent classes, subclasses, and superclasses allows for a level of abstraction for grouping objects. Think of a *class* as a template for objects. This helps you in managing very complex objects. This capability to group by class also allows objects to take advantage of similarities of behaviors and other characteristics they share.

VIP
Classes are templates for objects.

Encapsulation

One of the basics of the object-oriented model is the support of encapsulation. *Encapsulation* is when the data is bound to the object so that access to the data can only happen through the behaviors approved or accepted by that object. This has the direct benefit of protecting the data from illegal access.

From a developer's perspective, objects are an encapsulation of data and behaviors. They can be thought of as programming black boxes. Think of objects as collections of code and data that have the capability to function independently. This is a very powerful capability.

A question that springs up immediately is "does encapsulation violate the relational rule of data independence?" We think not. One of the pillars of object-oriented programming is encapsulation. Encapsulation includes the capability to access objects and their data only through the behaviors approved or accepted by a given object. This contradicts the fundamental principle of relational databases, known as *data independence*. According to the relational model as defined by Dr. Codd and Chris Date, any data can be accessed in an ad hoc, independent manner.

At first glance, you might think it was impossible to have data that was independent from the application while allowing encapsulation. One easily jumps to the conclusion that these two differences would make the relational model incompatible with the object-oriented model, but this is not the case.

In the object-oriented model, the data behaviors are stored within the database, and they are not external to the database. Since the data behaviors are within the database, this scheme does not jeopardize the independence of applications from the data. This is the basis of the law of data independence—the applications, be they SQL or other ad hoc tools, are independent of the data itself.

Database Triggers

We suppose a case could be made that relational databases have always had a form of encapsulation through the use of database triggers. But then, to support encapsulation, that would mean creating a trigger for every possible method of accessing the data. Our experience has taught us this would not be practical. In fact, if you were to try to implement encapsulation through database triggers, overall database performance would degrade.

Every time you accessed a table, a corresponding trigger would need to fire. This fact alone causes the database to do twice the work it normally would to access the data. The other problem we commonly see is that many times these triggers are not well written, a fact that will very quickly destroy database performance in itself. So in practice, we see very limited use of database triggers.

We do want to make the point that triggers are a very powerful tool within a relational database when used correctly. But they were never intended as a tool to give you the power of encapsulation.

Extensibility

Extensibility is the capability of an object-oriented database to add new objects and their associated behaviors without affecting the other objects and applications. Since data can be encapsulated with objects, this capability of extensibility gives the object model the capability to handle nonstandard data situations. This is a very powerful feature.

Inheritance

Think of *inheritance* as a form of code sharing. As a new class of objects is defined, it can be defined in terms of an existing class or what is known as the base class. So as lower-level objects are created, they inherit or access the data and behaviors associated with all classes above them.

The class of objects derived from the base class typically augments or redefines the existing structure and behavior of the base class. Another way of thinking of inheritance is that you typically create new classes as specializations of existing classes. You usually derive classes for the following reasons:

■   You want to implement the same code but have different behaviors associated with it. For example, a nurse class might be treated differently than a doctor class, even though they all belong to the class of hospital employees.

■   You might want to incrementally extend the behavior of the base class. Now that you have created a specialized class called doctor, you can tailor code segments to give the doctor class special abilities. This is a way to add functionality to the system.

■   You might want to provide for different implementations of the system.

VIP

Inheritance is the capability to create new classes of objects as specializations of existing classes.

There are two different types of inheritance:

- **Data inheritance:** This is when a data element can inherit additional attributes from other data elements in the class.

- **Function/object inheritance:** This is when an object can inherit data and attributes from another object in its class.

Think of inheritance as building blocks of code; you can take advantage of behaviors that have already been developed. Suppose you have created an object called "states." When you create another object called "east_of _Mississippi," it is able to inherit all the things the base class understands about states and build from there. Fact—all states have capitals; therefore, the east_of_Mississippi object, having inherited characteristics of the state class, has a capital.

Polymorphism

Polymorphism is the capability of two different objects to behave differently when receiving the same message. The concept of polymorphism parallels the real world, in which identical messages are received every day, yet they are reacted to differently.

Let's take the simple act of sitting on the beach in the sun for an hour. Some of us are very fair-skinned people. If we sit on the beach in the sun for an hour, we will come out looking as red as a boiled lobsta (remember, in New England lobster is pronounced "lobsta"). Some people are of Caribbean heritage; they look as tanned as can be. Yet we all received the same dose of sun.

VIP

Polymorphism is the capability of objects to react differently to an identical message. An object reacts differently according to the information supplied, and it understands the context of the information that has been input.

Object-Oriented Technologies Summary

The cornerstone of object-oriented technology consists of the following things:

- Objects
- Classes
- Encapsulation
- Extensibility
- Inheritance
- Polymorphism

As you can see, these types of capabilities allow for a very powerful database capability. This database can learn from itself and reuse elements when it makes sense. Additionally, it can deal with very complex objects at a very simple level. This overview of object-oriented technologies will help you better understand Oracle8i and where the future of database technologies is headed. Oracle8i is an implementation of an object-relational database whose beginnings are in relational technology. This database's future is an evolution into object-oriented technologies. This is just the tip of the iceberg of the object-oriented features in Oracle8. You should appreciate and understand that Oracle8i's capabilities to support mission-critical, enterprise-wide applications go beyond the capability to create objects. Using your foundation of object-oriented technology, let's take a closer look at Oracle8i.

Oracle8i—An Overview

The goal when building Oracle8i was to manage your corporate data, no matter what type of data it is. This includes structured data and nonstructured data. Oracle8i can store that data in the most appropriate model for your applications and situation. If that means the pure relational model, then leave it that way. If that means taking advantage of objects, then Oracle8i has object support. If it means storing it in a multidimensional format, that is fine, too. Whatever makes it easy for you to be successful in your enterprise, Oracle8i can handle.

Oracle Corporation recognizes that there are many ways corporations use technologies. For some, it is online transaction processing; for others, it is decision support. Whatever the needs of your business, Oracle8i has been developed to deal with your corporate applications. Table 3-1 illustrates features that Oracle Corporation built into the Oracle8i database that allow it to be your source of one-stop shopping for the enterprise.

Key Focus Areas of Oracle8i

The key areas of focus when building Oracle8i are expected to be the following:

- High-end online transaction processing (*OLTP*) and data warehouse requirements

- Object-relational extensions

- Performance, manageability, and functional enhancements throughout

It should be no surprise to anyone that Oracle wants to own the corporate enterprise database. Oracle wants to manage all your data. Oracle recognizes that to do this, to attain this goal, it must be able to manage very large databases; this is the key to managing the demanding needs of the data warehouse as well as large high-end OLTP systems. Today no one runs an airline reservation system on a relational database, yet with Oracle8i, this would be possible.

Oracle8i: How Many Users and How Big Can It Get

Today, of the 20 largest databases in the world, 15 run on DB2. Oracle8i will be changing the landscape. Today, Oracle8i can scale to support over 10,000 users. Today, Oracle8i can support a database over 100 terabytes (where a terabyte is 1,099,511,627,776 bytes) in size. These abilities are critical to supporting high-end OLTP environments and very large data warehouse projects. Oracle8i has greatly

Any	Supports
Data Type	Scalar, text, video, spatial, image, user-defined
Data Model	Relational, multidimensional, object-oriented
Application	Operations, decision support, collaboration, commerce

TABLE 3-1. *What Oracle8i Is Designed To Support*

improved availability features and utilities to improve manageability; these features are crucial to keeping very large databases running.

VIP

With Oracle8i, you can now support 10,000+ users on a single node with a database over 100 terabytes in size.

Partitioning and Parallelism

One of the easiest ways we have found to work on a complicated problem is to break it into smaller, simpler problems. That is what partitioning is all about—the ability to break the database into smaller, more manageable pieces, and then to work with those pieces independently. With Oracle8i, you now have this ability.

We find that when we want a job done quickly, we inevitably ask for help. A team effort will always accomplish the task much quicker than an individual working alone. This is what parallel execution is all about—the ability to break a job into many smaller jobs that can be worked on in parallel. Jobs that used to take hours can now be accomplished in minutes. Let's take a closer look at Oracle8i and partitioning.

ORACLE8I: TABLE AND INDEX PARTITIONING
With Oracle8i, you have now the ability to partition tables and indexes. With this ability to partition, Oracle now has provided you with the tools you need to work with very large tables and indexes.

VIP

Partitioning is the ability to break tables and indexes into smaller, more manageable pieces.

When a table or index is partitioned, the column definitions, the constraint definitions, and the index column definitions must stay the same. For example, if you **create index life_cereal** consisting of column corey_col, abbey_col, and ault_col, this definition of the index will be the same for each partitioned piece.

What can change, and most likely will, is the storage definition and other physical attributes. For example, you can fine-tune the storage characteristics for each separate partition.

VIP

Under Oracle8, partitions can have different physical attributes. In other words, partitions can be placed in physically different locations.

For example, you would typically break a very large table into separate partitions, each stored on a separate tablespace. You do this many times to achieve the following things:

- Allow for better I/O load balancing. This is why you would typically have each partition mapped to a physically separate disk drive.

- Improve and enhance backup and recovery capability. Oracle8i supports the concept of partition independence; we will go over this in more detail later in this chapter.

- Minimize the possibility of data corruption. A corruption is local to one partition.

- Assist the archiving process by allowing the oldest information to be stored in its own partition and more easily moved elsewhere.

The following listing illustrates the syntax for how to partition a table into one or more pieces:

```
create table …
( col1    number,
  col2    number,
  …                  )
partition by range ( col1, col2 )
  ( partition p1 values less than ( …,… ) tablespace p1,
    partition p2 values less than ( …,… ) tablespace p2);
```

Using data stored within a table, you are able to determine how and where the information will be loaded. For example, you might have all customers' last names beginning with the letters A–C go into partition one, and all customers that have a last name beginning with the letters D–Z go into partition two.

The following listing shows you an example of an index being partitioned into two pieces. All customers with last names less than N end up in tablespace ts1. All other customers end up in tablespace ts2. Notice the use of **maxvalue**:

```
create index customer_idx
    on customer (customer_last_name, customer_first_name)
  global partition by range (customer_last_name)
          (partition values less than ('N') tablespace ts1,
            partition values less than (maxvalue) tablespace ts2);
```

With Oracle8i, you also gain the ability to create both global indexes and local indexes. A *local index* is one that is only local to a particular partition. A *global index* is one that spans many partitions. It is outside the scope of this book to get into the many grueling details of local indexes versus global indexes and all the derivatives. Suffice it to say that when an index is localized to a particular partition, you can use this fact to your advantage. You can fine-tune performance on a particular partition. You can also minimize the impact of certain activities down to a particular partition.

Let's now take a closer look at the concept of partition independence. We hinted at some of this functionality when we talked about why you would partition.

PARTITION INDEPENDENCE   Oracle8i supports the concept of *partition independence*. As we discussed earlier in this chapter, partitioning can make backup and recovery easier. With Oracle8i, it is possible to recover just a partition, since it supports partition independence. This makes it possible to perform concurrent maintenance operations on different partitions of the same table or index. With Oracle8, it is also possible to support **select** and DML operations that are unaffected by maintenance operations.

This means it is possible to load data using the direct path load. This method of loading data writes directly to the partition and eliminates database logging. This is the fastest possible way to load data into an Oracle8i database. This is a critical capability to support very large databases. While the load is running, other partitions have applications issuing **select** and DML operations against them.

VIP

Oracle8i supports partition independence. This means operations such as database recovery or direct path loading can be happening on one partition while applications are running DML and SQL operations on other partitions.

Partition independence is particularly important for operations that involve data movement. Such operations may take a long time (minutes, hours, or even days). Partitioning can reduce the window of unavailability on other partitions to a short time (few seconds) during operations that involve data movement, provided there are no interpartition stored constructs (global indexes and referential integrity constraints).

This capability to take a database and break its tables and indexes into partitions is a very powerful capability. It makes it possible to deploy mission-critical applications on multiterabyte databases. It makes it possible to support thousands of users. To put it bluntly, partitioning is a very big deal.

The fact is, Murphy's law always strikes when you least expect it. Remember Murphy's law—"what can go wrong will, at the worst possible moment." The bigger the database, the more likely a problem. Another way of saying it—the good news is that your disk drives only have a 1 in 100 failure rate over a one-year period. The bad news is that you have 500 disk drives. The point is that you will have database disasters strike in very large databases. At times, you will have to rebuild portions of the database. With Oracle8, it is now possible to break the database into smaller, more manageable pieces and load those partitions without affecting the rest of the database. The capability to back up and recover independently is critical. Again, partitioning is a very big deal.

REFERENCING A PARTITION   With Oracle8*i*, partition names can optionally be referenced in DDL and DML statements. They can also be referenced when using import and export utilities. This capability to specify partition names in DDL and DML commands coupled with the concept of partition independence is why you can back up and recover partitions independently.

VIP
Oracle8i supports incomplete tablespace recovery. This should only be done with the help of trained experts. This is a very difficult operation to perform.

The following listing illustrates some SQL statements against partitioned information:

```
alter table sales drop partition prt4;
alter table sales add partition prt4 values
     less than ('970523') tablespace ts4;
alter table sales drop partition prt4;
alter table sales modify partition prt4 unusable local indexes;
alter table sales modify partition prt4 rebuild unusable local indexes;
alter table sales rename partition prt4 to sale_prt4;
alter table sales truncate partition prt4 drop storage;
alter index cust_idx rebuild partition prt4 nologging;
alter index cust_idx modify partition prt4 unusable;
export scott/tiger file=exp.dmp
     tables=(scott.sales:prt4, scott.sales:prt2)
```

As you can see from this listing, Oracle8*i* partition names can optionally be referenced in DDL and DML statements. Yes, it is now possible to manage 100-terabyte databases.

Parallelism

As we stated earlier, parallelism is the ability to break a task into many smaller jobs that can be worked on in parallel. Jobs that used to take hours can now be accomplished in minutes.

Oracle8*i* Parallel Server

Oracle8*i* supports many different forms of parallelism. Figure 3-1 illustrates the capability to have loosely coupled machines all talking to the same database and disk farm. When we use the term *loosely coupled*, we mean that machines do not share memory. This capability to configure Oracle8*i* in Parallel Server mode provides the customer a combination of high availability combined with high performance.

Oracle8*i* Parallel Server provides you with enhanced very high availability, since you now have two or more machines doing the work normally done by one. In Figure 3-1, we illustrate the fact that one machine is unavailable, yet you still have three other machines able to access the database. This configuration gives you high fault tolerance using a nonproprietary platform.

You also get the expanded capability or additional processing power. If your organization outgrows one machine's capability, add a second machine. Oracle8*i* Parallel Server scales in performance as you add additional nodes.

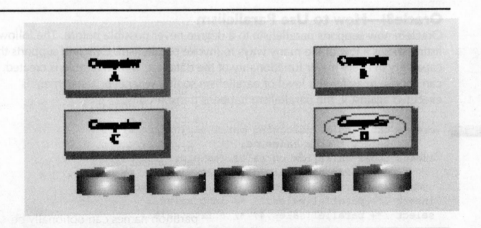

FIGURE 3-1. *Oracle8i Parallel Server*

Oracle8i—More Parallelism

Oracle8i supports parallel **select**, **insert**, **update**, **delete**, and **recovery**. This means that you can instruct the database to make certain operations work in parallel. An operation that is working in parallel works something like this:

1. The given task (**insert**, **update**, **delete**, **select**) is broken into smaller, separate tasks based upon the degree of parallelism chosen.

2. If the degree chosen was 3 for the given task (let's say **select** is broken into three separate **select** statements), each parallel **select** statement would work on a separate portion of the whole.

3. The tasks are executed.

4. The tasks are finished and the results are merged together.

5. The results are presented back to the user.

Figure 3-2 illustrates this process. If a typical **select** takes an hour, by having three separate tasks working on it, Oracle8i can bring its execution and processing time down substantially. Tasks that never could be run in a day can now be run in parallel in a fraction of the time.

Oracle8i—How to Use Parallelism

Oracle8i now supports parallelism to a degree never possible before. The following listing shows a few of the many ways to invoke parallelism. Oracle8i supports this capability in every major functionality of the database. When a table is created, you can choose to assign it a level of parallelism so that whenever a statement is executed against it, the parallelism happens transparently.

```
create table sales nologging parallel (degree 4) as
      select * from sales_ne;
create index sales_idx on sales (sale_dt)
      nologging parallel (degree 3);
update /*+ parallel(sales,4) */ sales set c1=c1+1;
insert /*+ parallel(sales,2) */ into sales …
select /*+ parallel(sales,4) */ * from sales;
```

Parallelism is completely configurable in Oracle8. You can now use it to help you get information out of the database in minutes; you can also use it to recover a database in parallel in a fraction of the time it used to take.

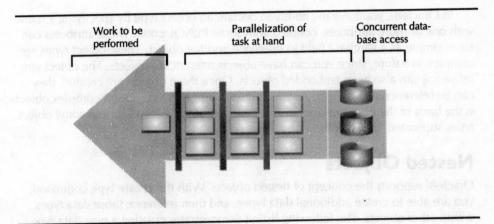

Work to be performed

Parallelization of task at hand

Concurrent database access

FIGURE 3-2.   *Parallel execution*

Oracle8*i* Backup and Recovery

The backup and recovery process has been reengineered in Oracle8*i*. It has more automation and more audit trails than ever before. In addition, Oracle is working more closely with third-party vendors to provide you with more options than ever before. Oracle realizes that in order to be successful in this arena, they need the best possible tools.

Oracle8*i*: Objects and New Database Objects

As we have discussed earlier, the relational model is used to represent data as a series of tables with columns and attributes. Oracle8*i* is an object-relational database. This means it has object-oriented technologies embedded within it. With this in mind, we would expect to be able to build complex object types in Oracle8*i* (complex in the sense we would expect you to be able to have objects within objects, and some ability to bind or encapsulate methods with those objects). Well, you won't be disappointed. Oracle8*i* does support complex object types.

VIP
A method is a procedure or function that is part of the object type definition and that can operate on the object type data attributes.

In Oracle8*i*, you have the ability to declare an object type by specifying a name with one or more attributes, coupled with some PL/SQL code. These attributes can be as simple as a varchar2 field to reference another object. These object types are complex in nature, since you can have objects referencing objects. The object you reference can also have embedded objects. Once these objects are created, they can be referenced elsewhere. As you can see, this ability to support complex objects is the basis of the object-relational database. Let's take a closer look at some object types supported in Oracle8*i*.

Nested Objects

Oracle8*i* supports the concept of *nested objects*. With the **create type** command, you are able to create additional data types, and then reference those data types within other objects. The following listing demonstrates creating a new data type called room_capacity_type:

```
create type room_capacity_type as object(
     auditorium_setting            integer,
     table_setting                 integer,
     standing_room_setting         integer)
/
```

The following listing references the newly created type in the conference_facility table. The type room_capacity_type exists with or without the table conference_facility. This type can be used in many different ways and in many different locations. This capability to extend the database with additional types is a very powerful capability. It is also a very powerful capability to help simplify the complexity of dealing with complex data types:

```
SQL*Plus 8.1.5.0.0 - Production on Fri Jun 19 07:56:01 2009
(c) Copyright 1999 Oracle Corporation. All rights reserved.
Connected to:
Oracle8i Enterprise Edition Release 8.1.5.0.0 - Production
With the Partitioning and Java Options
PL/SQL Release 8.1.5.0 - Production
SQL> create table conference_facility (
  2      room_name                   varchar2(20),
  3      room_settings               room_capacity_type);
Table created.
SQL> -- ** now let's insert into the table **
SQL> insert into conference_facility values (
  2      'GREAT HALL',  room_capacity_type(500, 200, 1000));
1 row created.
```

VIP
*Data types created with the **create type** command
exist independently of any table.*

VARRAY

A new type recognized in Oracle8*i* is VARRAY. An array is an ordered list of
elements. In Oracle8*i*, they are called VARRAY because the array is of variable size.
When we think of an array, we think of the mail boxes you see at old hotels when
you check in. Each room in the hotel would have a slot in this big box holding the
room keys. In Oracle8*i*, an *array* is an ordered set of built-in types or objects called
elements. Since the array is variable size, when you create it in Oracle8*i*, you must
always specify the maximum size. This listing uses VARRAY:

```
create type price as varray(100) of number
/
```

It is interesting to note that when you create this array in Oracle8*i*, the database
does not actually go out and allocate any database space; it merely defines a new
type and stores it in the system catalog. It is possible to reference this array in
another table, as the data type of a column. For example:

```
create table car (car_name varchar2(25), car_val price);
```

This ability to support arrays of variable size is a very nice enhancement in
Oracle8*i*. Many times in our careers as developers, this functionality would have
made our jobs much easier. We look forward to using this newfound ability to
manipulate order sets of objects.

TYPES Within TYPES

With Oracle8*i*, it is possible to use types within types. Another way of saying this is
that a type can be an attribute of another type. The following listing shows the
address type being referenced by the employee_type:

```
SQL*Plus 8.1.5.0.0 - Production on Fri Jun 19 07:56:01 2009
(c) Copyright 1999 Oracle Corporation. All rights reserved.
Connected to:
Oracle8i Enterprise Edition Release 8.1.5.0.0 - Production
With the Partitioning and Java Options
PL/SQL Release 8.1.5.0 - Production
```

```
SQL> create type address_type as object (
  2     street                    varchar2(40),
  3     city                      varchar2(30),
  4     state                     varchar2(2),
  5     zip_cd                    number(5))
/

Type created.
SQL> create type employee_type as object (
  2     name                      varchar2(30),
  3     hire_date                 date,
  4     address                   address_type,
  5     member procedure          give_raise,
  6     member function           get_salary return number)
/

Type created.
SQL>
```

This capability to create new types is a very powerful feature in Oracle8i. This is a great tool to help you standardize the types of like objects. By creating common types for frequently used items such as addresses, you can avoid a lot of issues down the road. We all know that standards are a wonderful tool for keeping production environments up and running. Types can be referenced across the database. The following listing shows types being used in a variety of different ways:

```
declare
    p1              person_type;
    addr            address;
    begin...
create procedure get_emp_id
        (employee              emp_type) as ...
create function get_emp (name varchar2)
        return emp_type as ...
```

Methods and Types

Another strength of Oracle8i is the capability to bind code to data. We call these *code segment methods*. Remember our definition of method. A *method* is a procedure or function that is part of the object type definition and can operate on the data attributes of the object type. This is approaching the capability of encapsulation, one of the foundations of object-oriented databases. The following listing shows a type definition linked to some methods:

```
SQL*Plus 8.1.5.0.0 - Production on Fri Jun 19 07:56:01 2009
(c) Copyright 1999 Oracle Corporation. All rights reserved.
Connected to:
Oracle8i Enterprise Edition Release 8.1.5.0.0 - Production
With the Partitioning and Java Options
PL/SQL Release 8.1.5.0 - Production
SQL> create type good_bad_type as object
    2        (good_guy              integer,
    3        bad_guy               integer,
    4        map member function good_or_bad return real,
    5        member procedure         normalize,
    6        member function         neutral (x good_bad_type)
    7        return good_bad_type)
/

Type created.
SQL>
```

As you can see by looking at this listing, Oracle8i gives you the very powerful capability to bind code and data together. In this example, we create a new data type that is specific to this business. Since it is a data type, we can reference it throughout our database, to ensure consistency. We also show the data type good_bad_type being bound together with some code. In this case, it is being bound together with a function called Neutral. We have code and data being tightly joined together. This is much more powerful than traditional database triggers. This ability to have objects within objects, code joined together with data, makes Oracle8i a very powerful tool.

Experience has shown us that standardization is a very desirable trait in a mission-critical environment. The ability to bind methods to types should help avoid many of the data consistency problems of the past. Perhaps it makes sense to develop a valid state lookup method and bind it to the state_type.

Object Views

Oracle8i object views are an extension of the traditional relational view mechanism that allows you to treat relational data as if it were object entities. Simply put, object views allow use of relational data in object-oriented applications. This means you can **select**, **update**, **insert**, and **delete** relational data as if the data were stored as object entities.

This means your current applications can coexist with new applications that use object-oriented features. With this mechanism in Oracle8i, you have the best of both worlds. You can continue to run your applications, at the same time building new applications that take advantage of object-relational features of Oracle8*i*. This allows for a gradual migration path. This is a very desirable feature as the databases continue to get bigger and bigger.

Materialized Views

Materialized views store the results of a query against one or more objects in a separate database table. They are synonymous with *snapshots*, and the keywords **materialized view** and **snapshot** can be used interchangeably. These views are especially handy in replication situations, in which *replication* involves the deliberate propagation of table data and its changes to remote sites. Oracle sees three main situations for setting up and using materialized views:

- Decision support, or data warehousing, in which precomputed results and aggregations (also referred to as *summarized data*) are accessed frequently as users go about their daily activities. The optimizer has been trained when to use materialized views to enhance performance of the data warehouse by recognizing and deciding to use materialized views.

- When distributed processing is used, materialized views are local copies of tables from remote sites, reflecting changes made to the base tables upon which they are based. In this context, *materialized view* is simply a new name for a pre-Oracle8*i* phenomenon referred to as a *snapshot*.

- In the mobile computing arena, materialized views are used to download a subset of data from a central server to mobile clients. Subsequent changes to the downloaded data on the client are sent back to the server via the same materialized view.

Oracle8*i* maintains a *materialized view log* that tracks changes (additions, modifications, and deletions) from the master site where the table resides, upon which a materialized view is based. Materialized views and their indexes can be partitioned, when the data within the view or index can be manually split among different data files or containers for Oracle8*i* data referred to as *tablespaces*.

Dimensions

Dimensions are logical schema objects that define a hierarchical relationship between columns. They contain no data, and the columns defined within the relationships can come from one or more tables. The hierarchy used to specify how multiple tables are connected define a **join key**. A common situation in which a dimension might be used is demonstrating the hierarchical relationships among day, date, month, and year.

Summary

By covering the foundation of an object-oriented database, we hope to give you an understanding of where Oracle8*i* is headed. It is the second pass at object-relational database (Oracle 8.0 was the first)—a very big second step in the right direction. Coming out of the gate, all the features of an object-oriented database are not there. But you have to learn how to crawl before you can walk.

We believe that Oracle has already crossed the biggest hurdle it had to face by implementing object views. It has provided a mechanism to support objects without breaking the existing applications. From this foundation, Oracle corporation can add additional object technology capabilities. Look to the features we have discussed, and you can see where Oracle is headed.

We feel objects are just a tiny part of the story to tell. Oracle now has a database that can support 100+ terabytes and over 10,000+ users on a node. It has **select**, **insert**, **update**, **delete**, and recovery parallelism and full partition support. If and when your 100+ terabyte database fails, you can restore just the failed partition. You can tune down to the partition itself. These are very powerful capabilities.

What's Next

Enough said! Let's now move on to a discussion of Oracle, the software, and highlight the means by which Oracle has crafted support for very large relational and object-relational databases. In the next chapter, we cover the gamut of objects stored in the Oracle8*i* database, from tables to synonyms.

CHAPTER

4

Architecture

fter memorizing Chapters 1 through 3, you now know about Oracle Corporation and some of the products it sells to its worldwide user community. We spent a great deal of time on the Oracle Server—it is the foundation of everything Oracle has out there. We feel the major reason Oracle is such a force in modern information technology is its staying power. Oracle Corporation has been down a number of times in its history but always bounces back up to greater heights. This chapter delves further into Oracle8*i* database architecture. After reading this chapter, you will understand the following:

- Components of an Oracle8*i* database
- Tablespaces
- Rollback segments
- Online redo logs
- Control files
- Processes associated with an Oracle8*i* database
- System global area (SGA)
- An Oracle8*i* instance

Terminology

The following definitions will arm you with the technical jargon to make it through this chapter:

- An *application* is a set of Oracle programs that solve a company's or person's business needs. In more day-to-day terms, the computer system that generates bills for a hydroelectric utility could be referred to as a billing application.

- An *instance* is a portion of computer memory and auxiliary processes required to access an Oracle database.

- *Objects* are software representations of real-world entities.

- A *datafile* is a file on your disk that stores information. For example, when working with a word processor, you could call your document a datafile.

- A *DBA* or database administrator is a technical wizard who manages the complete operation of the Oracle8*i* database. The DBA's job is highlighted in Chapters 14 and 18.

■ A *dirty data block* is a portion of computer memory that contains Oracle data whose value has changed from what was originally read from the database. If a personnel application read the name "Julie Cohen" into a data block in memory and the name was changed to "Julie Anderson," the block in memory containing the new name is called a *dirty data block*. Think of dirty data blocks as data sitting in memory that has been changed but not yet written back to the database.

■ A *hot data block* is a block whose data is changed frequently. In an inventory application, a popular part's quantity_on_hand would be in a hot data block because its value undergoes constant change.

■ *LRU* (least recently used) is an algorithm Oracle uses when it needs to make room for more information in memory than will fit in the memory space allocated. Let's say Oracle has five slots in memory holding information, and it needs to put some additional information into memory. Since the five slots are full, Oracle flushes the information that has sat idle for the longest period of time.

■ A *table* holds Oracle data. It contains space allocated to hold application-specific data in your database.

■ A *job* is a set of one or more tasks that run *attended* (that is, in the foreground) or *unattended* (that is, in the background). Oracle has a *job submission* facility that is used by portions of its distributed computing technology.

■ A *snapshot* is a copy of one or more tables from one site (called the *master*) stored on another site (called the *remote site*). Using the job submission facility in Oracle8*i*, these snapshots are refreshed periodically according to parameters entered when the DBA creates the snapshot.

■ A *tablespace* is a collection of one or more datafiles. All database objects are stored in tablespaces, so called because they typically hold a database object called a table.

■ *Rollback* is the activity Oracle performs to restore data to its prior state before a user started to change it. For example, you change the value for someone's location from "AL" to "MN" and then decide that you made a mistake—a rollback activity could change the location back to "AL."

■ *Undo information* is the information the database needs to undo or roll back a user transaction due to a number of reasons. For example, when you change a customer's credit limit from $2,000 to $3,000 USD, undo information is kept in case you decide not to save the change.

Why Bother to Learn the Architecture?

We have found in our travels that many users do not see the need for understanding the internal architecture of the Oracle database. They just go out and code the application (the official term for this is rapid prototyping). The Oracle relational database and its tools make application building look easy—much the way a pro athlete makes a sport look easy. However, we all know from experience that what looks easy in theory might not be easy in practice.

Here's an analogy to illustrate why you should take the time to understand the Oracle database architecture. It all started a year ago, when I helped the plumber put a new heating system in our home. By helping the plumber, I was able to bring the installation cost way down; being a Yankee at heart, I found that money was a very strong motivator to do manual labor! The heating system installed was forced hot water: after the water is heated, electric pumps move it through the pipes. During the installation process, I expended a great deal of effort bleeding the air pockets out of the heating system, as air prevents the heated water from circulating through the pipes. A few weeks later, the bedrooms were not getting enough heat. With some knowledge of the heating system, I was able to determine that an air pocket must be in the pipes. I took the time to bleed the air out, and, shortly after, heat was restored.

A month later, a "Nor'easta" (in Boston, lobster is pronounced "lobsta" and chowder is pronounced "chowda") snowstorm hit Boston and we lost our power. Within a few hours, without electricity to work the electric pumps, the house started to get very cold. With three small children at home, this was not a good situation. I kept thinking there must be a way to get the remaining hot water in the heating system to circulate through the pipes without electricity. Again, applying my limited knowledge of the architecture of a hot-water heating system, I came up with the solution: I opened the return pipes so that the cold water was replaced with the remaining hot water. Heat was then restored. Yes, Super Dad was able to Save the Day!

There is a point to the analogy: We are not plumbers. But a good understanding of how things were designed helped in ways we had never anticipated. With this in mind, you may want to take the time to read the rest of this chapter.

TIP

When starting to work with complex software such as Oracle, take the time to learn the architecture. Down the road, taking this time at the beginning will pay off.

What Is a Database?

We posed the question "What is a database?" to Scott Martin, one of the Oracle core developers who helped write the Oracle Parallel Server and who most recently engineered his own product called SQL*Trax. Scott replied: "It's a bunch of programs that manipulate datafiles." Scott's statement is absolutely correct. A database is a collection of datafiles and the software that manipulates it. So let's take a closer look at the Oracle database using Scott's definition as our starting point. We start at the datafile level.

Datafiles

Datafiles contain all the database data. The Oracle database is made up of one or more datafiles; datafiles are grouped together to form a tablespace. Especially important to note here is that the datafiles contain all of the data information stored in the database. Think of disk drives on a PC. The files contained on those disk drives represent all the information currently available to that PC.

User Data and System Data

Two types of data or information are stored within the datafiles associated with a database: user data and system data.

■ *User data* is your application data, with all of the applications' relevant information. This is the information your organization stores in the database. Table 4-1 shows typical types of user data.

Type of Data	Contains Information About
Customer information	Last name, first name, phone number
Product information	Product name, availability, price
Medical information	Lab results, doctor's name, nurse's name
Inventory information	Quantity in stock, quantity backordered
Financial information	Stock price, interest rate

TABLE 4-1. *Common Types of User Data*

■ *System data* is the information the database needs to manage the user data and to manage itself. For example, with system data, Oracle tells itself that the Social Security field in a table consists of all numbers and no letters and that it is a mandatory field. System data also tells Oracle the valid users of the database, their passwords, how many datafiles are part of the database, and where these datafiles are located. Table 4-2 shows typical system data.

What Is a Database? Summary of Points

To summarize what we have learned about databases:

■ A database is a collection of programs that manipulate datafiles.

■ Two types of information are stored in an Oracle database:

1. User data is your particular application data (such as a customer invoice).

2. System data is the data that the database needs to manage itself (such as the name and location of all the datafiles associated with a particular database).

Tablespaces—Oracle's Manila Folder

Since a database is a collection of datafiles, it's very important that you understand how an Oracle database groups these files together. It does this under the umbrella of a database object called a *tablespace*. Before you can insert data into an Oracle database, you must first create a tablespace, then an object within that tablespace to hold the data. When you create the object, you must include all the information

Type of Data	Contains Information About
Tables	The fields of the table and the type of information they hold
Space	Amount of physical space the database objects occupy
Users	Names, passwords, privileges
Datafiles	Number, location, last time used

TABLE 4-2. *Common Types of System Data*

about the type of data you want to hold. This is similar to the COBOL programmer defining a record layout. Look at the following code used to create the customer table; it illustrates how Oracle stores information about the type of data it will record. In the next listing, we give the table a name (in this case, customer), give a descriptive name to each element of information we wish to store (in this case, first_name or last_name), and tell Oracle the type of data we wish to capture (in this case, **number** and **varchar2**).

```
create table customer
     (first_name          varchar2(15),
      last_name           varchar2(15),
      phone_area_code     number,
      phone_number        number)
tablespace users;
```

Now that you understand why it is called a tablespace, let's try to understand why we need tablespaces to group datafiles together. The best analogy to explain a database, tablespace, datafile, table, and data is an image of a filing cabinet. Think of the database as the filing cabinet; the drawers within the cabinet are tablespaces; the folders in those drawers are datafiles; the pieces of paper in each folder are the tables and other database objects; the information written on the paper in each folder is the data. Tablespaces are a way to group datafiles.

Keep this in mind: As with your own filing cabinet, you would not intentionally put your homeowner's insurance policy in a drawer called "school records." On the other hand, you might put your homeowner's policy in a drawer called "insurance." The same commonsense rules should apply to naming the tablespaces within your database.

VIP
Do not mix application data in the same tablespace.
When you create tablespaces for your applications,
give them a descriptive name (for instance, your
federal tax data may be held in the
intern_rev_bound tablespace).

If you follow the previous recommendation, you will find out in no time how easy it is to manage your database—separate applications mean separate tablespaces.

VIP
Keep in mind the limits placed on the length of filenames when working with Oracle on multiple platforms of which one may be DOS. The eight-character filename and three-character extension in DOS may impact on the names of the datafiles you select.

Tablespace Names and Contents

Let's take a look at a typical database and the tablespace names you might see. Since you have a lot of freedom in Oracle when naming tablespaces, notice how we use a descriptive name for each tablespace that describes the type of data it contains. The names we give you are merely an accepted convention; your site's DBA is not required to use them. Remember—the whole point of tablespaces is to help you organize your database.

System Tablespace

The system tablespace is a required part of every Oracle database. This is where Oracle stores all the information it needs to manage itself, such as names of tablespaces and what datafiles each tablespace contains.

Temp Tablespace

The temp tablespace is where Oracle stores all its temporary tables. This is the database's whiteboard or scratch paper. Just as you sometimes need a place to jot down some numbers so you can add them up, Oracle also has a need for some periodic disk space. In the case of a very active database, you might have more than one temp tablespace; for example, TEMP01, TEMP02, and TEMP03.

Tools Tablespace

The tools tablespace is where you store the database objects needed to support tools that you use with your database, such as Oracle Reports, with its own set of tables (Oracle Reports is discussed in Chapter 9). Like any Oracle application, Oracle Reports needs to store tables in the database. Most DBAs place the tables needed to support tools in this tablespace.

Users Tablespace

The users tablespace holds users' personal information. For example, when you are learning how to use Oracle, you might want to create some database objects. This is where the DBA will typically let you place your database objects.

Data and Index Tablespaces

From here, anything goes. In some installations, you see tablespace names such as DATA01, DATA02, DATA03, which represent different places to hold data. In other sites, you might see DATA01, INDEX01, and so on. Think of a database index as the index in a book: To find a particular reference in the book, you look in the index for its location, rather than reading the whole book from page one. Indexes are special database objects that enable Oracle to quickly find data stored within a table.

In Oracle, looking at every row in a database is called a *full table scan*. (We expect that the term full table scan will go away over time, now that Oracle8 supports objects). Using an index search is called an *index scan*. Many other shops name their tablespaces after the application data they hold. For example, in a hospital, the tablespace names might be lab_system or research.

Rollback Tablespace

All Oracle databases need a location to store undo information. This tablespace, which holds your rollback segments, is typically called rollback or rbs. One of the primary reasons you use a database management system such as Oracle is for its capability to recover from incomplete or aborted transactions as part of the core functionality. Recovery is discussed in more detail in the "Redo Logs—The Transaction Log" section of this chapter.

Back to Scott's original definition of a database: You start to realize that a database is certainly made up of lots of datafiles. Creating tablespaces and adding space to existing tablespaces are covered in Chapter 14 and Chapter 18.

Tablespaces: Summary of Points

To summarize what we have learned about tablespaces:

- A tablespace is a collection of one or more datafiles.

- The following tablespaces are either required or common to many databases:

  - The system tablespace contains the information Oracle needs to manage itself and your data. This tablespace name is mandatory.

  - The temp tablespace is Oracle's scratch area. On certain occasions, Oracle needs disk space to manage its own transaction or a transaction on your behalf.

  - The tools tablespace stores the objects needed by tools that run against an Oracle database.

  - The users tablespace keeps users' personal database objects.

■ The rollback tablespace is where the database object rollback segments are typically stored.

■ The data and index tablespaces store your application data.

■ An index is a special type of database object. Oracle uses indexes to speed up data retrieval. We discuss indexes and how they enhance Oracle's performance in Chapter 13.

■ A full table scan means that Oracle reads every row of data associated with a given object.

■ Undo information is stored in a special database object called a rollback segment. A rollback segment is used to roll back the old value of a database object in case of a failure or aborted transaction.

Redo Logs—The Transaction Log

In addition to the datafiles associated with a tablespace, Oracle has other operating system files associated with it called *online redo logs*. Another common term for redo logs is transaction logs. These are special operating system files in which Oracle records all changes or transactions that happen to the database. As changes are made to the database, these changes occur in memory. Oracle handles these changes in memory for performance reasons. A disk I/O (input/output) is 1,000 times slower than an action in memory. Since a copy of all transactions is always recorded to the online redo logs, Oracle can take its time recording back to the original datafile the changes to data that occurred in memory. Eventually, the final copy of the change to the data is recorded back to the physical datafile. Since all the transactions are recorded in the online redo logs, the database is always able to recover itself from these transaction logs. It is a requirement that every Oracle database have at least two online redo logs.

How Redo Logs Work

Redo logs work in a circular fashion. Let's say you have a database with two online redo logs, logA and logB. As transactions create, delete, and modify the data in the database, they are recorded first in logA. When logA is filled up, a log switch occurs. All new transactions are then recorded in logB. When logB fills up, another log switch occurs. Now all transactions are recorded in logA again. This is shown in Figure 4-1.

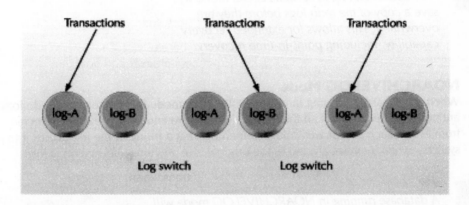

FIGURE 4-1. *How redo logs work*

VIP
Since redo logs are used in a cyclical fashion, when Oracle reuses logA, the transaction information sitting in logA is overwritten.

This point leads us into the discussion of how the Oracle database runs in either ARCHIVELOG or NOARCHIVELOG mode; these have a direct correlation to the online redo logs.

ARCHIVELOG Mode: Full Recoverability

When a database is running in ARCHIVELOG mode, all transaction redo logs are kept. This means that you have a copy of every transaction that runs against the database; so, even though the redo logs work in a circular fashion, a copy of the redo log is made before it is overwritten. In the event that the database needs to switch before the copy has been made, Oracle will freeze up until this action has completed. Oracle will not allow the old transaction log to be overwritten until it has a copy of it. By having a copy of all transactions, the database is now able to protect you against all types of failures, including user error or a disk crash. This is the safest mode to run your database in.

VIP

A database running in ARCHIVELOG mode will save a copy of the redo logs before they are overwritten. This allows for extended recovery capability, including point-in-time recovery.

NOARCHIVELOG Mode

When a database is running in NOARCHIVELOG mode (the default), old redo logs are not kept. Because not all the transaction logs are kept, you are only protected from events such as a power failure (remember that a fill-up of the log causes it to switch—when it circles around to the original, the previous information is lost).

VIP

A database running in NOARCHIVELOG mode will not save a copy of the redo logs before they are overwritten. NOARCHIVELOG mode allows for the bare minimum level of recovery. It is primarily designed to protect you from instance failure.

Redo Logs: Summary of Points

To summarize what we have learned so far about redo logs:

- An Oracle database is made up of two types of files:
  - Datafiles grouped together into tablespaces
  - Datafiles grouped under the family of redo logs

- A database must have at least two redo logs.

- A redo log contains all the transactions that have occurred against the database.

- Another common name for the redo log is the transaction log.

- The transaction logs are necessary to protect your data against loss. Their sole purpose is for recovery against unexpected failures.

- An Oracle database runs in two modes:

- ARCHIVELOG mode saves all transaction logs.
- In NOARCHIVELOG mode, old redo logs are not kept.

Control Files

Every database must have at least one control file, though it is highly recommended that you have two or more.

VIP
It is good to have two or more control files in case one is damaged while the database operates. If you have a single control file, you will be in trouble without an additional control file to keep the database accessible to your users.

A control file is a very small file that contains key information about all the files associated with an Oracle database. Control files maintain the integrity of the database and help to identify which redo logs are needed in the recovery process.

The best analogy we can think of to illustrate this point is getting your yearly car inspection. Every year in the state of Massachusetts, residents must get their cars inspected to make sure they meet all safety and pollution guidelines.

Use of Control Files

Before the database is allowed to begin running, it goes to the control file to determine if the database is in acceptable shape. For example, if a datafile is missing or a particular file has been altered while the database was not using it, then the control file informs the database that it has failed inspection. If this happens, as in a car inspection, you will not be allowed to continue until the problem is corrected.

VIP
If Oracle reads the control file and, based on the information it contains, determines the database is not in acceptable shape, it will not permit the database to run.

Whenever a database checkpoint occurs or there is a change to the structure of the database, the control file is updated. If you do not have a valid control file, your database will not start.

VIP

*Have at least two control files for your database and store them on different disks. In the event you lose all your control files, Oracle7/8 supports a **create controlfile** command that can, under most circumstances, be used to re-create a control file.*

Control File: Summary of Points

To summarize what we have learned so far about control files:

- Every database must have at least one control file. You are strongly advised to have at least two control files, and they should be on separate disks.

- All major changes to the structure of the database are recorded in the control file.

Programs

We have defined a database as being "a bunch of programs that manipulate datafiles." It's now time to discuss the programs; we prefer to call them processes because every time a program starts against the database, it communicates with Oracle via a process. Later in this chapter we talk about support processes required to run the Oracle database (see the section "Database Support Processes"). There are two types of Oracle processes you should know about: user and server.

User (Client) Processes

User processes work on your behalf, requesting information from the server processes. Examples of user processes are Oracle Developer (Chapter 9) and SQL*Plus (Chapter 7 and Chapter 12). These are common tools any user of the data within the database uses to communicate with the database.

Server Processes

Server processes take requests from user processes and communicate with the database. Through this communication, user processes work with the data in the database. The best analogy we have ever heard comes to us compliments of a company called J3 that makes training videos. A good way to think of the client/server process is to imagine yourself in a restaurant. You, the customer, communicate to the waiter who takes your order. That person then communicates the request to the kitchen. The kitchen staff's job is to prepare the food, let the waiter know when it is ready, and stock inventory. The waiter then delivers the meal back to you. In this analogy, the waiter represents the client process, and the kitchen staff represents the server processes.

Programs: Summary of Points

There are two types of programs or processes:

- One type is the user (client) process. Examples include SQL*Plus, Oracle Forms, and Oracle Reports—in other words, any tools you might use to access the database.

- Server processes take requests from client processes and interact with the database to fill those requests.

Database Support Processes

As we stated before, server processes take requests from user (client) processes; they communicate with the database on behalf of user processes. Let's take a look at a special set of server processes that help the database operate.

VIP
These database support processes operate and allow you to interact with the Oracle8i server regardless of the number of layers used in system design—it is the same for two- and three-tier architecture.

Database Writer (DBWR)

The database writer is a mandatory process that writes changed data blocks back to the database files. It is one of the only two processes that are allowed to write to the datafiles that make up your Oracle database. On certain operating systems, Oracle allows you to have multiple database writers. This is done for performance reasons.

Checkpoint (CKPT)

When users are working with an Oracle database, they make requests to look at data. That data is read from the database files and put into an area of memory where users can look at it. Some of these users eventually make changes to the data that must be recorded back onto the original datafiles. Earlier in the chapter, we talked about redo logs and how they record all transactions. When the redo logs switch, a checkpoint occurs. When this switch happens, Oracle goes into memory and writes any dirty data blocks' information back to disk. In addition, it notifies the control file of the redo log switch. These tasks are by the checkpoint process.

Log Writer (LGWR)

The log writer is a mandatory process that writes redo entries to the redo logs. Remember, the redo logs are a copy of every transaction that occurs in the database. This is done so that Oracle is able to recover from various types of failure. In addition, since a copy of every transaction is written in the redo log, Oracle does not have to spend its resources constantly writing data changes back to the datafiles immediately. This results in improved performance. The log writer is the only process that writes to the redo logs. It is also the only process in an Oracle database that reads the redo logs.

System Monitor (SMON)

System monitor is a mandatory process that performs any recovery that is needed at startup. In the parallel server mode (Oracle databases on different computers sharing the same disk farm—see Figure 4-2), it can also perform recovery for a failed database on another computer. Remember, the two databases share the same datafiles.

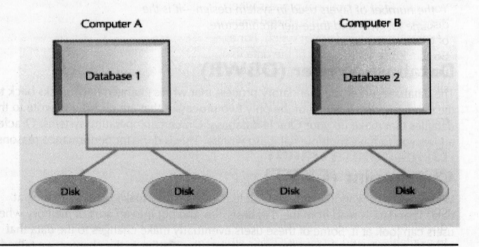

FIGURE 4-2. *Oracle in parallel server mode*

Process Monitor (PMON)

Process monitor is a mandatory process that performs recovery for a failed user of the database. It assumes the identity of the failed user, releasing all the database resources that user was holding, and it rolls back the aborted transaction.

Archiver (ARCH)

Archiver is an optional process. As we discussed earlier in the "Redo Logs—The Transaction Log" section, the redo (transaction) logs are written to in a sequential manner. When a log fills up, there is a log switch to the next available redo log. When you are running the database in ARCHIVELOG mode, the database goes out and makes a copy of the redo log. This is done so that when the database switches back to this redo log, there is a copy of the contents of this file for recovery purposes. This is the job of the archiver process. Similar to a copy machine, it makes a copy of the file.

Lock (LCKn)

Lock is an optional process. When you are running the Oracle database in the parallel server mode, you will see multiple lck processes. In parallel server mode (see Figure 4-2), these locks help the databases communicate.

Recoverer (RECO)

You only see this optional process when the database is running the Oracle distributed option. The distributed transaction is one in which two or more locations of the data must be kept in synch. For example, you might have one copy of data in Boston and another copy of the data in Mexico City. Let's say that while updating the data, the phone line to Mexico goes down due to a severe rainstorm, and a mud slide washes the phone line away. It is the job of the reco process to resolve transactions that may have completed in Boston but not in Mexico City. These transactions are referred to as in-doubt until they are resolved by this reco process.

Dispatcher (Dnnn)

Dispatchers are optional background processes, present only when a multithreaded server configuration is used. At least one dispatcher process is created for every communication protocol (such as TCP/IP, and SNA) in use (D000, . . ., Dnnn). Each dispatcher process is responsible for routing requests from connected user processes to available shared server processes and returning the responses back to the appropriate user processes. Toward the end of this chapter, we spend more time discussing this important facility.

Job Queue Processes (SNPn)

These processes facilitate Oracle's snapshot technology. These processes wake up from time to time and refresh shapshots set to be updated periodically. The DBA can configure up to 36 of these processes, and, if more than one is spawned, the refresh of snapshots may be shared among available workers.

Queue Monitor Processes (QMNn)

This process is enlivened to support Oracle8i's Advanced Queuing (*AQ*) option, which integrates a message queuing system in Oracle. Using AQ, messages can be stored in the database for deferred or immediate delivery. Systems access the functionality delivered with AQ using Java, PL/SQL, or the likes of Visual Basic. AQ offers many features, including priority and ordering of messages within the queue, as well as the capability to send messages to local or remote queues.

Database Support Processes: Summary of Points

A number of support processes help communication between the user processes and the database server. These support processes are responsible for the following:

- Writing data back to the datafiles when a checkpoint occurs (dbwr)
- Ensuring dirty data blocks are written back to disk when a checkpoint occurs (ckpt)
- Reading from and writing to the redo logs (lgwr)
- Running any database recovery that may be required at startup (smon)
- Releasing resources that a user acquired if that user's session ends abnormally (pmon)
- Archiving a copy of a redo log when a log switch occurs when running ARCHIVELOG mode (arch)
- Managing locking in a parallel server configuration (lck)
- Recovering in-doubt transactions when using the Oracle distributed option (reco)
- Supporting Oracle's snapshot technology (snp)
- Supporting Oracle Advanced Queuing (qmn)

This list of processes we gave you is not the complete list. What we gave you are the processes you are most likely to see in 90 percent of the installations. If you understand the purpose behind these processes, you have the fundamentals you need to understand how the Oracle8 database works. If your shop is running the database in parallel server mode, then you will see some additional processes to help the database share locks. Let's now discuss memory structures, the way many processes communicate with each other.

Memory Structure—The Phone Line

Up to this point, we have talked about the datafiles and the programs. We have also talked about server processes and client processes. Now we will talk about how the client and server processes communicate to each other and themselves through memory structures. Just as the name implies, this is an area of memory set aside where processes can talk to themselves or to other processes.

Oracle uses two types of memory structures: the system global area, or SGA (think of it as an old-fashioned telephone party line or the conference calling option on your phone), and program global area, or PGA (think of this as an intercom system).

System Global Area (SGA)

SGA is a place in memory where the Oracle database stores pertinent information about itself. It does this in memory, since memory is the quickest and most efficient way to allow processes to communicate. This memory structure is then accessible to all the user processes and server processes. Figure 4-3 shows how the SGA is in the center of all communication.

Since the SGA is the mechanism by which the various client and server processes communicate, it is important that you understand its various components. The Oracle Server SGA is broken into the following key components.

Data Buffer Cache

The data buffer cache is where Oracle stores the most recently used blocks of database data. In other words, this is your data cache. When you put information into the database, it is stored in data blocks. The data buffer cache is an area of memory in which Oracle places these data blocks so that a user process can look at them. Before any user process can look at a piece of data, the data must first reside in the data buffer cache. There is a physical limit on the size of the data buffer cache. Thus, as Oracle fills it up, it leaves the hottest blocks in the cache and moves out the cold blocks. It does this via the least recently used (LRU) algorithm.

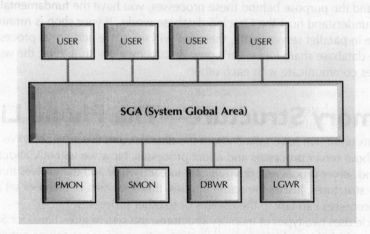

FIGURE 4-3. *SGA—the great phone line*

An important point to clarify: If a client process needs information that is not in the cache, the database goes out to the physical disk drive, reads the needed data blocks, and then places them in the data buffer cache. It does this so that all other client and server processes get the benefit of the physical disk read.

Dictionary Cache (Row Cache)
A dictionary cache contains rows out of the data dictionary. The data dictionary contains all the information Oracle needs to manage itself, such as what users have access to the Oracle database, what database objects they own, and where those objects are located.

Redo Log Buffer
Remember that another common name for the online redo logs is the transaction log. So before any transaction can be recorded into the redo log (the online redo logs are needed for recovery purposes), it must first reside in the redo log buffer. This is an area of memory set aside for this event. Then the database periodically flushes this buffer to the online redo logs.

Shared SQL Pool

Think of the shared SQL pool as your program cache. This is where all your programs are stored. Programs within an Oracle database are based on a standard language called SQL (pronounced "ess que ell" or "sequel"). This cache contains all the parsed SQL statements that are ready to run.

To summarize, the SGA is the great communicator. It is the place in memory where information is placed so that client and server processes can access it. It is broken up into major areas: the data cache, the redo log cache, the dictionary cache, and the shared SQL cache. Figure 4-4 shows the caches Oracle maintains in the SGA—we call the SQL cache the sqlarea; these two terms can be used synonymously.

Program Global Area (PGA)

PGA is an area of memory that is used by a single Oracle process. The program global area is not shared; it contains data and control information for a single process. It contains information such as process session variables and internal arrays. Like an intercom system in your home, the various parts of the process can communicate to each other but not to the outside world.

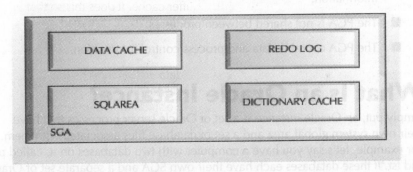

FIGURE 4-4. *SGA—a closer look*

Memory Structure: Summary of Points

To summarize what we have learned so far about memory structure:

- There are two types of memory areas:
  - System global area (SGA)
  - Program global area (PGA)
- The SGA is shared by all server and client processes.
- The SGA has four major components:
  - The data buffer cache is your data cache.
  - The dictionary cache (rows cache) is the information Oracle needs to manage itself.
  - The redo log buffer is the transaction cache.
  - The shared SQL pool is your program cache.
- Before a user process can look at information out of the database, it must first reside in the SGA.
- The SGA is the great communicator by which all processes can share information.
- The PGA is not shared between processes.
- The PGA contains data and process control information.

What Is an Oracle Instance?

Simply put, an Oracle instance is a set of Oracle server processes that have their own system global area and a set of database files associated with them. For example, let's say you have a computer with two databases on it, called prd and tst. If these databases each have their own SGA and a separate set of Oracle server processes, then you have two instances of the database. This is shown in Figure 4-5.

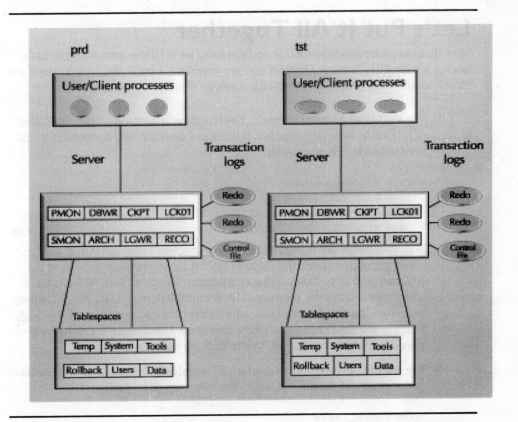

FIGURE 4-5. *Two Oracle instances*

So that the database does not get confused, each instance is identified by what's known as the SID (system identifier). On most UNIX computers, it is set by the variable "ORACLE_SID." Then each of the server processes is named to match the SID. For example, on the tst database, the processes would be named as follows:

```
ora_tst_dbw0
ora_tst_pmon
ora_tst_smon
ora_tst_lgwr
```

Let's Put It All Together

Now that we understand the Oracle architecture, we'll follow a transaction. Let's say we are strolling through Freeport and we approach a bank machine to see if we have enough money for a bottle of wine. Let's go through the transaction:

1. We ask for an account balance. The machine is running a program called SQL*Plus as the client process. It takes our question and formulates it into the following SQL statement:

```
select account_balance
  from bank_table
 where account_number = '1112222333'
   and account_type = 'SAVINGS';
```

2. SQL statements are passed to the server processes through the SGA. The server processes check the shared pool for the executable version of the program. If it's not there, it places a parsed "Ready to Run" version there and then executes the program. The account balance "Data Block" is then read from the datafiles and placed into the data cache portion of the SGA. Once in the data cache, the client process is able to read the balance and pass it back to the customer. We're told the balance is $325.00.

3. We see the balance and request a $25 withdrawal. The client process takes our request and formulates it into the following SQL statement:

```
update bank_table
   set account_balance = 300
 where account_number = '1112222333'
   and account_type = 'SAVINGS';
```

In closing, here is a summary of the processing that Oracle does with this update statement:

1. The client process passes the statement to the server process through the SGA.

2. The server processes look in the shared pool for an executable version of the program. If one is found, proceed to step 4; if not, proceed to step 3.

3. Process this SQL statement and move its executable version into the pool.

4. Execute the SQL statement.

5. Is the data this statement manipulates in the data cache? If it is, proceed to step 7; if it is not, proceed to step 6.

6. Read the data from the database file into the data cache.

7. Record the old value of the data in a rollback segment (the rollback segment holds the old balance of $325).

8. Create a copy of the transaction in the redo logs.

9. Change the data in the data cache to reflect the new balance of $300.

10. The bank machine signals through the SGA that all is complete.

11. Record the completion of the transaction in the redo log.

12. Free up the undo information in the rollback segment.

13. Deliver money to customer.

14. Buy a great bottle of wine for half the price we would pay in Boston!

VIP
In step 7 of this process, if the user cancels the transaction or the system comes down during the transaction, the information held in the rollback segment is used to restore the original balance.

VIP
As with every transaction, eventually the database writer writes the data cache copy of the data block back to the original datafile.

As you can see, a lot goes on for your client process to be able to access the database. After you work with Oracle for a while, its value becomes clear.

A Closer Look at the Multithreaded Server (MTS)

As we stated earlier, the multithreaded server allows numerous connections to the database to all share memory and resources. This minimizes the memory overhead associated with supporting many users.

NOTE
MTS is one of many features in Oracle8i that make it possible to support the 10,000+ concurrent user community. Not all clients will use MTS, but it is a component in the strategy to support such a large number of users.

Before we had the MTS configuration, each process that connected to the Oracle8i database required a separate process with its own allocation of memory. Due to the overhead of creating these connections, and maintaining these connections, this way of managing connections became a major performance bottleneck.

The multithreaded server configuration allows processes to share memory and connections. This eliminates much of the overhead associated with supporting large amounts of users trying to access the database. This is a major feature that allows Oracle to support a large number of users.

VIP

The multithreaded server feature is not necessarily the best way to go with all applications. Familiarize yourself with its features and speak with colleagues and fellow techies before running out and implementing it on all your Oracle8 instances.

The multithreaded server has pools of connections, called *shared server processes*, that are constantly established and that allow users to share those open connections. This method of connection is much faster than its predecessor, a dedicated connection. To help illustrate this concept, let's look at an example. Consider an order entry system with dedicated server processes. A customer places an order as a clerk enters the order into the database. For most of the transaction, the clerk is on the telephone talking to the customer and the server process dedicated to the clerk's user process remains idle. The server process is not needed during most of the transaction, yet the system is forced to support the connection, draining needed resources for other users. The multithreaded server configuration eliminates the need for a dedicated server process for each connection.

A pool of connections is maintained. As the clerk needs to talk to the database, that clerk is allocated a connection. The time and resources needed to create connections are eliminated. The time and resources needed to maintain the connection are shared by all users. This frees up very valuable, scarce resources.

To set up your system to use the multithreaded server, you must make some changes in the instance initialization parameter file, and then shut down and restart the database. The appropriate number of dispatcher processes for each instance depends upon the performance you want from your database, the host operating system's limit on the number of connections per process, and the number of connections required per network protocol.

The instance must be able to provide as many connections as there are concurrent users on the database system; the more dispatchers you have, the better potential database performance users will see, since they will not have to wait as long for dispatcher service. Think of dispatchers as like the dispatcher at your local taxi cab company. When you call up, the dispatcher answers the phone and assigns the work to a cab. The more dispatchers you have, the more calls can be answered.

We have discussed the multithreaded server on its own based on the importance of the feature and its mission—supporting lots of user connections very effectively. Just like the rest of the Oracle8 database, it is highly tunable. With Oracle8's capability to support 10,000+ concurrent users, perhaps more of us will end up experimenting and becoming fluent with MTS.

What's Next

We leave this chapter with two suggestions:

- Ingest the information we have discussed here, and look at your database configuration and try to recognize all the components we have highlighted. Walk through the chapter again, and as you cross into a new section, ensure you can identify the components as they appear in your database. For example, when we discuss database support processes, stop and run a program status command on your machine and identify every process by name.

- Keep running back to parts of this chapter as you read the rest of the book. It is remarkable how much you will understand about Oracle having this chapter as a foundation.

In the next chapter, we discuss the assortment of objects stored in the Oracle database and the jobs some special objects perform as your database operates.

CHAPTER
5

Database Objects

his chapter deals with all the major database objects you will
encounter while working with Oracle8i. Each of these objects has a
specific purpose or job to do. In this chapter, we will explain what
each object is used for and give you an example of how to use it.
We will provide details on tables, views, indexes, synonyms, and
snapshots, to name a few. In Chapter 1, we discussed how Oracle stores information
in one place. If a payroll application needs personnel information for a firm's
employees, rather than capture the required information itself, the payroll system
reads data from the personnel system. Since data is stored in one place and read by
all, we will also introduce object privileges in this chapter and show you how
privileges are used to control who can do what with data.

Terminology

The following definitions will arm you with the technical jargon to make it through
this chapter:

- A *table* is a database object that holds your data. Information about every
  table is stored in the data dictionary; with this information, Oracle allows
  you to maintain data residing in your table.

- *Database triggers* are programs that are stored in the database and run
  when something happens, such as data changes or user logins.

- A *view* allows you to see a customized selection of one or more tables, and
  it uses an SQL query that is stored in the database. When using views, the
  SQL statement that defines the view is executed as if you had coded the
  defining statement yourself.

- An *index* is a minicopy of a table. Index entries for a table allow Oracle
  rapid access to the data in your tables.

- A *synonym* is an alternate name for an object in the database. Think of a
  synonym as a nickname for an object—somewhat like calling a woman
  named Margaret by the name Maggie instead.

- *Grants* are privileges given out by owners of objects, allowing other users to
  work with their data.

- A *data type* is the format structure in which you plan to store your
  information. The types of data stored in Oracle8i datatypes include
  characters, numbers, images, and text.

■ A *user-defined data type* is a datatype by which you specify how the data is to be stored.

■ The *data dictionary* is maintained by Oracle and contains information relevant to the tables that reside in the database. For example, in a telecommunications system, the data dictionary records the fact that a North American area code is three digits long.

■ A *role* is a group of privileges that are collected together and granted to users. Once privileges are granted to a role, a user inherits the role's privileges by becoming a member of that role. This way, instead of updating every user's account on an individual basis, you can just manage the role.

■ A *remote database* is an Oracle8 instance that runs on a computer different than the one you may currently be logged into. Picture a network on which a database server resides in Newton and communicates with another server in Toronto. Users logged into the machine in Toronto may access a remote database in Newton using a network transport mechanism to enable the communication.

■ A *snapshot* is a read-only copy of data stored in one or more tables. Using Oracle8's scheduling features, the DBA instructs Oracle to regularly refresh a snapshot on a remote database from the contents of the data in the tables that serve as the inputs to the snapshot.

■ *Contention* occurs when two or more database users are waiting for data or a resource (such as memory required to perform a sort or CPU time to perform some calculation). Closely hooked to contention are situations that cause users to wait for one another to complete their activity before they can take their turn using the resource in question.

Tables—Where Oracle Stores Your Data

A *table* is the database object that holds your data. The data dictionary holds information about every table; Oracle uses its data dictionary to ensure the correct type of data (for instance, number or character) is placed in Oracle tables. The best analogy is to think of a table as a spreadsheet. The cells of the spreadsheet equate to the columns of the table. Just like the cells of a spreadsheet, the columns of a table have a data type associated with them. If the number data type is associated with a spreadsheet cell, then you will not be allowed to store letters in the spreadsheet cell.

The same applies to a table's columns. Table columns that are of a number data type cannot accept letters. Data types are covered in detail in Chapter 7.

The way you create tables in Oracle is through the **create table** command. Let's take a closer look at an example of this command in its simplest form:

```
SQL*Plus: Release 8.1.5.0.0 - Production on Mon Jun 14 21:35:29 2002
(c) Copyright 1999 Oracle Corporation.  All rights reserved.
Connected to:
Oracle8i Enterprise Edition Release 8.1.5.0.0 - Production
With the Partitioning and Java options
PL/SQL Release 8.1.5.0.0 - Production
SQL> create table customer
  2  (customer_id  number(10) not null,
  3   surname      varchar2(30) not null,
  4   first_name   varchar2(20),
  5   sales_region char(2),
  6   ytd_sales    number(10,2),
  7*  total_sales  number(14,2));
Table created.
```

In this example, we create a table called customer. The columns associated with the table are customer_id, surname, first_name, sales_region, ytd_sales, and total_sales. Each of these columns has a data type associated with it; let's look at each column in more detail as shown in Table 5-1.

Column	Data Type	Max Length	Notes
Surname	varchar2	30	Column cannot hold a name larger than 30 characters. The data type varchar2 tells the database that this column can accept letters, numbers, and special characters. In addition, varchar2 tells the database to store the information internally in a variable-length format. For example, the last name Lane takes less room to store than the last name Ellison. In other words, Oracle only uses the amount of space it needs to hold the name.

TABLE 5-1. *Columns and Notes on Data Types*

Column	Data Type	Max Length	Notes
Sales_region	char	2	Column can accept letters, numbers, and special characters. In addition, char tells the database to store the information internally in a fixed-length format. No matter how big the sales_region value is, it can take up no more and no less space than it takes to hold two characters.
Ytd_sales	number	12	Column contains up to 2 decimal places as part of the number. This ensures that the number is always a valid money amount. In addition, since they are numbers, you can add, subtract, multiply, and divide the contents. In fact, Oracle has an extensive set of mathematical functions you can apply to columns of data type number.
Total_sales	number	14	Same as ytd_sales.

TABLE 5-1. *Columns and Notes on Data Types* (continued)

VIP
A table is a database object that holds your data. It is made up of many columns. Each of those columns has a data type associated with it. This data type is the roadmap that Oracle follows so that it knows how to correctly manipulate the contents.

Oracle8*i* has introduced a new feature associated with tables that allows us to drop columns from existing tables. When you build tables, you define the columns; in the past, however, if your table definition required change, it was difficult. Oracle allowed us to add columns, but removing them was a different situation. The way you add columns to a table in Oracle is through the **alter table** command. Let's take a closer look at an example of this command in its simplest form:

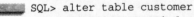

```
SQL> alter table customer
  2   add tax_exempt_ind varchar2(1);
Table altered.
SQL> describe customer
```

```
Name                            Null?     Type
------------------------------- --------  ----------------
CUSTOMER_ID                     NOT NULL  NUMBER(10)
SURNAME                         NOT NULL  VARCHAR2(30)
FIRST_NAME                                VARCHAR2(20)
SALES_REGION                              CHAR2(2)
YTD_SALES                                 NUMBER(10,2)
TOTAL_SALES                               NUMBER(14,2)
TAX_EXEMPT_IND                            VARCHAR2(1)
```

As expected, the column we have added to the table is shown in the previous listing. In our case we added the tax_exempt_ind column, a varchar2 column of length 1. We issued the **describe** command so that we could view the structure of the table. The **describe** command is one that can be used to view many objects; you can use it to look at views, stored procedure parameters, and other objects such as Oracle8i packages.

Then, after we've added the column, the boss says, "That's not what I wanted; we don't care about the tax exemption status of our customers. We charge everyone tax! Get rid of the column." Since you love your job, you need to find a way to get rid of the extra column. Well, Oracle8i now allows you to remove a column. Let's take a look at the **drop column** command:

```
SQL> alter table customer
  2   drop column tax_exempt_ind;
Table altered.
SQL> describe customer
Name                            Null?     Type
------------------------------- --------  ----------------
CUSTOMER_ID                     NOT NULL  NUMBER(10)
SURNAME                         NOT NULL  VARCHAR2(30)
FIRST_NAME                                VARCHAR2(20)
SALES_REGION                              CHAR2(2)
YTD_SALES                                 NUMBER(10,2)
TOTAL_SALES                               NUMBER(14,2)
```

So you can see that, using the **alter table** command with the **drop column** argument, we have removed the tax_exempt_ind column. That means you get to keep your job. Tables are the foundation of the database, and the flexibility that Oracle8i provides allows you to control your tables very closely. Let's look at user-defined data types to see how we can specify our own data types.

User-Defined Data Types

Databases objects, such as tables, have in the past been great repositories for holding data. The data in tables were stored in a simple data type, such as char,

number, varchar2, long, and so on. As you can see, these types perform the job;
but, as the applications get bigger and the need for standardization becomes more
important, user-defined data types will allow you to create these standards. Oracle8*i*
is an object-relational database management system (*ORDBMS*), which means that
users can define additional kinds of data, specifying both the structure of the data
and the ways of operating on it. User-defined data types make it easier for
application developers to work with complex data like images, audio, and video.
Object types store structured business data in its natural form and allow applications
to retrieve it that way. For that reason they work efficiently with applications
developed using object-oriented programming techniques. Let's look at how to
create a user-defined type:

```
SQL> create type indiv_details as object
  2  (name       varchar2(40),
  3   phone      varchar2(20),
  4   height     number(3),
  5   weight     number(4))
/
Type created.
```

We can now use the newly created type in a table. The following example
illustrates a simple use of the new user-defined data type, with the usage of the type
italicized in bold.

```
SQL> create table vendors
  2  (vendor_name     indiv_details,
  3   create_date     date,
  4   company_name    varchar2(30),
  5   postal_zip_code varchar2(9),
  6   prov_state_cd   varchar2(2));
Table created.
```

The new table, vendors, contains the column, vendor_name, which is the
defined as the type indiv_details. This column will contain the standard information
that we want to hold about a person. You can get a feel for where you can use
user-defined data types.

Database Triggers

A *database trigger* is a program that is associated with a database table. Triggers
are procedures that are stored in the database and run, or fire, when something
happens. This program is activated when an action is performed on a table. When

you create a database trigger, you decide when the program is run and the type of action on the table that will activate the program. When a database trigger is created, you specify when the trigger will fire—before or after a transaction. The primary reason for using database triggers is to validate data before it is saved in the database. The action types include inserts, deletes, and updates. With triggers you can do just about anything, including

- Checking your data before it is posted to the database

- Generating records in other tables based on the data that was just entered

- Implementing business rules in a trigger

Implementing business rules in a trigger is one of many Oracle8i features that you need to get your finger on. We recently implemented an application that provided for address maintenance. Within this application we needed to know if an address was an apartment building. By implementing a trigger on the address table, we could check the characteristics of an address. Relying on the business rule that defined a building, we created a record in the building table where one may not have previously existed. All of this was within a database trigger. Take a look at an example of a database trigger, so you can see the basic command structure.

```
SQL*Plus: Release 8.1.5.0.0 - Production on Sat Jun 19 10:35:01 2002
(c) Copyright 1999 Oracle Corporation.  All rights reserved.
Connected to:
Oracle8i Enterprise Edition Release 8.1.5.0.0 - Production
With the Partitioning and Java options
PL/SQL Release 8.1.5.0.0 Production
SQL> create or replace trigger display_new_sales
  2  before insert or update
  3  on customer
  4  for each row
  5  declare
  6      new_sales_amt  number;
  7  begin
  8      new_sales_amt := :new.total_sales-
  9                       nvl(:old.total_sales,0);
  9      dbms_output.put_line ('New sales amount: '||
 10                       new_sales_amt);
 11  end;
 12  /
Trigger created.
```

The preceding trigger has been created; let's look a little closer on the code so that we better understand how triggers are created. The numbers in the next list refer to the line counter in the previous listing.

1. This tells Oracle to create the trigger if it is a new trigger or to replace an existing trigger. We have named our trigger display_new_sales.

2. We have specified to fire this trigger when we **insert** or **update** a record. When a **delete** is performed, the trigger will not fire. The **before** clause tells the trigger to fire before a new record (in the case of **insert**) is created, or before an existing record is updated.

VIP
*You also have the option to fire the trigger **after** posting the data, but **before** triggers are more efficient and should be used wherever possible.*

3. This tells Oracle that this trigger has been assigned to the **customer** table.

4. The **for each row** argument tells the database to fire this trigger each time a row is either inserted or updated.

Lines 5 to 10 are the body of the trigger. In the body of a trigger you have access to the values for the fields that existed before the activity to which the trigger is keyed—this is the **:old** value. The **:new** is the value that the column will have after the transaction is complete. During a database trigger you always have access to the old and new values of a column. Now that we have looked at creating a database trigger, we guess that makes us database gunslingers, partner. Let's look at the trigger firing. This is one trigger that we can fire without a license.

```
SQL*Plus: Release 8.1.5.0.0 - Production on Sat Jun 19 10:40:30 3210
(c) Copyright 1999 Oracle Corporation.  All rights reserved.
Connected to:
Oracle8i Enterprise Edition Release 8.1.5.0.0 - Production
With the Partitioning and Java options
PL/SQL Release 8.1.5.0.0 Production
SQL> set serveroutput on
SQL> insert into customer
  2> values
  3>(11, 'CHADIRDJIAN','JACK','QC',15003.32,39540.75);
New sales amount: 39540.75
1 row created.
```

We did something special in the body of our trigger—we used a program that is included with the Oracle database. When we included the line that included **dbms_output.put_line**, this told Oracle that our program will output information to the user. This output is conditional on users setting their SQL*Plus session to show these types of output. It is your option to view these output values; if you choose to see the output, you simply issue the **set serveroutput on** command from within SQL*Plus. By default, Oracle does not display server output.

Okay, let's get back to the job at hand. We inserted a new record and Oracle completed the insert and returned the value of new sales to us. In our example, this amount of $39540.75 was the same as the amount included in the **insert**, since there was no previous value in the database; therefore, we assigned a value of zero to the old sales amount. Let's see what happens when we **update** the same record.

```
SQL> update customer
  2   set total_sales = 55240.00
  3   where customer_id = 11;
New sales amount: 15699.25
1 row updated.
```

We have successfully updated the customer record that we had previously created. Now our total sales are $55,240.00. The trigger fired and computed the new sales amount of $15,699.25. Wow, work never seemed so easy, but we have only touched the surface of database triggers. Not only can you execute triggers on table actions, but with Oracle8i you can fire triggers when users log into the database. This capability is valuable if you want to perform some auditing of user activity in the database.

VIP

Be careful when implementing triggers; if the trigger does not function as you expect, it can cause unexpected results in applications or user sessions that access the database.

Views—A Special Look at Your Data

A *view* is a database object that allows you to create a customized slice of a table or a collection of tables. Unlike a table, a view contains no data, just an SQL query. The data that is retrieved from this query is presented like a table. In fact, if you did not create the view, you would think you were dealing with a table. Like a table, you may **insert**, **update**, **delete**, and **select** data from a view.

VIP
*You can always **select** data from a view; but, in some situations, there are restrictions on other ways data in a view can be manipulated.*

Why Use Views?

It is important to know how to use views, since you will probably require views for one or all of the following reasons:

■ Views can provide an additional level of security. For example, you might have an employee table within your company, and you might want to **create** a view that allows managers to see information on only their employees.

■ Views allow you to hide data complexity. An Oracle database is made up of many tables. You can retrieve information from two or more tables by performing a join, and these joins can get very confusing for a typical end user and even a seasoned veteran. Many times, you will create a view that is the combination of many tables. For example, you might have a view that is a combination of the customer table and order table. Thus, the user of the database would only have to make a simple **select** off of the view called cust_ord. The user would never know that this might actually be based on two tables.

■ Views help you maintain naming sanity. Often, when we create column names for an Oracle table, we forget that people actually have to type them when wording SQL statements. For example, we might have a column named middle_initial_of_person. In the view, we could rename the column MI for middle initial.

■ Views allow the flexibility of changing the makeup of one or more tables that make up the view without the need to change application code. Suppose a view joins two tables, displaying three columns from one table and four from the next. If the first table is altered to contain an extra column, the view definition is not affected and any applications that reference the view require no attention.

Creating Views

You create a view using the command **create view** while connected to Oracle. Let's try creating a simple view, as shown in the next listing:

```
SQL*Plus: Release 8.1.5.0.0 - Production on Mon Jun 14 21:26:22 2001
(c) Copyright 1999 Oracle Corporation.  All rights reserved.
Connected to:
Oracle8i Enterprise Edition Release 8.1.5.0.0 - Production
With the Partitioning and Java options
PL/SQL Release 8.1.5.0.0 - Production
SQL> create view v_customer_sales_rgn
  2  as
  3  select surname,sales_region
  4    from customer;
View created.
```

Suppose there were a cust view, containing the last_name and state_cd from the customer table. Users could issue the command **select * from cust;** rather than **select last_name,state_cd from customer;**. When the command is issued, Oracle runs the SQL statement associated with the view. This query brings back the data from the customer table, missing any columns not mentioned in the **create view** statement. Since this view did not include the column sales, you can allow people access to the customer data without giving them access to the sensitive data stored within the sales column. As with a table, you have complete control over who has access to the view.

VIP
A view is just an SQL query that is stored in the database. The results of that query are returned in the form of a table.

Materialized Views

Materialized views are schema objects that can be used to summarize, precompute, and distribute data. They are especially important in data warehousing, decision support, and distributed or mobile computing.

In data warehouses, materialized views are used to precompute and store aggregated data such as sums and averages. Materialized views in these types of applications are typically referred to as summaries, since they usually store summarized data. They can also be used to precompute joins with or without summarizations. The cost-based optimization, used within the database to efficiently perform database tasks, can make use of materialized views to improve query performance by automatically recognizing when a materialized view can and should be used to satisfy another request. The optimizer transparently rewrites the request to use the materialized view. Queries are then directed to the materialized view and not to the underlying detail tables or views. This usually provides for improved performance and can lighten the load on your database, since it doesn't have to perform complex summarizations on large volumes of data but can now get the information directly from the materialized view.

Materialized views are similar to tables and indexes in several ways; for one, they consume storage space. These are not the same as views that do not consume space. They are also close to indexes, since they must be refreshed when the data in their master tables changes; and, when used for query rewrites, they improve the performance of SQL execution and their existence is transparent to SQL applications and users. Unlike indexes, materialized views can be accessed directly using a **select** statement. To read more about materialized views, refer to Chapter 19.

Indexes—A Quick Way to Speed Access to Your Data

Just like an index in a book, which helps you find information faster, an index placed on a table helps you retrieve your data faster. If your application is running slowly, a well-placed index will make it run quicker.

VIP
A well-placed index on a table will help the database retrieve your data faster.

It has been our experience that if you think of indexes as minitables, you will be able to understand how they work. Let's imagine we have the following table (the four dots in the listing represent the definitions of column d through column z, giving the table 26 columns):

```
SQL*Plus: Release 8.1.5.0.0 - Production on Mon Feb 29 22:06:42 2001
(c) Copyright 1999 Oracle Corporation.  All rights reserved.
Connected to:
Oracle8i Enterprise Edition Release 8.1.5.0.0 - Production
With the Partitioning and Java options
PL/SQL Release 8.1.5.0.0 - Production
SQL> create table sample_3
  2     (a    varchar2(30),
  3      b    varchar2(30),
  4      c    varchar2(30),
  ....
Table created.
```

VIP
*The discussion in the next few paragraphs is an
oversimplification of the advantages of using
indexes in many situations. It gives you a flavor of
savings that can be realized with indexes.*

Every time you want to read the information stored in column c, Oracle must also bring back the information stored in columns a, b, and d through z. As with every resource in a computer, there is a limit to how much it can physically do at any point in time. Let's suppose Oracle8i can retrieve the equivalent of four records' worth of information at a time. Given the makeup of sample_3, the four records being retrieved at once, as shown in Table 5-2, define a read buffer of 3,120 characters.

Even though you may only wish to see the information stored in column c, the database is forced to wade through all the information stored in the table; we have a solution to this problem, and it's called an index. Let's say you create an index on column c with the SQL statement **create index colc_ind on sample_3(colc);**. Oracle creates the index object. Think of this as a minitable that holds only the column c information from the table named sample_3. In addition, it will retrieve the information needed to point back to the actual row within the table called sample_3, where the particular column c information came from. Like Siamese twins, these two objects are now linked together. Whatever happens to one happens to the other. If you drop a column c item from the main table, you will also delete the corresponding index entry.

Now, say you want to retrieve just the information stored in column c of the table called sample_3. Oracle knows it can resolve that request from the index; so, rather than wading through the table, it just looks at the index. Oracle performs that same physical read, which was limited to four records' worth of information (or 3,120 characters at a time as shown in Table 5-2). By using the index just created, Oracle now only has to hold column c information. So instead of four records' worth of information, you can now get 104 records each read, since column c is 30 characters and the buffer can hold 3,120 characters. This is illustrated in Table 5-3. The "Rows retrieved" line in the table could actually read "Column c values retrieved."

Column length	CL	30
Columns retrieved	CR	26
Rows retrieved	RR	4
Buffer size		CL*CR*RR = 3,120

TABLE 5-2. *Fetching Column c Without an Index*

Buffer size	BU	3120	
Column length	CL	30	
Columns retrieved	CR	1	
Rows retrieved		CL/CR*BU =	104

TABLE 5-3. *Fetching Column c with an Index*

VIP
Index entries contain information only about the columns that are part of the index, not all the columns in a table.

That same read can bring back much more focused information. It's limited to looking at what you need and not required to wade through all the other columns in the table. Before moving on, let's look at some features of and uses for indexes, since indexes are so important.

Indexes Have a Sorted Order

By design, the data stored in a relational database has no particular order. The record you insert into a table goes into the next available slot. When you issue an SQL query looking for a particular date or range of dates (such as **select * from state where state_cd = 'MA';**), Oracle is required to look at every row of data in the table.

An index, on the other hand, is in a sorted order. If you have a date data type column in a table, you could create an index on that column. The index created by Oracle would contain all the dates in sorted order. It is typically much quicker for Oracle to go to the index, find all the records for a desired date, and then bring back the information to you.

Indexes Can Guarantee Uniqueness

There are two types of indexes you can create. You can create a unique index and a nonunique index. A unique index does not allow duplicates; a nonunique index allows duplicates. As we stated earlier, an index is like a Siamese twin to the table. If you create a unique index on column c in a table, then every time you try to insert a row into the actual table, the index will check to make sure that column c is still unique. The SQL statement **create index colc_ind on sample_3 (colc);** is used to create a nonunique index, and the statement **create unique index colc_ind on sample_3 table (colc);** creates a unique index.

Two Columns Are Better Than One

Oracle allows you to create concatenated indexes. These indexes are made up of more than one column. Many times, you realize when looking at your tables that you would never look at column a without looking at column b. So it makes sense to index both together using a concatenated index. Let's build a concatenated index using the SQL statement **create index colabc_ind on sample_3 table (cola, colb, colc);**. Once this concatenated index is built, Oracle manages the index just as it does with those built on single columns.

The where Clause and Your Indexes

Oracle determines which index it will use to satisfy a query by how the **where** clause is worded (that is, the columns referenced in the **where** and **and** part of an SQL statement). Oracle examines the available indexes and selects the index that will provide the quickest results.

VIP
*Oracle determines which indexes it will use by looking at the **where** clause of the SQL query.*

As your experience with formulating queries increases, you will find yourself becoming quite adept at wording SQL to allow Oracle to process queries using the available indexes.

Synonyms—A New Identity

Just as many actors change their names to make themselves easier to remember, and more recognizable, you can do the same for an Oracle table. When we created the table sample_3, the complete identity it received was the name of the owner of the table (such as ops$coreymj) and the table name. Then if you are connected to Oracle as ops$coreymj, when you issue an SQL query, Oracle is smart enough to realize you are connected as the user who owns the table. So behind the scenes, Oracle places the owner's name in front of the table name. Let's say you want to retrieve a column from the table and you issue the SQL query **select cola from sample_3;**, which Oracle translates into the following:

```
select colA from ops$coreymj.sample_3;
```

A synonym is a database object that allows you to create alternate names for Oracle tables and views. Using our sample_3 table as an example, suppose a user who did not own the table issued the command **select cola from sample_3;**. Oracle would not know what to do. However, if the user had a synonym for the table, Oracle could successfully execute the SQL statement using the synonym. This simple SQL statement illustrates how synonyms are used. When users who do not own a table wish to reference a table in an SQL statement, they must always use a synonym to refer to the table.

You may decide to set up synonyms for any Oracle table for a variety of reasons:

- You want to hide the true owner or name of a table.

- You want or need to hide the true location of a table. Some installations have one table in Boston and another table in Ottawa.

- You want to provide users with a table name less complicated than the real table name (such as s3 instead of sample_3).

With this in mind, let's create a synonym using the SQL statement **create synonym toast for ops$coreymj.sample_3;**. Now the following statements will bring back the same rows from the same table:

```
select cola from ops$coreymj.sample_3;
select cola from toast;
```

Private Synonyms and Public Synonyms

As you can see, you can use synonyms to give a table an alternate identity. This can greatly simplify SQL statement syntax. The synonym we created in the previous section is called a private synonym: normally, ops$coreymj is the only one that can use the synonym toast to point to the table ops$coreymj.sample_3. Another type of synonym is a public synonym, which all Oracle users are able to use. You can create a public synonym with the SQL statement **create public synonym tonic for ops$coreymj.sample_3;**. Any Oracle user can now refer to the table using the public synonym tonic. Now users can issue the statement **select cola from tonic;** and Oracle would know they really mean **select cola from ops$coreymj.sample_3;**.

Grants—May I Please Have Access?

Up to now in this chapter, we may have given the impression that every database user has access to every other database user's objects and their contents. This is not true in the real world. Oracle gives you extensive control over what a user can see, modify, delete, or change. It is one of the real strengths of the Oracle Server. Combine this with views, and you can even control what data a user can look at.

VIP

Grants are used to give one user privileges to work with another user's data. Once privileges have been granted, recipients of the grant have the ability to work with someone else's objects.

We will now discuss some types of privileges and show how they are granted to other users.

Granting Privileges to Users

Granting of object privileges allows users to work with database objects and their contents.

VIP

When users are granted privileges on other users' tables, before they can reference those tables in SQL statements, there must be a public or private synonym through which Oracle can identify the table.

Say user jrstocks owns a table called sample_b and gives all database users access to the table. Along comes user coreyam and runs a statement against the sample_b table, receiving the following error message:

```
select * from sample_b;
                 *
ERROR at line 1:
ORA-00942: table or view does not exist
```

Regardless of which privilege is being granted, there are three parts to each **grant** statement:

1. The keyword/privilege part is made up of the word **grant** followed by one or more privileges. When multiple privileges are placed in the same **grant** statement, they are separated by a comma.

2. The table name part starts with the keyword **on** and lists the table on which privileges are being given.

3. The recipient part lists one or more users who receive the privileges being given out.

Let's look at how four object privileges are given to users.

select

The select privilege allows other users to look at the contents of tables they do not own. The statement **grant select on sample_3 to public;** would allow all users to view the sample_3 table. The statement **grant select on sample_3 to ops$rosenberge,ops$abbeyms;** would allow the two users mentioned to look at sample_3. Notice that when more than one user receives a grant, the usernames are separated in the list by a comma.

VIP
When public is the target of any grant, all users of the database receive the privileges specified. If your database had 15,000 users, granting a privilege to public would be the same as issuing 15,000 grants separately (one to each user!).

insert

The insert privilege allows one to create rows in other users' tables. The statement **grant insert on sample_a to public;** allows all users to create new rows in sample_a. Oracle allows stacking of privileges in a single grant statement—the SQL statement **grant insert, select on sample_a to public;** is the same as the two statements **grant select on sample_a to public;** followed by **grant insert on sample_a to public;**.

update

The update privilege allows other users to modify or change data in tables they do not own. The statement **grant update on sample_a to teplownd;** would permit user teplownd to modify information in sample_a.

delete

The delete privilege permits users to delete rows of information from specified tables. We recommend using caution giving out this privilege, since it is very powerful. Picture the following that actually happened to one of our acquaintances. A programmer was connected to the production database while she thought she was logged in to a test database. She issued the command **delete from people_master;** and Oracle responded with

```
12003 rows deleted.
```

After the programmer exited SQL*Plus, the next program that accessed people_master looking for a personnel record for Rick Bower was told the record did not exist!

The command **grant delete,update,select on sample_a to public;**
gives the specified privilege to all database users. The command **grant
select,update,insert,delete on sample_a to teplownd,greerw;** allows users
teplownd and greerw to do the listed activities on the sample_a table.

Recipients of Grants

Throughout this section, we have shown a number of **grant** statements in which
the recipients were either public or an assortment of database users (for instance,
teplownd). Imagine an installation in which there are two distinct classes of users
for a financial management system. One class of user is allowed to approve travel
claims, cancel requisitions, and adjust quantities and unit prices on purchase orders.
The other class is your everyday run-of-the-mill user who can only create
requisitions. Say there was a list of 18 users in the first category, and over 900 in the
second. Oracle uses roles to help manage grants to multiple users; we discuss roles
in the next section.

Roles—A Way to Group Users Together

You can create a database object called a role, then grant privileges to that role, and
then grant that role to individual users. Sounds complicated, but it's very simple. For
example, let's create a role called nurse by issuing the SQL statement **create role
nurse;** and give the role some privileges by running the six commands:

```
grant insert on tableA to nurse;
grant insert on tableB to nurse;
grant insert, delete on tableC to nurse;
grant update on tableD to nurse;
grant delete on tableE to nurse;
grant select on tableF to nurse;
```

Now let's give some users the nurse role by running the following three
commands:

```
grant nurse to ops$abbey;
grant nurse to ops$teplownd;
grant nurse to ops$lane;
```

When we want to effect a change to these three users, we just have to change
the role nurse, and the users will automatically receive the change. If we want all
three users to be able to delete from tablef, for example, we would issue the SQL

statement **grant delete on tableF to nurse;**. All database users who have the role nurse would be affected by the new change.

Other Objects You May Encounter in Oracle8*i*

Up until now, we have discussed objects in the Oracle8*i* database that all (or at least most) readers will become familiar with. This section features a number of objects that are closely related to the two main objects (tables and views), but that some readers may never have the need or opportunity to create.

Snapshots

A *snapshot* is a recent copy of a table from another database or, in some cases, a subset of that table. The SQL statement that creates and subsequently maintains a snapshot normally reads data from a database residing on a remote server. In a distributed computing environment, DBAs define snapshots for one or both of the following reasons:

- Response time improves when a local read-only copy of a table exists—this can be many times faster than reading data directly from a remote database.

- Once a snapshot is built on a remote database, if the node containing the data from which the snapshot is built is not available, the snapshot can be used without the need to access the down database. Suppose the DBA has created a snapshot called zip_codes on a server in Boston. The data from which the snapshot is built is in Redwood Shores. If the Redwood Shores server is unavailable, the users of the Boston server can still access the zip_codes snapshot that resides in Boston.

The query that creates a snapshot closely resembles the code used to create a view as we discussed in the "Views—A Special Look at Your Data" section of this chapter. The secret to keeping a snapshot up to date is the specification of a refresh interval. When defining the snapshot, the DBA specifies this interval, and Oracle8*i* manages the propagation of data from the table(s) upon which the snapshot is built.

VIP
To define and incorporate snapshots into your applications, you must install Oracle8's distributed database feature.

Stored Objects

We first mentioned stored procedures, packages, and functions in the "Procedural Capabilities" section of Chapter 1. The code for these special objects is written using Oracle's procedural SQL offering called PL/SQL, featured in Chapter 8. Just as with tables and views, users of the Oracle8*i* database need privileges to run these code segments sitting in the database. Owners of stored objects must issue an SQL statement similar to the following to allow users to run their code:

```
grant execute on my_package to public; -- all users can execute the code
grant execute on my_func to nurse_role; -- role members can run the code
grant execute on my_procedure to tom_scholz; -- tom_scholz may run code
```

VIP
Just as with tables and views, users need a method to point to other users' stored objects before they can be executed. One of these ways is using a synonym.

Database Links

Database links are closely coupled to the distributed database feature. Database links allow users to work with data in remote databases without the need to know where that data resides. When a database link is created, login information to the remote database is supplied; and, each time the database link is used, a session is initiated on the distributed network to resolve the reference to a remote table or view. Interestingly enough, the ability to reference information without knowing (or caring) where it is stored is an extension of the relational theory of storing data once and reading it many times.

VIP
Database links are a key component in an Oracle8i phenomenon called location transparency. Using this feature and database links, programs end up using the same name for a table regardless of where it actually resides.

Sequences

Often in a relational or object-relational database, systems generate numeric column values that serve as primary keys. Sequences help relieve the need for disk I/O by caching numbers in memory, thereby making them available to systems requiring a sequentially numbered primary key. In the past, before sequences appeared, application developers had to get a number from a single column table containing the ever-growing numeric value. This led to contention for the table and required resources to lock the table while one session obtained the next available number. Unlike with tables or views, applications do not select a value directly from a sequence.

Clusters

Clusters allow for a different method of storing table data. When applications continually work with a set of two or more tables, the DBA may consider using a cluster to store the data from the tables so commonly joined together. Tables in a cluster share the same data blocks; this cohabitation of the same physical area in the database files can enhance performance as the clustered data is retrieved, viewed, and perhaps updated.

Viewing Object Information in the Data Dictionary

Information about all the objects we have discussed in this chapter is stored in the Oracle8*i* data dictionary. The next listing points you to the most frequently accessed data dictionary information about objects:

ALL_CATALOG	All tables, views, synonyms, sequences accessible to the user
ALL_INDEXES	Descriptions of indexes on tables accessible to the user
ALL_IND_COLUMNS	COLUMNs comprising INDEXes on accessible TABLES
ALL_OBJECTS	Objects accessible to the user
ALL_SEQUENCES	Description of SEQUENCEs accessible to the user
ALL_SYNONYMS	All synonyms accessible to the user
ALL_TABLES	Description of tables accessible to the user
USER_CATALOG	Tables, Views, Synonyms and Sequences owned by the user
USER_CLUSTERS	Descriptions of user's own clusters
USER_CLU_COLUMNS	Mapping of table columns to cluster columns
USER_INDEXES	Description of the user's own indexes
USER_IND_COLUMNS	COLUMNs comprising user's INDEXes or on user's TABLES
USER_OBJECTS	Objects owned by the user
USER_SEQUENCES	Description of the user's own SEQUENCEs
USER_SYNONYMS	The user's private synonyms
USER_TABLES	Description of the user's own tables
USER_TRIGGERS	Description of the database triggers created by the user, including the source code
USER_TYPES	Description of the user-defined datatypes owned by the user
USER_VIEWS	Description of the user's own views

We have found one of the most useful items of information you can glean from the Oracle8i data dictionary is the interobject dependencies. The data dictionary view shown in the next listing is queried to display dependency information:

```
SQL> desc user_dependencies
 Name                                Null?    Type
 ---------------------------------- -------- ----
 NAME                                NOT NULL VARCHAR2(30)
 TYPE                                         VARCHAR2(12)
 REFERENCED_OWNER                             VARCHAR2(30)
 REFERENCED_NAME                              VARCHAR2(64)
 REFERENCED_TYPE                              VARCHAR2(12)
 REFERENCED_LINK_NAME                         VARCHAR2(128)
 SCHEMAID                                     NUMBER
```

Inspect the output from the following query for a flavor of how useful we find this information:

```
SQL*Plus: Release 8.1.5.0.0 - Production on Mon Jun 14 21:26:22 1999
(c) Copyright 1999 Oracle Corporation.  All rights reserved.
Connected to:
Oracle8i Enterprise Edition Release 8.1.5.0.0 - Production
With the Partitioning and Java options
PL/SQL Release 8.1.5.0.0 - Production
SQL> select name, referenced_owner, referenced_type
  2     from user_dependencies
  3     where referenced_name = 'ASSIGNMENT';

NAME                 REFERENCED_OWNER REFERENCED_TYPE
-------------------- ---------------- --------------------
DEPARTMENT           DEPT             TABLE
GET_END_DATE         COMMON           PROCEDURE
DURATION             COMMON           TABLE
SQL>
```

This query tells us that the department and duration tables as well as the get_end_date procedure are dependent on the assignment table. When maintenance activities begin that may affect the structure of the assignment table, it would be wise to visit these objects to see what effect the changes may have on them.

What's Next

We have given you an introduction to the most common database objects and their use. This list is not complete, but we have highlighted what are by far the most common. Every day that we work with the Oracle Server, we learn something new.

As our experience has taught us, you will continually learn about Oracle's vast capabilities while you travel down its path. Just when you think you have learned it all, you will either discover a new product or something new you want to learn to do with an existing one.

The next chapter discusses how to install Oracle8*i* and a whole bunch of other Oracle products that interact with Oracle8*i*. Many of you may have Oracle and some of its products already installed on your personal computers. Nevertheless, Chapter 6 will teach you how to do it yourself next time. The focus of Chapter 6 is Windows NT, though Oracle is Oracle is Oracle; the look and feel of the installation routines are the same regardless of the size and manufacturer upon which they are run. Installation is where it all starts . . . carry on.

CHAPTER

6

Installation

his chapter deals with installing Oracle products and the Oracle8i Enterprise Edition. Installation can often be fraught with pitfalls; vendors address how their products are installed. Many times potential clients judge a company by the friendliness and completeness of the installer mechanism. Oracle has rewritten the installer for 8i, and our experience has shown that this has been a move in the right direction. At the end of this chapter, you will have experienced and become a little more familiar with installing the following products on a Windows NT Server or Workstation:

- Oracle8i Enterprise Edition

- Oracle WebDB version 2.0.5

- Oracle Developer version 6.0

- Oracle JDeveloper 2.0

- Oracle Enterprise Manager 2.0.4

- Oracle8i Client

NOTE
It is possible as the products evolve that the dialog boxes and the sequence of events covered in this chapter may change. This chapter is designed to give a flavor of the installation routines Oracle is now bundling with their products. When possible, we will quote part numbers on the CDs we used.

Terminology

The following definitions will arm you with the technical jargon you need to make it through this chapter:

- *Autorun* is the process whereby many CD-ROM drives automatically execute a program (normally called autorun.inf) when a CD is loaded into the drive.

- *ORACLE_HOME* is the directory name under which all the Oracle software is installed. Think of it as the home of the Oracle installation or as the location where the Oracle software resides on the machine upon which it is installed.

■ *HTML* stands for Hypertext Markup Language, the universal language used for the design of Web pages. It contains a combination of text and references to objects on Web sites, with tags embedded to handle display of images and links to other Web sites.

■ The *staging area* is made up of a number of locations on a disk (also called a directory structure) from which Oracle installs software. The files are sometimes stored in compressed format, to save disk space. Installation is often a two-stage process: from the distribution medium to the staging area, and then from the staging area to the ORACLE_HOME.

■ The CD-ROM upon which you find many vendors sending out their software is also referred to as the *distribution medium*.

■ The *structured query language*, abbreviated SQL, is the most widely used interface to relational databases; it is used for data definitions, data manipulation, and the preparation of queries. Standards and acceptable syntax are defined and agreed upon by many relational database vendors.

■ A *precompiler* takes third- (for instance, COBOL) or fourth-generation (for instance, C language) source code and translates Oracle's SQL calls to standard code that can be understood by the native language's compiler.

■ A *database administrator* or DBA is a technical wizard who manages the complete operation of the Oracle database.

■ A *DLL* is a dynamic link library used by all Windows software. These libraries contain routines that are enlivened at run time to manage the resources consumed by the programs.

■ The *ORACLE_SID* is an identifier unique to each Oracle database. When Oracle is installed, one specifies an ORACLE_SID to tell the database apart from others that may end up on the same machine. It's wise to choose a meaningful name for a database so that its purpose can be figured out from the ORACLE_SID (for instance, the SID "prd" may be used for production, and "tst" for a test database).

■ A *system administrator* is the person who manages computer resources and, with the DBA, manages hardware and computer peripherals.

■ A *local database* is one that resides on the same computer as the user. Accessing Personal Oracle8*i* from Windows 98 on the same machine is an example of a local database configuration.

■ A *remote database* is one that resides on a different computer than the one the user or developer is using. The remote database is accessed using a vendor's (for instance, Novell's) network software and Oracle's network product called Net8.

- The *desktop* is the environment found on personal computers that accesses local or remote databases. The Apple Macintosh and Microsoft Windows are examples of desktop computing.

- A *patch* is a fix applied to a program. Patches do not change the overall functionality of a program; they simply fix or enhance an existing product.

- *Product bundling* is a method a vendor uses to package software components. Suppose two kinds of breakfast cereals were packaged together for a marketing promotion and sold separately at other times; one could say the product bundling during the sale is different than under normal circumstances.

- *Three-tier architecture* refers to the next-generation client/server environment in which the first tier, the client, handles display and data entry activities, the middle tier (commonly referred to as the application server) is where all the programs reside, and the third tier is the data server, where all the application-specific data is stored.

The Oracle Universal Installer

Right from the start, you will find yourself using the Oracle Universal Installer, whether you are installing the Enterprise Edition, the Oracle Enterprise Manager, or other Oracle products. Readers who have seen or used the installer from previous versions of Oracle (primarily Oracle7 or 8.0) will find many things about the Universal Installer familiar. The thrust behind the rewrite of the installer is twofold:

- It is intended to standardize the installation across all platforms all the way from high-end UNIX servers to the desktop environments such as Windows 98 and NT.

- It is intended to satisfy complex component-based requirements utilizing a Java engine. The installer's portability across any Java-enabled platform adds credibility to the product's claim to be universal.

To get started, let's first consider installing the Oracle8i Enterprise Edition software on a Windows NT server. We recommend the following minimum configuration for the server:

- Windows NT Server 4.0 with Service Pack 3 or 4 configured with a swap file of at least 240MB

■ 96MB of memory

■ A Pentium II processor with a clock speed of at least 233 Mhz

NOTE
Oracle WebDB, Oracle Developer, and Oracle JDeveloper also interact with a pre-Oracle8i database and, therefore, do not yet use the Universal Installer.

Oracle8*i* Enterprise Edition

The session we use in this section of this chapter leads you through the basics of installing Oracle8*i* Enterprise Edition on an NT server. The examples, screen shots, and text relate to version 4.0 of the NT Server, with Service Pack 3.

NOTE
Many readers may have auto insert notification turned on for the local or network CD-ROM drive from which they are installing Oracle8i.

This section deals with installing the Oracle8*i* Enterprise Edition software. This is the most common activity using the Oracle Universal Installer. When the distribution medium is placed in the CD-ROM drive, the screen shown in Figure 6-1 will appear as the autorun program loads when the medium is inserted.

VIP
If the CD does not autorun, choose Run from the Start menu or Windows Explorer and invoke the autorun.exe application in the Autorun folder on the CD.

Notice there are three choices, with icons pointing to Oracle Web sites in the bottom-right corner. Because so much content has been deposited on vendors' Web sites, perhaps it's just a matter of time until little if any documentation comes on the CD with the software.

NOTE
The CD we used for this installation is part #A69464-01. You may be in possession of an earlier or later CD with the same software.

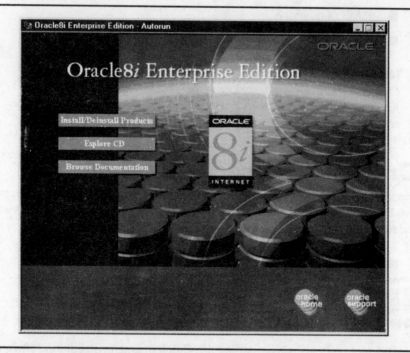

FIGURE 6-1. *Oracle8i Enterprise Edition autorun*

The Explore CD and Browse Documentation selections are shown in Figures 6-2 and 6-3. The Setup allocation shown in the former figure is where you may end up starting if the CD is not allowed to autorun or is already in your drive when you start the installation activity. Oracle has invested in HTML-based documentation. Depending on your system's default Internet browser, you will see the Oracle8*i* documentation menu displayed in Netscape Navigator as shown in Figure 6-3 or in any other browser of your choice. You may find the What's New section on the CD informative if you are upgrading from a previous release of Oracle's software or looking for specific features that led you to choose Oracle in the first place.

Finally, it's time to get on with the business at hand. Figure 6-4 shows the Universal Installer welcome screen. Readers familiar with previous versions of Oracle will find this radically different from the past. This screen is the focal point for just about all activities, be it

■   Deinstalling products

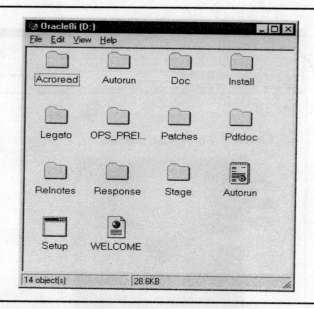

FIGURE 6-2. *The Oracle8i folder on the distribution medium*

◼ Viewing a list of installed products

◼ Carrying on to build a list of products to install

Figure 6-5 shows the File Locations dialog box with the installer. Here is the first place where decisions you make could have a profound effect on what happens further down the road. Look at the Source and Destination areas on this screen.

In the Source area of this screen, notice how the installer, by default, places the letter of your CD-ROM. Watch out when you have a mix of late version 8.0.*x* or 7.3.*x* software and Oracle8*i* as the name and location of the product-list file has changed. Oracle has always included a file on its distribution medium holding the names and version numbers of all the programs on the CD. In the Windows 95/98 environment this has always been windows.prd, and in NT it has been nt.prd. If you look for this list of products to install with the Universal Installer, the file will have the .JAR extension as shown in Figure 6-5.

And now, the fun begins. Oracle asks for an Oracle Home name and a location with full pathname. The pathname is built according to the entry you make for Home. The default name is "Ora81Home," and the default location is

FIGURE 6-3. *The Documentation menu*

"\Oracle\Ora81Home." Thus, if you entered the value "Oracle81" for the Home location, the installer would build a location of "\Oracle\Oracle81."

NOTE
If you will be installing Oracle WebDB, do not accept the defaults for Oracle Home and its location, as in that case the WebDB installer will not be able to find the database it is to be installed against.

When we installed Oracle8i for this book, we changed Oracle Home to "Ora81" and let the installer build the location as shown in Figure 6-5. After filling in values in this File Locations dialog box, you are ready to move on to the actual installation portion of this exercise. After clicking Next, a small window appears in the top-right corner of the screen with a progress indicator showing the products the installer is preparing.

FIGURE 6-4. *The Universal Installer welcome screen*

NOTE
During a number of follow-up installations using the Universal Installer, from time to time you may not see this progress indicator and the product preparation messages. If this is the case, the session should be terminated and the reason investigated.

Once the list of products has been prepared, the Installer will present you with an Available Products dialog box. The Oracle8*i* installer session displays the following choices:

■ *Oracle8i Enterprise Edition 8.1.5.0.0* installs an optional preconfigured starter database, product options, networking services, basic client software, and documentation for the server.

■ *Oracle8i Client 8.1.5.0* installs components that enable database application users to interact with an Oracle database. These components

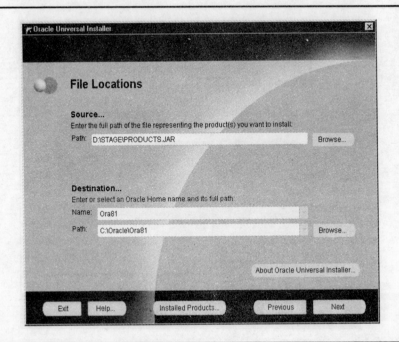

FIGURE 6-5. *The File Locations dialog box*

include networking services, basic client software, and documentation for the most common client/server configurations.

■ *Oracle Programmer 8.1.5.0* installs separately licensed development tools and interfaces for creating applications that access an Oracle database, including precompilers, networking services, basic client software, and documentation.

Figure 6-6 then appears, prompting you for your desired installation type. Notice how the Typical and Minimal choices list their respective megabytes required and Custom can make no suggestions. Armed with this information, you should take the opportunity to look around your server disks to ensure there is adequate space available.

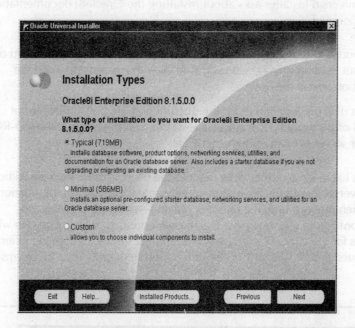

FIGURE 6-6. *The Installation Types dialog box*

When you click Next to carry on, Oracle displays a progress indicator toward the top-right corner of the screen, listing products as they are being added to the list that will be displayed on a subsequent screen. Be patient—this part of the Universal Installer's work could take a few, if not many, minutes. At this time, Oracle checks the NT server configuration; if it finds less than 96MB of memory, it will display a warning with the following suggestions:

■ If you are migrating a database from a previous release, upgrading an existing database, or building a custom Oracle8*i* database, it is suggested you need more memory.

■ If you are running Active Desktop, it will make the same recommendation.

■ If you are doing a Custom (with no database) or Minimal installation, it will inform you that you may not need the recommended 96MB.

Next, the Universal Installer asks about installing the Oracle8i documentation. You have the choice of

- Using your CD-ROM for viewing the documentation, which saves hard disk space but requires anyone who wants to view the material to insert the installation disc in the drive.

- Using a disk on your server for the documentation, consuming about 133MB of disk space. The advantage of this approach is that the CD-ROM on your server is freed up for other CDs.

What seems like a long journey now reaches the heart of the Enterprise Edition install. The Universal Installer is now ready to get some identification information from you and then proceed with the real task at hand—software copying and database creation! Figure 6-7 shows the Database Identification dialog box, in which you enter values for the Global Database Name and the Oracle System Identifier, always abbreviated to *SID*. This SID is one of the most frequently used acronyms in

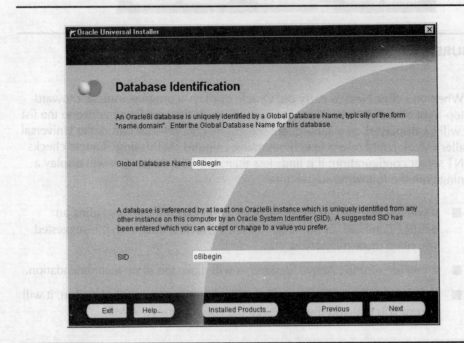

FIGURE 6-7. *The Database Identification dialog box*

the Oracle database software environment; it is used to reference database instances all the way from the desktop to the highest-range multiprocessor servers upon which Oracle operates. In the figure, notice how we have entered the text **o8ibegin** in the upper box, and the installer has built the Oracle SID automatically beneath.

Figure 6-8 shows a summary of the work the Universal Installer is about to perform. In the figure, it lists 72 new products—the number of products being installed will differ depending on the nature of the installation type you have chosen. A while back we spoke of the Available Products dialog box and listed the three options presented by the Universal Installer. The choice you made there (Oracle8*i* Enterprise Edition, Oracle8*i* Client, or Oracle8*i* Programmer) will impact on the names and numbers of products being installed.

Coffee time! The next screen displayed by the Universal Installer is shown while the installation work is being performed. Depending on the strength of your server (that is, the number and speed of your one or more CPUs), the screen with its progress indicator could take anywhere from 10 to 25 minutes to complete its work. As each piece in the puzzle is installed, Oracle lists the component name and advances the indicator as work completes. This is shown in Figure 6-9.

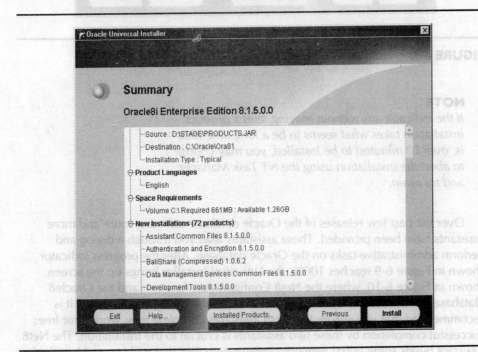

FIGURE 6-8.   *The Installation Summary screen*

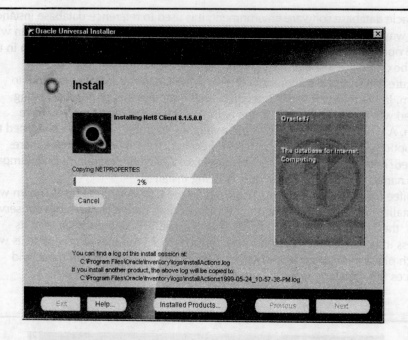

FIGURE 6-9. *Installation progress*

NOTE
If the indicator sits without moving, and a product installation takes what seems to be a long time (that is, over 10 minutes) to be installed, you may choose to abort the installation using the NT Task Manager and try again.

Over the past few releases of the Oracle database software, more and more assistants have been provided. These assistants lead you through a dialog and perform administrative tasks on the Oracle database. After the progress indicator shown in Figure 6-9 reaches 100%, the Universal Installer brings up the screen shown in Figure 6-10, where the Net8 Configuration Assistant and the Oracle8 Database Configuration Assistant are invoked. As the dialog box suggests, it is recommended that you ensure that both assistants complete their work error free; successful completion by these two assistants is crucial to the installation. The Net8 Assistant builds some initial network configuration files that will be used by clients as they interact with the Oracle8*i* database. These files help route requests from clients for connections to the database, holding necessary information such as the location of the Oracle software and the Oracle SID for the desired database. The Database Configuration Assistant constructs the Oracle8*i* database based on the SID entered in Figure 6-7 and the default names and locations of the starter database on the distribution medium.

Now spend a little time on the Database Creation Progress information that appears as the Database Configuration Assistant does its work. Notice, as shown in Figure 6-11, how there are three distinctive steps in this process:

1. *Creating and starting the Oracle instance.* This is where the services are defined to support the database on the server, and the services are started to allow, for instance initialization further in the process.

2. *Copying database files.* This is where the starter database files are copied from the distribution medium CD to the server's disk drives. Since this starter database is preconfigured, its files reside on the CD and are copied rather than re-created during this step.

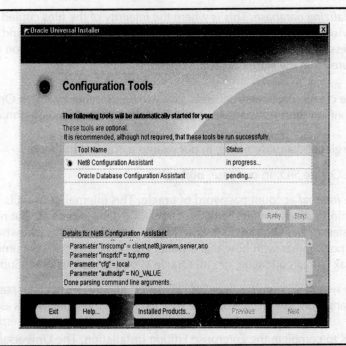

FIGURE 6-10.   *The Configuration Assistants dialog box*

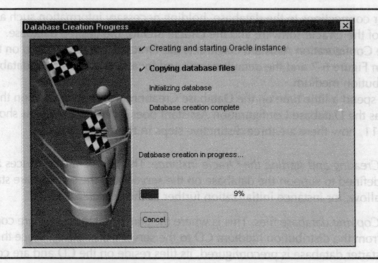

FIGURE 6-11. *Database Creation Progress*

3. *Initializing database.* This is where the integrity of the files copied in the previous step is verified, and the database instance is opened and accessibility is tested. Once this step completes successfully, you can rest assured that the starter database is usable.

Once the creation process succeeds, you will be presented with an Oracle Database Configuration Assistant Alert and the following tidbits of information:

■ The global database name, in our example, the text **o8ibegin**.

■ The Oracle SID, in our case, **o8ibegin**.

■ The *internal* account password of **oracle**. This internal account is used for administrative activities with the Oracle8*i* database such as, but not limited to, startup and shutdown. It would be wise to change this password. If you are not familiar with how this is done, check the Oracle8*i* documentation, speak with a colleague, or call Oracle World Wide Customer Support.

■ The *system* account password of "manager" and the *sys* account password of "change_on_install." It would be wise to change these passwords as well.

Click OK to complete the Enterprise Edition installation. The Universal Installer then presents you with an exit screen; as you are now done, click Exit to leave the installer. Oracle will ask for confirmation and then leave the Universal Installer.

Oracle Web DB

As discussed in Chapter 2, Oracle WebDB is a solution specifically designed to build, deploy, and manage Web-based database applications. An HTML interface allows users to work with an assortment of database objects, as well as DBAs to proactively monitor performance of individual components in a total Web-based solution built using WebDB. The following list includes the suggested hardware requirements for running this version of WebDB:

- Windows NT 4.0 with Service Pack 3 or Service Pack 4

- Oracle8*i* (release 8.1.5), though this version runs on releases 7.3.4 and 8.0.5 as well

- Netscape 4.0.7 or higher

- Oracle software SQL*Plus and SQL*Loader

NOTE
The part number for the CD used in this section of the chapter is A69323-01.

Many readers may have downloaded Oracle WebDB from the World Wide Web, while others may have received the CD from Oracle. The installation we feature here is from the CD. All aboard—Figure 6-12 shows the NT folder on this CD, where the setup program can be found. Select the "setup" program to begin.

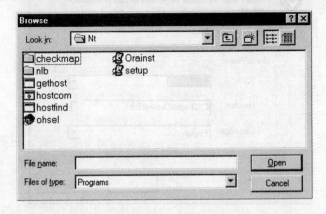

FIGURE 6-12. *The Oracle WebDB NT folder*

Oracle then brings up the Oracle Installation Settings dialog box, where you will be asked to specify information related to this session. Notice how the Company Name and Oracle Home Name will more than likely be filled in by the installer. We have set Oracle Home Name to "OraWebDB" and allowed the installer to fill in the directory name based on that entry. This dialog box is shown in Figure 6-13.

Next you will be asked the type of installation you desire, and choose from

- *Typical* installs all WebDB software components, including the WebDB packages, the WebDB listener, and the PL/SQL toolkit.

- *Custom* lets you choose which WebDB software components to install and allows you to configure each component selected.

The installer will then ask for WebDB to Oracle8i connection information, as shown in Figure 6-14. The Host Name is the name used for the server upon which the database resides; leave the entry "80" beside Port # as it works for most, if not all, WebDB installations.

NOTE
If you are installing WebDB against an Oracle8i database on which the SYS password has not been changed, it will be "change_on_install."

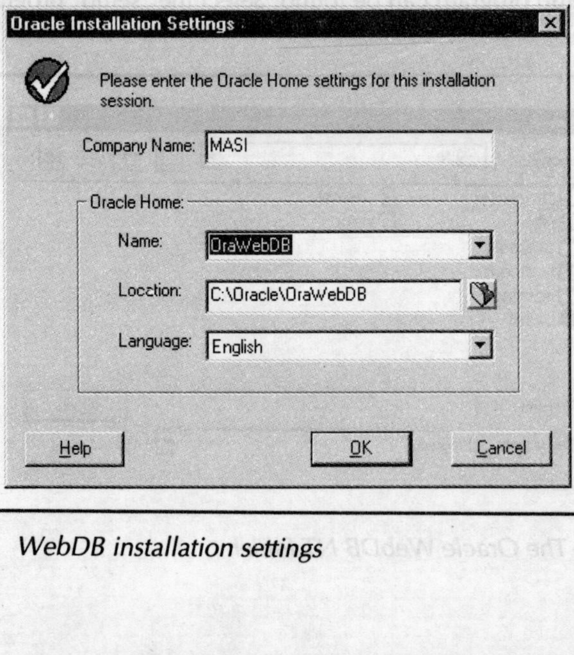

Oracle Installation Settings

Please enter the Oracle Home settings for this installation session.

Company Name: MASI

Oracle Home:

Name: OraWebDB

Location: C:\Oracle\OraWebDB

Language: English

Help   OK   Cancel

FIGURE 6-13. *WebDB installation settings*

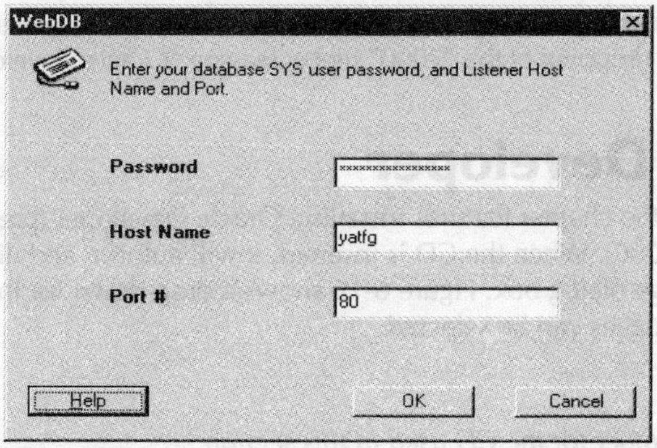

FIGURE 6-14. *The Oracle8i Connection dialog*

Armed with the information you have now supplied, the installer is ready to go off and do its real work. Product messages are displayed as the installation proceeds. During the WebDB Listener installation phase, the installer will pop up a Specify Database dialog box, asking you to select Oracle8*i*, 8.0.*x*, 7.3.3, or 7.3.4. Highlight the appropriate choice and click OK. Also, when the WebDB package installation is about to begin, the dialog box shown in Figure 6-15 appears. Before saying Yes to this question, keep in mind that the work will take from 10 to 15 minutes.

Pretty straightforward; for us, the installation of WebDB went without a glitch as long as we ensured we had not accepted the default Oracle Home location as discussed alongside Figure 6-5, earlier in this chapter. Next, we will have a look at installing Oracle Developer. This suite of products has undergone the most rapid product renaming we have seen with the Oracle software. Originally, the applications

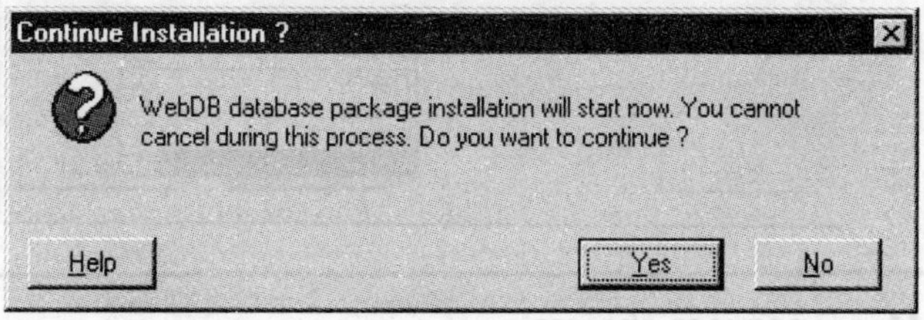

FIGURE 6-15. *WebDB package installation confirmation*

forming the heart of the product (that is, SQL*Forms and SQL*Reportwriter) were sold separately. Then along came CDE; CDE2; Developer/2000; and, never mind the millennium, the dropping of the "2000" piece, leaving "Oracle Developer."

Oracle Developer

This portion of the chapter features installing Oracle Developer (previously known as Developer/2000). When the CD is inserted, it will autorun and display the familiar language dialog box. Figure 6-16 shows a drop-down list in which a handful of languages can be selected.

NOTE
The part number for the CD used in this section of the chapter is A69616-01.

The next dialog box asks for the Company Name and the location of Oracle Home. If the two fields are filled in and you are happy with the results, click OK to move on or else enter values of your choice. The Oracle Developer Options dialog box appears next, with the following choices:

■ *Typical* installs most common Oracle Developer components and a basic set of networking utilities that allow access to a remote database server.

■ *Complete* copies the same basic components as Typical but also installs pieces for more advanced users or developers, such as the Oracle Graphics

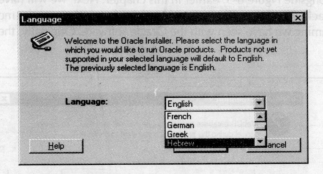

FIGURE 6-16. *Language choices*

database tables, the Oracle Developer Open Interfaces, and the Oracle Open Client Adapter for ODBC.

■ *Minimal* is used when the installation requirements dictate a streamlined set of components from the Typical install. For example, this option does not install full-blown Oracle Developer Forms, Graphics, and Reports.

■ *Custom* is chosen when the session will be customized to the installer's desires, manually selecting components to install and those to be ignored.

For this session, we will have a look at a custom installation. Figure 16-17 shows the familiar Software Asset Manager, displayed after the type of installation has been selected. Notice how many of the multiline products (for instance, Oracle Developer – Documentation) have already been expanded.

For this custom installation, we will select the following components:

■ Oracle Developer Form Builder 6.0.5.0.2

■ Oracle Developer Forms Runtime 6.0.5.0.2

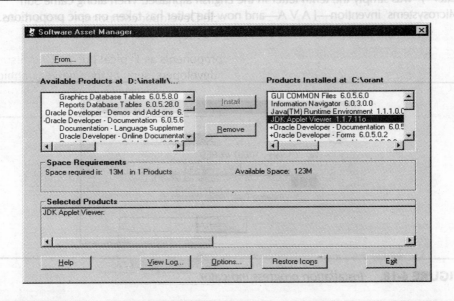

FIGURE 6-17. *The Software Asset Manager*

- Oracle Developer Procedure Builder 6.0.5.0.0

- Oracle Developer Query Builder 6.0.5.6.0

After selecting these products, click Install to get started. The next dialog with the installer will be looking for a directory within which to store Oracle Developer Forms. If you are happy with the suggested location, simply click OK; otherwise, enter your desired directory location before moving on. The next dialog box appears only when the installer detects that certain files distributed by Microsoft are not already on the workstation. Many of you may not see this at all, meaning these products are already installed. You will be prompted for a location of Oracle Developer Graphics and Oracle Developer Documentation, after which the work of copying files will commence. Sit back now and watch the show. The installer presents a progress indicator, as shown in Figure 6-18, as it goes about its work.

When the job completes, the Start menu Programs item will contain options for Oracle Developer 6.0, Oracle Developer 6.0 Demos, and Oracle Developer 6.0 Docs. Figure 6-19 shows the first of these program groups expanded, providing access to the Builder, Compiler, and Runtime environments for Oracle Developer Forms, as well as Graphics Runtime, the two modes of Procedure Builder, and the Query Builder.

It's now time to move on to the Oracle JDeveloper. Until a few years back, the letter "J" was simply the tenth letter in the English alphabet. Then along came Sun Microsystems' invention—J A V A—and now the letter has taken on epic proportions.

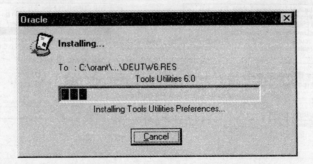

FIGURE 6-18. *Installation progress indicator*

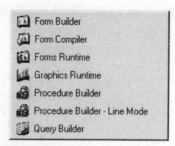

FIGURE 6-19. *Start menu programs for Oracle Developer 6.0*

Oracle JDeveloper

The Oracle JDeveloper we are using for this section of the installation chapter is release 2.0. We downloaded the software from the Oracle Technology Network Web site and unzipped the archive into the folder shown in the Windows Explorer in Figure 16-20. Double-click Setup to start the installation process.

The look and feel of the balance of the process should be very familiar to readers who have experience using the standard Windows installation routines. The next information box suggests that all open Windows programs should be closed, as well as the standard copyright statement threatening you with multicentury jail terms if you violate the licensing terms of this software.

Naturally, the installation directory defaults to "Program Files\Oracle\JDeveloper 2.0," though this may be changed. The next two screens prompt for the installation type from the following list:

■ *Typical* is the most common option selected, recommended for most readers.

■ *Compact* is installation of a minimum of the required and available options.

■ *Custom* allows the operator to pick and choose options to be installed; this is recommended for advanced users with some knowledge of product interdependences.

In line with the previous section on Oracle Developer, we are going to select Custom for this installer session. Figure 6-21 shows the Select Components products list, with the Oracle JDeveloper Program Files, Samples, and Documentation preselected. The JDeveloper Program Files include subcomponents with the following pieces, as shown in Table 6-1.

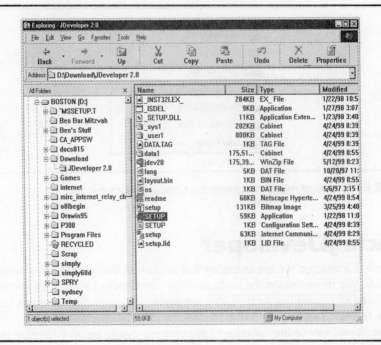

FIGURE 6-20. *Locating the setup program*

You will then be asked to select a program folder for the installation, with, surprise, surprise, "Oracle JDeveloper 2.0" as the default. The installer will then display the Copying Files confirmation screen, and Next will commence the journey. The installer displays the familiar progress indicator, as well as information on the screen in a series of splash screens, a sample of which is shown in Figure 6-22.

Component	Required Disk Space
Main program files	138,037KB
Samples	5,226KB
Documentation – HTML Help	34,08KB

TABLE 6-1. *JDeveloper 2.0 Components*

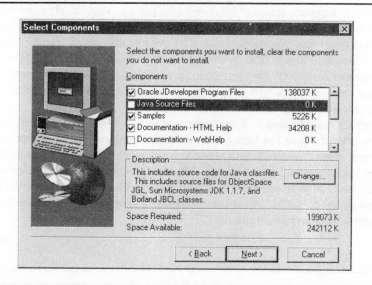

FIGURE 6-21. *The component selection product list*

FIGURE 6-22. *The Installation splash screen*

As setup completes, you will be asked whether you want to view the release notes; select or deselect the check box, as you see fit, and carry on. After the installation completes, control is released by the installer when you click Finish on the Setup Complete dialog box. You will notice a JDeveloper 2.0 option on Start menu Programs item, with the choices to read release notes and shortcuts to invoke JDeveloper itself. The first time JDeveloper is started, you will be presented with screens as shown in Figure 6-23.

Chapter 22 is dedicated to JDeveloper and will give you a high-level guided tour of the product. Java has become an industry-standard Web development environment. Pretty much all of us, even if not familiar with Java, have seen the message "Applet started" in the bottom-left corner of our favorite Web browser as a page loads. Time to move on to an old friend—Oracle Enterprise Manager, affectionately called *OEM*. This product has been around for some time, though it has undergone many incarnations.

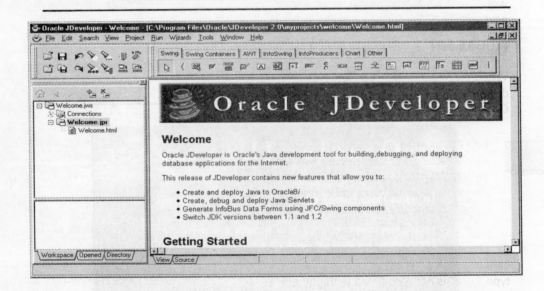

FIGURE 6-23. *Starting JDeveloper for the first time*

Oracle Enterprise Manager

Oracle Enterprise Manager is where many DBAs spend lots of time. Chapters 14 and 18, the heart of the book's DBA chapters, spend some time on a few of the tools in OEM. Before getting started with this installation, you must delve into two configuration issues briefly.

NOTE
The CD we used for this installation is part #A69135-02. You may be in possession of an earlier or later CD with the same software.

In a beginner's guide such as this, we have struggled with whether we should even bother looking at OEM installation. It took a while, but we realized we must look at the work the Universal Installer does for OEM—leaving out this discussion would be a serious omission. Bear with us and, if you follow our instructions in the next section, OEM installation will proceed just fine.

Preinstallation Tasks

When you installed the Oracle8*i* Enterprise Edition and asked for the starter database, the installer created an Admin\O8iBegin\pfile directory underneath OracleHome, with some initialization parameters in a file called init.ora.

NOTE
*The database SID we selected was **o8ibegin**; if you selected something else, the installer would have created an Admin\xxxx\pfile directory where the "xxxx" is that SID you selected.*

Using the Windows Explorer, proceed to that directory, and double-click the file called "init.ora." If the Windows Open With dialog box appears (that is, if the file type ".ora" is not associated with any executable), select Notepad and click OK to proceed. When the file is opened, proceed to the line resembling the next listing, and change the value **59** (or whatever is in your file) to **200**. The text after the "#" may or may not appear in Notepad, and it is just a comment.

NOTE
If your entry for processes is higher than 200, leave it as it is when you open the parameter file.

```
processes = 59   # INITIAL
```

Now proceed to the bottom of the file, and make the entry shown in the next listing.

```
max_enabled_roles = 32
```

These two values now need to be enlivened before Oracle Enterprise Manager is installed. This can be accomplished as follows.

1. Open up an MS-DOS Prompt window from the Start menu Programs item.

2. Enter the command **svrmgrl** to enter Oracle Server Manager as shown in this listing:

```
Oracle Server Manager Release 3.1.5.0.0 - Production
(c) Copyright 1997, Oracle Corporation.  All Rights Reserved.
Oracle8i Enterprise Edition Release 8.1.5.0.0 - Production
With the Partitioning and Java Options
PL/SQL Release 8.1.5.0.0 - Production
SVRMGR>
```

3. Enter the command **connect internal/oracle**; you should receive the feedback "Connected" from Oracle.

NOTE
*If you have ever changed the internal password (that is, to something other than "oracle"), enter your new password after the text **internal/**.*

4. Enter the command **shutdown immediate** and receive the feedback shown in this listing:

```
Database closed.
Database dismounted.
ORACLE instance shut down.
SVRMGR>
```

5. Enter the command **startup**; you should receive the following messages from Oracle.

```
ORACLE instance started.
Total System Global Area          36437964 bytes
Fixed Size                           65484 bytes
Variable Size                     19521536 bytes
Database Buffers                  16777216 bytes
Redo Buffers                         73728 bytes
Database mounted.
Database opened.
SVRMGR>
```

OEM Installation

The look and feel of the installer for this product is identical to that of the Enterprise Edition Universal Installer. When the CD is inserted in your drive, it should autostart and display the screen shown in Figure 6-24.

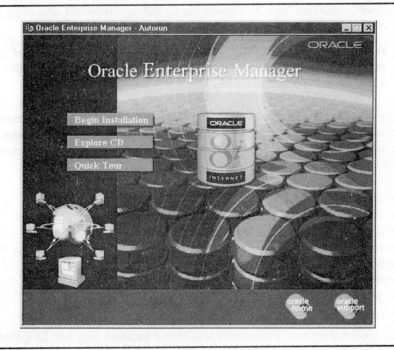

FIGURE 6-24. *The OEM installer autorun display*

The Quick Tour option on this screen invokes your Web browser, bringing up a menu where you can begin to familiarize yourself with the power of OEM or, if a seasoned user, get acquainted with version 2.0's new bells and whistles. The first menu off the Quick Tour offers you the following choices:

- *Getting to Work* gives you an overview of OEM, introduces the OEM console, and discusses the integrated applications and architecture of OEM.

- *How to Use the Console* looks at administrator accounts and introduces some features of OEM such as the Navigator, the Scheduler, and OEM Events.

- *How Enterprise Manager Works* looks at client operations/interaction with OEM, management servers, and security features and issues.

- *Stories from the Field* looks at some real-life situations and the role OEM plays in the reliability, availability, and serviceability of your corporate databases.

- *Why Use Enterprise Manager* is where you can look at how to become more productive, how to manage the Oracle environment, and some verbiage on OEM's specialized tools.

- *What's New in This Release* is where the new features are discussed, such as general interface changes from previous releases coupled with the three-tier architecture of OEM 2.0.

Clicking Begin Installation brings up the Universal Installer startup screen similar to that shown in previous Figure 6-4—remember the "U" stands for "universal." The File Location screen is displayed after clicking Next, again similar to the screen shown in Figure 6-5.

NOTE
Enter an Oracle Home location other than that used for the database. Later in the installation of OEM, you will be told that Oracle Enterprise Manager must be installed in its own Oracle Home if you accepted a suggested location that already contains other products.

If you have not entered a unique Oracle Home location, you will be informed later in the installation. The installer builds a list of products, and then the Universal Installer Available Products screen is displayed, as shown in Figure 6-25.

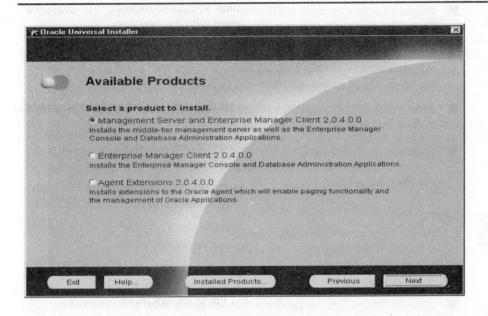

FIGURE 6-25. *Selecting a product to install*

NOTE
We recommend selecting the first option (Management Server and Enterprise Manager Client 2.0.4.0.0), as it will provide the easiest and most productive interface to your Oracle8i database.

The Installation Types screen is displayed next, offering Typical or Custom installations. The former choice installs the middle-tier management server as well as the Enterprise Manager console and database administration applications. The Typical installation occupies about 130MB of disk space. After you click Next, the installer will paint a progress indicator in the top-right corner of the screen and display messages as a summary of components to be installed is built. A summary screen is then displayed, with a tree-like hierarchy containing the following branches:

- *Global Settings* lists the location where products to be installed have been placed, the location of Oracle Home, and the type of installation being performed.

- *Product Languages* reflects the language chosen for running the product(s) being installed.

- *Space Requirements* lists the estimated space for the products chosen for installation. If not enough space is available on the specified target drive, the space requirement is shown in a different color.

- *New Installations* lists products that have never been installed before on the current machine.

- *Upgrades and Downgrades* lists products that currently exist on the machine but whose version numbers on disk differs from those on the distribution medium.

NOTE
If there are no products to be upgraded or downgraded, these bullets will not appear in the product summary screen.

- *Deinstallations* lists the products that are going to be removed before a different release will be installed from the distribution medium. The Universal Installer explicitly deinstalls a product before replacing it with a different version. Interestingly enough, the version of the Universal Installer that came on the CD with Oracle8i (which we installed first in this chapter) was 1.6.0.9.0, and the one that comes on the OEM medium is 1.6.0.7.0.

- *Already Installed* lists products that are already on the machine and have the identical version on the current distribution medium.

It's now time for the work to begin. The Universal Installer now paints an Install screen, with a progress indicator showing what is being done to what product. Log files are written to the Program Files\Oracle\Inventory\logs directory on your server. The installer builds a log filename with the time and date of the session so these logs can be differentiated from those written during a previous session. Once the installer is done copying files and running a number of configuration routines, it will invoke the OEM Repository Configuration Assistant, discussed in the next section.

OEM Configuration Assistant

There are four steps in this configuration assistant, requesting information about the OEM Repository that sits behind the scenes as you interact with OEM and its many tools. When you are performing a new install of OEM 2.0, only three of the four dialog boxes will be presented; the first two look for operator data entry, and the fourth is for information purposes only.

Selecting a Database

Figure 6-26 shows the first screen in this repository dialog. We entered the DBA privileged user **system** for User name and **manager** for the Password in the dialog box. The database within which the repository resides must be up and running while this configuration assistant goes about its work. You will have trouble connecting to the database to create the tables beneath the repository if the database is not accessible. The server we are using is called "yatfg," the port used for connection requests from OEM is 1521, and the Oracle SID we selected a while back is "o8ibegin."

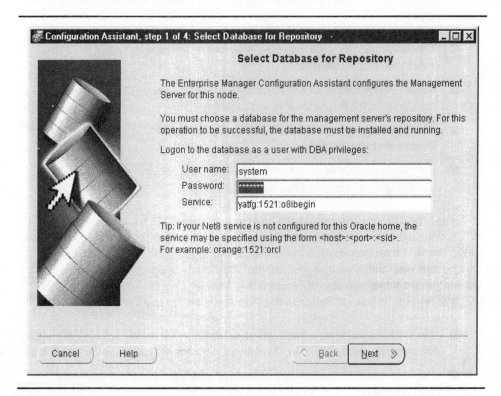

FIGURE 6-26.   *Selecting a database for a repository*

Repository Login Details

You now supply login information for the repository we referenced in the previous step. The user will be created by the assistant if it does not exist. As with many Windows dialog boxes, you will be asked to confirm the password after entering it in the Password field. Click Next to continue. We entered the User name of **yatfg** and the password **yatfg** to conform with the name of the server upon which we are running the database.

Create a Repository Summary

Figure 6-27 shows the details of the repository creation that is about to take place. The installer has checked to see if the YATFG user exists, and when it is not found, informs you that Create user is set to Yes. After the repository is created, the Oracle Management Server, or *OMS* for short, will be updated to reflect the existence of the o8ibegin database. Click Finish to complete the repository install.

A Configuration Action Progress dialog box will appear, with four pieces to the creation puzzle:

- *Create Repository User* sets up the owner as entered in Figure 6-27 as a valid user of the database.

- *Create Repository* is where the database tables and all other objects associated with the repository are created.

- *Populate Registry* is where the Windows NT Registry is updated to reflect the installation of OEM.

- *Set Configuration Parameters* is where the repository is populated with some database-specific information.

When the "Processing completed" message appears, click Close to carry on. When returned to the Configuration Tools screen, click Next to continue. That's all, folks! You will then be presented with the End of Installation information box, at which point you click Exit and then confirm that you are done. You are then returned to the screen shown in Figure 6-24. After exiting the Universal Installer, you will find the following items on the Windows Start menu for OEM 2.0:

- The DBA Management Pack, offering Instance Manager, Schema Manager, Security Manager, SQLPlus Worksheet, Storage Manager, and a quick tour

- The Extended Database Administration, offering Oracle8*i* interMedia Text Manager

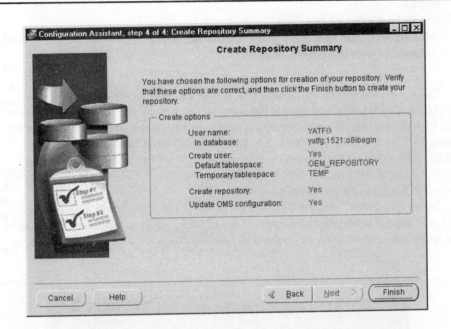

FIGURE 6-27. *The repository creation summary*

■ Oracle Enterprise Management, offering Enterprise Manager Configuration Assistant, Enterprise Manager Console, Enterprise Manager Documentation, Enterprise Manager Migration Assistant, Enterprise Manager Quick Tour, and Enterprise Manager V2 Readme

The last thing we will have a look at in this chapter is installation of the Oracle8*i* Client software. This product bundle contains an assortment of software required for the client to access the Oracle8*i* database. Typically, the base components are Net8, a player in the Oracle network connection mechanisms, the TCP/IP protocol adapter, and the developer and DBA query interface called SQL*Plus.

Oracle8*i* Client

When the Oracle8*i* Client CD is inserted, it will autorun as shown in Figure 6-28, with the Universal Installer's familiar trio of options—Install/Deinstall Products, Explore CD, and Browse Documentation.

NOTE
The CD we used for this installation is part #A69467-01. You may be in possession of an earlier or later CD with the same software.

Begin with the first option. Naturally, this being the Universal Installer, the Welcome screen presented next is the same as the screen you have come to know and love during this chapter. For this session, we have entered **Ora81Client** as the name for Oracle Home and the folder **C:\Oracle\Ora81Client** as that home's folder. After entering the necessary information, click Next to continue, at which point the Universal Installer builds its products list. When the list is built, the screen shown in Figure 6-29 will be displayed.

Select Oracle8i Client 8.1.5.0, and click Next. The Installation Types dialog box will appear next, offering a Typical install that installs components that enable database application users to connect to and interact with an Oracle database, as

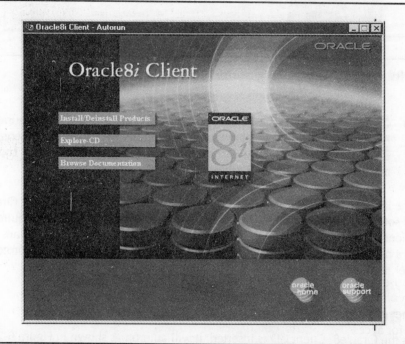

FIGURE 6-28. *The Oracle8i Client autorun*

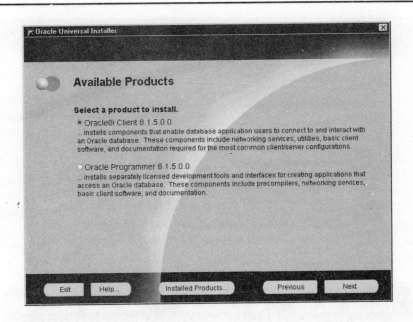

FIGURE 6-29. *Available products*

well as a Custom install that enables you to pick what you want to install. The
Typical install option will consume about 294MB; select it and click Next. The
next screen asks what you wish to do with the documentation—whether you want
it copied to your server or read from the CD. The choice is yours, though copying
the files to your server offers you more ongoing flexibility, even though it chews up
about 128MB of space. Click Hard Drive and then Next to continue. The familiar
product/processing messages will appear in the top-right corner of the screen while
the product summary screen is built, as shown in Figure 6-30.

Show time! The Install screen with the assortment of product messages now
appears as the Universal Installer goes about its work. As was the case with the
Enterprise Edition and OEM, the installation session is logged to a file underneath
Program Files\Oracle\Inventory\logs on your server.

The next dialog box that appears asks for information to set up a Net8 service
name for accessing the Oracle8*i* database. Remember, Net8 is a product that is
specifically designed to enable the connection between the client and the database
server. This screen is shown in Figure 6-31.

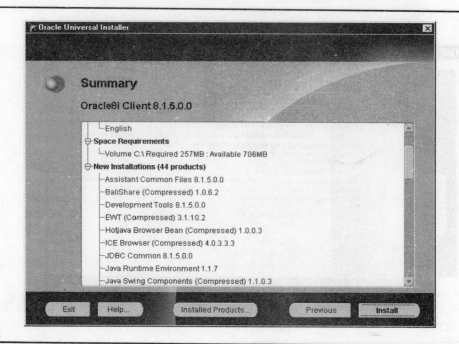

FIGURE 6-30. *The Oracle8i Client Product summary*

After you specify the Net8 service name, the following screen will ask for a network protocol, with TCP/IP (Internet Protocol) suggested as the default. Accept this protocol and click Next to continue. Step 3 requests a host name; in our case, it's **yatfg** (the name of the server upon which the database resides). Click Next to go on to step 4, whose screen is shown is Figure 6-32. This is where you specify whether the service being defined will access an Oracle8i or pre-Oracle8i database.

We're almost done—click Next to complete this configuration assistant, where you will be able to test the connection to the Oracle8i database you have just created. When the test screen appears, click Test to verify the connection. If the test does not succeed, select Change Login and enter **system** with the password **manager** to retry the test.

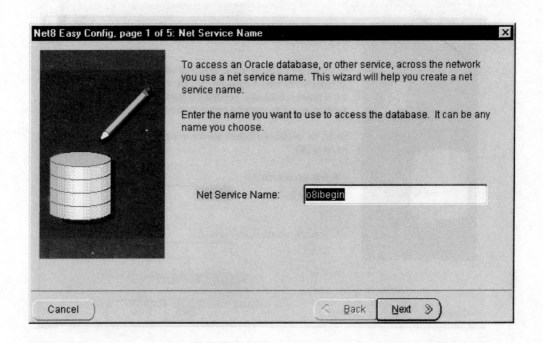

FIGURE 6-31. *Specifying a Net8 service name*

VIP
*If you have changed the SYSTEM password at any time before doing this Oracle8i Client install, use that password rather than **manager**.*

Click OK to dismiss the username and password dialog box, and then click Test once again. This is all shown in Figure 6-33.

The Configuration Tools information box appears next, showing how the Net8 Configuration Assistant and the Net8 Easy Config tools completed their work

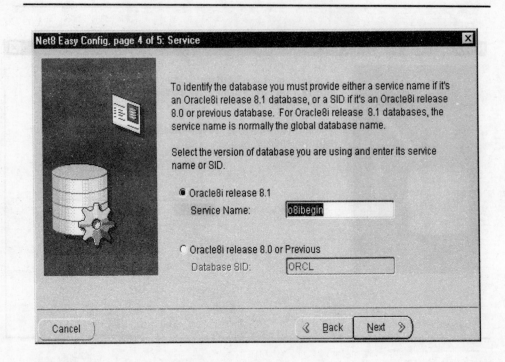

FIGURE 6-32. *Specifying a version of Oracle Server*

successfully; click Finish to bring up the End of Installation dialog box, and then exit the Universal Installer with the appropriate confirmation.

Now that was a handful! In a nutshell, we have just given you a taste of installing the Oracle8i server and an assortment of other products that interact with and support this server product. We know that your installation sessions may not resemble the screen shots and steps outlined in this chapter. If that is the case, we hope the material we have covered here familiarizes you with running the Oracle Universal installer.

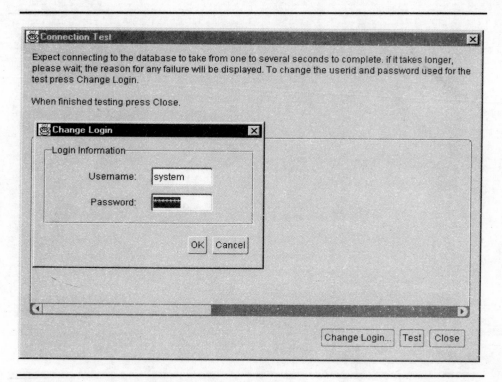

FIGURE 6-33. *Specifying a user name and password for test*

What's Next

In the remainder of the chapters, we will guide you through working with a number of Oracle products, and we'll offer some suggestions for using them effectively. Get yourself a cup of coffee—you could be here for a while.

CHAPTER
7

SQL 101

n this chapter, we teach you the basics of SQL. This could be the most important chapter of this book because if you understand SQL, you understand a relational database. Back when we started working with Oracle, this was the tool of choice for writing all the reports. Then came along another tool called RPT. If you have ever used RPT, you will understand why some people thought it might not have cut it as a robust, powerful reporting tool.

Today, you have lots of excellent choices for report writers. But if you just need to punch it, crunch it, and get it out the door, use SQL*Plus. SQL*Plus is Oracle's offering of a tool that can be used to manipulate Oracle data and prepare reports on the contents of that data. With Oracle's enhancements to the core SQL language, you have a great reporting tool. We have found that many of the reports we generate every day could be accomplished with SQL*Plus alone.

VIP
*SQL (Structured Query Language) is used by Oracle for all interaction with the database. SQL*Plus (one of many Oracle tools) is based on SQL, but it has some Oracle-specific features that can be used for writing reports and controlling the way screen and paper output is formatted.*

Some people don't use SQL*Plus for many of these tasks, for the same reason that some people find it easier to add up numbers with pencil and paper instead of a calculator. We are of the "keep it simple" camp—make it happen quick. Accordingly, SQL*Plus is our first choice for all reports. Only when our needs exceed the capability of SQL*Plus do we look for a better tool.

With this in mind, let's see what SQL*Plus can do. In this chapter, we will not try to teach you every nuance or detail about SQL*Plus; we will teach you what it takes to get at the information you need quickly. We will also teach you how to present this information in the best possible light. We will do this using a step-by-step process. First, we will teach you the two basic types of SQL statements. Next, we will create tables and populate those tables with data. Then, we will write some reports against those tables. This chapter will cover the following topics:

- DDL and DML: what they are and some practical examples of using them

- How to log in to SQL*Plus

- The most common setup parameters

- How to retrieve data from the database

- How to format data using SQL*Plus
- How to **update** and **delete** data stored in the database
- How to **create** a table and **insert** data into a table
- How to **alter** a table

Terminology

The following definitions will arm you with the technical jargon to make it through this chapter:

- *DDL*, or Data Definition Language, is the SQL construct used to define data in the database. When you define that data, entries are made in Oracle's data dictionary. Common DDL keywords are **create**, **revoke**, **grant**, **drop**, and **alter**.

- *DML*, or Data Manipulation Language, is the SQL construct used to manipulate the data in the database (rather than the definition of the data, done by DDL). Common DML keywords are **select**, **insert**, **update**, and **delete**.

- With Oracle, we use the word *commit* to indicate that data has been saved back to the database. Think of your favorite word processor. Each time you save your work, Oracle would refer to that action as committing your work.

- A *constraint* is a mechanism used to protect the relationship between data within an Oracle table or the correspondence between data in two different tables. Logic that insists that as a new employee is entered in the human resources application, his or her state of residence must be one of the 50 states in the U.S. is an example of a constraint.

- An *object* in the Oracle8 database is a thing of significance within which information is stored. We commonly speak of object types—tables and views being the two most common.

- If you try to get information out of an Oracle database using a program such as SQL*Plus, then this action is called a *query*.

- *Functions* are operations performed on data that alter the data's characteristics. For example, forcing the text "Abbeflantro" to uppercase using the SQL keyword **upper** is an example of performing a function on the text.

■ *Rollback* is the activity Oracle goes through when a session changes some data in the database and then for some reason decides not to commit the change. This is the act of restoring the information to the state it was in prior to the **update**, **insert**, or **delete** initiated by the user.

Two Types of SQL Statements

SQL statements fall into two major categories: DDL (Data Definition Language) and DML (Data Manipulation Language). Let's take a closer look at their differences and similarities.

DDL

Data Definition Language allows you to perform the following tasks:

■ Create a database object.

■ Drop a database object.

■ Alter a database object.

■ Grant privileges on a database object.

■ Revoke privileges on a database object.

It's important to understand that when you issue a DDL SQL statement, Oracle commits the current transaction before and after every DDL statement. Thus, if you were inserting records into the database and you issued a DDL statement like **create table**, then the data from the **insert** command would be committed to the database. Table 7-1 is a partial list of DDL statements.

VIP

Statements that fall into the category of DDL are autocommit; this means that when Oracle8i informs you with a message like "Revoke succeeded," the command is complete and cannot be rolled back.

In summary, SQL commands that **alter**, **drop**, **create**, and **grant** are the most frequently used examples of the Data Definition Language. Just as the name implies, DDL is the SQL statements that help define and create tables and privileges.

SQL Command	Purpose
alter procedure	Recompiles a stored procedure
alter table	Adds a column, redefines a column, changes storage allocation
analyze	Gathers performance statistics for database objects to be fed to the cost-based optimizer
alter table add constraint	Adds a constraint to an existing table
create table	Creates a table
create index	Creates an index
drop index	Drops an index
drop table	Drops a table from the database
grant	Grants privileges or roles to a user or another role
truncate	Deletes all the rows from a table
revoke	Removes privileges from a user or database role

TABLE 7-1.   *Partial List of DDL Statements*

VIP
Data Definition Language is the set of SQL commands that create and define objects in the database, storing their definitions in the data dictionary.

DML

Data Manipulation Language allows you to **insert**, **update**, **delete**, and **select** data in the database. Just as the name implies, DML allows you to work with the contents of your database. Table 7-2 is a partial list of DML statements.

In summary, DML statements are SQL commands that allow you to manipulate the data in the database. The most common SQL statements are **insert**, **update**, **delete**, and **select**.

SQL Command	Purpose
insert	Adds rows of data to a table
delete	Deletes rows of data from a table
update	Changes data in a table
select	Retrieves rows of data from a table/view
commit work	Makes changes permanent (write to disk) for the current transaction(s)
rollback	Undoes all changes since the last commit

TABLE 7-2. *Partial List of DML Statements*

VIP
*Data Manipulation Language is the set of
statements that allow you to manipulate the
data in the database.*

Now that we understand the two major types of SQL statements, let's get our feet wet. We will start by logging in to SQL*Plus. From there, we will try some of the more common DDL and DML statements.

SQL*Plus: Getting In

The easiest way to learn about SQL is by using SQL*Plus. So let's begin by logging in to SQL*Plus. For these examples, picture an Oracle username of **polly** whose password is **gone**. Enter SQL*Plus in one of two ways:

- From the Start menu, click Programs|Oracle – Ora81|Application Development|SQL Plus. You are prompted for a username and password in a Connect dialog box.

NOTE
*Since we are using Ora81 as the ORACLE_HOME,
the start menu option is Oracle – Ora81; yours may
be different if using a different ORACLE_HOME.*

■ From a DOS window,

 1. Enter the command **sqlplus polly/gone**. Oracle8*i* will open up a separate
     DOS window and display the herald as shown in the next listing:

```
SQL*Plus: Release 8.1.5.0.0 - Production on Sun Mar 17 15:32:10 2002
(c) Copyright 1999 Oracle Corporation.  All rights reserved.
Connected to:
Oracle8i Enterprise Edition Release 8.1.5.0.0 - Production
With the Partitioning and Java options
PL/SQL Release 8.1.5.0.0 - Production
SQL>
```

 2. Log in to SQL*Plus passing just the username, as in **sqlplus polly**, and
     you are prompted for the account password.

 3. Log in to SQL*Plus passing no parameters, as in **sqlplus**, and you are
     prompted for the account and password.

After entering SQL*Plus, you should see the SQL*Plus prompt: SQL>.

create Statement

The first phase of any database always starts with DDL statements, since it is
through DDL that you create your database objects. First, we will create four tables:
customer, state, X, and Y:

```
SQL> create table customer(
  2         last_name  varchar2(30) not null,
  3         state_cd   varchar(2),
  4         sales      number)
  5  tablespace custspace
  6  storage(initial 25k next 25k minextents 1);
Table created.
SQL> create table state (
  2         state_cd   varchar(2) not null,
  3         state_name varchar2(30));
Table created.
SQL> create table x (
  2         col        varchar2(30));
Table created.
SQL> create table y (
  2         col        varchar2(30));
Table created.
```

NOTE
In listings, numbers after the SQL> prompt string should not be entered by you. When you press ENTER to go to the next line, SQL*Plus puts those numbers there. The column definitions are bounded by a set of parentheses.

Data Types

By examining the **create table** scripts just shown, a few items become obvious. Not only do you have to give each table a name (such as customer), you must also list all the columns or fields (such as last_name, state_cd, and sales) associated with the table. You also have to tell the database what type of information that table will hold. For example, the column sales holds numeric information. An Oracle database can hold many different types of data. Table 7-3 is a partial list of the most common data types.

Data Type	Description
char(size)	Stores fixed-length character data, with a maximum size of 2,000
nchar(size)	Same as the char data type, except the maximum length is determined by the character set of the database (e.g., Eastern European, Korean, or American English)
varchar2(size)	Stores variable-length character data, with a maximum size of 4,000
nvarchar2(size)	Same as the varchar2 with the same caveat listed for the nchar data type
varchar	Currently the same as char
number(l,d)	Stores numeric data, where "l" stands for length and "d" for the number of decimal digits
blob	A binary large object, where maximum size is 4GB (gigabytes)
raw(size)	Raw binary data with a maximum length of 2,000 bytes
date	Stores dates from January 1, 4712 B.C. to December 31, 9999 A.D.
long	Stores variable-length character data up to 2GB (gigabytes)

TABLE 7-3. *Partial List of Data Types*

NOTE
Oracle8i offers an enhanced set of data types to handle very large objects, as well as a more robust mechanism to store numeric data. The large object data types are rolled together and referred to as LOBs (large objects).

VIP
When defining numeric columns with a length and number of decimal digits, the length defines the total number of digits, including integer and decimal. For example, the largest number that can be stored in number(4,2) is 99.99.

Remember that an Oracle database is made up of tables and that those tables are defined by the columns or fields within the table. Those columns or fields have an attribute that tells what kind of data they can hold. The type of data they hold tells the database what it can do to the contents—this is especially relevant in the sections in this chapter entitled "Using Functions with the Number Data Type," "Using Functions with the Character Data Type," and "Using Functions with the Date Data Type." For example, the number type tells Oracle it can add, subtract, multiply, or divide the contents.

What Is Null and Not Null?

If you look closely at the customer table, you will see the qualifier "not null" next to the last_name column. This means the database will not accept a row of data for that customer table unless the columns so defined have data in them. In other words, not null columns are mandatory fields. In the customer table, this means the last_name and state_cd fields must contain a value in order to insert a row of data into the table.

VIP
*Another way of thinking of not null is to use the word "mandatory." A **not null** column means data for that column can never be empty.*

What's a Null Value?

A common question people ask is "What is a null value?" Null is a column that contains no data. Think of it as a character string with a length of 0. Many times, people will load null into a column value if it is unknown. The most common mistake people make is to load null into a numeric column. The problem is 1 + null is null. So if you accidentally load null values into a numeric field, you can very quickly cause your reports to add up incorrectly.

VIP
Never use null to represent a value of zero in a numeric field. If you might perform arithmetic on a numeric column, give it a value of zero instead.

On the customer table **create** statement, notice the storage clause used to size the table. As well, we have used the **tablespace** clause to place the table in a certain tablespace in the database. The storage clause is discussed in more detail in *Oracle8 Tuning* (Corey, Abbey, Dechichio, and Abramson, Osborne/McGraw-Hill, 1997).

At the end of each line, you see a semicolon (;). This tells Oracle that you have finished entering the SQL statement and to begin execution.

describe

One of the nicest enhancements that Oracle has added to its implementation of SQL is the **describe** command. This command gives you a quick summary of the table and all its columns. In the next chapter, you will learn about stored PL/SQL packages and procedures. The **describe** command can also list the internal procedures of a package and the I/O arguments. The command **describe customer** yields the following output about the customer table:

Name	Null?	Type
LAST_NAME	NOT NULL	VARCHAR2(50)
STATE_CD	NOT NULL	CHAR(2)
SALES		NUMBER

NOTE
*The **describe** command can be shortened to **desc** in SQL*Plus.*

insert

Now that we have created some tables, let's use DML. We will start with the customer table. The statements **insert into customer values ('Teplow','MA', 23445.67);** and **insert into customer values ('Abbey','CA',6969.96);** create two rows in the customer table. Oracle responds with the following message for each set of column information created by the **insert** command:

```
1 row created.
```

The row-created message is returned once for each successful **insert**; the message informs you of the number of rows created. If there are many **insert** statements in a program, the output would resemble the following:

```
SQL> insert into customer values ('Nicholson','CA', 6989.99);
1 row created.
SQL> insert into customer values ('Martin','CA',2345.45);
1 row created.
SQL> insert into customer values ('Laursen','CA',34.34);
1 row created.
SQL> insert into customer values ('Bambi','CA',1234.55);
1 row created.
SQL> insert into customer values ('McGraw','NJ', 123.45);
1 row created.
```

insert with Columns Specified

Next, we insert data into the state table, using a slight variation on the **insert** command: we will specify the column names into which the data is inserted. This is very useful on a very large table for which you might not have all the data for every column in the table on the insert. A good example of not having all the data up front is a budget system in which you won't have the actual dollars spent data until the end of the month. Let's take a look at a program with this variation of the **insert** command that allows you to selectively load columns in a table:

```
SQL> insert into state (state_name, state_cd)
   2 values ('Massachusetts','MA');
1 row created.
SQL> insert into state (state_name, state_cd)
   2 values ('California','CA');
1 row created.
SQL> insert into state (state_name, state_cd)
   2 values ('NewJersey','NJ');
1 row created.
```

Let's finish up our inserts by loading data into tableX and tableY.

```
SQL> insert into X values ('1');
1 row created.
SQL> insert into X values ('2');
```

```
1 row created.
SQL> insert into X values ('3');
1 row created.
SQL> insert into Y values ('3');
1 row created.
SQL> insert into Y values ('4');
1 row created.
SQL> insert into Y values ('5');
1 row created.
```

select

The **select** command is how you retrieve data from an Oracle database. Simply put, you are telling the database which information you have selected to retrieve. This is the most common SQL statement you will see. The **select** command has four basic parts:

1. The word **select** followed by what you want to see (that is, the names of the columns in the tables mentioned in the next part). This is mandatory.

2. The word **from** followed by where you get it from (that is, the names of one or more tables in which the data resides). This is mandatory.

3. The word **where** followed by any selection criteria (that is, conditions that restrict the data that the statement retrieves). This is optional.

4. The words **order by** followed by the sort criteria (that is, a list of column names from part one that control how the data is presented). This is optional.

Let's issue our first **select** statement against a data dictionary view called user_tables:

```
SQL> select *
  2    from user_tables
  3    where table_name = 'CUSTOMER';
TABLE_NAME
------------------------------
TABLESPACE_NAME
------------------------------
CLUSTER_NAME
------------------------------
IOT_NAME                                        PCT_FREE  PCT_USED
------------------------------                 --------- ---------
INI_TRANS MAX_TRANS INITIAL_EXTENT NEXT_EXTENT
--------- --------- -------------- -----------
MIN_EXTENTS MAX_EXTENTS PCT_INCREASE FREELISTS
```

```
----------- ----------- ------------ ---------
FREELIST_GROUPS LOG B   NUM_ROWS      BLOCKS EMPTY_BLOCKS
--------------- --- -  ----------- -------- ------------
AVG_SPACE CHAIN_CNT AVG_ROW_LEN
--------- --------- -----------
AVG_SPACE_FREELIST_BLOCKS NUM_FREELIST_BLOCKS
------------------------- -------------------
DEGREE     INSTANCES  CACHE TABLE_LO SAMPLE_SIZE
---------- ---------- ----- -------- -----------
LAST_ANAL PAR IOT_TYPE    T S NES BUFFER_ ROW_MOVE GLO
--------- ---- ------------ - - --- ------- -------- ---
USE DURATION      SKIP_COR MON
--- --------------- -------- ---
CUSTOMER
SYSTEM
                                        10        40
     1       255       10240       10240
          1       121         50           1
          1 YES N
     1              1       N ENABLED
             NO              N N NO   DEFAULT DISABLED NO
NO                   DISABLED NO
```

Let's discuss what has just happened. Based on our criteria, the text **select** * tells Oracle to retrieve all the columns in the view. This is a special and very popular form of the **select** command.

VIP

*To see all the columns from a table, use the asterisk (*) with the **select** statement.*

In this chapter (and you may have noticed this elsewhere), we refer to the Oracle feature called a *view*. Think of a view as a subset of one or more tables. A view is a special database object that can be created to restrict access to certain columns or rows of data in a table. A view acts like a table in all other aspects (that is, in most cases, you can **update** or **insert** data using a view rather than a table). A good example of why you might use a view is to allow managers to see only their own employees' payroll records.

VIP

A view is a special database object that can be created to restrict access to certain columns or rows of data within a table.

select with Columns Specified

Rather than using the asterisk as we did in the previous section, we can specify one or more columns after the **select** keyword. The asterisk instructs Oracle to display all the columns from a table. Let's now issue this same **select** statement but specify a column we want to see:

```
SQL> select table_name from user_tables;
TABLE_NAME
------------------------------------
CUSTOMER
STATE
X
Y
4 rows selected.
```

where

Up to now, you have seen how the **select** command can be used to bring back all the columns (**select ***) or a subset of the columns (**select column1, column3**). What if you want to see only certain rows of your data? You do this with a **where** clause. For example, if you want to see all the customers with a state_cd of MA, you would issue the command **select last_name, state_cd, sales from customer where state_cd = 'MA';**. The output would resemble the following:

```
LAST_NAME                       ST    SALES
------------------------------- --    ---------
Teplow                          MA    23445.67
```

where Clause with and/or

A **where** clause instructs Oracle to search the data in a table and return only those rows that meet your criteria. In the preceding example, we asked Oracle to bring back only those rows that have state_cd equal to MA. This was accomplished by **where state_cd = 'MA';**.

Sometimes you want to bring back rows that meet multiple criteria. For example, you might be interested in the rows with a state_cd of CA and sales greater than 6,000. The statement **select * from customer where state_cd = 'CA' and sales > 6000;** produces the following output:

```
LAST_NAME                       ST    SALES
------------------------------- --    ---------
Abbey                           CA    6969.96
Nicholson                       CA    6989.99
```

In the preceding example, we wanted to retrieve rows that met all the criteria. What if you wanted to retrieve rows that met either criterion? Let's look at the statement **select * from customer where state_cd = 'CA' or sales > 6000;**. This produces the following output:

```
LAST_NAME                      ST    SALES
-----------------------------  --  ---------
Teplow                         MA  23445.67
Abbey                          CA   6969.96
Nicholson                      CA   6989.99
Martin                         CA   2345.45
Laursen                        CA     34.34
Bambi                          CA   1234.55
```

Notice how Teplow is displayed because his sales are greater than 6000, even though he is not from the state_cd CA. The **and** and **or** are known as logical operators. They are used to tell the query how the where conditions affect each other. The concept of logic as it applies to how Oracle evaluates multiple conditions could be a book in itself. Let's take the time to delve into some of the evaluation techniques. Table 7-4 explains how Oracle deals with **and** and **or** when they appear together in the same **where** clause.

The logic involved with multiple **and** and **or** words (referred to as compound conditions) can become confusing unless you look at each statement separately and walk slowly through its logic. For example, let's examine the statement **select last_name from customer where state_cd = 'MA' and state_cd = 'CA';**. With the two conditions connected by the **and** keyword, both conditions must be true for the compound condition to be true.

VIP
*Compound conditions connected by the **and** keyword must all evaluate to TRUE for the whole statement to be true.*

Operator	Reason
or	Returns TRUE when either one of the conditions is true
and	Returns TRUE only when both conditions are true

TABLE 7-4. *Logical Operators and/or*

Using the statement **select last_name from customer where state_cd = 'MA'
and state_cd = 'CA';**, let's look at a row whose state_cd value is MA. The first
condition evaluates to TRUE (since MA equals MA), and the second condition
evaluates to FALSE (since CA is not equal to MA). The logic of the statement says
that only rows whose state_cd is MA and CA at the same time can be displayed. Of
course, this is impossible, and thus the condition fails, since TRUE + FALSE =
FALSE. We deliberately created this **select** statement to show how complicated your
where clauses can become in relatively no time.

where Clause with NOT
Oracle also supports the ability to search for negative criteria. For example, you
might want to see all the customers who are not in state_cd MA. The statement
select * from customer where state_cd != 'MA'; (the characters != mean "not
equal" to SQL*Plus) would yield the output

```
LAST_NAME                        ST     SALES
-------------------------------- --  ---------
Abbey                            CA   6969.96
Nicholson                        CA   6989.99
Martin                           CA   2345.45
Laursen                          CA     34.34
Bambi                            CA   1234.55
McGraw                           NJ    123.45
```

where Clause with a Range Search
Oracle also supports range searches. For example, you might want to see all
the customers with sales between 1 and 10,000. This would be done using the
statement **select * from customer where sales between 1 and 10000;**, and the
output would resemble the following:

```
LAST_NAME                        ST     SALES
-------------------------------- --  ---------
Abbey                            CA   6969.96
Nicholson                        CA   6989.99
Martin                           CA   2345.45
Laursen                          CA     34.34
Bambi                            CA   1234.55
McGraw                           NJ    123.45
```

where Clause with a Search List
Oracle also supports the concept of searching for items within a list. For example,
you might want to see all the customers with a state code of NJ or CA. The

statement **select * from customer where state_cd in ('NJ','CA');** would show the
following:

```
LAST_NAME                       ST    SALES
------------------------------- --  ---------
Abbey                           CA    6969.96
Nicholson                       CA    6989.99
Martin                          CA    2345.45
Laursen                         CA      34.34
Bambi                           CA    1234.55
McGraw                          NJ     123.45
```

where Clause with a Pattern Search

Oracle also supports pattern searching through the **like** command. For example, you
could tell Oracle to retrieve all the last names that begin with the letter M by issuing
the statement **select * from customer where last_name like 'M%';**. The output
would resemble the following:

```
LAST_NAME                       ST    SALES
------------------------------- --  ---------
Martin                          CA    2345.45
McGraw                          NJ     123.45
```

You could also tell Oracle to look for all the last names that contain the
characters "tin" by entering the command **select * from customer where last_name
like '%tin%';**. It would return the following data:

```
LAST_NAME                       ST    SALES
------------------------------- --  ---------
Martin                          CA    2345.45
```

where Clause: Common Operators

As you can see from these many examples, Oracle has a very powerful set when it
comes to restricting the rows retrieved. Table 7-5 is a partial list of operators you
can use in the **where** clause.

order by

Let's take another look at the contents of the customer table. This time, we will
request the list sorted by last_name in descending alphabetical order. The command
select * from customer order by last_name desc; gives the following results:

```
LAST_NAME                       ST    SALES
------------------------------- --  ---------
```

```
Teplow          MA   23445.67
Nicholson       CA    6989.99
McGraw          NJ     123.45
Martin          CA    2345.45
Laursen         CA      34.34
Bambi           CA    1234.55
Abbey           CA    6969.96
7 rows selected.
```

Operator	Purpose	Example
=	Test for equality	select * from state where state_cd = 'MA';
!=	Test for inequality	select * from state where state_cd != 'MA';
^=	Same as !=	select * from state where state_cd ^= 'MA';
<>	Same as !=	select * from state where state_cd <> 'MA';
<	Less than	select * from customer where sales < 100;
>	Greater than	select * from customer where sales > 100;
<=	Less than or equal to	select * from customer where sales <= 10000;
>=	Greater than or equal to	select * from customer where sales >= 10000;
in	Equal to any member in parentheses	select * from customer where state_cd in ('MA','NJ');
not in	Not equal to any member in parentheses	select * from customer where state_cd not in ('MA','NJ');
between A and B	Greater than or equal to A and less than or equal to B	select * from customer where sales between 1 and 50;
not between A and B	Not greater than or equal to A and not less than or equal to B	select * from customer where sales not between 1 and 50;
like '%tin%'	Contains given text (e.g., 'tin')	select * from customer where last_name like '%tin%';

TABLE 7-5. *Common Comparison Operators*

As you can see, Oracle brought the list back in descending sorted order. We could have easily sorted the list in ascending order by issuing the command **select * from customer order by last_name;**. We could have also done a multilevel sort by issuing the command **select * from customer order by state_cd desc, last_name;**. This command would list customers sorted by state descending (that is, Vermont before Mississippi) and ascending by last_name.

VIP
*When no order (neither descending nor ascending) is specified in an **order by**, Oracle sorts ascending.*

Number Data Type

These fields contain only numeric data. Let's see what you can do to the columns of this type in a **select** statement. Table 7-6 highlights the most popular arithmetic operations and how they are worded in SQL*Plus.

As you can see in Table 7-6, you can certainly perform all the standard arithmetic operations: add, subtract, multiply, and divide. With Oracle, your ability to manipulate the contents goes far beyond the standard list. In addition to the operators mentioned, there is an extensive list of functions. Before we present that list, let's talk about what a function is.

Using Functions with the Number Data Type

A function manipulates the contents of a column in an SQL statement. When you are using a function in an SQL statement, the column value upon which the function is performed is changed as the column value is displayed. Displaying a

Operator	Operation Performed	Example
+	Addition	select ytd_sales + current_sales from customer;
–	Subtraction	select ytd_sales – current_sales from customer where state_cd = 'NJ';
*	Multiplication	select ytd_sales * commission from customer;
/	Division	select ytd_sales / 12 from customer;

TABLE 7-6. *Arithmetic Operators*

number column's absolute value is a good example of a function; a column that contains the number –321 has an absolute value of 321. In SQL*Plus, absolute value is indicated by placing parentheses around the column name, and the word "abs" in front, for example, abs(ytd_sales). Thus, an SQL statement worded **select abs(ytd_sales) from customer;** would display the value 321 when a ytd_sales column contained the value –321 or +321.

Table 7-7 shows some popular functions performed on number data type columns, how they are worded in SQL*Plus, and the values they display. Notice that the **select** statements in Table 7-7 use a table called dual. This table is owned by SYS and is used in situations where correct SQL syntax must be used (that is, it must contain a **from** portion) and no other table in the database is used in the statement.

Table 7-7 presents an extensive list of functions that can be performed on number data. This is only a partial list.

Function	Returns	Example	Displays
ceil(n)	Nearest whole integer greater than or equal to number	select ceil(10.6) from dual;	11
floor(n)	Largest integer equal to or less than n	select floor(10.6) from dual;	10
mod(m,n)	Remainder of m divided by n. If n=0, then m is returned	select mod(7,5) from dual;	2
power(m,n)	Number m raised to the power of n	select power(3,2) from dual;	9
round(n,m)	Result rounded to m places to the right of the decimal point	select round(1234.5678,2) from dual;	1234.57
sign(n)	If n = 0, returns 0; if n > 0, returns 1; If n < 0, returns –1	select sign(12) from dual;	1
sqrt(n)	Square root of n	select sqrt(25) from dual;	5

TABLE 7-7. *Common Functions on Number Data*

NOTE
*With Oracle8i on Windows NT, the SQL*Plus help
facility is in the Oracle documentation, and you will
be informed as shown in the next listing.*

```
SQL> help functions
SP2-0171: HELP not accessible.
SQL>
```

If you try to perform a numeric function on nonnumeric data, you will receive
an Oracle error. For example, the statement **select floor('ABC') from dual;** will
cause the following error because the data ABC is not numeric:

```
ERROR at line 1:
ORA-01722: invalid number
```

There is a whole different set of functions you perform with character data. Let's
take a look at what Oracle can do with a character string.

Character Data Type

These are fields that are entered as char, varchar, or varchar2 in the **create table**
statement. The character data type can be used to represent all the letters, numbers,
and special characters on your keyboard. There is a whole complete set of functions
you can use with the character data type.

Using Functions with the Character Data Type

Table 7-8 lists the most common functions you will perform with the character
data type.

The concatenation operator deserves special attention before moving onto the
discussion of the date data type. This is quite useful when you want to join two
character fields together. It is called an operator, though we include it in this section
on functions. Two vertical bars (II) indicate concatenation. The statement **select
'ABC' II 'DEF' from dual;** returns the text ABCDEF. Think of a form letter. The
statement **select 'Dear 'I Ilast_nameI I':' from customer;** would return the text
"Dear John:" for the row whose last_name was John.

Function	Returns	Example	Displays
initcap(*char*)	Changes the first character of each character string to uppercase	select initcap('mr. Teplow') from dual;	Mr. Teplow
lower(*char*)	Makes the entire string lowercase	select lower('Mr. Terry Baker') from dual;	mr. terry baker
replace(*char, str1, str2*)	Character string with every occurrence of *str1* being replaced with *str2*	select replace('Scott', 'S', 'Boy') from dual;	Boycott
soundex(*char*)	Phonetic representation of *char*. Commonly used to do fuzzy name searches. You can compare words that are spelled differently but sound alike	select last_name from customer where soundex(last_name) = soundex('ABEE');	Abbey
substr(*char,m,n*)	Picks off part of the character string starting in position *m* for *n* characters	select substr('ABCDEF',3,2) from dual;	CD
length(*char*)	Length of *char*	select length('Anderson') from dual;	8

TABLE 7-8. *Common Functions on Character Data*

Date Data Type

Date is the third most common type of data you find in an Oracle database. When we created the customer table, we could have easily included an additional column called sale_date, as in the following:

```
SQL> create table customer
  2  (last_name    varchar2(30) not null,
  3   state_cd     varchar2(2),
  4   sales        number,
  5   sale_date    date);
Table created.
```

In Oracle, the date data type really contains two values: the date and the time. This is critical to remember when comparing two dates, since Oracle always stores a time with the date. The default date format in Oracle is DD-MON-YY, where DD is the day, MON is the month, and YY is the two-digit year. The year portion of the date is stored as a four-digit year, where the first two digits are defaulted to the current date.

NOTE
Oracle supplies a century-specific date format mask DD-MON-RR, which is designed to preserve century digits when entering a two-character year. Please consult the Oracle8i Server SQL Reference for details under the date data type.

VIP
To ensure preservation of the four-digit year, it is wise to use the DD-MON-YYYY date format as much as possible.

Using Functions with the Date Data Type

Oracle has provided you a list of extensive functions to help you manipulate the date data type. For example, suppose you want to send out a reminder to a customer on the last day of the month for an unpaid invoice. If you want to print the letter and send it when appropriate, you would perform the function last_day to place the correct date in the reminder's header. Table 7-9 shows the most common date functions.

Special Formats with the Date Data Type

You can use a number of formats with dates. These formats are used to change the display format of a date. Table 7-10 shows some date formats and their output.

Function	Returns	Example	Displays
sysdate	Current date and time	Select sysdate from dual;	28-FEB-02 on February 28, 2002.
last_day	Last day of the month	Select last_day(sysdate) from dual;	31-MAR-02 on March 12, 2002
add_months(d,n)	Adds or subtracts n months from date d	Select add_months (sysdate,2) from dual;	18-MAY-02 on March 18, 2002
months_between (f,s)	Difference in months between date f and date s	Select months_between (sysdate, '12-MAR-02') from dual;	13 in April 2003
next_day(d,day)	Date that is the specified day of the week after today	select next_day (sysdate,'Tuesday') from dual;	03-JAN-02 on December 30, 2001

TABLE 7-9. *Common Functions on Date Data*

VIP
Be careful about using the format MM for minutes (you should use MI for minutes). MM is used for month; it will work if you try to use it for minutes, but the results will be wrong. This is a common pitfall; just ask Mark!

Date Arithmetic

Just as soon as you start working with the date data type, you will ask the question "How many days ago did we change the oil in the car?" Date arithmetic allows you to find this answer. When you add two to a date column, Oracle knows that you

Format	Returns	Example	Displays
Y or YY or YYY	Last one, two, or three digits of year	select to_char(sysdate, 'YYY') from dual;	002 for all dates in 2002
SYEAR or YEAR	Year spelled out; using the S places a minus sign before B.C. dates	select to_char(sysdate, 'SYEAR') from dual;	–1112 in the year 1112 B.C.
Q	Quarter of year (January through March = 1)	select to_char (sysdate, 'Q') from dual;	2 for all dates in June
MM	Month (01–12; Dec = 12)	select to_char(sysdate, 'MM') from dual;	12 for all dates in December
RM	Roman numeral month	select to_char(sysdate, 'RM') from dual;	IV for all dates in April
Month	Name of month as a nine-character name	select to_char(sysdate, 'Month') from dual;	May followed by 6 spaces for all dates in May
WW	Week of year	select to_char(sysdate, 'WW') from dual;	24 on June 13, 2002
W	Week of the month	select to_char(sysdate, 'W') from dual;	1 on October 1, 2002
DDD	Day of the year: January 1 is 001, February 1 is 032, etc.	select to_char(sysdate, 'DDD') from dual;	363 on December 29, 2002
DD	Day of the month	select to_char(sysdate, 'DD') from dual;	04 on October 4 in any year
D	Day of the week (1–7)	select to_char(sysdate, 'D') from dual;	5 on March 14, 2002

TABLE 7-10. *Common Formats Using Date Data*

Format	Returns	Example	Displays
DY	Abbreviated name of day	select to_char(sysdate, 'DY') from dual;	SUN on March 24, 2002
HH or HH12	Hour of day (1–12)	select to_char(sysdate, 'HH') from dual;	02 when it is 2 hours, and 8 minutes past midnight
HH24	Hour of day using 24-hour clock	select to_char(sysdate, 'HH24') from dual;	14 when it is 2 hours and 8 minutes past noon
MI	Minutes (0–59)	select to_char(sysdate, 'MI') from dual;	17 when it is 4:17 in the afternoon
SS	Seconds (0–59)	select to_char(sysdate,'SS') from dual;	22 when the time is 11:03:22

TABLE 7-10.   *Common Formats Using Date Data* (continued)

mean two days. Say the column sale_date contains 03-MAR-02; in this case, the SQL statement **select sale_date+10 from customer;** would return 13-MAR-02. Let's look at two more examples with date arithmetic.

VIP
*Date arithmetic can be one of the most frustrating operations in SQL*Plus. Oracle is very stringent with the rules on date formats upon which arithmetic can be performed.*

Oracle takes care of arithmetic that spans month or year boundaries. For example, the statement **select to_char(sysdate+14) from dual;** will return 06-JAN-03 on December 23, 2002.

Converting from One Column Type to Another

Many times, you may want to convert a data column from one data type to another (for instance, number to date or character to number). Oracle has three main conversion functions:

- **to_char** converts any data type to character data type. The statement **select to_char(8897) from dual;** returns a character data type answer containing the characters 8897.

- **to_number** converts a valid set of numeric character data (for instance, character data 8897) to number data type. The statement **select to_number('8897') from dual;** returns a number data type answer containing the number 8897.

- **to_date** converts character data of the proper format to date data type. This is the conversion that provides the most problems. The statement **select to_date('12-DEC-02') from dual;** succeeds, since 12-DEC-02 is a valid date format. However, problems arise if you pass the statement **select to_date('bad date') from dual;** to Oracle. The statement **select to_date('20021227','YYYYMMDD') from dual;** would return a date of 27-DEC-02 because the date mask in the to_date function and the data to be converted are valid dates. The statement **select to_date('20021236','YYYYMMDD') from dual;** would fail because there are not 36 days in December.

VIP
Using the to_date conversion mechanism can generate a wide assortment of Oracle errors when it receives bad date format data.

Update, Delete, and Alter

While the **select** statement will be the one you use the most, you will use these three commands regularly. Many SQL programs you write will have a mixture of these statements (such as **update**, **delete**, and **insert**) coupled with statements starting with the **select** keyword. Earlier in the chapter, we've seen how the insert statement works. In this section, we'll take a closer look at the **update** and **delete** commands. We've also added the DDL **alter** command.

update

Sometimes it is necessary to update data stored within a table. You do this via the **update** command. The command has three parts:

■ The word **update** followed by the table you want to change. This is mandatory.

■ The word **set** followed by one or more columns you want to change. This is mandatory.

■ The word **where** followed by selection criteria. This is optional.

For example, say you want to change all the sales figures to 0 in the customer table. You would issue the SQL statement **update customer set sales = 0;** and Oracle would respond with the number of rows updated. If you want to change only those customers from state_cd of MA to 0, you could use the SQL statement **update customer set sales = 0 where state_cd = 'MA';**. As you can see, the **update** command is a very powerful tool at your disposal.

delete

The **delete** command is used when you want to remove one or more rows of data from a table. The command has two parts:

■ The words **delete from** followed by the table name you want to remove data from. This is mandatory.

■ The word **where** followed by the criteria for the delete. This is optional.

Let's take a closer look at the **delete** command. If you want to remove all the customer records, you could issue the SQL statement **delete from customer;**. If you just want to delete records with customers from state_cd CA, you would use the SQL statement **delete from customer where state_cd = 'CA';**.

alter

After a table is created, you sometimes realize you need to add an additional column. You do this with the **alter table** command. For example, the statement **alter table customer add (sale_date date);** would successfully add the sale_date column to the customer table if it did not exist. Most of the time, you will use **alter** to add a column to a table. The statement **alter table x modify (col1 date);** is used to change the data type for a column that already exists in a table.

VIP

*Oracle8i is very strict with its rules about column contents when you wish to change the data type for a column if the column contains data when the **alter** is issued.*

You are allowed to stack the columns in the **alter table** statement. The command **alter table x modify (col1 date, col5 number(3,1));** is just as valid as two separate **alter** statements.

New with Oracle8*i*, you can remove columns that you don't want anymore with the **alter table** statement. For example, if you wanted to remove a newly added sale_date column from the customer table, the syntax used is shown in the next listing.

```
alter table customer drop column sale_date;
```

This would immediately remove the column from the table, allowing you to reclaim space that was used by the sale_date column.

VIP

*There are some strict rules governing what types of **alter table** statements are valid under what conditions. If you enter an invalid **alter table** statement, Oracle informs you and tells you why it is not valid.*

Joining Two Tables Together

In the real world, much of the data you need is in more than one table. Many times, you need to go to multiple tables. For example, let's say that in the customer table you only store the state code; then, if you want the state name, you would need to join the customer table to the state table. You do this by joining the tables together. By definition, relational databases such as Oracle allow you to relate (or join) two or more tables based on common fields. Most often, these fields are what we refer to as key fields.

There are two types of keys: primary and foreign. A primary key is what makes a row of data unique within a table. In the state table, state_cd is the primary key. The customer table also contains state_cd, which in this case is a foreign key. One table's foreign key is used to get information out of another (foreign) table. With this in mind, let's take a look at two tables, X and Y, first mentioned in the "create Statement" section of this chapter. The SQL statement **select * from x;** returns these rows:

```
col
---
1
2
3
```

The statement **select * from y;** returns these rows:

```
col
----
3
4
5
```

Let's see what happens when you join the two tables together. Oracle allows you to give tables an alternate name, called an alias. In this case, we are going to give tableX the alias right and tableY the alias left. Then, we can use the alternate names with the columns to keep things clear. The statement **select right.col, left.col from x right, y left where right.col = left.col;** yields the following output:

```
col col
--- ---
3   3
```

Notice the col column values in both tables were compared, and the SQL statement required both tables to match on their respective col column values. The only column value that matches both tableX and tableY is the row with the number 3 in the col column value. Hence, only one row is selected as the tables are joined.

Formatting the Output

Up to now, we have learned how to **create** and **alter** tables, **insert** data into the tables, **update** and **delete** from the tables, and convert from one data type to another. Now we'll learn how to put it all together and write a great report. In SQL*Plus, you can set many parameters to control how SQL*Plus output is displayed. You can see all the current settings by issuing the SQL*Plus command **show all**. The output from this command resembles the following:

```
appinfo is ON and set to "SQL*Plus"
arraysize 15
autocommit OFF
autoprint OFF
autorecovery OFF
autotrace OFF
blockterminator "." (hex 2e)
btitle OFF and is the first few characters of the next SELECT statement
cmdsep OFF
colsep " "
compatibility version NATIVE
concat "." (hex 2e)
copycommit 0
COPYTYPECHECK is ON
define "&" (hex 26)
describe DEPTH 1 LINENUM OFF INDENT ON
echo OFF
editfile "afiedt.buf"
embedded OFF
escape OFF
FEEDBACK ON for 6 or more rows
flagger OFF
flush ON
heading ON
headsep "|" (hex 7c)
instance "local"
linesize 55
lno 5
loboffset 1
logsource ""
long 80
longchunksize 80
newpage 1
null ""
numformat ""
numwidth 9
pagesize 1000
PAUSE is OFF
pno 1
recsep WRAP
recsepchar " " (hex 20)
release 801050000
repfooter OFF and is NULL
repheader OFF and is NULL
```

```
serveroutput OFF
shiftinout INVISIBLE
showmode OFF
spool OFF
sqlblanklines OFF
sqlcase MIXED
sqlcode 0
sqlcontinue "> "
sqlnumber ON
sqlprefix "#" (hex 23)
sqlprompt "SQL> "
sqlterminator ";" (hex 3b)
suffix "sql"
tab ON
termout ON
time OFF
timing OFF
trimout ON
trimspool OFF
ttitle OFF and is the first few characters of the next SELECT statement
underline "-" (hex 2d)
USER is "O8IBEGIN"
verify ON
wrap : lines will be wrapped
```

As you can see, there are many parameters you can set to alter your
environment. We are going to change the major ones.

Page and Line Size

The **set linesize** command tells Oracle how wide the page is. The most common
settings are 80 and 132. To set the line size to 80, enter the command **set linesize
80**. The **set pagesize** command tells Oracle how long the page is. The most
common settings are 55 and 60. To make it easier to see the page breaks,
you can set this parameter to 30 using the command **set pagesize 30**.

Page Titles

You can also tell Oracle how you want the page title to show up. The **ttitle**
command includes many options. We usually stick with the default settings:
the text shown in the title is centered on the line, and the date and page number are
printed on every page. To place the title on two lines, use the vertical bar character
(|) to get SQL*Plus to issue two lines. The command **ttitle 'Database
Technologies | Customer Report'** tells SQL*Plus to center the text "Database

Technologies" on the first title line, then to skip to line two and center the text "Customer Report."

Page Footers

The **btitle** command is used to place something on the bottom of every page. We recommend putting the program name there. Then, when users want you to change a report, all they need to tell you is the name on the bottom. This can help avoid a lot of confusion. The command **btitle '--- sample.sql ---'** tells SQL*Plus to center the text "--- sample.sql ---" at the bottom of every page. You can use the word **left** or **right** to place the text in **btitle** elsewhere than the center of the page; if no placement word is included in **btitle**, Oracle places the text in the center.

Writing SQL*Plus Output to a File

The **spool** command tells Oracle to save SQL*Plus output to a datafile. To use the spool command, you include the name of the output file. On Windows NT, for example, this can be done by entering the command **spool c:\report\out.lis**. Most operating systems append the text **.lst** to the end of the name you specify. For example, the command **spool report** will produce a file called report.lst.

VIP
*SQL*Plus adds an extension to the filename mentioned in the spool command. This extension can differ among operating systems.*

Say we have issued the commands **set linesize 70**, **set pagesize 23** and formatted the sales column using the command **col sales format 99999999**. We want to save the output of the SQL statement **select * from customer;** to a file. The output from that command is shown in Figure 7-1; this output would be captured in the filename specified with the spool statement. Notice that there are no decimal digits in the sales, since the column was formatted using 99999999.

To stop spooling, issue the command **spool off** or **spool out**. The latter closes the output file and prints it as well.

Formatting Columns in the Output

Most times, you need to format the actual column data. You do this through the **column** command. Let's issue two additional formatting commands and then reissue the query on the customer table.

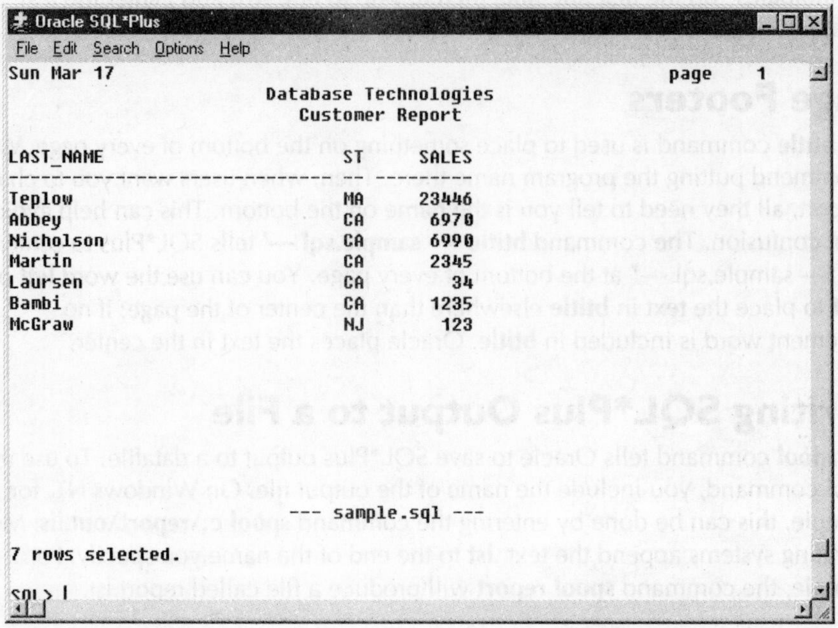

```
┌─────────────────────────────────────────────────────────────────┐
│ ♨ Oracle SQL*Plus                                    _ □ X       │
├─────────────────────────────────────────────────────────────────┤
│ File  Edit  Search  Options  Help                                │
│ Sun Mar 17                                         page    1      │
│                     Database Technologies                        │
│                       Customer Report                            │
│                                                                  │
│ LAST_NAME                        ST      SALES                   │
│ --------------------------------- --     ---------               │
│ Teplow                           MA        23446                 │
│ Abbey                            CA         6970                 │
│ Nicholson                        CA         6990                 │
│ Martin                           CA         2345                 │
│ Laursen                          CA           34                 │
│ Bambi                            CA         1235                 │
│ McGraw                           NJ          123                 │
│                                                                  │
│                                                                  │
│                     --- sample.sql ---                           │
│                                                                  │
│ 7 rows selected.                                                 │
│                                                                  │
│ SQL >                                                            │
└─────────────────────────────────────────────────────────────────┘
```

FIGURE 7-1.   *Sample formatted output*

The command **column last_name format a9 wrap heading 'Last | Name'** tells SQL*Plus that there should be only nine characters displayed in the last_name column. The 9 places a length on the display width of last_name, and the a tells SQL*Plus that it will be only character data. The wrap portion tells SQL*Plus that if a last_name shows up that is longer than nine characters, the extra characters should spill onto the next line. The heading portion tells SQL*Plus to print the heading "Last Name" on the report, split over two lines.

The command **column state_cd format a8 heading 'State | Code'** tells SQL*Plus to reserve eight positions for display of the state_cd and put the two-line heading "State Code" at the top of the state code column. Now the identical SQL statement **select * from customer;** will produce the output shown in Figure 7-2.

Hey—pretty slick! Now let's format the number field. The format clause indicates the number of places to use to display each number and where to insert the commas. The statement **column sales format 999,999,999,999.99 heading**

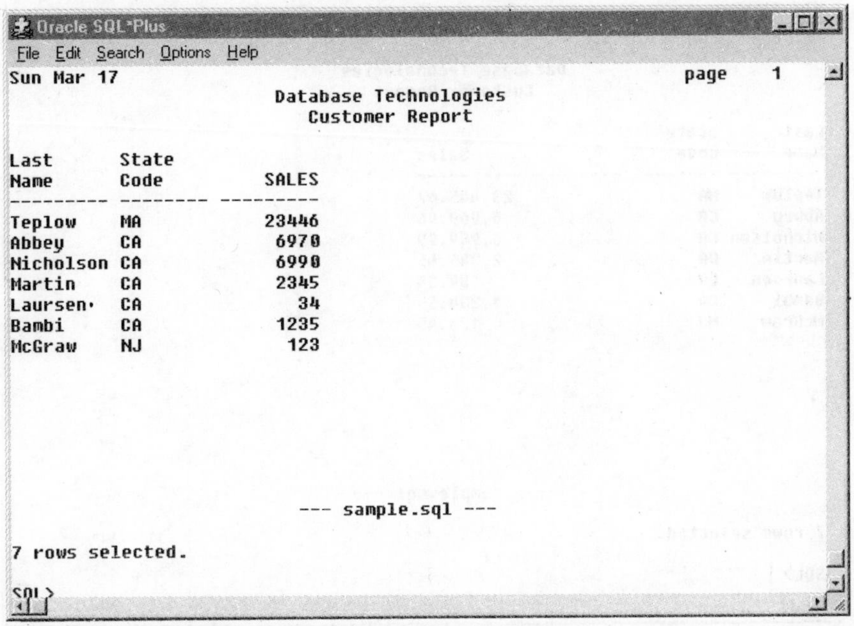

```
Oracle SQL*Plus                                          _ □ ×
File  Edit  Search  Options  Help
Sun Mar 17                                         page    1
                      Database Technologies
                        Customer Report

Last       State
Name       Code          SALES
--------   --------   ----------
Teplow     MA             23446
Abbey      CA              6970
Nicholson  CA              6990
Martin     CA              2345
Laursen·   CA                34
Bambi      CA              1235
McGraw     NJ               123




                    --- sample.sql ---

7 rows selected.

SQL>
```

FIGURE 7-2.   *Output with two-column formatting commands*

'Sales' tells SQL*Plus to print up to 12 integer digits and 2 decimal digits, using the commas to separate the thousands. The enhanced report output is shown in Figure 7-3.

Break Logic

Now let's add some break logic. One of the things SQL*Plus makes easy is dealing with breaking. As soon as you issue the break command, SQL*Plus is smart enough to manage all break logic for you.

Let's look at the SQL query **select state_cd, last_name, sales from customer order by state_cd, last_name;**, with the column format command **col sales format 999999.99**. Without using break logic, the output from this query is shown in Figure 7-4.

Let's issue the command **break on state_cd**, and the same query output changes to what is shown in Figure 7-5. Notice how the state_cd CA prints in line 1, is

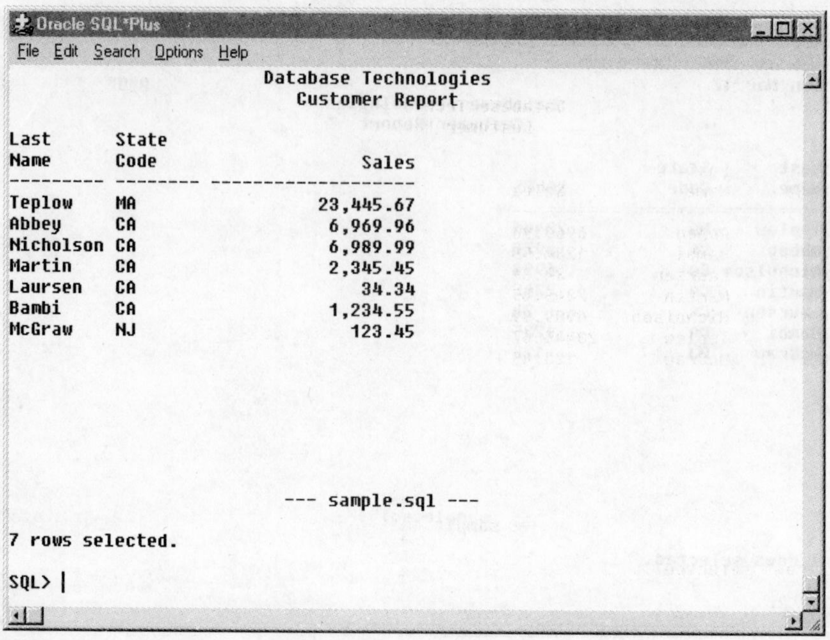

```
‡ Oracle SQL*Plus                                    _ □ ×
File  Edit  Search  Options  Help
                    Database Technologies
                      Customer Report
Last        State
Name        Code                     Sales
---------   --------    -------------------
Teplow      MA                   23,445.67
Abbey       CA                    6,969.96
Nicholson   CA                    6,989.99
Martin      CA                    2,345.45
Laursen     CA                       34.34
Bambi       CA                    1,234.55
McGraw      NJ                      123.45




                    --- sample.sql ---

7 rows selected.

SQL> |
```

FIGURE 7-3. *Output with all columns formatted*

suppressed in lines 2 through 5 (since the state_cd has not changed from line 1), and then prints again in lines 6 and 7 with different values.

VIP
*To implement break logic in SQL*Plus, you must order the query by the same column on which the* ***break*** *command is issued.*

To illustrate this point, the command **break on state_cd** followed by the query **select state_cd,last_name,sales from customer order by last_name;** would produce the output shown in Figure 7-6.

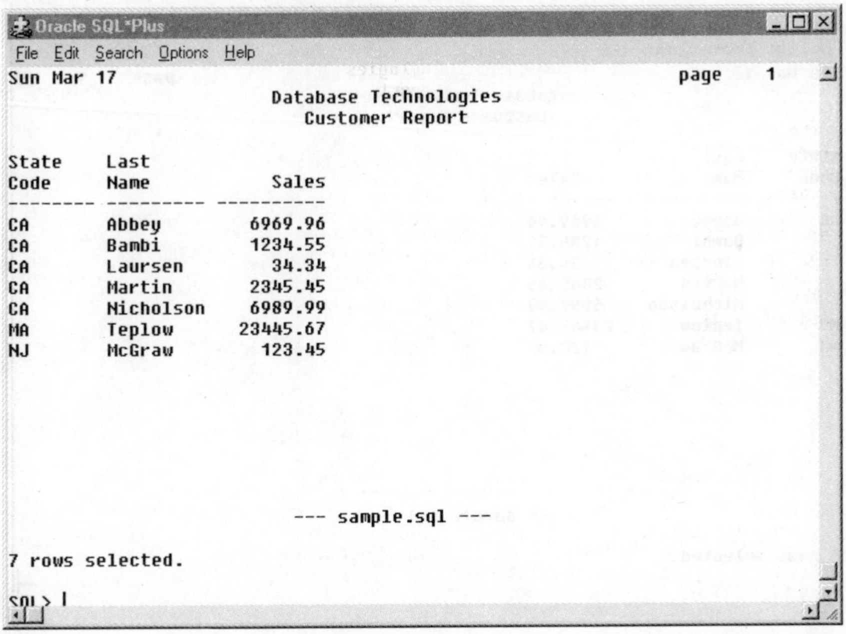

```
┌─────────────────────────────────────────────────────────────────────┐
│ ♨ Oracle SQL*Plus                                          _□×│
│ File  Edit  Search  Options  Help                                      │
│ Sun Mar  17                                         page     1    ▲│
│                        Database Technologies                           │
│                          Customer Report                               │
│                                                                        │
│   State     Last                                                       │
│   Code      Name            Sales                                      │
│   --------  ---------   ----------                                     │
│   CA        Abbey         6969.96                                      │
│   CA        Bambi         1234.55                                      │
│   CA        Laursen         34.34                                      │
│   CA        Martin        2345.45                                      │
│   CA        Nicholson     6989.99                                      │
│   MA        Teplow       23445.67                                      │
│   NJ        McGraw         123.45                                      │
│                                                                        │
│                                                                        │
│                                                                        │
│                          --- sample.sql ---                            │
│                                                                        │
│   7 rows selected.                                                     │
│                                                                        │
│   sol > |                                                          ▼│
└─────────────────────────────────────────────────────────────────────┘
```

FIGURE 7-4.   *Output without break logic*

Notice how ordering the query results by last_name has interfered with the desired output; the three CA states print first, then one NJ, followed by another CA entry.

Break and Skip

Let's take this one step further. Often when implementing break logic, we want to leave one or more blank lines before displaying the new break column value. This is done with the **skip** command. Let's reformat the sales column with the command **col sales format $999,999,999.99 heading 'YTD | Sales'** and reissue the break with **break on state_cd skip 1**. Now, the statement **select state_cd,last_name,sales from customer order by state_cd,last_name;** produces the output shown in Figure 7-7.

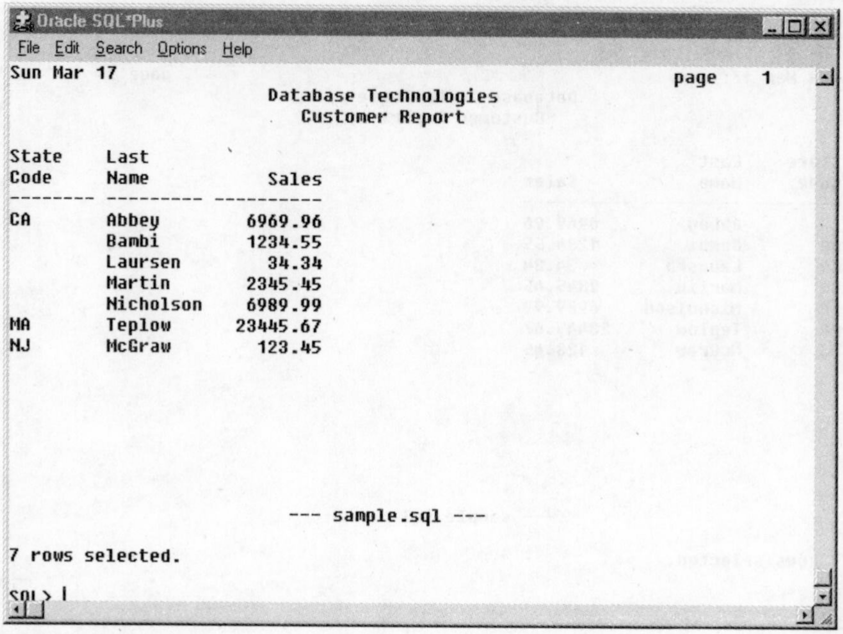

```
Oracle SQL*Plus                                              _ □ X
File  Edit  Search  Options  Help
Sun Mar 17                                          page    1
                     Database Technologies
                       Customer Report

State    Last
Code     Name           Sales
------   --------   ----------
CA       Abbey         6969.96
         Bambi         1234.55
         Laursen         34.34
         Martin        2345.45
         Nicholson     6989.99
MA       Teplow       23445.67
NJ       McGraw         123.45




                    --- sample.sql ---

7 rows selected.

SQL>
```

FIGURE 7-5. *Break report output*

Notice how Oracle suppresses printing of the state_cd every time. You could have easily told Oracle to compute total sales at each break. We discuss this in the next section.

Computing Column Values at Break

You just need to tell SQL*Plus what you want added up, using the **compute sum** command. Let's now issue the commands necessary to complete the formatting of the break and to compute the YTD totals.

The command **compute sum of sales on report** forces a report total at the end of the output. The word **report** is used here to trigger the sum of a number field to be

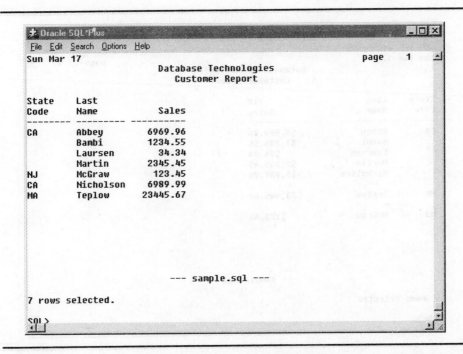

```
Sun Mar 17                                                    page    1
                         Database Technologies
                           Customer Report

State      Last
Code       Name           Sales
-------    -------    ----------
CA         Abbey         6969.96
           Bambi         1234.55
           Laursen         34.34
           Martin        2345.45
NJ         McGraw         123.45
CA         Nicholson     6989.99
MA         Teplow       23445.67




                      --- sample.sql ---

7 rows selected.

SQL>
```

FIGURE 7-6.   *Output with break on state_cd and ordered by last_name*

displayed at the end of a report. The command **compute sum of sales on state_cd** forces totals to be printed for a state when a new state code is printed.

To print the report total, we need to reset the break conditions with the command **break on report skip 1 on state_cd skip 1**. We change the SQL statement to sort the data by state_cd. Ordering the data by the same column mentioned in the break statement is necessary for break reporting.

NOTE
*You may have to increase the page size to get the output from this section to print on one page. Do so by entering the command **set pagesize 28**.*

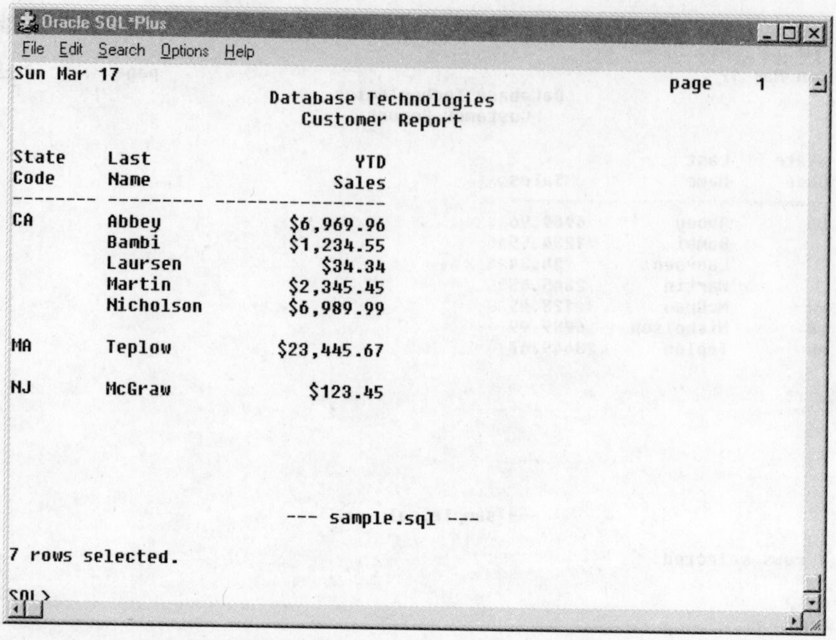

```
Oracle SQL*Plus                                          _ □ ×
File  Edit  Search  Options  Help
Sun Mar 17                                        page    1
                    Database Technologies
                     Customer Report

State    Last              YTD
Code     Name             Sales
------   --------    -------------
CA       Abbey          $6,969.96
         Bambi          $1,234.55
         Laursen           $34.34
         Martin         $2,345.45
         Nicholson      $6,989.99

MA       Teplow        $23,445.67

NJ       McGraw          $123.45




               --- sample.sql ---

7 rows selected.

SQL >
```

FIGURE 7-7.   *Break report output with one line after break*

The SQL statement is now **select state_cd, last_name, sales from customer order by state_cd, last_name;**. Figure 7-8 shows the break output after reformatting the sales column with the statement **col sales format $999,999,999.99 heading 'YTD I Sales'**.

Break Logic and Compute Sum Using Two Tables

Finally, let's utilize what we've learned in this chapter to show a final report. Recall the earlier "Joining Two Tables Together" section in which we discussed joins: You select data from more than one table and match column values from one against the other. Now, rather than printing the state_cd, let's print the state name instead.

We need the state_name column from the state table, and we can join the state table to the customer table via state_cd. The select statement becomes **select**

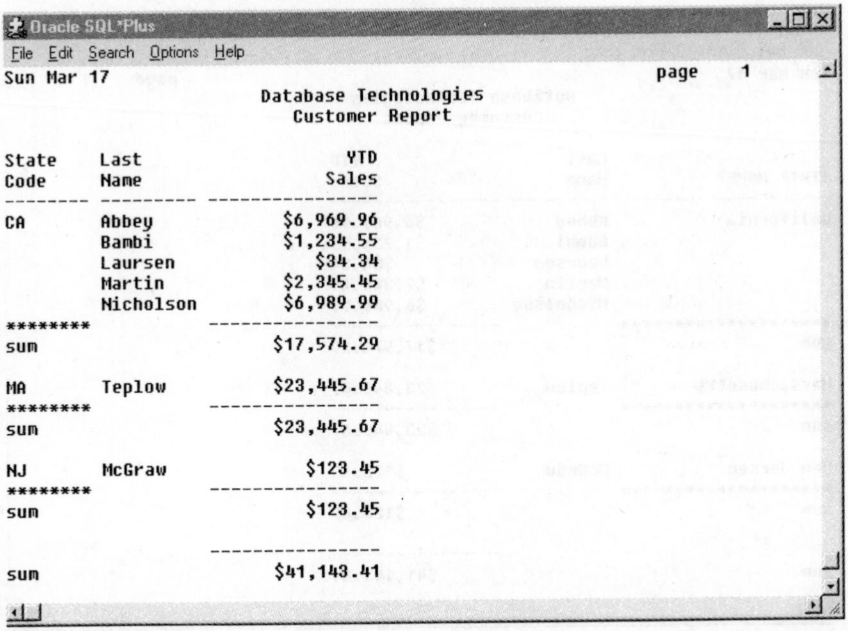

```
┌─────────────────────────────────────────────────────────────────┐
│ ⚓ Oracle SQL*Plus                                      _ □ ✕     │
├─────────────────────────────────────────────────────────────────┤
│ File  Edit  Search  Options  Help                                │
│ Sun Mar 17                                         page    1   ▲ │
│                        Database Technologies                     │
│                        Customer Report                           │
│                                                                  │
│    State     Last                  YTD                           │
│    Code      Name                Sales                           │
│    ────────  ────────        ───────────                         │
│    CA        Abbey            $6,969.96                           │
│              Bambi            $1,234.55                           │
│              Laursen             $34.34                           │
│              Martin           $2,345.45                           │
│              Nicholson        $6,989.99                           │
│    ********                 ─────────────                         │
│    sum                       $17,574.29                          │
│                                                                  │
│    MA        Teplow          $23,445.67                          │
│    ********                 ─────────────                         │
│    sum                       $23,445.67                          │
│                                                                  │
│    NJ        McGraw            $123.45                            │
│    ********                 ─────────────                         │
│    sum                         $123.45                           │
│                                                                  │
│                             ─────────────                        │
│    sum                       $41,143.41                       ▼  │
│  ◄│                                                      ►│    ⁄ │
└─────────────────────────────────────────────────────────────────┘
```

FIGURE 7-8. *Break report output with totals by state_cd and at end of report*

state_name, last_name, sales from state a,customer b where a.state_cd = b.state_cd order by state_name, last_name;. And since we are using the state_name column, we have to restate the break conditions to SQL*Plus using **break on report skip 1 on state_name skip 1**. We also need to define the compute sum statements for state_name and the report with **compute sum of sales on state_name** and **compute sum of sales on report**. We are now ready to issue the query joining the two tables, and the output produced is shown in Figure 7-9.

What's Next

Now, that was a chapter! You've come a long way! You are well on your way to becoming familiar with the power of SQL and Oracle's SQL*Plus. Not a bad report

```
┌─────────────────────────────────────────────────────────────────────────┐
│ ≜ Oracle SQL*Plus                                              _ □ X      │
│ File  Edit  Search  Options  Help                                         │
│ Sun Mar 17                                             page    1     ▲    │
│                     Database Technologies                                 │
│                       Customer Report                                     │
│                                                                           │
│                      Last              YTD                                 │
│ STATE_NAME           Name             Sales                               │
│ ─────────────────    ─────────    ─────────────────                       │
│ California           Abbey          $6,969.96                             │
│                      Bambi          $1,234.55                             │
│                      Laursen           $34.34                             │
│                      Martin         $2,345.45                             │
│                      Nicholson      $6,989.99                             │
│ *********************             ─────────────────                       │
│ sum                               $17,574.29                              │
│                                                                           │
│ Massachusetts        Teplow        $23,445.67                            │
│ *********************             ─────────────────                       │
│ sum                               $23,445.67                              │
│                                                                           │
│ New Jersey           McGraw           $123.45                            │
│ *********************             ─────────────────                       │
│ sum                                  $123.45                              │
│                                                                           │
│                                   ─────────────────                       │
│ sum                               $41,143.41                              │
│ ◄│                                                              ▼         │
└─────────────────────────────────────────────────────────────────────────┘
```

FIGURE 7-9. *Final report output*

writer, you say. No argument here. We have been using SQL*Plus since day one. It's a workhorse and always will be. As you experiment with its features, you will be amazed at how much you can do with it.

With this chapter, you now have a solid groundwork with SQL. Follow the next few chapters as we discuss more tools you need to be familiar with as you jump into Oracle at the deep end. We'll be back . . . .

CHAPTER

8

PL/SQL

rogrammers need to be able to assemble a set of data and process the results of a query one row at a time. Imagine arriving at the supermarket checkout counter with a cartload of groceries and insisting the checkout person pass everything over the bar code scanner at once. That person would have absolutely no control over what is being processed—it's all or nothing. Without the ability to manipulate data row by row, the programmer, depending on the application's requirements, could be likened to that poor checkout person—in other words, you could be that checkout person. With version 6, Oracle implemented a procedural processing language referred to as PL/SQL (pronounced "pea ell sequel") that will make your job a great deal easier. PL/SQL has programming constructs that resemble most programming languages.

There are two versions of PL/SQL: One is part of the database engine; the other is a separate engine embedded in a number of Oracle tools. We call them database PL/SQL and tool PL/SQL. They are very similar: both use the same programming constructs, syntax, and logic mechanisms. Tool PL/SQL has additional syntax designed to support the requirements of the tools. For example, to place a push button on a form to navigate to the bottom of the screen, the movement would be coded using PL/SQL in an Oracle Forms system. This chapter will deal with database PL/SQL.

In this chapter, you will learn about the following:

- Where Oracle uses PL/SQL

- PL/SQL character set

- Variables and PL/SQL reserved words

- Common data types

- Components of PL/SQL

- Cursors

- Coding conventions

- The look and feel of PL/SQL

- Dealing with compilation errors

- PL/SQL for the Internet

In the middle of some PL/SQL code examples in this chapter, we will use three dots (...) to indicate omissions. These dots are not part of the code; they indicate portions of code unnecessary to the point at hand.

Terminology

The following definitions will arm you with the technical jargon to make it through this chapter:

- An *executable* is the name of a program written using one of the assortment of computer programming languages. When you type the name of an executable, the program runs. For example, when you use SQL*Plus, you enter the command **sqlplus**.

- A *character set* describes the range of characters that a computer language supports and displays in reports. Most programming languages, including PL/SQL, can display just about any character set as text.

- *Arithmetic operators* are symbols used to define mathematical operations with data. Common operators are +, –, *, and / .

- *Relational operators* define states of comparison or choice, such as comparing two dates to see their relationship to one another. Common operators are >, <, and <>.

- *Variables* are programmer-defined names used to store information.

- *Reserved words* have special meaning to PL/SQL. They are reserved for use by Oracle and cannot be used as variable names. For example, the word "declare" means something special to PL/SQL and cannot be used as a variable name.

- A *data type* defines the class of a piece of information (data). In everyday terminology, we are used to classifying information as numeric or character. The character data type contains characters from a specific character set. The numeric data type contains the decimal digits 0 through 9.

- A *loop* is a construct in a computer program in which a segment of code is executed repeatedly.

- An *exit condition* is the part of a loop where a test is performed on data; and, if the test evaluates to TRUE, the loop terminates.

- *Control structures* influence the flow of processing in a computer program. If there were two different ways to process data, the mechanism used to decide which processing route to follow is a control structure.

- A *stored object* is a PL/SQL code segment saved in the database and used by developers and end users as Oracle systems operate. We spoke about the procedural capabilities of Oracle in Chapter 1 in the "Procedural

Capabilities" section. *Procedures, packages, functions,* and *database triggers* are all stored objects.

■ A *procedure* is a named set of PL/SQL stored in the database. It may or may not contain input and output arguments. It is an executable set of code.

■ A *function* is also a collection of PL/SQL that is stored in the database. The main distinction from a procedure is that a function must always return an output value.

■ A *package* is a collection of procedures and functions bundled together usually by virtue of similar functionality. All internal procedures and functions are recorded in the data dictionary as one singular stored package.

■ A *database trigger* is also stored executable PL/SQL. Database triggers are created to execute (fire) before or after an insert, update, or delete statement. These *data manipulation language* (DML) statements were discussed in Chapter 7.

■ The *Oracle Application Server* (OAS) is an add-on tool to the Oracle Database. The OAS is used to build Web-based database applications and to serve as the main engine between Web requests, the PL/SQL engine, and the database.

■ *HTML* (Hypertext Markup Language) is the Internet standard language for Web-based browsing. Text and graphics are sent from a Web server as HTML to be interpreted by the client-side browser.

■ HTML *tags* are used to mark up the HTML document. The tags act as commands to a Web browser, identifying, for example, which text is to be italicized. Tags are often built in pairs, the first one in a pair identifying the beginning point of an action eventually followed by a tag that terminates the action.

■ A *dynamic Web page* is an HTML document that is built on demand. In the OAS world, it is very often the result of the execution of a parameter-fed PL/SQL procedure that queries the database.

■ *WYSIWYG* is the acronym for "What you see is what you get."

■ A *cookie* is a string of text associated with your Web browser that is written to and read from by the Web server. Among many uses, cookies are used to control access to Web sites and maintain statistics about site usage.

■ In this chapter, the discussion about *persistent connections* refers to the state of connection between an application and the database. A transactional front end–based application will most often maintain a continuous connection with the database as the user navigates from form to form to complete a transaction. The result of a request for a Web page is an HTML document that does not maintain a persistent connection with the database. The use of cookies are one way you will learn to simulate persistency.

Why Do I Need to Know PL/SQL?

When we first started using PL/SQL, we looked around on the disk for an executable called plsql. We did not find one, so then we tried writing PL/SQL blocks in SQL*Plus. Lo and behold—there it was! If you have access to Oracle Forms or SQL*Plus, you have everything you need to start learning PL/SQL and develop your skills. When using Oracle stored procedures, database triggers, packages, or functions, all the coding is done using PL/SQL. You will not get very far with Oracle without knowing PL/SQL. It is the basis of all the programming you may end up doing in the following Oracle tools:

- Oracle Forms
- Oracle Reports
- SQL*Plus
- Oracle Graphics
- Oracle Application Server

If you want to become fluent with the Oracle product set, PL/SQL must become part of your skill set. If you have any programming experience with Ada, PL/SQL will seem very familiar. We will cover some introductory concepts, programming constructs, and PL/SQL for the Internet in this chapter. As you become more familiar with PL/SQL, you will be able to take advantage of its rich features.

PL/SQL Character Set

As with all other programming languages, there is a set of characters you use in PL/SQL. Just about any character you can enter from the keyboard is a PL/SQL character, yet there are rules about using some characters in some situations. In this section, you will learn details on

- Characters you may use when programming in PL/SQL
- Arithmetic operators
- Relational operators

■ Miscellaneous symbols

Characters Supported

When programming in PL/SQL, you are limited to the following characters:

■ All uppercase and lowercase letters

■ Digits 0 through 9

■ Symbols ( ) + – * / < > = !~ ; : . ' @ % , " # $ ^ & _ | { } ? [ ]

Some of these characters are for code; others serve as arithmetic operators (division, addition, exponents, and so on) and relational operators (equal and not equal). For example, in a communications application, the developer may use a variable named "area_code" to store a client's calling area. The choice "area_code" of the characters a r e a _ c o d e conform to the rules outlined in the "Variables" section of this chapter.

Arithmetic Operators

The following table shows the common arithmetic operators used in PL/SQL. If you are familiar with other high-level programming languages, this will not be new to you.

Operator	Meaning	Operator	Meaning
+	Addition	–	Subtraction
*	Multiplication	/	Division
**	Exponentiation		

Relational Operators

The next table shows the PL/SQL relational operators. If you have experience with any other programming languages, then you have probably seen these symbols before.

Operator	Meaning	Operator	Meaning
<>	Not equal	!=	Not equal
^=	Not equal	<	Less than
>	Greater than	=	Equal

Miscellaneous Symbols

To support programming in PL/SQL, the following symbols are used. This table shows a partial list of symbols; they are the most commonly used symbols and the ones you must know to start using PL/SQL.

Symbol	Meaning	Example
()	List separators	and NAME in ('Collins','Drab','Abramson')
;	End-of-statement	Procedure_name (arg1,arg2);
.	Item separator (in the example, it separates an account name from a table name)	select * from account.table_name;
'	Character string enclosure	if var1 = 'SANDRA' ...
:=	Assignment	rec_read := rec_read + 1;
||	Concatenation	full_name := 'Nahtan' || ' ' || 'Yebba';
– –	Comment delimiter	-- This is a comment
/* and */	Comment delimiters	/* This, too, is a comment */

Variables

Variables are names used in PL/SQL to process items of data. The programmer selects names to use for these variables based on the following rules:

- Variables must start with a letter (A–Z).

- Variables can be optionally followed by one or more letters, numbers (0–9), or the special characters $, #, or _.

- Variables must be no longer than 30 characters.

- There can be no spaces embedded in the variable name.

With these three rules in hand, let's look at some examples. Table 8-1 shows sample variable names and determines their validity.

Variable Name	Valid?	Reason
23_skidoo	No	Must start with a letter
Nature_trail	Yes	
nature-trail	No	Only special characters are $ # or _
love boat	No	Cannot contain any white space
a_very_insignificant_variable_name	No	Longer than 30 characters
me_____and$$$$$you	Yes	
lots_of_$$$$$$	Yes	
23	No	Must start with a letter

TABLE 8-1.   *Valid and Invalid Variable Names*

Reserved Words

Think of a reserved word as being copyrighted by PL/SQL. When choosing names for variables, you cannot use these reserved words. For example, the word "loop" means something to PL/SQL, and the second variable declaration in the following segment of code would be invalid.

```
declare
  employee varchar2(30);
  loop number;
```

You are not permitted to use a reserved word as a variable name. We do not recommend it, but if you want to, you may join two reserved words together (for instance, loop_varchar2) to build a variable name. A complete list of PL/SQL reserved words can be found in the Oracle8i documentation set.

Common Data Types

So far, we have discussed the characters that can be used when programming in PL/SQL, naming variables, and reserved words. Now we move on to the data itself. A PL/SQL program is written to manipulate and display many different types of data. Oracle, like all computer software, has data types (such as characters) divided into a number of subtypes. For example, some of the subtypes of the number datatype are integer (that is, no decimal digits allowed) and decimal (that is, number with one or more decimal digits). PL/SQL supports a wide range of data types. This section provides an overview of what you will run across most often and find most useful in your code. In this section, you will learn details on the following data types:

- varchar2
- number
- date
- Boolean

varchar2

This is a variable-length, alphanumeric data type. In PL/SQL, it can have a length of up to 32,767 bytes. The definition in the declare section is terminated by the semicolon (;), and all *varchar2* definitions are done to resemble

```
variable_name varchar2(max_length);
```

where the *length* in parentheses must be a positive integer, as in

```
vc_field varchar2(10);
```

It may be initialized (that is, set to its initial value) at the same time by using the syntax

```
vc_field varchar2(10) := 'STARTVALUE';
```

number

This data type can be used to represent all numeric data. The format of the declaration is

```
num_field number(precision,scale);
```

where *precision* can be from 1 to 38 characters, and *scale* represents the number of positions specified by precision that are for decimal digits. Keep in mind that the declaration

 `num_field number(12,2);`

describes a variable that can have up to ten integer digits (precision[12] - scale [2]) and up to two decimal digits.

date

This data type is used to store fixed-length date values. The declaration takes no qualifiers and is done as

 `date_field date;`

By default, Oracle displays dates in the format DD-MON-YY; thus, September 9, 2004, is displayed as 09-SEP-04. When programming with dates in PL/SQL, you must use this format. Would it be better to say you must match the default date format for the database unless you're using TO_CHAR or TO_DATE? Should we recommend that you always use your own formats as specified with TO_DATE/TO_CHAR so that it's independent of the default date format? That would make applications more portable and less dependent on the init.ora settings.

> **VIP**
> *Oracle has a date format mask DD-MON-RR that is to be used for preservation of dates entered with a four-character year. Please consult the SQL*Plus documentation set for details on using this mask to ensure Oracle does not drop the century digits as it stores dates.*

Boolean

This data type is a switch that holds the status **true** or **false**. When you use this data type, you test its status and then can do one thing if it is true, something else if false. For example, say you were trying to see if a corporation had distributed a 10K form for its 2000 fiscal year. Using a Boolean variable, it would be set to **true** if the form had been filed.

PL/SQL Components

We now move on to a discussion of how PL/SQL is put together. Using the knowledge from the previous few sections, we can start to formulate some living and breathing code examples. PL/SQL offers the standard set of procedural techniques that developers have been using since the dawn of computers: logic, looping, and error handling mechanisms.

In this section, you will learn details on the following topics:

- Block structured coding

- Variable declarations

- Control structures, including program control, if logic structures, and looping structures

- Handling exceptions

- "Do nothing" constructs

Block Structure

PL/SQL programs are written in blocks of code with separate sections for variable declarations, executable code, and exception (error) handling. PL/SQL can be stored in the database as a named subprogram, or it can be coded directly in an SQL*Plus window as an unnamed anonymous block. When storing PL/SQL in the database, the subprogram includes a header section in which the stored unit is named; the type of the program is declared; and then, optionally, **in**, **out**, and **in out** arguments are defined. Only the executable section, defined by **begin** and **end** statements, is mandatory. The **declare** and **exception** sections are optional.

The following are examples of an unnamed block and a stored procedure:

```
-- Unnamed Block
declare
  . . .
begin
  . . .
end;

-- Stored Procedure
create or replace procedure_name
```

```
as
-- The declare section automatically follows
-- the as statement and does not need to be coded
 . . .
 . . .
begin
 . . .

 . . .
exception
 . . .

 . . .
end;
/
```

PL/SQL blocks can be nested, creating numerous BEGIN/END blocks of code within the main **begin/end** block. The advantages will become more obvious later when we demonstrate how to control the flow of a program when errors occur. This discussion will take place in the exception section of this chapter. It is even acceptable to nest blocks within nested blocks or to have many **begin/end** blocks within one outer block. The following is an example of nested blocks:

```
create or replace procedure calculate_rebate
                          (pharmacy_id in number)
as
 . . .
 . . .
begin
 . . .
    begin
      . . .

      . . .
    end;
 . . .
 . . .
exception
 . . .
 . . .
end;
/
```

Starting with 8*i*, Oracle has introduced autonomous transaction handling. In earlier versions of PL/SQL, a **commit** or **rollback** statement in a subprogram would perform the same action on any transactions from the initiating program unit. By adding an autonomous transaction statement in the declaration section of an anonymous PL/SQL block, procedure, function, or database trigger, you assure that a **commit** or **rollback** statement in that block will have no effect on outstanding transactions from the initiating block. An autonomous transaction declaration in an anonymous block can only be made in the very first declaration section. Autonomous transaction declarations are not allowed in any nested blocks.

The following sample code illustrates how to create an autonomous transaction block:

```
declare
    pragma autonomous_transaction;
begin
    . . .
end;
/
```

The Declare Section

This part of PL/SQL blocks is where you define your variables. If you are familiar with COBOL, this is similar to working storage. You will see the common data types we discussed previously, plus the cursor variable type, which we cover in the next section. The following code is an example of a procedure's declare section.

When a stored object is created (named block), the **declare** section automatically follows the **as** keyword. When coding a block of PL/SQL code in SQL*Plus (anonymous block), you must specify DECLARE.

```
create or replace procedure samp (i_salary in number,
                                   i_city in number)
as
-- this is the declare section; since we are coding a
-- named stored object, the declare is implied, and
-- need not be mentioned
    accum1          number;
    accum2          number;
    h_date          date := sysdate;  - variables can be
                                      - initialized here
    status_flag     varchar2(1);
    mess_text       varchar2(80);
    temp_buffer     varchar2(1);
    -- cursors, such as the one below, will be
    -- discussed in the next section
    cursor my_cursor
    is
    select employee_number, last_name, first_name
```

```
     from employee a, department b
   where a.department_number = b.department_number
     and a.salary >  i_salary
     and b.location = i_city;
begin
  ...
  ...
end;
/
```

Control Structures

Control structures are the heart of any programming language. Since most systems are written to handle a number of different situations, the way different conditions are detected and dealt with is the biggest part of program control. This section provides you with details on the following topics:

- Program control

- Three types of the **if** logic structure

- Four types of looping structures

Program Control

Program control is governed by the status of the variables it uses and the data it reads and writes from the database. As an example, picture yourself going to the DMV (Department of Motor Vehicles) to renew your car registration. When you enter the building, you are presented with the instructions "Sticker renewals in Room 12-G." Once you find 12-G, you receive these instructions: "Cash/certified check ONLY in lines 1 and 2. All payment types accepted in lines 3 to 15." Your decision-making process begins with the question "Why am I here?" The program control for this decision-making example is shown in Table 8-2.

if Logic Structures

When you are writing computer programs, situations present themselves in which you must test a condition; when it evaluates to **true** you do one thing, when it evaluates to **false** you might choose to do something different. PL/SQL has three **if** logic structures that allow you to test true/false conditions. In most computer programs, many lines of code will test the value of a variable and, based on its value, perform one or more operations. In everyday life, we are continually bombarded with decision making; this is how you code decision making with PL/SQL.

Process or Decision to Make	Next Step	
Here for driver's license transactions	YES=5	NO=2
Here for car sticker renewal	YES=7	NO=3
Here for driving test	YES=6	NO=4
Oops, in the wrong building!	13	
Go to Room 12-A and carry on desired transaction	13	
Go to Room 12-B and carry on desired transaction	13	
Go to Room 12-G	8	
Paying by cash or certified check	YES=10	NO=9
Paying by check or credit card	YES=11	NO=12
Do cash or certified check transaction	13	
Do check or credit card transaction	13	
They don't take play money!	13	
Leave building		

TABLE 8-2. *Program Control Decision Making*

IF-THEN   This construct tests a simple condition. If the condition evaluates to TRUE, one or more lines of code are executed. If the condition evaluates to **false**, program control is passed to the next statement after the test. The following code illustrates implementing this logic in PL/SQL.

```
if var1 > 10 then
    var2 := var1 + 20;
end if;
```

The test (in this case, >) is a relational operator we spoke about in the "PL/SQL Character Set" section of this chapter. The statement could have been coded using the following instead, with the same results.

```
if not(var1 <= 10) then
    var2 := var1 + 20;
end if;
```

You may code nested **if-then** statements as shown in the following.

```
if var1 > 10 then
    if var2 < var1 then
      var2 := var1 + 20;
    end if;
end if;
```

Notice the two **end if** parts in the previous code—one for each **if**. This leads us into two rules about implementing **if** logic in PL/SQL.

GUIDELINE I
Each ***if*** *statement is followed by its own* ***then****. There is no semicolon (;) terminator on the line that starts with* ***if****.*

GUIDELINE 2
Each ***if*** *statement block is terminated by a matching* ***end if****.*

IF-THEN-ELSE   This construct is similar to **if** except that when the condition evaluates to **false**, one or more statements following the **else** are executed. The following code illustrates implementing this logic in PL/SQL.

```
if var1 > 10 then
    var2 := var1 + 20;
else
    var2 := var1 * var1;
end if;
```

Note that the same logic can be expressed the other way—adding 20 to var1 with the **else** and squaring var1 with the **if** branch of the statement.

```
if var1 <= 10 then
    var2 := var1 * var1;
else
    var2 := var1 + 20;
end if;
```

The statements can be nested, as shown in the following listing.

```
if var1 > 10 then
    var2 := var1 + 20;
else
    if var1 between 7 and 8 then
        var2 := 2 * var1;
    else
        var2 := var1 * var1;
    end if;
end if;
```

This leads us to two more rules about implementing **if** logic in PL/SQL.

GUIDELINE 3
*There can be one and only one **else** with every*
***if** statement.*

GUIDELINE 4
There is no semicolon (;) terminator on the
*line starting with **else**.*

IF-THEN-ELSIF   This format is an alternative to using the nested **if-then-else**
construct. The code in the previous listing could be reworded to read

```
if var1 > 10 then
    var2 := var1 + 20;
elsif var1 between 7 and 8 then
    var2 := 2 * var1;
else
    var2 := var1 * var1;
end if;
```

This leads us into one final rule about implementing **if** logic in PL/SQL.

GUIDELINE 5
*There is no matching **end if** with each **elsif**.*

In this code segment, the **end if** appears to go with its preceding **elsif**:

```
if var1 > 10 then
    var2 := var1 + 20;
elsif var1 between 7 and 8 then
    var2 := 2 * var1;
end if;
```

In fact, the **end if** belongs to the **if** that starts the whole block rather than the **elsif** keyword. Notice how the previous listings indent portions of the PL/SQL code to indicate to which conditions they belong.

> **NOTE**
> *We recommend you use the indentation convention—it is easier to follow and understand the flow of logic and control.*

The previous examples only illustrated one **elsif** statement; however, there can be multiple **elsif** statements in any **if** statement. It is also worth noting that an **else** statement is not required. The following example illustrates an **if** statement with multiple **elsif** statements.

```
if location = 'PHOENIX' then
    v_hockey_team_name := 'COYOTES';
elsif location = 'NEW YORK CITY' then
    v_hockey_team_name := 'RANGERS';
elsif location = 'OTTAWA' then
    v_hockey_team_name := 'SENATORS';
end if;
```

Examine the following two listings, which illustrate no indentation and indentation.

```
/* Code segment 1 - hard to follow. */
if var1 < 5 then var2 := 'y'; elsif
var1 = 5 then
var2 := 'n';
else var2 := null; end if;
/*                                    */
/* Code segment 2 - easier to follow. */
if var1 < 5 then
    var2 := 'y';    --statement is controlled by
                    --first test on var1 being true
elsif var1 = 5 then
    var2 := 'n';    --statement is controlled by
                    --second test on var1 being true
```

```
else
    var2 := null;    --statement is controlled by second
                     --test on var1 being false
end if;
```

Using the earlier DMV example, let's word the logic using PL/SQL. Depending on the value of "the_act", procedure 12a, 12b, or 12g will be called.

```
create or replace procedure license_transaction
                          (the_act in varchar2) as
begin
  if the_act = 'DLT' then
     12a;
  elsif the_act = 'DT' then
     12b;
  else
     12g;
  end if;
end;
/
```

Looping
Looping provides the ability to execute a process over and over again until complete. In a real-life situation, think of looping when you unload your groceries from your car—there are two loops in this activity. The first is the repetitive action of picking up one or more grocery bags and walking in your front door, returning to the car until there's no more grocery bags. The second is the repetitive whine that comes from your lethargic 16-year-old: "Why is it always me who has to help?" In general, looping is based on the logic shown in Table 8-3.

Process or Decision to Make	Next Step	
Set condition to enter loop (i.e., done_loop=N)	2	
End loop condition is true (i.e., done_loop=Y)	YES=6	NO=3
Process data	4	4
There is no more data to process	YES=2	NO=5
Set exit condition (i.e., done_loop=Y)	2	2
Done processing		

TABLE 8-3. *Looping Logic*

One of the problems with coding loops is making sure there is code to allow them to terminate when an exit condition has been satisfied. Unfortunately, all too many times, developers write endless loops (we have never done that, of course, but we know many who have). A good example of an endless loop is found in the instructions on your shampoo bottle: Rinse, Lather, Repeat. The best way to sum up looping and the major problems programmers may have with it is to quote from an online technology dictionary we once saw:

Definition of LOOP: See "Definition of LOOP."

Implementing loops in PL/SQL is discussed in the next few sections.

LOOP-EXIT-END LOOP   This construct contains three parts. Study this commented code to see how this is used.

```
cnt := 1;        -- Initialize the loop counter before
                 -- loop starts
loop             -- Part 1: Loop keyword starts the loop
  cnt := cnt + 1;  -- Part 2: Incrementing the loop
                 -- counter
  if cnt >= 100 then  -- Testing cnt for exit
                 -- condition.
    exit;        -- End loop condition met,
                 -- so get out.
  end if;        -- "end-if" to match previous
                 -- "if".
  ...
  ...
end loop;        -- Part 3: End loop keywords to end the
...              --         loop
...
...
```

LOOP-EXIT WHEN-END LOOP   This is similar to the previous example, except the exit condition is detected differently.

```
cnt := 1;        -- Initialize the loop counter before
                 -- loop starts
loop             -- Part 1: Loop keyword starts the loop
  cnt := cnt + 1;    -- Part 2: Incrementing the
                 -- loop counter
  exit when cnt >= 100; -- Test for exit condition by
                 -- examining "cnt"
  ...
  ...
  ...
```

```
end loop;           -- Part 3: End loop keyword
...                 --        to end the loop
...
```

WHILE-LOOP-END LOOP   With this construct, the exit condition is manually set somewhere inside the loop. The test for exit condition is accomplished by the comparison in the **while** part of the loop.

```
-- Initialize the loop counter before loop starts
cnt := 1;
-- Part 1: The "while" checks exit condition every
-- time before executing loop
while cnt < 100 loop
   -- Part 2: Code executed inside the loop
   ...
   cnt := cnt + 1;   -- Incrementing counter to arrive
   ...               -- at exit condition
   -- Part 3: End loop keyword to end the loop
end loop;
...
```

FOR-IN-LOOP-END LOOP   The final construct we examine allows repetitive execution of a loop a predefined number of times. There are three parts to the loop:

- The **for in** portion, in which the variable to track the looping is defined

- The one or more statements within the loop that are executed until the variable controlling the loop reaches the exit condition value

- The **end loop** portion that terminates the loop

The following shows an example of how this loop mechanism can be used:

```
for cnt in 1 .. 3 loop
   insert into tab1 values ('Still in loop',cnt);
end loop;
```

In the preceding code, the indexed variable "cnt" increments by one for each iteration of the loop.

Exceptions

Earlier in this chapter, we talked about PL/SQL block structured coding, and we introduced the concept of an **exception** section being optional in every block of code. The exception section is the PL/SQL method of dealing with error conditions.

Whenever an error occurs during the execution of a section of PL/SQL code, control automatically drops down to the executing blocks exception section. Table 8-4 lists common PL/SQL exceptions; by testing for these predefined exceptions, you can detect errors that your PL/SQL programs raise.

When a predefined error is encountered, it is trapped by the corresponding **when . . . then** statement in the exception section of the current block. The code that follows the **then** statement of the **when** clause is executed. After the **then** statement is executed, control passes to the line immediately following the **end** statement of the current block. If your error-trapped code just exited an inner nested block, the program will continue with the first line of the outer block that follows the inner block's **end** statement. Using nested blocks with their own exception sections is one way to control the flow of your programs.

If there is no associated **when** clause for the error in the current block and the **begin/end** block is nested, the program will continue to search for an error handler in each of the outer blocks until it finds one. When an error occurs and it has no associated error handler in any of the exception sections, the program will abort. Oracle has supplied us with a "catch all" error handler to trap errors that are not

Exception	Explanation
no_data_found	If a select statement attempts to retrieve data based on its conditions, this exception is raised when no rows satisfy the selection criteria.
too_many_rows	Since each implicit cursor is capable of retrieving only one row, this exception detects the existence of more than one row. (See the "Implicit Cursors" section, later in this chapter, where we define and discuss implicit cursors.)
dup_val_on_index	This exception detects an attempt to create an entry in an index whose column values already exist. For example, suppose a billing application is keyed on the invoice number. If a program tries to create a duplicate invoice number, this exception would be raised.
value_error	This exception indicates that there has been an assignment operation where the target field is not long enough to hold the value being placed in it. For example, if the text ABCDEFGH is assigned to a variable defined as "varchar2(6)", then this exception is raised.

TABLE 8-4. *Most Common Exceptions in PL/SQL*

predefined. The **when others then** error handler will trap all Oracle errors that fall out of the scope of the predefined errors. It's a good idea to display the error code and error message from within the **when others then** handler by using Oracle's *sqlcode* and *sqlerrm* functions.

> **GUIDELINE 6**
> *Always use a **when others** error handler. If you have other error handlers in an exception section, make sure that the **when others** clause is the last one. If you mistakenly code the **when others** clause first, it will trap all errors, even the other predefined errors.*

The following code illustrates a nested block and a couple of exception sections.

```
create or replace procedure
        veteran_info (i_vin in number,
                      o_spouse_exists  out boolean,
                      o_benefit_exists out boolean)
as
    v_benefit_amount     number(7,2);
    v_spouse_id          number(9);
begin
    --
    -- Find the veteran identification number
    -- for the spouse.
    --
    select spouse_vin
    into   v_spouse_id
    from   vin_xref
    where  client_vin = i_vin;
    --
    -- If a row was returned, set the output
    -- spouse flag.
    --
    o_spouse_exists := true;
      --
    begin        -- this will execute only if the
                 -- above select statement returned
                 -- exactly one row.
      --
      -- determine if the spouse receives a benefit.
      --
      select benefit_amount
      into   v_benefit_amount
      from   spouse_benefit
```

```
      where  spouse_vin = v_spouse_id;
      --
      -- If a row was returned, check the amount and
      -- set the output benefit flag accordingly.
      --
      if v_benefit_amount > 0 then
          o_benefit_exists := true;
      end if;
      --
   exception
     when no_data_found then
          -- The spouse existed in the outer block but
          -- they do not receive a benefit. Set the
          -- output flags.
          o_spouse_exists := true;
          o_benefit_exists := false;
   end;
   --
exception    -- This is the exception section for the
             -- outer block.
  when no_data_found then
       -- The veteran does not have a spouse. The first
       -- select statement failed to return a row. The
       -- inner block was not executed. Control passes
       -- to the exception section of the block being
       -- executed. Since a spouse does not exist, set
       -- both output flags to false.
   o_spouse_exists := false;
   o_benefit_exists := false;
end;
/
```

"Do Nothing" or "Null" Construct

Sometimes, especially when using **if** logic, you end up testing a condition; when that condition is **true**, you do nothing; when otherwise, you perform some operation. This is handled in PL/SQL in the following way:

```
if cnt >= 90 then
   null;
else
   insert into tab1 values ('Still less than 90',cnt);
end if;
```

The **null** keyword denotes performing no operation. The "null" construct is often used when you want to trap an exception, do nothing, and then continue in the next block without aborting the program unit.

Cursors

PL/SQL uses *cursors* for management of SQL select statements. Cursors are chunks of memory allocated to process these statements. Sometimes you define the cursor manually, and other times you let PL/SQL define the cursor. A cursor is defined like any other PL/SQL variable and must conform to the same naming conventions. In this section, you will learn about both explicit and implicit PL/SQL cursors. Using explicit cursors, you must declare the cursor, open it before using it, and close it when it is no longer needed. Using implicit cursors, you do none of these; you simply code your select statement and let PL/SQL handle the cursor on your behalf.

Explicit cursors combined with a loop construct are required to process select statements that will return more than one row. The cursor combined with the loop will allow you to process one row at a time. When a select statement is expected to return only one row, an implicit cursor will do fine.

Explicit Cursors

This technique defines a cursor as part of the **declare** section. The SQL statement defined must contain only **select** statements—there can be no **insert**, **update**, or **delete** keywords used. An explicit cursor must be used when a select statement might return zero or more than one row. In this section, you will learn how to do the following:

■ Name your explicit cursors

■ Prepare (or open) an explicit cursor for use

■ Fetch data using an explicit cursor

■ Release the cursor's memory when done with it

When using explicit cursors, you always code four components:

■ The cursor is defined in the **declare** section of your PL/SQL block.

■ The cursor is opened after the initial **begin** in the PL/SQL block.

■ The cursor is fetched into one or more variables. There must be the same number of receiving variables in the **fetch** as there are columns in the cursor's **select** list. For example, look at the following cursor definition:

```
declare
  l_first_name    varchar2(30);
  l_last_name     varchar2(30);
  l_ssn           number(9);
  -- In the person table, first_name and last_name are
```

```
     -- varchar2(20) and ssn is number(9)
     cursor region_cur is
        select first_name,last_name,ssn
           from person
           where region_number = region_number_in;
   begin
      open region_cur;
      fetch region_cur into l_first_name,l_last_name,l_ssn;
```

■ The cursor is closed after you are done using it.

The following listing puts these four parts together.

```
...
...
declare
   fname          varchar2(10);
   lname          varchar2(30);
   ssec_num       varchar2(8);
   cursor region_cur is
   select first_name, last_name, ssn
      from person
      where region_number = region_number_in;
begin
   open region_cur;
   fetch region_cur into fname, lname, ssec_num;
   while region_cur%found
   loop
      if ssec_num is null then
         insert into e_msg values (pin_in,'no ssnum');
      else
         insert into e_tab values (pin_in,sysdate);
      end if;
      fetch region_cur into fname, lname, ssec_num;
   end loop;
   close region_cur;
end;
...
...
/
```

Note the following points about explicit cursors:

■ The success or failure of the cursor (we call it "mycur" here) is determined
   by testing either **%found** or **%notfound**. The cursor returns success if it
   retrieves a row from the database based on its selection criteria. This test
   must be done before the cursor is closed.

```
if mycur%found then
   ...
end if;
if mycur%notfound then
   ...
   ...
end if;
...
...
fetch mycur into temp_buffer;
close mycur;
-- this will not work since the cursor has been closed.
if mycur%found then
   ...
   ...
end if;
```

■ If a cursor is repeatedly fetched in a loop construct, a running total of the number of rows retrieved so far can be found in the **%rowcount** system variable.

```
while counter < 100 loop
   fetch mycur into temp_buffer;
   if mycur%rowcount <= 50 then
      ...
   else
      ...
   end if;
counter := counter+1;
end loop;
```

■ All cursors must be fetched into one or more variables (depending on the number of columns in the cursor's select list). The following is not legal:

```
open mycur;
fetch mycur;
if mycur%found then
   ...
```

◢ The target variable(s) of the cursor must match the columns in the table being selected in data type:

```
-- This is correct
--
declare
```

```
    cursor mycur is          ,
      select pin,          /* Pin is numeric         */
            last_name      /* Last_name is character */
        from person
       where pin = pin_in;
    field1 varchar2(10);
    field2 number;
  begin
    open mycur;
    fetch mycur into field2, field1;
    ...
  -- This is incorrect because the variables data types
  -- are not the same as the columns being selected.
  --
  declare
    cursor mycur is
      select pin,          /* Pin is numeric              */
            last_name      /* Last_name is character data */
        from person
       where pin = pin_in;
    field1 varchar2(10);
    field2 number;
  begin
    open mycur;
    fetch mycur into field1, field2;
    ...
```

You will receive an error if you try to open a cursor that is already open or close a cursor that has already been closed. You can check the status of a cursor using **%isopen**, which evaluates to either **true** or **false**.

```
...
...
if mycur%isopen then
   null;
else
   open mycur;
end if;
```

If a PL/SQL block uses more than one cursor, each cursor must have a unique name.

The "Cursor For Loop"

This section wouldn't be complete without a brief introduction to the "cursor for loop." This construct asks you to disregard almost everything you've just learned about explicit cursors. The beauty of a "cursor for loop" is that you don't have to open the cursor, fetch, test for the existence of data (%found), close the cursor, or define variables to fetch into. The only similarity is that the cursor is defined in the declaration section. When the cursor is invoked, a record is automatically created with the same data elements that are in the select statement. The program continues to execute all the code inside the loop for each row retrieved by the cursor, and the cursor automatically closes when no more data is found. This method requires the least programming and results in fewer cursor construction errors.

Our previous example is rewritten here with a "cursor for loop."

```
...
...
declare
  cursor region_cur is
  select first_name, last_name, ssn
    from person
  where region_number = region_number_in;
begin
  for region_rec in region_cur
  loop
     -- NOTE: all columns in the select statement
     --       are automatically created as
     --       record_name.column_name
     --       (i.e. region_rec.last_name)
     if region_rec.ssn is null then
        insert into e_msg values (pin_in,'no ssnum');
     else
        insert into e_tab values (pin_in,sysdate);
     end if;
  end loop;
end;
...
...
/
```

Implicit Cursors

The following code segment uses implicit cursors. You place your **select** statement inline and PL/SQL handles cursor definition implicitly. There is no declaration of implicit cursors in the declare section.

```
...
begin
  if counter >= 20 then
     select last_name
       into lname
       from person
```

```
     where pin = pin_in;
  ...
  else
     ...
  end if;
end;
/
```

Note the following points that pertain to using implicit cursors:

■ There must be an **into** with each implicit cursor.

```
-- This is incorrect
if this_value > 0 THEN
   select count(*) from person;
end if;
-- This is OK
if this_value > 0 then
   select count(*) into cnter from person;
end if;
```

■ As with explicit cursors, the variables that receive data with the **into** keyword must be the same data type as the column(s) in the table.

■ Implicit cursors expect only one row to be returned. You must examine some of the exceptions, as discussed in Table 8-4. The most common ones to look out for are **no_data_found** and **too_many_rows**.

```
...
if counter >= 10 then
   begin
      select age
      into   v_age
      from   person
      where  pin = pin_value;
   exception
      when too_many_rows then
              insert into taba values (pin_value,
                                   sysdate);
      when no_data_found then
              null;
   end;
end if;
...
...
```

Which Approach to Use

We find using explicit cursors more efficient and recommend you use them for the following reasons:

- The success or failure is found by examining the PL/SQL system variable **%found** or **%notfound**. Code segments that use explicit cursors simply test one of these variables to detect success or failure of a select statement using an explicit cursor.

- Since the explicit cursor is manually defined in the **declare** section, the PL/SQL block can be more structured (the definitions are done in one place, and the code that uses the cursor is in another).

- The "cursor for loop" reduces the amount of code and is easier to follow procedurally.

- The best programmers use them!

PL/SQL Tables

Interesting enough, when looking at relational database theory, query results assembled by a join of two or more tables is a table itself. Often one needs to loop through a set of data using PL/SQL and compare values against a set of lookup values. PL/SQL allows one to load these lookup tables into memory, thereby reducing the I/O operations required to reference the lookup table values.

In many places throughout this book we have spoken of data types—character, alphanumeric, and numeric, to name a few. PL/SQL tables are declared with a user-defined data type **table**. Inspect the following code to see how a table of states of the union would be loaded for lookup purposes.

```
set serveroutput on size 100000
declare
   state_rec state%rowtype;   -- State_rec has same
                              -- makeup as a row from
                              -- the state table
 type just_names is table of state.name%type
        index by binary_integer; -- The local just_names
                                 -- table contains
   i binary_integer := 0;      -- "rows" with the same
                               -- makeup as each row
                               -- in state
   nametab just_names;
   begin
     for state_rec in      -- Notice how the rows are
```

```
                        -- fetched" from state by
                        -- this query embedded in the
                        -- for loop
        (select name from state)
    loop
      i := i+1;
      nametab(i) := state_rec.name;
      dbms_output.put_line (nametab(i));
    end loop;
  end;
/
```

The output for the first few rows of names read from the state table would be

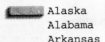

```
Alaska
Alabama
Arkansas
```

NOTE
PL/SQL tables are supported with release 2.3 of PL/SQL, but not by earlier versions.

The Look of PL/SQL

PL/SQL is a mixture of SQL*Plus and procedural code. Indentation, white space, and comments make the code more readable. Comment text is delimited by the slash-asterisk combination (/* comment */) or two dashes (- -), as in the following:

```
begin
   declare tfield varchar2(20);
   begin
       select desc_text
         into tfield
         from prod                /* Prod is a central */
        where pnum = 'FR4512';    /* lookup table owned */
                                  /* by planning        */
   end;
end;
/
```

or

```
begin
   declare tfield varchar2(20);
   begin
```

```
        select desc_text
          into tfield
          from prod              -- Prod is a central
         where pnum = 'FR4512';  -- lookup table owned
                                 -- by planning
    end;
end;
/
```

or

```
begin
   declare tfield varchar2(20);
   begin
       /*
        Prod is a central lookup
        table owned by planning
       */
       select desc_text
         into tfield
         from prod
        where pnum = 'FR4512';
   end;
end;
/
```

Inspect the following PL/SQL code segment and study the comments. They will illustrate how the pieces of PL/SQL go together.

```
create or replace procedure examine_order_details
                   (order_number_in in number)
as
   -- This is the start of a PL/SQL block. Local
   -- variables & explicit cursors are defined here
   cursor detail_cur is
   select product_number, quantity
   from   order_detail
   where  order_number = order_number_in;
   v_product_number  number;
   v_quantity        number;
begin
    -- This "begin" is the start of the code
    -- executed when the PL/SQL is invoked.
    open detail_cur;
    fetch detail_cur into v_product_number, v_quantity;
    while detail_cur%found
    loop
```

```
         -- "if" procedural logic
    if v_quantity > 100 then
         -- An implicit cursor
         insert into order_audit (order_number,
                                  product_number,
                                  quantity)
                 values (order_number_in,
                         v_product_number,
                         v_quantity);
    else
       null;
    end if;    -- "if" statement ends with "end if"
    fetch detail_cur into
         v_product_number,v_quantity;
    end loop;
    -- Each "begin" terminated by matching "end"
    -- keyword
    -- "/" terminates the PL/SQL block
end;
/
```

Built-In Packages

Oracle provides the developer with a set of tools to make our lives easier. One such example are the many built-in packages available to programmers. *Built-in packages* are prebuilt programs stored in the database that can be called from within any PL/SQL block of code, passing arguments if required. They can be used to accomplish the following types of tasks:

- Write output to a terminal window (dbms_output)

- Read and write directly to and from operating system files (utl_file)

- Execute dynamic SQL (dbms_sql)

The power of PL/SQL lies within many of the prewritten procedures. The section on "Dynamic HTML Concepts" will demonstrate how to use the built-in packages in the Web developers toolkit to build dynamic Web pages.

Compilation Errors

When a PL/SQL block is passed to Oracle for compilation, you may be informed of some errors. As we indicate in the previous listing, the slash (/) terminates the PL/SQL block and passes the code to Oracle. Inspect the following error-ridden compilation. Note that the errors raised by a PL/SQL compilation are not displayed until you code the statement **sho errors**.

```
sql> create or replace procedure temp (count in number) as
  2  begin
  3    declare cursor mycur is
  4      select count(*) from emp;
  5    begin;
  6      open mycur;
  7      fetch mycur;
  8    end;
  9  end;
 10  /
Warning: Procedure created with compilation errors.
SQL> sho errors
Errors for PROCEDURE TEMP:
LINE/COL ERROR
---- -----------------------------------
5/8      PLS-00103: Encountered the symbol ";" when expecting one of the
         following:
         begin declare exit for goto if loop mod null pragma raise
         return select update while <an identifier>
         <a double-quoted delimited-identifier> <a bind variable> <<
         close current delete fetch lock insert open rollback
         savepoint set sql execute commit forall
         <a single-quoted SQL string>
```

After removing the ";" from line 5, we tried once again to compile the code, only to discover there was yet another error.

```
sql> create or replace procedure temp (count in number) as
  2  begin
  3    declare cursor mycur is
  4      select count(*) from emp;
  5    begin
  6      open mycur;
  7      fetch mycur;
  8    end;
  9* end;
sql> /
Warning: Procedure created with compilation errors.
SQL> sho errors
Errors for PROCEDURE TEMP:
LINE/COL ERROR
---- -----------------------------------
7/16     PLS-00103: Encountered the symbol ";" when expecting one of the
         following:
         . into bulk
```

As your experience with PL/SQL increases, you will become quite adept at debugging your code based on the output of this **sho errors** command.

Code Examples

We will now present three simple requirements and show how to carry them out using PL/SQL. The comments embedded in these examples illustrate some of the points we have made throughout this chapter. Hopefully, the coding style we have used will help illustrate good coding techniques at the same time. Oracle reserved words have been capitalized, and indentation and comments are used to make the code more readable.

Example 1

Let's see how to figure out a person's date of birth by using his or her social security number. The code is commented to illustrate how PL/SQL works. We are using an implicit PL/SQL cursor.

```
create or replace procedure get_dob
        (ss_num in varchar2, dob out date)
as
begin                       -- Start of program.
    select birth_date      -- Implicit cursor.
      into dob             -- Dob and birth_date must
      from person          -- be of the same data type.
     where soc_sec_num = ss_num;
exception
    when no_data_found then
        error_notify (ss_num);      -- Call another
                                    -- procedure
end;
/
```

Let's study a few concepts based on the code in this listing:

- The line that defines the procedure has two variables enclosed in parentheses. The first contains the value of the social security number of the person whose date of birth we require. The second will receive the date and pass it back to the user that invoked the procedure.

- Notice the semicolon (;) terminators are missing on the **begin** and the **create or replace procedure as** lines of code. These two lines never have a semicolon.

Example 2

This example shows how to accomplish exactly the same result as in the preceding one, but using a function instead of a procedure. A function can receive as many variables as possible but returns only one value, as you will see in the listing. The code is similar but reads differently from the procedure.

```
create or replace function get_dob
                          (ss_num in varchar2)
      return date
as
   birthd     date;                  -- Local date field to
                                      -- hold birth date
begin
   begin
      select dob
         into birthd       -- "into" mandatory for
                            -- implicit cursor
         from person
      where soc_sec_num = ss_num;
   exception
      when no_data_found then
         begin
            error_notify (ss_num);   -- Call another
                                     -- procedure
            birthd := trunc(sysdate);
         end;
      when others then
         null;
   end;
   return birthd;
end;                        -- Termination of outer block
                            -- "/" terminates pl/sql block
```

Let's study a few concepts based on the code in this listing:

- Since we are using an implicit cursor, we do not define it in the **declare** section of the procedure.

- The error situation **no_data_found** is the implicit cursor method of doing what **%found** or **%notfound** does with explicit cursors.

- The **when_others** error check is a bucket that traps all other types of errors and returns control to the code that invoked the procedure.

Example 3

As area codes are split into pieces, some numbers stay with the old code, and some are moved to the new. Let's look at a procedure that loops through a list of the first three numbers of a phone number for a specified area code and changes the area code for those exchanges that do not have a row in static_exc (exchanges with a row in this table are to keep the old area code). This code will use an explicit cursor code using the "cursor for loop" method.

```
create or replace procedure ac_switch (oac in number,
                                       nac in number)
as
    l_change_sw        number(3);
    l_change_it        varchar2(1);
    cursor ac_cur
    is
    select distinct pref_3
    from    phone_nbr
    where   area_code = oac;
begin                              -- Main processing
    for ac_rec in ac_cur
    loop                           -- Start of loop
        l_change_it := 'N';
        begin                      -- "begin" of select
            select ''              -- with exception block
            into    l_change_sw
            from    static_exc
            where   area_code = oac
            and     pref_3 = ac_rec.pref_3;
        exception
            when no_data_found then
                -- The 3 digit prefix was not found in
                -- the exception table so the area code
                -- will need to be changed.
                    l_change_it := 'Y';
        end;                       - Close of inner block.
        if l_change_it = 'Y' then
            -- Change the old area code to the new
            -- area code for all rows with the prefix
            -- currently held in the ac_cur cursor.
            update phone_nbr
                set area_code = nac
            where area_code = oac
                and pref_3 = ac_rec.pref_3;
        end if;
    end loop;                      -- End of loop
end;                               -- End of main processing
/
```

Let's study a few concepts based on the code in this listing:

■ Note the use of the word **distinct** when the cursor is declared. Some readers may be familiar with the keyword **unique** as well; it cannot be used in PL/SQL, only SQL*Plus.

■ The **for ac_rec in ac_cur loop** statement continues to fetch rows matching the predicate of the select statement one row at a time into the ac_rec records pref_3 variable as long as there is data in the cursor. Once there is no more data in the explicit cursor result set, the cursor closes automatically.

■ The **select** statement that references static_exc is enclosed in its own inner **begin end** block. This is done when you need to check one or more exceptions in an implicit cursor.

PL/SQL for the Internet

This section is going to touch briefly on Oracle's Application Server and how to write PL/SQL code that will return dynamic HTML documents to a client Web browser. The PL/SQL will be stored in the database. It will be a combination of application logic and built-in package calls that will generate HTML tags, cookies, and more.

This section will start by giving a high-level overview of HTML, what it is and how it is interpreted. With an understanding of the fundamentals of HTML, the remainder of the section will attempt to familiarize you with the tools and the means to build a dynamic Web page. The section will be concluded by merging your knowledge of PL/SQL, cursors, and HTML together to produce an application that obtains data from the database that matches a passed parameters value.

HTML Basics

HTML is a markup language that uses embedded tags within the code, which are then interpreted by a Web browser to format and display the information. Back in the early days of PC word processing, before the WYSIWYG environment of Windows, if you viewed the source of a document, you might have seen a "bold on" tag before and a "bold off" tag after text that would print out in bold face. This method of marking up documents was used to assist the clerk with determining what the printed document would look like. HTML marks up a text document much the same way. It can be written using the native markup language with any text editor. Alternatively, Web authoring software can be used for point-and-click simplicity. Next time you browse to a Web page, view the page source from within your browser's menu and you will see all sorts of tags surrounding the text and graphics that you're currently viewing.

The example we have provided can be written exactly as you see it in a text editor on your computer and then displayed by entering the access path of the file in your Web browser. We have purposely provided you with an example that has no fancy backgrounds or images so you can try this on your own.

```html
<html>
<head>
<title>King and Queen Burgers and Shakes Inc.</title>
</head>
<body bgcolor="#808000">
<div align="center"><center>
<table border="0" cellpadding="2" width="100%">
  <tr>
    <td width="10%"></td>
    <td width="80%"><p align="center">
        <big>KING AND QUEEN RESTAURANTS</big></p>
      <p align="center"><em>
        <big>A Burgers and Shakes Experience</big>
      </em></p>
      <p align="center">HUMAN RESOURCES DEPARTMENT</p>
      <p align="center">1999 Vacation Leave</td>
    <td width="10%"></td>
  </tr>
  <tr>
    <td width="10%"></td><td width="80%"></td>
    <td width="10%"></td>
  </tr>
  <tr>
    <td width="10%"></td>
    <td width="80%"><div align="center"><center>
      <table border="0" cellpadding="2" width="100%">
      <tr>
        <td width="24%">Job Classification:</td>
        <td width="42%">Executive</td>
        <td width="34%"></td>
      </tr>
      </table></center></div>
    </td>
    <td width="10%"></td>
  </tr>
  <tr>
    <td width="10%"></td>
    <td width="80%"><div align="center"><center>
      <table border="0" cellpadding="2" width="100%">
      <tr>
```

```
          <td width="31%"><u><strong>Employee Name
            </strong></u></td>
          <td width="25%"><u><strong>Location
            </strong></u></td>
          <td width="20%" align="right"><strong>
            <u>Days Used</u></strong></td>
          <td width="24%" align="right"><u>
            <strong>Days Remaining</strong></u></td>
        </tr>
        <tr>
          <td width="31%">Drab, J</td>
          <td width="25%">Ann Arbor, MI</td>
          <td width="20%" align="right">6</td>
          <td width="24%" align="right">9</td>
        </tr>
        <tr>
          <td width="31%">Soble, M</td>
          <td width="25%">Tucson, AZ</td>
          <td width="20%" align="right">3</td>
          <td width="24%" align="right">12</td>
        </tr>
        <tr>
          <td width="31%">Lalonde, M</td>
          <td width="25%">San Francisco, CA</td>
          <td width="20%" align="right">10</td>
          <td width="24%" align="right">5</td>
        </tr>
        <tr>
          <td width="31%">Alsukairy, Z</td>
          <td width="25%">Boston, MA</td>
          <td width="20%" align="right">1</td>
          <td width="24%" align="right">14</td>
        </tr>
      </table>
      </center></div></td>
      <td width="10%"></td>
    </tr>
    <tr>
      <td width="10%"></td><td width="80%"></td>
      <td width="10%"></td>
    </tr>
  </table>
</center></div>

</body>
</html>
```

Figure 8-1 shows you how the HTML code appears in a Web browser. An explanation of the code follows so that you will have a better understanding before we move on to the section on building dynamic HTML.

Tags usually appear in pairs, encapsulating the text and graphics to be formatted. The very first tag defines the starting point of the markup, and the second tag defines where the formatting ends. The example begins with an **<html>** tag, which declares that all that follows is HTML. The last entry found in the text file is **</html>**, which closes the HTML that is interpreted by a Web browser.

In order to professionally lay out and align text and graphics in an HTML document, tables are a must. Simply put, a table is a grid, with rows and columns creating cells where text and graphics can be inserted. Our example even has a nested table within a cell of an outer table. A table is defined with an open table tag, **<table>** and a close table tag, **</table>**. Inside a table you will have table rows, which will be opened with a **<tr>** tag and closed with a **</tr>** tag. The columns inside a row are defined with table data tags. No surprises here, the table data open tag is **<td>** followed by a table data close tag **</td>**. In between the table data tags we have the data that will be displayed in the document (text, graphics, hyperlinks,

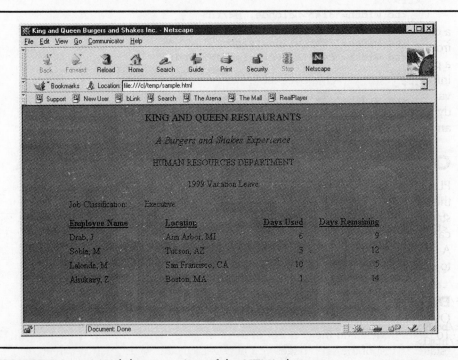

FIGURE 8-1. *A Web browser view of the HTML document*

and so on) and any formatting attributes that are supported (underlining, bold, italics, and so on).

The whole key to success in using tables is to get the tags in the right sequence. You always close tags in the reverse order that they appear in. Therefore, the table open tag isn't closed until all the table rows and table data tags have been coded. The following illustrates a simple table:

```
. . .
<table>
  <tr>
    <td>Marissa</td>
    <td>Amanda</td>
    <td>Shane</td>
    <td>Dalia</td>
  </tr>
  <tr>
    . . .
  </tr>
</table>
. . .
```

We know that we can extract data from the database one row at a time using a cursor. Imagine generating the King and Queen Restaurant examples HTML from a set of database tables. By passing the job classification of "executive" into a procedure, a cursor can retrieve each "executive" type employee's personal information from an employee table and his or her vacation balances from the vacation_leave table. As we get set to start discussing dynamic HTML, imagine dynamically creating an HTML row for each database row we retrieve with a cursor and placing it in between the right tags. It's as simple as that.

Oracle Application Server and PL/SQL

PL/SQL is the heart and soul of dynamic Web page creation using data found in the Oracle database. The savvy developer will build templates for a Web site of standard backgrounds, table layouts, navigation links, and more. These standards can all be created as separate modules that can be called every time a page is built. A combination of calls to these separate procedures and application logic will lead to professional HTML documents with dynamic information.

Dynamic HTML Concepts

Over the past number of pages, we keep casually dropping the term "dynamic." To better understand the concept of dynamic, we should explain what is meant by "static." Most of the Web pages you access are static. When you key in an HTML document URL in your browser, you access a file on the Web server that changes only when some Webmaster places a new file with the same name on a Web server. In contrast, when you call a PL/SQL procedure from the URL, depending on the changing data in the database or the parameters you pass in, the PL/SQL code builds the HTML document for you and returns a potentially different page for every request.

Developers Toolkit

Oracle has provided the developer with a set of built-in packages that will create the HTML tags, send or receive cookies, create front-end forms, and so much more. Let's look at a couple of these tools and see how they will help us access data and present it to a Web browser as an HTML document.

HTP   Using the procedures defined in the HTP built-in package in your application server PL/SQL code, you can generate HTML tags and return an HTML document to the calling Web browser. There are several HTP packaged procedures, as well as a general one that can be used to pass an HTML string in the absence of a suitable HTP procedure. The following sample code and output will illustrate how HTP can be used to generate Web pages.

```
create or replace procedure phrmc_info_web_page
                                (zip_in in number)
as
  cursor phrmc_cur is
    select name,contact,phone_number
      from pharmacy
     where zip = zip_in;
  begin
    htp.htmlopen;
    htp.headopen;
    htp.title('Health Information Corporation');
    htp.headclose;
    htp.bodyopen(cattributes => 'bgcolor="#808000"');
    htp.tableopen('border');
    htp.tablecaption('Pharmacy Information','center');
    htp.tablerowopen;
    htp.tableheader('Pharmacy Name');
    htp.tableheader('Contact Name');
    htp.tableheader('Phone Number');
    htp.tablerowclose;
    for phrmc_rec in phrmc_cur
        loop
          -- for each row in the cursor, create a new
          -- row of data in the web page.
          htp.tablerowopen;
          htp.tabledata(phrmc_rec.name);
```

```
        htp.tabledata(phrmc_rec.contact);
        htp.tabledata(phrmc_rec.phone_number);
        htp.tablerowclose;
     end loop;
  htp.tableclose;
  htp.bodyclose;
  htp.htmlclose;
end;
/
```

In the next section, we will demonstrate how to call this procedure from a Web form. The following is an illustration of the HTML that would be generated when the previous procedure is called. The pharmacy names, contact names, and phone numbers that appear in the HTML would change depending on the value of the zip_in parameter and the corresponding database rows. The next listing illustrates the Web browser view of the dynamically generated HTML.

```
<HTML>
<HEAD>
<TITLE>Health Information Corporation</TITLE>
</HEAD>
<BODY bgcolor="808000">
<TABLE border>
<CAPTION ALIGN="CENTER">Pharmacy Information</CAPTION>
<TR>
<TH>Pharmacy Name</TH>
<TH>Contact Name</TH>
<TH>Phone Number</TH>
</TR>
<TR>
<TD>A.B. Thrift Drug Mart</TD>
<TD>Arlene Broitman</TD>
<TD>(602)555-6565</TD>
</TR>
<TR>
<TD>Mirage Medical Center Pharmacy</TD>
<TD>John Collins</TD>
<TD>(602)555-4235</TD>
</TR>
<TR>
<TD>Number Five Drug Store</TD>
<TD>Mark Shore</TD>
<TD>(602)555-6706</TD>
</TR>
</TABLE>
</BODY>
</HTML>
```

Figure 8-2 shows the output of the HTML in the previous listing in our favorite Web browser.

Each call to an HTP-packaged procedure generated a corresponding tag, attributes, and text. The title of the page, caption, and table headings are hard-coded and would therefore be the same for every generation of this page. In the preceding example, there were three pharmacies in the pharmacy table that matched the input zip code. Since the "cursor for loop" code was entirely inside a set of table tags, a single HTML table was generated with one table row for each iteration of the loop. The htp.tableData procedure calls inside the htp.tableRowOpen and htp.tableRowClose procedure calls generated table data tags with actual data selected from the database. The data that was selected from the database was inserted in the HTML document by inserting the record type variable from the cursor.

It's as simple as that to generate dynamic pages. By passing in another value for the zip code, an entirely different document would be generated.

DYNAMIC FORMS   HTML forms generated by the Oracle Application Server aren't as elaborate as some other front-end development tools, but they serve their

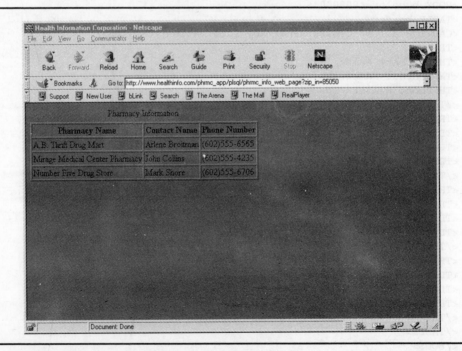

FIGURE 8-2.   *Dynamic HTML output in a browser*

purpose. Data validation usually needs to be performed by the called procedure, but some handy object-oriented JavaScript programming can hand some of this function off to be done on the client side. Drop-down lists can be created in an HTML form, and, if your database contains a table of values, a cursor call with a loop can be used to generate the lookup list of values for the form.

Now that we have a basic idea how to dynamically generate a Web page with data from the database, let's examine how to build a simple form. The form will call the previous examples procedure and pass in a ZIP code to be used in selecting data from the database.

```
create or replace procedure ZipForm
as
begin
  htp.htmlOpen;
    htp.headOpen;
    htp.title('Zip Code Entry Form');
    htp.headClose;
    htp.bodyOpen;
    htp.header
       (2, 'Pharmacy Information Zip Code Form');
    -- This is an example of how to embed an HTML
    -- tag using the htp.p procedure. The <br> tag
    -- produces white space. If you know how to code
    -- something in HTML, you can code the HTM string
    -- inside an htp.p procedure call. Using htp.br
    -- would produce the same results.
    htp.p('<br>');
    -- Open the 'formZip' form. The
    -- phrmc_info_web_page PL/SQL procedure by
    -- default is called via the GET method. The GET
    -- method shows the passed parameters in the URL
    -- while the POST method just displays the name
    -- of the called procedure without parameters.
    htp.formOpen
       ('phrmc_info_web_page',cmethod=>'GET');
    htp.tableOpen('border');
    -- Prompt user for Zip Code using a text field.
    -- The name of the text field must be the same
    -- as the input parameter in the procedure that
    -- is being called.
    htp.tableRowOpen;
    htp.tableData('Enter Zip Code: ');
    -- The htf function is used to embed an HTML tag
    -- inside another set of HTML tags. The following
    -- line creates a text entry field inside a set of
    -- table data tags. The text field is 5 characters
```

```
      -- wide on the page and will only accept a maximum
      -- of 5 characters of data.
      htp.tableData(htf.formText('zip_in', 5, 5));
      htp.tableRowClose;
      htp.tableRowOpen;
      -- The next line is passing actual HTML using the
      -- htp.p procedure. It is often simpler to mock up
      -- your page with a web authoring tool and then
      -- paste the HTML inside an htp.p call. This line
      -- will create a table data tag that spans two
      -- columns and inserts white space to separate the
      -- text field and label from the submit button.
      htp.p('<td colspan="2"> </td>');
      htp.tableRowClose;
      -- The next table row contains both a Submit and
      -- Reset button.
      htp.tableRowOpen;
      htp.tableData(htf.formSubmit);
      htp.tableData(htf.formReset);
      htp.tableRowClose;
      htp.tableClose;
      htp.formClose;
      htp.bodyClose;
  htp.htmlClose;
end;
/
```

This htp.formOpen procedure accepts the name of the procedure being
called. The form is closed after all other htp.form procedures are called with an
htp.formClose call. A text field is required to enter the zip code that will be passed
to the phrmc_info_web_page. The text field is given the same name as the input
parameter name of the procedure being called. This is how the Application Server
handles interrogation of the URL query.

The HTML generated by this procedure is shown in the following listing, and
Figure 8-3 illustrates how this simple Web form will appear in a Web browser.

```
<HTML>
<HEAD>
  <TITLE>Zip Code Entry Form</TITLE>
</HEAD>
<BODY>
  <H2>Pharmacy Information Zip Code Form</H2>
  <br>
  <FORM ACTION="phrmc_info_web_page" METHOD="GET">
    <TABLE  border>
      <TR>
        <TD>Enter Zip Code: </TD>
```

```
      <TD><INPUT TYPE="text" NAME="zip_in"
         SIZE="5" MAXLENGTH="5"></TD>
   </TR>
   <TR>
      <td colspan="2"> </td>
   </TR>
   <TR>
      <TD><INPUT TYPE="submit" VALUE="Submit"></TD>
      <TD><INPUT TYPE="reset" VALUE="Reset"></TD>
   </TR>
   </TABLE>
  </FORM>
 </BODY>
</HTML>
```

OWA_UTIL   In addition to the HTP and HTF built-in packages, Oracle has
provided the developer with a small arsenal of tools for collecting additional
information. OWA_UTIL is one of the Oracle-provided OWA utilities.

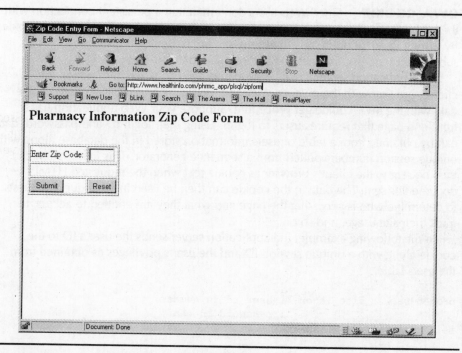

FIGURE 8-3.   *A simple form in a Web browser*

We've illustrated how to receive data from a form and build a page of dynamic data and a standard input/output example, but there is more. Suppose you wanted some information about what server is accessing your site, what type of browser is being used, the user's IP address, and so on. The owa_util.get_cgi_env procedure makes all of this possible.

The following example PL/SQL will collect the user's host name, IP address, and browser type, inserting the information into a database table. Once this information is in an Oracle table, it's readily available for the scrutiny of management, DBAs, and developers so that they can learn more about the users that are accessing the Web site.

```
. . .
insert into user_statistics
    (user_host, user_ip, user_browser, date_timestamp)
values
    (owa_util.get_cgi_env('REMOTE_HOST'),
     owa_util.get_cgi_env('REMOTE_ADDR'),
     owa_util.get_cgi_env('HTTP_USER_AGENT'),
     sysdate);
```

OWA_COOKIE   Since Web users don't maintain a persistent connection with the Web server, maintaining state across requests is often handled by using cookies. By storing information in the client browser and retrieving this information on subsequent requests, Internet applications can maintain state.

The application server's owa_cookie package can place information into a client's browser with the **owa_cookie.send** procedure and retrieve client cookie data with the **owa_cookie.get** procedure. Suppose your Web application has a front-end page that requires users to log in. Using their login ID and password, data can be obtained from a table of users information stored in the database along with unique session numbers pulled from a sequence generator. This information can then be sent to the client's browser as cookie text when the requested HTML document is sent. The data in the cookie can then be used in subsequent requests to determine who is accessing the page and what they are entitled to access, to track their site usage, and so on.

In the following example, the application server sends the user's ID to the cookie along with a unique session ID and the user's privileges as obtained from the users table.

```
procedure web_site_logon (i_user_id in number,
                          i_password in char)
is
    . . .
begin
```

```
    -- Validate user logging on. When a match is not
    -- found for the userid and password, the
    -- no_data_found exception for this block will
    -- handle the error.
    select userid, privileges
      into v_userid, v_privileges
      from site_user_info
     where userid = i_userid
       and password = i_password;
    -- If you reached this part of the code, the
    -- userid and password were valid. Obtain the
    -- next session id so it can be passed back to
    -- the clients browser.
    select session_id_sequence.nextval
      into v_session_id
      from dual;
    -- Send the text strings to the cookie in the
    -- mime header.
      owa_util.mime_header('text/html',FALSE);
      owa_cookie.send('userid', v_userid);
      owa_cookie.send('session_id', v_session_id);
      owa_cookie.send('privileges', v_privileges);
      owa_util.http_header_close;
    -- Build dynamic HTML document
      htp.htmlOpen;
    . . .
end;
/
```

With the user ID, session ID, and privileges stored in the browser's cookie, we give you the following example that illustrates how to retrieve those values. Once retrieved from the cookie, the data can then be interrogated. In the following example, when a user does not have administrator privileges, that user is denied access to the procedure and is sent an appropriate message.

```
procedure web_site_usage_statistics
is
    v_privileges         owa_cookie.cookie;
    v_user_privileges    varchar(1);
    e_unauthorized       exception;
    . . .
begin
    -- Get the users privileges from the cookie
      v_privileges := owa_cookie.get('privileges');
    -- Extract the value for privileges from
    -- v_privileges
      v_user_privileges := v_prvlgs_cookie.vals(1);
```

```
        -- If the users does not have administrator
        -- privileges, raise the unauthorized exception
          if v_user_privileges != 'A' THEN
          raise e_unauthorized;
        end if;
        . . .
exception
        . . .
      when e_unauthorized then
          -- Call another procedure that will send an
          -- access denied message to the client web
          -- browser.
          messages.unauthorized;
      . . . .
  end;
  /
```

What's Next

As far back as version 6, Oracle made a commitment to PL/SQL, which has evolved into the standard programming language in all Oracle tools. We have discussed the basics of PL/SQL and shown you some bottom-line functionality and features to get you started. Work with PL/SQL, and in little or no time, you will find yourself comfortable with a remarkably powerful programming language. As you read on and look at Oracle Developer, you will see how the tool PL/SQL is used.

CHAPTER
9

Oracle Developer

n this chapter, we will further round out your knowledge of Oracle8*i* in a little bit different way—by looking at the development environment we call Oracle Forms. We looked at installing Oracle Developer 6.0 in Chapter 6. Using Form Builder, programmers can build applications that provide users access to information stored in a database.

NOTE
We feature version 6.0 of Form Builder; though the name may be new (formerly known as Oracle Forms), this is an established product and immensely popular in the development community.

There is already a widespread acceptance of release 6 as a solid application development environment, now with deployments on client/server and Internet/intranet platforms. There is a gamut of GUI (graphical user interface) products on the market; Form Builder, part of the Developer 6 suite of products, is Oracle's offering.

In this chapter, we will also briefly discuss the Developer tool called Report Builder (it, too, has had a name change—previously known as Oracle Reports). The version we feature in this chapter, version 6, has a sophisticated programmer interface and has been significantly enhanced to offer you the ability to publish reports onto the Web.

When you are done reading this chapter, you will know about the following topics:

- What Form Builder is and the direction Oracle Developer is heading

- How to prepare your workstation to run Form and/or Report Builder

- How to build a few basic forms and a report

- Screen formatting in Form Builder

Terminology

The following definitions will arm you with the technical jargon you need to make it through this chapter.

- *ActiveX* replaces OLE as the term for COM-based technologies. OLE, once again, refers to object linking and embedding in compound documents.

- *Applet Viewer* is a component that client machines use to view applications running on the Forms Server.

■ A *block* is a container for items in Form Builder. Blocks can be related to tables in the database.

■ Asking Oracle to convert PL/SQL code into executable format is referred to as *compiling* PL/SQL.

■ *Comma insertion* is used to format numeric data for display purposes. It places commas in large numbers to make them more readable to the user (for instance, the number 83892029 is displayed as 83,892,029).

■ *Inheritance* allows the creation of objects in Oracle Forms that take on the look and feel and processing associated with other objects. Using inheritance, changes made to the referenced object affect the objects that have inherited its properties.

■ *Interface items* are objects in Form Builder with which the operator interacts. Enterable fields, push buttons, check boxes, and radio buttons are all interface items.

■ *JavaBeans* are program units that are written in Java and conform to the JavaBean specification.

■ Form Builder uses *locking* to preserve the integrity of data. Locking ensures that more than one user is not allowed to modify the same item of information at the same time.

■ *OLE2*, or Object Linking and Embedding version 2, allows dynamic sharing of objects between two OLE2-compliant software programs. Using Microsoft Word for Windows (OLE2-compliant), you can embed a Microsoft Excel (OLE2-compliant) spreadsheet in a document; when the contents of the spreadsheet change, the OLE2 link gives Word immediate access to the changes.

■ *Stored procedures* are PL/SQL subprograms in the database that can be called by name from an application.

■ *Tabular* is the default layout displaying labels at the top of the page and rows of data underneath the labels.

■ *Wizards* automate frequently performed tasks such as creation of a data block or chart in Form or Report Builder.

■ *WYSIWYG* stands for "what you see is what you get." In all GUI products, the look of your information on the screen is exactly the way printed output will look. For example, if you bold text in a WYSIWYG word processor, the text is bolded on the screen.

■ *Zero suppression* replaces leading zeros with spaces in numeric data for display purposes. Using zero suppression, the number 00003487 would be displayed as 3487 (that is, with four blanks in front of the number where the zeros used to be).

What Is Form Builder?

Form Builder version 6 has evolved to become a very intricate part of Developer, Oracle's new generation of tools for application development on the World Wide Web. With this integrated software, programmers can develop applications for an internal company intranet or the Internet, while still keeping in touch with existing client/server implementations.

Form Builder is a feature-rich application building tool that produces production-quality screens utilizing data stored in a database. You can embed graphics, sound, video, word processing documents, and spreadsheets through the use of OLE2. Other components that can be embedded, which are new in version 6, are JavaBeans and ActiveX components. This is part of Oracle's efforts to ensure that the objects already developed, whether internally in your company or by a third party, can be utilized and reused in Form Builder. Oracle has emphasized programmer productivity with Developer: Form Builder is a fully mouse-driven interface, with the capability to do most of the development without a great deal of coding. Let's look a bit more at Oracle Developer 6 and the Internet computing three-tiered model.

Application Tiers and Oracle Developer

Application development is now moving from high-volume client/server applications commonly known as two-tier to "multitier" (often referred to as "three-tier" or "n-tier") architecture implementations. Do not let the terminology alarm you; the definition of a tier is simply a logical-component level. We have discussed multiple tiers in many places around this work. For example, the existing client/server or two-tier application architecture is typically defined in this way:

■ The client, or first tier, is primarily responsible for presentation (a GUI interface).

■ The server or second tier is primarily responsible for supplying the data to the client (Oracle database).

The issue with the two-tier architecture and why application development is moving away from it is "Where do application logic and business rules reside?"

Typically, the answer to this question was either at the client, at the server, or both. Figure 9-1 shows two-tier application architecture.

A multitier architecture supplies the logical-component level for the application logic and business rules. This tier is implemented by using an *application server*. An application server can take many forms, anything from

- A Transaction Processing Monitor, defined as a subsystem that groups together sets of related database updates and submits them together to a relational database.

- A Message Queue, which queues messages from an application so that some other part of the application (or some other application) can then read the message. If needed, this reader of the message can respond, again by sending a message into the queue that's later read by the original sender or even by another application elsewhere.

- A CORBA/COM (Common Object Request Broker Architecture/Common Object Model)–based solution (commonly called an ORBS—Object Request Broker). These automate many common network programming tasks.

Oracle has its own application server, which supports the multitier architecture that delivers the benefits of both client/server and Web in a single application. In a

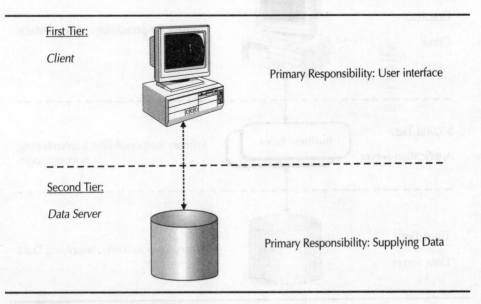

First Tier:

Client

Primary Responsibility: User interface

Second Tier:

Data Server

Primary Responsibility: Supplying Data

FIGURE 9-1. *Two-tier architecture*

Web application, application logic and business rules are focused on the middle tier—the application server—instead of on the desktop machines. Figure 9-2 depicts a multitier application architecture.

Development of multitier applications does not have to be as difficult as it sounds, and we will see later in this chapter what Oracle has done to help the programmer create this type of application. Get out your stethoscope; we are about to see if your PC is capable of running Developer 6.

Preparing Your Workstation to Run Form or Report Builder

The following must be done before running Form Builder:

■ You must have access to a local or remote Oracle database. To access a remote database, you or your database administrator must have installed Net8 and be able to successfully connect to the database.

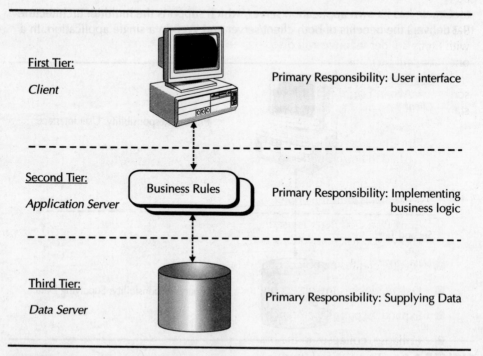

First Tier:

Client

Primary Responsibility: User interface

Second Tier:

Application Server

Business Rules

Primary Responsibility: Implementing business logic

Third Tier:

Data Server

Primary Responsibility: Supplying Data

FIGURE 9-2. *Three-tier architecture*

NOTE
The work involved in setting this up may have to be done by a more senior resource or with help from Oracle Worldwide Customer Support.

■ You must have already loaded your network software if you are accessing a remote database. If you are using a local Personal Oracle8*i* database, this is not necessary.

That's all! For development of applications for the Web, Oracle comes with a preloaded applet viewer, which mimics the Web environment, enabling the programmer to see how an application will look and act on the Web. You haven't seen anything yet. Before getting started actually using the product, let's look at its main components and some of the design tools with which you will become familiar.

Form Builder—A Quick Tour

Before diving into Form Builder, look at the assortment of buttons and tools you will be using. Form Builder calls the collection of buttons along the top of its screen the toolbar and the collection of tools down the side of its screen the tool palette. Figure 9-3 shows the various buttons. There are many more buttons and tools you can use with Form Builder than we will discuss in this chapter. We will only touch on the ones you will be using.

Let's briefly look at the Form Builder specific buttons on the left side of the screen, shown in Figure 9-3. It is not necessary to spend any time on the Windows standard buttons (that is, New, Open, Save, Cut, Copy, and Paste):

■ Run Client/Server is used to compile an executable file from the application created in Form Builder to be run on a client/server platform.

■ Run Web brings up the Oracle Developer Server to run the application as an applet within the applet viewer.

■ Run Form Debugger is used to run your form in debug mode. This mode allows you to create debug actions, such as breakpoints and debug triggers.

■ Create, creates an object of the type for the branch highlighted.

■ Delete, deletes the object highlighted.

■ Expand, expands the branch highlighted to the next detail level below.

■ Collapse, collapses to the branch level highlighted.

■ Expand All, expands to all levels of detail below the branch highlighted.

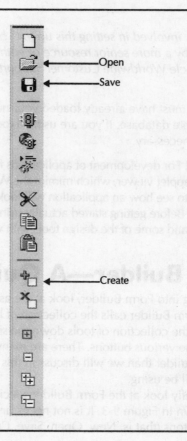

FIGURE 9-3. *Form Builder buttons*

■ Collapse All, collapses all levels of detail into the branch highlighted.

Now, let's look at the Form Builder's five main components; then we'll delve into the part each plays in the interface to Form Builder:

■ Object Navigator

■ Property palette

■ Layout editor

■ PL/SQL editor

■ Object Library

Object Navigator

The most important of the five is the Object Navigator. This navigator is shared by
all of the Developer tools. Learning to utilize its functions will allow for a smooth
transition to the other tools. The Object Navigator is used primarily to move quickly
between the other three interfaces. Its other purpose is drag-and-drop application
development. Using the Object Navigator, you can access objects and libraries both
on disk and in the database. By dragging these objects into your Form Builder
workspace, you have added their functionality to your form.

Property Palette

As important as the Object Navigator is, the Property palette is where you spend
most of your development time, setting object attributes or characteristics. The
nature of the characteristics you define using a Property palette depends on what
type of object is being designed (say, the Property palette for a module, a canvas
view, or a block). Figure 9-4 shows a property sheet for the module MODULE1.
Here you define characteristics of modules, such as the module's title, and fine-tune
the canvas screen coordinates. You can achieve a lot of different looks, and most of
them are determined by individual tastes. It is very important to carefully plan out
what the screens are going to look like at the beginning of a project, especially
when several developers are involved.

As you move through the entries on most Property palettes, you will find three
ways to change properties:

■ Some properties are set by typing information into the text entry box that is
   highlighted when the property is selected. The Name property shown in
   Figure 9-4 is set this way.

■ Some properties are set by clicking the down arrow that appears when the
   property is highlighted. A drop-down menu appears from which the
   property characteristics are chosen. The Class Type property shown in
   Figure 9-4 is set this way.

■ Some properties are set by clicking a More button that appears when the
   property is highlighted. A dialog box appears within which the property
   characteristics are set. The Subclass Information property shown in Figure
   9-4 is set this way.

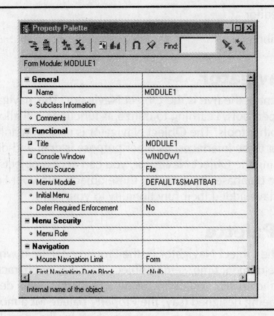

FIGURE 9-4. *The Property palette*

VIP
When you type in an entry for a property (such as the name of a canvas view), press ENTER to update the property you have just changed in the Property palette. Leave the property sheet by clicking the Exit-X.

Layout Editor

The Layout editor is where you design the look and feel of your canvases or screens; this is what the client or user is going to interact with. If the layout of a canvas (screen) is pleasing to the eye, you are halfway there. While working with canvas views, you can control the application's color, size, font, data access, and style. Think of the Layout editor as where you paint your application's objects, with the entire screen as your canvas. Figure 9-5 shows a canvas within the Layout editor.

You create a new canvas in the Object Navigator by highlighting Canvases and clicking the Create tool on the Object Navigator tool palette. You control what type of canvas it will be in the canvas property sheet. The property sheet can be reached in the Object Navigator by highlighting Canvases and then choosing Tools from the main menu and then Properties.

Object attributes can be added, modified, or removed using the Form Builder Property palette. The Layout editor is fully *WYSIWYG*—standing for what you see is what you get.

NOTE
A colleague of ours, Dr. Paul Dorsey, coined the acronym WYSISWYG—what you see is sort of what you get.

This is where you place all of the objects for the particular screen that is being developed.

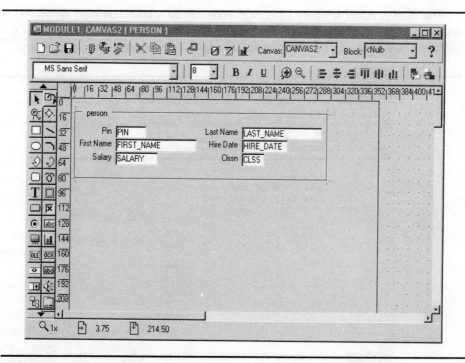

FIGURE 9-5.   *The Layout editor*

PL/SQL Editor

The PL/SQL editor is where the application will take on its specialized functionality. You can control exactly what the program can and cannot do based on the work you do in this editor. This is where all of the form's triggers and procedures are edited and compiled. It is also where database procedures can be accessed, modified, and compiled. The PL/SQL editor is accessed by selecting the PL/SQL Editor menu option under the Program menu in the Form Builder console. A PL/SQL editor screen is shown in Figure 9-6.

NOTE
If there is a plus (+) sign beside Program Units on the Object Navigator, double-click it to display any defined program units. You can edit individual program units by then double-clicking the icon.

The PL/SQL editor is where all PL/SQL code can be added, modified, removed, and compiled. All work is done in the PL/SQL editor regardless of the type of PL/SQL object you are working with (for instance, a trigger, a stored procedure, or a library).

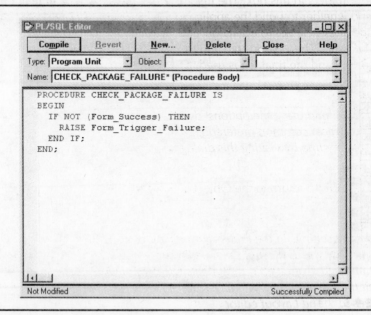

FIGURE 9-6. *The PL/SQL editor*

Object Library

In any development environment, you will always have standards to which you want your developers to adhere, as well as common objects, which can be reused throughout the development effort. The Object Library provides an easy method of reusing objects and enforcing standards across the entire development organization.

Now that you have had a look at the tools you will be using in this chapter's exercises, as well as the Object Navigator, Layout editor, Property palette, PL/SQL, and Object Library, let's discuss setting options in Form Builder. You can customize the look and feel of Form Builder according to your preferences by setting options.

Setting Options

The first area to look at is setting options. This is where you set aspects of Form Builder to suit your individual tastes. The menu at the top of the designer screen is where you start:

1. Click Tools on the menu at the top of the screen. This menu is available anywhere from any Form Builder screen.

2. Click Preferences to open the dialog box shown in Figure 9-7. There are four folders in this box. The first is to set General options such as printers and whether to build the application before running. The Access option specifies whether to open and save modules to the file system or to the database. The Wizards tab allows you to select what wizards are available to use, and the final tab is used to set Runtime options.

NOTE
We recommend using the options' defaults. They reflect the most common preferences and can be changed anytime by visiting this dialog box.

3. Click OK to return to the Object Navigator.

NOTE
The default settings in the Preferences dialog box will suit your needs most of the time. When you run programs right from the Form Builder, you may wish to visit the Preferences dialog box and make some changes in the Runtime Options folder.

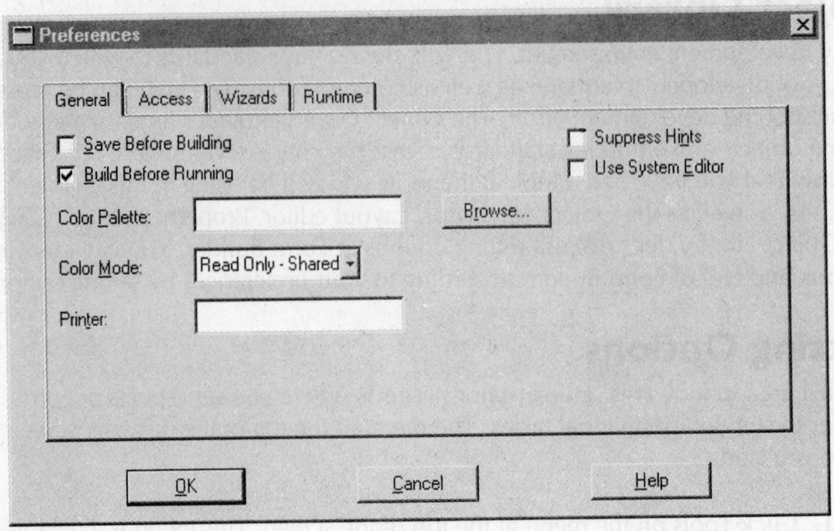

FIGURE 9-7. *Form Builder Preferences*

Working with Form Builder Files

In this section, you will learn how to do the following:

- Create and save a new form

- Open an existing form

- Change the name of a form

After clicking the Form Builder icon in the Oracle Developer 6.0 program menu, Form Builder will appear. When the Welcome dialog appears, click "Build a new form manually" and then Click the OK button. The form name MODULE1 will be highlighted in the Object Navigator. At this point, you can open an existing form or begin working on a new one.

Creating a New Form

After loading Form Builder, you are ready to begin creating an application. By default, the Form Builder starts with a new form ready to go (with the name MODULE1). If you have done some work on a form and wish to start a new form, select New on the File menu at the top of the screen. Alternatively, you can highlight the text Forms at the top of the Object Navigator and double-click the Create tool on the Object Navigator tool palette.

TIP

If after loading Form Builder you immediately open an existing form, the MODULE1 form created by default is removed automatically.

Opening an Existing Form

To open a form that already exists, select Open on the File menu at the top of the screen. The Open dialog box appears, as shown in Figure 9-8. Alternatively, you may click the Open tool on the Object Navigator tool palette. Double-click a filename, or click a filename to highlight it and then click OK to open the report. The title of the form in the Object Navigator will change to show the name of the form you have opened.

TIP

The quickest way to open a form is to use the shortcut key CTRL-O. This brings up the same dialog box shown in Figure 9-8.

Open				? ✕
Look in:	Forms60			
java	Fmgus.msb	lewbfnim.res	lewbtysp.r	
Userexit	Fmlus.msb	lewbipim.res	lewbtytv.re	
Fmcus.msb	Fmmus.msb	lewblpim.res	lewbupim.i	
Fmdbusw.res	Fmrpcweb.res	lewblvim.res	lewbweim.	
Fmdus.msb	Fmrusw.res	lewbmdim.res	lewblbkim.re	
Fmdwel.res	Fmrweb.res	lewbqpim.res	lewlcaim.re	
Fmfus.msb	lewbdpim.res	lewbtbim.res	lewlfnim.re	

File name:		Open
Files of type:	All Files (*.*)	Cancel

FIGURE 9-8. *The Open Form dialog box*

Saving a Form

To save a form you have been working with, select Save on the File menu at the top of the screen, or click the Save tool on the Object Navigator tool palette. If this is the first time you are saving a form, Form Builder displays the Save As dialog box shown in Figure 9-9. Enter a filename for the report, and then click Save to complete the save. If Oracle Forms knows the name of the form you are working with (that is, if you have saved it previously in the same session), it saves the form without opening the Save As dialog box.

TIP
The quickest way to save a form is to use the shortcut key CTRL-S. *If Oracle does not know the name of the report you are saving, it will open up the dialog box shown in Figure 9-9.*

Changing the Name of a Form

If you wish to change the name of a form, select Save As on the File menu at the top of the screen. Form Builder brings up the dialog box shown in Figure 9-9. Enter a new filename and then click Save to complete the save using the new name.

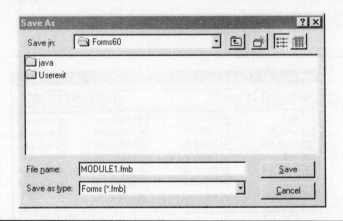

FIGURE 9-9. *Saving a form*

The Right Mouse Button

The right mouse button has special meaning for Form Builder. It allows quick access to the Layout editor, PL/SQL editor, and Property palettes. For example, when you click the right button while the mouse cursor is on a Form in the Object Navigator, a menu appears, as shown in Figure 9-10.

In addition, clicking the right button while the mouse cursor is on a canvas shows the menu in Figure 9-11. Notice how the available options in these menus are context sensitive: the SmartTriggers and SmartClasses options are inactive.

NOTE
If you have your mouse defined with the right button as the primary one, you would use the left button to accomplish what we discuss in this section. Most mouse software allows you to redefine the two mouse buttons.

FIGURE 9-10.   *Form Options*

Cut	Ctrl+X
Copy	Ctrl+C
Paste	Ctrl+V
Property Palette	
Layout Editor	
Object Library	
Data Block Wizard	
Layout Wizard	
LOV Wizard	
SmartTriggers	▶
SmartClasses	
Help	

FIGURE 9-11. *Canvas options*

Sample Data

Hopefully, most, if not all of you, will be able to run off to Osborne/McGraw-Hill's
Web site (*http://www.osborne.com*) and dig up this seed data. For the few who
cannot do so, we have included it here just in case. If there are any fellow workers
who "owe you one," typing this in for you could be a good way for them to pay you
back.

```
rem * -----------------------------------------------------------
rem *  Script to set up tables used in Chapter 9 from
rem *  Oracle8i: A Beginner's Guide
rem * -----------------------------------------------------------
set echo on
drop table person;
drop table clssn;
drop table bonus;
drop table factory;
drop table commission;
create table person (
     pin              number(6),
     last_name        varchar2(20),
     first_name       varchar2(20),
     hire_date        date,
     salary           number(8,2),
     clssn            varchar2(5));
```

```
create table clssn (
    clssn          varchar2(5),
    descr          varchar2(20));
create table bonus (
    emp_id         number(4),
    emp_class      varchar2(2),
    fac_id         varchar2(3),
    bonus_amt      number);
create table factory (
    fac_id         varchar2(3),
    descr          varchar2(20),
    prov           varchar2(2));
create table commission (
    sales_id       number(3),
    qtr            varchar2(1),
    comm_amt       number(8,2));
insert into person values
    (100110,'SAUNDERS','HELEN','12-DEC-87',77000,'1');
insert into person values
    (100120,'FONG','LYDIA','11-MAY-88',55000,'3');
insert into person values
    (100130,'WILLIAMS','FRANK','09-DEC-82',43000,'4');
insert into person values
    (100140,'COHEN','NANCY','14-AUG-93',44000,'4');
insert into person values
    (100150,'STEWART','BORIS','11-NOV-91',48000,'4');
insert into person values
    (100160,'REDMOND','KENNETH','01-FEB-92',32000,'5');
insert into person values
    (100170,'SMYTHE','ROLLY','11-JUL-83',33000,'5');
insert into person values
    (100180,'FRANKS','HENRY','31-JUL-83',55000,'3');
insert into person values
    (100190,'GREENBERG','JOE','30-MAR-86',21000,'6');
insert into person values
    (100200,'LEVIS','SANDRA','06-DEC-89',18000,'7');
insert into person values
    (100210,'APPOLLO','BILL','12-APR-89',44000,'4');
insert into person values
    (100210,'JENKINS','SALLY','12-DEC-87',44000,'4');
insert into clssn values ('1','Manager');
insert into clssn values ('2','Chief');
insert into clssn values ('3','Leader');
insert into clssn values ('4','Analyst');
insert into clssn values ('5','Clerk');
insert into clssn values ('6','Trainee');
insert into clssn values ('7','Part time');
insert into bonus values (123,null,'AE',2000);
```

```
insert into bonus values (124,null,'AF',2200);
insert into bonus values (125,null,'AH',1200);
insert into bonus values (126,null,'AH',1200);
insert into bonus values (127,null,'AF',1200);
insert into bonus values (128,null,'AT',1500);
insert into bonus values (129,null,'AT',1100);
insert into bonus values (130,null,'AU',1400);
insert into bonus values (131,null,'AE',200);
insert into bonus values (132,null,'AF',220);
insert into bonus values (133,null,'AG',120);
insert into bonus values (134,null,'AG',200);
insert into bonus values (135,null,'AG',200);
insert into bonus values (136,null,'AU',1400);
insert into bonus values (137,null,'AH',100);
insert into bonus values (138,null,'AU',1400);
insert into factory values ('AE','Northeast','ON');
insert into factory values ('AF','Northwest','MN');
insert into factory values ('AH','Southeast','ON');
insert into factory values ('AT','Central','MN');
insert into factory values ('AU','South','CA');
insert into commission values (10,1,140);
insert into commission values (10,2,10);
insert into commission values (10,3,null);
insert into commission values (10,4,810);
insert into commission values (20,1,1200);
insert into commission values (20,2,200);
insert into commission values (20,3,500);
insert into commission values (20,4,100);
insert into commission values (30,1,40);
insert into commission values (30,2,19);
insert into commission values (30,3,340);
insert into commission values (30,4,null);
commit;
```

Working with Form Builder— A Primer

Now that the introductions are over, you are ready to build your first application. Not only are you ready to build your first application, you are also now able to run it as if it were on a client/server or Web platform! In this version of Form Builder, Oracle has come out with some real nifty wizards. As a programmer that has been through too many rewrites of applications developed by someone who sat through a sales presentation showing how easy it is to develop an application, we were never a fan of wizards. The code produced by wizards would always be cryptic and complex. Oracle has changed this view.

At the very start when you open Form Builder, you are presented with the option of generating an application, as shown in Figure 9-12. Ensure that the Use the Data Block Wizard radio button is highlighted. All items used in Form Builder, whether they come from a table in the database or not, must be in a block; let's build a simple application and follow the wizard through its steps.

NOTE
It is possible that, depending on what you are doing with this wizard and when it is invoked, the series of screens you encounter may be somewhat different than what you see here.

NOTE
We will be using the data shown in the "Sample Data" section of this chapter.

1. Click OK on the startup screen and off you go.

2. A welcome screen is presented to you stating you are about to start creating a data block. Click Next to get to the Data Block Wizard screen shown in Figure 9-13.

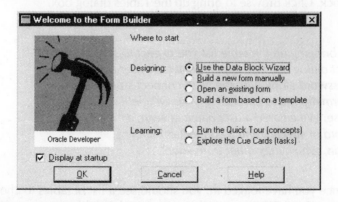

FIGURE 9-12. *Wizard welcome*

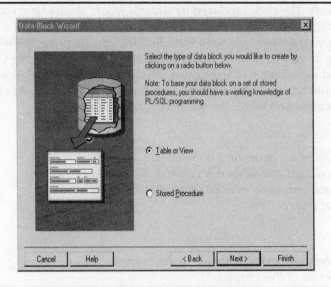

FIGURE 9-13. *Data Block Wizard screen 1*

3. The dialog box in Figure 9-13 explains whether your data block will go against a Table or View or Stored Procedure. Select Table or View, and click Next to continue.

4. The wizard asks you to choose a table or view as the source for your data block. Click Browse to bring up the Tables dialog box.

VIP
*Before bringing up the table list you expect to see, a connect dialog box will appear; enter the user name and password along with the Net8 connect string you normally use to connect to your Oracle8i database. We entered a user name of **sean**, a password of **speedo**, and a connect string of **o8ibegin**, which may differ from yours.*

5. Once you have logged in, you should see a list of tables to choose from Figure 9-14. This screen allows you to select tables, synonyms, or views of the current user or other users if you have been granted permission.

6. Highlight the PERSON table and click OK.

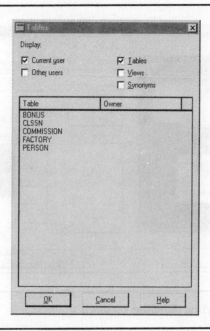

FIGURE 9-14.   *List of available tables*

7. You are now taken back to the data block screen you saw in step 4. This time we have selected a table, and the list of columns available are on the left under the Available Columns. You can move these columns over as database items individually by highlighting them and clicking >; but, for present purposes, click >> (the multicolumn select button), bringing all displayed columns over from Available Columns to Database Items. This is shown in Figure 9-15. Click Next to carry on.

8. A quick pat on the back from Oracle is then displayed while asking if you would like to continue on with a second wizard to assist you on doing your application layout. When responding to this question, ensure the option "Create the data block, then call the Layout Wizard" is selected, and click Finish.

9. Another welcome screen pops up, this time for the Layout Wizard; click Next.

10. You are then asked if you will be using a new Canvas; the Canvas Type is shown in Figure 9-16. Leave as is, and Click Next.

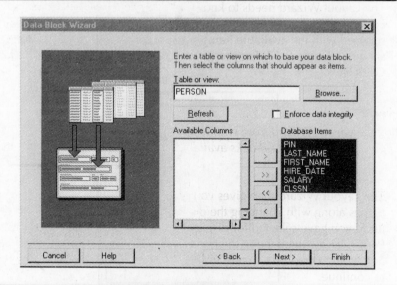

FIGURE 9-15. *Selecting database columns*

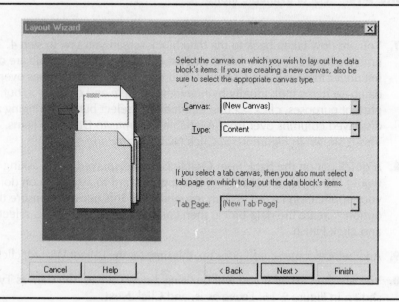

FIGURE 9-16. *Choosing canvas and canvas type*

11. The Layout Wizard needs to know the data block you will be using. Fortunately, it already knows, and the PERSON data block should be selected with the available items for display listed in Available Items, as shown in Figure 9-17. For present purposes, select them all by Clicking >>. Click Next.

NOTE
Using the Layout Wizard from within Forms Builder
will give a list of all Data Blocks available.

12. The Layout Wizard then gives you an opportunity to give more meaningful names along with changing the display width and height to the database items you have selected for display. Let's change the PIN display to, say, Person ID by highlighting the text beside the Name in the Prompt field and typing **Person ID**. Figure 9-18 shows where this is done. Click Next to continue.

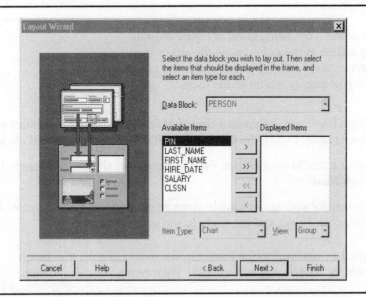

FIGURE 9-17. *Choosing columns for layout*

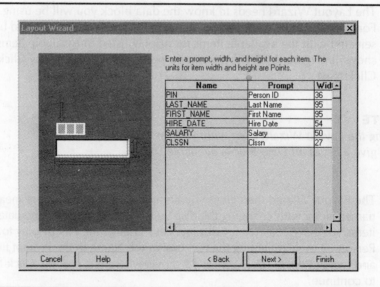

FIGURE 9-18. *Changing column names in a data block*

VIP
*Think of the work being done in Figure 9-18 as
giving aliases to the columns on the selected canvas.
We recommend doing this everywhere to give more
meaningful display names to the users.*

13. From here, you are given a choice of Form or Tabular presentation or
    layout style. Ensure the Form radio button is highlighted, and click Next.

14. Enter a title to your Frame. Type in **Person**, as shown in Figure 9-19, and
    click Next.

15. Hurray for you again! Oracle announces you have done it again. To get by
    this, click Finish and get ready to see your creation.

You are then returned to the Form Builder main console, the design
environment for developing applications. Try running your application.

1. Click the menu option Program, as shown in Figure 9-20, on the top of the
   Form Builder main console.

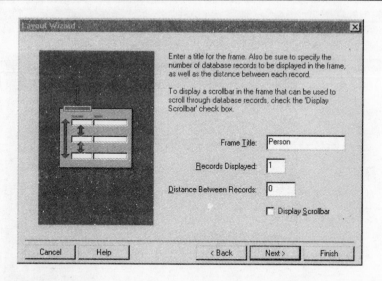

FIGURE 9-19.   *Naming a data block in the Layout Wizard*

2. Click Client/Server (hold on, we'll get to the Web next). Presto! Here is your application you worked so hard to bring to life!

3. Bring down the Query menu from the top of the screen, and then select Execute to see your first record, as shown in Figure 9-21. Three words come to mind now—cool huh?

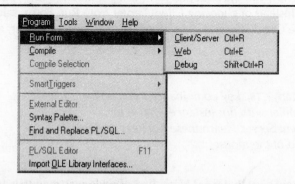

FIGURE 9-20.   *Running the application*

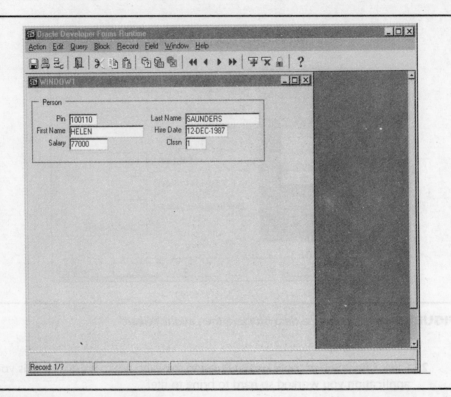

FIGURE 9-21. *Beautiful form*

Okay, okay, let's look at this using the Web. Close the application by clicking the Exit-X. Let's now run the beautiful form using a different run option than shown in Figure 9-20. Instead of choosing Client/Server from Run Form, select Web. This will bring up the Oracle Form Builder Runtime Web applet viewer, as shown in Figure 9-22.

NOTE
There are many CTRL key combinations you will become familiar with (for instance, CTRL-R for running Client/Server); learn these hot keys and use them instead of the mouse.

Okay, see how easy that was? Not a line of code was manually written, and you have created an application that can be run on both the client/server and Web platforms. Let's look at some bells and whistles of the Form Builder tool.

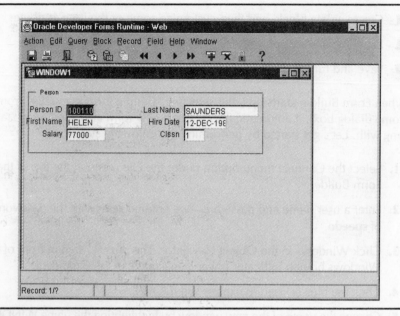

FIGURE 9-22. *The Runtime Web applet viewer*

More Hands-On Experience with Form Builder

Let's build a few simple forms from scratch to illustrate how to develop screens with Form Builder. We entered a user name of **sean**, a password of **speedo**, and a connect string of **o8ibegin**, which may differ from yours.

NOTE
Again, we will be using the data shown in the "Sample Data" section of this chapter.

Exercise #1

In this exercise, you will start from the beginning and work through some important steps in creating a new form. We will show you how to do the following:

■ Create a window.

■ Create a content canvas.

■ Create a data block, and then customize some of the item attributes.

■ Label the items displayed.

■ Save and run the form.

When Form Builder starts up (after selecting "Build a form manually" from the Welcome dialog box), it automatically creates a new form and window to start working with. Let's get started by performing the following steps:

1. Select the Connect menu option under the File menu at the top of the Form Builder.

2. Enter a user name and password—we entered **sean** with the password of **speedo**.

3. Click Windows in the Object Navigator. The plus (+) sign in front of the Windows branch indicates lower levels that can be expanded.

4. Click the plus (+) sign to expose WINDOW1.

5. Change the name of the new window by highlighting the name WINDOW1, and changing it to **person**. You have just created your first window (fun, eh?).

6. Click the Canvases branch on the Object Navigator. Form Builder creates the initial canvas and calls it CANVAS1.

7. Again, you want to change this name to something more meaningful, so click once on the highlighted name and change it to **person**. By utilizing these same names, you are quickly able to determine where all of the objects are located.

8. Highlight the Data Blocks branch in the Object Navigator, and then click Create. You will be given a choice of creating the data block manually or using the wizard. Let's be daring and try it manually this time.

9. Right-click the new block created, and bring up the Property palette.

10. Under General, change the Name to **person**. Once changed, **person** should appear under the Data Blocks branch.

11. Again using the Property palette, under the Database property, enter **person** as the Query Data Source Name.

12. Highlight the Items branch under the Data Block and click Create. Using the Property palette, you can change the name and other attributes. Enter the following items with the properties as shown in Table 9-1.

Item	Property Category	Property	Value
PIN	General	Name	PIN
		Item Type	Text Item
	Data	Data Type	Number
		Maximum Data Length	7
	Database	Column Name	PIN
	Physical	Canvas	CANVAS1
LAST_NAME	General	Name	LAST_NAME
		Item Type	Text Item
	Data	Data Type	Char
		Maximum Data Length	20
	Database	Column Name	LAST_NAME
	Physical	Canvas	CANVAS1
FIRST_NAME	General	Name	FIRST_NAME
		Item Type	Text Item
	Data	Data Type	Char
		Maximum Data Length	20
	Database	Column Name	FIRST_NAME
	Physical	Canvas	CANVAS1
HIRE_DATE	General	Name	HIRE_DATE
		Item Type	Text Item
	Data	Data Type	Date
	Database	Column Name	HIRE_DATE
	Physical	Canvas	CANVAS1

TABLE 9-1. *Property Palette Data Entry Values*

Item	Property Category	Property	Value
SALARY	General	Name	SALARY
		Item Type	Text Item
	Data	Data Type	Money
	Database	Column Name	SALARY
	Physical	Canvas	CANVAS1
CLSSN	General	Name	CLSSN
		Item Type	Text Item
	Data	Data Type	Char
		Maximum Data Length	5
	Database	Column Name	CLSSN
	Physical	Canvas	CANVAS1

TABLE 9-1. *Property Palette Data Entry Values* (continued)

13. Click the Layout Editor option under the Tools menu within the Form Builder console. You see only one item; where are the others you have just defined? Do not despair, all the items that you have defined are together on the same area on the canvas, Figure 9-23. Take your mouse and drag these items to where you would like to see them on the screen.

14. Let's quickly put labels with your displayed items. Click the text button, which looks like a capital T, located on the Layout editor tool palette; then click the canvas where you would like the label, and type in the label. Repeat this for each item you want labeled. Once complete, your canvas should look like that shown in Figure 9-24.

15. Save the form by pressing CTRL-S to open the Save As dialog box. Enter the name **form1**, and then click OK.

NOTE
When we discussed Form Builder Options earlier in the "Setting Options" section, we accepted the default by telling Form Builder to Generate Before Run. This is why we do not have to generate here.

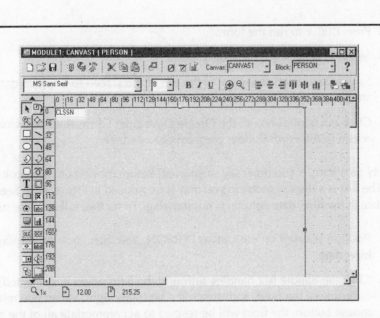

FIGURE 9-23. *Canvas view*

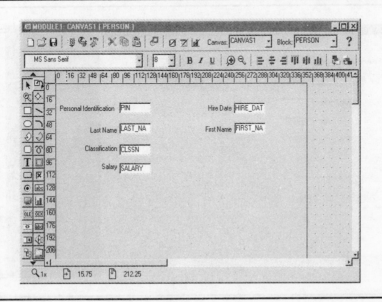

FIGURE 9-24. *Canvas with labeled Items*

16. Press CTRL-R to run the form.

17. Select Execute from the Query menu.

18. Select Execute on the menu at the top of the screen to bring up data, as shown in Figure 9-25.

19. Click the control box in the Oracle Developer Forms Runtime window to return to the Form Builder programmer interface.

Pretty nice form, if you don't say so yourself! Before moving on, let's look at two items. The first is a display problem you may have noticed in Figure 9-25. See how the entire date in the **hire_date** column is not showing? To fix this, follow these steps:

1. Position yourself on the canvas PERSON, and then click the display area for **hire_date**.

2. Click the handle (six handles surround the field when it is selected) on the right side of the field, and stretch it a bit to the right. When you release the mouse button, the field will be resized to accommodate all of the data in **hire_date**.

3. Save the form by pressing CTRL-S.

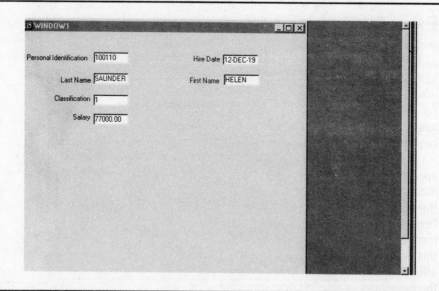

FIGURE 9-25. *Form1*

4. Look at the changes by pressing CTRL-R.

5. Click the Exit-X in the Oracle Developer Forms Runtime window to return to the Form Builder console.

Let's also look at a quick way to customize item attributes on a canvas view.

1. Navigate to the PERSON canvas by clicking in its window if it is still visible, or double-clicking its button in the Object Navigator.

2. Hold down CTRL and click each field on the canvas. Each field shows six handles after all fields are selected.

3. Place the cursor on the canvas, and press the right mouse button. Choose Property Palette from the menu that appears.

4. Select Background Color property (under the Color property), and type in Green.

5. Close the Property palette by clicking its Exit-X.

6. Save the form by pressing CTRL-S.

The next time you run the form, its background color will be green. This completes your first exercise.

Exercise #2

In this exercise, you will learn what a master-detail relationship is, when to use it, and how to create it. A master-detail relationship is an association between two base table blocks; the parent is called a master block, and there is a detail block whose records are associated with the parent's. The master-detail relationship in Form Builder ensures that the detail block displays only those records that are associated with the current record in the master block and coordinates querying between the two blocks.

The primary reason for a master-detail relationship is to enable the users of your application to access multiple detail records of information linked by a common master record. A good example of this is an invoice. The record of the customer in the customer master file is the master record. The order placed consists of many items—the detail record. The two pieces of information are linked together to give the users greater visibility and usability of the information. Form Builder provides this unique feature to make developing applications easier. Since Form Builder allows definition of this link between the two types of records as a standard feature, the developer is able to concentrate on other areas of the application. Now you will create this type of relationship with Form Builder:

1. Click the Form Builder shortcut in the Oracle Developer 6.0 folder of the Windows Program Manager. When the Form Builder console has finished loading, follow steps 1 through 15 from the previous section ("Exercise #1") to create your first block.

NOTE
*Alternatively, you can open the previous form, click File and then Save As to change its name, and save it under the name **form2** (or whatever name you choose).*

2. Let's now create the second block. Position yourself on the Object Navigator by selecting Object Navigator from the Window menu at the top of the screen, and then click Data Block.

3. With the Data Block text highlighted, click the Create tool on the Object Navigator tool palette to open the New Data Block Options dialog box.

4. Under General, change the Name to **clssn**. Once changed, **clssn** should appear under the Data Blocks branch.

5. Again using the Property palette, under the Database property, enter **clssn** as the Query Data Source Name.

6. Highlight the Items branch under the Data Block, and click Create. Using the Property palette you can change the name and other attributes. Enter the following items with the properties, as shown in Table 9-2.

7. Highlight the Relations branch under the **clssn** data block and double-click. A dialog box to add a new relationship will be brought up. Enter **person** in the Detail Block field and **person.clssn = clssn.clssn** in the Join Condition field, as shown in Figure 9-26, and click OK. Form Builder will then generate triggers for the **clssn** data block to handle the master-detail relationship, as shown in Figure 9-27.

8. Click the Layout Editor option under the Tools menu within the Form Builder console and adjust the **clssn** and the **descr** items to be at the top of the canvas. Then save the form by pressing CTRL-S.

9. Press CTRL-R to run the form. When the form appears, select Execute from the Query menu at the top of the screen. Figure 9-28 shows the screen after the query executes.

Item	Property Category	Property	Value
CLSSN	General	Name	PIN
		Item Type	Text Item
	Data	Data Type	Char
		Maximum Data Length	5
	Database	Column Name	CLSSN
	Physical	Canvas	CANVAS1
DESCR	General	Name	DESCR
		Item Type	Text Item
	Data	Data Type	Char
		Maximum Data Length	20
	Database	Column Name	DESCR
	Physical	Canvas	CANVAS1

TABLE 9-2. *Property Palette Data Entry Values for clssn Data Block*

10. Select Next from the Record menu at the top of the screen until the **descr** item shows "Leader."

11. Select the menu option Next under the Block menu on top of the screen.

12. Select Next from the Record menu on the top of the screen. Notice that the data scrolls to the next **person** who's **clssn descr** is "Leader."

13. Click the Oracle Developer Forms Runtime Exit-X to return from where you came. Press CTRL-W to close the form.

Click the Form Builder console Exit-X to return from where you came. You have now built a master/detail form, something you will do time and time again with Oracle Forms.

This completes your hands-on exercises. You have built three forms, manually and via the wizards. You have saved, run, modified them, and modified them again.

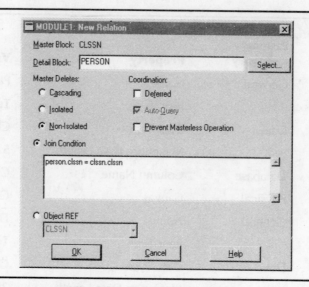

FIGURE 9-26. *Defining a master-detail relationship*

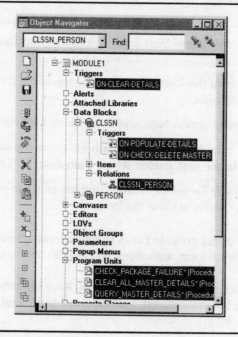

FIGURE 9-27. *Data Block triggers*

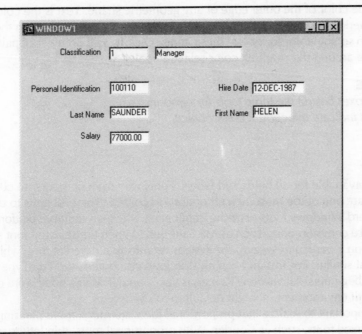

FIGURE 9-28. *Master-detail execution*

Let's move on to screen formatting. Since Oracle Forms runs on PCs, the assortment of colors, fonts, graphics, and fill you have become familiar with can be used here as well.

Screen Formatting with Form Builder

We will now round out our discussion on the Form Builder by discussing screen presentation issues. Forms should be designed to have a look that is pleasing to the eye as well as being functional. Let's talk about color and fonts and then move on to how to embed a graphic in one of your forms. Color, fonts, and graphics are just a few of the options that a developer can use to ensure usability and acceptance of a Form Builder application.

Color

There are three areas of color that can be controlled: fill, line, and text. Fill is the color of the background, and it is represented by the Fill Color tool on the canvas tool palette. The line color is represented by the Line Color tool on the tool palette;

this sets the color of the outer edge of any geometric shape. Text is the color of the alphanumeric characters, and it is represented by the Text Color tool on the tool palette. To set the color for one of these items, click its tool on the tool palette, and then move around the resulting color selection palette.

NOTE
The boxes beside the three tools for choosing colors indicate the current color choice.

Fonts

Fonts are available for all fields and labels. Fonts vary from computer to computer, and they are one of the most difficult options to control. The best fonts to use are the standard Windows fonts or, if the application will span multiple platforms, one of the more common ones, such as MS Sans Serif. When the selected font is not available on a particular system, the system defaults to a different font, which may not be that similar. For instance, on all Windows computers, the TrueType Font (TTF) (for beginners) Times New Roman is very popular. If this book were read into a Motif environment, it might default to MS Sans Serif.

It is important to realize that proportional fonts are much more pleasing to the eye than fixed fonts, such as Courier. With proportional fonts, thin letters such as "I" take less space than wider letters such as "G." The text in this paragraph uses proportional fonts. Using fixed fonts, all letters, regardless of their widths, take up the same amount of horizontal space. To change the font of an item,

1. Select the item to change by clicking it.

2. Select Font from the Format menu at the top of the screen.

3. Scroll through the Font dialog box, select the desired font, and select any desired attributes, such as bold and italic.

4. Click OK to choose the selection you have made. When you return to the canvas view, the font for the selected item changes.

VIP
Experience dictates you should use underline and bold sparingly. They may look nice during design but can be a nuisance when a screen goes to production.

When you need to use special fonts and text attributes, keep in mind that all attributes may not be supported by the computer configuration on all your clients' machines.

Graphics

Graphics are pictures that are typically used for splash or logo screens. A splash screen is a window that comes up briefly while the application is loading. It can be used to announce the entrance to an application or as a distraction as processing occurs in the background. For instance, if there is a need to do extra setup or security checks that take several seconds to complete, a developer may want to include a splash screen to let end users know that processing is occurring or to distract them from the time it takes to complete that processing. Another use of graphics is the inclusion of the company logo. To use a graphic in your form, follow these step:

1. Create an image object on your canvas. Select Import from the File menu at the top of the Form Builder console, selecting the Image option. When the Import Image dialog box appears, enter the filename of the image or drawing to import, or use the browser to select the file to import.

2. Click OK to import the image or drawing.

We now move on to Form Builder Runtime, leaving you with one last point that, unfortunately, should restrict just how fancy you may get with screen design. As with all fun things in life, enjoy these options (colors, fonts, and graphics) in moderation. Too much of any of the available screen formatting techniques will cause unpleasant side effects and possible performance slowdowns—especially when you start developing for the Internet. Also remember, you are not the only one who will have to stare at your application for long periods of time. It may be a good idea to get a second opinion on the aesthetics of your screen design.

It's now time to take a look at deploying the forms built with the Form Builder. As we all know, there are two deployment environments—client/server and Web. Deployment to the Web is a multistep process requiring some Web deployment experience. Some steps require working with the Web gurus in your installation. For that reason, we will stick to a very rudimentary (but simple!!) deployment in a client/server environment.

Form Builder Runtime—Client/Server

This part of Form Builder is used to run menus and screens. It is invoked by clicking the Forms Runtime icon in the Oracle Developer 6 program group. When you are presented with the Runtime welcome screen, do the following to run a form:

1. Enter the name of the form to run, or browse and then select the one you want.

2. Once you have selected a form (for example, form1), click OK.

3. Enter your user name and password when asked to connect to the Oracle8*i* database.

4. Go about whatever you need to do with the form, and then exit Oracle Developer Forms Runtime Exit-X to return to the Form Builder console.

After developers code Form Builder programs, the source code is compiled and becomes part of the set of application code delivered to the end user. The end user invokes Oracle Developer Forms Runtime within an application to work with the network of system screens and menus.

Working with the Report Builder

As we have said all along, the Form Builder is one of many integrated tools in Oracle's Developer suite. The Report Builder is another. Report Builder is a feature-rich reporting tool that produces production-quality output using data sources such as the Oracle8*i* database. Developers are able to embed graphics, sound, video, and a wide assortment of visual aids in screen and hard-copy (printed) output.

A lot of the techniques you have picked up previously in this chapter can be applied to Report Builder, since it has a look and feel and operator interface in common with Form Builder.

How Report Builder Processes Queries—A Primer

The key importance to Report Builder is performance. Report Builder can be a very complex product, yet you can design useful and sophisticated output with little or no programming. A network of nested **select** statements can produce the desired results in a short time period. Nested **select** statements are a series of SQL statements in which column values from a high-level query (called the parent query) are passed down for further processing to a lower-level query (referred to as the child query). A query that is a child of a higher-level query can in turn be the parent of a query at a lower level. Table 9-3 shows an example of how Report Builder handles this processing. The information in the Type column indicates a parent (P) or child (C) query.

There is a significant difference in the way these queries are worded; usually when more than one table is referred to in an SQL statement, you place both table names in the **from** line of that statement. The parts of SQL statements are discussed in Chapter 7 and Chapter 12. Asking SQL to process a statement using more than one table is called a join operation. The column values in the tables are compared against one another using a join condition. Rows whose column values match one another appear as the results of the query. Most join conditions are done using equality as the relational operator, though conditions using other operators (such as >, <, or <>) are possible. The following listing shows how a common join condition is worded.

```
select oname,location,province,
       desc_e,desc_f       /* The columns come from both tables.*/
  from offices,locations   /* For a row to be fetched, its        */
 where offices.location =  /* location column values must be      */
       locations.location; /* the same in both tables.            */
```

Query Name	Query Text	Type	Column Values
Q_1	Select oname, location, province from offices	P	Passes oname to Q_2 Passes location to Q_3
Q_2	Select oname, leader_name, leader_rank from leaders	C P	Receives oname from Q_1 Passes leader_rank to Q_4
Q_3	Select location,desc_e, desc_f from locations	C	Receives location from Q_3
Q_4	Select leader_rank, rank_weight, rank_desc, from ranking	C	Receives leader_rank from Q_2

TABLE 9-3. *Parent/Child Query Example*

In Table 9-3, notice how the SQL text in Q_2 mentions the column oname but does not equate it to the value passed from its parent query (Q_1). Also, Q_3 does not equate location to the value it receives from its parent (Q_1). Finally, Q_4 does not explicitly equate leader_rank to the value it receives from its parent (Q_2). Thus, when a row is selected from Q_1, it passes down its oname column value to Q_2 and its location column value to Q_3. Also, when a row is selected in Q_2, it passes its leader_rank column value to Q4.

Report Builder—Hands On

As with the Form Builder, Oracle has included wizards to assist in quicker development of reports. Let's create report showing only the **persons** who are leaders. You will again be using tables from our sample database discussed and presented in the "Sample Data" section of this chapter. We entered a user name of **sean**, a password of **speedo**, and a connect string of **o8ibegin**, which may differ from yours.

At the very start when you open Report Builder, you are presented with the option of generating a report, as shown in Figure 9-29. Ensure that the Use the Report Wizard radio button is highlighted.

NOTE
It is possible that, based on what you are doing with this wizard and when it is invoked, the series of screens you encounter may be somewhat different than what you see here.

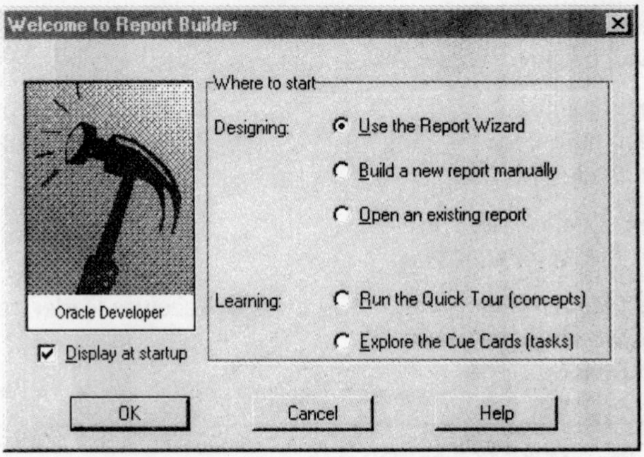

Welcome to Report Builder

Where to start

Designing:
- ⦿ Use the Report Wizard
- ○ Build a new report manually
- ○ Open an existing report

Learning:
- ○ Run the Quick Tour (concepts)
- ○ Explore the Cue Cards (tasks)

Oracle Developer

☑ Display at startup

[OK]   [Cancel]   [Help]

FIGURE 9-29. *Wizard Welcome*

I. Click OK on the startup screen and off you go.

2. A welcome screen is presented to you stating you are about to start creating a report. Click Next to get to the Report Wizard screen shown in Figure 9-30.

3. Enter Leaders in the Title field and click Next to continue.

4. Enter the SQL statement **select last_name,first_name from person where clssn = 3** as displayed in Figure 9-31. Click Next to continue.

5. Choose all available fields shown in Figure 9-32 for display by clicking >>. Click Next to go on.

6. The next screen allows the user to create calculated fields. We do not have any in this example, so click Next to continue.

7. The next screen allows the user to modify the labels displayed with the fields generated by the wizard. You again will take the default and click Next to continue.

8. The Report Wizard now gives the user an opportunity to select either a predefined template supplied with the Report Builder, choose one you may

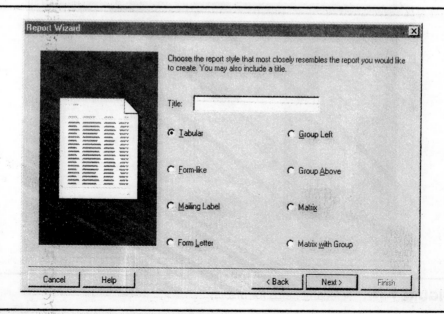

FIGURE 9-30. *Report Wizard screen 1*

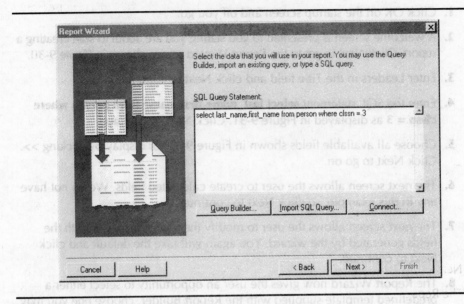

FIGURE 9-31. *The SQL Query statement*

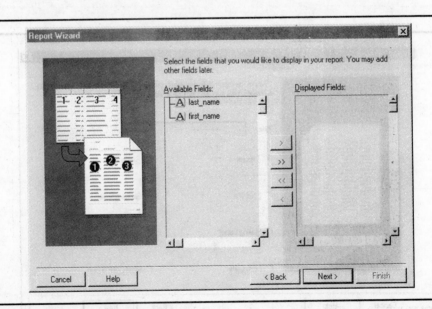

FIGURE 9-32. *Selecting fields for display*

have designed yourself, or use no template at all, as shown in Figure 9-33. You will once more accept the default and click Next to continue.

9. Oracle gives you one more pat on the back for such a great job you are doing. Great work! Now to see what you have produced, click Finish and it will bring up your report running in the Report editor Live Previewer showing our leaders, as shown in Figure 9-34.

10. That's it. Click the Report editor Live Previewer Exit-X, which will return you to the Report Builder console and then the console's Exit-X to leave Report Builder.

You have now built a report.

What's Next

Form Builder has reinforced Oracle's position as one of the major players in the GUI data entry environment and now in Web application development. We have shown you some basics and have, hopefully, tickled your fancy, and now you can't wait to try bigger and better things, right? The next chapter deals with SQL*Loader,

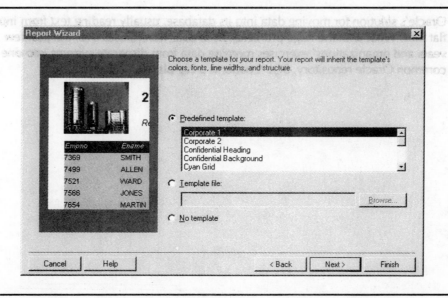

FIGURE 9-33. *Choosing report templates*

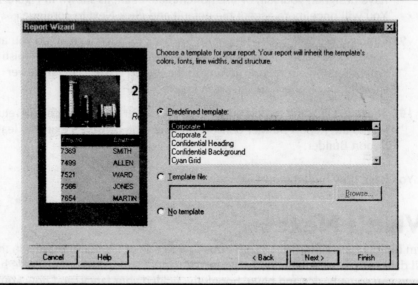

FIGURE 9-34. *A report of leaders*

Oracle's solution for moving data into its database, usually reading text from input flat files. What with the huge proliferation of data warehouses over the past few years and organizations' exercises merging data from disparate systems into one common Oracle repository, SQL*Loader is a big player.

CHAPTER
10

Loader

his chapter introduces SQL*Loader, the tool used to move data from another data source into the Oracle database. In this chapter, we'll also offer some advice on using this tool effectively. When existing systems are converted to Oracle, SQL*Loader ensures that all the data is moved from an old system's format into Oracle's format. By the end of this chapter, you will know details on the following topics:

- Using Loader in a DOS window and the parameters it requires

- The parts of a Loader control file

- The files written by Loader as it runs

- Using the Load Wizard from the OEM Schema Manager

- Bells and whistles of SQL*Loader

SQL*Loader is pretty much the same regardless of the computer you are using. It behaves the same way whether you're running Oracle8*i* on a Sun Enterprise, an HP minicomputer, or Oracle8*i* in Windows NT.

Terminology

The following definitions will arm you with the technical jargon you need to make it through this chapter.

- A *text file* contains alphanumeric data that is made up of the numerals 0–9, the uppercase and lowercase characters A–Z, and the special characters ~[-]!@#$%^&*()_ +=|\?/>.<,"':;{[]}. You use text files to move data between different operating systems and computer types.

- A *control file* provides information to a program in the format of keywords and values. For example, when you're using SQL*Loader, the keyword **bad=** tells where to place the data that for some reason is not loaded into the Oracle database.

- A *record* is a row of information made up of all the data elements stored in an Oracle table. For example, in an inventory application, each occurrence of a part_id and part_description is called a record. The next table illustrates this concept:

Record #	Part id	Description
1	ABW34E	Thingimajigg
2	ABW45W	Whatchamicallit
3	ABW77H	Gitgatgiddle
4	ABW99K	Framazan

■ A *unique key* is used to uniquely identify each record in an Oracle table. There can be one and only one row with each unique key value.

■ *GUI* stands for graphical user interface, the familiar mouse-driven point-and-click scenario used with Windows applications.

■ A *fixed-length* record is one that is made up of the same number of fields, with the same field length for each record in a file. The data shown in the next listing contains fixed-length records.

```
Comfortably Numb          Waters           The Wall
Bring the Boys Back Home   Waters/Gilmour   The Wall
Eclipse                    Waters           Dark Side of the Moon
Lost For Words             Gilmour          Division Bell
Dogs of War                Waters           Ummagumma
```

■ A *variable-length* record is one that is made up of the same number of fields with some form of field delimiter separating fields in a file. The data shown in the next listing contains variable-length records, using the comma to separate fields. With variable-length records, alphanumeric data is commonly surrounded by double quotes.

```
"Comfortably Numb","Waters","The Wall"
"Bring the Boys Back Home","Waters/Gilmour","The Wall"
"Eclipse","Waters","Dark Side of the Moon"
"Lost For Words","Gilmour","Division Bell"
"Dogs of War","Waters","Ummagumma"
```

What Is SQL*Loader?

SQL*Loader reads files and places the data in the Oracle database based on the instructions it receives from a control file. The control file tells SQL*Loader where to place data, and it describes the kinds of data being loaded into Oracle. It can filter records (that is, not load records that do not conform), load data into multiple tables at the same time, and generate a unique key or manipulate data before placing it in an Oracle table.

Moving data out of your existing system into Oracle is a two-step process. First you create a text file copy of your existing data using your current software, and then you load the data from that text file into Oracle using SQL*Loader.

Sometimes SQL*Loader is called Oracle Loader; we use the two product names synonymously. Over the past few years, Oracle has taken the "SQL*" prefix off most of its products and replaced it with the company name. Since you may use SQL*Loader to move data into one or more tables, throughout this chapter we will also use the words "table" and "tables" interchangeably. Let's get going.

SQL*Loader in a DOS Window

By the end of this section, you will know how to invoke SQL*Loader and the most common parameters supplied when SQL*Loader is invoked. To invoke SQL*Loader, enter the command **sqlldr** from an MS-DOS window. If you do not include any parameters, you are given online help: The output will resemble what is shown in the following listing:

```
SQL*Loader: Release 8.1.5.0.0 - Production on Tue Jun 1 10:00:30 2004
(c) Copyright 1999 Oracle Corporation.  All rights reserved.
Usage: SQLLOAD keyword=value [,keyword=value,...]
Valid Keywords:
    userid -- ORACLE username/password
   control -- Control file name
       log -- Log file name
       bad -- Bad file name
      data -- Data file name
   discard -- Discard file name
discardmax -- Number of discards to allow      (Default all)
      skip -- Number of logical records to skip (Default 0)
      load -- Number of logical records to load (Default all)
    errors -- Number of errors to allow         (Default 50)
      rows -- Number of rows in conventional path bind array or
              between direct path data saves
              (Default: Conventional path 64, Direct path all)
  bindsize -- Size of conventional path bind array in bytes (Default 65536)
    silent -- Suppress messages during run
              (header,feedback,errors,discards,partitions)
```

```
      direct -- use direct path                  (Default FALSE)
     parfile -- parameter file: name of file that contains parameter
                specifications
    parallel -- do parallel load                 (Default FALSE)
        file -- File to allocate extents from
skip_unusable_indexes -- disallow/allow unusable indexes or index
                         partitions  (Default FALSE)
skip_index_maintenance -- do not maintain indexes, mark affected
                          indexes as unusable  (Default FALSE)
commit_discontinued -- commit loaded rows when load is discontinued
                       (Default FALSE)
     readsize -- Size of Read buffer             (Default 65535)
PLEASE NOTE: Command-line parameters may be specified either by
position or by keywords.  An example of the former case is 'sqlload
scott/tiger foo'; an example of the latter is 'sqlload control=foo
userid=scott/tiger'.  One may specify parameters by position before
but not after parameters specified by keywords.  For example,
'sqlload scott/tiger control=foo logfile=log' is allowed, but
'sqlload scott/tiger control=foo log' is not, even though the
position of the parameter 'log' is correct.
```

NOTE
*On most platforms, the name of the executable for SQL*Loader is **sqlldr**. In the documentation, it may still be called **sqlload**.*

Isn't it odd that even though the cross-platform command name is sqlldr, the Oracle help uses the command name of sqlload?

There is a long list of parameters; however, most sessions will be started with commands similar to **sqlldr username control=cfile.ctl**. In the following sections, we will discuss **userid** and **control** plus a few more keywords from the previous listing that, if used, influence how SQL*Loader runs. Afterward, we will present a few examples and show the command lines to accomplish the desired results.

NOTE
The keywords discussed in the next few sections have no specific order. If you provide keywords and values on the command line, they can be in any order.

Userid

Userid must be the user name and password for an account that owns the table being loaded or that has access to someone else's table for loading. If you omit the password, Oracle will prompt you for it as the session begins. Along with the control parameter, this is one of the two required inputs to SQL*Loader.

TIP
*Let SQL*Loader prompt you for the password in order to protect your password confidentiality.*

Normally, rather than include the keyword userid on the command line, you include an Oracle user name and let SQL*Loader prompt for the password. Thus, the command **sqlldr username** is the same as **sqlldr userid=username**; in both cases, you are prompted for the control filename, then the account password.

Control

Control names a file that maps the format of the input datafile to the Oracle table. The format of the control file is discussed in the "SQL*Loader Control File" section, later in this chapter. If you do not include the control keyword when calling SQL*Loader, you are prompted, as in the following:

```
sqlldr blast
control = person
Password:
SQL*Loader: Release 8.1.5.0.0 - Production on Tue Jun 1 10:00:30 2004
(c) Copyright 1999 Oracle Corporation.  All rights reserved.
```

Parallel

Running SQL*Loader in parallel can speed up the time SQL*Loader takes to complete and, in situations where there are large amounts of input data, shrink runtimes dramatically. Invoking SQL*Loader with **parallel=true** runs multiple sessions, loading data simultaneously into the same table. The parallel sessions' data is merged by Oracle in a number of temporary tables and then inserted as a single unit of data. This parameter defaults to false; a parallel session is started by coding **parallel=true** as Loader is invoked.

Direct

When using a direct load, data is assembled in memory in the same format as Oracle data blocks, and the data block is copied directly into data blocks in the target datafile. This parameter defaults to false; to run a direct load, code **direct=true**. The direct load runs faster than conventional loads, especially when accompanied by **parallel=true**.

VIP
*If you choose **direct=true** for an SQL*Loader session,
and for some reason the load aborts, any indexes on
the target table will be left in direct load state and
will have to be dropped and re-created.*

Skip

This parameter defaults to **0**. If you code a positive integer value, SQL*Loader skips over the specified number of rows and starts loading with the record immediately after the specified number. This may prove useful in large loads. For example, you might browse the log file for a load that was supposed to move 1,000,000 rows into Oracle and find that the table has run out of space and received only 275,000 rows. Rather than redo the load from scratch, for the next session you could include the parameter **skip=275000**.

Load

This parameter defaults to **all**. If you code a positive integer value, Oracle will load that exact number of rows and then quit. You may want to use this if you want a subset of a very large amount of data moved into a development or test database for a system on its way to production.

Log and Bad

These two parameters are not normally mentioned on the command line. They inherit their filenames from the name of the control file used for the session. The command **sqlldr control=person.ctl** would log the session to **person.log** and write records that contain bad data into the file **person.bad**.

Discard

Sometimes you place one or more conditions on the input data; in this case, records that do not pass the condition(s) are discarded. If you include this parameter followed by a filename, these discarded records are written to the specified file. See the "Discard File" section, later in this chapter, where we give an example of placing a condition on a load session.

Example 1

Pretend you want to invoke an SQL*Loader session using the parameters and parameter values from the following table. Say it's a large load, and you want to run multiple load sessions at the same time.

Component	Value
User name	smith
Password	baby
Control file	portnoy
Load	all records
Parallel	Yes
Direct	No

The command to accomplish the load as described in the previous table would be **sqlldr smith/baby control=portnoy parallel=true**. Note that there is no filename extension on the file **portnoy**, so SQL*Loader assumes that the control filename is **portnoy.ctl**. By excluding the parameters load and direct, they assume their defaults (that is, all and false, respectively).

Example 2

This time we want to load an additional 1,000 records into a table. Record numbers 1 to 499 were loaded in a previous session. To speed things up, we wish to use the direct load path with parallel sessions.

Component	Value
User name	esther
Password	cool
Control file	cullen.crl
Skip	500
Direct	Yes
Load	1000
Parallel	yes

The command to accomplish the load described in the previous table would be **sqlldr esther/cool control=cullen.crl parallel=true direct=true skip=500 load=1000**. Note the filename extension on the file **cullen** since it is not the SQL*Loader **.ctl** default.

Example 3

For this example, suppose you wanted to load records number 501 to 520 using the direct path load mechanism. This also illustrates how SQL*Loader prompts for missing components of a parameter (that is, SQL*Loader expects a user name and password after the userid parameter, but we only supply the user name).

Component	Value
User name	janet
Skip	500
Direct	Yes
Load	20

Notice in this example that we will not supply a password or the name of the control file when invoking SQL*Loader. The command would be **sqlldr janet direct=true load=20 skip=500**. Oracle will prompt for the missing parameters, as shown in the following listing:

```
control = montreal
Password:
SQL*Loader: Release 8.1.5.0.0 - Production on Tue Jun 1 10:00:30 2004
(c) Copyright 1999 Oracle Corporation.  All rights reserved.
```

SQL*Loader Control File

We will now move on to building the control file. The control file sets up the environment for a Loader session: it tells Loader where to find the input datafile; which Oracle table the data should be loaded into; what, if any, restrictions to place on which data is loaded; and how to match the input data to the columns in the target table. When you're just getting started with SQL*Loader, the control file is the area that can cause the most problems. If the control file has errors, the SQL*Loader session stops immediately. Let's look at the four main parts of an SQL*Loader control file, as shown in Figure 10-1, focusing on the format and the instructions each part gives to SQL*Loader.

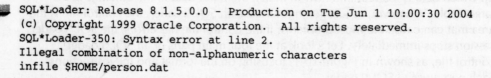

FIGURE 10-1. *An SQL*Loader control file*

Part 1: Load Data

The keywords *load data* start most SQL*Loader control files, regardless of
the contents of the rest of the control file. They serve as a starting point for the
rest of the control file, and nothing else. Think of these two keywords as the title
page of a book.

Part 2: Infile

This line names the input file. Notice in Figure 10-1 how the input filename is
enclosed in single quotes. Though the quotes are not mandatory here, they are
required in some situations. For example, in UNIX, let's say the input file
description line is infile $HOME/person.dat. The dollar sign causes the following
error to be raised:

```
SQL*Loader: Release 8.1.5.0.0 - Production on Tue Jun 1 10:00:30 2004
(c) Copyright 1999 Oracle Corporation.  All rights reserved.
SQL*Loader-350: Syntax error at line 2.
Illegal combination of non-alphanumeric characters
infile $HOME/person.dat
```

TIP

*We recommend enclosing the input filename in
single quotes. Get in the habit in case you find
yourself working with SQL*Loader under
circumstances where they are mandatory.*

Part 3: Into Table

This line instructs SQL*Loader where to place the data as it is loaded into Oracle. There are four modifiers to the into table portion of the control file:

1. **Insert** is the default and expects the table to be empty when the load begins.

2. **Append** adds new rows to the table's existing contents.

3. **Replace** deletes the rows in the table and loads the new rows.

4. **Truncate** behaves the same as replace. Normally, you will not code the insert qualifier with SQL*Loader, since it is the default. The most common error you may encounter is when you try to load data into a table that contains rows, and you have not included append, replace, or truncate on the into table line. If this happens, SQL*Loader returns the following error:

```
SQL*Loader: Release 8.1.5.0.0 - Production on Tue Jun 1 10:00:30 2004
(c) Copyright 1999 Oracle Corporation.  All rights reserved.
SQL*Loader-601: For INSERT option, table must be empty.  Error on PERSON
```

Part 4: Column and Field Specifications

This section of the control file matches characters in the input file to the database columns of the target table. There are four parts to each line in this specification: the column name in the target table, the keyword position, the start and end character positions, and the data type of those characters in the input file. In Figure 10-1, the data in the input file starts in position 1 and goes to position 42, using every character in the input record. The position keyword followed by character number specifications becomes more meaningful when you wish to load parts of each line in the input file rather than the entire line. Picture the following column and field specifications in a control file:

```
(first_name position (01:14) char,
 surname    position (15:28) char,
 clssn      position (29:36) char,
 hire_date  position (40:46) date 'YYMMDD')
```

Whichever characters lie in positions 37 through 39 are ignored.

Loading date fields into Oracle deserves special mention. Oracle dates default to the format DD-MON-YY, where DD stands for the day, MON for the three-character month name, and YY for the two-digit year. If the data in the input file is not in this format (and it usually isn't), you must tell Oracle how the dates appear in that file. Suppose the following four lines were fed into SQL*Loader:

```
BORIS          ABBEFLANTRO    AU2        830101
NANCY          BESDESMITH     MX         840926
FRANCIS        DEFWAYNO       DX         860422
NORMAN         NADROJIAN      CR5        860422
```

The column and position section of the control file would be

```
(first_name position (01:14) char,
 surname     position (15:28) char,
 clssn       position (29:36) char,
 hire_date   position (37:42) date 'YYMMDD')
```

VIP
The date format you specify in the control file is the format of the data in the input file, not the format you want Oracle to use for storage.

Since there are rules for dates (for instance, the month 13 is impossible, as is the day 31 in the month of June), Oracle will reject data in the input file that violates these rules. Examine the errors returned while loading data into the created column in a table using the date format YYMMDD:

```
BORIS          ABBEFLANTRO    AU2        831501
NORMAN         NADROJIAN      MX         860422
NANCY          BESDESMITH     DX         840926
FRANCIS        DEFWAYNO       CR5        870229
Record 1: Rejected - Error on table PERSON, column HIRE_DATE.
ORA-01843: not a valid month
Record 4: Rejected - Error on table PERSON, column HIRE_DATE.
ORA-01847: day of month must be between 1 and last day of month
```

The first record is rejected because there is no month number 15 (831501). The fourth record is rejected because there is no day number 29 in February 1987 (870229): 1987 was not a leap year.

SQL*Loader Outputs

As SQL*Loader runs, it writes a number of files that are used to figure out how successful the load was. By default, SQL*Loader writes a log file and, based on the success or failure of the load and the parameters used when it is invoked, may write a bad file and a discard file. Unless specified otherwise, these two extra files have the same name as the control file with the extensions **.bad** and **.dsc**, respectively.

Log File—Complete Load

The output shown in the following listing was produced by a session using the command sqlload control=person. SQL*Loader does not put the line numbers in the log file—we put them there for referencing in our discussion. The log file produced is called person.log.

```
 1  SQL*Loader: Release 8.1.5.0.0 - Production on Tue Jun 1 10:00:30 2004
 2  (c) Copyright 1999 Oracle Corporation.  All rights reserved.
 3  Control File:   person.ctl
 4  Data File:      person.dat
 5  Bad File:       person.bad
 6  Discard File:   none specified
 7  (Allow all discards)
 8  Number to load: ALL
 9  Number to skip: 0
10  Errors allowed: 50
11  Bind array:     64 rows, maximum of 65536 bytes
12  Continuation:   none specified
13  Path used:      Conventional
14  Table PERSON, loaded from every logical record.
15  Insert option in effect for this table: REPLACE
16  Column Name                   Position   Len  Term Encl Datatype
17  ----------------------------- ---------- ----- ---- ---- ------------
18  FIRST_NAME                       1:14    14              CHARACTER
19  SURNAME                         15:28    14              CHARACTER
20  CLSSN                           29:36     8              CHARACTER
21  HIRE_DATE                       37:42     6              DATE YYMMDD
22  Table PERSON:
23  2609 Rows successfully loaded.
24  0 Rows not loaded due to data errors.
25  0 Rows not loaded because all WHEN clauses were failed.
26  0 Rows not loaded because all fields were null.
27  Space allocated for bind array:                3584 bytes(64 rows)
28  Space allocated for memory besides bind array:  52603 bytes
29  Total logical records skipped:     0
30  Total logical records read:        2609
31  Total logical records rejected:    0
32  Total logical records discarded:   0
33  Run began on Fri Mar 12 10:44:14 2004
34  Run ended on Fri Mar 12 10:44:16 2004
35  Elapsed time was:     00:00:02.12
36  CPU time was:         00:00:00.54
```

Lines 1 and 2 are the SQL*Loader herald displayed at the top of all log files. Lines 3 to 15 report on the parameters that were in effect as the session ran. Lines 16 to 21 report the column and table information as specified in the control file. Lines 22 to 26 show the number of rows loaded successfully, as well as the number rejected. Lines 27 through 36 show the size of some of the SQL*Loader memory structures, start and stop times of the session, and the CPU time accumulated.

NOTE
*The length of your SQL*Loader control file depends on the outcome of the session and the amount of table and column information displayed.*

Log File—Incomplete Load

When one or more rows are rejected because of invalid data, SQL*Loader writes the bad rows to its bad file. The log file from an incomplete load is similar to the output shown earlier produced by a complete load, but with additional information.

Rejected Row Explanations

As SQL*Loader writes rejected rows to its bad file, it makes an entry in the session log file similar to the following:

```
Record 222: Rejected - Error on table PERSON.
ORA-00001: unique constraint (PERSON.U_FIRST_LAST) violated
```

The target table insists each first_name and surname combination must be unique; thus, the data in record 222 is rejected, since it contains duplicate first_name and surname information. In the following listing, record 87 has no value in the first_name position in the input record, and the row is rejected:

```
Record 87: Rejected - Error on table PERSONNEL.
ORA-01400: mandatory (NOT NULL) column is missing or NULL during insert
```

Finally, record 1189 has been rejected, since the month number columns contain the number 14, which is not a valid month. The full date lies in columns 37 to 42 in the input data file; thus, positions 39 and 40 are expected to contain a two-digit month number.

```
Record 1189: Rejected - Error on table PERSON, column HIRE_DATE
ORA-01843: not a valid month
```

The log file displays the Oracle error number with some descriptive text to help you zero in on the reason.

Load Statistics

When one or more rows are rejected, the statistics change to reflect those numbers:

```
Table PERSON:
   2903 Rows successfully loaded.
   3 Rows not loaded due to data errors.
   0 Rows not loaded because all WHEN clauses were failed.
   0 Rows not loaded because all fields were null.
```

VIP
*You should verify that all the records in the input file
were read by summing the numbers in the load
statistics section of the log file. The result should
equal the number of lines in the input file.*

Bad File

This file is only written when one or more rows from the input file are rejected. In our example, we invoked SQL*Loader using the command **sqlload / control=person**. Thus, rejected rows, if any, are placed in a file called person.bad. The format of the rows in the bad file is the same as in the input file. For example, record 1189 would be written to this bad file:

```
FWUFFEROO     DES          FE8      851429
```

There is no descriptive information in the bad file, so you must match the log file error messages with the bad file information.

VIP
*If you use the same control file for successive
SQL*Loader sessions, deal with the rows in each
run's bad file before running the next session—the
file is overwritten each time.*

Here's a story of how not checking the bad file affected one of our clients. This client ran three SQL*Loader sessions using the same control file. The input to the three sessions was accrec1.dat, accrec2.dat, and accrec3.dat, each containing 11,000 records. The first run loaded 11,000 records successfully and created no bad file. The second run loaded 10,811 rows successfully and wrote 189 rows to the bad file. The client did not deal with the rows written to the bad file and instead ran the third session, which wrote a bad file containing 42 rows. The 189 rows written to the bad file by the second session were lost and were never loaded properly. When the client's employees started to use the data on their applications, they wondered why information was missing!

Discard File

The control file shown in Figure 10-1 instructed SQL*Loader to attempt to load all records in the input file. In the following listing, the control file uses the **when** keyword to discard rows whose clssn column positions contain the text "CR4."

```
load data
infile 'person.dat'
into table personnel
when clssn <> 'CR4'
(first_name position (01:14) char,
 surname    position (15:28) char,
 clssn      position (29:36) char,
 hire_date  position (37:44) date 'YYYYMMDD')
```

The discard file is not created unless the **discard=** parameter is used when invoking SQL*Loader. We now move on and have a brief look at using SQL*Loader from the OEM Load Wizard embedded in the Schema Manager.

SQL*Loader from OEM

SQL*Loader from OEM is simply a wizard that will ask for input, and then submit a job through OEM and accomplish your desired load activity. You must connect to an Oracle Management Server (*OMS*) to be able to successfully start the Load Wizard. Thus, invoking this Load Wizard is a two-step process:

■ From Start Menu|Programs|Oracle Oem|Oracle Enterprise Management, invoke the Enterprise Manager Console option. This will bring up the dialog box shown in Figure 10-2. Enter the appropriate login credentials, in our case **sysman** with a password of **oem**. Notice the drop-down pick list of OMSs on the screen.

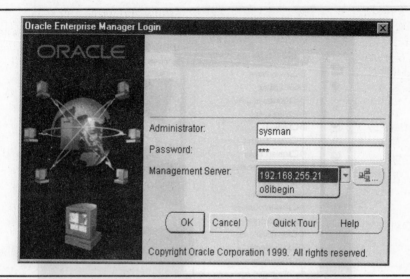

FIGURE 10-2. *Logging in to an OMS*

VIP
*There is some important setup work to be done
before you can successfully open the OEM Main
console. It is beyond the scope of this chapter. A
more senior experienced DBA will have to perform
this setup for you, or work with Oracle Worldwide
Customer support.*

■ Proceed to the Tools option at the top of the OEM Main Console; then
 select Database Applications|Schema Manager from the drop-down menu
 that appears. This will park you at the Oracle Schema Manager main
 console, as shown in Figure 10-3.

The next display you will see is screen 1 of the Load Wizard, shown in Figure 10-4.
The second screen in this Wizard asks for the name and location of the
SQL*Loader control file. It's just as well we looked at this before covering the OEM

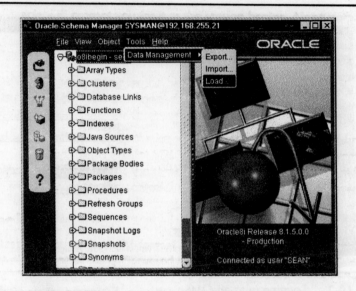

FIGURE 10-3. *The Schema Manager main console*

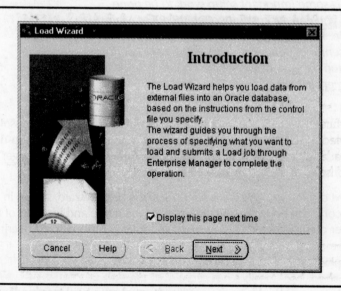

FIGURE 10-4. *Screen 1 of the Load Wizard*

Loader interface, because you are now an expert on the creation and makeup of control files. There is no Browse button, so simply enter the folder and name of the control file to be used.

The third screen in the Wizard is where you specify the file containing the data to be loaded into the Oracle8*i* database. This is shown in Figure 10-5.

Last, and by all means least, is where you specify the load method and, if so inclined, dictate Advanced options for the ensuing load session. There are three load methods with the Load Wizard, but, for this exercise, we are only going to concern ourselves with one of these three—the first in the next list:

1. The Conventional Path method formulates an SQL **insert** statement for every row in the input data file—this is the tricycle approach, though the most common workhorse.

2. The Direct Path method builds data blocks in memory and stuffs them when full into the database, rather than generating an **insert** statement for each row—this is the bicycle approach, faster than the trike.

3. The Parallel Direct Path method is all the Direct Path is and then some. This is the motorcycle.

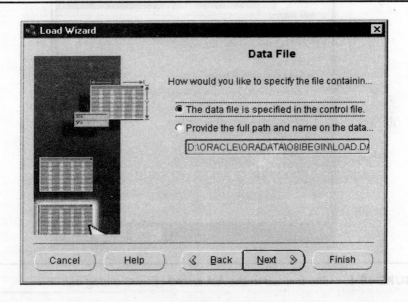

FIGURE 10-5.   *Specifying an input file for the Load Wizard*

To specify additional options, click the Advanced button on the Load Method screen, bringing up a three-tab folder, as shown in Figure 10-6. The first two check boxes allow you to specify values for **skip=** and **errors=** as though you were running SQL*Loader in the DOS window in the previous section.

Before wrapping up this discussion about SQL*Loader, let's mention a bit about the other two tabs in this dialog box:

- The Tuning tab is where you specify the number of rows to load before committing to the database. Think of *commit* in the same way as saving. You also can specify the amount of memory to be used to accommodate record creation in the target tables(s), as well as the size of the read buffer.

- The Optional Files tab is where you dictate the name and location of the Bad file (where error records are written), the Discard file (for records that may pass data validation but cannot be written to the database, as mentioned in the "Discard File" section of this chapter), and the Log file for the session being initiated.

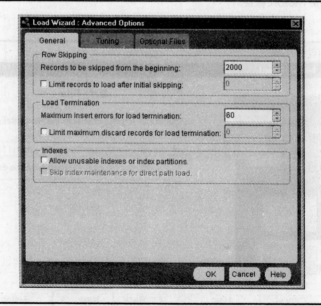

FIGURE 10-6. *The first tab in the Advanced options dialog box*

After specifying advanced parameters for the loader session, click OK to return to the Load Method screen. You click two buttons now to perform the load:

1. Click Next to bring up a dialog box in which you can specify the time for the loader work to be scheduled. You can also specify you want the load to repeat after a specified time interval or perhaps once a week or once a month.

2. Click Finish if you want the work to be performed immediately.

When you are all done, you will be returned to the OEM Main Console, and you will see the job you have just created with details similar to those shown in Figure 10-7.

All in all, it's been quite a chapter! SQL*Loader is a bona-fide workhorse in the Oracle8i solution for moving data into the database. The *Oracle8i A Beginner's Guide* train is leaving the station; let's get on board for the next chapter in the journey.

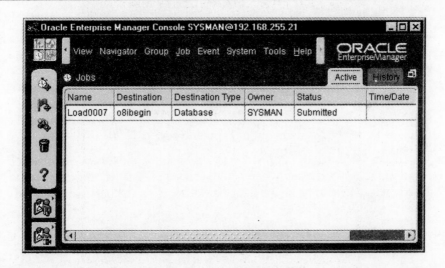

FIGURE 10-7. *OEM SQL*Loader job details*

What's Next

We have introduced you to SQL*Loader and shown you how it is used to move data from text files into Oracle database tables. The material we covered here just skims the surface, but you now have enough information to use SQL*Loader for most load session requirements. SQL*Loader contains a wealth of additional functionality you can use for more sophisticated sessions. Experiment with SQL*Loader and investigate its power—you will use it from day one. Armed with the knowledge, why not carry on?

CHAPTER
11

Application Tuning 101

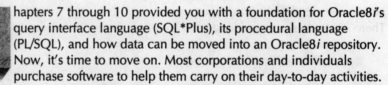hapters 7 through 10 provided you with a foundation for Oracle8i's query interface language (SQL*Plus), its procedural language (PL/SQL), and how data can be moved into an Oracle8i repository. Now, it's time to move on. Most corporations and individuals purchase software to help them carry on their day-to-day activities. All of us expect systems written using this software to operate efficiently—we expect them to ingest gobs of information and do exactly what we want them to do quickly. Realistically, we can only expect them to do this if the applications are tuned. Tuning is a process whereby applications are optimized to run as quickly as possible and use as few computer resources as possible.

Oracle, like all other vendors, provides tools with which to write custom applications. In this book, we discuss some of the tools Oracle provides for this purpose: SQL*Plus (Chapters 7 and 12), Oracle Developer (Chapter 9), JDeveloper (Chapter 21), and PL/SQL (Chapter 8). Developers (also called programmers) who write code with these Oracle products will want to write code that uses the Oracle8i Server efficiently. All too often, when a new computer system is installed, the users complain about how slow the system is and how long it takes to get responses to queries on its screens. By the end of this chapter, you will have some basics on the following:

- Why applications should be tuned
- The two main components in the tuning process
- How Oracle stores data
- How Oracle processes SQL statements
- The shared pool or shared SQL area
- Writing SQL statements to use the shared pool
- Using indexes to access data more efficiently
- Taking advantage of parallel processing
- Ways to reduce wait situations

Why Tune Oracle Systems?

As new applications come on board, we hear constant complaining about how poorly they perform. As applications are written, you should attend to their

performance and make it as important a component as the programming itself.
There are many short- and long-term benefits to tuning applications:

■ Well-tuned applications require less attention down the road.

■ Your end users will be happier with the system's performance and its
capability to process more data in less time.

■ Applications that have been tuned make more efficient use of resources on
your computer.

There is only a finite amount of computing power on any computer. This is
especially crucial in a multiuser system when more than one person is using the
system simultaneously. The throughput of your systems will be better with tuned
applications. Throughput is a measurement of the amount of data your systems are
capable of processing in a given time period. The more time you spend tuning
applications, the more information they will be able to ingest and send back to you
as reports, graphs, and onscreen query results.

Tuning applications can be a time-consuming and frustrating exercise; but, using
the ideas and guidelines in this chapter, you will get the most bang for your buck. In
Chapter 13, we discuss more technical details of the tuning process.

Terminology

The following definitions will arm you with the technical jargon to make it through
this chapter:

■ A *query* is a request for information from the database. For example, when
you press the green key (commonly the one that tells the machine which
account you wish to work with) on the automatic teller machine, you are
requesting a balance from your checking account.

■ *Query results* are the data that satisfy a query. The account balance
displaying on the ATM screen is an example of query results.

■ *Disk access* is the act of reading information from the database files on disk.

■ A *wait situation* arises when a user process is "standing by" while resources
or data it requires are being tied up by other user processes.

■ A *view* is a subset of one or more tables' data assembled in memory to satisfy the results of an SQL statement. One example of a view is a list of all employees in the western region of a company; the table on which that view is built contains all the employees regardless of their locations.

■ A *synonym* is a name stored in the data dictionary used to refer to tables and views. Think of a synonym as a nickname for tables and views.

■ A *public synonym* is created by the DBA (database administrator), pointing at an object somewhere in the database. Any user can refer to that object using the public synonym.

■ A *data dictionary* is maintained by Oracle containing information relevant to the database. It is used by Oracle to find out who is allowed to log in to the database, what datafiles are associated with the database, and other information required to permit your systems to operate. Additionally, Oracle stores information about what the data in the database looks like. For example, Oracle's data dictionary defines the fact that a North American area code is three digits (including no letters or special characters) and that the states and provinces are two letters (no numbers or special characters).

■ An *object* is an umbrella definition encompassing all data source names stored in Oracle's data dictionary. Objects are usually tables, but they can also be views or synonyms.

■ A *cache* is a portion of memory that Oracle reserves to do a specific job as the database operates. The caches contain data that has been read from the database, information about the SQL statements that have been processed, and other information required to run the instance.

■ An *execution plan* is the "map" that Oracle builds to get at the data that satisfies a user's query. The plan is built using statistics about the data that reside in the data dictionary. When Oracle builds an execution plan, it looks for the shortest and least costly route—somewhat like using the ABCFHI route rather than the ABDEGHI route, as shown in Figure 11-1.

■ A *block* is the smallest unit of storage that Oracle uses. The block size of the database is set when the database is created and can range from 2K (2,048 bytes) up to 32K (32,768 bytes). Oracle maintains a list in memory of free data blocks and places new information created by your applications in them.

■ The operation that reads data from and writes data to disk is called *I/O* (input/output).

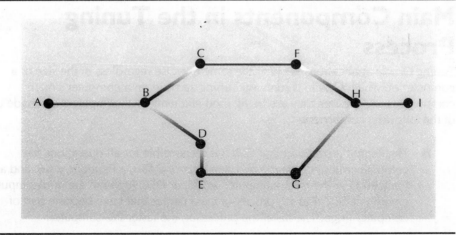

FIGURE 11-1.   *Two paths to get from A to I*

- Oracle assigns a *rowid* to data as it places it in data blocks. The rowid uniquely identifies each row in the database.

- An *index* is a structure separate from a table that contains one or more column values from a table plus the rowids of the rows with those values.

- A *select list* is the group of columns mentioned in the SQL statement, following the **select** keyword up to the list of objects referenced in the **from** portion of the statement. In the following SQL statement, the boldfaced text is called the select list:

```
select last_name, first_name, date_of_birth
  from person
 where pin = 100720;
```

- A *secure database operation* is an Oracle database operation usually restricted to DBA users. Creating a tablespace, creating new users, and managing rollback segments are examples of secure database operations.

- A *system privilege* is given to users and allows them to perform secure database operations. For example, the system privilege **select any table** allows the recipient to select data in any object anywhere in the database.

Main Components in the Tuning Process

Tuning Oracle applications is much the same exercise regardless of the size of a computer on which Oracle is running. Tuning zeros in on a computer's main components and ensures they are being used efficiently. All computers are made up of the following components:

- The central processing unit (CPU) is responsible for all operations the computer will undertake. You often hear of a 486, a Pentium, a K6, and a Pentium III in the microcomputer world, or DEC Alpha in the minicomputer environment. These are processor class names that have become part of computer lingo. The faster the processor, the faster the computer.

VIP

With the advent of computers with more than one CPU, parallel processing alone has taken a giant leap toward speeding execution of applications.

- Secondary storage devices such as hard drives, floppy disk drives, tape drives, DVDs, and CD-ROMs are used to save information that applications create as they operate.

- Computer memory is where programs operate and commonly requested data waits in anticipation of the next request for information.

- The other peripherals that complete the requirements are a computer monitor and a keyboard.

VIP

The two main components in the tuning process are reading information from memory and reducing I/O operations.

The next section of this chapter will discuss the roles that reading information from memory and reducing I/O operations play in the tuning process.

Memory

Since all computers contain a finite amount of memory, making optimal use of memory is a contributing factor to tuning. In this section, we will discuss the basics on the following:

■ How all data is routed through memory

■ The communication lines from the database to the users

■ The shared SQL area

■ The key to efficient use of memory

As Oracle runs, it receives requests for data from users. The data sits in an assortment of datafiles on disk. The flow of information among users, memory, and the database is outlined in Figure 11-2.

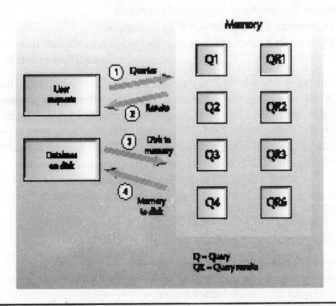

FIGURE 11-2. *Flow of information among database, memory, and users*

Notice the four communication lines:

■ User to memory (UM): Requests for data initiated by applications are assembled in memory, where Oracle decides the most efficient way to get to the desired data.

■ Memory to user (MU): Results of queries are transferred from memory to the user session that made the request.

■ Disk to memory (DM): As requests are received, data that satisfies the request is transferred to memory.

■ Memory to disk (MD): Data that has been changed or created is written to disk.

There is no direct communication between the database and the users. All reads, writes, and changes to data pass through Oracle memory structures. This stresses the importance of using memory efficiently.

VIP

Oracle keeps the results of previously executed queries in memory until the space they occupy is required for results to more recent queries.

Oracle maintains a shared SQL area in memory, also referred to as the shared pool. All SQL statements are executed from this pool. When an SQL statement is passed to Oracle, before loading an SQL statement into this pool, Oracle searches this pool for an identical statement. If it finds a match, the new statement is discarded and the one already in the pool is executed in its place. We'll refer to the preparation for execution and placement in the shared pool as the *preparation phase*.

When an SQL statement is passed to Oracle for execution, it must first be placed in the shared pool. Oracle executes SQL statements after loading them into the shared pool.

VIP

Oracle keeps prepared SQL statements in the shared pool. These statements are executed when an identical request is received from a user.

How the Communication Lines Are Used to Process Queries

Let's look at the way Oracle would process five queries from user processes using the four communication lines UM, MU, DM, and MD introduced in Figure 11-2. The indicator PR stands for "prepare SQL statement" in Table 11-1.

Query	Processing	Reason
Q1	UM MU	This query can be satisfied in memory, since the prepared SQL statement Q1, as well as its query results QR1, still resides in the memory cache.
Q2	UM MU	This, too, can be satisfied in memory, since the prepared SQL statement Q2, as well as its query results QR2, still resides in memory.
Q3	UM MU	This, too, can be satisfied in memory, since the prepared SQL statement Q3, as well as its query results QR3s, still resides in memory.
Q4	UM MD DM MU	The prepared SQL statement Q4 resides in the shared pool. The results for the query, however, have long since been removed from memory. This situation requires that a new data request to read data from disk be executed and the results, placed in memory. The information will then be returned to the user.
Q5	UM PR MD DM MU	There is no SQL statement in memory. Therefore, this request needs to prepare the SQL statement, read the data from disk, put the results in memory, and then return the data to the user. As you can guess, this is the most undesirable situation to have, since the SQL must be prepared and then data must be read from disk.
Q6	UM PR MU	There is no matching prepared SQL statement, though the query results QR6 are still in memory.

TABLE 11-1. *Query Processing Using Memory*

The memory shown in Figure 11-2 is the shared pool; it contains prepared SQL statements Q1, Q2, Q3, and Q4 as well as query results QR1, QR2, QR3, and QR6, which are still in memory. The Processing column values in the table show the communication lines from Figure 11-2 that are used to process each query and return its results.

The processing for queries Q1, Q2, and Q3 are the most desirable, since there is no disk access. Next most desirable is processing Q6; even though the SQL statement has to be prepared, there is no disk access. Q4 requires disk access; even though the prepared statement is still in memory, its query results are not in memory. Oracle prepares the statement issued by Q5 and must retrieve its results from disk.

VIP
Access to data in memory is quicker than access to data on disk. It is desirable to get as much information as possible from memory.

VIP
If you can write SQL statements that match those sitting in the pool, the preparation phase can be skipped. Avoiding the preparation phase is the single most important area to attend to when tuning Oracle applications.

Disk Access

Reading information from disk is referred to as disk access. Minimizing disk access is important given the operations the computer performs when reading from disk. It takes time to position the reader above the exact spot on the disk where the data resides, and the time to transfer the data to memory can become quite significant. In this section, we will discuss the basics on the following:

■ How Oracle stores data

■ How Oracle accesses your data

■ How to minimize disk access

We mentioned in the previous section how all data is transferred from disk to memory before being made available to users. I/O is required to make this transfer. Oracle places data in blocks in the datafiles that make up the database. When a data block is too full to hold any more data, Oracle places its data in the other blocks in the datafile. Its address or rowid can identify each row in a data block.

Oracle fetches data for your queries using one of the two methods discussed in the next few sections. We now discuss using indexes to help minimize disk access. When we show you how Oracle processes data with and without an index, you will begin to see their advantages when attending to application tuning.

Processing with an Index

If an index exists, and an SQL statement is worded in a way to take advantage of the index, the index is searched first. Oracle reads the index and processes according to the steps shown in Table 11-2.

VIP

The number of I/O operations to process a query using an index can be significantly lower than the number required to process a query without an index.

Think of an index as an address book: The rows of data are the names in that book, and the rowids are the street addresses. If you know that the Jacobs live at 234 Rideau, you can proceed directly to the location of their house. If you know the Jacobs live on Rideau but you don't have their address, you would have to go from house to house until you found them. Oracle goes through the same exercise when using indexes. Indexes provide rapid access to your data.

Figure 11-3 shows a very simple example. Suppose the column values shown for tableA are in the column named ID. IndexA contains ID column values plus the location of the first column with that ID value (for instance, the first row with ID=15 can be found in location 005).

The user passes an SQL statement to Oracle on tableA looking for the data in the row with ID=15. Oracle reads entries in indexA to find where it should look in the

Process	Next Step	
Are there more rows in the table?	YES=2	NO=4
Do the columns in this row match the selection criterion?	YES=3	NO=1
Mark the data for inclusion in the query results.	1	
Display query results.		

TABLE 11-2. *Processing without an index*

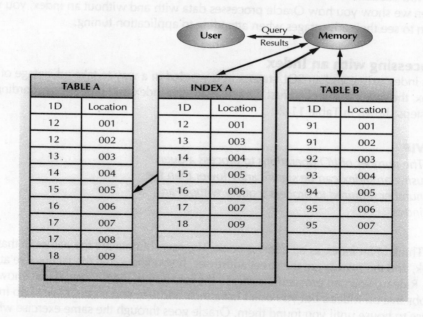

FIGURE 11-3. *Tables with and without an index*

table data to find the desired row. If Oracle read indexA from start to finish, it would encounter the address for ID=15 in the fourth entry in the index and proceed to get the data from the row at address 005. If indexA did not exist, Oracle would read tableA and find the ID=15 in the fifth row in the table. This example shows how Oracle would need to perform one additional I/O if indexA did not exist.

Processing Without an Index

When no index exists that can be used to satisfy a query, Oracle does a full table scan. It reads every row in a table and evaluates column values against the selection criterion. It discards rows that do not qualify and includes rows that do. Oracle reads every row in the table, processing according to the steps in Table 11-2.

I/Os Required with and Without an Index

Now that we have discussed processing with and without an index, let's examine a real-life example. Let's say a table holds the following information:

```
book_number                          varchar2(20)
publisher                            varchar2(40)
year_printed                         varchar2(4)
```

and there are 80,000 rows in the table. Oracle has packed 40 book records into each data block. Thus, data blocks numbered 0001 to 2000 contain book information. Suppose Oracle has placed a book with ISBN 882122-3 in data block number 0807. If the table has an index, fetching that book's data would require two I/O operations—the first to read the index entry and get the rowid of where the 882122-3 row is stored, and the second to retrieve the book's publisher and year in print. If there were no index, Oracle would have to read the table's data starting with data block 0001 until it reached a data block with the desired ISBN (data block 0807). Thus, without an index, fetching the book's data would require, in theory, 807 I/O operations!

NOTE
Actually, it would require 2,000 I/O operations because Oracle would check to see if any of the other blocks had the same ISBN. Remember, uniqueness isn't enforced in this case, since there is no (unique) index.

Using Statements in the Shared Pool

As we stated near the start of this chapter, using memory efficiently is a large contributor to the application-tuning process. Coupled with using indexes (which results in minimizing disk access), this practice puts you well on your way to tuning applications. In this section, we will discuss some of the basics on the following:

- How Oracle processes SQL statements
- How to word SQL statements to reuse ones already in the pool
- How to implement coding conventions
- How to store code in the database

Steps in SQL Statement Processing

When Oracle receives an SQL statement, it runs an internal routine to compute the statement's value. To illustrate computing a value, let's run a very simple routine using the U.S. cities shown in Table 11-3.

You will notice in Table 11-3 that each city/state combination has been assigned a six-digit ID. Let's pretend the ID is the same as the identifier that Oracle assigns to every table as it is created. Now we will look at some SQL statements that use these

City	State	ID
Portland	ME	446721
Portland	OR	978219
Springfield	MA	893417
Springfield	MO	662198

TABLE 11-3. *U.S. Cities, States, and Identifiers*

city names as table names, and we'll figure out the value of each statement. You can see how the statement

```
select col1, col2, col3, col4
   from PORTLAND            /* OR in this case */
 where col5 > col6;
```

is not the same as

```
select col1, col2, col3, col4
   from PORTLAND            /* ME in this case */
 where col5 > col6;
```

The value of the city coded in the former statement is 978219, and the one in the latter is 446721. Similarly, in the next three statements, the first two statements are the same, but the second and third are not:

```
select col1, col2, col3, col4
   from SPRINGFIELD         /* MA in this case */
 where col5 > col6;
select col1, col2, col3, col4
   from SPRINGFIELD         /* MA in this case */
 where col5 > col6;
select col1, col2, col3, col4
   from SPRINGFIELD         /* MO in this case */
 where col5 > col6;
```

The value of the city coded in the first two statements is 893417, and the value in the third statement is 662198.

VIP
*Using the same name for objects in an SQL
statement is not enough; the names must evaluate to
the same object in the database.*

Table 11-4 gives a thumbnail sketch of how a statement is evaluated when sent
for processing. The computing of a statement's value is shown as the first step.

Ideally, statements should be processed using steps 1, 2, 3, and 8. Statements
passed to Oracle that do not pass the tests in both steps 2 and 3 are processed using
steps 1, 2, 3, 4, 5, 6, 7, and 8. Wording SQL statements in such a way to take the
1–2–3–8 path is more efficient than taking the 1–through–8 path.

Wording SQL Statements to Reuse Ones in the Pool

In this section, we will discuss adopting coding conventions and storing code in the
database. When SQL statements are passed to Oracle for processing, the secret is to

	Process	Next Step	
1.	Compute the value of the statement.	2	
2.	Is there a statement in the shared SQL pool with the same value?	YES=3	NO=4
3.	Is there a statement in the pool that matches character by character?	YES=8	NO=4
4.	Prepare statement for execution.	5	
5.	Make room for the new SQL statement in the shared pool.	6	
6.	Place statement in the shared pool	7	
7.	Update the map of the shared pool showing the new values and location in the pool	8	
8.	Execute the statement		

TABLE 11-4. *Simplified Steps for Parsing an SQL Statement*

The guidelines we now present help ensure that SQL statements you generate can
find a match against one already prepared and sitting in the shared pool

reuse a statement already in the pool rather than forcing Oracle to prepare each new statement as it is received. We stated previously that Oracle reuses statements in the shared pool if it receives one identical to one already in the pool. In the next two sections, we discuss standardizing the format of the code you write and using centralized code stored in the Oracle data dictionary.

Coding Conventions

We will present one of many possible schemes for coding SQL statements. Adopt this method if you like the looks of it.

NOTE
Establishing and using a coding convention is more important than the actual style you decide to use.

Once you have a convention in place, you can start coding SQL statements to take advantage of ones already in the shared pool. To get the most out of this discussion, you should have read Chapter 7 and/or Chapter 12.

The **select** statement in SQL is made up of five parts. Using the following code, let's review the components of a statement.

```
select col1, col2, sum(col3)    /* Part 1 */
   from fiscal_year             /* Part 2 */
  where col1 > col2             /* Part 3 */
    and col1 > 10               /* Part 3 */
  group by col1, col2           /* Part 4 */
  order by col1;                /* Part 5 */
```

These are the five component parts of an SQL statement:

- The **select** keyword that starts the statement, followed by the list of columns being displayed in the query results

- One or more tables from which the data is obtained

- One or more conditions that determine which values are desired

- The **group by** keyword followed by one or more column names on which some summarizing is to be done as the data is fetched

- The **order by** keyword followed by a list of one or more columns that determine the sorting method for the desired rows

The guidelines we now present help ensure that SQL statements you code can find a match against one already prepared and sitting in the shared pool.

FORMATTING THE PARTS OF THE SQL STATEMENT   Rather than letting the statement spill haphazardly onto the next line at column 80, do the following:

```
select col1, col2, sum(col3)
  from fiscal_year
 where col1 > col2
   and col1 > 10
 group by col1, col2
 order by col1;
```

NOTE
*You could take a plastic ruler and line it up with the **select** keyword to ensure that all other lines' keywords align with the letter "t" from **select**. The | (vertical line) in the next listing represents that ruler.*

```
select|col1, col2, sum(col3)
  from|fiscal_year
 where|col1 > col2
   and|col1 > 10
 group|by col1, col2
 order|by col1;
```

GUIDELINE 1
*Use a separate line for each part of the SQL statement. Align the first keyword in each line to end in the same column as the **select** keyword on the first line.*

UPPERCASE OR LOWERCASE?   Lowercase code is easier on the eyes than either mixed case or all uppercase. Some installations decide to use uppercase for all SQL special words and lowercase for all others. The problem is that developers forget which is which. You could easily end up with the following two statements:

```
SELECT col1, col2
  FROM fiscal_year;
```

and

```
select COL1, COL2
  from FISCAL_YEAR;
```

Both statements are written by developers trying to ensure they conform to the uppercase and lowercase convention. Using mixed case, it's just too easy to forget which is which.

GUIDELINE 2
Use lowercase characters in all SQL statements.

COMMAS EMBEDDED IN THE STATEMENT   We find the code easier to read with a space after the comma. For example, we find the first line easier to read than the second in the following:

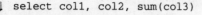

```
select col1, col2, sum(col3)

select col1,col2,sum(col3)
```

GUIDELINE 3
*Put commas right beside the text they follow, and
leave one space afterward.*

COMMAS AS THE LAST CHARACTER ON A LINE   In some cases, developers like to place the trailing comma on one line as the first character in the next line:

```
select col1, col2
       ,col3
```

We prefer to see it the following way:

```
select col1, col2,
       col3
```

GUIDELINE 4
*When a comma is the last character on a line, put it
on that line rather than skipping to the next line and
then inserting the comma.*

FORMATTING CONTINUATION LINES   When the same part of an SQL statement continues onto the next line, line them up as in the following listing:

```
select col1, col2, sum(col3), col4, col5, sum(col6),
       col7, col8, col9, col10, col11, col12, col13
```

GUIDELINE 5
*Start lines in column 8 that belong to the same part
as the previous line.*

FORMATTING THE STATEMENT QUALIFIERS   When you are formatting
the **where** and **and** part of the SQL statement (also referred to as the predicate), the
placement of each **and** should resemble

```
where
   and
   and
   and
   and
```

GUIDELINE 6
*When you have the **where** followed by one or more
lines that start with **and**, start the former in column 2
and the latter in column 4.*

FORMATTING PARENTHESES   Syntax requires the use of parentheses in
many SQL statements. The most common spot is where a function (such as finding
the largest value with **max** or taking the first three characters of a 10-character string
with substr) is used as a column in a select list, as in

```
select col1, col2, sum(col3)
```

GUIDELINE 7
*Leave no spaces on either side of parentheses when
they appear in SQL statements.*

STATEMENT TERMINATOR   This statement terminator is the signal to Oracle
that you are done coding your statement and wish to begin processing. You may use
the semicolon (;) or the forward slash (/).

GUIDELINE 8
*Use the semicolon (;) terminator for SQL*Plus
statements. When your programs contain a mixture
of SQL*Plus and PL/SQL, you must terminate a
group of PL/SQL statements with a slash (/). Reserve
using the slash for that purpose.*

FORMATTING OPERATORS   When you compare column values in your SQL statements, you most commonly use the equal sign (=). Other operators, such as <> for not equal or > for greater than, are coded like the equal sign.

GUIDELINE 9
Leave a space on either side of operators used anywhere in SQL statements.

SQL statements are easier to read with spaces, as shown in the following example:

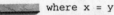

```
where x = y
  and d = c
  and j = p
```

rather than

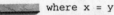

```
where x=y
  and d=c
  and j=p
```

VIP
Design your coding conventions (or use the ones we've recommended) and stick to them. Passing statements for processing that are identical to ones already in the pool helps tune your applications.

EXAMPLES   Theory is all fine and dandy, including the guidelines we have outlined. Seeing them put into practice will crystallize the theory we speak about in the previous section. Let's look at two more complex examples; they are commented to highlight the implementation of the guidelines we have presented.

```
rem *************** Example #1 *******************

rem * The decode in the column list starts back in column 8 so the code
rem * in parentheses within the decode is not broken onto two lines.
rem * There is a single space left after each comma as well as
rem * no space before the opening parenthesis in the decode.
select fy_code, prd.prod_num, prd.sdesc_e, proj_num, prj.sdesc_e,
       comm_amt, comm_amt*1.10,
       decode(fiscal, 'Y', 'multi', 'single'), bud_class
  from prod prd, project prj, bud_mast bud
 where prd.prod_num = prj.prod_num
   and bud.rpt_cat = prd.rpt_cat
 order by fy_code, prd.prod_num;

rem *************** Example #2 *******************
```

```
select max('&1'), max('&2'), max(sysdate), max('DETAIL'), max(a.sr),
       b.sdesc_e,
       /*  Note how the parentheses have no spaces on either side  */
       /*  and there is one space after each comma but nothing     */
       /*  before.                                                 */
       nvl(round(sum(nvl(a.comm_amt, 0)), 0), 0),
       nvl(round(sum(nvl(a.precomm_amt, 0)), 0), 0),
       nvl(round(sum(nvl(a.budget_orig, 0)), 0), 0),
       nvl(round(sum(nvl(a.budget_rev,0)), 0), 0),
       nvl(round(sum(nvl(a.exp_accr, 0)), 0),0),
       nvl(round(sum(nvl(a.exp_accr_comm, 0)), 0), 0),
       nvl(round(sum(nvl(a.free_bal, 0)), 0), 0),
       nvl(round(sum(nvl(a.adj_bal, 0)), 0), 0)
  from fms_financials a, fms_control_obj b
 where b.cobj_type = 'SR'        /* The first word in each line ends in  */
   and b.cobj_code = a.sr        /* column 8.                            */
   and b.fy_code = '&2'
   and a.repname = '&1'          /* All the where and and lines line     */
   and a.fy_code = '&2'          /* up with one another.                 */
   and a.qualifier = 'SRDETAIL'
 group by a.sr, b.sdesc_e;
```

Storing Code in the Database

Oracle provides the capability to store segments of code in the database. As your applications operate, this code is read from the database and passed to the shared pool for processing like any other SQL statement. This code can be written in PL/SQL or Java.

VIP

Code read from the database will almost always match a code segment already prepared and resident in the shared pool.

Suppose you work at a library and you want to be able to generate an electronic reminder to the front desk every morning that identifies the borrower, book title, and author of books more than seven days overdue. You may have a number of applications that can initiate these reminders by clicking an Overdue Note button on a lending information screen. Each of those screens may have its own code behind the scenes handling overdue notice generation, or each screen may invoke a routine similar to the following:

```
create or replace procedure overdue_notice (borrower_ident char) as
   l_book_name     varchar2(40);
   l_book_ident    number;
   l_due_date      date
```

```
-- Get any overdue book numbers for current person
cursor mycur is
  select book_name, book_ident, due_date
    from overdue_notes
   where borrower_id = borrower_ident;
begin
  open mycur;
  fetch mycur into l_book_name, l_book_ident, l_due_date;
  while mycur%found loop
    -- Create an overdue notice
    insert into overdue_notes
         values (book_ident, book_name, borrower_ident,
                 book_title, was_due, sysdate, user);
       fetch mycur into l_book_name, l_book_ident, l_due_date;
  end loop;
end;
/
```

The following SQL text places the PL/SQL in the database:

 `create or replace`

 NOTE

*Use the **create or replace** syntax when storing objects in the Oracle8i database to avoid having to drop the procedure, package, or function before creation.*

 VIP

Design your applications to take advantage of code stored in the database. Look at all your business processes and centralize common procedures. Study existing applications and convert their centralized processing routines into code segments stored in the database.

IMPLEMENTING STORED PROCEDURES   In conjunction with the DBA you work with, there are some things to do before you can store procedures in the database and start using them. It is not simply a matter of deciding to use stored procedures. You must consult with your DBA, or the implementation may not work for the reasons outlined here:

- Stored procedures occupy space in the **SYSTEM** tablespace in your database. You may have to work with the DBA to ensure the space in this tablespace is sufficient. The DBA may have allocated space for this system tablespace before stored procedures were investigated.

■ You must give other users privileges to execute your procedures by issuing a command similar to **grant execute on overdue_notice to public;**.

■ In most cases, the DBA creates a public synonym for your stored procedure; for example, **create public synonym overdue_notice for polly.overdue_notice;**.

VIP
We have found that programs that manipulate data should be written using PL/SQL. Programs that require significant logic (decisions) benefit from the use of Java.

CALLING STORED PROCEDURES   Stored procedures can be executed from a PL/SQL block (we discuss PL/SQL blocks in Chapter 8), as in

```
-- other PL/SQL statements followed by
if sysdate - :due_back >= 6 then
   overdue_notice (borr_ident);
end if;
```

Stored procedures can be executed from SQL*Plus (we discuss SQL*Plus in Chapter 7 and Chapter 12), as in

```
-- other SQL statements followed by
execute overdue_notice ('A45R');
```

NOTE
When calling procedures, packages, and functions, one must pass the correct number of parameters with the appropriate data type to the stored object. Otherwise, the program will not run and Oracle will send you a friendly Oracle error, telling you that you have supplied the wrong number of parameters for the program. So the moral of the story: Be careful and hold hands when crossing the street.

Triggers, Functions, and Packages

Besides stored procedures, Oracle provides for three other kinds of centralized code that is stored and read from the database: *triggers, functions,* and *packages.*

■ Triggers are associated with tables and run transparently when predefined events happen to the data in the table. For example, you may use a database trigger to log the fact that an accounts receivable clerk has lowered the amount owing on an outstanding account.

■ Functions accept a number of parameters and pass a single value back to the calling program. For example, the validation of a ZIP code could be done with a function. The routine would be invoked with a ZIP code, and the function could pass back true or false depending on whether the ZIP code is valid.

Look at the next listing to see how a user-defined function is set up and then used in an SQL statement:

VIP
You can embed your own functions in SQL statements in the same way you use Oracle8i SQL functions on number, date, or character data.

```
SQL> create or replace function is_yorn (in_char varchar2)
  2  return number is
  3  begin
  4    if in_char = 'A' then
  5        return 1;
  6    else
  7        return 0;
  8    end if;
  9  /
Function created.
SQL> select last_name,first_name,a.status,c.inc_date
  2    from person a,cstat b
  3   where a.c_code = b.c_code
  4     and is_yorn(a.status) = 1
  5     and a.pin = 100782;
LAST_NAME            FIRST_NAME              STATUS     INC_DATE
-------------------- ----------------------- ---------- -----------
JOHANSSEN            FREDERIQUE              A          23-MAY-2001
```

■ Packages are single program units that contain procedures and functions. By grouping them together, the developer defines a set of routines that are commonly invoked together or one after another.

Refer to *Oracle8 Tuning* (Corey, Abbey, Dechichio, and Abramson; Osborne/McGraw-Hill, 1998), in particular, Chapter 8 ("Application Tuning"), where writing generic code using procedures, triggers, functions, and packages is discussed in more detail.

Parallel Processing

With the advent of bigger and more powerful computers, multi-CPU machines have begun appearing that leverage the Oracle8*i* Parallel Query feature, also called *PQO*. Oracle8*i* can parallelize many operations using PQO; in Chapter 10, we spoke of running SQL*Loader in parallel. The Oracle8*i* Server can parallelize sorts, joins, table scans, table population, and index creation operations. PQO is ideal in the following situations:

- Processing queries that access a large amount of data by scanning very large tables (normally in excess of 1,000,000 rows)

- Processing queries that join more than one very large table; the gain using parallelization is especially evident when tables with millions of rows are accessed together to assemble query results

- Processing that involves creation of large indexes, bulk loads, summarization operations, and copying large amounts of data between Oracle8 objects

- Processing queries on machines that fall into the SMP (symmetric multiprocessor) or MPP (massively parallel processors) category, and clusters (more than one computer working together and accessing the same set of disks and a central database)

- Processing queries whose data resides in many datafiles on many different disk drives or different table partitions

- Processing on machines where the CPU is typically underutilized or on intermittently used CPUs (classically, these CPUs check in with an average utilization of less than 40 percent)

- Processing queries alongside sufficient memory to support additional memory-intensive processes such as sorts

It is the responsibility of the application developer to approach the DBA and work closely with other resources to identify operations that can be processed in parallel.

VIP

There must be more than one CPU on a machine to enable the benefits of parallel processing. When looking at parallelization, do not experiment with the feature on a single-CPU machine, since it will degrade performance.

Determining How Much to Parallelize

It is the DBA's responsibility to set up an Oracle8i instance to leverage the power of PQO. Since the application developer knows system data better than most DBAs, you must work with the DBA to define a degree of parallelization for objects to fully utilize PQO. Oracle will compute a default degree of parallelization based on the number of disks upon which a table's data resides. Before deciding how much to parallelize, the developer and DBA need to do the following:

- Look at the nature of the way the user community accesses a system's data. Typically, when queries retrieve information from the same set of tables and when multiple user processes are running concurrently, you reduce the degree of parallelization.

- Decide the nature of the systems that access the Oracle8i database. Ask questions and figure out the balance between decision support system (DSS) access and OLTP (online systems) access. These two genres of systems have different processing requirements, and thus their different goals may influence how much parallelization it makes sense to implement.

- Look at implementing parallel-aware features of the Oracle8i cost-based optimizer (affectionately called *CBO*). We discuss CBO in Chapter 13 and look at ways the DBA and the application developer can work together to leverage Oracle8i enhancements that instruct the optimizer to be more parallel-aware.

Let's cap this chapter about application tuning by looking at ways to reduce waits for data and resources. Waits normally involve one of two situations that are caused by

- User processes queuing behind one another as they look for precious sort space and CPU time

- User processes tying up records in the Oracle8i database that are required by other user processes to allow them to go about their work

Reducing Wait Situations

The Oracle Server technology supports just about all its suite of tools. Installations continue to use a wide assortment of front-end tools to work with data stored in Oracle's data repository. Reducing wait situations is an attainable goal regardless of the hodgepodge of tools one uses to get at Oracle.

VIP

Enhance the speed of your online applications by minimizing the frequency and length of wait situations.

The next few sections outline a few ways to decrease the time spent waiting for resources in use by other users.

COMMIT Your Work Often

Regardless of what tool you use with Oracle, save your work often. If a user works with an Oracle Forms–based application, either commit programmatically or enliven a *Save* key on data entry screens. In SQL*Plus, after each **insert**, **update**, and **delete**, after each statement, issue a **commit** (or the more popular **commit work** one sees in PL/SQL). When you save your work often, you release all the resources (locks, latches, redo space, and so on) required until you complete your transaction. Reducing resources frees them up for other users and reduces their wait times. Interestingly enough, the other all-important feature of saving your work often is that you run less risk of losing work you have so carefully completed!

Let Oracle Do Its Own Locking

Oracle will issue the least restrictive lock it requires to accomplish a task you have asked it to perform. Don't lock manually with the SQL *lock* verb. Oracle does a fine job on its own. Its lock manager does the best job when left on its own. With the emergence of *tpo* (the transaction processing option) in version 6, the default lock became share update. With *share update* locks, different transactions can update different rows in the same Oracle data block concurrently.

Close Down Unused Application Windows

Terminal inactivity robs valuable resources from other users who may need them to go about their work. When users allow their terminals to sit and not do anything, they are still tying up a bottom-line amount of shared memory required to support their sessions, even though they are not doing anything. Freeing up that memory by leaving an unattended session will reduce wait time for resources with other users.

Use Multitasking Sparingly

It is tempting to open up multiple sessions in many windows when using a GUI front end. It is not unheard of when users find themselves in a deadly embrace with themselves. That is, they have multiple windows open attempting to update the same data that sits uncommitted on another window. If you practice good housekeeping with your Windows applications, you will reduce your own wait times.

VIP
In cooperation with your database administrator, investigate the occurrences of wait situations as your applications operate using the v$waitstat data dictionary view belonging to SYS.

What's Next

After reading this chapter, you've come a long way! Perhaps you (as we were one time) are just getting started on the road to application tuning. We have provided you with some bottom-line theory and pointed you in the right direction to get started. Even though the points we make are the basics of application tuning, they are applicable to all developers regardless of how long they have been using Oracle.

In Chapter 12, we will cover some advanced SQL concepts, and we'll show you some more complex examples. The SQL language is a powerful programming environment; after reading Chapter 12, you will be well on your way to exploiting some of its remarkable functionality.

CHAPTER
12

Advanced SQL

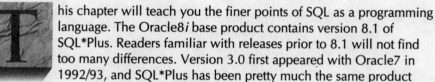his chapter will teach you the finer points of SQL as a programming language. The Oracle8*i* base product contains version 8.1 of SQL*Plus. Readers familiar with releases prior to 8.1 will not find too many differences. Version 3.0 first appeared with Oracle7 in 1992/93, and SQL*Plus has been pretty much the same product ever since with a few enhancements. Our experience has shown that SQL is a very flexible programming tool once you master some of its more advanced features: for example, one of our favorite tricks is using SQL to write SQL. We will show you how to use this feature, plus a number of others that will put you on the fast track to becoming a skilled SQL developer. Here is a list of the major items we will discuss:

- Grouping results from an SQL statement

- Using subqueries (queries within queries)

- Using SQL*Plus to generate SQL and create datafiles for other programs

- Using **decode** and **new_value**

- Defining variables in SQL*Plus

- Passing values into SQL*Plus

- Advanced **repheader** features

- Set theory in SQL*Plus

- Structured programming

- Using an editor in SQL*Plus

- Handling nulls in SQL*Plus

This chapter is intended to teach you more about Oracle8*i* and its SQL implementation; and, when you have finished with it, you will be able to create very sophisticated reports. You will also be able to determine when it is appropriate to use SQL*Plus or when it makes more sense to use a different tool, like Oracle Reports.

Terminology

The following definitions will arm you with the technical jargon you need to make it through this chapter:

- A *command file* contains a series of commands that are read by a program such as SQL*Plus. The work accomplished by a command file is the same as if you had typed commands interactively one after the other.

■ *Functions* perform operations on data that alter the display or data type of the data. For example, reformatting the date 11-DEC-2001 to be displayed as December 11, 2001 is done by using a function.

Functions That Group Results

These functions allow you to group sets of data together for the purpose of getting summary information. When you group rows together, think of this as an operation that lumps similar types of information together as the information is retrieved from the database. Table 12-1 lists the most common group functions, using the customer table we introduced in Chapter 7.

After looking at the most common group functions, let's move on and look at how they can be applied. A large number of the queries you write in SQL*Plus perform group functions as the data is retrieved from the database. Mastering the use of functions is fundamental to your understanding of the power of SQL and SQL*Plus.

Using the group by Clause

We discussed in Chapter 1 how the relational database model works with sets of rows. These sets can also be thought of as a group. You may use the functions described in Table 12-1 with or without the **group by** clause. When you don't mention the **group by** clause in a query, such as **select max(sales) from customer;**, you are telling the database that you want to treat all the rows in the table as one group. For example, you might want to know the average sales of all your customers or the total sales for all customers. The query **select avg(sales) from customer;** gives

Function	Returns	Example
Avg(column_name)	The average value of all the values in column_name	select avg(sales) from customer;
Count(*)	The number of rows in a table	select count(*) from customer;
max(column_name)	The maximum value stored in column_name	select max(sales) from customer;
min(column_name)	The minimum value stored in column_name	select min(sales) from customer;

TABLE 12-1. *Most Common group by Functions*

you the average, and **select sum(sales) from customer;** gives you the total sales for all customers. This is useful, but many times you are really interested in looking at your data in predetermined classes or groups. For example, to know the average sales by state, we use the query **select state_cd, avg(sales) from customer group by state_cd;**. Most people understand the purpose of the **group by** statement at first but have trouble implementing it. You must ensure that the **group by** clause references the correct number of columns in each SQL statement.

VIP
*When using **group by**, whatever columns are not mentioned in the **group by** portion of the query must have a group function on them.*

When you omit the group function from a selected data element or fail to include an element in the **group by** clause, the query will fail to execute. If we issue the statement **select last_name, state_cd, sum(sales) from customer group by last_name;**, the following error is returned:

```
ERROR at line 1:
ORA-00979: not a GROUP BY expression
```

Since the column state_cd is not included in the **group by** clause, it must have a group function on it. In other words, we must use a function such as **max( )**, **min( )**, **sum( )**, **count( )**, or **avg( )**. If you can't find a group function you want to use on a particular column, then move that column to the **group by** clause.

Using the having Clause

Just as you have search conditions (for instance, where state_cd = 'MA') for individual rows of a query, you can use the **having** clause to specify a search condition for a group of rows. For example, suppose you only wanted to see the states with more than 300 customers. Using the **having** clause, the query would be **select state_cd, avg(sales) from customer group by state_cd having count(state_cd) > 300;**.

VIP
*The **having** clause allows you to specify a search condition for a group of rows. The traditional **where** search condition works with an individual row, not a group of rows.*

Query Within a Query

Another powerful capability of SQL is having a query within a query; which is also known as using a subquery. The format for using a subquery is

```
{main query text} where {condition}
          ({sub query text});
```

For example, the main query in the following data looks at the customer table, the subquery at state:

```
select last_name,sales
  from customer
 where state_cd =
          (select max(state_cd)
              from state);
```

Note that the subquery is enclosed in parentheses. In addition, the condition in the **where** clause is resolved based on the results of a query. In other words, your **where** clause contains an SQL statement itself. Say you only want to see the sales of customers that exceed the average of all sales for the whole company. You would enter the query **select state_cd, sales from customer where sales > (select avg(sales) from customer);**. As you can see, the ability to have a query within a query is very powerful. You are enabled to build SQL statements that return data based on the information stored in the database. While your database changes, the same static query can return different results. Suppose you had determined beforehand that the average sales figure was $12,800 and you had worded the previous query **select state_cd, sales from customer where sales > 12800;**. You'd be in trouble if the average sales figure changed—you would have to change the query.

VIP
Using subqueries allows you to write SQL statements that can stay the same as your data changes (which it always does!).

Running SQL statements with embedded subqueries can affect performance. You will find, as your experience with subqueries increases, that you will need to work closely with your DBA to optimize statements with subquery processing.

Creating Datafiles for Other Programs

One of the most common programs we see people write is one that will feed data from an Oracle8i database into a spreadsheet. Let's use SQL*Plus to do this. Most spreadsheets require data in which each item is separated by a comma. Character-type data needs to be enclosed in single or double quotes. If we need single quotes, the following code will do this for us:

```
SQL*Plus: Release 8.1.5.0.0 - Production on Sun Jun 30 18:14:41 2002
(c) Copyright 1999 Oracle Corporation.  All rights reserved.
Connected to:
Oracle8i Enterprise Edition Release 8.1.5.0.0 - Production
With the Partitioning and Java options
PL/SQL Release 8.1.5.0.0 - Production
SQL> rem * Make spreadsheet data program
SQL> set heading off
SQL> set pagesize 0
SQL> set feedback off
SQL> set echo off
SQL> spool out.dat
SQL> /* Notice you need to select four single quotes to */
SQL> /* put a single quote in the output data file      */
SQL> select ''''||last_name||''''||','||''''||
  2     state_cd||''''||','||sales
  3     from customer;
SQL> spool off
```

VIP

Since the single quote means something special to Oracle8i (that is, it starts and ends a literal), you must select four of them together if you want the single quote character in your query results.

If we need double quotes, the following will work:

```
SQL*Plus: Release 8.1.5.0.0 - Production on Sun Jun 30 18:17:36 2002
(c) Copyright 1999 Oracle Corporation.  All rights reserved.
Connected to:
Oracle8i Enterprise Edition Release 8.1.5.0.0 - Production
With the Partitioning and Java options
PL/SQL Release 8.1.5.0.0 - Production
SQL> set heading off
SQL> set pagesize 0
SQL> set feedback off
```

```
SQL> set trimspool on
SQL> set echo off
SQL> spool out.dat
SQL> /* Notice how you place a double quote between two single */
SQL> /* to place a double quote in the output data file        */
SQL> select '"'||last_name||'","'||state_cd||'",'||sales
  2  from customer;
SQL> spool off
```

The output would be

```
'Teplow','MA',23445.67
'Abbey','CA',6969.96
'Nicholson','CA',6989.99
'Martin','CA',2345.45
'Laursen','CA',34.34
'Bambi','CA',1234.55
'McGraw','NJ',123.45
```

with single quotes, or

```
"Teplow","MA",23445.67
"Abbey","CA",6969.96
"Nicholson","CA",6989.99
"Martin","CA",2345.45
"Laursen","CA",34.34
"Bambi","CA",1234.55
"McGraw","NJ",123.45
```

with double quotes. Table 12-2 discusses the lines in the program to make the spreadsheet data.

NOTE
*The **set trimspool on** command only works in SQL*Plus with a version number greater than or equal to 3.2 (which comes with Oracle8i, 8, 7.3 and 7.2). You have always been able to trim blanks from screen output; this is how it is done as data is written to a file.*

As you can see from Table 12-2, SQL*Plus is a very flexible tool. It is also a very easy tool to create datafiles with. Getting data into and out of an Oracle8*i* database is typically very easy from the Oracle side.

Component	Meaning
set heading off	Since you are creating a datafile, you do not want headings.
set pagesize 0	You do not want page breaks, so you set this to zero for datafile output.
set linesize 80	You set this to the size of the longest line in your output datafile.
set trimspool on	Tells SQL*Plus to trim trailing blanks off spooled output.
set feedback off	Suppresses SQL*Plus from telling you how many rows are retrieved to satisfy the query.
set echo off	Tells SQL*Plus not to echo the SQL statement as it is run.
spool out.dat	Tells SQL*Plus to send the results of the query to a file named out.dat.
spool off	Tells SQL*Plus to close the output datafile.

TABLE 12-2. *Discussion of Lines of Code from a Spreadsheet Data Creation Program*

SQL Creating SQL

There is no reason why you cannot get SQL to create SQL programs. In fact, this is a technique most DBAs find very useful. The following SQL code will generate an SQL file called out.sql that will contain SQL statements:

```
SQL*Plus: Release 8.1.5.0.0 - Production on Sun Jun 30 10:56:42 2002
(c) Copyright 1999 Oracle Corporation.  All rights reserved.
Connected to:
Oracle8i Enterprise Edition Release 8.1.5.0.0 - Production
With the Partitioning and Java options
PL/SQL Release 8.1.5.0.0 - Production
SQL> set heading off
SQL> set pagesize 0
SQL> set feedback off
SQL> set echo off
SQL> spool out.sql
SQL> select 'set pagesize 55' from dual;
SQL> select 'grant select on  '||table_name||'  to public;'
  2    from user_tables;
SQL> spool off
```

As you can see, we have a program that creates another SQL program. The first **select** references the dual table. This is a table owned by Oracle user SYS that contains only one row. We use it in this case to load a setup command for the output file called out.sql; we then follow up with the **grant** statements. You have all the elements you need to generate numerous SQL programs from SQL programs. Let's say this code was run from an Oracle account that owned a customer and state table. The contents of out.sql would be

```
set pagesize 55
grant select on CUSTOMER to public;
grant select on STATE to public;
```

The decode Statement

The **decode** statement is how you implement if-then-else logic in SQL*Plus. (We discussed how this is done in PL/SQL in Chapter 8.) One of the most powerful functions within SQL*Plus is the **decode** statement. Most people shy away from it due to its ugly syntax. As soon as you add other functions onto the columns, you can very quickly get what we call "ugly SQL." Like a small dog, its bark is far worse than its bite. With that in mind, let's take a look at the format for a **decode** statement:

```
decode (column_name,comparison,action,comparison,action,. . .
        else action)
```

The **decode** statement compares the column contents to the comparison field. If they are equal, then **decode** does the action. If they are not equal, **decode** goes on to the next comparison. If none of the comparisons match, then the else action is performed.

Suppose we want to write a query that would categorize our customers by region, so that customers on the east side of the Mississippi come under the heading East, and customers on the west side of the Mississippi come under the heading West. Let's take a look at how to do this with **decode**:

```
column region format a20 heading 'Region'
column sales  format 999,999,999,999,999.99
compute sum of sales on report
compute sum of sales on region
break on report on region
select decode(state_cd, 'MA', 'East',
                        'NJ', 'East',
                        'CA', 'West',
                  'Middle of River'),sales
from customer
order by 1;
```

The logic expressed by this listing is as follows:

```
if state_cd = 'MA' then
   display 'East'
elsif state_cd = 'NJ' then
   display 'East'
elsif state_cd = 'CA' then
   display 'West'
else
   display 'Middle of River'
end if
```

This example demonstrates the power of using **decode**. Unlike a subquery (or a **select** within a **select**), which will abort if no rows are found, the **decode** statement has the else clause, which can handle exceptions. The bottom line is that the **decode** function is very powerful and can be used to implement logic in SQL*Plus.

Defining Variables in SQL*Plus

In SQL*Plus, it is possible to define variables that can then be used further on in the same program. Think of a variable as a table column with one row of data. Like a table column, a variable has a type (number or character), and, like a table column, it contains data. Think of a variable as a single row of data from a table with one column. The key thing to remember is that a command file can have one or more SQL queries within it. By using the SQL*Plus **define** statement, we are able to define a variable that can be referenced in all SQL statements in the command file. So let's see how you define variables, using the following code as an example:

```
define rpt_cd = "MA"
select sales from customer where state_cd = '&rpt_cd';
```

VIP
Though this is not mandatory, enclose the text assigned to variables in double quotes. This allows you to embed spaces in the value.

We have assigned the variable named "rpt_cd" the value MA. Thus, when issuing a query, we can prefix the variable name with an ampersand (&) and enclose it in single quotes. To view all variables that have been defined, enter the word **define** by itself. Say we have defined the three variables "rpt_cd," "sales_amt," and "cust_start." The command define would present the following output:

```
DEFINE RPT_CD        = "MA" (CHAR)
DEFINE SALES_AMT     = "18000" (CHAR)
DEFINE CUST_START    = "A" (CHAR)
```

To see the value of one variable, enter **define** followed by the name of the variable. If you entered **define sales_amt**, you would be told

```
DEFINE SALES_AMT        = "18000" (CHAR)
```

NOTE
All variables, regardless of the data type assigned, are character data.

If for some reason you wish to clear the value of a variable, enter the word **undefine** followed by the variable name. If you issue the command **undefine sales_amt**, then the command **define sales_amt**, you are informed the variable has been cleared as shown in the next listing:

```
SP2-0135: symbol sales_amt is UNDEFINED
```

NOTE
The define and undefine words may be abbreviated to def and undef.

Substitution Variables in SQL*Plus

Many times when we are running a query, we do not know beforehand what value the user wants to use in the report. When the report is started, you want to type in a value to be used for the report. You do this by placing an ampersand (&) in front of the section of code you want replaced. For example, let's have Oracle8*i* prompt us for the value of "rpt_cd." The SQL statement would be **select sales from customer where state_cd = '&rpt_cd';**. When this statement is executed, Oracle8*i* asks you to supply the value for "rpt_cd." Then the query runs based on the report code you supply. This way, you are able to build a report without knowing the user's specific needs.

Many times you want to avoid being prompted multiple times for a variable you use more than once. An easy way to do that is by using double ampersands. This tells Oracle8*i* to ask for the variable once and issue a **define** command on it. For example, the statement **select state_cd, avg(&&rptcol), max(&&rptcol) from customer group by state_cd;** will prompt for the value of "rptcol" only once (the three dots at the end of the old and new lines represent code not relevant to the listing):

```
Enter value for rptcol: sales
old   1: select state_cd, avg(&&rptcol), max(&&rptcol) . . .
new   1: select state_cd, avg(sales), max(sales) from . . .
ST AVG(SALES) MAX(SALES)
```

```
-- ---------- ----------
CA    3514.858     6989.99
MA   23445.67    23445.67
NJ     123.45      123.45
```

VIP

When a variable has been defined with the &&
*convention, you must **undefine** the variable if you*
want to give it a different value.

We all know that presentation is everything. The default prompt would not be
acceptable for the typical end user we encounter. You use the **prompt** and **accept**
commands to get a more descriptive prompt. Examine the following:

```
clear screen
prompt *********************************************
prompt Enter "ALL" to see all your tables
prompt Or Enter a Partial table name
accept tname prompt "Enter ALL/Partial Tablename....:"
select table_name
  from user_tables
 where table_name like '%&tname%'
    or upper('&tname') = 'ALL';
```

When this is run, the following output is produced for the same user who owns
a customer and a state table:

```
*********************************************
Enter "ALL" to see all your tables
Or Enter a Partial table name
Enter ALL/Partial Tablename....:ALL
old   3:   where table_name like '%&tname%'
new   3:   where table_name like '%ALL%'
old   4:      or upper('&tname') = 'ALL'
new   4:      or upper('ALL') = 'ALL'
TABLE_NAME
------------------------------
CUSTOMER
STATE
```

As you can see, Oracle8*i* generates the prompt statements and places the input
you give it into a variable called "tname"; it then uses the value of "tname" in

the **where** clause. You should also pay special attention to the use of the word "ALL." It has a special meaning in this case. If you enter ALL at the prompt, then the condition upper('&tname') = 'ALL' becomes 'ALL' = 'ALL', which is true. Thus every row is retrieved. If you do not enter ALL, then the database will only retrieve the table names that meet the entered criteria. This is a very powerful technique. Also notice the **clear screen** command that clears the screen before displaying the first prompt. This is used to make the prompt present better on the screen.

Sometimes you want to prompt the user for inputs and then pass those directly to SQL on the command line. This is also a very easy thing to do. If you name the variables in your program "&1," "&2," and so on, Oracle8*i* will take data passed into it on the command line and assign it to the variables "&1," "&2," and so on. For example, suppose we have an SQL program named test.sql containing the following:

```
select state_cd, sales from customer
  where sales > &1
    and state_cd = '&2';
```

If we wish to report on all data where the sales are greater than $1,000 and the state is CA, we could call the preceding program with the command

```
sqlplus username/password @test 1000 CA
```

and the output would be

```
old   1: select state_cd, sales from customer where sales > &1
new   1: select state_cd, sales from customer where sales > 1000
old   2: and state_cd = '&2'
new   2: and state_cd = 'CA'

ST     SALES
--  ----------
CA    6969.96
CA    6989.99
CA    2345.45
CA    1234.55
```

NOTE
*Oracle8i displays old and new lines as it substitutes values for variables. This display can be suppressed with the SQL*Plus command* **set verify off***, which can be abbreviated to* **set ver off***.*

If you are already in SQL*Plus, you use the **start** command to run a program, and pass variables after the name of the program. The **start** command tells Oracle8*i* to get the command file, load it, and then execute it (using any parameters that you enter with the **start** command).

```
start test.sql 1000 CA
```

As you can see, SQL*Plus has numerous capabilities when it comes to passing parameters. By passing values to SQL*Plus as you invoke a program, you can write one SQL query and have it satisfy a number of users' needs. In addition, you can very easily interface it with other programs.

NOTE
*Most operating systems allow using the @ sign rather than the word **start**. What's the difference between the two, you ask? Four keystrokes!*

New SQL*Plus Features

In this section, we cover a few new features of SQL*Plus. Some of the features mentioned here were first delivered with Oracle8 and apply as well to Oracle8*i*. Report header and footer commands are the most noticeable change, so let's look at these and a few other differences before delving more into writing SQL*Plus reports. Most of the enhancements to SQL*Plus are designed to reflect new data types and some of the techniques for handling very large objects. The last item in this section highlights a few of the Oracle8*i*-specific additions.

Header and Footer Commands

We looked at the **ttitle** and **btitle** commands in Chapter 7 when we wrote the Database Technologies customer report. The command **repheader** places and formats a specified report header at the top of each report, or it lists the current **repheader** definition. Its corollary is the **repfooter** command, which places and formats a specified report footer at the bottom of each report or lists the current **repfooter** definition.

Storing the SQL*Plus Environment

Often, developers or DBAs prefer to set up their own environment in SQL*Plus. Using the new command **store**, you can save attributes of the current SQL*Plus environment in a host operating system file (a command file). Then, the next time you log in to SQL*Plus, you can run that command file to restore the environment, as shown here.

```
SQL*Plus: Release 8.1.5.0.0 - Production on Sun Jun 30 10:56:42 2002
(c) Copyright 1999 Oracle Corporation.  All rights reserved.
Connected to:
Oracle8i Enterprise Edition Release 8.1.5.0.0 - Production
With the Partitioning and Java options
PL/SQL Release 8.1.5.0.0 - Production
SQL> -- Restore the environment so painstakingly set up; note that the
SQL> -- filename ends in the ".cmd" text which is nonstandard and
SQL> -- must be included.
@D:\Oracle\Ora81\resenv.cmd
```

set autotrace

The **set** command now has an **autotrace** clause. The **autotrace** clause displays a report on the execution of successful SQL DML statements (**select**, **insert**, **update**, or **delete**). The report can include execution statistics and the query execution path. We will discuss **autotrace** in Chapter 13 while looking at the **explain plan command.**

serveroutput

While using PL/SQL as featured in Chapter 8, you can display text to the terminal using the **put_line** command that is part of the dbms_utility package owned by SYS. To enliven output from **put_line**, the **set serveroutput** command now has a **format** clause. You can use **wrapped**, **word_wrapped**, or **truncated** with the **format** clause.

Oracle8i-Specific Enhancements

There are a handful of new commands in SQL*Plus with Oracle8i. Table 12-3 highlights some of these enhancements.

In addition to all of these wonderful new SQL*Plus features, a few more commands are introduced with Oracle8i. All these new commands can be found in the Oracle8i Server documentation in the SQL*Plus Release 8.1.5 Enhancements section.

repheader—the Whole Header and Nothing but the Header

Up to now, you have only seen examples in which we use the default behavior of the **repheader** command. As you know, the **repheader** command is used to print a title at the top of each page. In Chapter 7, we showed you the default behavior of **ttitle**,

Command	Desired Action	Syntax
Startup	Start up, mount, and open the database. Immediately shut down the current database, restarting it without opening or mounting it using a parameter file.	startup startup pfile=*parmfile* force nomount
Shutdown	Normal shutdown of the current instance. Immediately shut down a database, close and dismount the database.	shutdown shutdown immediate
Set describe	Set how many levels deep you can recursively describe an object.	set describe depth 10 (valid depth range 1–50 or all)
Show parameters	Display all initialization parameters. Display initialization parameters that match a string.	show parameters show parameters *partial_string*
Show sga	Display particulars of the System Global Area for the current instance.	show sga

TABLE 12-3. *SQL*Plus Enhancements in Oracle8*i

because from experience we have found this to be sufficient for the majority of your needs. However, there comes a time when you want more. Perhaps you need a clerk's name in the heading, or page numbers on the left. Regardless, there is much more you can do with the **repheader** command, at which Table 12-4 takes a closer look.

NOTE
The bold formatting command may not work on all operating systems.

The best way to understand these advanced formatting features is to use them. So let's do a more sophisticated **repheader** command:

```
set linesize 62
repheader left 'Michael Abbey Systems International Inc.' -
skip center -
'An Oracle Systems Consulting Company' -
right 'Page: ' format 999 sql.pno -
skip center bold 'Customer Report'
```

Option	Meaning
col *n*	Indents to position *n* of the current line.
skip *n*	Skips to the start of a new line; if you enter 0, then it goes to the beginning of the line.
left, right, center	Left align, right align, or center align.
bold	Displays data in boldface.
format char	Specifies the format model to be used (similar to the format command with col).
sql.lno	The current line number.
sql.pno	The current page number.
sql.user	The name of the user logged in to SQL*Plus.

TABLE 12-4. *Advanced Formatting for repheader*

The title would then show up on any report as

```
Michael Abbey Systems International Inc.
        An Oracle Systems Consulting Company  Page:   1
            Customer Report
```

The hyphen (-) in **repheader** represents a line continuation, and the **skip** word instructs **repheader** to skip the specified number of lines (or one line, if a number is omitted). As you can see, you can get pretty sophisticated with this command.

VIP
Oracle8i documentation suggests using the **repheader** *command to format an SQL*Plus report title rather than* **ttitle**, *and the same with* **repfooter**. *Use whichever you wish, though the default* **ttitle** *is more rich than the* **repheader** *default.*

column—the Whole Column and Nothing but the Column

As you have seen from previous examples, the **column** command controls how your data is displayed. Just like the **ttitle** command, you have lots of options with

column. We will now present a summary of the extra formatting commands for number and then character data.

NOTE
*The **column** command can be abbreviated to **col**, and the **format** command, to **form**.*

Formatting Number Data

The **format** command determines how the information from the database will be displayed. Table 12-5 highlights the most useful formats for number data.

Format Character	Example	Description
9	Format 999999	Determines the display width based on the number of digits entered. When you have a number overflow, it will display '######'. You will not see any leading zeros.
0	09999 99990	Displays leading zeros. When value is zero, it displays a zero instead of a blank space.
$	$99999	Places a dollar sign in front of the number.
B	B99999	Displays a zero as a blank.
MI	99999MI	Displays a minus sign when the value is negative.
PR	99999PR	Places <> around a negative number.
	99,999	Places a comma in the position specified.
	999.999	Places a decimal point where specified and rounds appropriately.

TABLE 12-5. *Common Number Formats Used with the column Command*

The next listing shows some of these formats in action:

```
SQL> column sales format 999,999,999.99
SQL> select sales from customer;
Michael Abbey Systems International Inc.
    An Oracle Systems Consulting Company                Page:    1
                        Customer Report
            SALES
    ----------------
        23,445.67
         6,969.96
         6,989.99
         2,345.45
            34.34
         1,234.55
           123.45
7 rows selected.

SQL> column sales format $099999
SQL> select sales from customer;
Michael Abbey Systems International Inc.
    An Oracle Systems Consulting Company                Page:    1
                        Customer Report
SALES
--------
 $023446
 $006970
 $006990
 $002345
 $000034
 $001235
 $000123
7 rows selected.
SQL>
```

Formatting Character Data

Character data can be harder to deal with. For example, say you want to print a report in which the number of characters across a page is 80. The report lists names and salaries. Some of the names (for example, Alexander Springhurst, at a length of 21 characters) are longer than others (for example, Sue Ray, at a length of 7 characters). If you allocate the necessary space to accommodate short names, the long names could be broken over multiple lines and become hard to read.

Wrapping and Truncating Character Data

The following three words can be used to format character data and are useful when a report needs to display character data that is longer than the width of the column display you have set.

- **wrap:** This command tells SQL*Plus to display the specified number of characters, then go to the next line and continue. Using our long name example, if the full_name column were formatted using the column expression **column full_name format a18 wrap**, the name would appear as

```
Name                City
------------------  ----------------
Alexander Springhu  Winnipeg
rst
```

- **word_wrap:** This command tells SQL*Plus to display the specified number of characters but move a word to the next line rather than split the word into pieces. Using the column expression **column full_name format a18 word_wrap**, the name would appear as

```
Name                City
------------------  ----------------
Alexander           Winnipeg
Springhurst
```

- **truncate:** This command tells SQL*Plus to display the specified number of characters and ignore the rest. Using the column expression **column full_name format a18 truncate**, the name would appear as

```
Name                City
------------------  ----------------
Alexander Springhu  Winnipeg
```

Justify Left, Center, or Right

This controls the centering of the column heading (not the data in the column). By default, a number column heading is right-justified, and a character heading is left-justified. The following listing illustrates how these affect a column heading display format using the statement **select state_name from state;**:

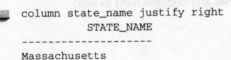

```
column state_name justify right
        STATE_NAME
--------------------
Massachusetts
```

```
California
NewJersey
col state_name justify center

      STATE_NAME
    -------------------
Massachusetts
California
NewJersey
```

new_value

You can create a variable that will hold data from a column using **new_value**. Once a variable is defined, you can then place its value into a **repheader** command. This is useful when you want to create a master/detail report with a value from the report appearing in the heading. To place a value in the heading, you must always reference a column from your query (in our example the column state_cd) in the **break** command, with the **skip page** option. For example, using the SQL statement **select state_cd, last_name, sales from customer order by 1;**, examine the following output:

```
column state_cd new_value rpt_cd
repheader left 'STATE CD: ' rpt_cd skip 1
break on state_cd skip page
STATE CD: CA
ST LAST_NAM SALES
-- -------- ------------
CA Abbey        6,970
   Nicholson    6,990
   Martin       2,345
   Bambi        1,235
   Laursen         34

STATE CD: MA
ST LAST_NAM SALES
-- -------- ------------
MA Teplow      23,446

STATE CD: NJ
ST LAST_NAM SALES
-- -------- ------------
NJ McGraw         123

7 rows selected.
```

You could also use this technique to put today's date in the heading. Examine the following code to see how today's date is put in a report title using **new_value**:

```
column today new_value today_date
select to_char(sysdate,'HH24:MM:SS DD-Mon-YYYY') today
  from dual;
repheader center 'Michael Abbey Systems International Inc.' -
       skip left today_date -
       right 'Page: ' format 999 sql.pno skip
select sales from customer;
```

When this is run, the date appears on line two of the title (format resembling 14:54:17 26-Mar-2002), with the page number on the left side of the same line.

```
             Michael Abbey Systems International Inc.
14:54:17 26-Mar-2002                               Page:     1
    SALES
----------
   23445.67
    6969.96
    6989.99
    2345.45
      34.34
    1234.55
     123.45
```

SQL*Plus Set Theory

The nice thing about a relational database is that you write SQL queries that act upon sets of data versus a single row of data. Not having to issue a read makes it very, very powerful. SQL by design has a very strong relationship to math theory. There is a series of set functions that work very nicely with an Oracle8i database using SQL*Plus. We will discuss these set operators in the next few sections, using tables x and y (both have a single column of character data type). The next listing shows the contents of these tables:

```
select * from x;

COL
---
1
2
3
4
5
```

```
6
6 rows selected.
select * from y;
COL
---
5
6
7
3 rows selected.
```

union

Using this operator in SQL*Plus returns all the rows in both tables with no duplicates. In the previous listing, both the tables have columns with the value of 5 and 6. The query **select * from x union select * from y;** returns the following results as expected:

```
COL
---
1
2
3
4
5
6
7
7 rows selected.
```

union all

Using this operator in SQL*Plus returns all the rows in both tables with duplicates. The query **select * from x union all select * from y;** returns the following results:

```
COL
---------
        1
        2
        3
        4
        5
        6
        5
        6
        7
9 rows selected.
```

intersect

Using this operator in SQL*Plus returns all the rows in one table that also reside in the other. Using tables x and y, the column values 5 and 6 are in both tables. The query **select * from x intersect select * from y;** returns the following results as expected:

```
COL
---
  5
  6
```

minus

Using this operator in SQL*Plus returns all the rows in the first table minus the rows in that table that are also in the second table. Using tables x and y, the column values 5 and 6 are in both tables. The query **select * from x minus select * from y;** returns the following results, as expected:

```
COL
---
  1
  2
  3
  4
```

VIP
When using these set operators with Oracle8, the data types of the column(s) in both tables must be the same.

The following error occurs if the data types differ (using table z, whose single column is number data type):

```
select * from x union select * from z
       *
ERROR at line 1:
ORA-01790: expression must have same data type as corresponding expression
```

Structured Code Techniques

SQL is a programming language like any other: to do it right requires care. The first thing we recommend you do is have an SQL script with common setup information and the most common column definitions. Look at the following example:

```
rem ****************
rem * setup.sql
rem ****************
rem This script contains common setup information and
rem formatting information I use for many sql scripts
rem Michael Corey     05/23/2001     Created
rem Michael Abbey     10/23/2001     Changed pagesize to 60,
rem                                  to add additional
rem                                  5 lines for new printer.
rem Standard set-up
set echo off
set pagesize 60
set linesize 80
rem *************************************
rem * common column format statements
rem *************************************
column bytes heading 'Bytes' format 999,999,999.99
column kbytes heading 'K Bytes' format 999,999,999.99
column less1 heading 'Under 1|Minute' format 999,990
column sales heading 'Sales|Ytd' format 999,999,999,999,999.99
column state_cd heading 'St|Cd' format a2
column state_name heading 'State|Name' format a20 truncate
column sum(sales) heading 'Sales|Ytd' format 999,999,999,999,999.99
column sum(bytes) heading 'Bytes'       format 999,999,999.99
column table_name heading 'Table|Name' format a20 wrap
rem *******************
rem * End of script
rem *******************
```

This command file holds the most common setup items (**pagesize** and **linesize**) and the most common column format statements. The next step is to write your SQL query and invoke the preceding program to format and set up the report. This is done in the following listing:

```
SQL*Plus: Release 8.1.5.0.0 - Production on Sun Apr 21 20:16:41 2002
(c) Copyright 1999 Oracle Corporation.  All rights reserved.
Connected to:
Oracle8i Enterprise Edition Release 8.1.5.0.0 - Production
With the Partitioning and Java options
PL/SQL Release 8.1.5.0.0 - Production
SQL> rem *****************************************
SQL> rem *     customer.sql
SQL> rem *****************************************
SQL> rem * This report gives a complete customer listing
SQL> rem * Mike Corey  10/23/2001
SQL> rem * Call in standard setup residing in central repository
SQL> @D:\ORACLE\Ora81\setup.sql
```

```
SQL> rem * Set the report title and page footer
SQL> repheader center 'Database Technologies Inc.' skip -
     center 'Customer Report'
SQL> repfooter center '*** customer.sql ***'
```

By using a standard setup file, you merely execute it first. This sets up the environment. Then your program (that is, customer.sql) contains the query to get the data, any **break** logic (the **break** statement), any totals you want to display, and the **repheader** and **repfooter** commands the report uses (we discussed **btitle** in the "Page Footers" section of Chapter 7; **repfooter** behaves the same as **btitle**). You don't spend a lot of time formatting the data; instead, you spend your efforts on the program logic needed to accomplish the task.

Notice that the **btitle** name is the name of the command file. The reason for this is when an end user calls you up about a report, you can easily tell what the source code is. In real life, many SQL statements you use for your reports will tend to be slight variations of each other. By putting the report title in the footer of the report, you can zero in on which report needs attention. This technique is illustrated in the next listing:

```
SQL> repfooter skip 2 center '**** my_report.sql ****'
```

Command Line Editing

When you are working with SQL*Plus, it becomes apparent very quickly that Oracle8*i* holds the last command executed in a buffer. To access that buffer, you merely have to enter a slash (/) and press the ENTER key. This action will cause the last SQL query entered to run again. Many times when building these command files, if you are like most of us, you have fat-fingered the typing and need to make a minor change. We find in these cases that it's much easier to use the command line editor you get with SQL*Plus than retyping the whole line. Even though this editor is very crude, it has always served a very useful purpose. You can make changes very quickly to the SQL buffer and then execute an SQL statement once again. Table 12-6 takes a look at the core commands.

The key to this editor is knowing what the current line is: the only line that you are able to change. With that in mind, let's try a few things. Let's look at our query by entering the command **list**:

```
1    select state_cd, last_name, sales
2    from customer
3*   order by 1
```

The asterisk tells us what the current line is. So let's change the current line to line one. From now on, we will use the abbreviated form of the command

Editor Command	Purpose
(a)ppend	Add text to the end of the current line.
(c)hange /old/new/	Replace old text with new text in the current line.
(c)hange /text/	Remove the text from the current line.
Del	Delete the current line.
(i)nput text	Add a line after the current line.
(l)ist	Show all the lines in the buffer.
(l)ist n	Show line number n in the buffer.
(l)ist m n	Show line numbers starting with line m and ending with line n.

TABLE 12-6. *SQL*Plus Line-Editing Commands*

(presented in parentheses in Table 12-6). Type the command l 1 (the letter "l" followed by the number one), and SQL*Plus lists line one:

```
1*  select state_cd, last_name, sales
```

Now the current line is set at line one. Let's change state_cd to customer.state_cd. You enter the command **c/state_cd/customer.state_cd/** and SQL*Plus responds with

```
1*  select customer.state_cd, last_name, sales
```

Now let's list the entire query again using the command **l**:

```
1   select customer.state_cd, last_name, sales
2   from customer
3*  order by 1
```

Let's remove the **order by** statement. Since we are pointing to line three, we just enter the delete command **del** and then list our query with the command **l**:

```
SQL> l
  1   select customer.state_cd, last_name, sales
  2       from customer
  3*  order by 1
SQL> del
```

```
SQL> l
  1  select customer.state_cd, last_name, sales
  2*   from customer
SQL>
```

Notice how SQL*Plus leaves the current line as line two after doing the delete we requested. With the edited command in the SQL buffer, we can run it again using the command **r** or by typing the slash (/) character. Either produces the following query output:

```
ST LAST_NAME
-- ------------------------------
MA Teplow
CA Abbey
CA Nicholson
CA Martin
CA Laursen
CA Bambi
NJ McGraw
```

Your last SQL query is kept in the buffer until you exit SQL*Plus.

Arrrghh! We Need a Real Editor

As we said, this command line editor is great for simple tasks. But it only allows you to edit the SQL query itself. Many times, a lot of formatting and setup is required to make a simple SQL query into a usable report. That job is best done with a full editor. There is a command in SQL*Plus that lets you define your favorite editor for use directly from SQL*Plus. The command is formatted as **define _editor=** **"editor_name"** where editor_name is the name of the program that runs your favorite editor. In UNIX, that editor may be vi, in VMS it may be edt, or in NT it could be Notepad.

You can set up any editor of your choice. To use the editor you define in this manner, type the command **edit** or abbreviate it to **ed**. Oracle8*i* will then issue the command you have used in the **define _editor** command.

NOTE
*The SQL Worksheet in Oracle Enterprise Manager can be used for many activities we discuss here with SQL*Plus. Most of the formatting commands only work in SQL*Plus.*

Nulls in SQL*Plus

The ever elusive "null" character deserves even more special attention as you move up to Oracle8*i*. When a column value in a table is not known, one says "it is null." With Oracle8*i*, the length of a column that contains a null value is null, though earlier versions have answered zero to the same question.

Problems with Nulls in Comparison Operations

The only way to allow true preservation of null data is using the keywords **is null** and **is not null** as shown in the next listing.

```
select count(*)
  from mytab
 where cola is null;
select count(*)
  from mytab
 where cola is not null;
```

The query **select count(*), comm_amt from comm group by comm_amt;** returns the following output:

```
COUNT(*)   COMM_AMT
---------  ---------
      12       1200
       7       1700
       8
```

You can quickly get into trouble when using other constructs for **null** comparisons. Picture a table whose comm_amt column contains the following data:

Column Value	Number of Rows
Null	8
1200	12
1700	7

Now the fun begins: Let's try issuing the SQL statement **select count(*) from comm where comm_amt < 1700;**, and the result is a count of 12. This result is determined from the not null values in the comm_amt column containing the value

1200. Note how the rows whose value is null are not counted. Oracle does not know the value of the comm_amt column whose value is null; null is meaningless and indeterminate, and hence the null column value rows are not returned. This leads into the next discussion about how to do comparisons using null column values.

Using NVL for Null Comparisons

The **nvl** function is the solution to the null column value comparison problem. Picture the following enhanced statement to retrieve bona fide counts from our comm table:

```
SQL> select count(*),nvl(comm_amt,0) from comm group by nvl(comm_amt,0);
  COUNT(*) NVL(COMM_AMT,0)
 --------- ---------------
         8               0
        12            1200
         7            1700
```

The **nvl** function substituted the value "0" into all rows whose comm_amt column value was null. Using this newfound functionality, let's issue our previous query to find out how many rows have a comm_amt value less than 1700.

```
SQL> select count(*) from comm where nvl(comm_amt,0) < 1700;
  COUNT(*)
 ---------
        20
```

Let's finish off this brief discussion of nulls by looking at the right and the wrong way to do character string comparisons against null column values. Your ability to deal with null column values will lead to a better comprehension of Oracle8i data stored as null values.

The Null=Null Comparison Anomaly

By not using the **is null** and **is not null** syntax, you can easily get yourself into more trouble. Picture the following statements, commented to illustrate the point each makes:

```
SQL*Plus: Release 8.1.5.0.0 - Production on Sun Apr 21 20:16:41 2002
(c) Copyright 1999 Oracle Corporation.  All rights reserved.
Connected to:
Oracle8i Enterprise Edition Release 8.1.5.0.0 - Production
With the Partitioning and Java options
```

```
PL/SQL Release 8.1.5.0.0 - Production
SQL>
SQL> -- Oracle8i cannot resolve the equality condition since the ''
SQL> -- represents a zero length character string BUT NOT a null value
SQL>
SQL> select 12 from dual where null = '';
no rows selected
SQL>
SQL> -- One would think that Oracle8i would allow equality comparison
SQL> -- between two '' strings, but not so! Watch out!
SQL>
SQL> select 12 from dual where '' = '';
no rows selected
SQL> -- Even though the comparison is coded correctly with the null
SQL> -- keyword,
SQL> -- the null on the left side of the = is meaningless as is the one on
SQL> -- the right; 2 meaningless values can't be compared against one another
SQL> select 12 from dual where null = null;
no rows selected
SQL>
SQL> -- This in the only way to do it properly to get the desired results
SQL>
SQL> select 12 from dual where null is null;
        12
---------
        12
SQL>
SQL> -- Let's do the same sort of thing using the nvl function
SQL>
SQL> select 12 from dual where nvl(null,'X') = nvl(null,'X');
        12
---------
        12
SQL>
```

VIP
*Many developers and DBAs find the way Oracle
handles null values frustrating; obviously, there is
nothing you can do about it other than familiarize
yourself with the convention, and be prepared with
that knowledge if any query results are suspicious.*

What's Next

What we have given you in this chapter are all the pieces to become really productive with SQL and SQL*Plus. We did not intend for this book to be the complete guide to programming in SQL; rather, it's a guide to the most useful techniques and commands. Armed with our introductory chapter on SQL, you now have an understanding of how to word queries and how to format SQL*Plus report output. Remember, SQL is the foundation of Oracle. The better you know it, the better you will be able to use Oracle.

In the next chapter, we will discuss some advanced concepts about application tuning. You will be able to add some more SQL skills to your repertoire as we look at ways to write efficient SQL queries and take advantage of its truly remarkable features.

CHAPTER
13

Advanced
Application Tuning

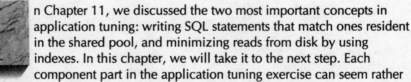 n Chapter 11, we discussed the two most important concepts in application tuning: writing SQL statements that match ones resident in the shared pool, and minimizing reads from disk by using indexes. In this chapter, we will take it to the next step. Each component part in the application tuning exercise can seem rather insignificant on its own, but, considered in the light of the whole tuning methodology, it is a worthwhile contributor.

Tuning applications should begin with the programmer and the very first line of code and continue throughout the system lifecycle. There are always many different ways to do something with a given requirement—the good way, and all the others. It is not enough just to know how to use Oracle. Tuning your applications will enable you to get the best performance out of Oracle. When your applications are tuned, they use fewer resources, which has a ripple effect. Efforts to tune the Oracle software could be wasted without your taking the time to tune applications. In this chapter, we will highlight the following issues that pertain to application tuning:

- The twin optimization approach used to process SQL statements

- The three phases in SQL statement processing

- Naming variables in Oracle tools

- The data access path chosen by Oracle

- Primary key constraints

- Looking at the contents of the shared pool

- Explain plan and autotrace

- The tkprof facility

We will discuss ways to maximize your available resources and focus on the areas of tuning your applications that will benefit you the most.

Terminology

The following definitions will arm you with the technical jargon you need to make it through this chapter:

- An *access path* is the method Oracle determines to get at your data. It chooses this path in accordance with a number of evaluation processes over which we have no control.

- The *execution plan* is a roadmap to the data involved in every SQL statement; it is built by Oracle according to a set of predefined optimization techniques.

- *Locks* are internal mechanisms Oracle maintains to ensure the integrity of your data. For example, when a user starts to change the information in a personnel record, Oracle issues a lock to ensure that no one else can make changes until the first user is finished.

- The *environment* is a section of memory allocated to each session on a computer. This memory contains session-specific information, such as the user's name, the system identifier of the user's database, and a list of directories to search for programs when the user issues a command.

- *ORACLE_HOME* is the location on one of your disks (a directory) under which the Oracle software resides. It is defined at installation time, and it becomes part of the environment as Oracle operates.

- When you inspect a series of characters (say, the text ahdjek9kk) for the occurrence of one or more characters (say, k9), the characters you are looking for are referred to as the *lookup string*.

- The *optimizer* is a set of internal Oracle routines that decides the most efficient access path to your data. These routines are run when Oracle is trying to arrive at the most efficient way to access data to satisfy an SQL statement.

- A *unique* or *primary key* refers to one or more column values in a table that can uniquely identify each row in a table. Picture a primary key as one's social insurance number, used by the Canadian government to identify each resident of Canada (even though a study once found over 700 people had the same social insurance number—guess the Department of Employment and Immigration was not using Oracle then!). For one or more columns to be a primary key, the values cannot be duplicated anywhere else in the table's data.

- A *host character* is placed in an SQL*Plus program to drop back to the operating system to issue a command. Execution of the SQL script is suspended until the operating system command completes. You are then returned to SQL*Plus.

Optimization

Advanced application tuning requires an understanding of how Oracle optimizes SQL statements. Oracle uses one of two approaches to accomplish this. With the rule-based approach, Oracle ranks data access path efficiency in accordance with a set of rules. With the cost-based approach, which is the Oracle8 default, Oracle examines the data in one or more tables in the SQL statement and selects the access path that will cost the least (that is, that will use the least resources and take the least amount of time).

NOTE
We recommend that, armed with the material we cover in this chapter about the cost-based optimizer (or CBO), you use CBO after gathering statistics on your data using the approach we outline.

VIP
If you are running version 10.7 or lower of the Oracle Applications (such as Financials, HR, or Assets), continue to use the rule-based optimization approach. Very few, if any, routines in the Applications have been tuned using cost-based approaches; the rule-based approach works best with these systems.

By the end of this section, you will understand the advantages of each approach and have a good feel for which one you should use.

The Cost-Based Approach

When using the cost-based approach, Oracle optimizes an SQL statement to cost the least. "C," "B," and "O" were once some of the three most dreaded letters a technically savvy Oracle software professional could say. Cost-based optimization involves weighing a number of factors that can affect the performance of an SQL statement and arriving at the execution plan that "costs" the least. In this context, cost is a measurement of many factors including the amount of computer resources (such as I/O and CPU consumption) and the time to complete execution. As database administrators update their Oracle environments to use CBO, a number of issues can spring up. Let's highlight some of those issues and allow you to get the best bang for your buck out of this approach.

In some ways, CBO is magic (or seems to be); in other ways, it isn't. When you go out and decide what groceries to buy for yourself and your family, you weigh factors such as cost, appearance, and your like or dislike of certain commodities. For CBO to work its magic, it needs information such as the number of rows in each table, the distribution of keys within a table's primary key column(s), and the number of data blocks allocated to and occupied by the table's rows. The trick to getting this information is deciding how often it should be collected, and ensuring that when the statistics are collected, no errors are encountered. Let's look at the three (actually, there are four, with one cluster-related object we are not covering) data dictionary views whose contents are populated by the statistic collection keyword **analyze**. What follows are the important columns for CBO; since they are part of Oracle's data dictionary, they are never updated manually.

USER_TABLES

num_rows	number
blocks	number
chain_cnt	number
avg_row_len	number
degree	varchar2(10) -- of parallelism
sample_size	number -- size of sample when estimating statistics
last_analyzed	date
partitioned	varchar2(3) -- may optimize differently if partitioned

USER_INDEXES

distinct_keys	number
avg_leaf_blocks_per_key	number -- this and the next give CBO an idea
avg_data_blocks_per_key	number -- of index entry distribution
status	varchar2(8)
num_rows	number
sample_size	number -- if index stats were estimated
last_analyzed	date
degree	varchar2(40)
partitioned	varchar2(3)

USER_TAB_COLUMNS

num_distinct	number
low_value	raw(32) -- column value in second lowest index entry
high_value	raw(32) -- column value in second highest index entry
num_nulls	number -- Oracle8 keeps statistics on NULLs
last_analyzed	date
sample_size	number -- is analysis estimated rather than computed

Gathering Statistics in SQL*Plus

There are many ways to collect statistics for CBO, many of which most readers may be familiar with. I recommend estimating statistics on tables, and computing statistics for indexes. The lock requested for computing statistics is very restrictive, and if it cannot be acquired, the statement will fail with error ORA-00054, as shown next.

```
ORA-00054    resource busy and acquire with NOWAIT specified
Cause:       The NOWAIT keyword forced a return to the command
             prompt because a resource was unavailable for a LOCK
             TABLE or SELECT FOR UPDATE command.
Action:      Try the command after a few minutes or enter the
             command without the NOWAIT keyword.
```

Let's now examine the **analyze** command using a few examples. We recommend estimating statistics on tables according to the following:

1. Estimate statistics for all tables using a sample percentage of rows.

2. Sample using 20 percent of the rows in the table; Oracle randomly selects the rows to include in the sample.

Thus, a few **analyze** statements for a handful of tables resemble

```
analyze table lumberjack estimate statistics sample 20 percent;
analyze table mountie estimate statistics sample 20 percent;
analyze table suspenders estimate statistics sample 20 percent;
```

We recommend computing statistics for all indexes; the following listing shows a few index collection SQL statements.

```
analyze index lumberjack_pk compute statistics;
analyze index mountie_pk compute statistics;
analyze index suspenders_pk compute statistics;
```

Let's look at two SQL statements whose output can be captured and passed to Oracle to analyze tables and indexes in any user's schema.

```
SQL*Plus: Release 8.1.5.0.0 - Production on Sun Jun 30 18:17:36 2002
(c) Copyright 1999 Oracle Corporation.  All rights reserved.
Connected to:
Oracle8i Enterprise Edition Release 8.1.5.0.0 - Production
With the Partitioning and Java options
PL/SQL Release 8.1.5.0.0 - Production
SQL>
SQL> -- Tweak the SQL*Plus environment by suppressing headings,
SQL> -- feedback about number of rows fetched, and echoing of commands
SQL> -- to the screen.
SQL> set pages 0 feed off echo off
SQL> -- Capture output to ana_all.sql
SQL> spool ana_all.sql
SQL> prompt set echo on feed on
SQL> spool ana_all
SQL> select 'analyze table '||owner||'.'||table_name||
  2    ' estimate statistics sample 20%;'
  3    from all_tables
  4    where owner = upper('&1');
SQL>
SQL> select 'analyze index '||owner||'.'||
  2  index_name||' compute statistics;'
```

```
  3    from all_indexes
  4    where owner = upper('&1');
SQL> spool off
```

When this program terminates, you are left with a series of SQL statements written to the file ana_all.sql. Run this in SQL*Plus to collect statistics for the schema defined by the substitution variable passed to the program.

Gathering Statistics Using PL/SQL Procedures

Oracle8*i* introduces a new packaged subprogram called DBMS_STATS belonging to SYS. Dozens of pages are dedicated in the documentation to discussing this package; in this section, let's do a high-level overview to simply get you started, concentrating on the three main parts of DBMS_STATS.

- Gather_schema_stats collects statistics for a whole schema based on the parameters entered.

- Gather_table_stats does the same for the desired table, offering more control if desired over collection of statistics for parts of a schema.

- Gather_index_stats is the lowest level of breakdown in this package for assembling statistics for one or more indexes within a specified schema without touching their corresponding tables.

Gather_schema_stats

The following listing shows the hierarchy of the most common parameters passed to this procedure. Then Table 13-1 discusses some of these parameters in more detail.

VIP
When this procedure is invoked, parameters are accepted in a sequential manner. Thus, if you do not wish to specify a value for a parameter (for example, **degree***), you must pass the keyword* **null** *fifth on the command line.*

```
DBMS_STATS.GATHER_SCHEMA_STATS (
ownname           VARCHAR2,
estimate_percent  NUMBER DEFAULT NULL,
block_sample      BOOLEAN DEFAULT FALSE,
method_opt        VARCHAR2 DEFAULT 'FOR ALL COLUMNS SIZE 1',
degree            NUMBER DEFAULT NULL,
granularity       VARCHAR2 DEFAULT 'DEFAULT',
cascade           BOOLEAN DEFAULT FALSE);
```

Parameter	Default	Notes
Ownname	None	Current schema is analyzed if invoked with **null** keyword.
Estimate_percent	None	If **null** is passed, statistics are computed for the schema rather than estimated.
Block_sample	False	A value of **true** instructs Oracle to build a random sample of blocks rather than rows.
Degree	Degree set for table	Instructs Oracle to gather statistics using the specified number of parallel processes (if one passed) or the same as the table if nothing passed.
Cascade	False	If set to **true**, statistics are gathered on indexes as well as tables within a given schema.

TABLE 13-1. *Important gather_schema_stats Parameters*

The next commented listing looks at two invocations of dbms_stats.gather_schema_stats.

```
dbms_stats.gather_schema_stats ('SPEEDO',null,null,null,null,null,true);
-- Compute statistics for the SPEEDO schema since the second parameter
-- is null. Indexes are included since cascade receives the value true.
dbms_stats.gather_schema_stats ('SPEEDO',20,true,null,2,null,null);
-- Estimate statistics for the SPEEDO schema using a block sample of
-- 20 percent with 2 parallel analysis processes. Do not cascade down
-- to indexes.
```

Gather_table_stats

The next listing shows the expected parameter list when this procedure is invoked. The parameters underlined are the same as those used for gather_schema_stats. Table 13-2 discusses the most used parameters in addition to those these two procedures have in common.

NOTE
The three "stat" parameters in the next listing are not used in most statistic collection exercises and will not be discussed.

Parameter	Default	Notes
Tabname	None	Name of table being analyzed.
Partname	Null	If the table is partitioned, this parameter defines the partition being analyzed.

TABLE 13-2. *Gather_table_stats Parameters*

```
DBMS_STATS.GATHER_TABLE_STATS (
ownname            VARCHAR2,
tabname            VARCHAR2,
partname           VARCHAR2 DEFAULT NULL,
estimate_percent   NUMBER DEFAULT NULL,
block_sample       BOOLEAN DEFAULT FALSE,
method_opt         VARCHAR2 DEFAULT 'FOR ALL COLUMNS SIZE 1',
degree             NUMBER DEFAULT NULL,
granularity        VARCHAR2 DEFAULT 'DEFAULT',
cascade            BOOLEAN DEFAULT FALSE,
stattab            VARCHAR2 DEFAULT NULL,
statid             VARCHAR2 DEFAULT NULL,
statown            VARCHAR2 DEFAULT NULL);
```

Let's look at a few sample calls to gather_table_stats as shown in the next listing.

```
dbms_stats.gather_table_stats ('BEN_OH','CLASSIC',null,20);
-- This will collect statistics on the CLASSIC table in the BEN_OH
-- schema, estimating using a row sample of 20 percent.
dbms_stats.gather_table_stats ('BEN_OH','CLASSIC','VERITABLE');
-- This will collect statistics on the VERITABLE partition in the
-- CLASSIC table in the BEN_OH schema. Since estimate_percent is
-- not passed, it defaults to null, causing statistics to be
-- computed rather than estimated.
```

Before moving on, let's look at one last piece of DBMS_STATS for collection of statistics on indexes.

Gather_index_stats

The next listing shows the arguments when invoking this procedure. The arguments underlined are common to one if not both of the previous two procedures and are not discussed again. The **indname** argument is simply the name of the index on the specified table name in the appropriate schema.

```
DBMS_STATS_GATHER_INDEX_STATS (
     ownname            VARCHAR2,
     indname            VARCHAR2,
     partname           VARCHAR2 DEFAULT NULL,
     estimate_percent   NUMBER DEFAULT NULL,
     stattab            VARCHAR2 DEFAULT NULL,
     statid             VARCHAR2 DEFAULT NULL,
     statown            VARCHAR2 DEFAULT NULL);
```

The next listing illustrates a few usages of the gather_index_stats procedure.

```
dbms_stats.gather_index_stats ('AR','AR_CUSTOMER_TRX_LINES_U1');
-- Statistics are computed for the specified index in the AR schema.
dbms_stats.gather_index_stats ('AR','AR_CUST_LINES_N11','P2000',10);
-- Statistics are estimated for the specified index in the AR schema,
-- only for the P2000 partition, using a 10% row sample.
```

Controlling Usage of CBO

DBAs can control how CBO is used using one of the following approaches:

1. By the instance (that is, for all SQL statements passed to Oracle for processing)—the init.ora entry **optimizer_mode** sets the default optimization approach. Common values are **all_rows**, **first_rows**, and **choose**. Classically, reporting-based applications that work with complete sets of rows as they operate are the best candidates for the first. Screen-based systems in which users retrieve a set of rows but most of the time only work with the first set of those rows are candidates for the second approach. The **choose** keyword causes Oracle to behave according to the following logic:

   ■ If no statistics are available for all tables involved in an SQL statement, Oracle will use the rule-based approach.

   ■ If at least one table involved in an SQL statement has statistics, Oracle will estimate statistics on the fly for the other objects using the **all_rows** goal.

2. By the session—while using SQL*Plus, the **alter session** command is passed to Oracle and the optimizer runs according to the specified approach until either the session ends or another **alter session optimizer_goal** statement is encountered. The next listing illustrates this convention.

```
SQL*Plus: Release 8.1.5.0.0 - Production on Sun Jun 30 18:17:36 2002
(c) Copyright 1999 Oracle Corporation.  All rights reserved.
Connected to:
```

```
Oracle8i Enterprise Edition Release 8.1.5.0.0 - Production
With the Partitioning and Java options
PL/SQL Release 8.1.5.0.0 - Production
SQL> alter session set optimizer_goal = ALL_ROWS;
Session altered.
......
...... Whole bunch of SQL statements
......
SQL> alter session set optimizer_goal = CHOOSE;
Session altered.
SQL>
```

3. By the statement—developers embed hints to the SQL statements they are formatting, using one of two conventions.

- With the /* beginning and */ ending comment block indicators as in

  ```
  select /*+ choose */ name, address ....
  ```

- With the – comment leaders as in

  ```
  select --+ choose
          name, address ....
  ```

These two conventions are identical to one another except that one uses the double-dash facility, which causes any text on the same line to be treated as part of the comment. The funny thing about hints is that they are simply comments, so if one makes a coding error, Oracle gives no notification or syntax error.

Methodology for Statistic Collection

Let's look at a few guidelines about statistic collection that will enable collection and storage of valid, current statistics for CBO. Regardless of how you prefer to collect statistics, intervention may be required from time to time to ensure the operation completes successfully.

GUIDELINE #1
Inspect the listing file produced by the analysis program.

All too many times, we hear of installations painstakingly collecting statistics on objects and not ensuring that the job runs successfully. If one or more objects contain archaic stats, they could adversely contribute to the selection of a nonoptimal execution plan. To assist the process that inspects the listing produced by the analysis job, we suggest doing the following:

1. When building the script that collects statistics, use the semicolon terminator for each statement. This offers more flexibility than the forward slash (/) terminator, as you will see in the next step. In other words, use the convention shown in bold in the next listing rather than that shown in italics.

```
analyze table jess estimate statistics sample 20 percent;
analyze table jess estimate statistics sample 20 percent
/
```

2. Using some text searching software (the example we show uses a freeware **tsearch** program in Windows NT), search the output listing looking for the **analyze** keyword on any lines that are not terminated by the semicolon as illustrated in the following listing. The command **tsearch analyze -e ";" d:\orawork\analyze\ana_all.lst > fail.sql** produced the following output (the **-e ";"** tells **tsearch** to exclude lines found with the text "analyze" and a semicolon):

```
analyze index flounder_pk compute statistics
analyze index bowie_david compute statistics
```

Then the output trapped in fail.sql can be run in SQL*Plus to analyze objects whose statistic collection failed the first time.

GUIDELINE #2
*Use the SQL*Plus method of statistic collection.*

When using SQL*Plus, you end up passing statements to Oracle for each object in the schema individually. The success or failure of one statement has no effect on other statements. When using dbms_stats, it may be all or nothing.

GUIDELINE #3
*Use an automated notification mechanism to ensure
one intervenes when required to ensure all the
desired objects have been successfully analyzed.*

Whether you use a host-based e-mail facility, use a gateway from your server to your office mail system, or run the collection program on a client and then hook output dissemination to the client-based network transport, you must send output from the statistic collection to two or more locations. Do not take for granted that the analyze job ran with 100 percent successful completion.

The Rule-Based Approach

Oracle ranks access paths on a weight of 1 to 15 and then chooses the access path with the lowest rank. Think of ranking as going into a grocery store and inspecting the Granny Smith apples. As you pick them up, you turn them over, look for bruises, and examine the color of the skin. Ones you like the most are ranked with the number "1," whereas those you prefer the least are ranked with the number "15." Just as in the rule-based approach to optimizing, the rank number affects whether the apple is chosen or discarded in favor of one with a better (or lower) rank.

VIP
The material included in this section is discussed briefly in the Oracle8i documentation set. Oracle has done its best to declare rule-based optimization obsolete, while keeping rule-based optimization for systems' backward compatibility.

When retrieving data, Oracle can find the location of a desired row fastest if it knows its rowid (each row can be uniquely identified by its rowid). The rowid provides immediate access to data; it identifies its exact location. Picture the rowid as the address of each piece of data stored in the Oracle database.

Access path rankings are determined by the available indexes and how the SQL statement is worded. Let's look at the most common rule-based access path weights and their meanings. For the next few sections, we will refer to the part of the SQL statement using **where** and one or more instances of **and** as the where/and part of the statement.

VIP
The lower the rank of the access path chosen to satisfy a query, the faster and more efficient the processing.

Rule-Based Access Path Rank 1

This path is available when the **where** keyword equates the rowid to a single value. For example, the statement

```
select *
  from fin_mast
 where rowid = 'AAAADCAABAAAAVUAAA';
```

would be ranked using this weight. In the SQL statements that you write for your applications, you never know rowids, so this path is not explicitly used very often. However, if you are using Oracle tools such as Oracle Forms and you retrieve a row of information onto a screen, its rowid is fetched as well. When you update the row and save the information back to the database, Oracle Forms passes an SQL statement to Oracle using this rowid construct. You may have seen this if you have ever received an Oracle error from Oracle Forms (yes, Oracle errors do happen):

```
Oracle error occurred while executing KEY-COMMIT trigger:
update tabA set name=:nam,address=:addr ........ where rowid=:rowid
```

Oracle knows the rowid of the record on the screen you are attempting to update, and it uses this access path to perform the update.

Rule-Based Access Path Rank 4

This path is available when all columns in a unique or primary key are referenced by your SQL statement in equality conditions. Let's look at the following table:

Column	Part of Primary Key
street_name	Y
house_number	Y
City	N

The SQL statement

```
select *
  from street_master
 where street_name = 'ROBSON'
   and house_number = '2802';
```

could take advantage of this access path; all the columns in the primary key are mentioned in the **where/and**, and they are compared using equality. The SQL statement

```
select *
  from street_master
 where street_name = 'ROBSON'
   and house_number >= '2802';
```

could not take advantage of this access path, since the comparison condition performed on the house_number column is not equality (there is a greater than or equal to comparison). Likewise, the statement

```
select *
  from street_master
 where street_name = 'ROBSON';
```

does not use all the primary key columns in the **where/and** and cannot be ranked with this weight.

Rule-Based Access Path Rank 8
If the statement's **where** clause mentions all the columns in a composite index and performs equality comparisons, this access path will be used. Remember, a composite index is one built on more than one column in a table.

Rule-Based Access Path Rank 9
This access path is used if the **where/and** portion of the SQL statement uses one or more single-column indexes. If more than one single-column index is used, the conditions must be connected with **and**. For example, consider the fin_mast table indexed on fin_id. The following SQL statement uses this access path:

```
select max_out
  from fin_mast
 where fin_id = '1234M';
```

If there is also an index on the fin_rel column of the same table, the following statement will not use this access path, since the conditions are connected using **or**, not **and**.

```
select max_out
  from fin_mast
 where fin_id = '1234M'
    or fin_rel is not null;
```

Rule-Based Access Path Rank 15
The full table scan is used for any SQL statement that does not satisfy the criteria for other weighted access paths. Each record in the table is read sequentially; those that qualify for all selection criteria are chosen, and those that do not are discarded.

The rule-based access path weights not discussed in this section are beyond the scope of this book.

Why CBO Over Rule-Based Optimization
Whether you are a database administrator for an OLTP system or a data warehouse administrator for a decision support system, fluency with the cost-based optimizer is mandatory. In the early days of CBO, installations reported that their SQL queries

were taking longer than they used to using the rule-based approach. We believe that if you systematically analyze your objects and find a robust way to ensure the work is accomplished as planned, CBO will work well for you. If you don't think it is, speak with Oracle about your problems, and, if you have your "house in order," you will find most of the time that CBO works as well if not many times better than its archaic predecessor.

When Oracle7 first appeared in late 1992, the cost-based approach was touted as a dream come true. Developers no longer had to expend much energy optimizing SQL statements. At run time, Oracle would decide an execution plan based on statistics in the data dictionary. Since the cost-based approach is able to optimize statements based on the current data volumes and distribution of indexed column values, execution plans are more dynamic. As the data changes, so will the selected optimal plan.

To help invest in the cost-based approach, Oracle has provided a technique called *hints.* Using hints, you can influence choices made by cost-based optimization and experiment with different access paths to your data. Oracle has done its homework. Users have been provided with a new optimization technique and can now influence Oracle choices by using these hints. We offer the following guidelines to help you choose between the rule-based and cost-based optimization approaches:

■ Applications that have migrated from earlier versions of Oracle (version 6 and earlier offer only rule-based optimization) should be left running rule based.

■ Experiment with the cost-based approach and familiarize yourself with using optimizer hints coupled with new hints in Oracle8*i* that expand on the set of hints used with Oracle7/8.

■ New application development and tuning exercises should use the cost-based approach.

■ Tune SQL statements using the tools we introduce in the next section of this chapter: **explain plan** coupled with a few of the members of the Oracle Expert family of performance monitoring tools embedded in the Oracle Enterprise Manager.

SQL Statement Processing

All SQL statements are processed in three phases—parse, execute, and fetch—regardless of the tool (for instance, Oracle Forms or Oracle Reports) that passed it to Oracle for processing. Let's look briefly at these phases.

Parse

Parse is the most time-consuming of the three phases, and the most costly. In the section of this chapter covering the shared pool, we will discuss ways to avoid parsing SQL statements prior to execution. During this phase, the optimizer does its job of selecting the most efficient access path and execution plan. Using the following SQL statement as an example, let's look at the tasks involved in this phase.

NOTE
This section offers an oversimplified explanation of the parse phase of SQL statement execution. It gives you a flavor of the amount of work involved. It is not the way Oracle directly processes your SQL statements.

```
select a.class_group,descr,sum(mon_amt+tue_amt+wed_amt+thu_amt+
                                fri_amt+sat_amt+sun_amt)
  from timesheets a,classes b
 where a.class_group like 'CS%'
   and a.class_group = b.class_group
group by a.class_group,a.descr;
```

The next four sections illustrate some of the processing required to parse every SQL statement.

Word Meaning

Oracle examines the code from the bottom to the top. It finds different kinds of words in the statement: words it knows as part of its own lingo (such as **select** or **where**), words that refer to your tables and their columns (such as timesheets a or class_grp), and all other miscellaneous words and punctuation (such as commas and parentheses). Table 13-3 outlines the decisions Oracle has to make using the last four lines of the previous listing.

Once Oracle works through the statement, bottom to top, it can start to put the whole thing together. Considering what it found, it deduces the following:

■ The objects in the SQL statement are timesheets and classes, using the aliases "a" and "b," respectively. Therefore, column names using one of those prefixes must reside in the appropriate object.

■ The columns enclosed in parentheses all belong to the timesheets object. Since they are being summed in the statement, they all must be defined as numeric.

	Component	Decision Made	Action Taken
1.	a.descr	Not a reserved word	Store until the prefix "a" can be resolved
2.	a.class_group	Not a reserved word	Store until the prefix "a" can be resolved
3.	by	Reserved word	
4.	group	Reserved word	
5.	b.class_group	Not a reserved word	Store until the prefix "b" can be resolved
6.	a.class_group	Not a reserved word	Store until the prefix "a" can be resolved
7.	and	Reserved word	
8.	'CS%'	Text enclosed in quotes	Nothing more to do
9.	like	Reserved word	
10.	a.class_group	Not a reserved word	Store until the prefix "a" can be resolved
11.	where	Reserved word	
12.	classes b	Not a reserved word	Must be an object name and its alias
13.	timesheets a	Not a reserved word	Must be an object name and its alias
14.	from	Reserved word	

TABLE 13-3. *Parse Phase Decisions*

Resolve Object Names

After learning what it has, Oracle then tries to find out what objects and columns are in the statement. Table 13-4 shows the decisions that must be made. The numbers in the Item(s) column are the component numbers from Table 13-3.

Item(s)	Assumptions	Error If Not True
13	The user must have access to an object called timesheets.	Table or view does not exist
12	The user must have access to an object called classes.	Table or view does not exist
5	The classes table must contain a class_group column.	Invalid column name
10, 6, and 12	The timesheets table must contain a class_group column.	Invalid column name
1	The timesheets table must contain a class_group column.	Invalid column name

TABLE 13-4. *Resolving Object Names*

Syntax Checking

Oracle checks the following to ensure that the statement is syntactically correct:

- **Parentheses:** Some portions require parentheses.

- **Commas:** Members of lists are usually separated from one another by commas.

- **Location of reserved words:** Oracle checks the placement of these words and verifies they are in the proper order and do not appear more times than permitted.

SQL statement syntax is verified, and the objects mentioned in the statement are resolved.

Determination of the Execution Plan and Data Access Path

The execution plan is determined after the optimizer evaluates the available access paths. The choices the optimizer makes are influenced by the tables accessed in the SQL statement and the way the statements are worded. We discussed cost-based and rule-based optimization approaches earlier in this chapter. The execution plan selected by Oracle during the parse phase is influenced by the optimization approach in use.

VIP

*Over 75 percent of application tuning can be
realized by avoiding the parse phase altogether.
By using ready-parsed statements already in
the shared pool, you are more than three-quarters
of the way there.*

As we discussed in Chapter 1, the shared pool consumes a significant part of the memory allocated to running the Oracle database. To use ready-parsed statements in the shared pool, you may need to allocate more memory to the shared pool.

VIP

*You may have to work closely with your database
administrator (DBA) to ensure that there is adequate
space in the shared pool to accommodate an
optimal number of ready-parsed SQL statements.*

Let's spend a little time on the data access path. When the optimizer parses an SQL statement, it evaluates possible access paths in order to use the best access path. To some degree, users can help the optimizer choose an access path through deliberate wording of SQL statements.

Let's use the following scenario to illustrate the concepts of access path and optimizer. Suppose you need to get from Montreal to Boston. Your goals are to realize as little wear and tear on your vehicle as possible, spend as little money as possible, and avoid traffic in any large urban centers along the way. The assortment of possible routes is similar to the access path. As with your data, there is a fixed number of ways to get from one end to the other (for example, if a road has not been built, you cannot include it in your plans). In the midst of selecting the best route, you decide where the fewest bottlenecks are, and you avoid routes that pass through states with higher gasoline prices. You weigh the costs and benefits of each potential route and decide which is best.

With Oracle, this decision-making process is the job of the Oracle optimizer. In more detailed technical discussions of application tuning, we would highlight ways to influence Oracle while it chooses the most efficient access path to your data. For discussions on some of these issues, consult other publications, such as *Oracle8 Tuning* (Corey, Abbey, Dechichio, and Abramson; Osborne/McGraw-Hill, 1997).

VIP

*Oracle chooses the access path that will yield the
fastest results and consume the least amount of
computer resources.*

Execute

The reads and writes required to process the statement are performed during the execute phase. Oracle now knows how it will get at the data (based on the execution plan determined during the parse phase). It knows the optimal access path (as determined during the parse phase), and it is armed with all the information necessary to fetch the data that qualifies based on the selection criteria in the SQL statement. Locks are obtained, as required, if the SQL contains any update or delete operations.

Fetch

All rows that have qualified are retrieved during the fetch phase. If the query requires sorting, this is done now. The results are formatted and displayed according to the query's instructions.

VIP
The golden rule about processing SQL statements is this: parse once, execute many times. By reusing parsed statements in the shared pool, you have made the biggest step toward application tuning.

Naming Variables

You need to adopt a standard convention when naming variables in your programs. Using the same name across SQL statements coupled with the coding conventions discussed in Chapter 1 helps ensure that SQL statements you pass to Oracle will match ones already in the shared pool. When using a tool such as Oracle Forms, you must standardize the names of variables, especially block names. We discuss coding conventions in Chapter 11. The same theory holds when choosing names for variables in your SQL and PL/SQL programs.

When you are programming using Oracle Forms, a block groups a number of fields on the screen together, permitting creation, modification, and deletions to database data. Fields within blocks and the block name together form what is referred to as *bind variables*. Referencing a block name and a field name prefixed by a colon allows direct manipulation of values in fields on a form. Standardizing block names allows SQL statements using these bind variables to match statements already in the shared pool. For example, the first pair of statements in the following listing match, whereas the second pair differ. The same bind variable is used in the first two statements; the latter two may be referring to the same data, but they use different bind variable names.

```
select count(*) into :people.class_count from classif where class_1 =
:people.classif;
```

```
select count(*) into :people.class_count from classif where class_1 =
:people.classif;
select last_name||' '||first_name into :person.full_name from person;
select last_name||' '||first_name into :person.fnam from person;
```

VIP
Even if two bind variables with different names
(such as ":nam" and ":name") hold the same data
(for instance, the name Wilson), they are still treated
as different variables.

TIP
We recommend using block names that match the
table name they refer to. When the same table is
referenced in more than one block in a program,
call the blocks table_name_1 and table_name_2.

What Should Be Indexed?

Where to use indexes is a difficult decision. Using indexes properly contributes to the application tuning process. Toward the end of this chapter, in "Tools of the Tuning Trade," we show you how to assess what indexes are used as your applications operate. Indexes are optional structures maintained by Oracle that provide rapid access to your data. When you create an index, you specify the table name and one or more columns to keep track of. Once an index is created, Oracle maintains it automatically as data is created, changed, and deleted from your tables. The following rules help you decide when to create indexes:

■ You should index columns that are mentioned in the **where** or **and** sections (also referred to as the predicate) of an SQL statement. Suppose the first_name column in a personnel table is displayed as query results, but never as part of the predicate. The column, regardless of what values it contains, should not be indexed.

■ You should index columns that have a range of distinct values. Here's the rule of thumb: if a given value in a table's column is present in five percent or less of the rows in the table, then the column is a candidate for an index. Suppose there are 36,000 rows in a table with an even distribution (about 12,000 each) of values through one column in the table. The column is not a good candidate for an index. However, if there are between 1,000 and 1,500 rows per column value in another column in that same table (between 3 percent and 4 percent of the rows), then that column is a candidate for an index.

- If multiple columns are continually referenced together in SQL statement predicates, you should consider putting these columns together in an index. Oracle will maintain single-column indexes (those built on one column) or composite indexes (those built on more than one column). Composite indexes are also referred to as concatenated indexes.

Primary Key Constraints

Relational database theory dictates that one or more columns in a table that can uniquely identify each row in that table is the object's *primary key*. Creating primary keys for tables in the Oracle8*i* database assists the application tuning process, since primary key definitions in the data dictionary ensure uniqueness between rows in a table. In addition, this alleviates the need for developers to implement their own individual methods for uniqueness checking.

VIP
Data retrieval using entries stored in a primary key is faster than using an index that does not contain unique values.

Suppose that a person table uses its id column as a primary key, and the constraint has been set up using the code

```
alter table person add constraint person_pk primary key (id)
   using index storage (initial 1m next 1m pctincrease 0)
   tablespace prd_indexes;
```

While processing the following SQL statement:

```
select last_name,first_name,salary
   from person
 where id = 289;
```

Oracle would proceed directly to the person_pk index when looking for a certain id column value. If it did not find the right index entry, Oracle would know the row does not exist. The primary key index offers the following two attractions:

- Since each entry in the index is unique, Oracle knows there can only be one entry with the desired value. If the desired entry is found, the search terminates at once.

- The sequential search of the index can be terminated as soon as an entry greater than the desired one is encountered; if a greater primary key index entry (in this case, anything over 289) is encountered, then the desired entry cannot exist.

Tools of the Tuning Trade

We have discussed SQL statement processing, execution plans, access paths, optimization, and indexes. We now show you how to peek at the contents of the shared pool. Once you know how to inspect the SQL statements in the pool, you can start coding SQL to match the statements already there. Then with a brief introduction to tools supplied with Oracle, you will be armed with enough knowledge to start, or continue, tuning applications. In this section, you will learn details on the following:

- How to issue an SQL statement to display the shared pool contents

- Using **explain plan** and **autotrace** to analyze the access path Oracle chooses to access your data

- How to present output from **explain plan** in a readable, tree-like fashion

- How to use SQL trace and the tkprof utility to report on SQL statement processing and CPU utilization

Seeing What Is in the Shared Pool

So far we have talked (or have we nattered at you on and on!) about the shared pool. We will now take the time to show you how to look around the pool and view its contents. Seeing the current contents of the shared pool may help you to make decisions about standardizing as outlined in this chapter as well as Chapter 11. A data dictionary view called v$sqlarea will serve our purpose. You are interested in a column called sql_text. The following code shows you what is in the shared pool:

```
rem *  The sql_text column is 1,000 characters wide so
rem *  set it to 80 for this display
col sql_text format a80
select sql_text from v$sqlarea where lower(sql_text)
      like lower('%'||'&text'||'%');
```

TIP
When comparing text against the values of the sql_text column in v$sqlarea, force your lookup string and the sql_text column to the same case (using one of the SQL functions lower and upper).

When this is run, you will see something similar to the following (the code you see will, of course, depend on what is happening in your database when the query is issued).

```
SQL> select sql_text from v$sqlarea where lower(sql_text)
  2           like lower('%'||'&text'||'%');
Enter value for text: last_name
old   2:        like lower('%'||'&text'||'%')
new   2:        like lower('%'||'last_name'||'%')
SQL_TEXT
-------------------------------------------------
select last_name||' '||first_name into :person.fname from person
select last_name||' '||first_name into :person.fnam from person
SQL>
```

NOTE
The v$sqlarea view is owned by Oracle user SYS, and you must be granted access to the v$ views manually.

explain plan

This utility inspects the indexes being used during the execution of **select**, **insert**, **update**, and **delete** statements. The output is presented as a list of operations describing the access mode for each table in the statement and the indexes Oracle used during processing. All too often, indexes are created on tables and never get used. The **explain plan** utility is the way to detect which indexes are being used and the indexes you could just as well do without.

VIP
*Before you can run **explain plan**, you must own or have access to a table called plan_table. A script called utlxplan.sql in the %ORACLE_HOME%/ rdbms\admin directory creates this table for you.*

This is how to run **explain plan** on the following SQL statement:

```
select ob.entity entity_code, ob.region region_code,
       r.region_desc_e, r.region_desc_f,
       ob.branch branch_code, b.branch_desc_e, b.branch_desc_f,
       ob.responsibility rc_code, res.rc_desc_e, res.rc_desc_f,
       ob.gl_summary_code, gls.gl_summary_desc_e,
       gls.gl_summary_desc_f,
       ob.fiscal_year, ob.budget_actual_ind,
       ob.budget_version_id,
       ob.period_1, ob.period_2, ob.period_3, ob.period_4,
       ob.period_5, ob.period_6, ob.period_7, ob.period_8,
```

```
       ob.period_9, ob.period_10, ob.period_11, ob.period_12,
       ob.period_13,
       ob.year_1, ob.year_2, ob.year_3
  from nc_operating_budget ob,
       nc_region r,
       nc_branch b,
       nc_responsibility res,
       nc_gl_summary_code gls
 where ob.region = r.region_code
   and ob.branch = b.branch_code
   and ob.responsibility = res.rc_code
   and ob.gl_summary_code = gls.gl_summary_code
   and ob.budget_version_id = '1004'
   and ob.budget_actual_ind = 'B';
```

1. Save the SQL statement to a file by entering the command **save sql_test replace** (we use the filename **sql_test**, but use whatever you want).

2. Edit the file called sql_test.sql and insert the text **explain plan set statement_id = 'statement_id' for** in front of your SQL statement. The **statement_id** is a 1-character to 30-character name used to uniquely identify the code. The file **sql_test.sql** now contains (using a sample statement_id of **ST_ID**):

```
explain plan set statement_id = 'ST_ID' for
select ob.entity entity_code, ob.region region_code,
       r.region_desc_e, r.region_desc_f,
       ob.branch branch_code, b.branch_desc_e, b.branch_desc_f,
       ob.responsibility rc_code, res.rc_desc_e, res.rc_desc_f,
       ob.gl_summary_code, gls.gl_summary_desc_e,
       gls.gl_summary_desc_f,
       ob.fiscal_year, ob.budget_actual_ind,
       ob.budget_version_id,
       ob.period_1, ob.period_2, ob.period_3, ob.period_4,
       ob.period_5, ob.period_6, ob.period_7, ob.period_8,
       ob.period_9, ob.period_10, ob.period_11, ob.period_12,
       ob.period_13,
       ob.year_1, ob.year_2, ob.year_3
  from nc_operating_budget ob,
       nc_region r,
       nc_branch b,
       nc_responsibility res,
       nc_gl_summary_code gls
 where ob.region = r.region_code
   and ob.branch = b.branch_code
   and ob.responsibility = res.rc_code
```

```
         and ob.gl_summary_code = gls.gl_summary_code
         and ob.budget_version_id = '1004'
         and ob.budget_actual_ind = 'B';
```

3. Run the following SQL script (we call it **expl.sql**) by entering the command **@expl statement_id**, using the statement_id name from when you loaded your SQL into the plan_table:

```
rem *  File name: expl.sql
spool expl
select decode(id,0,operation||' Cost = '||position,
        lpad(' ',2*(level-1))||level||'.'||position)||' '||
        operation||' '||options||' '||object_name||' '||
        object_type Query_plan
   from plan_table
connect by prior id = parent_id
     and statement_id = upper('&1')
   start with id = 0 and statement_id = upper('&1');
spool off
```

4. Interpret the output in the file expl.lst.

NOTE
The name of the file is based on the spool statement in the code shown in the previous listing. The filename extension .lst may be different on your platform.

The next listing shows the output of the statement loaded in this exercise. The two operations in the listing are

■ Hash join is one of many mechanisms Oracle8*i* uses when tables are joined together. It involves building a list of matching column values in memory and using that structure to assemble rows from the tables that qualify based on the query's election criteria.

■ Table access full is the act of scanning a table's columns from start to finish, reading every row one after another.

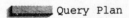Query Plan
```
-----------------------------------------------------------------
   SELECT STATEMENT    Cost = 620
     2.0 HASH JOIN
       3.1 TABLE ACCESS FULL NC_BRANCH
       3.2 HASH JOIN
```

```
4.1 TABLE ACCESS FULL NC_REGION
4.2 HASH JOIN
   5.1 TABLE ACCESS FULL NC_GL_SUMMARY_CODE
   5.2 HASH JOIN
      6.1 TABLE ACCESS FULL NC_RESPONSIBILITY
```

VIP

*As you become more experienced with **explain plan**, you will notice that some operations almost always appear with each other. For example, prior to most index range scans, you will find a table access by rowid operation.*

Using set autotrace

set autotrace provides a more automated way of using **explain plan** with your SQL statements. The process of explaining statements was streamlined starting with release 7.3 of Oracle using the **autotrace** feature. The next listing shows the format of the set command to start autotracing your SQL.

```
SQL> set autotrace
Usage: SET AUTOT[RACE] {OFF | ON | TRACE[ONLY]} [EXP[LAIN]]
[STAT[ISTICS]]
```

Note how the command can be abbreviated to **set autot**. To set the SQL environment to automatically trace statements, issue the command **set autotrace on**. If you receive the following error message, you will have to ensure you have access to a plan_table to allow the set command to succeed.

```
SQL> set autotrace on
SP2-0613: Unable to verify PLAN_TABLE format or existence
SP2-0611: Error enabling EXPLAIN report
```

When the **set autotrace** command succeeds, you will get no feedback from Oracle. Now after each statement is issued, Oracle will produce trace output similar to that shown in the following session.

NOTE

We have cut out the results of the query and simply shown the output displayed as a result of autotrace being turned on.

```
SQL*Plus: Release 8.1.5.0.0 - Production on Sun Jun 30 18:17:36 2002
(c) Copyright 1999 Oracle Corporation.  All rights reserved.
Connected to:
Oracle8i Enterprise Edition Release 8.1.5.0.0 - Production
With the Partitioning and Java options
PL/SQL Release 8.1.5.0.0 - Production
SQL> select ob.entity entity_code, ob.region region_code,
  2          r.region_desc_e, r.region_desc_f,
  3          ob.branch branch_code, b.branch_desc_e, b.branch_desc_f,
  4          ob.responsibility rc_code, res.rc_desc_e, res.rc_desc_f,
  5          ob.gl_summary_code, gls.gl_summary_desc_e,
  6          gls.gl_summary_desc_f,
  7          ob.fiscal_year, ob.budget_actual_ind,
  8          ob.budget_version_id,
  9          ob.period_1,ob.period_2,ob.period_3,ob.period_4,
 10          ob.period_5,ob.period_6,ob.period_7,ob.period_8,
 11          ob.period_9,ob.period_10,ob.period_11,ob.period_12,
 12          ob.period_13,ob.year_1, ob.year_2,ob.year_3
 13     from nc_operating_budget ob,
 14          nc_region r,
 15          nc_branch b,
 16          nc_responsibility res,
 17          nc_gl_summary_code gls
 18    where ob.region = r.region_code
 19      and ob.branch = b.branch_code
 20      and ob.responsibility = res.rc_code
 21      and ob.gl_summary_code = gls.gl_summary_code
 22      and ob.budget_version_id = '1004'
 23      and ob.budget_actual_ind = 'B';


Execution Plan
----------------------------------------------------------
   0      SELECT STATEMENT Optimizer=CHOOSE (Cost=620 Card=5989
          Bytes=2084172)
   1    0   HASH JOIN (Cost=620 Card=5989 Bytes=2084172)
   2    1     TABLE ACCESS (FULL) OF 'NC_BRANCH'
              (Cost=1 Card=24 Bytes=960)
   3    1     HASH JOIN (Cost=602 Card=5989 Bytes=1844612)
   4    3       TABLE ACCESS (FULL) OF 'NC_REGION'
                (Cost=1 Card=13 Bytes=520)
   5    3       HASH JOIN (Cost=586 Card=5989 Bytes=1605052)
   6    5         TABLE ACCESS (FULL) OF 'NC_GL_SUMMARY_CODE'
                  (Cost=2 Card=140 Bytes=12180)
   7    5         HASH JOIN (Cost=511 Card=5989 Bytes=1084009)
   8    7           TABLE ACCESS (FULL) OF 'NC_RESPONSIBILITY'
                    (Cost=28 Card=2745 Bytes=310185)
   9    7           TABLE ACCESS (FULL) OF 'NC_OPERATING_BUDGET'
                    (Cost=218 Card=5989 Bytes=407252)
```

```
Statistics
------------------------------------------------------------
      6077  recursive calls
      1083  db block gets
      3676  consistent gets
       288  physical reads
    143064  redo size
    788276  bytes sent via SQL*Net to client
     45007  bytes received via SQL*Net from client
       395  SQL*Net roundtrips to/from client
         1  sorts (memory)
         0  sorts (disk)
      5872  rows processed
```

SQL Trace and tkprof

These facilities provide performance information on SQL statements. It reports on times spent on the parse, execute, and fetch phases of statement execution. One Oracle technique that allows applications to perform well is the capability to keep significant amounts of data and data dictionary information in memory. As they operate, your applications will find a large part of the information they need in memory. If application-specific information can be found in memory, the I/O involved to retrieve that information can be bypassed. SQL trace also informs you of the percentage of logical reads (those satisfied by memory reads) and physical reads (those satisfied by reads from disk). To use SQL trace and tkprof, one of the following must be done:

1. Ensure the timed_statistics entry in your initialization parameter file is set to true, or enter the following command in SQL*Plus:

   ```
   alter session set timed_statistics = true;
   ```

NOTE
*If this parameter is not set to **true**, change it and then restart the database to activate the changed value.*

2. Enter the text **alter session set sql_trace = true;** at the top of your SQL program.

3. Run the SQL program to produce a trace file to be fed to tkprof. For this exercise, the name of the trace file is ora00140.trc.

NOTE
The location of the trace file is defined by the initialization parameter file entry user_dump_dest. For help finding the name of the trace file, see the next section, "Finding Which Trace File Is Yours."

4. Run the command **tkprof ora00140.trc output=ora00140.out explain=system/manager** to produce formatted SQL trace output.

5. Examine the output produced by tkprof. You then begin to see how much time Oracle is spending retrieving your data. When tkprof output is coupled with explain plan, you are presented with formatted output similar to the following (with the "..." representing text we cut from the output trace file).

```
TKPROF: Release 8.1.5.0.0 - Production on Mon Jul 6 20:47:48 2009
(c) Copyright 1999 Oracle Corporation.  All rights reserved.
Trace file: ora00140.trc
Sort options: default
*************************************************************
count    = number of times OCI procedure was executed
cpu      = cpu time in seconds executing
elapsed  = elapsed time in seconds executing
disk     = number of physical reads of buffers from disk
query    = number of buffers gotten for consistent read
current  = number of buffers gotten in current mode
           (usually for update)
rows     = number of rows processed by the fetch or execute call
*************************************************************
alter session set sql_trace=true
call     count    cpu elapsed disk query current  rows
-------  ------  ----- ------- ---- ----- -------  ----
Parse        0   0.00    0.00    0     0       0     0
Execute      1   0.00    0.00    0     0       0     0
Fetch        0   0.00    0.00    0     0       0     0
-------  ------  ----- ------- ---- ----- -------  -----
total        1   0.00    0.00    0     0       0     0
Misses in library cache during parse: 0
Misses in library cache during execute: 1
Optimizer goal: CHOOSE
Parsing user id: 5  (SYSTEM)
*************************************************************
alter session set timed_statistics=true
```

```
call      count      cpu elapsed disk query current  rows
-------   ------    ----- ------- ---- ----- ------- ----
Parse         0     0.00    0.00    0     0       0     0
Execute       1     0.00    0.00    0     0       0     0
Fetch         1     0.00    0.00    0     0       0     0
-------   ------    ----- ------- ---- ----- ------- -----
total         2     0.00    0.00    0     0       0     0
Misses in library cache during parse: 1
Optimizer goal: CHOOSE
Parsing user id: 5  (SYSTEM)
****************************************************************
BEGIN DBMS_APPLICATION_INFO.SET_MODULE(:1,NULL); END;
call      count      cpu elapsed disk query current  rows
-------   ------    ----- ------- ---- ----- ------- ----
Parse         2     0.01    0.03    0     0       0     0
Execute       2     0.02    0.02    0     0       0     2
Fetch         0     0.00    0.00    0     0       0     0
-------   ------    ----- ------- ---- ----- ------- -----
total         4     0.03    0.05    0     0       0     2
. . .
. . .
select ob.entity entity_code, ob.region region_code,
       r.region_desc_e, r.region_desc_f,
       ob.branch branch_code, b.branch_desc_e, b.branch_desc_f,
       ob.responsibility rc_code, res.rc_desc_e, res.rc_desc_f,
. . .
. . .
   and ob.budget_version_id = '1004'
   and ob.budget_actual_ind = 'B'
call      count      cpu elapsed disk query current  rows
-------   ------    ----- ------- ---- ----- ------- ----
Parse         1     0.07    0.07    0     0       0     0
Execute       2     0.00    0.00    0     0       0     0
Fetch       393     2.29    3.24  288  1718     602  5872
-------   ------    ----- ------- ---- ----- ------- -----
total       396     2.36    3.31  288  1718     602  5872
Misses in library cache during parse: 1
Optimizer goal: CHOOSE
Parsing user id: 5  (SYSTEM)
Rows      Row Source Operation
-------   -------------------------------------------------
   5872   HASH JOIN
     24    TABLE ACCESS FULL NC_BRANCH
   5872   HASH JOIN
     13     TABLE ACCESS FULL NC_REGION
```

```
  5872     HASH JOIN
   140       TABLE ACCESS FULL NC_GL_SUMMARY_CODE
  5872       HASH JOIN
  2745         TABLE ACCESS FULL NC_RESPONSIBILITY
  5872         TABLE ACCESS FULL NC_OPERATING_BUDGET
    10    SORT ORDER BY
    10     FILTER
    11      FIXED TABLE FULL X$KSUSESTA
     2       SORT AGGREGATE
   196        FIXED TABLE FULL X$KSUSD
 . . .
 . . .
 Rows    Execution Plan
 -------  ---------------------------------------------------------
     0    SELECT STATEMENT    GOAL: CHOOSE
  5872     HASH JOIN
    24       TABLE ACCESS    GOAL: ANALYZED (FULL) OF 'NC_BRANCH'
  5872       HASH JOIN
    13         TABLE ACCESS    GOAL: ANALYZED (FULL) OF 'NC_REGION'
  5872         HASH JOIN
   140           TABLE ACCESS    GOAL: ANALYZED (FULL) OF
                   'NC_GL_SUMMARY_CODE'
  5872           HASH JOIN
  2745             TABLE ACCESS    GOAL: ANALYZED (FULL) OF
                     'NC_RESPONSIBILITY'
  5872             TABLE ACCESS    GOAL: ANALYZED (FULL) OF
                     'NC_OPERATING_BUDGET'
 . . .
 . . .
Trace file: ora00140.trc
Trace file compatibility: 7.03.02
Sort options: default
     1   session in tracefile.
    13   user  SQL statements in trace file.
   581   internal SQL statements in trace file.
   594   SQL statements in trace file.
    23   unique SQL statements in trace file.
     5   SQL statements EXPLAINed using schema:
           SYSTEM.prof$plan_table
             Default table was used.
             Table was created.
             Table was dropped.
  5459   lines in trace file.
```

The technical ins and outs of this output are too much to handle in this book. Suffice it to say that, by looking at the Parse, Execute, and Fetch lines that appear in bold type, you can get a grasp of how your SQL statements are performing. Run tkprof, examine the results, and try to get the times for the three processing phases to an absolute minimum.

Finding Which Trace File Is Yours

Picture yourself figuring out which trace file to use for tkprof. You go to the directory where the trace files are deposited and find hundreds of files all starting with ora_ and ending with .trc. You issue the directory command for your operating system and sit back and watch the show—screens and screens of filenames. Use the following technique to help you find which trace file is yours. The simple "dir" command is used on NT followed by inspection of the output for the appropriate time and date of the desired trace file. Most of the time, you will end up sending the output to a file with the "> {file_name}" convention.

```
C:\Oracle\Admin\O8ibegin\Udump> date
The current date is: Mon 07/06/2009
Enter the new date: (mm-dd-yy)
C:\Oracle\Admin\O8ibegin\Udump> dir *.trc
 Volume in drive C is PINK_FLOYD
 Volume Serial Number is 2627-1D06
 Directory of C:\Oracle\Admin\O8ibegin\udump
03/20/09  09:21a      <DIR>          .
03/20/06  09:21a      <DIR>          ..
04/25/06  11:47a              26,092 ORA00076.TRC
07/06/09  10:35a             330,848 ORA00140.TRC
02/05/09  04:05a               1,559 ORA00206.TRC
01/32/09  11:35p               1,559 ORA00296.TRC
               4 File(s)        30,769 bytes
                     231,523,089,408 bytes free
C:\Oracle\Admin\O8ibegin\Udump>
```

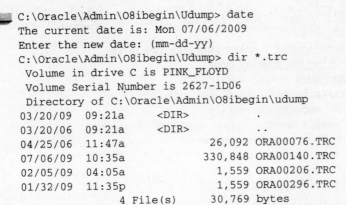

VIP

*If you turn on sql_trace during testing and program development, make sure the **alter session** statement is removed before the programs are turned over to the users. Forgetting to remove them can be disastrous! The statement will end up generating many, many megabytes of trace files.*

What's Next

A wealth of information is available in technical publications, newsletters, magazines, and books on Oracle to help you get the most out of your applications. One of life's golden rules is so applicable when working with Oracle: do it right the first time. In an earlier book, *Oracle8 Tuning*, the following sentiments were quoted:

- You know, one of the things I like so much about Oracle is that it is so tunable.

- You know, one of the things I hate so much about Oracle is that it is so tunable.

When it comes to tuning your applications, you will find this to be all too true. By reading the likes of Chapters 9, 11, and 12, we trust that you have become better equipped to write efficient Oracle applications using Oracle Developer and use some more sophisticated SQL syntax. In subsequent chapters of this book, you will read details on important database administrator (DBA) duties and round out your understanding of Oracle8*i*. We touch on database tuning, which, alongside application tuning discussed here and in Chapter 11, provides for optimal system performance and efficient use of your computer's resources.

CHAPTER 14

DBA 101

n this chapter, we will discuss what you need to know to become a database administrator (DBA). The work of the DBA contributes to the effective operation of all systems that run with the Oracle database. The DBA offers technical support to everyone and is expected to become fluent in all technical issues that arise with the Oracle software. The DBA is responsible for the following:

- Day-to-day operations of the Oracle database

- Installation and upgrades of Oracle software

- Performance tuning

- Backup and recovery strategies

- Consultation with data administration personnel

- Consultation with developers

We will show you the main tool of the trade—Oracle Enterprise Manager. With this tool, we will show you how to do the following:

- Start the database

- Shut down the database

- Create new users

- Drop existing users

- Create tablespaces

- Add more space to a tablespace

We will lead you through some important concepts and guide you through the DBA's job using code samples. We will introduce some new terminology and then use those technical terms as part of the DBA lingo in the rest of the chapter. This is designed to be an introduction, so we will not get into much technical detail. If you have problems, or if procedures do not work as expected, something may be wrong with your configuration or the way the Oracle8*i* software has been installed. Chapter 18 covers these and some additional topics in more detail.

Becoming a Database Administrator

You may have already worked with Oracle as a developer, also called a programmer or programmer analyst. Or you may be starting from scratch with Oracle. As you become a DBA, you will find yourself becoming the focal point for all your installation's Oracle issues. The major components of your new role include the following responsibilities:

- Installation and upgrades of the Oracle Server and all its associated products

- Allocation of resources to support Oracle, including memory, disk space, and user account management, to name a few items

- Backup and recovery

- Tuning the Oracle database for optimal performance

- Liaising with Oracle Worldwide Customer Support to deal with technical issues requiring Oracle's intervention

- Staying current with Oracle's emerging product line and with new additions that may complement your existing applications

At the end of this chapter, you will have the knowledge to start working as a DBA. We strongly recommend that you read this book cover to cover, paying special attention to the following chapters that are of special interest to the DBA:

- Chapter 4
- Chapter 6
- Chapter 16
- Chapter 17
- Chapter 18

We also recommend reading *Oracle8 Tuning* by Corey, Abbey, Dechichio, and Abramson (Osborne McGraw-Hill, 1997) and the *Oracle8 DBA Handbook* by Kevin Loney (Osborne McGraw-Hill, 1997). These two works will enhance your understanding of the DBA role and will help you become an effective DBA. Both cover important issues such as the architecture of the Oracle database, database design, application tuning, and DBA roles and responsibilities. In this chapter, we are going to discuss some theory related to the DBA's work load, and then look at some examples using Oracle Enterprise Manager 2.0 and Server Manager.

Terminology

The following definitions will arm you with the technical jargon you need to make it through this chapter.

■ *GUI* (graphical user interface) programs allow users to interact with them by clicking an assortment of icons, menus, check boxes, radio buttons, and so on. Products such as MS Word, WordPerfect for Windows, and Personal Oracle8*i* are GUI based.

■ An *instance* is a set of support processes and memory allocated for accessing an Oracle database. Throughout your experience as a DBA, you will hear the terms Oracle instance and Oracle database. Use these two terms synonymously.

■ *Startup* is the action of placing an Oracle instance in a state that allows users to access the database to carry on their business. Startup initiates processes required for users to access the database, and it reserves a portion of your computer's memory within which Oracle operates.

■ The command *connect internal* with the appropriate password information, logs you in to the database as Oracle user SYS. One accesses the database in this fashion to perform activities such as startup and shutdown.

■ *Shutdown* is the action of taking an Oracle instance from a state that allows users to access the database to a dormant state; when the database is shut down, we say that it is closed. Shutdown terminates the processes required for users to access the database, and it releases the portion of your computer's memory within which Oracle was operating.

■ A *user name* is assigned to people when they require access to the Oracle database. It is also referred to as one's logon ID.

■ A *password* accompanies every user name and must be supplied to Oracle to connect to the database.

■ A *user* is associated with a person that is allowed access to an Oracle database. Many people are familiar with logging in to a local area network at work by entering accounting information with a user name and password.

■ A *role* is a logical grouping of one or more Oracle users who end up performing similar tasks while they work with Oracle data. Suppose a handful of users in personnel required the same set of privileges to work with sensitive data that no other user had access to. You would group these users together in a role and make these people members of that role.

■ A *profile* is a set of resource consumption limits assigned to users of the Oracle database. Unless they are restricted by the DBA, users automatically have no limits on the resources they can consume so that they are not prevented from completing their day-to-day work.

■ A *job* is a set of one or more computer programs that perform a task. If you use Microsoft Word, you could say that saving your word processing document is a job.

■ *O/S* is a short form for operating system. An operating system is a collection of programs that permit a computer to manage the flow of information between its processor, peripherals (for instance, keyboard, screen, and hard disk), and memory.

■ *Batch* is a facility available on most mini- and mainframe computers that runs jobs for you unattended; the jobs are submitted to batch using an O/S-specific command. As batch jobs execute, they do not tie up your screen and terminal.

■ A *tablespace* is a container for data in an Oracle database. It is made up of one or more datafiles, whose size and component locations are dictated by the DBA. This phenomenon is called *space management*.

Oracle Enterprise Manager— A Quick Tour

This product, affectionately referred to as *OEM*, first appeared with Oracle 7.3 and has developed into a solid database administration tool—and then some. Since this is the first time we have really had a look at it, let's take a few minutes to look at what OEM can do for you, the database administrator. When OEM was installed on your machine, you had to choose a location for the software, other than the ORACLE_HOME used by the Oracle8*i* database. We selected the folder called C:\Oracle\Oem20 and will use this throughout the samples contained in this chapter.

The OEM Console

Prior to OEM release 2.0, DBAs connected to the Enterprise Manager and used a user-dependent repository. That repository was simply a set of Oracle database objects within which management data was stored, as well as configuration preferences. With the onslaught of centralized management of a wide variety of Oracle8i databases on a distributed network, OEM 2.0, this organization has changed. Now an administrator superuser called SYSMAN is created, and other users are enrolled using the System|Manager Administrators option off the menu bar at the top of the console. The screen that is displayed when the OEM console is opened is shown in Figure 14-1.

Notice the tree-like structure under the OEM Navigator. Let's have a look at the three folders displayed in the upper-left pane of the OEM main console, two of which are displayed in Figure 14-1:

- The Databases folder, when expanded, shows many of the types of objects that we end up working with using some of the DBA Management Pack tools discussed in the next section. OEM uses the standard Windows interface with "+" and "−" signs to indicate what has been or is capable of being expanded or collapsed. Lower in the Databases folder, you can manipulate schema objects owned by anyone in the database, expanding

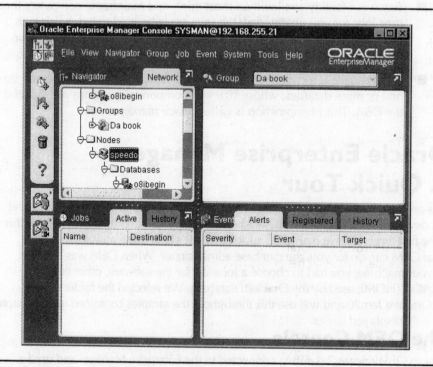

FIGURE 14-1. *The OEM main console*

tabs to display information on objects by user. A right-click on most items in expanded lists brings up options for further manipulation of that object. In Figure 14-1, if a node were selected in the Nodes folder, a right-mouse button would display the databases within the responsibility of the person using OEM. You can then connect to or disconnect from the selected database, run a related tool against that instance, or invoke a backup or data management interface tool.

■ The Groups folder is where you can define groups of targets; some installations may choose to define those groups based on the name of the Administrator, whereas others may decide to group by geographical location of the servers in the network.

■ The Nodes folder is where each server in the network is registered, along with the one or more databases that reside on each node.

As you open the OEM Main Console and start to go through the definition process, thereby populating the tree displayed in Figure 14-1, you will notice many n-way relationships between the branches in the tree and their subordinate folders. For example, the Databases folder defines an Oracle instance (such as prd.world or aob.world), and when the Nodes folder is expanded, it may show node "oaghp1" with a Databases folder beneath defining the same two instances. It's time to move on to the tools in the DBA Management Pack. Afterward, we will guide you through a number of activities using these very tools. Before getting started with OEM (some people say "Don't start with OEM!"), take a brief look at the user interface. Here are a few highlights, referencing Figure 14-1:

■ The four icons in the upper left-hand corner of the screen are fast paths to expanding the like-positioned pane in the main console. They can be used to hide or show each of the four panes; they are toggled by clicking each. As you work more with OEM 2.0, you will find you spend more time with some panes than others. The shortcut keys CTRL-SHIFT-X can also be used, where the "X" refers to N for Navigator, E for Event, J for Jobs, and G for Group.

■ The arrow configuration at the top right-hand corner of each pane is a toggle, switching between full-screen and windowed for each pane.

■ The ellipses (...) between each pair of panes vertically and horizontally are the familiar Windows resizing handles, used to change the dimensions of displayed panes.

■ The upper icon of the two on the left side of the console can be used for quick access to one of the subordinate managers (that is, Security, Schema, Instance, Storage, or Worksheet).

Roll up your sleeves—soon it will be time to get to work.

DBA Management Pack Tools

Here is where you will spend most of your time as the DBA; like it or not, the GUI interface is very powerful and is used more widely than many of its predecessors. The Start Menu|Oracle Oem20 options include the following DBA tools:

- Instance Manager is where you perform administrative activities on the database such as shutdown, startup, and session monitoring. You can tweak configurations for the initialization parameter file (many times referred to as "init.ora") and resolve pending transaction conflicts in a distributed Internet computing environment.

- Schema Manager is where you work with the assortment of objects in the Oracle8*i* repository such as tables, indexes, triggers, and views, to name a few. Through the Tools menu at the top of the manager's console, you can access the Export, Import, and SQL*Loader tools. We do not use the Schema Manager in this chapter; its main console is shown in Figure 14-2.

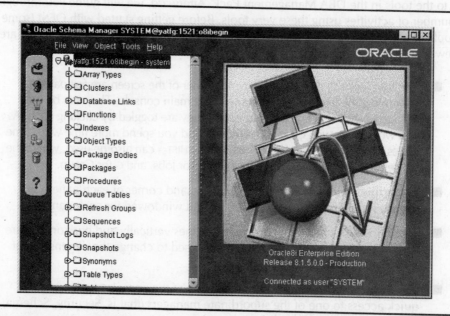

FIGURE 14-2. *The Schema Manager main console*

NOTE
The OEM Console must be open for some of the DBA Management Pack tools to be used in release 2.0.4, featured in this section and elsewhere in this book.

■ Security Manager is where you, the DBA, work with users, roles, and profiles. Basically, a *user* can be thought of as a Username/Password combination that is allowed to connect to the Oracle8*i* database. A *role* is a logical grouping of one or more users and can be the target of the granting of privileges to work with data in the database. A *profile* is a set of limits that can be defined and given out to control resource consumption by users as they interact with the Oracle8*i* instance.

■ Storage Manager is where DBAs work with the assortment of objects that make up the infrastructure of the Oracle8*i* database. You will more than likely spend most of your time here interacting with the Tablespace and Datafile folders. A *tablespace* is a container of one or more data files within which all Oracle data resides.

■ SQL*Plus Worksheet is where the DBA interacts with the database somewhat like using SQL*Plus itself, as discussed in Chapters 7 and 12. The startup screen for the SQL*Plus Worksheet is shown in Figure 14-3.

VIP
*Not all of the SQL*Plus commands mentioned in Chapters 7 and 12 work in SQL*Plus Worksheet. Most formatting commands (like **column** and **format**) do not work in SQL*Plus Worksheet as they do in SQL*Plus.*

Invoking Oracle Enterprise Manager

OEM is started from the Windows NT Start menu, or by clicking the appropriate icon in the Oracle Enterprise Manager folder. There are two ways to invoke OEM—one, by connecting to a defined management server, the other, directly to a remote database. The connection information required for either is different. Let's look at the two methods and the information they require.

Connecting to an Oracle Management Server

The Oracle Management Server (or *OMS*) must be configured before connections will succeed. The configuration exercise may need to be carried out by an

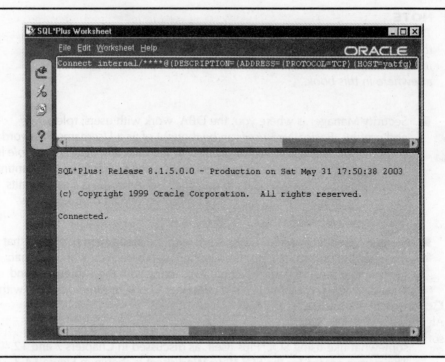

FIGURE 14-3. *The SQL*Plus Worksheet*

experienced DBA in your installation, or by someone who has successfully carried out the activity before for OEM 2.0.

VIP

The error dialog "VTK –1000: unable to connect to management server XXXX. Please verify that you have entered the correct name and status of the Oracle Management Server" indicates the OMS is not properly configured.

If the OMS is properly configured and able to accept connection requests, supply the following information to access the service:

■ Beside Administrator, enter the administration management name for connecting to the specified OMS. You are not actually hooking up to a database; rather, you are logging in as an administrator of network resources being serviced by an instance of OMS. The default administrator delivered with OEM 2.0 is **sysman**.

■ Password is where you enter just that. The default password for **sysman** is **oem_temp**.

NOTE
*You may be prompted to change the password for **sysman** the first time you log in if you use the default password **oem_temp**.*

■ Management Server is where you enter the name of the node upon which the OMS is running. You may pick from a list of management servers if such a list exists, by clicking the screen's icon shown underneath the Management Servers dialog box in Figure 14-4.

Connecting Directly to a Database Instance
Although connecting directly does not offer access to more than one database, sometimes it seems to be the preferred connection method to OEM. By contrast,

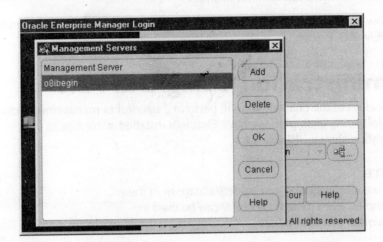

FIGURE 14-4. *Defining management servers*

since OMS offers access to network resources defined in that server configuration, it enables multiple database access. When you connect directly to a database, you are asked for the following information:

- **User name** is where you enter the name of the user whose account you use to connect to the database.

- **Password** is the password that was assigned when the user was created.

- **Service** refers to a connect string to be used to hook up to a remote database.

VIP
Using either the Net8 Configuration Assistant or Net8 Easy Config, you will have to successfully create a Net8 alias for the database to which you will be connecting before accessing OEM in the specified fashion. If you cannot do this, ask a more senior person for assistance or speak with Oracle Worldwide Customer Support.

- **Connect As** refers to the mode with which you wish to log in to the repository. Most of the time, you select the "Normal" option, though the SYSOPER and SYSDBA options in the drop-down menu are used to perform startup and shutdown, for example.

Whew! That was a handful. Let's get on with the work at hand—administration using OEM 2.0. Enjoy!

Administration Using OEM 2.0

In this section of the chapter, we will perform a handful of management activities. For the following examples, we have Oracle8i installed according to the configuration shown in Table 14-1.

NOTE
We are administering an Oracle8i database in these examples, even though OEM 2.0 can be used to administer pre-8i databases.

Item	Details
Folder where database is installed (i.e. ORACLE_HOME)	C:\Oracle\Ora81
Node name of NT machine	yatfg
Database identifier (i.e., ORACLE_SID)	o8ibegin
Internal password	Oracle

TABLE 14-1. *Location and Identification Information*

Start Up the Database

The tool we use for this activity is the Instance Manager. Invoke the tool, and get ready to supply appropriate login information. Enter the following login information:

1. Beside Username, we entered **internal** as the account with which to connect to the database.

2. Beside Password, we entered **oracle**, though it may be different if you have changed the password.

3. Beside Service, we entered **yatfg:1521:o8ibegin** to describe the target database to which we wish to connect.

4. Beside Connect as, we selected SYSDBA from the pick list.

VIP
*Since we are attempting to start a database, you must Connect as either **SYSDBA** or **SYSOPER**. We connected directly to the database for these exercises, not to the Oracle Management Server.*

After entering login information as the Instance Manager is invoked, do the following to start the Oracle8*i* database:

1. Double-click the Database icon to bring up the screen shown in Figure 14-5. The red light reflects the status of the database. If you were to bring

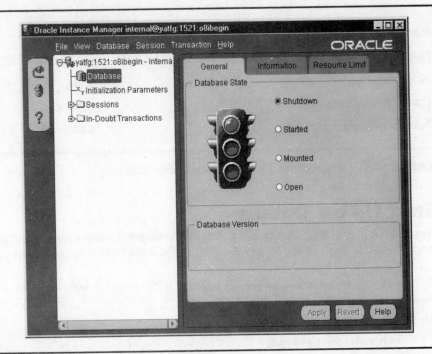

FIGURE 14-5. *Instance Manager database status*

up the Information tab of this folder, you would be told that the database is not mounted, and there is no SGA information for the same reason.

2. Select Started from the General tab of this folder, and then click Apply to proceed.

3. When presented with the Startup Options dialog box, next, you will probably see the Local parameter file option selected, with the text "<local init.ora>" filled in beneath. Click Browse and locate the appropriate initialization parameter file. Enter **C:\Oracle\Ora81\DATABASE\inito8ibegin.ora** as the startup filename.

4. Click OK to proceed. If the name you entered for the Local parameter file is not valid (for instance, if the file is not located where you are telling the Instance Manager), you will be informed in an alert box. After the instance is started, dismiss the information box that appears, and you will be returned to the screen shown in Figure 14-5, except in this case the green light will be on with Started selected by default.

5. Leave the Instance Manager by clicking the Exit-X in the top-right corner of the screen, or by composing the standard Windows close hot key combination ALT-F4.

The database is now open and available for user connections.

Shut Down the Database

This task is similar to the previous one, save for the activity at hand. Perform steps 1 and 2 as in the "Startup the Database" section. When the General tab appears, it will indicate that the database is Started. This is shown in Figure 14-6.

To shut down the database, do the following:

1. Select Shutdown, and click Apply to carry on.

2. When the Shutdown Options dialog box appears, ensure the Immediate option is selected, and then click OK to proceed.

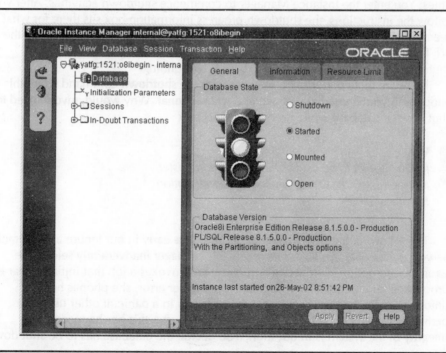

FIGURE 14-6. *Instance status with the database started*

NOTE
A discussion of the Shutdown options follows immediately after this exercise. It is best not leave this stone unturned long after these options are first mentioned.

3. After the Shutdown progress is dismissed, click OK to return to the General tab.

4. Leave the Instance Manager by clicking the Exit-X or pressing ALT-F4.

The database is now closed and inaccessible to the regular user community.

Shutdown Options/Problems
Shutting Down the Database

Early into your tenure as a DBA, you may run across a situation we have seen many times: You enter the Instance Manager to commence shutdown activities. After you follow the instructions, the shutdown progress information box sits there for what seems like an eternity. You are tempted to (and in many cases do) proceed to the NT Task Manager and end the Instance Manager task abnormally. Since the shutdown did not complete, the database is left running.

There are three options you may use with the **shutdown** command when this happens to you: **immediate**, **abort**, and **transactional**. Why would anyone need to shut down a database while users are connected?

VIP
*If you happen to be using OEM 2.0 to administer a pre-Oracle8 database, the **Transactional** option is not available.*

The following incident happened to one of us early in our tenure as an Oracle Server professional: An accounts receivable manager inadvertently selects the wrong menu option from her system menu and invokes a job that initiates year-end processing for a number of accounts. Noticing her error, she phones her IT (Information Technology) contact, who calls you in a panic. If other users are permitted to carry on with their regular business after this has happened, the integrity of the system is in question. You decide the database has to be shut down immediately before more harm is done. You log in to the OEM Instance Manager, and then commence shutdown, and guess what—mouse cursor hourglass syndrome! You return to your O/S and ask for a program status for the machine, and you find out that 17 users are logged in to the database doing various things.

CAUTION
*When any users are logged in to the database, you cannot close that database using the **shutdown** command without using the **immediate**, **abort**, or **transactional** option.*

Let's look at these three shutdown options.

Immediate Option

This is done by selecting **Immediate** in the Shutdown Options dialog box. The database will not close at once—after Oracle performs some cleanup, the database will shut down. The sessions that were accessing the database are terminated gracefully, and any resources in use by those sessions are methodically freed up. When Oracle completes this work, the database will be shut down. Think of shutdown immediate as a small child's caregiver carrying the youngster up to bed, reading to the child, preparing the blanket and pillow, and then putting the child to bed and leaving the room.

NOTE
*Shutdown with the selection of **Immediate** is the most common way you will shut down your database when a normal shutdown does not work. The length of time for a **shutdown immediate** to complete depends on the number of users on the database when the command is issued. Be patient.*

Abort Option

This is done by selecting **Abort** in the Shutdown Options dialog box. The database will close at once. The sessions that were accessing the database are terminated abruptly. Think of that child in the previous scenario. **Shutdown abort** is like walking up to that same child, pointing your index finger up at the stairs, and saying "*Go to bed, now.*"

CAUTION

Shutdown abort should be used as a very last resort. You may wish to get some advice from colleagues before using this command.

With this advice in mind, there are definitely situations in which you will have to use **shutdown abort**; you will have to use it from time to time when the need arises.

NOTE

*After doing **shutdown abort**, you may wait less than a minute, a few minutes, or as much as a few hours for the database to respond after initiating a startup activity in the Instance Manager. If your database has not started in what you feel is "an expected amount of time," speak with a skilled colleague or Oracle before taking corrective action.*

The amount of time it takes the database to restart after a shutdown abort is an extension of what was going on (that is, the number of users connected and how much activity they were in the midst of doing) when the **shutdown abort** command was issued.

VIP

*On a number of occasions, we have seen a database take six to eight hours to start after a **shutdown abort** was issued when there was a great deal of activity.*

Transactional Option

This Oracle8-only feature asks for an amount of time in seconds and then waits that specified length of time before shutting the database. If the time is left blank in the Shutdown Options dialog box, the Instance Manager will wait until the last database transaction completes before finishing the shutdown activity.

Enough said about shutdown—let's look at some operations with users in the OEM Security Manager.

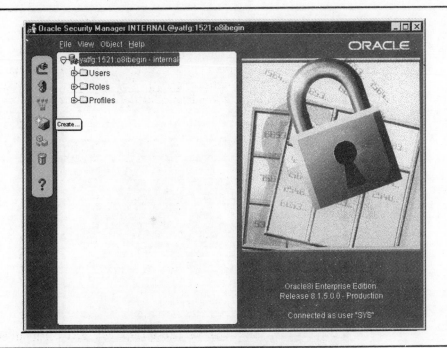

FIGURE 14-7. *Starting the user create process in the Security Manager*

Granting Access to a User

Enabling access is accomplished from the Security Manager using, in this case, the Create icon, as shown in Figure 14-7. This is the Security Manager main console, from which you can create, modify, or remove Users, Roles, or Profiles. Let's get started.

1. Click the Create icon to bring up a dialog box asking exactly what it is you want to create—a profile, a role, or a user.

2. Highlight User, and click Create to continue. This will bring up the Create User dialog box, as shown in Figure 14-8. Notice that there are five tabs to this folder. The discussion in this section is limited to the General folder.

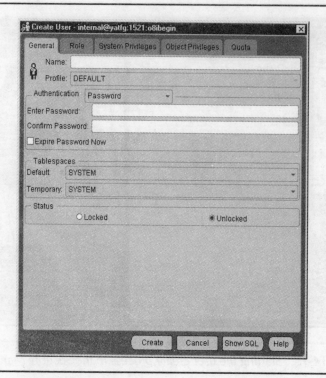

FIGURE 14-8. *The Create User dialog box*

3. Enter the Name **polly**.

4. Tab down to the Enter Password field, and enter the text **gone**. After that data entry is complete, ensure that the Profile is still set to DEFAULT and that the Authentication is still set to Password.

5. In the Confirm Password field, enter the same text, **gone**.

6. Accept the Default Tablespace suggested of SYSTEM, and then bring up the drop-down menu and one from the Temporary Tablespace list and select TEMP. This is shown in Figure 14-9. A *default tablespace* can be set up for users so that they can create objects in that tablespace without having to specify one. A *temporary tablespace* is used when a user needs to sort data for satisfying a query or perhaps build some intermediary tables during the assembly of query results.

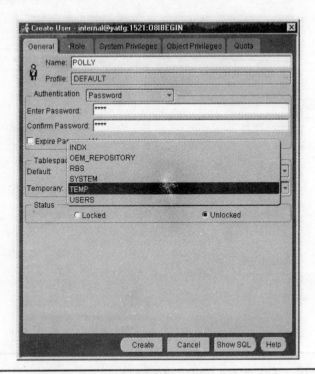

FIGURE 14-9. *Assigning a temporary tablespace*

VIP
Set up a dedicated temporary tablespace and point users there for sorting rather than using the SYSTEM tablespace.

7. Proceed to the System Privileges tab, and scroll down to CREATE SESSION in the Available privileges.

8. Click the down arrow as shown in Figure 14-10 to transfer CREATE SESSION to the Granted box.

9. Click Create to finish, and then acknowledge the information displayed when the user has been successfully created. When you are returned to the

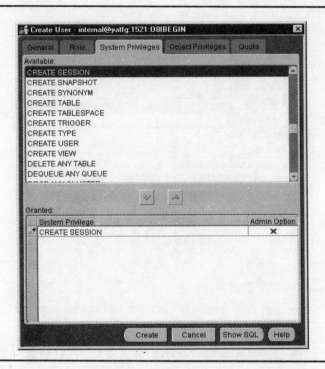

FIGURE 14-10. *Giving out system privileges*

Users folder in the Security Manager's main console, you will see that polly
exists, with an account status of OPEN, an expiry date of NONE,
authentication type PASSWORD, default tablespace SYSTEM, and
temporary tablespace TEMP.

10. Leave the Security Manager by clicking the Exit-X or ALT-F4.

User polly can now connect to the database. The SQL that we just passed to the
database using the Security Manager was pretty much the same as **create user polly
identified by gone;** followed by the statement **grant create session to polly;**. If you
were to have selected the Show SQL option, you would have seen SQL statements
resembling those in the next listing.

```
CREATE USER "POLLY" PROFlLE "DEFAULT" IDENTIFIED BY "GONE"
DEFAULT TABLESPACE "SYSTEM" TEMPORARY TABLESPACE "TEMP" ACCOUNT UNLOCK;
GRANT CREATE SESSION TO "POLLY";
GRANT "CONNECT" TO "POLLY";
ALTER USER "POLLY" DEFAULT ROLE ALL;
```

VIP
At this point, the user will be able to connect only to the database within which he or she was created. If you manage more than one database in OEM, the user must be created manually in each instance.

Revoking Access from a User

Again, revoking access is done in the Security Manager. After successfully connecting to the manager, you have a number of different ways to accomplish this task. Let's look at one of them:

1. Double-click the Users folder to display a list of users on the right pane in the Security Manager main console.

2. Right-click the user to be removed, in this case, POLLY.

3. Select the Remove option from the drop-down menu displayed, as shown in Figure 14-11.

4. When presented with the remove user dialog box, click Yes to complete this activity.

NOTE
If the user to be removed owns objects in the database, you will be reminded and must confirm that you want the user's objects removed as well.

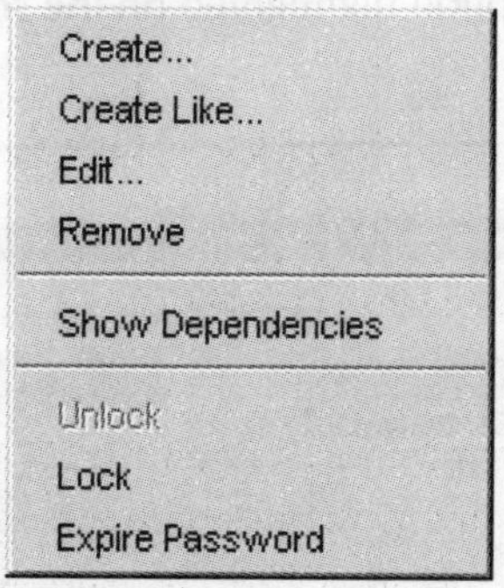

```
Create...
Create Like...
Edit...
Remove

Show Dependencies

Unlock
Lock
Expire Password
```

FIGURE 14-11.   *Starting the drop user activity*

5. Click the Exit-X to leave the Security Manager.

User polly's access to the database is now removed. This is the same as issuing an SQL statement similar to **drop user polly;**. If, for whatever reason, polly created any tables in the SYSTEM tablespace since the account was created, when trying to remove access to the database, you will be presented with the dialog box shown in Figure 14-12.

There are two ways to deal with this situation:

1. Click Yes in the dialog box shown in Figure 14-12, keeping in mind that the CASCADE option the text refers to will cause all the objects in the polly schema to be dropped as well before the user account is removed.

2. Run off to SQL*Plus and manually drop all objects belonging to polly, and then return to the Security Manager and attempt to remove polly once more.

Creating a Tablespace

This is accomplished using the OEM Storage Manager. In this exercise, we are going to create an empty tablespace using two datafiles. After connecting to the Storage Manager, do the following:

1. Click the "+" sign to expand the Tablespaces folder. This is for information purposes only, not required for this activity.

2. Right-click Tablespaces, and then select Create from the drop-down menu that appears. This will bring up the dialog box shown in Figure 14-13.

3. Enter the name **my_data1** for the name of the tablespace. Since the tablespace will hold tables, not being solely used for temporary objects, we leave the Permanent option highlighted on the screen.

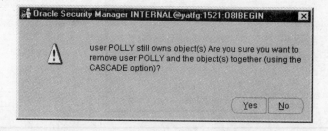

FIGURE 14-12. *The objects belonging to user warning*

FIGURE 14-13. *The Create Tablespace dialog box*

4. Since this is a new tablespace, no information will be displayed in the Datafiles section of the screen. Click Add to start defining the datafiles that will come together to make up the tablespace.

5. When the dialog box appears, enter the filename **p:\oracle\oradata\ o8ibegin\my_data1_1.dbf** or one using your own naming convention. The filename we entered may be different than what you use on your server.

VIP
Even though the filenames mean nothing to Oracle, it is wise to give the database files names corresponding to the tablespace to which they belong.

6. Move to the Size field, and enter the number **10**.

7. Click KBytes to bring up the drop-down menu shown in Figure 14-14, and select MBytes. This means we are adding a 10MB datafile to the new tablespace. Then click OK.

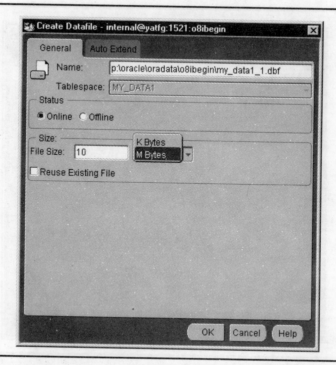

FIGURE 14-14. *Selecting a space measurement for the new tablespace*

8. Go through the same exercise but enter the filename **j:\oracle\oradata\ o8ibegin\my_data1_1.dbf** as the filename this time, with a size as well of **10** and a measurement of MBytes.

9. Click Create to finish this exercise; when returned to the Storage Manager main console to edit the MY_DATA1 tablespace we have just created, you should find its characteristics to be as shown in Figure 14-15.

10. Leave the Storage Manager by clicking the Exit-X or ALT-F4.

Adding Space to an Existing Tablespace

This activity is accomplished much in the same way that the tablespace was originally created and the first datafile defined. Here we go:

1. Right-click the tablespace name on the Storage Manager main console. Select Edit on the drop-down menu that appears.

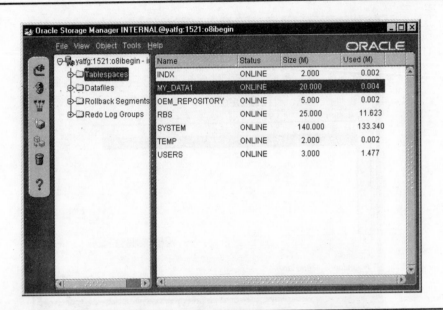

FIGURE 14-15. *Tablespace MY_DATA1 details*

2. When the dialog box appears as shown in Figure 14-16, click the Add button to specify details about the datafile being added to MY_DATA1.

3. When the datafile characteristics dialog box appear as shown in Figure 14-14, enter the new datafile name **x:\oracle\oradata\o8ibegin\ my_data1_2.dbf**.

4. Specify **10** as the size, using MBytes as the unit of measurement.

5. Click OK to return to the tablespace definition screen.

6. Click Create to finish adding the additional datafile to the MY_DATA1 tablespace.

7. Leave the Storage Manager by clicking the Exit-X or ALT-F4.

Now, that was a mouthful, n'est-ce pas? Speaking of mouthfuls, see if you can get your hands around using Server Manager as discussed in the next section of this chapter.

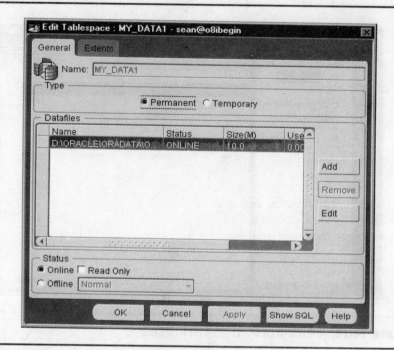

FIGURE 14-16. *Adding space to the MY_DATA1 tablespace*

Server Manager

This tool runs on any terminal, regardless of its capability to support graphics. You can run jobs unattended using line-mode Server Manager, which has been bundled with the Oracle Server for the past few releases. Many DBAs prefer using Server Manager rather than OEM—you decide. To run Server Manager, open an MS-DOS window via the Start | Programs | MS DOS Prompt or by Start | Run | *cmd* on the Start menu.

NOTE
The commands shown in bold in this section are operator entered and must be terminated with a semicolon to begin execution.

While working with Server Manager, sometimes you get "stuck" when it displays a series of numbers on the screen when you are tying to type in subsequent lines in a command to be executed. The next listing shows you what to do about this.

```
Oracle Server Manager Release 3.1.5.0.0 - Production
(c) Copyright 1997, Oracle Corporation.  All Rights Reserved.
Oracle8i Enterprise Edition Release 8.1.5.0.0 - Production
With the Partitioning and Java options
PL/SQL Release 8.1.5.0.0 - Production
SVRMGR> select
    2>
    3>
    4> /
*
ORA-00936: missing expression
SVRMGR>
```

An even cleaner way to deal with this is to enter a period or dot on a line by itself. Control will be passed back to the Server Manager prompt without the Oracle error, as shown in the previous listing.

VIP
The internal password we are using in this section is
oracle. If you have changed yours from this default,
use the password you changed it to instead.

Invoking

The command **svrmgrl** starts Server Manager and displays the following output:

```
Oracle Server Manager Release 3.1.5.0.0 - Production
(c) Copyright 1997, Oracle Corporation.  All Rights Reserved.
Oracle8i Enterprise Edition Release 8.1.5.0.0 - Production
With the Partitioning and Java options
PL/SQL Release 8.1.5.0.0 - Production
SVRMGR>
```

VIP
The name of the program that runs Server Manager
with pre-Oracle8i may, depending on the platform
you are using, differ from svrmgrl. For example, with
release 8.0 on NT, the command was svrmgr30.

connect internal

After starting Server Manager, enter **connect internal/oracle**; Oracle responds with

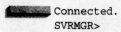

```
Connected.
SVRMGR>
```

You must connect to the Oracle database to perform all operations in Server Manager. If you simply enter the command **connect internal** without a password, Oracle will prompt for the password and not echo the entry to the screen.

Startup

After starting Server Manager, follow these steps:

1. Enter **connect internal/oracle**.

2. Enter **startup**. Oracle responds with the following:

```
ORACLE instance started.
Database mounted.
Database opened.
Total System Global Area        4393640 bytes
             Fixed Size           46112 bytes
          Variable Size         3929736 bytes
       Database Buffers          409600 bytes
          Redo Buffers            8192 bytes
SRVRMGR>
```

The database is now started. We also refer to the database as being open or up after this activity completes successfully. Using Server Manager to start your database is actually a three-step process—the **startup** command performs three distinct steps, as listed here:

```
startup nomount
alter database mount;
alter database open;
```

As you start your database with Server Manager, if any step in the startup process abends (that is, does not complete successfully), the database is left in the condition it was in when the last step successfully completed. What follows is an example of how this difference can affect your clients and what to do about it. Let's say your production database is shut down every morning at 2:00 A.M. for system backups. After the backups complete, you start the database with the command svrmgrl @startup_prd.sql. The startup_prd.sql file has the code

```
connect internal
startup
exit
```

In the morning, the users start logging in to the database and receive the following error message:

```
ERROR: ORA-01033: ORACLE initialization or shutdown in progress
```

You attempt to connect to the database, but you get the same message. For some reason, one of the three operations Server Manager has performed during startup has aborted, leaving the database in its previous state. Perhaps the alter database mount operation has failed, and the database has been left unmounted.

NOTE
*If you use Server Manager to start your database, rather than using the **startup** command, you may wish to enter the three commands **startup nomount**, then **alter database mount;**, then **alter database open;** separately, receiving feedback from Oracle as shown in the next listing.*

```
Oracle Server Manager Release 3.1.5.0.0 - Production
(c) Copyright 1997, Oracle Corporation.  All Rights Reserved.
Oracle8i Enterprise Edition Release 8.1.5.0.0 - Production
With the Partitioning and Java options
PL/SQL Release 8.1.5.0.0 - Production
SVRMGR> startup nomount
ORACLE instance started.
Total System Global Area                       36437964 bytes
Fixed Size                                        65484 bytes
Variable Size                                  19521536 bytes
Database Buffers                               16777216 bytes
Redo Buffers                                      73728 bytes
SVRMGR> alter database mount;
Statement processed.
SVRMGR> alter database open;
Statement processed.
SVRMGR>
```

Shutdown

After starting Server Manager, follow these steps:

1. Enter **connect internal/oracle**.

2. Enter **shutdown**. Oracle responds with the following:

```
Database closed.
Database dismounted.
ORACLE instance shut down.
SVRMGR>
```

The database is now closed. In this example, we simply coded **shutdown** by itself without any of the options discussed in the section "Shutdown Options/Problems Shutting Down the Database," earlier in this chapter. If we were to use one of those options (that is, **immediate** or **abort**), the results would be the same.

Exiting

To exit, enter **exit** at the SVRMGR> prompt. Oracle responds with

```
Server Manager complete.
```

Granting Access to a User

To set up a new user, start Server Manager and then follow these steps:

1. Enter **connect internal/oracle**.

2. Enter the command **grant connect to polly identified by gone;** and receive the response from Oracle:

```
Statement processed.
SVRMGR>
```

3. Enter the command **grant create session to polly;** and receive the same response from Oracle.

4. Enter **exit** to leave line-mode Server Manager.

In this example, *polly* is the user name and *gone* is the password. Thus, user polly may connect to the database after supplying the password *gone*.

Dropping a User

After starting Server Manager, follow these steps:

1. Enter **connect internal/oracle**.

2. Enter the command **drop user polly;** and receive Oracle's response:

```
Statement processed.
SVRMGR>
```

3. Enter **exit** to leave Server Manager.

When this completes, polly will no longer be able to access the database. If polly owns any objects when the **drop user** command is executed, you will receive the Oracle error shown in the next listing; simply add the **cascade** word to the **drop user** command, and the user will be dropped after the objects are removed.

```
SVRMGR> drop user polly;
*
ORA-01922: CASCADE must be specified to drop 'POLLY'
```

NOTE
*There are other ways to revoke access to the database from users; familiarize yourself when necessary with the **drop user cascade** SQL statement to be used where appropriate.*

Creating a Tablespace

After starting Server Manager, follow these steps:

1. Enter **connect internal/oracle**.

2. Enter the command **create tablespace my_index1 datafile 'g:\oracle\ oradata\o8ibegin\my_index1_1.dbf' size 20m, 'i:\oracle\oradata\ o8ibegin\my_index1_2.dbf' size 20m;** and receive the following response from Oracle:

```
Statement processed.
SVRMGR>
```

3. Enter **exit** to leave line-mode Server Manager.

We have created a 40MB tablespace, split between two equal-sized 20MB datafiles. Every time you start the database, it will now acquire the my_index1 tablespace.

Adding Space to an Existing Tablespace

We will now add another 10 megabytes (10,485,760 bytes) of space to the my_index1 tablespace. When this completes, we will have a total of 60MB allocated. After starting Server Manager, follow these steps:

1. Enter **connect internal/oracle**.

2. Enter the command **alter tablespace my_index1 add datafile 'x:\oracle\oradata\o8ibegin\my_index1_3.dbf' size 20m;** and receive feedback from Oracle:

```
Statement processed.
SVRMGR>
```

3. Enter **exit** to leave Server Manager.

The my_index1 tablespace now has an additional 20MB. You will probably use Server Manager from day one. It works everywhere and provides a quick method of accomplishing many DBA-related tasks. Time to wrap this one up and move on.

What's Next

Armed with the routines we examined in this chapter, you now know how to work with some of the Database Management Pack tools in the Oracle Enterprise Manager, as well as Server Manager, to perform the following tasks:

- Connect to the database
- Start up the database
- Shut down the database
- Grant access to a user
- Revoke access from a user

■ Create a tablespace

■ Add space to an existing tablespace

This is enough to get started, and this is also what you will have to do beginning with day one. To find out more about the DBA working with the Oracle database, read Chapter 18. Happy DBAing! Our next saga will take us down the export and import road. As you move from Oracle neophyte to intermediate beginner, these two utilities will become part of your Ora-psyche almost immediately. Get to know them—they are two of your best friends.

CHAPTER
15

Export and Import

xport and import are the most widely used utilities supplied with the Oracle software. All DBAs, whether seasoned or just getting started, need to be fluent with these two utilities. In Chapter 16, we discuss the role they play in making copies of your Oracle data. Knowing how to use them and why to use them (see the "What Export and Import Can Do for You" section in this chapter) will help further your understanding of Oracle as a whole. There are a number of ways to run export and import:

- In a DOS window, using the command **exp** or **imp**, and supplying parameters and values that dictate the nature of the activity being carried out.

- From the Oracle Enterprise Manager (*OEM*) console, by invoking the Schema Manager and then the Export or Import wizard.

NOTE
Since this is a hands-on chapter, you may not find that everything works exactly as shown in the following pages. There is setup that has to be done to enliven some of the screens and allow your activities to succeed. As Oracle8i matures, unfortunately it gets more complex, requiring some technical intervention before a lot of the new bells and whistles work.

We cover both approaches in this chapter, with the DOS window approach first, followed by the OEM wizard-based scenario.

NOTE
We believe the old-fashioned way, that is, using the DOS window to manually type commands and supply parameters and values, offers a more well-rounded foundation for export and import.

In the balance of pages in this chapter, we will discuss the following:

- Uses for export and import

- Similarities and differences between export and import

- Methods of operation

■   Modes of operation

■   Error handling and problem-resolution techniques

Terminology

The following definitions will arm you with the technical jargon you need to make it through this chapter.

■   A program runs *interactively* when it enters into a series of questions requiring the operator's response.

■   Programs are said to be *parameter driven* when you code a number of keywords and supply values for each parameter when the program is invoked.

■   An *instance* is a separate set of processes and memory structures required to support an open Oracle database.

■   An *extent* is a chunk of space in a tablespace that Oracle allocates to tables when they require additional space for new or changed data.

■   *Defragmenting* a table is a process whereby you take all the data from all the extents allocated to the table and pack it into one larger extent. Figure 15-1 shows what defragmentation involves.

■   *Roles* are used by Oracle to group user accounts together and thereby empower a collection of users to manipulate data or perform restricted activities with the database.

What Export and Import Can Do for You

Export and import empower the DBA and application developers to make dependable and quick copies of Oracle data. Export (invoked using the command **exp**) makes a copy of data and data structures in an operating system file. Import (invoked using the command **imp**) reads files created by export and places data and data structures in Oracle database files. These two handy utilities are used primarily in these ways:

■   As part of backup and recovery procedures (refer to Chapter 16 for details).

■   For moving data between different instances of Oracle. You may export data from your production database and use import to move all or part of the data in that export file into your development database.

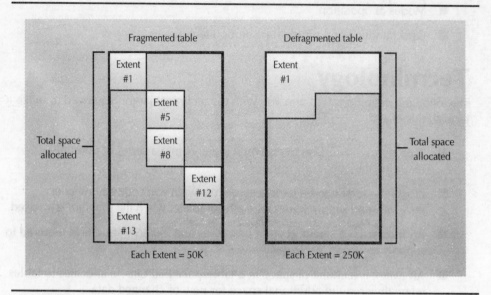

FIGURE 15-1. *Defragmenting extents allocated to a table*

■ To move all or part of a user's data from one tablespace to another. Suppose userA has data residing in two tablespaces, tablespaceA and tablespaceB. You could move all of the data out of tablespaceB and place it in tablespaceA using export and import.

NOTE
There must be enough space in tablespaceA to accommodate the data being moved from tablespaceB. Import itself will not always add additional disk space to tablespaceA if it is not already there.

■ When the need arises to rebuild an existing database, export and import are the only way to preserve the current database data before it is re-created.

NOTE
After performing a full database export, a number of SQL statements and some additional SQL scripts have to be run before the new database is ready for import to reinstate the database's data.

Similarities Between Export and Import

Export and import behave in the same way, and learning one of the two will put you more than 80 percent of the way to mastering both products. These two tools are similar in the following ways:

- Both can be run interactively or can read run-time parameters from a file.

- Both accept keywords (parameters started with keyword_value=) or positional parameters (those that mean something based on their order on the command line).

- Both work with Oracle read-only copies of data and data structures.

- Both are used to move data among different Oracle accounts and hardware platforms.

Differences Between Export and Import

Even though export and import are similar, there are some differences. Some parameters are used only with export; others, only with import. For example, the **fromuser** and **touser** parameters are only used with import. Likewise, the **compress** parameter is only coded when using export. These parameters are discussed in the "Parameter-Driven Export" and "Parameter-Driven Import" sections in this chapter.

- Import may report on a wide assortment of Oracle errors, since it is creating and loading data into Oracle database files.

- Export is sensitive to the amount of free space on a disk drive to which the export file is being written.

Even though these differences exist, export and import methods and modes of operation are the same. These two areas are the subject of the next two main sections in this chapter.

Methods of Operation

The methods we are about to discuss apply to export and import. Learning and experimenting with different methods is part of your job as a DBA. In this section, we will discuss

- Invoking interactive export with no parameters

- Invoking interactive import with no parameters
- Answering prompts to lead to the ultimate success of import and export
- Running parameter-driven export and import
- Using the **parfile** keyword parameter
- Mixing interactive and parameter-driven methods

When running export and import interactively, Oracle presents you with a list of questions. With export, the answers you give to those questions affect what is written to the export file. With import, these answers affect what data is retrieved from the export file. When export and import are parameter driven, you instruct Oracle what you want written to or read from the export file by means of values supplied with these parameters. Think of the parameter-driven method as a form you fill out when requesting reimbursement for expenses from a health insurance company; the questions you answer can affect the amount of coverage you are permitted. Later in this chapter, we discuss parameters that can be fed to export and import.

Interactive Export: Invoking with No Parameters

The next listing shows an example of the dialog between export and the user when export is invoked without any parameters.

```
C:\> exp
Export: Release 8.1.5.0.0 - Production on Tue Jun 1 14:17:47 2003
(c) Copyright 1999 Oracle Corporation.  All rights reserved.
Username: richard/head
Connected to: Oracle8i Release 8.1.5.0.0 - Production
With the Java option
PL/SQL Release 8.1.5.0.0 - Production
Enter array fetch buffer size: 4096 > 102400
Export file: EXPDAT.DMP >
(1)E(ntire database), (2)U(sers), or (3)T(ables): (2)U > t
Export table data (yes/no): yes >
Compress extents (yes/no): yes >
Export done in WE8ISO8859P1 character set and WE8ISO8859P1 NCHAR
                character set
About to export specified tables via Conventional Path ...
Table(T) or Partition(T:P) to be exported:
            (RETURN to quit) > dw_nhappening
. . exporting table          DW_NHAPPENING          1998544 rows exported
Table(T) or Partition(T:P) to be exported: (RETURN to quit) >
Export terminated successfully without warnings.
```

You are asked to supply the information in the Meaning and Response column of Table 15-1 before Oracle commences the export.

VIP
*When defragmenting a table, answer **yes** to the compress extents prompt.*

Prompt Received from Oracle	Meaning and Response
Username	The user name and password of the person running the export.
Enter array fetch buffer size	The size of the chunk of memory to use as a work area while export writes data to the export file. Normally, one enters values between **10240** (also called 10k) and **10485760** (also called 10m).
Export file	The name of the export file. Defaults to expdat.dmp but can be changed.
(2)U(sers), or (3)T(ables)	Oracle wants to know which method you wish to run. You will be asked for names of one or more users if you choose 2 or the names of one or more of your own tables if you answer 3.
Export table data (yes/no)	Instructions on what to write to the export file. Oracle always writes SQL statements necessary to create exported objects to the export file. Answering **yes** to this prompt tells Oracle to export the data in the objects as well.
Compress extents (yes/no)	Oracle wants to know if the **create table** statements written to the export file should include an initial space request capable of holding all the existing table data.
Table(T) or Partition(T:P) to be exported	The name of the table or partition name of a partitioned table to be exported.

TABLE 15-1. *Dialog When exp Is Invoked with No Parameters*

Interactive Import: Invoking with No Parameters

The next listing illustrates an Oracle8*i* dialog when invoking import without any parameters.

```
C:\> imp
Import: Release 8.1.5.0.0 - Production on Tue Jun 1 14:27:47 2003
(c) Copyright 1999 Oracle Corporation.  All rights reserved.
Username: richard/head
Connected to: Oracle8i Release 8.1.5.0.0 - Production
With the Java option
PL/SQL Release 8.1.5.0.0 - Production
Import file: EXPDAT.DMP >
Enter insert buffer size (minimum is 8192) 30720>
Export file created by EXPORT:V08.01.05 via conventional path
import done in WE8ISO8859P1 character set and WE8ISO8859P1
                NCHAR character set
List contents of import file only (yes/no): no >
Ignore create error due to object existence (yes/no): no > yes
Import grants (yes/no): yes >
Import table data (yes/no): yes >
Import entire export file (yes/no): no > yes
. importing RICHARD's objects into RICHARD
. . importing table      "DW_NHAPPENING"       1998544 rows imported
Import terminated successfully without warnings.
```

You are asked to supply the information in the Meaning and Response column in Table 15-2 before Oracle commences the import.

VIP
*If you answer **no** to the ignore create errors due to object existence prompt, then Oracle will not bring the table data in for tables that exist. Nearly all the time, you will answer **yes** to this prompt.*

How Answers to Prompts Affect Further Dialog

After using export and import interactively, you will notice that the chain of questions that follow your responses depends on your answers. In the last listing, we responded **yes** when asked if we want to import the entire export file. Suppose

Prompt Received from Oracle	Meaning and Response
Username	The user name and password of the person running the import.
Import file	The name of the file you want to import to read. Defaults to expdat.dmp but can be changed.
Enter insert buffer size (minimum is 4096)	The size of the chunk of memory to use as a work area while import writes data to the database. Normally, one enters values between **10240** (also called 10k) and **10485760** (also called 10m).
List contents of import file only (yes/no)	Oracle will list the SQL statements written to the import file if you answer **yes**. If you answer **no**, import will bring the data and data definitions into the database.
Ignore create error due to object existence (yes/no)	Oracle wants to know what it should do when it encounters an object in the import file that already exists. If you answer **yes**, Oracle ignores the fact that an object exists and brings in its data anyway. Answering **no** causes Oracle to report an error and then move on to the next object when it encounters an object that already exists.
Import grants (yes/no)	Oracle wants to know whether to run the grant statements written to the import file after an object is imported.
Import table data (yes/no)	Oracle wants to know if it should bring in the table data (yes) or just run the SQL statements to create objects (no).
Import entire export file (yes/no)	Oracle wants to know if the complete file or only specified portions should be imported. If you answer **yes**, the import starts at once. If you answer **no**, Oracle will ask questions about what you wish to import.

TABLE 15-2. *Dialog When imp Is Invoked with No Parameters*

instead of **yes**, we answered **no**. Oracle would then change the series of questions based on that negative response. This is illustrated in the next listing, with the changes italicized and bolded.

```
C:\> imp
Import: Release 8.1.5.0.0 - Production on Tue Jun 1 14:33:13 2001
(c) Copyright 1999 Oracle Corporation.  All rights reserved.
Username: jones/baby
Connected to: Oracle8i Release 8.1.5.0.0 - Production
With the Java option
PL/SQL Release 8.1.5.0.0 - Production
Import file: EXPDAT.DMP >
Enter insert buffer size (minimum is 8192) 30720>
Export file created by EXPORT:V08.01.05 via conventional path
import done in WE8ISO8859P1 character set and WE8ISO8859P1
               NCHAR character set
List contents of import file only (yes/no): no >
Ignore create error due to object existence (yes/no): no > yes
Import grants (yes/no): yes >
Import table data (yes/no): yes >
Import entire export file (yes/no): no > no
Username: richard
Enter table(T) or partition(T:P) names. Null list means
       all tables for user
Enter table(T) or partition(T:P) name or . if done: dw_nhappening
Enter table(T) or partition(T:P) name or . if done:
. importing RICHARD's objects into RICHARD
. . importing table      "DW_NHAPPENING"        234077 rows imported
Import terminated successfully without warnings.
```

How Answers to Prompts Affect Success or Failure

In addition, export and import behave in different ways based on the responses given to the dialog. The most common situation that comes up is related to the question shown in the next listing.

```
Ignore create error due to object existence (yes/no): yes >
```

NOTE
When run interactively, export and import suggest a response to most questions. Accept the suggested response by pressing ENTER.

Notice how the default answer to the question is **yes**. You will find as you use these utilities that the default answers Oracle suggests are usually the ones you will end up using. To translate the question in the previous listing into English, inspect the following logic.

```
Ignore create errors due to object existence ???
if answer = yes then
    if import encounters create table and table already exists then
        bring in the table data anyways
    else {table does not exist in database at time of import}
        create table and bring in data
    end if
else {response to question = no}
    if import encounters create table and table already exists then
        raise Oracle error and go on to next table
    else {table does not exist at time of import}
        create table and bring in data
    end if
end if
```

In this example, the success or failure of importing a table is affected by the answer to the question about ignoring create errors due to object existence.

TIP
Use the interactive method when getting started with export and import and experiment with different answers to Oracle's questions. This is the quickest way to familiarize yourself with using these utilities.

Parameter-Driven Export

In the parameter-driven export method, the **exp** command is issued with one or more parameters passed on the command line. This method is the most flexible. We recommend becoming fluent with this method early in your career as a DBA, as you will use it from day one. The format of the command is

```
exp keyword1=value1 keyword2=value2 keyword3=value3
```

By using keyword parameters, you instruct Oracle what to write to the export file. A quick list of keywords, their meanings, and their default values can be obtained by issuing the command **exp help=y** from your operating system prompt. The following shows the output from this command.

```
C:\Oracle\Ora81\Bin> exp help=y
Export: Release 8.1.5.0.0 - Production on Tue Jun 1 14:41:30 2088
(c) Copyright 1999 Oracle Corporation.  All rights reserved.
You can let Export prompt you for parameters by entering the EXP
command followed by your username/password:
     Example: EXP SCOTT/TIGER
Or, you can control how Export runs by entering the EXP command followed
by various arguments. To specify parameters, you use keywords:
    Format:  EXP KEYWORD=value or KEYWORD=(value1,value2,...,valueN)
    Example: EXP SCOTT/TIGER GRANTS=Y TABLES=(EMP,DEPT,MGR)
             or TABLES=(T1:P1,T1:P2), if T1 is partitioned table
USERID must be the first parameter on the command line.
Keyword  Description (Default)        Keyword      Description (Default)
------------------------------------------------------------------------
USERID   username/password           FULL         export entire file (N)
BUFFER   size of data buffer         OWNER        list of owner usernames
FILE     output files (EXPDAT.DMP)   TABLES       list of table names
COMPRESS import into one extent (Y)  RECORDLENGTH length of IO record
GRANTS   export grants (Y)           INCTYPE      incremental export type
INDEXES  export indexes (Y)          RECORD       track incr. export (Y)
ROWS     export data rows (Y)        PARFILE      parameter filename
CONSTRAINTS export constraints (Y)   CONSISTENT   cross-table consistency
LOG      log file of screen output   STATISTICS   analyze objects (ESTIMATE)
DIRECT   direct path (N)             TRIGGERS     export triggers (Y)
FEEDBACK display progress every x rows (0)
FILESIZE maximum size of each dump file
QUERY    select clause used to export a subset of a table
The following keywords only apply to transportable tablespaces
TRANSPORT_TABLESPACE export transportable tablespace metadata (N)
TABLESPACES list of tablespaces to transport
Export terminated successfully without warnings.
```

Table 15-3 discusses the most important and often-used export parameters.

VIP

*Use the **log** parameter on all parameter-driven exports. If something goes wrong, you need to study the log file to clean up the mess that may be left over by an unsuccessful export.*

Parameter-Driven Import

The **imp** command is issued with one or more parameters passed on the command line. Parameter-driven import provides the most flexible and robust method for using import as part of your new skill set. The format of the command is

```
imp keyword1=value1 keyword2=value2 keyword3=value3
```

Parameter	Meaning/Notes	Default
Userid	The Oracle user name and password of the account running the utility. If you supply just the user name, Oracle will prompt you for the password.	None
Buffer	The data buffer size in bytes. If you request too big a size, Oracle will carry on with whatever it can obtain.	4096
File	The name of the file being written to. If you do not specify a filename extension, Oracle assumes the .dmp extension.	Expdat.dmp
Compress	Write storage parameters to the export file that would place all table data in one extent when the data is imported.	Y
Grants	Write SQL grant statements to the export file.	Y
Indexes	Write SQL create index statements to the export file.	Y
Triggers	Instructs Oracle whether or not to write trigger creation statements to the export file.	Y
Rows	Export the data in the tables' rows as well as the definition of the underlying objects.	Y
Constraints	Write SQL statements to the export file needed to re-create declarative integrity when the objects are imported (for example, primary key and references statements).	Y
Log	Instructs Oracle to write the screen I/O from the export to a disk file.	None
Full	Controls whether Oracle writes SQL statements to the export file to re-create all the system associated datafiles, tablespaces, rollback segments, etc.	N
Owner	Provides a list of Oracle accounts whose objects are to be written to the export file.	None
Tables	Provides a list of tables whose definitions or data are to be written to the export file.	None

TABLE 15-3. *Export Parameters and Their Defaults*

Parameter	Meaning/Notes	Default
Recordlength	Length in bytes of the record written to the export file.	Operating system–specific
Inctype	Type of incremental export being performed.	None
Record	Instructs Oracle to track the type of incremental export being written in some data dictionary views. This information is used when performing an import from an incremental export file.	Y
Parfile	The name of a file containing parameters to be fed to export.	None
Consistent	Instructs Oracle to maintain cross-table consistency. This ensures that export will make copies of table data as of the time the export started even if tables being exported are being used while the export runs.	N
Statistics	Write SQL analyze statements to the export file.	Estimate
Direct	Causes export to extract data by reading the data directly, bypassing the SQL command processing layer. This method can be much faster than a conventional path export.	N
Feedback	Specifies that export should display a progress meter in the form of a dot for each *x* number of rows exported.	0

TABLE 15-3.   *Export Parameters and Their Defaults* (continued)

By using keyword parameters, you instruct Oracle what to bring in from the export file. A quick list of keywords, their meanings, and their default values can be obtained by issuing the command **imp help=y** from your operating system prompt. The following shows the output from this command.

```
C:\Oracle\Ora81\Bin> imp help=y
Import: Release 8.1.5.0.0 - Production on Sat Jun 5 08:10:02 2001
(c) Copyright 1999 Oracle Corporation.  All rights reserved.
You can let Import prompt you for parameters by entering the IMP
command followed by your username/password:
     Example: IMP SCOTT/TIGER
```

Or, you can control how Import runs by entering the IMP command followed
by various arguments. To specify parameters, you use keywords:

```
     Format:  IMP KEYWORD=value or KEYWORD=(value1,value2,...,valueN)
     Example: IMP SCOTT/TIGER IGNORE=Y TABLES=(EMP,DEPT) FULL=N
              or TABLES=(T1:P1,T1:P2), if T1 is partitioned table
USERID must be the first parameter on the command line.
Keyword  Description (Default)        Keyword       Description (Default)
------------------------------------------------------------------------
USERID   username/password            FULL          import entire file (N)
BUFFER   size of data buffer          FROMUSER      list of owner usernames
FILE     input files (EXPDAT.DMP)     TOUSER        list of usernames
SHOW     just list file contents (N)  TABLES        list of table names
IGNORE   ignore create errors (N)     RECORDLENGTH  length of IO record
GRANTS   import grants (Y)            INCTYPE       incremental import type
INDEXES  import indexes (Y)           COMMIT        commit array insert (N)
ROWS     import data rows (Y)         PARFILE       parameter filename
LOG      log file of screen output    CONSTRAINTS   import constraints (Y)
DESTROY  overwrite tablespace data file (N)
INDEXFILE write table/index info to specified file
SKIP_UNUSABLE_INDEXES  skip maintenance of unusable indexes (N)
ANALYZE  execute ANALYZE statements in dump file (Y)
FEEDBACK display progress every x rows(0)
TOID_NOVALIDATE  skip validation of specified type ids
FILESIZE maximum size of each dump file
RECALCULATE_STATISTICS recalculate statistics (N)
The following keywords only apply to transportable tablespaces
TRANSPORT_TABLESPACE import transportable tablespace metadata (N)
TABLESPACES tablespaces to be transported into database
DATAFILES datafiles to be transported into database
TTS_OWNERS users that own data in the transportable tablespace set .
Import terminated successfully without warnings.
```

Table 15-4 discusses each of the import parameters.

VIP
*Use the **log** parameter on all parameter-driven
imports. If something goes wrong, you need to study
the log file to clean up the mess that may be left
over by an unsuccessful import.*

The parfile Keyword Parameter

This parameter deserves special attention. You may feed keyword parameter values
to export and import by using this parameter with a filename afterward. The format
of the **parfile** parameter is either of the following:

```
imp parfile=my.parfile
```

Parameter	Meaning/Notes	Default
Userid	The Oracle user name and password of the account running the utility. If you supply just the user name, Oracle will prompt you for the password.	None
Buffer	The data buffer size in bytes. If you request too big a size, Oracle will carry on with whatever it can obtain.	30720
File	The name of the file being read from. If you do not specify a filename extension, Oracle assumes the .dmp extension.	Expdat.dmp
Show	Tells Oracle whether to perform the import or simply show the contents of the export file.	N
Ignore	Instructs Oracle on how to deal with SQL create statements in the export file. If set to N, Oracle reports an error when trying to create a table that already exists. If set to Y, Oracle ignores the error condition raised when attempting to run a create table for one that already exists.	N
Grants	Execute the SQL grant statements in the export file.	Y
Indexes	Execute the SQL create index statements in the export file.	Y
Rows	Import the data in the tables' rows as well as the definitions of the underlying objects.	Y
Log	Instructs Oracle to write the screen I/O from the import to a disk file.	None
Destroy	Instructs Oracle to not overwrite a datafile during a full database import if a datafile contains a tablespace belonging to any database.	N

TABLE 15-4. *Import Parameters and Their Defaults*

Parameter	Meaning/Notes	Default
Indexfile	Instructs Oracle to write all create table, create index, and create cluster statements to a user-supplied operating system filename. The table and cluster statements are commented out.	None
Charset	The character set of the data in the export file.	NLS_LANG value in initialization parameter file
Full	Controls whether Oracle executes the SQL statements in the export file to re-create all the system associated datafiles, tablespaces, rollback segments, etc.	N
Fromuser	The owner(s) of the data that was written to the export file.	None
Touser	The user(s) into which the data should be imported.	None
Tables	A list of table names to be imported.	None
Recordlength	Specifies the length of each record in the export file. May be necessary when moving data between platforms with different default record lengths.	Operating system–specific
Inctype	The type of incremental export being read. Values are either RESTORE or SYSTEM.	None
Commit	Instructs Oracle whether or not to commit after each array insert. This is very useful when importing large amounts of data that may cause rollback segment errors.	N
Feedback	Specifies that import should display a progress meter in the form of a dot for each x number of rows imported.	0
Parfile	The name of a file containing parameters to be fed to import.	None

TABLE 15-4. *Import Parameters and Their Defaults* (continued)

or

```
exp parfile=my.parfile
```

You place a list of parameters in the file (in this case, "my.parfile") following the parfile keyword. This could be the contents of "my.parfile" being fed into export:

```
userid=wall/the tables=(waters,wright,mason)
buffer=102400 compress=y grants=y
```

This could be the contents of "my.parfile" being fed into import:

```
userid=delicate/thunder fromuser=pulse touser=strat
buffer=102400 grants=y
```

Both parameter files are a free-form format. The export parameter file shows two parameters on the first line, then three parameters on the second. You could as easily have done either of the following things:

```
userid=diamond/crazy tables=(dogs,war)
buffer=102400 grants=y
compress=y
```

or

```
compress=y
userid=diamond/crazy
tables=(dogs,war)
buffer=102400
grants=y
```

Mixing Interactive and Parameter-Driven Methods

You may invoke export and import with a mixture of the two methods by doing the following:

```
exp floyd/pink buffer=102400 compress=n
```

As soon as Oracle encounters at least one keyword parameter on the command line, it starts the import or export immediately and does not enter into the interactive dialog. For example, invoking import with the command **imp mason/nick file=boogie** would start import without stopping to prompt for further parameter values. You must

be careful when calling export or import this way. Let's say you want to perform a full
database export. You call export with the command

```
exp system/not_manager buffer=102400 rows=n
```

Oracle would not prompt you for any other parameters and would carry on with
a user export.

> **TIP**
> *Experiment with export and import so that you are
> not caught off-guard by their behavior when you
> least expect it.*

Export and Import Modes

You can run export and import in one of three modes, depending on what you want to
accomplish. For example, if you want to create a copy of a table belonging to userA in
userB's area, you would use one mode. On the other hand, if you want to preserve a
complete copy of userA's data, you would use a different mode. By the end of this
section, you will know details on the following:

- Table-mode export and import
- User-mode export and import
- Full database export and import

Table-Mode Export

When using table-mode export, you tell Oracle the names of one or more tables to
export. Oracle writes the table data to the export file. The command

```
exp userid=amanda/scholz tables=(feeling,ride,mast)
file=fm.dmp
```

exports the three tables whose names are enclosed in parentheses belonging to
Oracle user amanda. The export file is called fm.dmp.

> **NOTE**
> *When listing more than one table after the **tables**
> keyword, the names are separated by commas and
> the whole list is enclosed in parentheses.*

User-Mode Export

In user-mode export, Oracle exports all of a user's objects, including views, synonyms, triggers, procedures, database links, and tables. User-mode export is commonly used to defragment a tablespace. After all the user's objects are exported, the tablespace can be dropped and re-created. The command

```
exp userid=beatles/rusty owner=(john,paul,george,ringo)
```

exports the four users whose names are enclosed in parentheses. The export file is called expdat.dmp.

> **NOTE**
> *When listing more than one owner after the owner keyword, the **owner** names are separated by commas and the whole list is enclosed in parentheses.*

Full Database Export

When using full database export, all users' data and database support file (datafiles, tablespaces, rollback segments, and so on) creation statements are written to the export file for every database user except SYS. This export file can be used for a full database import. The command

```
exp userid=system/not_manager full=y grants=y indexes=y
```

writes the full database export to a file called expdat.dmp.

> **NOTE**
> *Not every database user will be able to use the **full** keyword when trying to initiate a full database export. Many full database exports are run using the Oracle SYSTEM account.*

Table-Mode Import

When using table-mode import, you tell Oracle the names of one or more tables to import. Oracle writes the table data to the database. The command

```
imp userid=fletcher/frank tables=(blowup,redmond,flowers)
```

imports the three tables whose names are enclosed in parentheses belonging to Oracle user fletcher. The export file is called expdat.dmp.

VIP
*If the userid **fletcher** imports tables in an export file owned by another user, then the tables would be created under the **fletcher** schema, not that other user's schema.*

NOTE
*When listing more than one table after the **tables** keyword, the names are separated by commas and the whole list is enclosed in parentheses.*

User-Mode Import

In user-mode import, Oracle imports the specified users' objects, including views, synonyms, triggers, procedures, database links, and tables. User-mode import is commonly used after a tablespace has been re-created during a defragmentation exercise. The command

```
imp userid=blaster/caster fromuser=(per_man,acc_man)
touser=(per_man,acc_man) file=two_users
```

imports the two users whose names are enclosed in parentheses. The export file is called two_users.dmp.

NOTE
*When listing more than one user after the **fromuser** or **touser** keyword, the names are separated by commas and the whole list is enclosed in parentheses.*

Full Database Import

Full database import runs in two phases. During the first phase, all database support file (datafiles, tablespaces, rollback segments, and so on) creation statements in the export file are executed. When this phase is complete, the complete structure of the database is in place. The second phase brings users' objects into their appropriate tablespaces. The command

```
imp userid=system/beto full=y file=full_tst
```

performs a full database import from a file called expdat.dmp.

NOTE

*Not every database user will be able to use the **full** keyword when trying to initiate a full database import. Most full database imports are run using the Oracle SYSTEM account.*

VIP

*After creating a brand new database with the SQL **create database** command, when running a full database import from the system account, the password will be **manager**, regardless of what it was when the full database export was run.*

Switching Among Modes

We have devised a hierarchy of export files to illustrate how an export file written using one mode can be used by import in another mode. By assigning a weighting factor to each mode of export (3=full, 2=user, 1=table), you may use a file produced by a higher-numbered mode to run import in a lower- or equal-numbered mode. Table 15-5 summarizes which export files can be used for the three modes of import.

Thus, a full database export file can be used to do a table-mode, user-mode, or full database import. A user-mode export file can be used to do a user-mode or table-mode import. A table-mode export file can only be used to do a table-mode import.

Requirement	Can Export File Written by Export Mode Be Used?		
	Table	User	Full
Table mode import	Y	Y	Y
User mode import	N	Y	Y
Full database import	N	N	Y

TABLE 15-5. *Export Modes Used in Different Import Modes*

When to Use Each Mode

Table 15-6 illustrates what export and import can do for you, including a few scenarios and the suggested mode to use with export and import. Although the tasks can easily (and sometimes better) be accomplished using SQL*Plus, we use export and import here.

Requirement	Export Mode	Import Mode	Reason
Defragment user's tablespace	User	User	We need to get all the user's objects; table mode would ignore view, synonyms, procedures, etc.
Move a copy of the personnel table from development to test	Table	Table	We want one table. This can also be accomplished using the user mode, but table mode is faster.
Move a copy of the salary table from a full database export of production into development	Full	Table	The table we are looking for is in the full database export file. By importing in table mode, we extract only the desired table and data.
Recover the objects belonging to user from last night's full database export after inadvertently dropping a user	Full	User	We need all of the user's objects. Since he or she no longer exists in the data dictionary, we are unable to collect a list of them and run in table mode. User mode will extract all the user's objects from the full database export file.
Move the personnel system views from one user to another user	User	User	A table export does not extract SQL view creation statements. You must do this in user mode.

TABLE 15-6. *Export and Import Scenarios*

Using Export and Import with Partitioned Tables

The objects of most export or import sessions are tables, and with the partitioning capabilities of Oracle8i, you can specify partitioned objects as source data. Exports of selected partitions are accomplished using partition-level export, and a command similar to the following:

```
exp system/ahbeto file=export.dmp
tables=(scott.b:px, scott.b:py, mary.c, d:qb)
```

where the table names include partitions **px** and **py** belonging to table **b** owned by user **scott**, table **c** belonging to user **mary**, and partition **qb** belonging to the user running the export.

NOTE
Each partition name must be specified with its corresponding table name.

Oracle8i partition-level import imports one or more exported partitions of a table or the export of a nonpartitioned table into a partitioned or nonpartitioned target table. Import reads from the dump file only the data rows from the specified source partition(s). These specifications are delivered on the command line as import is invoked, or read from a parameter file.

VIP
Partition-level import will not bring rows into a specified target partition if the rows in the export file fall outside the allowable range within which the target partition was defined.

Source and target partitions must have the same table name. In other words, data from one partition of a table can be imported into only another partition of the same table.

Requirements for Running Export and Import

As the DBA, you must ensure that the two programs **exp** and **imp** are accessible to you and your developers. The requirements for a few common environments are outlined in the following table.

Operating System	Requirements
Windows	The executables must be in a directory in the current path and the appropriate values must be set in the Windows Registry to permit the programs and required libraries to be found at initialization.
VMS	World must have read and executed permissions (W=RE).
UNIX	The executables' file permissions must be set to 744 (execute for all users).

Error Conditions and Their Solutions

Yes, you are going to have problems with export and import. We all do! Most of them are a result of coding errors. This section of the chapter will show you how to deal with errors caused by the following situations:

- Trying to run export or import when the database is not open
- Trying to read an export file written by a DBA user
- Trying to run a full database export or import with insufficient privileges

Oracle Not Running

The Oracle instance you are using export or import against must be running to use these programs. The following message is encountered if the instance is not running:

```
C:\Oracle> exp userid=mexico/beto full=y
Export: Release 8.1.5.0.0 - Production on Tue Jun 1 14:57:02 2002
(c) Copyright 1999 Oracle Corporation.  All rights reserved.
EXP-00056: ORACLE error 1034 encountered
ORA-01034: ORACLE not available
EXP-00222:
System error message 2
System error message: No such file or directory
EXP-00005: all allowable logon attempts failed
EXP-00000: Export terminated unsuccessfully
```

Reading Your DBA-Created Export File

When you, as the DBA, create an export file, only other DBA-privileged users may read that file for import regardless of the mode (table, user, or full) used to create the export. The following will occur if a user (no DBA role) tries to read an export file you created as the DBA.

```
C:\Oracle> imp userid=mexico/beto full=y
Import: Release 8.1.5.0.0 - Production on Tue Jun 1 14:58:42 2001
(c) Copyright 1999 Oracle Corporation.  All rights reserved.
Connected to: Oracle8i Release 8.1.5.0.0 - Production
With the Java option
PL/SQL Release 8.1.5.0.0 - Production
Export file created by EXPORT:V08.01.05 via conventional path
IMP-00013: only a DBA can import a file exported by another DBA
IMP-00000: Import terminated unsuccessfully
```

Unable to Initiate a Full Database Export

You must start a full database export from your account with the DBA role or an account that you have given the role **exp_full_database**.

```
C:\Oracle> exp userid=mexico/beto full=y
Export: Release 8.1.5.0.0 - Production on Tue Jun 1 14:59:30 2002
(c) Copyright 1999 Oracle Corporation.  All rights reserved.
Connected to: Oracle8i Release 8.1.5.0.0 - Production
With the Java option
PL/SQL Release 8.1.5.0.0 - Production
EXP-00023: must be a DBA to do Full Database export
 (2)U(sers), or (3)T(ables): (2)U >
```

Relationship Between Parameters

You will soon learn that certain parameter values with export and import cannot be coded together. The most common occurrence is with export running in table mode. Suppose you wanted to export one table from userA and two tables from userB in the same export session. The first cut at calling export may be done using the following command:

```
exp userid=fin_man/drowssap owner=(userA,userB)
    tables=(table1A,table1B,table2B)
```

After you press ENTER, Oracle responds with

```
EXP-00026: only one parameter (TABLES, OWNER, or FULL) can be specified
EXP-00222:
System error message 2
EXP-00000: Export terminated unsuccessfully
```

and the export aborts.

In the next listing, you see that Oracle insists you enter the **fromuser** and **touser** parameters in the call to import, issue the keyword **full=y**, or provide some table names using the **tables=** keyword parameter.

```
D:\ORANT\BIN> exp userid=mexico/beto file=prod
Export: Release 8.1.5.0.0 - Production on Tue Jun 1 14:59:30 2002
(c) Copyright 1999 Oracle Corporation.  All rights reserved.
Connected to: Oracle8i Release 8.1.5.0.0 - Production
With the Java option
PL/SQL Release 8.1.5.0.0 - Production
Export file created by EXPORT:V08.01.05
IMP-00031: Must specify FULL=Y or provide FROMUSER/TOUSER or TABLE
          arguments
IMP-00021: operating system error - error code (dec 2, hex 0x2)
IMP-00000: Import terminated unsuccessfully
```

Examples

We now introduce some real-life export and import situations, and we will present a listing of the parameter file to use with each. As you become more fluent in using these utilities, you will specify the **parfile=** keyword more and more and place the appropriate parameters in a file.

Sample Scenario I

Export my person, acc_rec, fin_mast, and letters tables into a file called recs. The contents of the parameter file would be

```
userid=mexico/beto file=recs tables=(person,acc_rec,fin_mast) buffer=10240
```

Import userA's objects into userB's schema using export file frank. Some of the objects already exist in userB's schema, but we want to bring the data in for existing objects as well.

```
userid=mexico/beto ignore=y file=frank buffer=102400 fromuser=userA touser=userB
```

Sample Scenario 2

Export three of userA's tables and two of userB's tables.

```
userid=mexico/beto
tables=
(userA.table_1,userA.table_2,userA.table_3,userB.table_1,userB.table_2)
```

Sample Scenario 3

Make a copy of the tables exported in the previous example in userC's schema.

```
userid=userc/drowssap fromuser=(userA,userB) touser=(userC,userC)
```

Export and Import from OEM

Export and Import from OEM are simply two wizards that will ask for input and then submit a job through OEM and accomplish your desired export or import activity.

NOTE
*Getting into the Export and Import Wizards in OEM using the Schema Manager is the same as invoking SQL*Loader, as we described in Chapter 10. Thus, we will refer you to a few figures from that chapter in the next few paragraphs.*

You must connect to an Oracle Management Server (*OMS*) to be able to successfully start either of these wizards. Thus, invoking one of these wizards is a two-step process:

■ From Start Menu I Programs I Oracle Oem I Oracle Enterprise
Management, invoke the Enterprise Manager Console option. This will
bring up the dialog box shown in Figure 10-2. Enter the appropriate login
credentials, in our case **sysman** with a password of **oem**. Notice the
drop-down pick list of OMSs on the screen.

VIP
*There is some important setup work to be done
before you can successfully open the OEM main
console. It is beyond the scope of this chapter. A
more senior experienced DBA will have to perform
this setup for you, or work with Oracle Worldwide
Customer support.*

■ Proceed to the Tools option at the top of the OEM main console, then select
Database ApplicationsISchema Manager from the drop-down menu that
appears. This will park you at the Oracle Schema Manager main console,
as shown in Figure 10-3.

Now that you are looking at the Schema Manager main console, you select
Tools I Data Management I Export (or Import) to invoke either the Export or
Import Wizard.

The Export Wizard

The Export Wizard Introduction screen, as shown in Figure 15-2, can be disabled by
un-selecting the "Display this page next time" check box. Whatever you end up
requesting through this wizard will be run as a job in OEM when the dialog is
complete. Click Next to move to the next screen.

The next screen is where you specify the name and location of the file to be
written by export. When the Export File location dialog box appears, if there is more
than one filename displayed, the Maximum File Size button will be enabled where
the size can be coded in KBytes, MBytes, or GBytes. After entering a filename, click
Next to continue; the Export Type dialog box, as shown in Figure 15-3, appears
next. The three types listed, with their accompanying explanations, resemble the
same three types discussed in the "Export and Import Modes" section, earlier in this
chapter.

After specifying the Export Type, move on, by clicking Next, to display the
Associated Objects dialog box. This is where you can instruct export to

■ Export the grants that have been given out on the objects that will be
exported. *Grants* are privileges that owners of objects give to other users
that allow them to manipulate objects' data.

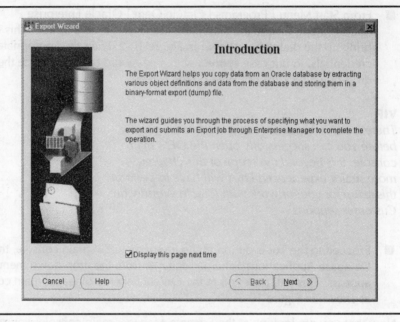

FIGURE 15-2. *The Export Wizard Introduction*

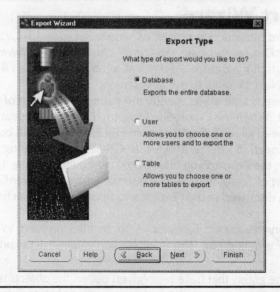

FIGURE 15-3. *The Export Type dialog box*

■ Export the index definitions for the objects being exported. Export does not actually bring out the index structures themselves—it simply writes SQL statements in the export file to create the indexes if so instructed.

■ Export the data itself as well as the SQL statements required to create the objects participating in the export.

■ Export any constraints that may have been defined on the objects being exported. *Constraints* are sets of rules that define the interrelationships between objects in the Oracle8*i* database. Just as with the indexes, selecting this causes SQL statements to be written to the export file.

The wizard then brings up the dialog box shown in Figure 15-4, in which you tell OEM when you want the export to run. Notice how, since we selected On Day of Month in the Run Job section of Figure 15-4, a calendar has appeared upon which we can select the desired day. The available data entry here depends on what measure (Interval, Day of the Week, or Day of the Month) has been selected.

Just about done. To complete the submission of the export job, click Finish. Had we selected the job to be run Immediately, upon returning to the OEM Main Console, we would see the job details in the console's Job pane. Import's turn ...

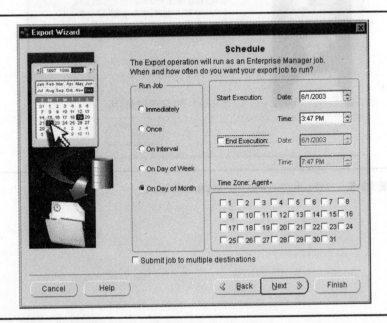

FIGURE 15-4. *Specifying when export should be run*

The Import Wizard

The Import Wizard begins with the Introduction shown in Figure 15-5.

You are then presented with a screen in which you can specify the name and location of the export file you wish to import. Next, you will see a status window appear, similar to that shown in Figure 15-6. There really isn't much to the Import Wizard. Whatever is in the export file you selected, as shown in Figure 15-4, is what controls the nature of the import.

When OEM has submitted the import job, it has begun running, and terminated successfully, the Next button onscreen shown in Figure 15-6 becomes active. Click Next to display an import job confirmation screen; then exit.

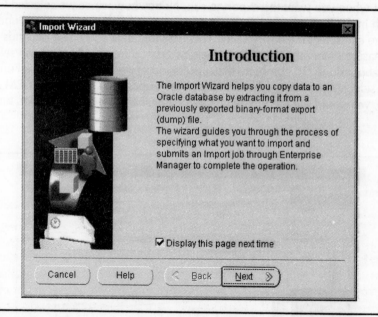

FIGURE 15-5. *Introduction to the Import Wizard*

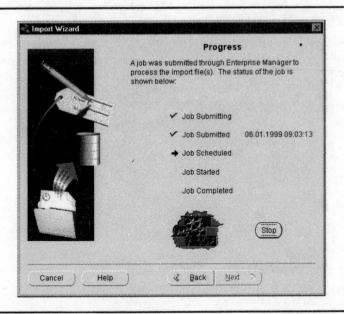

FIGURE 15-6.   *The Import Status window*

What's Next

We have stressed throughout this chapter the importance of export and import and how they are integrated into your DBA skill set. In Chapter 16, we will highlight how to use these utilities as part of your backup and recovery procedures. Export and import have been around for years—they are dependable and integral to the set of utilities you receive with the Oracle Server product. Very early in your career as a DBA, you will wonder how you could ever live without them. In one of our other works, we very proudly stated, "Back up and take a good look at backup; the secret about backup is getting your backup and getting your database back up." How true!

CHAPTER
16

Backup and Recovery

h yes! Backup and recovery—two of the biggest issues with any system, regardless of the software. Oracle has implemented sophisticated backup and recovery mechanisms that allow you to protect your precious data in case all or part of your database is inoperable. By the time you finish this chapter, you will be able to implement a standard backup and recovery plan for your installation. We include details on the following topics:

- Making image backups of your database

- Leaving the database open and accessible while making backups

- Running the database in ARCHIVELOG mode

- Performing complete and incomplete database recovery

- Integrating backup with export and import

All too often, DBAs look at backup and recovery procedures only when it's too late. One of our clients lost a production database before they "got around" to taking the time to implement routines that would have allowed the necessary protection. Keep in mind that there are two steps to initiating backup and recovery procedures. The first (the backup step) makes copies of the Oracle data; the second (the recovery step) copies the data created from the backup step and restores the database to its operable status.

Terminology

The following definitions will arm you with the technical jargon you need to make it through this chapter.

- A *checkpoint* causes information to be written from memory to the database files to which they belong. During this activity, the state of the datafiles, redo logs, and control files is synched, and the instance is in a consistent state.

- Oracle keeps an internal transaction log referred to as the *SCN* or system change number. Using an internal set of rules, Oracle assigns an SCN to transactions and, when performing a log switch, records the highest SCN in each redo log as it is archived.

■ The Oracle database is in a *consistent state* when the information in the control files (for instance, the last time the datafiles were updated) is the same as the information contained in the datafiles themselves.

■ A tablespace is *online* when it is accessible to the users of the Oracle instance. In contrast, when a tablespace is *offline,* it is available for maintenance and cannot be accessed by the user community until it is brought back online.

Protection Provided by Backup

We need to spend some time explaining some concepts and theory before we discuss how and what to back up. Essentially, Oracle offers two types of backup protection. After we discuss both and present a complete backup plan, you will know how to secure your installation with bulletproof protection against just about anything.

Protection Against Loss of an Object

Backing up data with export and import (which will be discussed in the "Export and Import Backup" section coming up) provides protection against loss of objects. How could that happen, you ask? Picture yourself as a developer for a large bank in Germany. You use Oracle's network product, Net8, which allows you to work with databases on a remote machine. You have just finished some cleanup before final installation of a new system in production, and you connect to the production database using Net8. You are called out of the office for a few minutes, and when you come back, you realize that you have forgotten to remove a table from the development database; so you enter the command **drop table account_master;**. Less than five minutes later, your phone rings, and guess what? The account_master table is missing in production. Now, how did that happen?

VIP
Export and import provide protection against loss of tables that get dropped inadvertently from the database. In other words, they provide protection against loss of all or part of one or more tables.

When a table needs to be recovered from an export file, bring it back using the table mode of import (this is discussed in Chapter 15 in the "Switching Among Modes" section). If the export was made at 2:00 A.M. and a table is inadvertently dropped at 3:00 P.M. the next day, any new or changed rows in the table after 2:00 A.M. are not restored as the table is re-created. Sound impossible? Believe us, it happens.

VIP
While import allows protection against losing a table, the import will only restore the table to the condition it was in when the export file was written.

Protection Against Loss of the Database

Protection against loss of the database also means protection against loss of a datafile or tablespace. This protection is related directly to the redo or transaction logs we discuss in many places throughout this book, especially the "Redo Logs—The Transaction Log" section of Chapter 4. Picture the following situation that happened to us a few years ago. It's morning, and everyone is happily working with the database. There is a phone call to the help desk from a user saying that Oracle is asking her for her user name and password. Interesting! When she usually logs in to the machine, the first screen she sees is the main menu for her system. We investigate, and find out that Oracle is not running! We look around and do some exploring, and we receive the following message from Oracle:

```
ERROR: ORA-01034: ORACLE not available
ORA-09243: smsget: error attaching to SGA
```

Panic! Something has gone wrong with one of the disks, and Oracle has shut itself down. This illustrates the second type of backup protection. In this situation, there is a problem with the hardware (disk pack, in this case) and we may have lost the datafiles on the bad disk. Unlike losing one or more objects, here the physical structure of the database is damaged.

Protection for this type of problem is provided by running the database in ARCHIVELOG mode, which will provide you with roll-forward capabilities. The redo or transaction logs record every transaction against the database. By saving copies of the redo logs before they are overwritten, they can be reapplied to the database as if the transactions had been entered by the users. We discuss what can be done when an instance runs in ARCHIVELOG mode in more detail in the "Recovery" section in this chapter.

VIP
ARCHIVELOG provides protection against an assortment of hardware problems that happen periodically. You can restore a backup of the database and recover all the transactions, since the backup was written using your archived redo logs.

Preparing for Backups with Database Open

One of the biggest mistakes DBAs make when managing backups for the Oracle databases is writing what they think are useful backups that turn out to be useless. This is most commonly caused when a DBA neglects to enliven the appropriate log mode and carries out backups with the database running. The secret to backing up an open database is ensuring that the files that are part of the backup are consistent as they are copied to disk or tape. Under normal circumstances this is impossible, since Oracle writes information to the various database tablespace files as users work with objects in those containers. Look at the following logic to see how Oracle maintains interfile consistency as it backs up one or more tablespaces in an open database.

```
if database is in archivelog mode then
    if backup is turned on for selected tablespace
        loop until tablespace is taken out of backup mode
            write information destined for that tablespace to
                the online redo logs
        end loop
        take tablespace out of backup mode
        dump appropriate information from redo logs to tablespace
            now out of backup mode
    else
        write information directly to appropriate tablespace data
            files as systems operate
    end if
else
    allow online tablespace backup with no intervention (thereby
        the DBA ends up writing an unusable backup)
end if
```

The secret here involves a two-step process:

1. Initiating a process that will archive online redo logs as they fill. This process is best started in such a way that every time the database is started, the archiver is spawned automatically.

2. Place the Oracle database in ARCHIVELOG mode.

Let's look at how to first initiate the archiver process using a text editor and Server Manager and then place the database in ARCHIVELOG mode.

Starting the Archiving Process

This is a two-step process:

- Modify the instance initialization parameter file, enlivening the appropriate entries to facilitate automatic archival.

- Recycle the database. When we speak of *recycling a database*, we mean shutting it down and then restarting.

Let's get started using the following steps.

1. Locate the desired initialization parameter file in the Explorer.

VIP
On the server we used when writing this chapter, ORACLE_HOME is defined as C:\Ora81, and we are working with the o8ibegin database. Thus, in our case, we will look at the file init.ora in the C:\Ora81\Admin\O8ibegin\Pfile folder. The folder you use on your server may differ.

2. Double-click the filename and, if asked by the Explorer to select a program with which to open the parameter file, choose Notepad. You will then be positioned at a window similar to that shown in Figure 16-1. We have paged down to the section where the series of parameters that start with log_ are positioned. When the o8ibegin database was built, the installer created some instance-specific entries for the last two of the three parameters shown.

3. Remove the leading # sign and space on the first line of the three log_ entries. This instructs Oracle8i to bring up the automatic archiver process each time the database is started.

4. Remove the leading # sign and space from the second line, and then change the entry from log_archive_dest_1 to **log_archive_dest**.

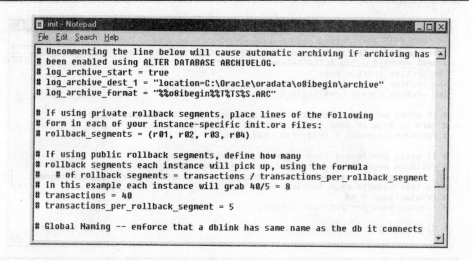

```
init - Notepad                                                    _ □ ×
File  Edit  Search  Help
# Uncommenting the line below will cause automatic archiving if archiving has  ▲
# been enabled using ALTER DATABASE ARCHIVELOG.
# log_archive_start = true
# log_archive_dest_1 = "location=C:\Oracle\oradata\o8ibegin\archive"
# log_archive_format = "%%o8ibegin%%T%TS%S.ARC"

# If using private rollback segments, place lines of the following
# form in each of your instance-specific init.ora files:
# rollback_segments = (r01, r02, r03, r04)

# If using public rollback segments, define how many
# rollback segments each instance will pick up, using the formula
#   # of rollback segments = transactions / transactions_per_rollback_segment
# In this example each instance will grab 40/5 = 8
# transactions = 40
# transactions_per_rollback_segment = 5

# Global Naming -- enforce that a dblink has same name as the db it connects  ▼
```

FIGURE 16-1. *Archiver process parameters*

NOTE
*The parameter log_archive_dest_1 is valid, though
for the purposes of this discussion, we concentrate
on log_archive_dest. Using the former convention,
you can specify up to five destinations for archived
redo logs.*

5. Remove the double quote ("location=) from the start of the value and the trailing quote at the end of the line. The entry then becomes C:\Oracle\Oradata\o8ibegin\archive.

6. Remove the leading # sign and space from the beginning of the next line, and change the parameter value to **o8ibegin_%s.arc**.

7. Quit Notepad, saving the changed parameter values on the way out. The lines we have just worked on are shown in Figure 16-2.

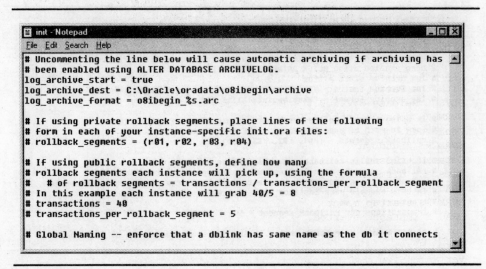

```
init - Notepad
File  Edit  Search  Help
# Uncommenting the line below will cause automatic archiving if archiving has
# been enabled using ALTER DATABASE ARCHIVELOG.
log_archive_start = true
log_archive_dest = C:\Oracle\oradata\o8ibegin\archive
log_archive_format = o8ibegin_%s.arc

# If using private rollback segments, place lines of the following
# form in each of your instance-specific init.ora files:
# rollback_segments = (r01, r02, r03, r04)

# If using public rollback segments, define how many
# rollback segments each instance will pick up, using the formula
#    # of rollback segments = transactions / transactions_per_rollback_segment
# In this example each instance will grab 40/5 = 8
# transactions = 40
# transactions_per_rollback_segment = 5

# Global Naming -- enforce that a dblink has same name as the db it connects
```

FIGURE 16-2.   *Archiver process changed parameters*

Scary stuff! Not really. The problem you may run into is specifying an invalid destination for your archived redo logs. Be careful. The pattern we used for log_archive_format will build archived redo logs starting with the folder "C:\Oracle\Oradata\o8ibegin\archive" and ending with the filename "o8ibegin," an underscore, the log sequence number and the suffix ".arc".

Placing the Database in ARCHIVELOG Mode

This recycles the database to enliven the changes we just made to the initialization parameter file, as well as placing the instance in ARCHIVELOG mode. After opening a DOS window and starting Server Manager with the command **svrmgrl**, do the following.

1. Connect to the instance using the command **connect internal/oracle**.

2. Close the database using the command **shutdown**.

3. Issue the command **startup mount** to ready the database for the pending log mode switch.

4. Enter the command **alter database archivelog;**.

5. Enter the command **alter database open;** to make the instance available to the users.

The next listing shows the dialog and the responses from Oracle.

```
Oracle Server Manager Release 3.1.5.0.1 - Production
(c) Copyright 1997, Oracle Corporation. All rights reserved.
Oracle8i Enterprise Edition Release 8.1.5.0.0 - Production
With the Partitioning and Java options
PL/SQL Release 8.1.5.0.0 - Production
SVRMGR> connect internal/oracle
Connected.
SVRMGR> shutdown
Database closed.
Database dismounted.
ORACLE instance shut down.
SVRMGR> startup mount
ORACLE instance started.
Total System Global Area        8030448 bytes
Fixed Size                        44584 bytes
Variable Size                   7510728 bytes
Database Buffers                 409600 bytes
Redo Buffers                      65536 bytes
Database mounted.
SVRMGR> alter database archivelog;
Statement processed.
SVRMGR> alter database open;
Statement processed.
```

The status of archive logging can be checked anytime using the command **archive log list;**. The output from this command is shown in the next listing.

```
SVRMGR> archive log list
Database log mode              Archive Mode
Automatic archival             Enabled
Archive destination            C:\Oracle\Oradata\o8ibegin\archive
Oldest online log sequence     345552
Next log sequence to archive   345564
Current log sequence           345564
SVRMGR>
```

After this brief overview of tweaking the environment to permit the writing of consistent backups when the Oracle database is open, let's look at the role played by export and import in a total backup strategy.

Export and Import Backup

We discuss export and import in Chapter 15 (we thought these two utilities were so important that they warranted their own chapter). If you refer to the "Export and

Import Modes" section in Chapter 15, you will see how export and import play a role in most standard backup procedures.

Classically, most backups are done in the quiet hours. When deciding how to use export as part of your backup, examine what we call your "window of opportunity." This window is the amount of time during which everything is quiet on your computer (that is, there are no reporting jobs or system backups running to interfere with the resources required to do an export), and no users are accessing the database. Most of our clients have a window of between six and seven hours. In some situations, however, that window is as small as 30 minutes or as large as nine hours. We suggest you use export according to the guidelines in the next two sections as part of your backup routines.

VIP

If you can do a full database export within this window of opportunity, the full database export must be part of your Oracle backups.

When the Window Is Long Enough

If the window is long enough to accommodate a nightly full database export, run the command **exp parfile=full_nightly.parfile;** the parameter file contents are the following:

```
userid=system/manager full=y file=full_sys
buffer=102400 log=full_sys grants=y indexes=y
```

Run this export every night, and you will have all the protection you could ever want against losing an object.

When the Window Is Not Long Enough

One important question needs to be answered when deciding what to export and when: "Which tables experience the highest activity?" With the answer to that question, you can decide to export those tables on a regular basis and other not-so-active ones less frequently. Examine Table 16-1 to see how this could be mapped to the largest and most strategic data in a communication company's database.

Armed with this information, you then produce the code that will run the export routines. You always add two more parts to the backup procedures, as shown in Table 16-2. Part 5 exports all the data not done in parts 1 through 4, and part 6 makes a copy of the makeup of the database but does not export any data.

Table Name	Owner	Approximate Size	Part
Customers	b_cust	8,000,000	1
Phones	b_numbers	12,000,000	2
loc_master	b_inventory	615,000	3
Interurban	b_ld	7,500,000	4

TABLE 16-1.   *Large Objects' Part of an Export Cycle*

VIP
Based on your configuration, you may have more or fewer parts after you analyze your requirements.

Use the following guidelines when implementing the procedures (the part numbers referred to are from Tables 16-1 and 16-2):

■ Each part (numbered 1 to 4) must complete successfully before the next component runs. Thus, if part 2 does not complete on a Tuesday night, part 2 is run again Wednesday night, and part 3 waits one more night for its turn.

■ These procedures must run unattended; thus, export must be run using the **parfile=** parameter (discussed in Chapter 15). Using part 3 from Table 16-1 as an example, the export command would be **exp parfile=sys_part3.parfile**, and the parameter file would contain the following:

```
userid=b_inventory/secure file=sys_part3 buffer=102400
grants=y indexes=y log=part3_systables=loc_master
```

Component	Part
Other data not part of 1 to 4	5
Full system no rows	6

TABLE 16-2.   *Other Parts of Database to Export*

- Part 5 exports all the data not done in parts 1 through 4.

- Part 6 runs every night and writes an export file containing all the SQL statements required to re-create your database. No data is written to the export file during this operation. Assuming the job runs from the Oracle SYSTEM account using the command exp parfile=full_no_rows, the contents of the parameter file are

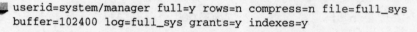

```
userid=system/manager full=y rows=n compress=n file=full_sys
buffer=102400 log=full_sys grants=y indexes=y
```

Keep a log of your export backups. A sample is shown in Table 16-3. Notice how part 3 was scheduled to run June 13 but did not complete. As a result, part 3 was rescheduled to run June 14. Had part 3 run to completion on the 13th, part 4 would have run on the 14th. Even though parts 5 and 6 run nightly, you still should track their successful completion.

Date	Part Scheduled	Completed	Written to Tape
June 11	1	Y	Y
June 11	5	Y	Y
June 11	6	N	N
June 12	2	Y	Y
June 12	5	Y	Y
June 12	6	Y	Y
June 13	3	N	N
June 13	5	Y	Y
June 13	6	Y	Y
June 14	3	Y	Y
June 14	5	Y	Y
June 14	6	Y	Y
June 15	4	Y	Y
June 15	5	Y	Y
June 15	5	Y	Y

TABLE 16-3. *Export Log*

Recovery from an Export File

Once the export files are written as described in the previous sections, restoring one or more objects from the export is done when required. Let's look at a few situations that may come up and how to use import to rebuild one or more missing objects.

NOTE
We recommend doing object restoration from the Oracle SYSTEM account.

Restoring a Single Object

Using the appropriate export file as input, follow these steps to restore the complete contents of the loc_master:

1. Log in to SQL*Plus using the SYSTEM account, and enter the command **truncate table b_inventory.loc_master;** to clean out the table. If the table has been dropped, the truncate command will return Oracle error "942:table or view does not exist."

2. Leave SQL*Plus, and enter the command **imp userid=system fromuser=b_inventory touser=b_inventory commit=y file=sys_part3 buffer=102400 tables=loc_master ignore=y log=sys_rest**. You will be prompted for the password missing from the command line.

NOTE
*Use the parameter **commit=y** to ensure that the import runs to completion. When you are restoring a large table, this ensures Oracle has enough rollback segment space to handle a large import.*

3. Log in to SQL*Plus as the b_inventory user and verify the grants on the table by issuing the command **select grantee, privilege from user_tab_privs_made where table_name = 'LOC_MASTER';**. If there seem to be some privileges missing, ascertain what they are and give them out again.

Restoring Multiple Objects

This exercise is similar to the previous section, except that you have to delete rows from more than one table before bringing the table back from the export file. In addition, the command used to invoke import is **imp userid=system fromuser=(b_inventory,b_cust) touser=(b_inventory,b_cust) commit=y file=sys_part2 buffer=102400 tables=(loc_master,customers) ignore=y**

log=sys_rest. You will be prompted for the password missing from the command line. In this command, the Oracle user names owning the tables are listed with **fromuser** and **touser** in parentheses separated by commas. The tables being brought back are listed in parentheses separated by commas as well.

Image Backups

Let's move from export and import to image backups. Image backups play an important role in your backup and recovery procedures. They make copies of some or all of your datafiles, redo logs, and control files. In this section, we will discuss making consistent (cold) backups and online (hot) backups.

Consistent (Cold) Backups

Cold backups are made with the database closed. Any file, be it datafile, redo log, or control, is part of this backup. Usually, disk space permitting, the files are copied somewhere on a disk and then backed up to tape during the quiet hours in the middle of the night. We recommend running the following program in SQL*Plus, as it will create output that can be used to make a cold backup. The bold text in the following listing may change to suit your database.

```
SQL*Plus: Release 8.1.5.0.0 - Production on Sun May 11 12:20:12 2002
(c) Copyright 1999 Oracle Corporation.  All rights reserved.
Connected to:
Oracle8i Enterprise Edition Release 8.1.5.0.0 - Production
With the Partitioning and Java options
PL/SQL Release 8.1.5.0.0 - Production
SQL> -- You must have select privileges on the v$parameter
SQL> -- v$logfile v$datafile and v$controlfile data
SQL> -- dictionary views belonging to SYS to run
SQL> -- this program
SQL> set pages 0 feed off echo off timi off
SQL> col a new_value b
SQL> col c new_value d
SQL> select value a,sysdate c
  2      from v$parameter
  3    where name = 'db_name';
SQL> spool cold.backup
SQL> prompt g:
SQL> prompt cd \oradb\backups
SQL> prompt
```

```
SQL> prompt Cold backup for "&b" database on &d ...
SQL> prompt
SQL> prompt rem Redo logs
SQL> prompt
SQL> select 'copy '||member
  2      from v$logfile;
SQL> prompt
SQL> prompt rem Datafiles
SQL> prompt
SQL> select 'copy '||name
  2      from v$datafile;
SQL> prompt
SQL> prompt rem Control files
SQL> prompt
SQL> select 'copy '||name
  2      from v$controlfile;
SQL> spool off
SQL> exit
```

In the listing, the name of the output file is cold.backup; if this does not conform to the file naming rules on your computer, the spool command filename will have to be changed. The output from the listing is shown next.

```
g:
cd \oradb\backups
Cold backup for "o8ibegin" database on 12-JUN-2001 ...
Rem Redo logs
copy g:\Oradata\o8ibegin\log1orcl.dbf
copy t:\Oradata\o8ibegin\log1orcl.dbf
Rem Datafiles
copy d:\Oradata\o8ibegin\dbs1o8ibegin.dbf
copy e:\Oradata\o8ibegin\tempo8ibegin.dbf
copy d:\Oradata\o8ibegin\userso8ibegin.dbf
copy g:\Oradata\o8ibegin\toolso8ibegin.dbf
Rem Control files
copy g:\Oradata\o8ibegin\ctl1o8ibegin.dbf
copy d:\Oradata\o8ibegin\ctl2o8ibegin.dbf
```

VIP
*Note how we are using long filenames with this
database. If these ever get shortened to names using
the tilde convention (as in dbs1o8~1.dbf), there will
be big problems!*

Online (Hot) Backups

Hot backups are made with the database running in ARCHIVELOG mode. Hot backups do not copy the online redo logs, since they are being archived and backed up as part of your nightly backups anyway. The database is open, and an online backup can be performed while the users are working with the database. Hot backups are done by placing a tablespace in backup mode, copying it somewhere else on disk or to tape, and then taking the tablespace out of backup mode. After the tablespaces are backed up in this manner, you can back up your control file.

VIP
You can provide users with 24-hour database availability by running in ARCHIVELOG mode and making hot backups. Even though the database is open and may be in use, the backup is consistent and may be used for recovery, as discussed later in this chapter.

Sample Hot Backup

Table 16-4 shows a database against which we will be doing a hot backup.

Tablespace	Datafile(s)
System	d:\Oracle\Oradata\o8ibegin\dbs1.dbf
Users	d:\Oracle\Oradata\o8ibegin\users1.dbf
	e:\Oracle\Oradata\o8ibegin\users2.dbf
Temp	d:\Oracle\Oradata\o8ibegin\temp.dbf
Rollback_segs	d:\Oracle\Oradata\o8ibegin\rbs1.dbf
	g:\Oracle\Oradata\o8ibegin\rbs2.dbf
Tools	i:\Oracle\Oradata\o8ibegin\tools.dbf

TABLE 16-4.   *Database for Backing Up*

The following SQL*Plus script can be used (make modifications where necessary if your operating system is not Windows NT):

```
SQL*Plus: Release 8.1.5.0.0 - Production on Sun May 11 12:20:12 2002
(c) Copyright 1999 Oracle Corporation.  All rights reserved.
Connected to:
Oracle8i Enterprise Edition Release 8.1.5.0.0 - Production
With the Partitioning and Java options
 PL/SQL Release 8.1.5.0.0 - Production
SQL> -- We inform Oracle that we are backing up a tablespace
SQL> -- before doing the copy. This is done one tablespace
SQL> -- at a time. After the tablespace is put in backup
SQL> -- mode, make a copy of its datafile(s). By forcing
SQL> -- a checkpoint after each tablespace is backed up,
SQL> -- we synch the registering of the backup internally
SQL> -- to Oracle.
SQL>
SQL> alter tablespace tools begin backup;
Tablespace altered.
SQL> $ copy i:\Oracle\Oradata\o8ibegin\tools.dbf d:\backups\tools.dbf
SQL> alter tablespace tools end backup;
tablespace altered.
SQL> alter system checkpoint;
System altered.
SQL> alter tablespace temp begin backup;
Tablespace altered.
SQL> $ copy d:\Oracle\Oradata\o8ibegin\temp.dbf d:\backups\temp.dbf
SQL> alter tablespace temp end backup;
Tablespace altered.
SQL> alter system checkpoint;
System altered.
SQL> alter tablespace rollback_segs begin backup;
Tablespace altered.
SQL> $ copy d:\Oracle\Oradata\o8ibegin\rbs1.dbf d:\backups\rbs1.dbf
SQL> $ copy g:\Oracle\Oradata\o8ibegin\rbs2.dbf d:\backups\rbs2.dbf
SQL> alter tablespace rollback_segs end backup;
Tablespace altered.
SQL> alter system checkpoint;
System altered.
SQL> alter tablespace users begin backup;
Tablespace altered.
```

```
SQL> $ copy d:\Oracle\Oradata\o8ibegin\users1.dbf d:\backups\users1.dbf
SQL> $ copy e:\Oracle\Oradata\o8ibegin\users2.dbf d:\backups\users2.dbf
SQL> alter tablespace users end backup;
Tablespace altered.
SQL> alter system checkpoint;
System altered.
SQL> alter tablespace system begin backup;
Tablespace altered.
SQL> $ copy d:\Oracle\Oradata\o8ibegin\dbs1.dbf d:\backups\dbs1.dbf
SQL> alter tablespace system end backup;
Tablespace altered.
SQL> alter system checkpoint;
System altered.
SQL> alter database backup controlfile to
  2    'd:\backups\control.bkp' reuse;
Database altered.
```

Recovery

So far in this chapter, we have discussed export and import, the role they play in
your backup procedures, and how to restore an object from an export file. We have
also discussed image backups. Now comes the meat of this chapter: recovery. Strap
yourself in; this is the heart of Oracle's backup and recovery strategy, and it can
prove quite stimulating!

In this section, we will lead you through some exercises and show you how to
perform recovery. You will need a "practice" database to do these exercises.
Following is a sample create database script you can use as a skeleton SQL script to
build your own database. It is included to get you started; the text that is bolded
needs modifications to suit your configuration:

```
Oracle Server Manager Release 3.1.5.0.1 - Production
(c) Copyright 1997, Oracle Corporation. All rights reserved.
Oracle8i Enterprise Edition Release 8.1.5.0.0 - Production
With the Partitioning and Java options
PL/SQL Release 8.1.5.0.0 - Production
SVRMGR> connect internal/oracle
Connected.
SVRMGR> spool scratch.log
SVRMGR> set echo on
SVRMGR> startup nomount pfile=c:\Oracle\database\initprac.ora
SVRMGR> create database prac
  2    datafile 'd:\Oracle\database\dbs1prac.dbf'    size 50m
  3    logfile  'd:\Oracle\database\log1prac.dbf'    size 300k,
  4             'd:\Oracle\database\log2prac.dbf'    size 300k
  5         maxlogfiles    20
  6         maxlogmembers   4
```

```
    7           maxdatafiles   30
    8           maxinstances   1
    9           maxloghistory 100;
Statement processed.
SVRMGR> create rollback segment temp
    2        tablespace system
    3     storage (initial 50k minextents 20 maxextents 20);
Statement processed.
SVRMGR> shutdown
SVRMGR> startup pfile=c:\Oracle\database\initprac.ora
SVRMGR> alter tablespace system default storage (pctincrease 0);
SVRMGR> set echo off
SVRMGR> set termout off
SVRMGR> @c:\Oracle\Ora81\rdbms\admin\catalog.sql
SVRMGR> @c:\Oracle\Ora81\rdbms\admin\catproc.sql
SVRMGR> connect system/manager
SVRMGR> @c:\Oracle\Ora81\rdbms\admin\catdbsyn.sql
SVRMGR> connect internal/oracle
SVRMGR> shutdown
```

The following checklist outlines what was done before running the **create database** script in the previous listing:

- The initialization parameter file initprac.ora has been created in the appropriate location.

- The command **set ORACLE_SID=prac** has been executed.

- The NT service to support the prac database instance has been defined.

VIP
Without this added infrastructure in place, the database will not be operational.

What Is Recovery?

Recovery is a process whereby an image backup of the database (done, let's say, at 7:00 A.M.) is rolled forward to a later point in time (let's say 2:00 P.M.) using the archived redo logs. Roll forward applies changes recorded in the redo logs; then, using the rollback segments, it undoes any transactions that were recorded in the redo log but were not committed. We discussed the redo logs in Chapter 4, pointing out how they record all activities against the database. Say a system had been used by 12 people between 7:00 A.M. and 2:00 P.M. Everything these people did to the database was written to the redo logs; thus, the redo logs are a mirror image of the activities of those 12 people during those seven hours.

Redo Log Types

There are two types of redo logs: online redo logs and archived redo logs. Online redo logs are the pool of two or more redo logs written to as the database operates. We discussed in Chapter 3 how Oracle cycles between the online redo logs. When running the database in ARCHIVELOG mode, before reusing a redo log, Oracle copies it elsewhere and adds it to the pool of archived redo logs. Every redo log is allocated a sequence number when Oracle does a log switch. In Table 16-5, we show how the status of redo logs cycles between active, being archived, and inactive.

In Table 16-5, after the second log switch, a redo log belonging to group 1 is archived, and that copy is referred to as an archived redo log. Notice that when the fourth log switch occurs, redo log group 1 becomes active once again, and any information in the log is overwritten. This is not a problem, since the previous contents of the redo log have become an archived redo log.

Types of Recovery

Every time you start the database, Oracle looks through its online redo logs to see if there is any recovery it should perform based on the information in those logs. If it finds any information, it applies it to the database before it is opened. This feature is

Event	Log Sequence	Redo Log Group	Status
log switch #1	23418	1	Active
		2	Inactive
		3	Being archived
log switch #2	23419	1	Being archived
		2	Active
		3	Inactive
log switch #3	23420	1	Inactive
		2	Being archived
		3	Active
log switch #4	23421	1	Active
		2	Inactive
		3	Being archived

TABLE 16-5. *Cycle of Redo Logs Through Four Log Switches*

called automatic database instance recovery. When you take a mixture of archived and online redo logs and recover all or part of the database, this is called either complete media recovery or incomplete media recovery.

Complete media recovery can be performed on the database, a tablespace, or one or more datafiles. Recovery stops with the application of the most recent redo log. Incomplete media recovery can only be performed on the whole database. The term "incomplete" is used because, with this type of recovery, not all of the redo logs are applied. You specify when the recovery process is to stop; when Oracle applies enough redo logs to reach that point, the recovery stops. Table 16-6 summarizes what can be recovered using complete and incomplete recovery.

Performing Complete Recovery

We will now lead you through a complete recovery session. The database we are recovering has the following makeup:

Tablespace	Datafile(s)
System	d:\Oracle\Oradata\o8ibegin\dbs1book.dbf
Rollback	g:\Oracle\Oradata\o8ibegin\rbook.dbf
Users	d:\Oracle\Oradata\o8ibegin\users.dbf
Tools	h:\Oracle\Oradata\o8ibegin tools.dbf
Temp	h:\Oracle\Oradata\o8ibegin temp.dbf

NOTE
*This is not the same database as the prac instance
we showed the **create database** code for in the
previous listing. It is deliberately a different
database.*

In this scenario, the database is backed up at 4:40 A.M. nightly. The archived redo logs are copied to the directory d:\Oracle\Oradata\o8begin\archive. Image

Recovery Type	Database	Datafile	Tablespace
Complete	X	X	X
Incomplete	X		

TABLE 16-6. *What Can Be Recovered Using Complete and Incomplete Recovery*

backups are written to the directory d:\sys\backups and written to tape from there at 6:00 A.M. At noon, there is a problem with one of the disk packs, and the database shuts itself down.

Before doing the recovery, you must restore the image backup from wherever it resides to the correct location on your disks. Using our sample database, the following five commands copy the image backup to its proper location:

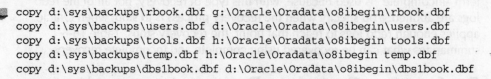

```
copy d:\sys\backups\rbook.dbf g:\Oracle\Oradata\o8ibegin\rbook.dbf
copy d:\sys\backups\users.dbf d:\Oracle\Oradata\o8ibegin\users.dbf
copy d:\sys\backups\tools.dbf h:\Oracle\Oradata\o8ibegin tools.dbf
copy d:\sys\backups\temp.dbf h:\Oracle\Oradata\o8ibegin temp.dbf
copy d:\sys\backups\dbs1book.dbf d:\Oracle\Oradata\o8ibegin\dbs1book.dbf
```

To perform the complete recovery, follow these steps:

1. Invoke line-mode Server Manager with the command **svrmgrl**.

2. Enter the command **connect internal/oracle**, followed by **startup mount**.

3. Check the status of the database by entering the command **alter database open;** and receive the following feedback from Oracle:

```
alter database open
*
ORA-01113: file 1 needs media recovery
ORA-01110: data file 1: 'd:\Oracle\Oradata\o8ibegin\dbs1book.dbf'
SVRMGR>
```

4. Enter the command **recover database;** and receive the following feedback from Oracle:

```
ORA-00279: Change 9964 generated at 12/21/01 14:37:06 needed...
ORA-00289: Suggestion : d:\Oracle\Oradata ... archive\arch_383.arc
ORA-00280: Change 9964 for thread 1 is in sequence #383
Specify log: {<RET>=suggested | filename | AUTO | CANCEL}
```

5. Press ENTER to accept the log filename presented (d:\Oracle\Oradata\ o8ibegin\archive \arch_383.arc, in this case).

As Oracle suggests each archived redo log filename, keep pressing ENTER to accept the suggestions made. When the recovery is complete, Oracle presents you with this message:

```
Log applied.
Media recovery complete.
SVRMGR>
```

You then issue the command **alter database open;** and the database recovery is complete! Bravo—nice job.

When presented with the name of the first redo log to apply, you could have entered the word auto (notice it is one of the suggestions in the specify log prompt), and Oracle would have run the recovery without need for further intervention. The last log file prompt is shown here, and the recovery complete message follows.

```
ORA-00279: Change 10029 generated at 12/21/01 14:43:13 needed...
ORA-00289: Suggestion : d:\Oracle\Oradata ... archive\arch_399.arc
ORA-00280: Change 10029 for thread 1 is in sequence #399
ORA-00278: Logfile 'd:\Oracle\Oradata\o8ibegin ... no longer...
Log applied.
Media recovery complete.
SVRMGR>
```

Performing Incomplete Recovery

Incomplete recovery is one of the most interesting features of Oracle's recovery mechanisms. Review the exercise we went through in the previous section, in which Oracle asked for names and locations of archived redo logs, and then look at the following listing:

```
ORA-00308: cannot open archived log 'd:\Oracle\Oradata ... arch_399.arc'
ORA-27041: unable to open file
OSD-04002: unable to open file
O/S-Error: (OS 2) The system cannot find the file specified.
SVRMGR>
```

Uh oh! Oracle wants archived redo log file with sequence number 387—panic (why did you want to be a DBA anyway?). Confident that Oracle just messed up, you try the job again and, lo and behold, it happens again. No problem. Just drop back to the operating system, find the missing log file, and all will be well. You issue the command **dir/w** and receive the following output:

```
arch_382.arc   arch_386.arc   arch_391.arc   arch_395.arc   arch_399.arc
arch_383.arc   arch_388.arc   arch_392.arc   arch_396.arc   arch_400.arc
arch_384.arc   arch_389.arc   arch_393.arc   arch_397.arc   arch_401.arc
arch_385.arc   arch_390.arc   arch_394.arc   arch_398.arc
```

Notice that the file arch_387.arc is not there. This is why incomplete recovery exists.

VIP
Incomplete recovery recovers the database to a point in time in the past. In our example, the database can only be recovered to the transaction at the end of archived log sequence number 386.

There are three ways to perform incomplete recovery: change-based recovery, cancel-based recovery, and time-based recovery. We will run through each one in the next sections. Hold on.

Change-Based Recovery

To do change-based recovery, you need to know the highest system change number (SCN) written to the archived redo log just before the missing log. You can then issue the recovery statement recover database until change scn_number; where the scn_number is that SCN written to archived redo log file sequence number 386 (that is, one less than the missing log sequence number 387). You can get that SCN information from a view called v$log_history owned by Oracle user SYS, which looks like the following:

```
RECID           NUMBER
STAMP           NUMBER
THREAD#         NUMBER
SEQUENCE#       NUMBER
FIRST_CHANGE#   NUMBER
FIRST_TIME      DATE
NEXT_CHANGE#    NUMBER
```

NOTE
Since v$log_history stores the first SCN for each archived redo log, you need to decrease the first_change# from the next highest sequence# log file by 1. Since we are looking for the last SCN for sequence number 386, we use sequence# 387 as the desired log file number.

Using the query **select first_change#-1 from v$log_history where sequence# = 387;**, you can find out the desired SCN. The output from this query is the following:

```
FIRST_CHANGE#-1
--------------------
           9999
```

Now that you know the SCN, let's perform the recovery, using these steps:

1. Invoke line-mode Server Manager with the command **svrmgrl**.

2. Enter the command **connect internal/oracle**, followed by **startup mount**.

3. Enter the command **recover database until change 9999;** and receive feedback from Oracle similar to when you started complete recovery.

4. Enter the word **auto** in response to Oracle's suggestion for the first archived redo log. Oracle stops recovery before it looks for arch_387.arc and informs you of the following:

```
ORA-00289: Suggestion : d:\Oracle\Oradata\o8ibegin ...
ORA-00280: Change 9999 for thread 1 is in sequence #387
ORA-00278: Logfile ' d:\Oracle\Oradata\o8ibegin ... no longer ...
Log applied.
Media recovery complete.
SVRMGR>
```

The final step in this recovery exercise is to open the database. After we have covered all three incomplete recovery types, we will show you how to open the database in the section called "Opening the Database After Incomplete Media Recovery."

Cancel-Based Recovery

Cancel-based recovery proceeds until you enter the word **cancel** to a prompt Oracle gives you suggesting the name of an archived redo log. So far in our discussions, you have seen the following prompt from Oracle:

```
Specify log: {<RET>=suggested | filename | AUTO | CANCEL}
```

Using the cancel option as the prompt suggests, let's do our recovery again. You are logged in to Server Manager and have issued **connect internal** and then **startup mount**. When you enter the command **recover database until cancel;**, Oracle suggests the name of the first archived redo log it requires. Press the ENTER key to accept the name, and keep going until Oracle asks for a log with the sequence number 387. Enter the word **cancel**, and recovery stops, as Oracle tells you the following:

```
ORA-00289: Suggestion : d:\Oracle\Oradata\o8ibegin ...
ORA-00278: Logfile 'd:\Oracle\Oradata\o8ibegin ...' no ...
Specify log: {<RET>=suggested | filename | AUTO | CANCEL}
cancel
Media recovery cancelled.
```

Again, the final step in this recovery exercise is to open the database, which we will cover in the "Opening the Database After Incomplete Media Recovery" section following our discussion of all three incomplete recovery types.

Time-Based Recovery

To use time-based recovery, you need to know the time recorded in v$log_history for archived redo log sequence 387 (the missing redo log). By issuing the query **select to_char(first_time,'YYYY/MM/DD:HH24:MI:SS') from v$log_history where sequence# = 387;**, you get the following time:

```
TIME
-------------------
2008/12/21:14:42:04
```

Let's do the recovery now. You are logged in to Server Manager and have issued **connect internal** and then **startup mount**. When you enter the command **recover database until time '2008/12/21:14:42:04';**, Oracle suggests the name of the first archived redo log it requires. Enter the reply **auto** and Oracle applies archived redo logs until the sequence number 387. You are then told the following:

```
ORA-00280: Change 9999 for thread 1 is in sequence #387
ORA-00278: Logfile ' d:\Oracle\Oradata\o8ibegin ...' no ...
Log applied.
Media recovery complete.
```

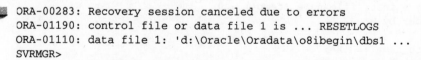

VIP
When using time-based recovery, the format for the time is YYYY/MM/DD:HH24:MI:SS and it is enclosed in single quotes.

Opening the Database After Incomplete Media Recovery

Before we tell you how to do this, we need to go over some pseudo-legal stuff. The command we are about to show you must *never be run against any database (other than your practice database) without speaking with Oracle worldwide customer support.* Issuing this command against a database after incomplete media recovery will allow you to open the database but *the backup you recovered from will not be usable.* If you attempt a recovery again using the same image backup, you will receive the following error:

```
ORA-00283: Recovery session canceled due to errors
ORA-01190: control file or data file 1 is ... RESETLOGS
ORA-01110: data file 1: 'd:\Oracle\Oradata\o8ibegin\dbs1 ...
SVRMGR>
```

The problem is that Oracle knows when the database was last opened with the resetlogs option, and any backups written before that time are unusable. We cannot stress this enough. The command **alter database open resetlogs;** is used to get a database open, but it can be very dangerous.

VIP
*Do not use the command **alter database open resetlogs;** without speaking with Oracle worldwide customer support FIRST!*

You have been warned.

A Complete Backup Plan

We now present a sample backup plan, using a combination of export and image backup. The database is running in ARCHIVELOG mode and the window of opportunity is about two hours.

Even though the makeup of the database is fairly static, we use the following SQL and PL/SQL script to write the program to do the hot backup (the bold text may have to be changed if your operating system is other than Windows NT):

```
set serveroutput on size 100000
set echo off feed off pages 0
spool hot.backup
select 'File created '||to_char(sysdate,'dd-Mon-yyyy hh24:mm:ss')
  from dual;
prompt
begin
  declare
    target_dir varchar2(100) := 'g:\oracle\backups';
    source_file varchar2(100);
    ts_name varchar2(100);
    prev_ts_name varchar2(100);
    cursor mycur is
      select file_name,lower(tablespace_name)
        from sys.dba_data_files
      where instr(file_name,'temp') = 0
      order by 2;
  begin
    prev_ts_name := 'X';
    open mycur;
    fetch mycur into source_file,ts_name;
    while mycur%found loop
      if ts_name <> prev_ts_name then
        dbms_output.put_line ('#######################');
        dbms_output.put_line ('# Tablespace '||ts_name||'. . .');
        dbms_output.put_line ('#######################');
        dbms_output.put_line ('sqlplus '||
        '@d:\Oracle\sysman\start.sql '||
                              ts_name);
      end if;
      dbms_output.put_line ('copy '||source_file||' '||target_dir);
      prev_ts_name := ts_name;
      fetch mycur into source_file,ts_name;
```

```
       if ts_name <> prev_ts_name then
          dbms_output.put_line ('sqlplus '||
          '@d:\Oracle\sysman\end.sql '||
                                 prev_ts_name);
       end if;
     end loop;
     dbms_output.put_line ('sqlplus @d:\Oracle\sysman\end.sql '||
                             prev_ts_name);
   end;
end;
/
```

The output from this PL/SQL code resembles the following:

```
File created 19-May-2002 11:05:20
######################
# Tablespace rollback_data. . .
######################
sqlplus @d:\Oracle\sysman\start.sql rollback_data
copy D:\ORACLE\O8IBEGIN\RBS1O8IBEGIN.DBF g:\oracle\backups
sqlplus @d:\Oracle\sysman\end.sql rollback_data
######################
# Tablespace system. . .
######################
sqlplus @d:\Oracle\sysman\start.sql system
copy G:\ORACLE\O8IBEGIN\DBS1O8IBEGIN.DBF g:\oracle\backups
sqlplus @d:\Oracle\sysman\end.sql system
######################
# Tablespace temporary_data. . .
######################
sqlplus @d:\Oracle\sysman\start.sql temporary_data
copy F:\ORACLE\O8IBEGIN\TEMPO8IBEGIN.DBF g:\oracle\backups
sqlplus @d:\Oracle\sysman\end.sql temporary_data
######################
# Tablespace user_data. . .
######################
sqlplus @d:\Oracle\sysman\start.sql user_data
copy F:\ORACLE\O8IBEGIN\USERS1O8IBEGIN.DBF g:\oracle\backups
sqlplus @d:\Oracle\sysman\end.sql user_data
```

The program **start.sql** referenced in this listing puts a tablespace in backup mode. It contains the code

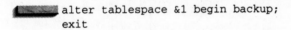
```
alter tablespace &1 begin backup;
exit
```

The program **end.sql** takes a tablespace out of backup mode. It contains the code

```
alter tablespace &1 end backup;
exit
```

NOTE
*The &1 text sequences in start.sql and end.sql allow passing of a parameter to each program. Since you place a tablespace name after **alter tablespace**, the &1 would translate to a tablespace name.*

In the "Substitution Variables in SQL Plus" section of Chapter 12, we showed how the & character is used. By placing the &1 substitution variable in a SQL*Plus program, you can pass a value to a program. Thus, the command sqlplus @start system is expanded into the following:

```
SQL> alter tablespace &1 begin backup;
old    1: alter tablespace &1 begin backup;
new    1: alter tablespace system begin backup;
SQL>
```

Notice how the text system from the command sqlplus @start system is accepted into the program and replaces the substitution variable &1. The complete backup plan we have presented here is to be used as a starting point. As you can see by examining Table 16-7, export, import, and hot backups play a role when developing a full backup strategy. Backup and recovery are two of the most popular topics at Oracle technical conferences. Users and Oracle Corporation personnel present papers and lead workshops on these ever-so-important topics.

What's Next

Perhaps you have noticed the amount of ground we have covered in this chapter. We believe that with guidance you can start doing some remarkably intense work with Oracle8*i* from day one as a DBA. In the next chapter, we will discuss tuning the Oracle8*i* database to help you get maximum performance from this robust software.

	Component	TIME	Notes
1	Export	2:00 A.M.	Full database export from the SYSTEM account.
2	Hot backup	3:30 A.M.	Same as the 12:05 P.M. and 8:00 P.M. backups, except all archived redo logs are moved to another directory.
3	Tape copy	5:00 A.M.	Image backup is written to tape as well as the directory to which the archived redo logs were moved at 3:30 A.M.
4	Control file	6:30 A.M.,	Control file contents are written to a trace file using the command **alter system backup controlfile to trace;**.
5	Export	7:30 A.M.	Full database export with **rows=n compress=n** whose output can be used to create the structure of the database (i.e., the tablespaces, rollback segments, and users).
6	Hot backup	12:05 P.M.	All tablespaces in the database except temp and ones containing objects protected by the nightly export.
7	Hot backup	8:00 P.M.	Same as 12:05 P.M. hot backup.

TABLE 16-7. *Full Backup Procedures*

CHAPTER
17

Database Tuning

his chapter deals with tuning your database, not your applications. We will discuss the major items that will allow you, as a database administrator, to get an extra 20 to 30 percent throughput from your Oracle-based systems. We do touch briefly on the cost-based approach to SQL statement processing, as it can have a profound effect on how your database performs.

But first, let's discuss what database tuning cannot do. It is not a substitute for good application design—remember that old saying, "Garbage in leads to garbage out." A system that is designed badly will perform badly. The bottom line: good performance out of your database starts with good application design. With this in mind, we will take a look at the key steps you can take to get that extra boost of performance from your system.

In this chapter we will cover the following subjects:

- The initialization parameter file init.ora

- Which key initialization file settings to change

- How to determine current initialization parameter file settings

- How to change the current initialization file settings

- The key input/output stream

- Key tablespaces and their contents

- How indexes work

Terminology

The following definitions will arm you with the technical jargon to make it through this chapter:

- A *database administrator*, or DBA, is responsible for the technical management of a database, including installation, performance tuning, and computer resource management. The DBA classically serves as an advisor on application design to maximize system throughput.

- The *initialization parameter file* (commonly called init.ora) is read by Oracle when starting the database; its values help determine resource utilization. The best analogy to this is your registry file in Windows or your autoexec.bat file when you boot your PC.

- A *database instance* is an amount of main memory and a set of support processes required to access an Oracle database.

- A *cache* is a segment of computer memory allocated to holding specific pieces of information. For example, while Oracle operates, it maintains a data cache that contains most recently read data.

- A *table* is defined in Oracle's data dictionary, and it groups rows of information together in the database. A list of your fellow workers' names, numbers, and hire dates is an example of a table.

- An *index* is a structure Oracle uses to permit rapid access to your tables.

- The *optimizer* is an internal routine Oracle8*i* uses to ensure the data qualifying for a query are retrieved in the most efficient manner. SQL statement optimization is key to turning screens with mouse hourglasses into screens full of data waiting for entry.

Initialization Parameter (init.ora) File

Many tools are available to you for tuning the database; the initialization parameter file is a good place to start. At startup, every database reads its initialization parameter to configure itself. Think of this file as the key to a lock. Before you can enter the room, you must first use the key. Before a database instance can start up, it must read the initialization parameter file. There are over 100 different changeable entries, all affecting how your database and processes that run against your database work. By making changes to this file, you will change the way your database uses and allocates resources.

VIP

All changes you make to the initialization parameter file only take effect the next time the database is started.

Let's investigate working with entries in the initialization parameter file; first we look at the types of entries in the initialization parameter file, then at working with those entries using the Oracle Enterprise Manager (*OEM*) Instance Manager with Oracle8*i*. Next, we look at doing the same work with Server Manager and a simple text editor.

VIP

Regardless of which way you decide to do it, it is wise to note previous values before making changes in case the new parameter values have a negative rather than a positive effect on performance tuning.

Types of Entries in the Initialization Parameter File

The initialization parameter file is like any other text file on your computer—pick your favorite editor and make the changes. The order of the entries within the initialization parameter file does not matter.

VIP
If you do not have an entry listed in your initialization parameter file, Oracle configures the missing value to a default setting.

There are three types of initialization parameter file entries:

- **Strings** A number of parameters are enclosed in single quotes, some are in double quotes, and some need not be in any quotes. Most of the string parameter values you enter will need no quotes. If one requires quotes of either type and you leave them out, Oracle will inform you when you start the database.

- **Integer** Some parameters accept integer values. There are no quotes.

- **Boolean** Some parameters accept the value TRUE or FALSE with no quotes.

Oracle8*i* Instance Manager—Viewing Settings

Viewing of settings can be done from the OEM Instance Manager. Invoke the Instance Manager and then enter the appropriate database login information.

VIP
*When working with initialization parameters in OEM, the results are stored locally and referred to as **configuration files**. In the Instance Manager, you can specify which configuration set you want to use as the database is started.*

When presented with the Instance Manager main console, click the Initialization Parameters folder to display the screen shown in Figure 17-1.

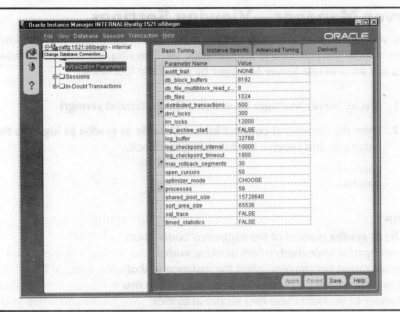

FIGURE 17-1. *The initialization parameters folder*

Notice how there are four property sheets underneath this folder.

1. Basic Tuning parameters are normally standard between different instances of the Oracle8*i* database. The Value shows the current setting.

2. Instance Specific parameters are specific to the instance being viewed. The control_files entry displaying the text "C:\Oracle\Oradata\O8ibegin\ ctlorcl..." and the db_name parameter displaying the value "oracle" are examples of this type of entry. For different instances, these values would most likely be different, though not necessarily always.

3. Advanced Tuning parameters are those that are adjusted on an as-needed basis, not quite as often as the Basic parameters. For example, the buffer_pool_recycle parameter might be adjusted to improve the performance of large table scans.

4. Derived parameters have been computed by Oracle according to other parameter values or operating system settings.

Server Manager—Viewing Settings

Before you begin making changes to the initialization parameter file, it is important you know how the parameters are currently set. The simplest way to see how the entries are set is to use Server Manager by doing the following:

1. Invoke Server Manager by entering the command **svrmgrl**.

2. Enter the command **connect internal/oracle as sysdba** to log in to the database, and receive the following feedback.

   ```
   Connected.
   SVRMGR>
   ```

VIP

*The **as sysdba** portion of the suggested connection command is important; when working with initialization parameters, often the instance is shut down and started. You should be connected in this manner to perform these two secure activities.*

After supplying these login credentials, you are at the right spot to view initialization parameters, as discussed in the next two sections.

Viewing All Parameter Values

To view all the parameters, enter the command **show parameters**. This displays all the possible entries and values in the initialization parameter file. The parameters are listed in alphabetical order, and the top of the output resembles the following:

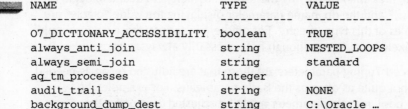

```
NAME                          TYPE          VALUE
------------------------       -----------   -------------
O7_DICTIONARY_ACCESSIBILITY   boolean       TRUE
always_anti_join              string        NESTED_LOOPS
always_semi_join              string        standard
aq_tm_processes               integer       0
audit_trail                   string        NONE
background_dump_dest          string        C:\Oracle …
backup_tape_io_slaves         boolean       FALSE
```

Viewing Some of the Parameter Values

Often you are only interested in a particular type of parameter. For example, you might be interested in all the parameters that contain the word "buffer." Once connected to the instance in Server Manager, enter **show parameters**, followed by another word. Oracle will do a character match on the word. For example, to see all the parameters that contain the word "buffer," you type the command **show parameters buffer** and receive output similar to the following:

```
NAME                        TYPE       VALUE
--------------------------  ---------  ------------------
buffer_pool_keep            string
buffer_pool_recycle         string
db_block_buffers            integer    400
log_buffer                  integer    32768
use_indirect_data_buffers   boolean    FALSE
```

Initialization Parameter File—What to Change

In this section, we list the key parameters you should consider tweaking. In our experience, these are the parameters that need changing 99 percent of the time.

db_block_buffers

This is your data cache. Before any process can look at, inspect, correct, or delete a piece of data, it must first reside in this data cache. The higher the value of the cache, the more data blocks Oracle is able to hold in memory. The lower the value, the fewer data blocks it can hold. If the data is not in memory, Oracle issues the needed I/O requests to obtain the data. I/O is one of the slowest operations a computer can do.

To summarize, the larger the number you choose for db_block_buffers, the larger your data cache. A large data cache is a very desirable situation. In fact, in a perfect world, you might want to make your db_block_buffers large enough to hold your entire database. In this situation, the need to go to the actual disk might be eliminated.

VIP

Set the db_block_buffers as high as possible for your operating environment in order to hold as much data in memory as possible.

This parameter is a memory hog. It very quickly increases the size of the SGA. Do not allow the SGA to go beyond 50 percent of the available memory of the computer.

shared_pool_size

This is your program cache and data dictionary cache. The data dictionary is information that Oracle needs to manage itself. For example, when a user logs in to the database, a number of data dictionary tables are referenced to determine the validity of the user's request to log in. Before that user can look at a row of information, a number of data dictionary tables are referenced to determine that database user's privileges. The program cache is where Oracle stores programs that work with the database. For example, every SQL statement you run in SQL*Plus must be placed into the program cache before it can be executed.

The larger the cache, the more likely your statement will be found in memory. The smaller the cache, the more often Oracle has to place the program into memory. A program cannot make requests from the database until it has been placed into this cache.

VIP

Set the shared_pool_size as high as possible. It is very desirable for performance reasons to have a program cache that is very large.

Again, this parameter is a memory hog. It very quickly increases the size of the SGA. Do not allow the SGA to go beyond 50 percent of the available memory of the computer.

sort_area_size

This is the parameter that controls the allocation of chunks of memory for sorting activities. SQL statements that include the **order by** and **group by** clauses generate sort activity. In addition, activities like **create index** also generate sort activity.

When the Oracle database cannot acquire enough memory to complete the sort, it completes the process on disk. An inadequate value for this parameter causes excessive sorts on disk (disk access is very slow compared to memory access). It has been our experience that the default setting is too low. We typically start off by doubling it.

VIP

Try doubling your sort_area_size parameter value. The default value is much too small.

The value coded for sort_area_size is allocated on a per-user basis. It does not take effect until you restart the database.

processes

This parameter defines the maximum number of processes that can simultaneously connect to an Oracle database. The default value of 50 is only acceptable for a very small system. Keep in mind that the Oracle background processes are included in this number. In addition, if an application spawns processes recursively, all the spawned processes count toward this number.

The only reason you keep this value low is to limit the number of users for a business reason or because of hardware/software capacity issues. Otherwise, it is highly recommended that you overestimate this value.

NOTE
We recommend setting this parameter to 200 when Oracle8i is installed. Our experience shows that this value is more than sufficient for most implementations.

open_cursors

This parameter is the maximum number of cursors a user can have open at a time. Think of a *cursor* as a chunk of memory that Oracle allocates to the user process for SQL statements. The default value for this is much too small. When you run out of cursors, your application stops. We recommend setting this value to 2500 to start with.

VIP
Set this value very high to start. If it is set too low, your application will come to a stop.

database_writers

This parameter controls the number of processes that write information to the database concurrently; on most platforms, you have the option of having multiple database writers. This greatly improves your ability to write information to the database. If you are on an operating system that supports additional database writers, the first thing you should do is increase the number of database writers that are activated. Many DBAs are under the misconception that this is limited by the number of CPUs; this is not true. In fact, we recommend you set database_writers to two per datafile.

VIP
If you are on an operating system that supports additional database writers, the first thing you should do is increase the number of database writers.

timed_statistics

This parameter tells the database to record additional information about itself as it is running. This is quite useful information in a test environment; in a production environment, we recommend you turn it off. Since this is additional overhead, it has a performance impact on your system.

optimizer_mode

This parameter has a major impact on how your database chooses to execute SQL statements. You have four possible choices for this parameter:

- **FIRST_ROWS or ALL_ROWS:** These two modes instruct Oracle to use the cost-based optimizer (*CBO*) approach (discussed as well in the "Cost-Based Approach" section of Chapter 13). With this setting, Oracle takes into account table sizes when you issue SQL statements. For example, your database knows that your customer table has 10,000 rows of information and your phone_type table has three rows. It takes this into account when executing SQL statements.

- **RULE:** This is the way Oracle databases have traditionally determined how SQL statements would execute. There is a weighting system that Oracle uses to determine how a SQL statement will execute. For example, a table that contains an index will be favored over a table that has no indexes.

- **CHOOSE:** This is the default setting. This tells the database to use the cost-based optimization approach when you have the necessary information. Without that information, use the rule-based method.

WHAT APPROACH TO USE FOR EXISTING SYSTEMS   If not already using the cost-based optimizer approach with your Oracle systems, we recommend looking at its performance after implementing a statistic collection system similar to one we discussed in the "Methodology for Statistic Collection" section of Chapter 13. Many systems that have been around since Oracle versions 5 and 6 perform well with the rule-based optimization. It can prove disastrous to suddenly switch the optimization approach without adequate preparation.

VIP

*For systems that were designed and tuned using the rule-based approach, set **optimizer_mode=rule** in your initialization parameter file. Gather statistics for the database objects and benchmark the performance of CBO before switching.*

WHAT APPROACH TO USE FOR NEW SYSTEMS   We unequivocally recommend using the cost-based approach with new system development. CBO is sensitive to the row counts in application tables, and to the distribution of column values in those tables; inspect the information in Table 17-1 to see the access path used by Oracle and CBO to process a query against the last_name (an indexed column) in a 2,450,000-row table.

When tuning the performance of the applications as well as the instance, using CBO can improve throughput of online and reporting systems based on its flexible nature of processing SQL statements. The first word (cost) in the name of this optimization approach is key to understanding why Oracle sometimes performs a full table scan and other times decides to first do an index lookup and then go fetch the qualifying rows' information.

VIP

After weighing the cost of alternative access paths, the cost-based optimizer will choose a path that costs the least, where cost is a measurement of resource consumption.

Changing Parameter Values in Oracle8*i* Instance Manager

To change a parameter value, simply park yourself in the appropriate property sheet, and place the cursor in the Value column to make changes. Making a change to dml_locks in the Basic Tuning folder is shown in Figure 17-2.

The value in effect for dml_locks is now 300, and we are going to change it to 600. When the change has been made, the new value entered is displayed on the Basic Tuning property sheet.

Selection Criterion	Qualifying Rows	% Qualifying	Access Path
last_name like 'J%'	187,501	7.65	Full table scan
last_name like 'JO%'	87,232	3.56	Index range scan
last_name like 'JOR%'	19,231	0.78	Index range scan
last_name = 'JORDAN'	4,891	0.19	Index range scan

TABLE 17-1.   *Comparison of Percentage of Qualifying Rows and Access Path*

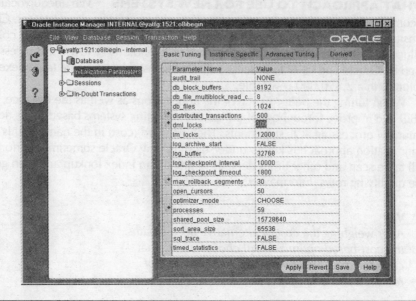

FIGURE 17-2. *Changing parameter values*

NOTE
*There may be operating system–specific maximums
that can be set for certain parameters. Consult
documents related to your specific operating system
for details.*

Changing Entries Using a Text Editor

With this in mind, we now give you an example of each type of entry. We include
db_block_buffers (integer type), db_name (string type), and log_archive_start
(boolean type):

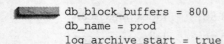

```
db_block_buffers = 800
db_name = prod
log_archive_start = true
```

It all sounds so simple. Take your favorite editor, change the entry, and you are
on your way. Well, almost. Here are the pitfalls:

■ **Fat fingers (also called typos)**   If you make one, the entire initialization parameter file is rejected. In other words, your database won't start until the typo is corrected.

■ **Domino effect**   In some situations, a change to one parameter affects other parameters.

VIP
Changing parameter values in the initialization parameter file is no trivial exercise. Look at the effects changes may have on other parameters, and make changes with caution.

With all this in mind, one word describes how you should proceed: s l o w l y. Tuning a database takes time. At first, it is best if you make one change at a time. Edit the file, and then try to start the database. This way, if you have made a typo, you at least know which entry is causing the database not to start. As you will see, Oracle is not always very gracious in telling you where the problem is. Use Server Manager and issue the **show parameters** command to see what changes have occurred. Try to develop your own checklist to help you determine if your changes are improving performance. We refer you to *Oracle8 Tuning* by Corey, Abbey, Dechichio, and Abramson (Osborne McGraw-Hill, 1997) for details on how to tune your database.

Viewing the Current Size of the SGA

As you make changes to the initialization parameter file, the changes affect how the database uses resources. One of the things you realize early on in the tuning process is that tuning is all about trade-offs. The more memory Oracle uses, the less memory is available for other processes. Many of the changes to the initialization parameter file affect the size of the SGA and how much memory the current database needs to operate. The command **show sga** tells you the current allocation of memory for the database:

```
Total System Global Area      4817701 bytes
Fixed Size                      28376 bytes
Variable Size                 3904532 bytes
Database Buffers               819200 bytes
Redo Buffers                    65596 bytes
```

VIP
The Oracle database is one of many processes that must live, share, and breathe all available resources. With this in mind, the SGA should never take over 50 percent of the available memory of the computer.

Spooling Results

Many times you will find it helpful to spool the results of your Server Manager session. We find it especially helpful to capture the output of the **show parameters** command; you can then use this output for your first attempt at customizing an initialization parameter file. By using the captured output as a starting point, you eliminate "fat fingers" (typos).

VIP
A misspelled entry in the initialization parameter file will prevent the database from starting up.

To start recording your actions while in Server Manager, do the following:

1. Enter the command **spool file_name** where the filename conforms to the rules of your computer. Oracle redisplays the SVRMGR> prompt after the spool file is opened.

2. Go about your job in Server Manager, and then close the file by entering the **spool off** command; Oracle closes the output file and redisplays the Server Manager prompt.

This is the output from the **show sga** command spooled to "example.log":

```
SVRMGR> show sga
Total System Global Area          4767460 bytes
            Fixed Size              36432 bytes
         Variable Size            3846292 bytes
      Database Buffers             819200 bytes
          Redo Buffers              65536 bytes
SVRMGR> spool off
```

I/O Stream

What is a database? A database is a place where information is organized, received, and dispensed. A disk drive is the physical location where a database holds information. To take this one step further, the major task of a database is to read and write data to the disks. The problem you face is that I/O (input/output) from a disk drive is slow. In fact, it is one of the slowest operations a computer can do. Even though CPUs keep getting faster and faster by comparison, I/O has not kept up the pace. Let's now take a look at some things you can do to minimize your I/O.

Tables and Indexes

All the data you place in an Oracle database is stored in an object called a *table*. Whenever a request is made to the database to read or write information, a record is read from a table or inserted into a table. There is another database object called an *index* (we also discuss indexes in the "Data and Index Tablespaces" section of Chapter 4). As we explained earlier, an index is used to speed up access to particular columns of information in a table. Think of an index as a minitable. For example, let's say you create an index on the customer table on the column last_name.

There are two major reasons why an index access is faster:

- When you read a record from a table, you must read in every column of information associated with that table. If you had a very large customer table with 300 fields associated with it, even though you just want the last_name column, you are forced into the additional overhead of reading every column of the table. For example, a concatenated index on last_name, first_name only contains two columns. It is faster to read two columns than 300 columns.

- Indexes are in presorted order. While data in an Oracle table is stored in the order it was loaded, data in an Oracle index is stored in a sorted order. This is part of the requirement of an index.

There are two major things you can do to improve your database's capability to access data. The first is to properly index your tables. In the long run, this will have the greatest impact on performance. The second is to make sure your tables and indexes are stored on separate physical devices. We recommend you create a separate tablespace to hold tables. In addition, you should create another tablespace to hold indexes.

VIP
Put tables on a separate disk from their indexes.

This point is important even if you have a limited number of disks at your disposal (say, one to three). Separating tables from their indexes allows for quicker access, since reading and writing to the index and the table may happen simultaneously.

VIP
Large tables in your database should have at least one index on them.

When we say "large," we mean tables with anything over 1,000 rows; our experience dictates that over 90 percent of the tables in an Oracle database are indexed.

VIP
Create separate tablespaces to hold data and indexes.

System Tables

Before an Oracle application can even look at a table or its contents, it must first talk to the Oracle data dictionary. The data dictionary contains information as to what is stored in the database, where it is stored, and who has the privilege to look at it. The tables and database objects that make up the Oracle data dictionary are owned by a database user called SYS. They are stored in a tablespace called system. This is a major I/O stream for the database. In a perfect world, you would place the system tablespace on its own disk drive.

VIP
Do not allow other users to place database objects in the system tablespace.

Temporary Segments

Temporary segments are objects the database periodically creates to help it finish transactions. For example, when you issue an SQL statement with a **group by** clause, the database will likely create some temporary objects to help it in its work. It is very important that you keep temporary objects in their own tablespace. By doing so, you will eliminate the performance problems associated with having temporary segments mixed with other database objects.

VIP
Create a separate tablespace to hold temporary segments.

Rollback Segments

A rollback segment is a database object that holds information when a user does an **insert**, **update**, or **delete**. This rollback information is recorded so that the database can undo or roll back the transaction in the case of failure. Since all transactions are not equal in size, these rollback segments have a tendency to grow and shrink.

VIP
Create a separate tablespace for your rollback segments.

Online Redo Logs

The online redo logs are your transaction logs. Every action that occurs in an Oracle database is recorded into these special files called online redo logs (discussed as well in the "Redo Logs—The Transaction Log" section of Chapter 4).

VIP
Since I/O can be one of the slowest operations, place online redo logs on a separate disk.

Summary

I/O is one of the slowest operations a computer can do. However, it is also one of the most important operations. In a perfect world, you would place every tablespace in a database on a separate disk drive. We don't live in a perfect world, but you should still create these separate tablespaces, even if they are on the same disk. Then, utilizing the tools available to you within Oracle and the operating system, balance the I/O load as best you can. If, over time, you are able to obtain additional disk drives, then you are ready for them.

What's Next

Tuning is a double-edged sword. Be careful how you handle it. Tuning is about choices. Each choice has its good points and its bad points. If you increase db_block_buffers to expand the data cache, then you are able to hold more data in memory. On the other hand, the system now has less free memory to do its own work. So, as you go down the tuning path, you will constantly have forks in the road to consider.

We have introduced you to the two major areas of database tuning: the initialization parameter file and tuning the I/O stream. We talked about the most common items to change in the initialization parameter file. In the "I/O Stream" section, we stressed the fact that I/O is slow. We encouraged you to look closely at indexes and a standard strategy for laying out your database. Now it's up to you. Tune slowly. The tortoise wins this race every time.

Our next chapter, "Advanced DBA," will prove helpful to your expanding knowledge of the Oracle database. We guide you through some advanced tasks you will be responsible for as a DBA and show you how to . . . better still, keep reading!

CHAPTER
18

Advanced DBA

erhaps, up until now, you have been quite content with not being a DBA. Well, it looks like somebody stole the DBA and, guess what, you're the new DBA! In Chapter 14, we pointed you in the right direction. We showed you how to do some DBA stuff you will be asked to do from day one (if not sooner). We discussed and walked you through how to start the database, shut down the database, create a tablespace to hold Oracle data, add more space to a tablespace, grant access to a user, and revoke access from a user.

NOTE

All the code samples and exercises we lead you through in this chapter work error free. If you receive some errors while running this material, there is probably some setup that has not been run successfully.

Database administration is pretty much the same regardless of the hardware you are using—Windows NT on a Pentium, an Amdahl mainframe, or an IBM AIX. Oracle releases port-specific documentation that highlights the differences you can expect to run across on different hardware platforms. These manuals are referred to as the port-specific System Release Bulletin (SRB) and Installation and Configuration Guide (ICG). There is a wealth of information on everything discussed in this chapter in the Oracle8*i* Server Administrator's Guide. Database installation and tuning are two DBA responsibilities that are not discussed in this chapter; they are highlighted in Chapter 6 and Chapter 17. By the end of this chapter, you will know more terminology, as well as some advanced details on how to do the following:

- Start up the database

- Perform additional user management

- Perform additional tablespace management

- Manage redo log file groups

- Add control files

- Drop control files

- Find your way around the data dictionary

- Classify error messages

- Work with Oracle Corporation's Worldwide Customer Support

In Chapter 14, we showed you how to use Oracle Enterprise Manager (*OEM*) and Server Manager to perform the basic DBA activities; this chapter uses Server Manager for the discussion on Startup, then OEM for all the hands-on work.

Terminology

The following definitions will arm you with the technical jargon you need to make it through this chapter:

- The *archiving status* of the database controls what Oracle does with redo log files before it reuses them. When this status is ARCHIVELOG, Oracle automatically copies a redo log file to a destination you specify before it is reused. When the status is NOARCHIVELOG, Oracle does not save a copy of each redo log file before it is reused. This is discussed in more detail in Chapter 16.

- A tablespace is *online* when it is accessible to all users and, therefore, available for storage of new objects, and for querying and modifying data.

- The *system tablespace* holds all the data dictionary information required to access the database. It must be online and accessible when the database is open.

- A tablespace is *offline* when its data is unavailable for any access. An offline tablespace must be brought back online before users may access it again.

- *Backup* is a procedure that makes a secondary copy of Oracle data (usually on tape) and helps provide protection against hardware, software, or user errors; backup minimizes data loss if and when problems arise.

- *Recovery* is a procedure whereby data is read from a backup in an effort to restore the database to a past or current point in time.

- *Redo logs* are written by Oracle and contain a record of all transactions against a database. They are written automatically as Oracle operates.

- The *active redo log group* is the group to which Oracle is currently writing information. All members of the active group are written to simultaneously.

- *Rollback* is the event that Oracle performs when, for an assortment of reasons, a transaction is not completed. The rollback restores the data to the state it was in before the transaction started.

- A *rollback segment* is a portion of a tablespace that contains undo information for each transaction in the database; this undo information is kept until a transaction is committed or rolled back.

- An *extent* is a chunk of space in a datafile of an Oracle database; it is measured in bytes, kilobytes (1,024 bytes), or megabytes (1,048,576 bytes). Extents are allocated based on keywords used when objects (for example, tables and rollback segments) are created.

- A database is *up* when it has been opened and is accessible to users. A database is *down* when it has been closed and is inaccessible to users.

VIP
*Throughout this chapter, we connect to the database as **internal** with the password **oracle**. If you have changed the internal password, use it rather than ours.*

Startup Options

Most of the time, when you start up your database, you simply start Server Manager, connect to the database, and type **startup** to get things going. In this section, we will discuss additional startup options, using these options in Server Manager, and when you may need or want to use one of these options.

Startup Normal

This is the default startup mode (you almost always omit the word **normal**). We showed you how to start up the database in Chapter 14. Use the output in the next listing as a reference point for the following discussion on startup options.

```
Oracle Server Manager Release 3.1.5.0.0 - Production
(c) Copyright 1997, Oracle Corporation.  All Rights Reserved.
Oracle8i Enterprise Edition Release 8.1.5.0.0 - Production
With the Partitioning and Java options
PL/SQL Release 8.1.5.0.0 - Production
SVRMGR> connect internal/oracle
SVRMGR> startup
ORACLE instance started.
Total System Global Area        8030448 bytes
Fixed Size                        44584 bytes
Variable Size                   7510728 bytes
Database Buffers                 409600 bytes
Redo Buffers                      65536 bytes
Database mounted.
Database opened.
SVRMGR>
```

Startup Mount

This mode is used to change the archiving status of the database or perform recovery. The database is not open, and, therefore, access by users is not permitted. After starting Server Manager, do the following:

1. Enter **connect internal/internal**.

2. Enter **startup mount**, and receive feedback from Oracle, as shown in the next listing. Notice that there is no message about opening the database after it is mounted.

```
ORACLE instance started.
Total System Global Area         8030448 bytes
Fixed Size                         44584 bytes
Variable Size                    7510728 bytes
Database Buffers                  409600 bytes
Redo Buffers                       65536 bytes
Database mounted.
SVRMGR>
```

3. Enter **exit** to leave Server Manager.

The database is left in a mounted condition; users are not able to log in when it is in this state.

Startup Nomount

This mode is used to re-create a control file (discussed in the "Control File Responsibilities" section of this chapter) or re-create the database from scratch. The database is not open; and, therefore, access by users is not permitted. After starting Server Manager, do the following:

1. Enter **connect internal/oracle**.

2. Enter **startup nomount**, and receive feedback from Oracle, as shown in the next listing.

```
ORACLE instance started.
Total System Global Area         8030448 bytes
Fixed Size                         44584 bytes
Variable Size                    7510728 bytes
Database Buffers                  409600 bytes
Redo Buffers                       65536 bytes
SVRMGR>
```

3. Enter **exit** to leave Server Manager.

The response from Oracle is similar to when the database is started and mounted, except the database mounted and database opened messages are suppressed.

Startup Restrict

This mode is used to start up the database, but access is restricted to a privileged set of users that you have defined. The output from this command is the same as when the database is started up in nonrestricted mode. The database is open; but if nonprivileged users attempt to log in, they will obtain the error message shown in Figure 18-1.

The current status of the database can be gleaned from looking at the data dictionary view v$instance, described in the next listing. The *LOGINS* column will show the status with value of either RESTRICTED or ALLOWED.

```
Column Name                             Null?      Type
-----------------------------------  --------   ----
INSTANCE_NUMBER                                  NUMBER
INSTANCE_NAME                                    VARCHAR2(16)
HOST_NAME                                        VARCHAR2(16)
VERSION                                          VARCHAR2(17)
STARTUP_TIME                                     DATE
STATUS                                           VARCHAR2(7)
PARALLEL                                         VARCHAR2(3)
THREAD#                                          NUMBER
ARCHIVER                                         VARCHAR2(7)
LOG_SWITCH_WAIT                                  VARCHAR2(11)
LOGINS                                           VARCHAR2(10)
SHUTDOWN_PENDING                                 VARCHAR2(3)
DATABASE_STATUS                                  VARCHAR2(17)
```

Let's discuss changing the database access mode from restricted to unrestricted. The first is done with the database open; the other, by restarting the database.

Change Status with Database Open

After starting Server Manager, do the following:

1. Enter **connect internal/oracle**.

2. Enter **alter system disable restricted session;** and receive feedback from Oracle, as shown in the next listing.

   ```
   SVRMGR> alter system disable restricted session;
   Statement processed.
   SVRMGR>
   ```

3. Enter **exit** to leave Server Manager.

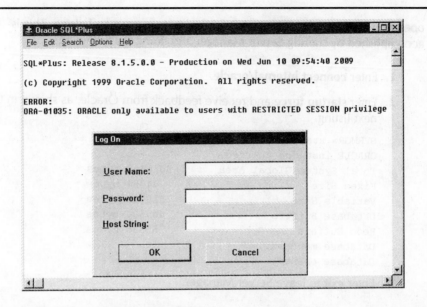

FIGURE 18-1. *Restricted session access denied*

When this is done, the database is running in unrestricted access mode and users will be able to log in once more.

Change Status by Restarting the Database
After starting Server Manager, do the following:

1. Enter **connect internal/oracle**.

2. Enter **startup**.

3. Enter **exit** to leave Server Manager.

Regardless of the method you choose, the database will be open and ready for access by all once the steps are completed. The key here is that when the database is started with no additional parameters (that is, with the command **startup** alone), regardless of the status of the instance when the **shutdown** was initiated, the status will be unrestricted when the database restarts.

Startup Force
This option is used in the rare situation when you are unable to shut down a database. It shuts the database and then starts it with no options; the startup

operation is the same as having issued the **startup** command alone. This is accomplished by starting Server Manager and doing the following:

1. Enter **connect internal/oracle**.

2. Enter **startup force** and receive feedback from Oracle, as shown in the next listing.

```
SVRMGR> startup force
ORACLE instance started.
Total System Global Area          8030448 bytes
Fixed Size                          44584 bytes
Variable Size                     7510728 bytes
Database Buffers                   409600 bytes
Redo Buffers                        65536 bytes
Database mounted.
Database opened.
```

3. Enter **exit** to leave Server Manager.

When this operation is complete, your database will be open and accessible to the user community.

Startup pfile

This option with the **startup** command does not affect the mode of the database operation; it defines the name and location of the initialization parameter file (**pfile**). As we have discussed elsewhere, the initialization parameter file is read by Oracle as it opens a database. Oracle expects the default initialization parameter file to be in a location and called a name that is dependent on the hardware on which the database operates. In Oracle8i for NT, for example, Oracle builds the default initialization parameter filename according to the following:

1. Start with the active ORACLE_HOME location, **C:\Oracle\Ora81** in our case.

2. Suffix that location with the **Database** folder.

3. Append the filename made up of the text **init** followed by the ORACLE_SID (making **init o8ibegin**) followed by the filename suffix of **.ora**. Thus, the default initialization parameter filename for our example would become c:\Oracle\Ora81\Database\Inito8ibegin.ora.

If you wish to start your database using an initialization parameter file other than the default, follow these steps after starting Server Manager:

1. Enter **connect internal/oracle**.

2. Enter **startup pfile=*parameter_file_name*** and receive feedback from Oracle as shown in the next listing.

```
SVRMGR> startup pfile=g:\Oracle\Ora81\pfile\inito8ibegin.ora
ORACLE instance started.
Total System Global Area       8030448 bytes
Fixed Size                       44584 bytes
Variable Size                  7510728 bytes
Database Buffers                409600 bytes
Redo Buffers                     65536 bytes
Database mounted.
Database opened.
SVRMGR>
```

NOTE
Fill in the appropriate parameter filename with the pfile option, replacing the bold and italicized text after the "=" sign.

3. Enter **exit** to leave Server Manager.

From time to time, you may use the **pfile** option to start your database with some initialization parameter file values different than usual. For example, when running a large data load, you may wish to instruct Oracle to allocate much more memory for sorting than you normally request.

NOTE
If you have started your database using the pfile option, remind yourself to shut it down and use the regular initialization parameter file when the job completes.

Nothing will go wrong if you leave your database running with an initialization parameter file other than the file you normally use.

VIP
More than 99 percent of the time, you will start up a database with no options.

Operation Modes

Table 18-1 summarizes the operating modes and indicates what can be accomplished with the database in each mode—open, mount, nomount, and closed. If you attempt to issue an SQL command and the database mode of operation does not support the command, Oracle will inform you.

Shutdown Options

When an Oracle database is not running, we refer to it as down. You shut down the database for a number of reasons. Some installations bring the database down for

Mode	Activities That Can Be Accomplished
closed	Add, drop, or move a control file (with modifications made in the initialization parameter file to reflect the changes)
	Back up the database—all datafiles, online redo logs, and control files
nomount	Create a database
	Create a control file
mount	Perform database, datafile, or tablespace recovery
	Rename any database file
	Change redo log archival mode (ARCHIVELOG or NOARCHIVELOG)
	Add, drop, or rename redo log groups or redo log file members
open	All users can access the database and go about their normal business
	Export full database, one or more users, or specific database objects
	Import full database, one or more users, or specific database objects

TABLE 18-1. *Operating Modes*

backups. Certain Oracle software requires that Oracle be shut down while you are running the upgrade or installation session. In Chapter 14, we talked about **shutdown normal**, **immediate**, and **abort** (a discussion of shutdown is not complete without mentioning these two extra options). There is nothing more frustrating than being told to shut down your database with the **shutdown** command only to find it does not work!

VIP
*Refer to the "Shutdown Options" section in Chapter 14—there is some **very** important and useful information there pertinent to this section.*

VIP
You will use shutdown immediate more than 90 percent of the time.

As a last resort, you may have to use the **shutdown abort** command. Sometimes, there are situations when nothing else works, and you have no choice.

CAUTION
If you shut down a database with the abort option, start it up immediately; then do a normal shutdown. Experience dictates this is the best way to care for a database shut down with this abort option.

Additional User Management Responsibilities

Coupled with the tasks discussed in Chapter 14, the exercises we highlight in this section will round out your user management skills. By the end of this section, you will know how to do the following:

- Give privileges to a user, allowing him or her to perform secure operations

- Create a profile and assign it to one or more users

- Create a role and sign up one or more users to that role

Let's get started with the Oracle Enterprise Manager interface. The next three sections assume that you have brought up the Security Manager.

VIP
We connected directly to the database rather than the Oracle Management Server, as shown in Figure 18-2.

Giving Privileges to Database Users

Privileges, when given out to users, allow them to perform activities in the Oracle8*i* database they would be unable to do without them. To give privileges to a user, do the following:

1. From the Security Manager main console, right-click Users to bring up the menu shown in Figure 18-3.

2. Select the Add Privileges to User option on the ensuing drop-down menu to display the dialog box shown in Figure 18-4.

3. Highlight a user in the Users list; in our case, we chose user OUTLN.

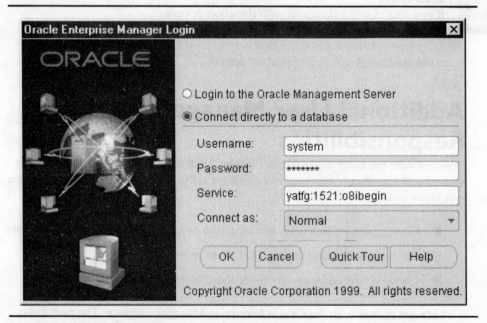

FIGURE 18-2. *Connecting directly to the database*

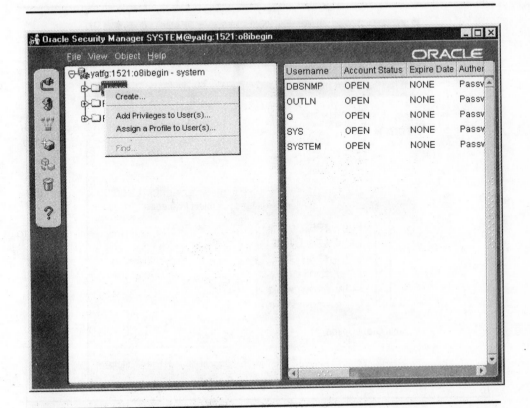

FIGURE 18-3. *The User Maintenance menu*

4. Highlight one or more privileges in the Role tab of the dialog box. We chose AQ_ADMINISTRATOR_ROLE, AQ_USER_ROLE, and SELECT_CATALOG_ROLE.

5. Move to the System Privileges tab, and select one or more privileges to be given to the same user. We highlighted the EXP_FULL_DATABASE and IMP_FULL_DATABASE privileges.

6. Move to the Object Privileges tab, and expand the desired owner to show a tree-like list, as shown in Figure 18-5.

7. Click Apply to pass the SQL off to the database for execution.

8. Click the Exit-X twice to leave this dialog box in the Security Manager.

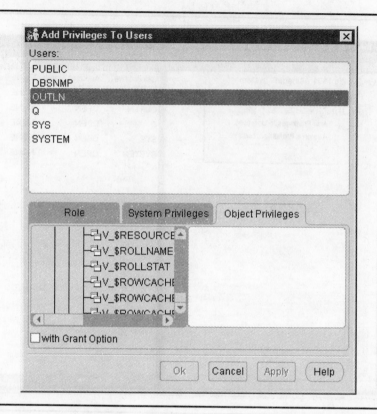

FIGURE 18-4. *Add Privileges to Users*

Creating and Assigning a New Profile

For the sake of this exercise, we have decided that the users of the database spend long periods of time doing nothing, and we would like to disconnect them from the server after 15 minutes of inactivity. Let's do this one a little differently: Start by highlighting the Profiles folder on the Security Manager main screen, and then do the following:

1. Click the Create icon, as shown in Figure 18-6.

2. Ensure the Profile option is highlighted on the ensuing menu box, and then click Create.

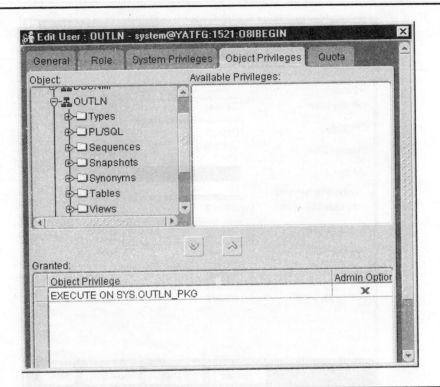

FIGURE 18-5.   *Object privileges*

3. Give the new profile a name; in our case, we entered **o8ibegin_ltd**.

4. Proceed to the Idle Time position in the Details area, and then select **15** from the pick list displayed, as shown in Figure 18-7.

5. Click Create to finish the task at hand and be presented with a confirmation dialog box.

When you return to the Security Manager console, expand the list under the Profiles folder; you will notice that the new profile just created appears.

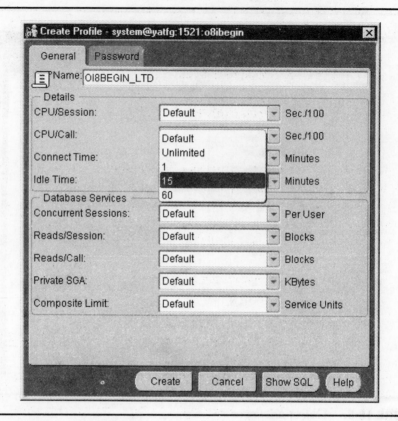

FIGURE 18-6.   *Create a profile icon*

Creating and Assigning a New Role

We continually use roles as database administrators to make the activity of granting object privileges easier to manage. To start, proceed to the Object option across the top of the screen and then do the following:

1. Select Create from the drop-down menu that appears.

2. Select Role from the ensuing dialog box.

3. Enter a name for the role on the screen that then appears, as shown in Figure 18-8.

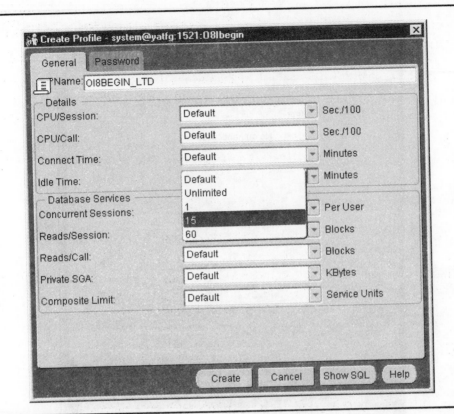

FIGURE 18-7. *Specifying an environment for new profile*

VIP
For some unknown reason, we could not do any data entry for Name on the General tab of the Create Role dialog box. We had to select one of the other three tabs and then return to the General tab where the field was then active.

NOTE
We have selected the Show SQL button on Figure 18-8 to display the SQL statements that are passed to the database when clicking Create or OK on most screens. This can be a learning experience, helping you become familiar with the SQL built by the pieces in the Database Management Pack in OEM 2.0.

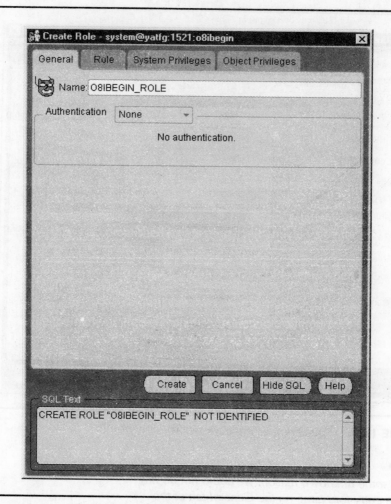

FIGURE 18-8. *Creating a new role*

4. Click Create to accomplish the role creation.

Now when you're granting privileges on application tables to users, rather than giving out the grants individually, you simply give them to the o8ibegin_role role, as shown in the next listing using Server Manager. This could have been done as well using the Security Manager.

```
Oracle Server Manager Release 3.1.5.0.0 - Production
(c) Copyright 1997, Oracle Corporation.  All Rights Reserved.
Oracle8i Enterprise Edition Release 8.1.5.0.0 - Production
With the Partitioning and Java options
PL/SQL Release 8.1.5.0.0 - Production
SVRMGR> connect internal/oracle
Connected.
SVRMGR> grant o8ibegin_role to ops$masii;
Statement processed.
SVRMGR> grant o8ibegin_role to ops$skiast
Statement processed.
SVRMGR> rem Now when privileges are given to the o8ibegin_role role, ops$masii
SVRMGR> rem and ops$skiast assume the privileges based on their membership
SVRMGR> rem in the o8ibegin_role role.
SVRMGR> grant select, insert, update, delete on spoon to o8ibegin_role;
Statement processed.
SVRMGR>
```

Additional Tablespace Maintenance Responsibilities

In Chapter 14, we discussed creating a tablespace and adding more space to one that already exists. By the end of this section, you will also know how to move the datafile that makes up a tablespace (that is, how to rename a datafile) as well as drop a tablespace. For the following few sections, we assume you have connected to the database and have positioned yourself at the Storage Manager console to start the work.

Adding More Space to a Tablespace

Either by plan, or when forced to do so in anticipation of something like a large data load, you may need more space in an existing tablespace. This can be accomplished one of two ways:

- Adding an additional datafile to the suite of files already making up the existing tablespace

- Growing one of the additional existing files already allocated to the tablespace

Let's look at doing this both ways—first from the Storage Manager (resize approach) and then from Server Manager (adding another datafile approach).

Resizing an Existing Datafile
From the Storage Manager main console, do the following:

1. Expand the database name, showing the Tablespaces folder.

2. Right-click the desired tablespace, and then choose Edit from the menu that drops down, as shown in Figure 18-9.

3. When the Edit Tablespace dialog box appears, highlight the datafile that you wish to resize.

4. Click Edit to bring up the dialog box shown in Figure 18-10.

5. Proceed to the File Size field, and enter the new size in measurements of KBytes or MBytes—we changed **2048 KBytes** to **3 MBytes**, thereby changing the file size from 2MB to 3MB.

6. Click OK to return to the Edit Tablespace screen.

7. Click Apply to commence the resizing operation, with the SQL built from the previous steps shown in Figure 18-11.

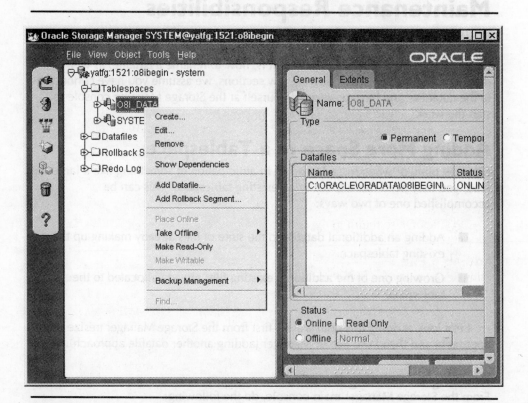

FIGURE 18-9. *The Tablespace drop-down menu*

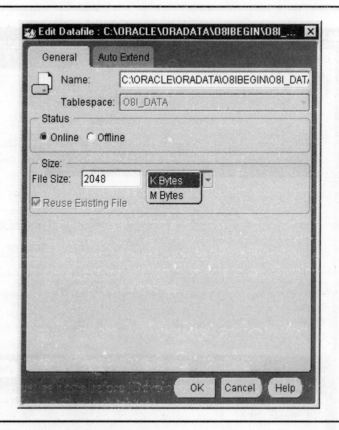

FIGURE 18-10. *The Edit Datafile dialog box*

    8. Click OK to return to the Storage Manager opening screen.

Adding a File
Using Server Manager, let's look at this operation. Hold on tight ...

    1. Invoke Server Manager by entering the command **svrmgrl**, bringing up the herald shown in the next listing.

```
Oracle Server Manager Release 3.1.5.0.0 - Production
(c) Copyright 1997, Oracle Corporation.  All Rights Reserved.
Oracle8i Enterprise Edition Release 8.1.5.0.0 - Production
With the Partitioning and Java options
PL/SQL Release 8.1.5.0.0 - Production
```

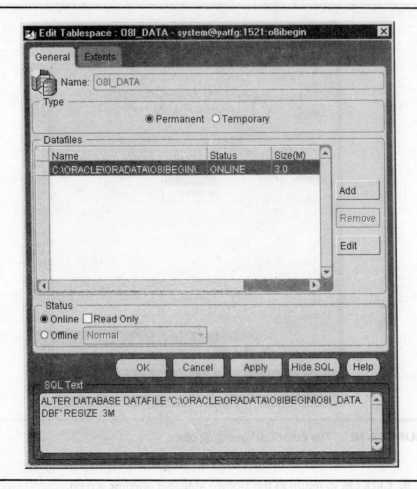

FIGURE 18-11. *SQL to resize datafile*

2. Enter the command **connect internal/oracle** and receive the following feedback from Oracle.

```
Connected.
SVRMGR>
```

3. Enter the command **alter tablespace o8I_data add datafile 'C:\Oracle\Oradata\O8ibegin\O8i_data2' size 1m;**, and receive the following feedback from Oracle.

```
Statement processed.
```

The o8i_data tablespace now has two datafiles—the original as well as the second file we just added. Let's now look at dropping a tablespace.

Dropping a Tablespace

Once a user's data is no longer required, you may want to get rid of the data and even the tablespace the data now resides in. Let's look at dropping a tablespace using the Storage Manager in the following steps:

1. Expand the Tablespaces folder in the Security Manager's main console.

2. Highlight the tablespace to be dropped.

3. Click the Remove icon (the Trash Can) on the left side of the console to bring up the confirmation dialog box shown in Figure 18-12.

4. Click Yes to complete the operation.

VIP
PLEASE BE CAREFUL: when dropping a tablespace and clicking Yes on the information box shown in Figure 18-12, the DATA IN THE TABLESPACE BEING DROPPED ARE GONE; TOAST; ARE NO MORE; GIVEN UP THE GHOST; PASSED ON; HISTORY!!!

We actually prefer using Server Manager for this activity—it is a lot more friendly and will warn you if data resides in the affected tablespace. This is shown in the next listing.

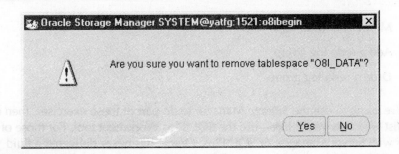

FIGURE 18-12. *Remove tablespace confirmation*

```
SVRMGR> drop tablespace o8i_data;
drop tablespace o8i_data
*
ORA-01549: tablespace not empty, use INCLUDING CONTENTS option
SVRMGR>
```

If you encounter this error message when trying to drop a tablespace, there are two ways to proceed:

■ Add the **including contents** keywords to the **drop tablespace ...** command.

■ Manually drop all the tables in the tablespace, and then reissue the same **drop tablespace** statement.

VIP
Dropping a tablespace does not erase the datafile it was using. The datafile must be removed using an operating system command. Erase the datafile from the dropped tablespace immediately. If you decide to do this some other time, more than likely you will forget!

Managing Redo Log Groups

Oracle writes transaction information to redo log files. Picture a redo log as a passbook that records all changes to the database as if it were a checking account. With Oracle, we speak of redo log file groups. If you define more than one member for a redo log group, Oracle writes to each member simultaneously. This protects you against problems if a redo log file is damaged; Oracle continues to write to another member of the group that is still intact. In this section, we will discuss how to do the following:

■ Mirror your redo logs

■ Add a redo log group

■ Drop a redo log group

We're going to use the Storage Manager to do part of these exercises, then do a little twist we know you'll like—use the SQL*Plus Worksheet tool. For those of you familiar with Server Manager, or SQL*Plus, Oracle has never delivered a fluid command history feature with any tool the DBA has ever used. Along comes the SQL*Plus Worksheet—ta da! Here we go!

Mirrored Redo Logs

When instructed, Oracle will maintain mirrored copies of all online redo logs. A *redo log group* is made up of one or more equal-sized redo log files. Each redo log group is assigned a number when created, and Oracle writes to all members of each group at the same time. In the next section, we show you how to add a new redo log group to set up this mirroring. When the database operates in ARCHIVELOG mode, Oracle archives only one member of a redo log group before the whole group is reused.

TIP

*Have at least two members in each redo log group.
If Oracle ever has difficulty writing to one member
of a redo log group, it will carry on, satistied to write
to another member of the same group.*

The status of your database redo log groups and members is viewed by starting with the main console of the Storage Manager. Click the Redo Log Group folder, causing the desired information to be displayed, as shown in Figure 18-13. Notice how there are two redo log groups, each with a single member.

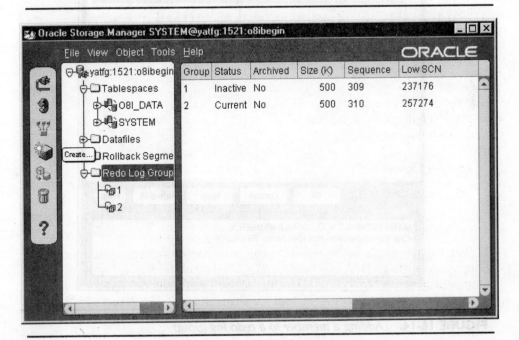

FIGURE 18-13. *Redo Log Group status*

Let's now add a member to each of these groups by doing the following:

1. Highlight Group 1, and then right-click and choose Edit from the choices that appear.

2. When the Edit Redo Log Group:1 screen appears, position the cursor at the next available line, and enter the name of the additional member for redo log group 1. This is shown in Figure 18-14 with the SQL statement displayed at the bottom.

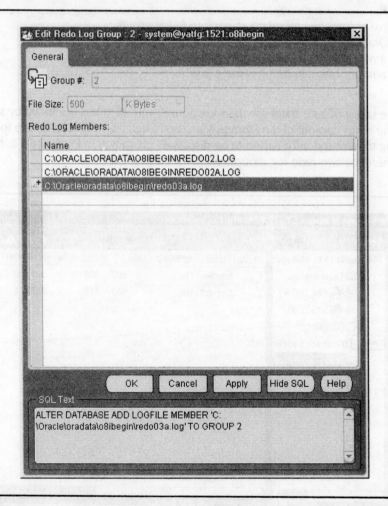

FIGURE 18-14. *Adding a member to a redo log group*

3. Click Apply to complete the task, and then Cancel to return to the previous screen.

Use the following conventions when setting up mirrored redo logs:

■ Ensure there are the same number of members in every redo log group.

VIP
Armed with this suggestion, we recommend you go back and add another member to redo log group 2, since in the last exercise we added another member to group 1.

■ Ensure each member of each redo log group is the same size.

■ Embed the member number and group number in the name of each redo log file. For example, the second member of redo log group 1 in Figure 18-14 is called **redo01a.log**, thereby preserving the group **01** text embedded in the other member's filename.

■ Whenever possible, place members of each redo log group on separate disks. For example, the two members of redo log group 1 in Figure 18-14 could be on separate drives if more than one resides on your NT server.

NOTE
*You may have difficulty when you try to add a third member to your redo log groups. The parameter **maxlogmembers** controls the number of members in a redo log group.*

The value of **maxlogmembers** can be increased by re-creating the database control file.

NOTE
*If you wish to increase the value for **maxlogmembers**, you can re-create your control file, as discussed in the "Building a New Control File" section, later in this chapter.*

Adding a New Redo Log Group

For this exercise, we need to add redo log group 3 with two members of 500K each. After invoking the SQL*Plus Worksheet, do the following:

1. Enter a username, password, and service to connect directly to the database. We entered **internal**, **oracle**, and a service of **yatfg:1521:o8ibegin**. This is shown in Figure 18-15.

2. Click OK to finish the login activity.

3. Enter the SQL text shown in Figure 18-16 to add redo logfile group 2, and then press F5 to pass the command to the database.

4. Exit the SQL*Plus Worksheet by clicking the Exit-X.

Notice in Figure 18-16 how the names of the redo log file members are enclosed in single quotes. In addition, the two redo log file member names are separated by a comma and enclosed in parentheses. We now have three dual-membered redo log groups associated with the database.

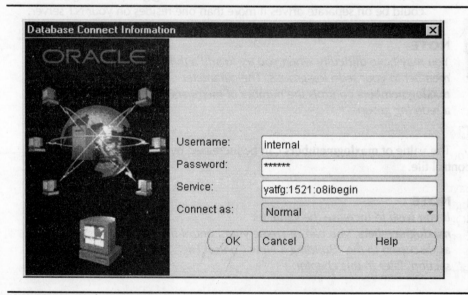

FIGURE 18-15.   *Signing onto the SQL*Plus Worksheet*

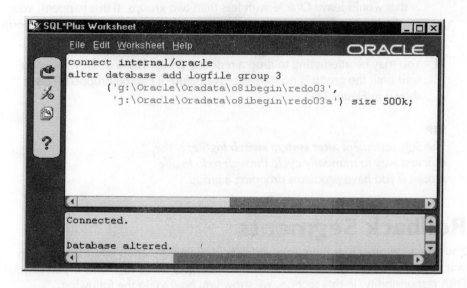

FIGURE 18-16.   *Adding logfile group 3*

TIP
*When building a redo log file member name, embed
the group number and member number in the
filename. That is why we named the files redo03
and redo03a in this exercise.*

Dropping an Existing Redo Log Group

You have just upgraded your hardware, and you find yourself with one less disk for
Oracle and its associated database files. You used to have three disks, and now you
have two. On the SQL*Plus Worksheet, enter the command **alter database drop
logfile group 3;**. Redo log group 3 is no longer part of the database. Note how the
SQL statement in the previous sentence makes no mention of any redo log file
member names as the group is dropped.

Problems Dropping Redo Log Groups

Two problems commonly occur when attempting to drop a redo log group. If one of these
happens to you, follow our advice and then reissue the command to drop the group.

■ You may be attempting to drop a redo log group (let's call it redo log group 2) that would leave Oracle with less than two groups. If this happens, you must add a third group before you can drop group 2. When you drop group 2, that leaves groups 1 and 3, which satisfies Oracle's requirements.

■ You may be attempting to drop a redo log group that is active. You must wait until the group is no longer active before it can be dropped. This is shown in Figure 18-17.

VIP
*The SQL statement **alter system switch logfile;** is the quickest way to manually cycle through redo logfile groups if you have problems dropping a group.*

Rollback Segments

You may remember that these segments are used to store undo information when you update or delete data in Oracle tables. Managing these segments is part of your DBA responsibility. In this section, we show you how to do the following:

■ Acquire a rollback segment using the initialization parameter file.

■ Create a rollback segment.

■ Change the status of a rollback segment.

■ Drop a rollback segment.

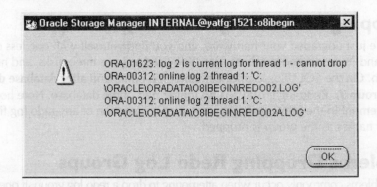

FIGURE 18-17. *Problems dropping a redo logfile group*

Acquiring a Rollback Segment

Oracle8*i* uses the term "configuration files" synonymously with what we have called "initialization parameter files." There are two ways to acquire a rollback segment:

■ At instance startup time, ensuring the rollback segment you wish to acquire is mentioned in the initialization parameter file in the "rollback_segments" entry

■ Bringing the rollback segment online from the Storage Manager

Let's look at the latter method, which will be used more frequently. Once positioned at the Storage Manager console, do the following:

1. Click the Rollback Segments folder on the main console, which expands listing any rollback segments that have been created.

2. Right-click the rollback segment you wish to acquire.

3. Choose Place Online from the menu that drops down.

When returned to the console, the segment brought online is so indicated.

| Create... |
| Create Like... |
| Edit... |
| Remove |
| Show Dependencies |
| Shrink |
| Place Online |
| Take Offline |

FIGURE 18-18.   *Acquiring a rollback segment*

Creating a Rollback Segment

We discussed rollback segments in greater detail in Chapter 4. As the DBA, you will quickly become more familiar with the nuances of working with them. From the Storage Manager main console, perform the following steps to create a rollback segment:

1. Right-click the Rollback Segment folder to display the drop-down menu.

2. Click Create.

3. When the dialog box appears, as shown in Figure 18-19, fill in the segment name and pick the tablespace name within which it is to reside.

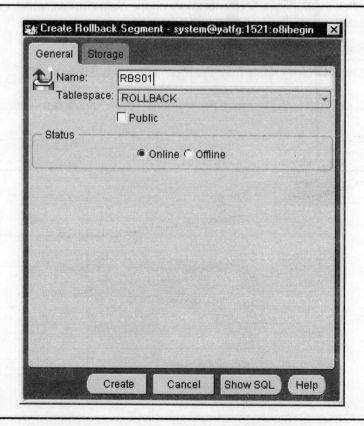

FIGURE 18-19. *The Create Rollback Segment general tab*

4. Proceed to the Public check box, and deselect the option, thereby making the **rbs01** rollback segment private.

5. Ensure the Online option is highlighted.

6. Proceed to the Storage tab, and enter **100** beside Initial Size and Next Size, allowing the KBytes measurement to stay active.

7. In the Maximum Number section of the dialog box, enter the number **20**, as shown in Figure 18-20. Notice how the SQL is shown, as you have clicked the Show SQL button beforehand.

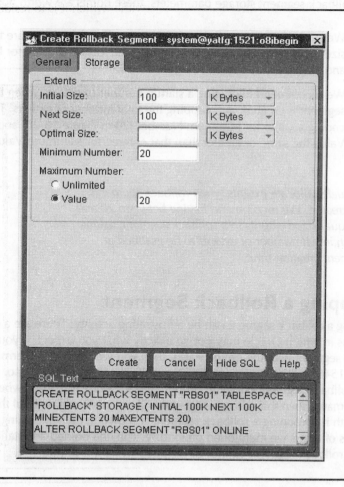

FIGURE 18-20. *Specifying rollback segment storage particulars*

When you are returned to the console, the rollback segment you just created appears in the list. The name of the rollback segment must be unique, and the tablespace you are placing it in must be accessible.

VIP
We recommend that you build one or more tablespaces to hold nothing other than rollback segments. This is the default behavior of Oracle8i.

Before moving on, let's spend a few minutes on the rationale behind the entries for the rollback segment storage parameters; these points are worth noting:

- We suggest ensuring all the extents in a rollback segment are the same size—this is accomplished by entering the identical value for Initial Size and Next Size, as shown in Figure 18-20.

- We recommend allocating a startup number of extents when the rollback segment is created, and capping the total number of extents. This is done by coding a value for Minimum Number (**20** in Figure 18-20) and a Maximum Value the same or greater than that entered for Minimum Value.

VIP
Manually allocate extents when rollback segments are created. We recommend having between 20 and 40 equal-sized extents in a rollback segment, asking for an initial number of extents to be grabbed at segment creation time.

Dropping a Rollback Segment

Dropping a rollback segment can be a frustrating activity: There are a number of situations in which Oracle may not do exactly what you expect. If you try to drop a rollback segment with the online status, then you will receive the error message "ORA-01545: rollback segment 'RBS3' specified not available." Also, if you try to take a rollback segment offline to drop it, and someone is using it when you issue the command, then the rollback segment will not come offline until that user is done with it. Dropping a rollback segment is shown in the next listing, fraught with the types of errors we mentioned previously. The line bolded and italicized tells us that the rollback segment cannot be dropped while it is online.

```
Oracle Server Manager Release 3.1.5.0.0 - Production
(c) Copyright 1997, Oracle Corporation.  All Rights Reserved.
Oracle8i Enterprise Edition Release 8.1.5.0.0 - Production
With the Partitioning and Java options
PL/SQL Release 8.1.5.0.0 - Production
SVRMGR> connect internal/oracle
Connected.
SVRMGR> drop rollback segment rbs01;
drop rollback segment rbs01
*
ORA-01545: rollback segment 'RBS01' specified not available
SVRMGR> alter rollback segment rbs01 offline;
Statement processed.
SVRMGR> drop rollback segment rbs01;
Statement processed.
SVRMGR>
```

The Initialization Parameter File

This file can be one of the most mystifying components of the Oracle8i database. Many articles in magazines and presentations at technical conferences deal with this file and what it does for the Oracle database. This section will discuss details on the following:

■ What the initialization parameter file is used for

■ Format of parameters in this file

■ Displaying values of entries in this file

■ Changing parameters in this file

■ Parameters most commonly changed

This file is read by Oracle when an instance is started. It is also called *init.ora* or the *pfile*. There are entries in this file that are specific to the database you wish to access, and they control the environment Oracle will set up during startup. The parameters in this file can be used to do the following:

■ Define the name and location of files used by the database

■ Control the size of portions of computer memory allocated to support the database configuration

■ Specify the number of concurrent sessions that may access the database

When Oracle starts the database, much of its operating environment is based on the values of entries in this file. When entries list the name and location of files the instance needs to open at startup, these files are checked. Oracle needs to ensure the files mentioned exist where they are supposed to and can be accessed without error. In addition, the settings of some of the parameters in this pfile affect the performance of your database.

Format for Entries in the Initialization Parameter File

There are two kinds of parameters in this parameter file (hereafter referred to as pfile):

- Explicit parameters have an entry in the pfile.

- Implicit parameters do not appear in the pfile and assume the default until (if ever) you place a value for them in the pfile.

In the next listing, all the values except the first (dml_locks) have no entry in the pfile. These parameters are allowed to assume their defaults until a value for each is hard-coded in the pfile.

```
dml_locks                       integer 1200
gc_db_locks                     integer 75
gc_files_to_locks               string
gc_rollback_locks               integer 20
gc_save_rollback_locks          integer 20
row_locking                     string default
temporary_table_locks           integer 80
```

The format for parameters is

```
pfile_keyword = keyword_value
```

For some entries, you need to enclose parameter values in appropriate punctuation such as parentheses, ( ), or double quotes, " ". If parameters span more than one line, they require a continuation character, as follows:

```
rollback_segments = (rollback_disk1,rollback_disk2, rollback_disk3, \
                     rollback_disk4)
```

Examining Contents of the Initialization Parameter File

This section returns to Server Manager again; OEM can be used to do the following, but we suggest staying familiar with your options and continually popping back and forth between tools. A complete list of parameters (implicit and explicit) is available by doing the following in Server Manager:

1. Enter **connect internal/oracle**.

2. To see a list of the values for all entries, enter the command **show parameters**. Oracle displays a list, the end of which is shown in the next listing.

```
sort_area_size                       integer 65536
sort_multiblock_read_count           integer 2
sql92_security                       boolean FALSE
sql_trace                            boolean FALSE
standby_archive_dest                 string  %ORACLE_HOME%\RDBMS
star_transformation_enabled          string  FALSE
tape_asynch_io                       boolean TRUE
text_enable                          boolean FALSE
thread                               integer 0
timed_os_statistics                  integer 0
timed_statistics                     boolean FALSE
transaction_auditing                 boolean TRUE
transactions_per_rollback_segment    integer 75
use_indirect_data_buffers            boolean FALSE
user_dump_dest                       C:\Oracle\admin\o8ibegin\udump
utl_file_dir                         string
```

You can look at a subset of parameters (implicit and explicit). For this exercise, we want all the parameters that contain the word "sort." After starting Server Manager, follow these steps:

1. Enter **connect internal/oracle**.

2. Enter the command **show parameters sort** and receive the feedback from Oracle as shown in the next listing.

```
nls_sort                             string
sort_area_retained_size              integer 0
sort_area_size                       integer 65536
sort_multiblock_read_count           integer 2
```

Changing Parameter Values

When Oracle is first installed on all platforms, it builds an initialization parameter file to start the database. As your knowledge of Oracle grows, you may change some initialization parameter entry values. Some of them can be changed; others must be left as is. Details about changing pfile parameter values are covered in the Oracle8i Server Administrator's Guide (commonly referred to as the OSAG). The manual gives advice and recommendations about what can be changed and the acceptable range of values. For example (used with permission of Oracle Corporation), the following advice is given about the **shared_pool_size** entry.

```
Parameter type:      string
Parameter class:     static
Default value:       If 64 bit, 64MB, else 16MB
Range of values:     300 Kbytes - operating system-dependent

SHARED_POOL_SIZE specifies the size of the shared pool in bytes. The
shared pool contains shared cursors, stored procedures, control
structures, Parallel Execution message buffers among others. Larger values
improve performance in multi-user systems. Smaller values use less memory
```

Perhaps the most important advice given is whether you are permitted to even change a parameter value; many should be left as is and never changed.

NOTE
Changes to any entries in the initialization parameter file will not take effect until the next time the database is started.

Parameters Most Commonly Changed

Over 130 parameter values are recorded in the data dictionary view v$parameter. This view lists the values in effect as the database operates, and it serves as the source for the query output displayed by the **show parameters** command. Table 18-2 highlights the four entries in the initialization parameter file you will change most often.

NOTE
When you change an entry in the pfile, comment the old one with the "#" character. This will help you keep track of what changed, why, and when.

Parameter	Meaning	Most Common Changes
Shared_pool_size	The number of bytes of memory allocated to the shared pool	As the size of your concurrent user community grows, you may increase this value periodically.
Rollback_segments	The name of one or more rollback segments to acquire when the database is started	When transaction volume increases or decreases over a period of time, you may add or remove the name of a rollback segment from this list.
Sessions	The maximum number of concurrent sessions that may access the database	Needs increasing as more and more users come onboard.
Processes	The maximum number of concurrent processes that may access the database	Needs increasing as more and more users come onboard.

TABLE 18-2. *Parameters Most Commonly Changed*

Control File Responsibilities

Coupled with the initialization parameter file, control files are read by Oracle every time you start the database. Their file information is vital to opening the database. In this section, you will learn details on the following:

■ How Oracle uses the control file

■ Adding a new control file

■ Dropping an existing control file

■ Moving an existing control file

■ Building a new control file

As the DBA, you will bear complete responsibility for managing control files. Think of control files as the transmission in your car. When both behave themselves, they require no attention; but when both misbehave, they can cause major headaches!

Use of the Control File

Every Oracle database has one or more control files. The control file holds information about the database creation time, the name of the database, and the locations and names of all files used when the database is running. You instruct Oracle to maintain as many copies of a database control file (usually two or more) as you deem necessary. The control files are written to as Oracle operates, and they are key to database startup and shutdown. Every time you perform maintenance operations, such as adding a datafile or configuring redo log file groups, the control files are automatically modified to reflect the change. Some control file maintenance is performed with the database down; some maintenance is performed with the database in a nomount status. When you start the Oracle database, the control file is opened first. Oracle then verifies the existence and status of all the files needed to operate, and it ensures all redo log files are accessible. As the DBA, you are responsible for ensuring Oracle can open its control files when it needs them. As we discuss in the "Building a New Control File" section, later in this chapter, making a copy of the control file is included in your backup procedures.

Adding a Control File

You may decide to add a control file when a new disk is added to the disk farm. This can be accomplished in a number of different ways; we are going to look at the solution that offers the most flexibility. Using Server Manager and a text editor on the NT Server machine, do the following to add a control file:

 1. Shut down the database using Server Manager or the OEM Instance Manager.

 2. Using the NT Explorer, open the instance initialization parameter file. In our case this was **C:\Oracle\Admin\O8ibegin\Pfile\init.ora**.

VIP
The initialization parameter file is actually
C:\Oracle\Ora81\Database\Inito8ibegin.ora; this
file, however, contains a single line pointing us at
the file mentioned in the first point in this list.

 3. Proceed to the control_files= line as shown in the next listing.

```
control_files = ("F:\Oracle\oradata\o8ibegin\control01.ctl", \
                 "T:\Oracle\oradata\o8ibegin\control02.ctl")
```

 4. Add the additional control filename as the third line in the entry, which becomes something like

```
control_files = ("F:\Oracle\oradata\o8ibegin\control01.ctl", \
                 "T:\Oracle\oradata\o8ibegin\control02.ctl", \
                 "X:\Oracle\oradata\o8ibegin\control03.ctl")
```

5. Copy one of the existing control files to the location, in our case, on drive X:, and then rename the copied file to its new name. These commands are shown in the next listing:

```
copy control01.ctl X:\Oracle\oradata\o8ibegin
X: cd\Oracle\oradata\o8ibegin
move control01.ctl control03.ctl
```

6. Save the changed initialization parameter file and then restart the database.

VIP
We recommend entering comments for this and all other activities; one never knows how long it will be until you revisit one of these screens, and the comments can sometimes help explain why you ended up doing something a certain way.

Dropping a Control File

Once in a while, you may find yourself with one less disk at your disposal. This requires you to drop one of your control files that was positioned on that disk. We are going to do this a bit differently to illustrate how there always seems to be more than one way to go about accomplishing something with Oracle8*i*; let's get started.

1. Open up an MS-DOS window, and then enter the command **svrmgrl** to start Server Manager.

2. Enter **connect internal/oracle**.

NOTE
*The secure password is **oracle** by default, but may have been changed by you or a colleague.*

3. Enter **shutdown immediate** to shut down the database.

4. Enter **exit** to leave Server Manager.

5. Proceed to the directory where the database initialization parameter file is located.

6. Edit the file looking for the entry that specifies **control_files =**. The parameter value could resemble the following (suppose the bold and italicized name is the one to be removed).

```
control_files = ("F:\Oracle\oradata\o8ibegin\control01.ctl", \
                 "T:\Oracle\oradata\o8ibegin\control02.ctl", \
                 "X:\Oracle\oradata\o8ibegin\control03.ctl")
```

7. Remove the name of the control file to be dropped. The parameter value then becomes

```
control_files = ("F:\Oracle\oradata\o8ibegin\control01.ctl", \
                 "T:\Oracle\oradata\o8ibegin\control02.ctl" )
```

8. Follow steps 1 and 2, and then enter **startup** to start the database.

9. Enter **exit** again to leave Server Manager.

10. Erase the unwanted control file.

Your database is now running with one less file in its pool of control files.

Moving an Existing Control File

If your system administrator needs to change the name of a disk where you have a control file, you, too, will have to inform Oracle of the name of the new location. Again, let's do this in Server Manager. This can be accomplished by following these steps:

1. Open an MS-DOS window, and then enter the command **svrmgrl** to start Server Manager.

2. Enter **connect internal/oracle**.

3. Enter **shutdown** to shut the database.

4. Enter **exit** to leave Server Manager.

5. Proceed to the directory where the database initialization parameter file is located.

6. Edit the file, looking for the entry that specifies **control_files =**. The parameter value could resemble the following (suppose the bold and italicized name is being moved).

```
control_files = ("F:\Oracle\oradata\o8ibegin\control01.ctl", \
                 "T:\Oracle\oradata\o8ibegin\control02.ctl", \
                 "X:\Oracle\oradata\o8ibegin\control03.ctl"))
```

7. Change the name of the second control file, at which point the entry becomes

```
control_files = ("F:\Oracle\oradata\o8ibegin\control01.ctl", \
                 "H:\Oracle\oradata\o8ibegin\control02.ctl", \
                 "X:\Oracle\oradata\o8ibegin\control03.ctl"))
```

8. Move the original control file into its new location using the command:

move *T:\Oracle\oradata\o8ibegin\control02.ctl*
H:\Oracle\oradata\o8ibegin

9. Follow steps 1 and 2, and then enter **startup** to start the database.

10. Enter **exit** again to leave Server Manager.

VIP
*The database **must** be closed when performing this
and the previous task.*

As the database starts, it reads the control_files value from the initialization
parameter file using the control file in the new location as created in step 8.

Building a New Control File

If and when a control file is damaged, Oracle cannot open your database. This is
why, in a number of places throughout this book, we recommend you have more
than one control file. If the need arises to build a control file, you place the
following routine somewhere in your nightly backup procedures.

```
svrmgrl < bcft.sql
```

where "bfct.sql" contains the following three lines:

```
connect internal/oracle
alter database backup controlfile to trace;
exit
```

VIP
*The first line in "bfct.sql" contains the login
information to the instance using the **connect
internal** command. Please ensure when using a
program similar to this that the privileges on the
file are set such that all users of the server cannot
read this file.*

This writes a trace file in the directory defined by the initialization parameter file entry user_dump_dest. The trace file will have the text "ora_" as the prefix and the text ".trc" as the file extension. Embedded in this trace file will be the SQL statements required to build a control file from scratch. The output of this command is shown in the next listing.

```
Dump file C:\Oracle\admin\o8ibegin\udump\ORA00065.TRC
Fri Jun 12 16:53:11 2009
ORACLE V8.1.5.0.0 - Production vsnsta=0
vsnsql=d vsnxtr=3
Windows NT V4.0, OS V5.101, CPU type 586
Oracle8i Enterprise Edition Release 8.1.5.0.0 - Production
With the Partitioning and Java options
PL/SQL Release 8.1.5.0.0 - Production
Windows NT V4.0, OS V5.101, CPU type 586
Instance name: o8ibegin
Redo thread mounted by this instance: 1
Oracle process number: 10
Windows thread id: 65, image: ORACLE.EXE
*** SESSION ID:(9.12) 2009.06.12.16.53.11.974
*** 2009.06.12.16.53.11.974
# The following commands will create a new control file and use it
# to open the database.
# Data used by the recovery manager will be lost. Additional logs may
# be required for media recovery of offline data files. Use this
# only if the current version of all online logs are available.
STARTUP NOMOUNT
CREATE CONTROLFILE REUSE DATABASE "O8IBEGIN" NORESETLOGS NOARCHIVELOG
    MAXLOGFILES 32
    MAXLOGMEMBERS 2
    MAXDATAFILES 32
    MAXINSTANCES 16
    MAXLOGHISTORY 506
LOGFILE
  GROUP 1 (
    'H:\ORACLE\ORADATA\O8IBEGIN\REDO01.LOG',
    'F:\ORACLE\ORADATA\O8IBEGIN\REDO01A.LOG'
) SIZE 500K,
  GROUP 2 (
    'F:\ORACLE\ORADATA\O8IBEGIN\REDO02.LOG',
    'H:\ORACLE\ORADATA\O8IBEGIN\REDO02A.LOG'
  ) SIZE 500K
DATAFILE
  'F:\ORACLE\ORADATA\O8IBEGIN\SYSTEM01.DBF',
  'F:\ORACLE\ORADATA\O8IBEGIN\TEMP01.DBF',
  'G:\ORACLE\ORADATA\O8IBEGIN\USERS01.DBF',
  'D:\ORACLE\ORADATA\O8IBEGIN\ROLLBACK.DBF'
CHARACTER SET WE8ISO8859P1
```

```
;
# Recovery is required if any of the datafiles are restored backups,
# or if the last shutdown was not normal or immediate.
RECOVER DATABASE
# Database can now be opened normally.
ALTER DATABASE OPEN;
# No tempfile entries found to add.
#
```

There are three distinct parts to this statement, which give you a better understanding of the use of the control file:

■ The name of the database and its environment, for instance, the database name and the maximum number of members in a redo log group

■ The location and size of all redo log groups and their members

■ The location and size of all the datafiles associated with the instance

TIP
Make this routine part of your daily backup procedure immediately. It can prove a lifesaver many times during your career as a DBA.

We use this routine as part of all backup procedures we have placed at all our clients' installations. We use the SQL statements in the trace file created with this feature regularly.

Getting the Most from Your Error Messages

Unfortunately, something *will* go wrong when you're working with software. In this case, Oracle feeds an error message back to you with a message number followed by some descriptive text about the problem. Most of the time, you will also get a suggestion or two about how to fix the problem. In this section, we will discuss the following:

■ Obtaining error message text online

■ Recognizing Oracle internal errors and what to do with them

As the DBA, you will become familiar with common error conditions, where to look for their resolutions, and what to do about them. As time marches on, you will surprise even yourself with how quickly you react to common messages. You will begin to spout error text at coffee breaks: "I looked where the clerk told me, and then got 942'ed" or "If I get asked to take on any more responsibilities before vacation, I'm gonna 1547." The Oracle8i Server Error Messages and Codes Manual will start following you around.

Online Error Messages

Oracle8i error messages can be deciphered from the hard copy or electronic copy included with the software. The company bundles HTML-based electronic documentation, as well as Adobe Acrobat. The main reason, we feel, for using the former is that you have your browser open anyway; the reason for using the latter is one word that starts with an "S"—S E A R C H. Let's look at the Adobe approach to using the online error message facility. Figure 18-21 shows the HTML-based menu for the Oracle8i Server Reference documentation.

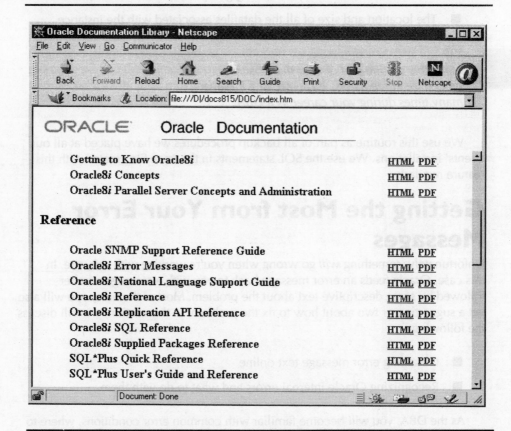

FIGURE 18-21. *The Oracle8i documentation menu*

To use the Adobe interface, click the PDF link beside Oracle8*i* Error Messages, bringing up the screen shown in Figure 18-22.

NOTE
Depending on your browser setup, you may be presented with a warning about a possible security hazard. If this happens, click Open It, and carry on.

Hang on tight—it gets really cool now! Select Tools and then Find from the menu at the top of the screen shown in Figure 18-22, or press the CTRL-F key combination, to bring up a search box. Suppose we were trying to track down an error with the text shown in the next listing:

```
package STANDARD
```

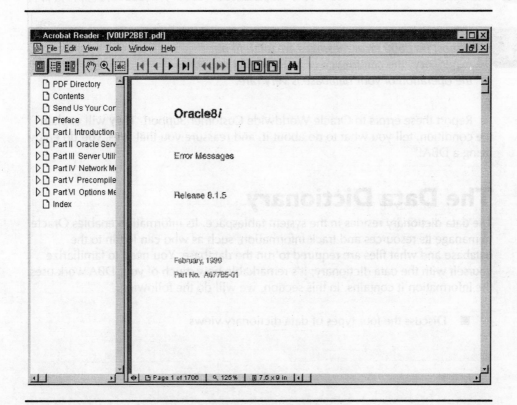

FIGURE 18-22.   *Error message welcome in Adobe*

When the Acrobat Find dialog box appears, enter the text from that listing, and then click Find to begin. At near the speed of light, Adobe will search all the error messages for the entered text, bringing up results when encountered. If you are not happy with the results from a find, press CTRL-G to do it again. If there are too many hits on the lookup string, narrow the search by entering more text or more specific text to look for.

ORA-00600 Internal Errors

Getting one of these errors is the "rite of initiation" to being a DBA, of sorts. The 0600 error is a "catch-all" message returned when Oracle encounters some internal difficulty. It is a generic message followed by up to six arguments enclosed in brackets, [ ]. The majority of the arguments in the square brackets are numbers, but sometimes you may find text. The arguments 12387 and 34503 shown in the example that follows should point Oracle support to the exact reason the error was raised.

```
ORA-00600: internal error code, arguments: [12387], [34503],[],[],[],[]
```

VIP
Almost no 0600 error messages are fatal. In our experience, the occurrence of an 0600 that impedes the operation of your database is very rare.

Report these errors to Oracle Worldwide Customer Support. They will explain the condition, tell you what to do about it, and reassure you that "yes, you do enjoy being a DBA!"

The Data Dictionary

The data dictionary resides in the system tablespace. Its information enables Oracle to manage its resources and track information, such as who can log in to the database and what files are required to run the database. You need to familiarize yourself with the data dictionary; it's remarkable how much of your DBA work uses the information it contains. In this section, we will do the following:

■ Discuss the four types of data dictionary views

■ See how objects appear in a different user's snapshot of the dictionary

■ Highlight the most important dba and v$ views

You will become more fluent with the makeup of the data dictionary in a surprisingly short time period. There is no magic in the Oracle database. Just about everything is stored somewhere in a table, or it can be displayed on the screen in some format. The Oracle8*i* data dictionary belongs to user SYS. The data dictionary is your friend—get to know it.

Types of Dictionary Views

You now need to concern yourself with types of dictionary views. Their names start with the prefixes shown in Table 18-3, and the pieces of their names are connected with the underscore character "_".

The following list shows how the information in these views is interrelated.

```
SQL> select * from dict where table_name like '%OBJECTS';
TABLE_NAME                        COMMENTS
--------------------              ------------------------------------
ALL_OBJECTS                       Objects accessible to the user
DBA_OBJECTS                       All objects in the database
USER_OBJECTS                      Objects owned by the user
SQL>  select * from dict where table_name like '%_QUOTAS';
TABLE_NAME                        COMMENTS
--------------------              ------------------------------------
DBA_TS_QUOTAS                     Tablespace quotas for all users
USER_TS_QUOTAS                    Tablespace quotas for the user
SQL> select * from dict where table_name like '%_SYNONYMS';
TABLE_NAME                        COMMENTS
--------------------              ------------------------------------
ALL_SYNONYMS                      All synonyms accessible to the user
DBA_SYNONYMS                      All synonyms in the database
USER_SYNONYMS                     The user's private synonyms
```

Most Useful dba and v$ Views

Unless you put access in place, users do not have privileges to view information in the v$ and dba views belonging to SYS. You need to grant **select** to everyone to

Dictionary View Prefix	Meaning
all	Returns information on all objects accessible to a user.
user	Returns information on all objects owned by a user.
dba	Returns a database-wide list (for all users) similar to the user category.
v$,	Dynamic performance views updated by Oracle as it runs. Performance information and the status of files and memory being used by Oracle are available by querying these views.

TABLE 18-3. *Main data Dictionary View Types*

allow them to see these views; the information they contain is invaluable to the novice as well as the seasoned DBA. These are the most useful dba_views, and the ones you need to become familiar with in order to get started.

```
TABLE_NAME            COMMENTS
------------------    ----------------------------------------
DBA_DATA_FILES        Information about database files
DBA_DB_LINKS          All database links in the database
DBA_EXTENTS           Extents comprising all segments in the database
DBA_FREE_SPACE        Free extents in all tablespaces
DBA_INDEXES           Description for all indexes in the database
DBA_IND_COLUMNS       COLUMNs comprising INDEXes on all TABLEs and
                      CLUSTERs
DBA_OBJECTS           All objects in the database
DBA_ROLLBACK_SEGS     Description of rollback segments
DBA_SEGMENTS          Storage allocated for all database segments
DBA_SEQUENCES         Description of all SEQUENCEs in the database
DBA_SYNONYMS          All synonyms in the database
DBA_TABLES            Description of all tables in the database
DBA_TABLESPACES       Description of all tablespaces
DBA_TAB_COLUMNS       Columns of all tables, views, and clusters database
DBA_TAB_GRANTS        All grants on objects in the database
DBA_TAB_PRIVS         All grants on objects in the database
DBA_TS_QUOTAS         Tablespace quotas for all users
DBA_USERS             Information about all users of the database
DBA_VIEWS             Text of all views in the database
```

Table 18-4 highlights the most useful v$ views, and the ones you need to become familiar with to get started.

View	Contains
v$datafile	Information on the datafiles used by the database; same as the information in the control file(s).
v$librarycache	Information on management of SQL statements in the shared pool.
v$lock	Information about locks placed on objects by sessions that access the database. Locks are used to prevent users from changing data in the database another user may have already started changing.
v$log	Information extracted from the control file about redo logs.
v$logfile	Information about the location and names of the instance redo log files.
v$parameter	The values of all entries in the initialization parameter file.
v$process	Information regarding current processes.
v$rollname	Rollback segment information.
v$rollstat	Statistics about online rollback segments.
v$rowcache	Information about data dictionary activity/performance in memory.
v$session	Information about active sessions.
v$sesstat	Statistics about active sessions reported in v$session.
v$sqlarea	Statistics about cursors currently held in the shared pool. Cursors are chunks of memory opened by Oracle for the processing of SQL statements.
v$statname	The meaning of each statistic reported in v$sesstat.
v$sysstat	Systemwide statistics based on currently active sessions.
v$waitstat	Details on situations encountered when more than one session wants access to data in the database. There can be wait situations when more than one session wishes to manipulate the exact same information at the same time.

TABLE 18-4. *Most Useful v$ Views*

Working with Oracle Worldwide Customer Support

As the DBA, you will end up being the central contact point for your organization and technical support requests. To expedite the logging of support calls, Oracle needs the following information when you call:

- Your appropriate customer number for the configuration and tool for which you require support.

- A complete list of version numbers; telling support you are using Oracle version 8 is helpful, but knowing it's 8.1.5 is better, and 8.1.5.1 is better still (if the version number even goes to this fourth qualification level). This is especially true with the Oracle tools: there are significant differences between using Oracle Forms versions 4.0.13 and 4.5.

- A list of any Oracle errors that caused your logging the support request. These can begin with an assortment of prefixes such as **ora**, **frm**, or **dba**.

- Descriptive information about "what was going on" when the error was detected.

Oracle will do one of four things when you call. We prefer the first solution (by far the most frequent).

1. Tell you what to do to remedy the situation, and send you on your way a satisfied, enthusiastic customer.

2. Keep you online while they search a number of support databases looking for a similar situation and, after finding a match, provide you with a number of workarounds.

3. Keep you online while they search a number of support databases looking for a similar situation, and, after finding no match, get back to you in an amount of time that varies directly with the severity of your call (that is, if the problem inhibits smooth operation of your business, you will be dealt with in a shorter period of time).

4. Record pertinent information and call you back at some later time.

Feel free to call and check on the status of your call whenever you feel the need.

"But I Can't See the Forest for the Trees"

You are poised to embark on a journey into the unknown. This DBA job you are starting (or is it "have been saddled with") is not going to wreck your social life. No, contrary to what you have heard, you will not be up until all hours of the night wrestling with the database. Yes, people will come to you for answers. Why do you think it's called Oracle? Perhaps they were thinking of you: you are the oracle that sees, says, and solves all.

Become fluent with what we have discussed in this chapter. Read technical magazines. Attend user conferences (ever wanted to go to Japan? Europe? or perhaps Australia?). Frequent Oracle forums and information services on CompuServe, the Internet, and World Wide Web servers. If you don't understand something or you are boggled by a new routine, idea, or concept, just ask! Between the two of us, we have over 20 years of experience using Oracle. We still learn things from each other. Believe it: we know a developer (thanks Lise!) who showed us some tricks with SQL*Forms version 3 a while back that we had never been aware of. If you figure out how to do something that you are excited about, let everybody know. One of the interesting things about Oracle is that it is such a complex product, you may just have mastered doing something that four other DBAs all over the world have been tearing their hair out trying to figure out for the past two years. Enjoy!

What's Next

Now that was a handful; you are now a seasoned Oracle8*i* DBA, waiting for your next assignment. Should you decide to accept this mission, we have two things to say to you—good luck and welcome aboard. The next chapter has a look at Oracle8*i* features tailored to data warehousing. We believe that after you have grown familiar with these features, as soon as you have the opportunity to work on a warehousing system, you will be able to ensure it does not turn into a data outhouse instead!

CHAPTER
19

Data Warehouse
Features

ince the beginning of time we have provided reports and information to the masses. Whether that information was in the form of smoke signals, stone tablets, or hand-written records, information sharing has been around for ages. Today we call this collecting and sharing of information *data warehousing.* In this chapter, we will briefly discuss the concept of data warehousing and highlight some of the features of Oracle8*i* that blend so nicely with this approach to information management. Data warehousing and the management of large volumes of static data are distinct features of the Oracle8.*x* database management solution. Release 7.3 (circa early 1996) delivered many of the bells and whistles that have continued to mature with Oracle8*i.*

To put it simply, a data warehouse is a device that turns data into information. We systematically collect information from one or many data sources, collate the information in a central repository, and then provide the information in a simple structure. This then allows end users to ask questions and improve the way they do business. A data warehouse helps people make better and more informed decisions, but it can't make those decisions for you. You can still make bad decisions even with good information.

One thing you must know before you embark on any data warehousing project is that the user is King or Queen. The data warehouse project that ignores the needs and input of the end user is a project on a path to failure. If you would like to build the Titanic of data warehouses, exclude your user. If you want to build the user's "Dream of Fields" (it's a play on words), then you must involve them in every aspect of the creation of the warehouse. The design of a warehouse is a special task, one that is best managed by those who are generally less "normal" than your regular operational system design. The design and deployment of the warehouse is a paradigm shift from the systems we designed for years to meet operational needs.

So why do we need to create data warehouses? The warehouse forms one component of modern reporting architectures. The goal of reporting is usually to aid in decision support. We need to address certain needs when it comes to reporting, and the warehouse helps us achieve these. Users of reporting system needs the following:

- Accessibility: Can I get my information when I need it?

- Timelessness: How long after something happened can I see it?

- Format: Can I present the data the way I need to?

- Integrity: Can I believe the data that I get?

It's hard not to see that such concerns bring into question the competence of the information technology (*IT*) department. Even more important, answering such questions can have a huge impact on the profitability of the company. Providing support to these types of requests will help you build a new future for your organization.

Defining the data warehouse is basic to understanding how to create a data warehouse that will improve your organization, so let's move on to a definition. *Data warehouses* are databases that are created for the sole purpose of reporting. Data warehouses have four distinct characteristics that differentiate them from operational systems. They are

- Subject oriented: The warehouse is organized around a specific business process such as purchasing.

- Integrated: The warehouse is integrated so that we can relate one subject against another, so that, for instance, we could perform purchasing versus sales analysis.

- Nonvolatile: The warehouse is static; it is not changing like an operational system. We load data on a regular basis into the warehouse, but we do not change data that already exists in the database. So if we had $500 of sales in January 2000, and I read the data in 2005, the information will still read as $500.

- Time based: The basic power of the warehouse is that the information contained in it is based on specific point-in-time loads. The loads may be daily, weekly, monthly, or based on some other time period, but whatever that time is, we include this with the data in the warehouse. The warehouse shows your business information at many points in time, whereas your operational system shows you information at the time you look at the information.

Each of the preceding points defines the nature of the data in a warehouse. The warehouse becomes the place in your business that people have the information needed to support strategic and tactical decisions that you may need to make.

Critical to the success of any project is assembling the right team. Just like the teams that win the Super Bowl, the World Series, and the Stanley Cup, the data warehouse team is composed of many different skills sets that work toward a common goal of building the right data warehouse for your organization. Data warehouses cannot be prebuilt; they must be built to the needs and requirements of an organization.

Oracle8*i* is a product that suits the data warehouse approach very well. Oracle's strategy to support data warehousing and very large databases (*VLDBs*) helps us to create a foundation for the warehouse that is reliable and provides the performance required. Oracle8*i* contains many new features that are critical to the warehouse. This chapter discusses many of these features that you will use during the development and implementation of your data warehouse.

NOTE
Headings will display the appropriate version numbers (7, 8, or 8i) to indicate which version of the database introduced the features that we discuss in this chapter.

Let's first look at some terminology.

Terminology

The following definitions will arm you with the technical jargon you need to make it through this chapter:

- A *data warehouse* is a data repository designed to support the decision-making process for an organization. Unlike with its operational system counterpart, the information can be stored many times in many different locations. Its primary purpose is to provide management with the information it needs in order to make intelligent business decisions.

- A *CPU* is the central processing unit of a computer that is responsible, in conjunction with the operating system, for coordinating work and managing the resources available as software operates.

- An *operational system* (commonly referred to as OLTP) is a partner with a business's data warehouse. These systems allow employees to go about their daily business. For example, let's suppose a company maintains a large inventory of automobile supplies. The system that manages part supply, reorder, and stock depletion notification is an OLTP system. The system that allows executives to analyze customer purchasing habits and make long-term business decisions is in the decision support arena where the data warehouse resides.

- An *enterprise-wide data warehouse* is a homogeneous collection of data designed to facilitate the decision-making process across a company's business units.

- A *full table scan* involves reading an Oracle table from start to finish. Each row of information is read sequentially, from beginning to end.

- An *index range scan* is an operation in which Oracle selects rows from a table by scanning the index and then fetching rows from the table whose column values match a query's selection criteria. The scan is two-phase: first the index, then the data. Under many circumstances, an index range scan can be many times faster than a full table scan.

■   A *data mart* is a subset of an organization's decision support information
    that focuses on a specific area of interest. The data mart caters to a smaller
    portion of an organization's user community and has a time-to-market that
    is far shorter than that of the enterprise-wide data warehouse.

■   *Data normalization* involves ensuring data is stored in only one place and
    updated centrally. When data is normalized, it conforms to the relational
    model we discussed in Chapter 1.

■   *Denormalizing* is a process used throughout the data warehouse that
    involves undoing a data normalization exercise. When data warehouse
    architects look at the reporting and analysis requirements of their user
    community, they go through a systematic denormalization of OLTP data to
    satisfy the community's reporting needs.

■   *Data mining* is a knowledge discovery in a database exercise. Data mining
    efforts analyze vast quantities of information, looking for patterns and trends
    in behavior that can be used by organizations when they are designing
    targeted marketing initiatives and new product releases.

■   *OLAP* stands for online analytical processing and relates to a set of end-user
    query tools that allow drill-down, aggregation, and collection of various
    levels of summarization. OLAP tools facilitate slicing and dicing of data
    warehouse information in ways unique to the decision support
    requirements of users of an information warehouse.

■   *Parallelization* is a process whereby work to be performed by a computer is
    split among different processes. These processes work simultaneously on a
    task, and the results of the work are merged when complete to appear the
    same as if the work had been done by only one process.

■   A *star schema* is a set of tables in the data warehouse that are organized
    around a single table with a multipart key that is known as the *fact table*.
    The smaller tables that form the components of the multipart key are called
    dimension tables. You can think of a dimension table as a lookup or
    reference table. The star schema is also know as a star join.

■   *Cardinality* is the measure of the number of distinct values in a column,
    versus the total number of rows in a table. Therefore, a column with 10,000
    distinct values in a one million–row table will have a cardinality of 0.01,
    which would be considered a low cardinality. Whereas a column with
    10,000 distinct values in a table of 100,000 rows would have a cardinality
    of 10, which we consider moderate to high cardinality.

Oracle has built a number of warehouse-centric enhancements into its Oracle8*i*
offering. These features are designed to speed the mechanisms involved in storing

vast amounts of data, as well as Oracle8's capability to retrieve that information. The details of all the features are too many and too technical to discuss at great length in this work, but we encourage you to look at *Oracle8 Data Warehousing* (Corey, Abbey, Abramson, and Taub, Osborne/McGraw-Hill, 1998) for a more detailed look at Oracle's offerings in this arena. Let's highlight a few features to give you a flavor of some Oracle internal mechanisms specially designed to enhance the performance of the Oracle7/8i software supporting the data warehouse.

NOTE
The material we cover in this chapter is more advanced than most covered elsewhere in Oracle8i A Beginner's Guide. Oracle8i specifics for data warehousing are technical, requiring our delving into their more advanced details.

Bitmap Indexing (7.3.2 and 8)

Many decision support queries are worded in the following way: "How many people who purchased an automobile bought a ____ within the same calendar year?" or "What is the likelihood that marketing efforts in the northeast quadrant of the continent will____?" These are translated by a query tool into SQL statements similar to **select count(*) from auto_sales where car_year = other_part_year;** and **select count(sales) from sales_summary where quadrant = 'NE';**.

Indexes are used by Oracle to provide rapid access to information. Think of an index on an Oracle table as the index to a book, because Oracle uses an index in the same way as you may use the index to an encyclopedia to locate a desired topic. Bitmap indexing is simply a stream of bits, where each bit corresponds to a row in a table. Picture a simplified example to satisfy the query just shown. Bitmap indexes provide us with some significant benefits in Oracle8 and 8i, including

- **Improved response time for large ad hoc queries:** The user community often complains about the length of time it takes to get results back when working with large amounts of data; mechanisms in Oracle8i address these specific concerns.

- **A reduction in space utilization compared to other indexing methods:** Space is a small problem that becomes larger as the space on your machine gets smaller. So anything that we can do to reduce the amount of space that is occupied in the database is advantageous. Bitmap indexes occupy less space than standard b-tree indexes and, therefore, reduce your space usage.

■ More efficient data loads: When loading data into the databases, we look to find additional efficiencies. Bitmap indexes in Oracle8*i* provide for more efficient loading of data into the database using SQL*Loader.

Bitmap indexes provide the most benefit when the cardinality of the table is considered low. Also, columns that contain repeat values where the value repeats more that 100 times are considered candidates for the index. Additionally, as we will discuss later in this chapter, the star query optimization performs best with bitmap indexes.

The building of a bitmap index is a two-step process:

1. Decide the number of unique values in the desired column (looking at Table 19-1, there are five values in car_year and three values in other_part_year).

2. Build a compressed bit stream for each value in the bitmap indexed column. To take this one step further, Oracle decides it will need five bit streams for car_year, and three for part_year. One bit in each stream represents one row in the underlying object.

Using the same data shown in Table 19-1, Oracle would build five bit streams on the former column, and three on the latter. Tables 19-2 and 19-3 show these bit stream indexes.

Row Number	Car_Year	Other_Part_Year
1	2001	2001
2	2001	2002
3	2002	2001
4	2000	2001
5	1999	1999
6	2001	2001
7	1997	2002
8	1998	1999

TABLE 19-1. *Years of Purchase*

Row Number	1998 Stream	1999 Stream	2000 Stream	2001 Stream	2002 Stream
1	0	0	0	1	0
2	0	0	0	1	0
3	0	0	0	0	1
4	0	0	1	0	0
5	0	1	0	0	0
6	0	0	0	1	0
7	0	0	1	0	0
8	1	0	0	0	0

TABLE 19-2. *Bitmap Index for Purchase Data*

Oracle8*i*'s bitmap indexing implementation allows rapid access to statistics about warehouse data, since the search on a compressed bitmap index can execute in a fraction of the time required to search data based on a more traditional indexing approach.

Row Number	1999 Stream	2001 Stream	2002 Stream
1	0	1	0
2	0	0	1
3	0	1	0
4	0	1	0
5	1	0	0
6	0	1	0
7	0	0	1
8	1	0	0

TABLE 19-3. *Bitmap Index for Other Parts Purchases*

Optimizer Histograms (7.3.2 and 8)

So many queries sent off to a data warehouse for processing are requests for rollups of large amounts of numeric data. Questions like "How many people in the sales organization in the southern hemisphere earned commissions of over $7,500 last year—break down by the four major geographical areas and display running totals for each quadrant" can best be answered after the data warehouse administrator builds histograms on parts of the warehouse data.

VIP
*Optimizer histograms are only beneficial on table columns with a nonuniform distribution of data that are frequently used in the **where** portion of an SQL statement.*

Histograms in Oracle

Histograms are nothing new to mathematics. In the Oracle arena, they were introduced in Oracle 7.3, and the implementation of the technology has matured with each subsequent release of the Oracle Server. Bitmap indexes record the distribution of data within an Oracle table and can enhance SQL statement processing in situations where there is nonuniform distribution. Inspect the next listing, which shows a histogram with the same weight to each bucket.

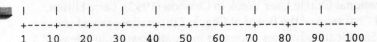

The optimizer would easily deduce that the data is distributed evenly throughout the table, and thus the number of records in the table whose column values lie between 41 and 50 is exactly the same as those between 91 and 100. Suppose the histogram looked like this.

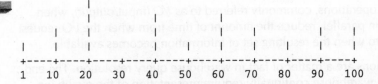

Using this histogram, without even reading the table or index data, one can see that twice as many rows fall into the 50–60 range as do the 70–80 range (using the upper bound of the bucket as the determining factor). Before moving on, let's briefly look at how optimizer histograms are built.

Building the Histogram

The SQL **analyze** command with the following syntax is used to build a histogram.

```
analyze table outlet
   compute statistics for columns province size 10;
```

Let's pick apart the statement:

1. The table name (shown in italics) is usually owned by the user collecting information for the histogram.

2. The column name upon which the histogram is being built (shown underlined) is specified prior to the number of buckets.

3. The number of buckets (shown in bold) is specified at the end of the statement. The bucket size is not required; if it is not included, it defaults to **75**.

Investigate optimizer histograms if they seem appropriate for your applications. Their implementation in Oracle8i could have a positive effect on your data warehouse applications. Next on the agenda is parallelization.

Parallelization

As far back as International Oracle User Week in Orlando (1993), Larry Ellison, President, CEO, and Chairman of the Board at Oracle Corporation, talked about *parallel everything*. Significant advances appeared in parallelization in release 7.1 in early 1994. As the size of Oracle databases increases, parallelization of operations is a significant component of the support for these very large databases that Oracle8i provides. The following operations highlight the type of processes that, when parallelized, contribute to improved performance and response times of information repositories using Oracle.

- Read/write operations, commonly referred to as *I/O* (input/output), when performed in parallel, reduce the amount of time from when the I/O request is initiated to when the resulting set of information becomes available.

- Sort operations are a matter of fact in warehouse query resolution. The end users of the warehouse continually require presentation of the qualifying data in various ways. Oracle7 and Oracle8i are capable of taking advantage of multi-CPU machines, leveraging their capability to perform tasks in parallel.

Oracle8*i* includes automatic parallel execution tuning. This capability is initiated by your friendly DBA, who will set some values in the initialization parameter to enliven Oracle8*i*'s strategic parallel processing capabilities. With this set up properly, the database is aware that it should tune itself to optimize parallel query functions.

VIP
Databases that have already been configured and optimized for parallel operations may not see any significant benefit from automated parallel tuning.

The familiar adage "more bang for the buck" comes to mind when looking at parallelization features, as does "two heads are better than one."

Query Processing

More and more hardware vendors are releasing these multi-CPU machines, and we have worked on a number with multiple processors. Oracle8*i* allows the database administrator to control how aggressively the optimizer will attempt to parallelize query processing. In a nutshell, this is a simplified version of how Oracle processes queries in parallel:

1. It inspects the degree of parallelization for the objects involved in the join operation. The *degree of parallelization* defines how you would like Oracle to try to separate the SQL utilizing multiple CPUs to complete the requested task. You define the degree of parallelization when you create the table or index. This degree is set as illustrated in the following two listings (with the keywords in bold).

```
-- Set degree of parallelization at creation time
create table account (acc_num      number,
                       owner_id     number,
                       address_id   number,
                       ...
                       ...
                       ...)
     parallel (degree 8);
```

```
-- Set degree of parallelization later or change a degree
-- previously set
alter table account parallel (degree 16);
```

2. It looks to see if the instance is running with multiple parallel query processes and, if it is, selects one of these processes to act as dispatcher for the parallel processing.

3. The dispatcher partitions the workload among the number of parallel query processes up to the number specified in the table's degree of parallelization. Suppose there are 16 parallel query processes, and a table's degree of parallelization is 8. Oracle uses the following logic to determine how many query processes to use, while inspecting the number of CPUs, the number of disks the data resides on, and the degree of parallelization for the tables:

```
if more than 1 CPU on machine then
   if degree of parallelization set for table then
      if table(s) data resides on only one disk then
         process query using one and only one server process
      else
         if number of available query server processes >= that degree
            dispatch that number of query server processes to process query
         else
            dispatch as many query server processes as are available
         end if
      end if
   else
      process query using one and only one server process
   end if
else
   process query using one and only one server process
end if
```

4. It assembles qualifying data, receiving chunks from each participant query process. As the participating query server processes finish their work, each passes qualifying data back through the dispatcher process.

5. It merges the chunks of data into a consistent set of qualifying data under the supervision of the dispatcher.

6. It passes the data back to the user process that initiated the query.

Picture a situation when, for whatever reason, the work passed off to parallel query process P001 was not as intensive as that passed to process P002. As a result, say P001 finished its work early while P002 was only half done with its task. Oracle uses a dynamic load balancing system such that query processes that finish early will rob work from processes involved in retrieving data from the same query.

VIP
*This dynamic load balancing is one of the most
important characteristics of a successful approach to
parallel query processing.*

Load Operations

In a data warehouse, large volumes of data end up being moved into the warehouse
during partial or complete refreshes. We've dedicated Chapter 10 to loading your
data, directing you here to look at how to parallelize loader routines. Suppose you
wanted to load 7,000,000 rows into a table in your warehouse, and the data resided
in a fixed-length text file. The next listing shows a few lines from that file.

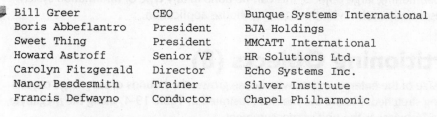

```
Bill Greer           CEO          Bunque Systems International
Boris Abbeflantro    President    BJA Holdings
Sweet Thing          President    MMCATT International
Howard Astroff       Senior VP    HR Solutions Ltd.
Carolyn Fitzgerald   Director     Echo Systems Inc.
Nancy Besdesmith     Trainer      Silver Institute
Francis Defwayno     Conductor    Chapel Philharmonic
```

Notice the number of characters reserved for name, position, and company;
hence the term fixed length. To perform a parallel load (using three parallel
processes in this example, though you can use more or less), do the following:

1. Extract the data from its source repository into three separate output files.
   Select a column from the source data such that, for example, records whose
   state code starts with A to H are in one file, I to M in another, and N to Z in
   the third.

2. Create three separate control files to feed to SQL*Loader. We discussed the
   control file in Chapter 10 and have included some examples.

   ```
   Initiate three SQL*Loader sessions to run concurrently.
   sqlldr userid=tom/scholz control=parr1 parallel=true
   sqlldr userid=tom/scholz control=parr2 parallel=true
   sqlldr userid=tom/scholz control=parr3 parallel=true
   ```

From our experience, load sessions run in parallel complete in significantly less
time even though they are loading data into the same table(s) concurrently.

Table and Index Creation

Data warehouse load and data transformation personnel continually create tables and indexes as the repository is refreshed. You can parallelize these two operations using parallel processing and the following syntax.

```
create table blah_blah (...) parallel (degree 2);
create index blah_blah_1 on blah_blah (...) parallel 2;
```

Previously, in the "Query Processing" section, we spoke of setting a degree of parallelization for a table. There, the parallel keyword was used in the **parallel (degree..)** construct, whereas here it is simply **parallel *n***, where ***n*** is an integer representing the number of parallel processes to utilize. Let's move on and talk about partitioning large objects; this can be done in any type of information system but is especially useful with the data warehouse application.

Partitioning Objects (8)

As the size of the enterprise data warehouse grows, the bounds of very large objects are being stretched. Picture the metrics illustrated in Table 19-4, using the megabyte (1,048,576 bytes) as the unit of measurement.

NOTE
Using this table, think of an exabyte as 1,152,921,504,607,000,000 bytes—perhaps some of us will have the opportunity to support a 16-exabyte data warehouse some day!

Measure		Units	Of
Megabyte	=	1,024	Kilobytes
Gigabyte	=	1,024	Megabytes
Terabyte	=	1,024	Gigabytes
Petabyte	=	1,024	Terabytes
Exabyte	=	1,024	Petabytes

TABLE 19-4. *Units of Measure*

It does not take too long to realize the sheer size of many data warehouse implementations when you start talking about a repository in the neighborhood of a few hundred terabytes (the same as a few thousand gigabytes or a few ten thousand megabytes). Some day-to-day operational system repositories' data swells well into many gigabytes, if not terabytes, but generally it is your data warehouse that will easily achieve that size. Oracle8*i* mechanisms address very large database requirements using a scheme of partitioning we will touch on in the next few sections. *Partitioning* is the deliberate separation of a very large object into smaller, more manageable chunks. Oracle8*i* permits partitioning of data and index segments using some of the syntax we are about to cover.

Why Partition Objects?

Partitioning is a smart approach because breaking up large objects provides so many benefits, including

- Less chance of losing data when it is partitioned: The chance of experiencing total data destruction in a partitioned object is exponentially lower than in a nonpartitioned object.

- Ease of load balancing: The breakup and deliberate separation of partitions can assist in the process we all go through of ensuring there is a balance of read/write operations between all the disks upon which our Oracle8*i* database resides.

- Backup and recovery: When an Oracle8*i* database design maps pieces of partitioned objects across multiple data files, it becomes easier to plan an optimal backup and recovery strategy.

- Ease of archiving: When objects are partitioned by column values, older data can be more easily moved offline as time marches on. Say an organization partitions by fiscal year and is committed to keeping the current and two previous years accessible at all times. As the calendar flips from December 31, 2002, to January 1, 2003, the data in the 1996 fiscal year can be easily moved to the archives.

Partitioning is one of the biggest trends in the industry regarding management of very large databases. All the vendors are getting on the bandwagon, not just Oracle.

Working with Partitioned Objects

We looked at some of the syntax for creating partitioned objects in a few other places around this book. Let's look at the flexibility offered by a partitioned object approach and how it fits so nicely into the management of very large objects. The following is a sample of five common operations you can do with partitioned tables and other objects:

- Table partitions can be moved from one device to another to assist the I/O balancing exercise. The **alter table account move partition p2...;** keywords are the heart of this operation.

- Index partitions can be moved as well, except the movement of one or more pieces of a partitioned index requires rebuilding the index or each partition individually. The **alter index account_1 rebuild partition p2;** construct is how this is accomplished.

- Partitions can be added to tables and indexes using **alter table account add partition p2;**. When a partition is added to an existing partitioned table, the corresponding indexes, if any, are further partitioned to match.

- Table partitions can be dropped after deleting their rows. This is accomplished using the **alter table account drop partition p3;** command. Index partitions cannot be manually dropped; they are dropped implicitly when the data they refer to is dropped from the partitioned table.

- Rows can be truncated from a partition using the **alter table account truncate partition p3;** command. The corresponding index partitions are truncated at the same time as the table to which the index belongs.

Materialized Views (8*i*)

A *materialized view* is a database object that is used to store summary and precomputed results in the data warehouse. Materialized views provide significantly faster data warehouse query processing. The time necessary to calculate these summarizations is performed in advance of the data request.

Materialized views allow the optimizer to determine if it should retrieve data from the lower-level tables (atomic data), resulting in potentially costly join and aggregation operations, or from the precreated view. The database automatically rewrites the query to access the materialized view when this is the appropriate choice. The optimizer will use the materialized view to improve the query performance. The optimizer can automatically recognize that it can make use of the view. The optimizer will then rewrite the query so that it accesses data contained in the materialized view. By performing this task, the optimizer assures that the query no longer accesses the underlying data during the query. This processing is done completely behind the scenes by the database, without the user knowing that it has occurred. This query rewrite facility is totally transparent to the application, which is not aware of the existence of the materialized view.

VIP
In case you are unsure of which materialized views to create, Oracle provides a set of advisory functions in the DBMS_OLAP package to help in designing and evaluating materialized views for query rewrites. Setting up this package and providing access to it are jobs for your DBA.

Let's look a little deeper into a bit of the work involved in setting up one of these views.

Dimensions

The first step in order to create a materialized view is to define dimensions. Dimensions in the Oracle8*i* world represent the levels of data, such as how many classrooms make up a school or how many stores make up a sales region. Dimensions can be thought of as lookup tables. We use dimensions as windows into our data.

VIP
You must define dimensions if you plan to use materialized views.

Let's look at how we define and create a dimension so we can then create a view using this dimension. We will create a date dimension, because when it comes to data warehousing, all we have is time—time to design, time to build, the time and date associated with the data. Time is critical to the warehouse, so the example that follows defines a date dimension that you can use for no extra charge in your own data warehouse.

```
create table dw_date (
    calendar_date       date,
    month               number(2),
    quarter             number(1),
    year                number(4),
    week_num            number(2),
    day_name            varchar2(10),
    fiscal_year         number(4),
    fiscal_quarter      number(1),
    month_name          varchar2(15));
```

```
create dimension date_dimension
    level cal_date    is dw_date.calendar_date
    level month       is dw_date.month
    level quarter     is dw_date.quarter
    level year        is dw_date.year
    level week_num    is dw_date.week_num
    hierarchy time_rollup (
            cal_date            child of
            month               child of
            quarter             child of
            year                )
    hierarchy weekly_rollup (
            cal_date            child of
            week_num            child of
            year                )
    attribute cal_date determines dw_date.day_name
    attribute month determines dw_date.month_name;
```

As you can see, we have created the base table dw_date, and from that we then define the dimension that makes up the date_dimension dimension. This example shows you how to create dimensions when the data is all stored in a single dimension table.

VIP
You can create dimensions from normalized dimension tables, by defining joins within the dimension definition.

In the dimension creation script, we have defined the levels within the dimension. In Figure 19-1, you can see the dimension levels that we defined in the script.

Now that we have created our dimensions, we can move on to creating our dimensional view. The question is what dimension are we entering? A dimension of time and space may very well be the answer.

Creating a Materialized View

A materialized view is not a view in terms of the view that we all know and love. The similarity between a materialized view and a standard view is that they are both defined in advance by a DBA and a developer and are then made available to the users. In the case of the standard view, the data is retrieved to satisfy the view at request time. The materialized view's data is retrieved and summarized from the database in advance of a query. Also, a materialized view requires storage space in the database, but the standard view uses Oracle's temporary space area.

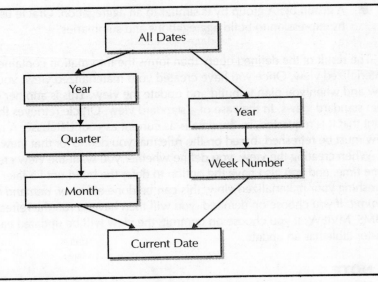

FIGURE 19-1. *The time dimension hierarchy*

So, therefore, we must create the view and define how often we want the information in the materialized view updated. The create statement for the materialized view usually contains some, if not all, of the following:

- A subquery: This is a query within a query, an example of which would be a query that finds all the sales for all the cities in the state of Alaska. The main query finds the sales data, and we then link it with the query that finds all the cities.

- A join: This is when you link two tables together using common database columns. An example of this is a customer ID that would exist in the customer table and a sales table. By joining the customer table with the sales table through the customer ID, you can display the customer's name along with the sales amount. This is much more meaningful than showing the customer ID.

- An aggregation: Simply put, this is a summary. An aggregation is totals, summed up under one or many columns. For example, you may want a summary that provides you the sales by state and then by store, but the data you have is at the individual sales level. So, by summing up the sales amount by state and store, you can find out the total sales for the combination.

■ **A group by:** A group by is similar to an aggregation. Oracle uses the group by expression to build aggregations and summaries.

The result of the defined query then forms the information contained in the materialized view. Once you have created your materialized view, you must define how and when you plan to build and update the view. This is another difference from standard views. In the case of a standard view, Oracle retrieves the data at the point that it is requested, so the data is as current as your database. A materialized view must be refreshed, based on the rule that you define for that view.

When creating the view, you define whether you want the view created at the same time, and you also have the option to defer the build until a later time. As for refreshing your materialized view, this can be done either *on demand* or *on commit*. If you choose on demand, you will then have to run the refresh package DBMS_MVIEW; if you choose on commit, the view will be updated each time the master table has an update.

NOTE
When selecting a refresh mode (complete or incremental), remember that a complete refresh will wipe all the information in the existing view and then repopulate the new data from the detail tables. An incremental will only update changed data.

So let's look at an example of the script needed to create a materialized view; this is shown in the next listing. The line numbers are there for the purposes of the discussion that follows; they are not part of the actual SQL statement.

```
1      create materialized view daily_company_sales
2         tablespace daily_mat_views
3         pctfree 0
4         build immediate
5      refresh complete on demand
6      enable query rewrite
7      as
8      select transaction_date, company_num,
9             sum(gross_sales) as daily_gross_sales,
10            sum(discount_amt) as daily_store_discount_amt,
11            sum(tax_amount) as daily_store_tax_amt,
12            sum(gross_sales-discount_amt-tax_amount) as daily_net_sales
13         from daily_sales
14      group by transaction_date, company_num;
```

That's a lot of syntax; so, before moving on, let's look at some details using the line numbering in the listing.

- Line 2: The data for the view will be stored in the daily_mat_views tablespace. A *tablespace* is a collection of one or more datafiles within which tables are stored.

- Line 4: This is where we specify that the view should be built at once rather than at some point in the future.

- Line 5: This is where we specify whether we want to rebuild the view when we decide or automatically.

- Line 6: This tells Oracle that if the optimizer senses that a query could use this view instead of the source data table, the optimizer can then rewrite the new query internally to run the query against the materialized view.

- Lines 8 to 14: This is the query that is used to create and maintain the materialized view. This defines the source of the view.

NOTE
The owner of the materialized view must have the space necessary to store the view's base table and associated index.

In the data warehouse world, we often created summary tables that were equivalent to a materialized view. We often wrote special programs to perform the updates and then needed to support this functionality through scheduled updates. Materialized views and the benefits that they provide can be used against currently existing summary tables. Through the **prebuilt** option, you can use data that has been previously created by your previous summarization routines. So remember the new old saying, "Don't reinvent the wheel, convert it to a materialized view."

Transportable Tablespaces (8*i*)

This feature has nothing to do with the Transporter that Captain Kirk and Captain Picard have used to fly around the galaxy. The question of why the Captain of a Starship always beamed down to the surface with his away team, is one that we will not answer here, but feel appropriate to ask. *Transportable tablespaces* allow you to move a subset of your Oracle database into another Oracle database. This is not unlike using the export and import utilities, but it is much simpler than that. It is more like unplugging your television in one room and moving it to the new room. Alright, it is a little more complicated than disconnecting and reconnecting a TV, well for some of us; but the capability to move tablespaces from one database to another is a valuable feature, especially in a data warehouse environment.

Transportable tablespaces can be used for a variety of reasons including the following ones:

- Archiving data efficiently

- Loading data from operational systems into a data warehouse

- Loading data from an enterprise data warehouse into a data mart

- Publishing data to internal and external users

Transportable tablespaces provide us with some much-needed functionality. The capability to archive tablespaces has always been a challenge; but with transportable tablespaces, you can now archive one or more tablespaces by creating a transportable tablespace set that is to be archived. A *transportable tablespace set* consists of datafiles for the set of tablespaces being transported and a file containing the required details for the set of tablespaces. The capability to quickly transport data is always an issue for data warehouse systems. Whether you are loading data from your operational system or a data warehouse, the capability to create the transportable set and then simply copy the files to the other database can provide you with a quick method for moving data. Once you copy the set from one database to the other, you then "plug in the data." Finally, the capability to provide data sets to your users can provide some important functionality. Think of creating a transportable tablespace set especially for the sales department that contains only sales-related data. You can then update the sales database with only the data that they specifically require.

Moving data with transportable tablespaces can be much faster than the import/export utility, because transporting a tablespace only requires the copying of datafiles and integrating the tablespace structural information.

NOTE
When you are transporting tables and their associated indexes, indexes do not require rebuilding after transport.

The process to create and move a transportable tablespace requires you to perform the following tasks that we have illustrated in Figure 19-2.

As Figure 19-2 illustrates, the process involved in creating and then moving the transportable tablespace set is a relatively easy process. Just like most things in Oracle, you can do things two different ways—the hard way or the easy way. The

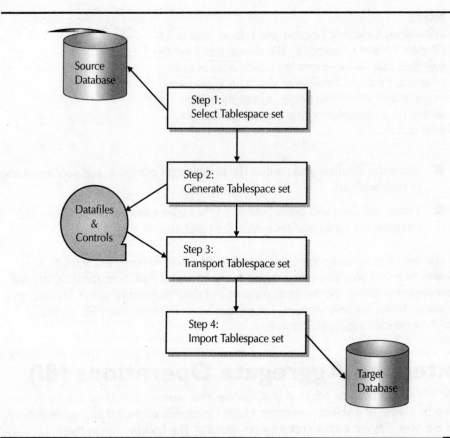

FIGURE 19-2. *The transportable tablespace process*

best option is—the envelope please—the easy way. To achieve the goal of the
"easy way," you must carefully plan the tablespaces that you will include in your
set. If you are moving tablespaces that contain data, you also want to include the
tablespaces that include your indexes. Later in this section, we will discuss how to
check that the set of tablespaces that you have selected to transport is considered a
valid list. Moving transportable tablespaces to their target database involves the
following steps:

■ Pick the list of tablespaces to transport.

■ Generate the transportable tablespace set using the Oracle8*i* export utility.

NOTE
We discuss Oracle8i's export and import utilities in Chapter 15 and Chapter 16. We do not touch on the role they play in transportable tablespaces in those chapters; they will familiarize you with import and export if and when you decide to use them with setting up and implementing transportable tablespaces.

■ Move the datafiles and control file to the target platform, and you are ready to rock and roll.

■ Initiate the Oracle8*i* import utility on the target platform, which then will integrate the new datafiles within the database.

You may end up using the transportable tablespace features of Oracle8*i* from day one. Many of you may never take advantage of this new functionality. We see many opportunities in the decision support and data warehouse arena—hence, this discussion in the last few sections. Let's move on to the next "new kid on the block"—extended aggregate options.

Extended Aggregate Operations (8*i*)

Oracle8*i* allows users to develop SQL queries that perform functions similar to the **group by** clause of a **select** statement. Using Oracle8*i*'s extended aggregate options, you are now playing with a **group by** on steroids! The bottom line to these extensions equals

■ **Rollup** creates subtotals at any level of aggregation needed, from the most detailed up to a grand total.

■ **Cube** is an extension similar to **rollup**, enabling a single statement to calculate all possible combinations of subtotals. These summaries are widely used in data warehouses providing timely analysis information.

While these same operations can be done using SQL (remember the **group by** clause), the SQL was difficult to generate, and the **select** statements took long periods of time to complete. These new functions allow users to perform aggregate operations with less effort and greater efficiency. Let's look in a little more detail at these two functions, with a small taste of the SQL syntax involved.

Rollup

Rollup and **cube** are simple extensions to the **select** statement's **group by** clause. **Rollup** creates subtotals at any level of aggregation needed, from the most detailed up to a grand total. The action of **rollup** is straightforward—it creates subtotals that "roll up" from the most detailed level to a grand total, following a grouping list specified in the **rollup** clause. **Rollup** takes as its argument an ordered list of grouping columns, using a three-step process:

1. It calculates the standard aggregate values specified in the **group by** clause.

2. It creates progressively higher-level subtotals, moving from right to left through the list of grouping columns.

3. It creates a grand total.

Rollup will create subtotals at *n*+1 levels, where *n* is the number of grouping columns. For instance, if a query specifies **rollup** on grouping columns of year, month_name, and company (that is, *n*=3), the result set will include rows at four aggregation levels. The next listing shows how **rollup** is used. The line numbers are not part of the syntax but have been placed in the listing for referencing in the verbiage following.

```
1    select d.year,d.month_name month,s.company_num,
2           sum(s.gross_sales)                          as tot_sales,
3           sum(s.discount_amt)                         as tot_discount,
4           sum(s.tax_amount)                           as tot_tax,
5           sum(s.gross_sales-s.discount_amt-s.tax_amount) as tot_net_sales
6      from daily_sales s,report_date d
7     where s.transaction_date = d.calendar_date
8     group by rollup(d.year,d.month_name,s.company_num,s.franchise_area);
```

Let's look at a few important pieces in the syntax of this listing before moving on:

■ Line 1: The **s.** and **d.** prefixes on the column names dictate what tables the columns are being extracted from.

■ Lines 2 to 4: Notice that the SQL is performing a summarization of columns from the daily_sales table, and, therefore, the **as ...** syntax is used to name the data as it is assembled.

■ Line 6: This is where the table names are listed, using aliases—**s** for daily_sales and **d** for report_date.

- Line 8   this is the heart of using **rollup**, where the function is applied to the columns listed in parentheses.

The results of this query, shown in the next listing, show you how these values roll up under the date dimension that we created earlier in the chapter.

```
YEAR MONTH         COMPANY_NUM TOT_SALES TOT_DISCOUNT   TOT_TAX TOT_NET_SALES
---- ------------- ----------- --------- ------------ --------- -------------
2001 APRIL                 100   1250.38       131.29    206.99        912.10
2001 APRIL                 200   2877.50       265.50    372.49       2239.51
2001 APRIL                       4127.88       396.79    579.48       3151.61
2001                             4127.88       396.79    579.48       3151.61
                                 4127.88       396.79    579.48       3151.61
7 rows selected.
```

As you can see in the output list of the rollup grouping, the values have been summarized at the year, month, and company levels and the levels of aggregation. The year, the year-month, and a grand total for the sample data set have all been calculated for us. Let's move on and see the **cube** function, which is the same but different from the **rollup** function.

Cube

Cube is an extension similar to **rollup**, enabling a single statement to calculate all possible combinations of subtotals. **Cube** can generate the information needed in cross-tab reports with a single query. A *cross-tab report* is an intersection report of rows from two or more tables, with the cells being summary values corresponding to a calculation for the row and the column. The easiest way in Oracle8*i* to generate the full set of subtotals needed for cross-tabulation is to use the **cube** function. **Cube** allows a **select** statement to calculate subtotals for all the combinations of a group of dimensions. It also calculates a grand total. This is the set of information typically needed for all cross-tabular reports, so **cube** can calculate a cross-tabular report with a single **select** statement. Like **rollup**, **cube** is a simple extension to the **group by** clause. Let's look at how you initiate a **cube** query:

```
select d.year,d.month_name month,s.company_num,
       sum(s.gross_sales)                         as tot_sales,
       sum(s.discount_amt)                         as tot_discount,
       sum(s.tax_amount)                           as tot_tax,
       sum(s.gross_sales-s.discount_amt-s.tax_amount) as tot_net_sales
  from daily_sales s,report_date d
 where s.transaction_date = d.calendar_date
 group by cube(d.year,d.month_name,s.company_num,s.franchise_area);
```

The syntax is similar to that shown when we discussed **rollup**, except that the results of this query show you how these values cube under the date dimension that we created earlier in the chapter. Notice that this data is the same data set that we used during the **rollup** example, yet the resulting combinations are much more complete. These data combinations allow for many ways to look at your data, which form the basis for data analysis. We call this *slice and dice analysis*, since you can slice and dice the data in so many different ways.

YEAR	MONTH	COMPANY_NUM	TOT_SALES	TOT_DISCOUNT	TOT_TAX	TOT_NET_SALES
2002	APRIL	100	1250.38	131.29	206.99	912.10
	APRIL	100	1250.38	131.29	206.99	912.10
2002	APRIL	200	2877.50	265.50	372.49	2239.51
2002	APRIL	200	2877.50	265.50	372.49	2239.51
2002	APRIL		2877.50	265.50	372.49	2239.51
	APRIL		1250.38	131.29	206.99	912.10
	APRIL		4127.88	396.79	579.48	3151.61
2002		100	1250.38	131.29	206.99	912.10
2002		100	1250.38	131.29	206.99	912.10
2002		200	2877.50	265.50	372.49	2239.51
2002		200	2877.50	265.50	372.49	2239.51
2002			2877.50	265.50	372.49	2239.51
2002			1250.38	131.29	206.99	912.10
2002			4127.88	396.79	579.48	3151.61
	APRIL	100	1250.38	131.29	206.99	912.10
	APRIL	100	1250.38	131.29	206.99	912.10
	APRIL	200	2877.50	265.50	372.49	2239.51
	APRIL	200	2877.50	265.50	372.49	2239.51
	APRIL		2877.50	265.50	372.49	2239.51
	APRIL		1250.38	131.29	206.99	912.10
	APRIL		4127.88	396.79	579.48	3151.61
		100	1250.38	131.29	206.99	912.10
		100	1250.38	131.29	206.99	912.10
		200	2877.50	265.50	372.49	2239.51
		200	2877.50	265.50	372.49	2239.51
			2877.50	265.50	372.49	2239.51
			1250.38	131.29	206.99	912.10
			4127.88	396.79	579.48	3151.61

28 rows selected.

The preceding results show you all the various data combinations that would be seen in a cross-product table. The data provides details as well as aggregates at the various levels as defined in the date dimension. Let's now look at how we would rank data using the **top-n** function.

Top-n

How many times have you asked who are the 10 top hockey players? Who are the 10 best salespeople in your organization? Or the top 10 ways Canadians are different from Americans? Alright, all but the last question can be answered from data in our database. The **top-n** query provides us with the functionality that allows us to easily determine rankings that would have been difficult to do in Oracle before Oracle8*i*. To illustrate the concept, we have run the query shown next; the line numbers are not part of the syntax:

```
1    select rownum as rank,
2           transaction_date as date,
3           company_num,
4           daily_net_sales
5      from (select transaction_date, company_num,
6                  sum(gross_sales) as daily_gross_sales,
7                  sum(discount_amt) as daily_store_discount_amt,
8                  sum(tax_amount) as daily_store_tax_amt,
9                  sum(gross_sales-discount_amt-tax_amount) as daily_net_sales
10              from daily_sales
11            group by transaction_date, company_num
12            order by sum(gross_sales-discount_amt-tax_amount) desc);
```

Before looking at the output from this **top-n** query, let's discuss a bit of the syntax in the previous listing:

- Line 1: This is the heart of **top-n** query processing, where you specify the columns you would like back from the daily_sales table.

- Lines 5 to 12: The source of the ranking, this query is used by Oracle to provide the **top-n** query the data it needs to rank the data.

This query returned the following data. As you can see, the database ranked the data from the highest values to the lowest and provided us with a list of our top sellers:

```
    RANK DATE        COMPANY_NUM DAILY_NET_SALES
--------- ----------- ----------- ---------------
       1 01-APR-2002         200         1275.87
       2 02-APR-2002         200          963.64
       3 01-APR-2001         100          467.59
       4 02-APR-2002         100          444.51
```

Let's have a look at one last data warehouse–centric feature of Oracle8*i*—star query optimization—and how it benefits processing queries against large information repositories.

Star Query Optimization (7.3 and 8)

In many data warehouses, designers build a star schema that can be characterized by a very large table (called the *fact* table) and two or more smaller tables (called *dimension* tables) that contain information about attributes in the large fact table. These dimension tables used to be called lookup tables. The optimizer recognizes queries built on a star schema when it encounters the following:

■ There is a join operation (merging data from two or more tables) where one table is very large compared to the other tables involved in the operation.

■ There is a network of foreign keys sitting in the very large table pointing at all of the smaller dimension tables.

■ The very large table has a primary key constraint (that is, an index built on more than one column).

Once Oracle detects these three characteristics of a query, special star query processing routines come into play. The cost-based optimizer uses a transformation technique to process star queries; this transformation specifically rewords a query (without changing the intent) to take advantage of speed-enhancing objects such as bitmap indexes discussed previously in this chapter.

VIP
*When supporting an Oracle8i database, star query transformation and processing routines will come into play when the initialization parameter file entry STAR_TRANSFORMATION_ENABLED is set to **true** and the instance restarted.*

The star transformation is a good example of why Oracle's optimization approach is called *cost based*. The optimizer decides the cost of using or not using the transformation by

■ Generating the best plan it can produce without the transformation and placing it away for safekeeping

■ Applying the transformation (if enabled), if applicable, and generating the best plan using the transformed query

■ Comparing the cost estimates of the best plans for the two versions of the query

■   Selecting the transformed or nontransformed plan, whichever is best (that is, whichever costs the least)

Most works that discuss data warehouse design, management, and deployment spend time talking about the star schema and why it makes so much sense in the decision support environment. We have found that the star schema and star query are paired well with Oracle8*i* and provide the power and simplicity that you need in our data warehouse environment.

What's Next

Data warehousing—a new phenomenon or simply a new way of saying an old thing? We lean toward the latter choice. We believe that what makes data warehousing seem so new is the sheer volume of data being managed in the present day. In the next chapter, we will look at WebDB, Oracle's newest offering in the Internet world. It is products like WebDB that will further empower you, by allowing you to deliver simple yet powerful applications to users via the Web. So let's move forward and look at WebDB and how we can provide functionality via the Web. Just remember to keep your hands in the vehicle at all times.

CHAPTER
20

WebDB

he advent of the Internet has spawned a need for tools that allow users and database administrators to quickly develop and deploy applications to the Web. WebDB is a product that allows organizations to streamline the development and maintenance of Web access with a simple interface with numerous functions. Oracle has followed the *KISS* (Keep It Simple, Stupid) principle when it came to developing WebDB. They have provided us with a tool that allows users and administrators who have only a limited amount of experience with the WebDB product to quickly become productive. They have further enabled experienced users to tap into the power provided within the database and the product by, for instance, integrating Java into their applications. WebDB offers all of this plus the power of the database to hold your application and drive the content of your Web pages.

WebDB stores all the data needed for the Web pages in the database. So whenever the content of your Web page changes, the page as viewed through the browser will reflect the new content. This relates not only to the data, but also headers, footers, graphics, and site navigation. This provides developers with the ability to quickly respond to the ever-changing needs of the Internet, intranets, and extranets that we use on a daily basis. Most of us work with organizations that have Web pages. It's difficult to find any company or any kid over the age of 10 who does not have a Web page today. Oracle has built WebDB allowing organizations or kids to move at Internet speed to meet users' needs as they change.

WebDB is a product that is related to Oracle Developer (discussed in Chapter 9) and Oracle JDeveloper (discussed in Chapter 21), but it is easier to use and exploit its features. WebDB allows user to create and generate Web pages, it enables administrators to manage the database and its objects, and it does all this from a simple Web browser. WebDB is an access method to your Oracle database, and all you need to exploit it is a browser like Netscape Communicator. You will also find that if you work in a heterogeneous database environment, WebDB will allow you to access these databases through a gateway in your Oracle database. A *heterogeneous database environment* is one in which there are databases from more than one vendor such as Oracle (of course) and something like SQL*Server (imagine that!). This ability to mix databases without your users knowing or caring is critical for users working in today's heterogeneous database world.

We now have an Internet tool that is easy to use and is database driven. You need to ask yourself, "Are these the features I'm looking for?" If we think of Oracle's current Web development tools, we can equate them to a family that has three sons—a wise son, a contrary son, and a simple son.

- Oracle Developer is the wise son, the oldest—let's call him Ed—he is the one who can do anything and perform complex logic tasks. The only problem is that Developer has had some serious identity issues. He wanted to change his name, just as everyone was getting used to it. However, the experience that has been gained over Developer's many years and many versions has allowed it to be built into a solid product. Oracle Developer is the son who can do everything you would ever ask and is still able to create a cool Web page. Developer allows you to create Web forms but still provides you with Old Faithful, client/server forms, with little effort. I told you it was wise.

- The contrary son is JDeveloper—let's call him Dan—he is the one who works out on the edge, balancing new technology and structured programming, but still having time to play some golf. Dan, who is our JDeveloper developer, delivers Web solutions using technology that has been built specifically for the Web. With Java at its core, JDeveloper allows you to develop, debug, and run Web forms and applications. JDeveloper is still a developing product and, as such, could still use a little refinement. We see JDeveloper's potential today, and we see it growing along with its cousin the Internet (Bob).

- That brings us to the simple son, David. The simple son of the Oracle development Web toolkit would have to be WebDB. On the surface, WebDB is a simple product to use, to manage, and to develop applications with. It is a stay-at-home product, as it leverages the database to store all of its objects. By storing all of its stuff in the database, WebDB allows you to leverage the reliability and recovery abilities of your Oracle database. David, our WebDB developer, can deliver applications to the Web quickly, using a mixture of data maintenance, reporting, graphs, and queries to meet the needs of the many. The simple son may not be that simple but at least has the skills necessary to administer a database.

Let's now look more closely at WebDB, the newest Oracle arrival. First, we'll have a look at WebDB's architecture. As we pointed out in Chapter 4, learning the architecture that supports software can prove helpful in getting up to speed on how a system operates. It can also have huge benefits down the road if and when anything goes wrong.

Terminology

The following definitions will arm you with the technical jargon to make it through this chapter:

- A *URL*, or uniform resource locator, specifies the location of an object on the Web.

- *HTML*, or Hypertext Markup Language, is a set of tags and rules used to develop hypertext documents and can be read and understood by a Web browser, like Netscape.

- *ASCII*, or American Standard Code for Information Interchange, is a code for representing English characters as numbers, with each letter assigned a number from 0 to 127. For example, the ASCII code for uppercase M is 77. Most computers use ASCII codes to represent text, which then makes it possible to transfer data from one computer to another.

- A *Web server* is a computer that delivers (serves up) Web pages. Every Web server has an IP address and possibly a domain name. For example, if you enter the URL *http://www.oracle.com/home.html* in your browser, this sends a request to the server whose domain name is oracle.com. The server then fetches the page named home.html and sends it to your browser.

- *Oracle's Web Application Server* is a Web server dedicated to answering requests that come in through the requested Web address. The Web Application Server can connect to database servers.

- The *Web listener* is the portion of the Web Application Server that receives HTTP requests. You can use the Oracle Web Application Server manager to create multiple Web Listener processes and assign each to accept connections on a different set of ports.

- *WebDB packages* are programs set up within the database to allow WebDB to generate Web pages based on information requests or Web pages generated from within WebDB.

- In client/server applications, a client may be designed to be especially small so that the bulk of the data processing occurs on the server. A *thin client* is a term used for computers, such as network computers and Net PCs, that are designed to serve as the clients for client/server architectures. A thin client is a network computer without a hard disk drive, whereas a *fat client* includes a disk drive.

- The *DBA* is the Database Administrator. It is the DBA who is responsible for ensuring that the database is running smoothly. Their responsibilities include managing the database, backing up and restoring the database, and tuning the database and applications accessing the database.

■ The *WEBDB_DEVELOPER* role is a set of database privileges required to develop applications within WebDB.

■ A *table* is a database object that holds your data. Information about every table is stored in the data dictionary; with this information, Oracle allows you to maintain data residing in your table.

■ A *schema* defines the tables, the fields in each table, and the relationships between fields and tables within the database.

■ A *procedure* is a program that is written using PL/SQL that may be stored in the database.

■ A *function* is a PL/SQL subprogram that executes an operation and returns a value at the completion of the operation. A function can be either built in or user named.

■ An *index* is a structure associated with a table; it is used by the database to locate rows of a table quickly; it can be used to guarantee that every row is unique.

■ A *package* is used as a method of encapsulating and storing related procedures, functions, and other package constructs together as a unit in the database.

■ A *trigger* is a stored procedure that is executed when an **insert**, **update**, or **delete** statement is issued against the table associated with the trigger.

■ A *commit* is an internal Oracle command that tells the database to permanently write data to the database.

■ *Data access pages* are Web pages that you build to allow users to access the data within the database via the Web. You can use these pages to **query**, **insert**, **update**, or **delete** data.

■ We define the *master-detail* relationship as a many-to-one relationship between blocks on a form or groups on a report. The master block is based upon the table with the primary key; the detail block is based upon the table with the foreign key.

■ A *list of values* is a list of the valid values for a field. It is used in WebDB to simplify data entry for the end user.

■ The terms *drill up* and *drill down* relate to how you structure data from summary to detail. You can initially display your data in a summarized view, but by allowing your users to drill into the data, you can then let them view the data that was used to build the summary.

- The *System Global Area* (SGA) is the memory allocated to Oracle to run and manage its internal processes and user processes. Every instance of an Oracle database has its own SGA; they are not shared.

- *Storage parameters* are the values used by Oracle to store your object, such as a table or an index, in the database.

- A *tablespace* is a logical portion of an ORACLE8*i* database used to allocate storage for table and index data. Each tablespace corresponds to one or more physical database files.

- *Rollback segments* provide the database with the information needed to revert back to original data after data has been added or changed.

- *Locks* control access to the database. A lock blocks other users from updating information in the database until the data is committed to it.

WebDB Architecture

The architecture of WebDB has been developed by Oracle as a highly flexible product. They have achieved this by developing the entire product using PL/SQL (see—we told you PL/SQL is not dead!). This means that it runs in any Oracle database from version 7.3.4 to Oracle8*i*.

NOTE
As discussed in Chapter 6, you do not use the Universal Installer when installing WebDB because the Universal Installer does run with database versions earlier than 8i.

WebDB is a product that functions under a standard three-tier architecture. To access WebDB, you simply point your browser to the Oracle WebDB URL. Users do not require any additional software. WebDB supports Java, so you can extend the functionality of your application. There is no need for Net8, or any two-tier client/server configuration—a browser and nothing but a browser is all you need.

The users communicate with WebDB through different Web server options depending on how the WebDB administrator determines the most appropriate technology choice. The administrator has numerous options for communicating to the database server:

- Through a Web listener specifically built for the WebDB product

- Through Oracle's Application Server or through some other Web server product

These options can be configured to support WebDB. In this book we will only discuss the WebDB listener services that are available.

To complete the final tier, all WebDB packages are installed in the database when you install the product. All work created by the WebDB Developers and Administrators—such as queries, forms, and ultimately Web sites—is stored in the database. Since pictures are worth so many words, let's look at Figure 20-1, to see how WebDB is structured.

NOTE
From the WebDB material in Chapter 6, you may recall that some time was spent during installation as the process spawned an assortment of MS-DOS windows showing where these packages were installed.

As you can see in Figure 20-1, WebDB does not require a great deal of overhead to run. This economy is achieved by providing a thin client to our users, by allowing access to WebDB applications via a Web browser. The performance is extremely good, due to the fact that the product requires such a low overhead; however, you are limited by the speed of your connection to the Internet and the

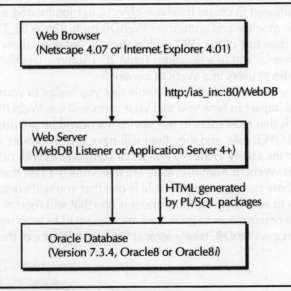

FIGURE 20-1. *WebDB architecture*

user traffic on your Web site. All the advantages of a thin client are contained within this product, as well as a simple method for maintaining Web sites from a central or remote location.

This architecture provides WebDB administrators with the ability to manage the objects in the database and the content of their Web sites through the same interface provided to the users. Web administrators manage the database and the Web objects through their Web browser as well.

Let's move on now and take a closer look at WebDB. If you have not yet installed WebDB, refer to Chapter 6 for a look at how to install and set up WebDB. WebDB is a very comprehensive tool, so let's get started and look at the various tasks that can be performed using the product.

WebDB Users

Using WebDB is a relatively simple task, if you want it to be, or a more complex job—depending on what you plan to use the tool for in your organization. The only prerequisite for using WebDB is that you have a pulse and an Oracle account.

The account we speak of in this context is not your run-of-the-mill Oracle account; this is a special account. To simply use WebDB, you must be either a DBA or a WEBDB_DEVELOPER. The DBA role is your standard Oracle DBA role with some added WebDB spice; it provides you with significant access to the database and some powers that you may not care to provide to your general user community. In the WebDB world, the DBA is provided with full access to all menu and screen options and is allowed to create database objects, to monitor and administer the database, and to monitor and administer WebDB itself. The WEB_DEVELOPER role is more limited than that of the DBA within WebDB but does allow users access to many WebDB menus and functionality. Table 20-1 summarizes the privileges that each role provides to users in a WebDB context.

As you can see from Table 20-1, the role that you assign to your users has a significant impact to how you and your users will use WebDB. What we have found is that most users in our environment will be provided with the WEBDB_DEVELOPER role, and they then will have specific grants within WebDB to provide them the ability to access and build components with other users' database objects. WebDB Administrators are few—this is a task that carries significant database privileges, so this role is one that you will control more closely. Setting up users to access your environment is one that will require planning, but it does allow your organization to grow and manage small to large applications. Since you can now access WebDB, take a look at the user interface of the product.

DBA Role	WEBDB_DEVELOPER Role
Access to all WebDB menus	Access to WebDB menus except administration, monitoring, and site building options
Browse any object in any schema in the database	Browse any object in your own schema or any objects that you have been granted access to by another user
Create WebDB components in your own schema or in any schema for which you have been granted "Build In" privileges	Create WebDB components in your own schema or in any schema for which you have been granted "Build In" privileges
Access to all DBA functions through the DBA menus. This provides you with the ability to create, modify, and drop users. Monitor the database performance and administer the database and its objects	No equivalent
The facilities to manage WebDB configuration and user privileges	No equivalent

TABLE 20-1. *Summary of WebDB Roles*

NOTE
In a number of places throughout this chapter, we quickly discuss carrying on some sort of activity with WebDB. Unlike throughout Chapter 9, in some places we summarize what we have done rather than walk you through step by step.

Navigating WebDB

The navigation within WebDB is a task that requires significant amounts of practice. You must be careful, when you start using WebDB, that you ensure that your mouse-button finger has been prepared for this job. You may wish to take a second at this point in the book and do a little stretching with your preferred mouse finger. Don't worry, we will wait for you to finish your training before we continue. Are you done? Don't forget to cool down, it's probably more important than the exercise itself. Now that you are ready to navigate WebDB, let's go over the steps to access the WebDB menus and task screens.

1. Open a Web browser (preferably Netscape Communicator 4.07 or greater).

2. Enter the Web address used to access your WebDB (this address is defined when the WebDB product is installed).

3. Log in to WebDB by supplying your user name and password.

4. Enjoy the ride, but please no standing on the bus.

Anyone who browses the Web today accesses WebDB in many places around the Internet. The key to accessing WebDB is knowing the correct URL to supply to your browser. In our case, the address we have used is *http://ias_inc:80/WebDB*. The address breaks down this way (in our case):

- *http://* is the standard first level of most Web addresses.

- *ias_inc:80* is the Web server name.

- *WebDB* is the site name.

VIP
When you install WebDB, the installation will supply you with the URL used to access the WebDB menus.

Make sure you provide your Web browser with the exact address the WebDB application is expecting. Once you have successfully connected to WebDB, you will be presented with a menu containing the tasks that can be performed. Figure 19-2 illustrates the default startup menu that will be presented to you after you successfully connect to WebDB.

The WebDB main menu provides you with your initial choices within WebDB. The view that you see in Figure 20-2 shows the choices that you see as a Web administrator or DBA. When you have the DBA role provided to you, all options in the menus are available to you. Let's look at each of the options in the default main menu and see where each takes you. Depending on the level of customization that the Web Administrator decides upon, your default menu will be similar or customized to your individual site.

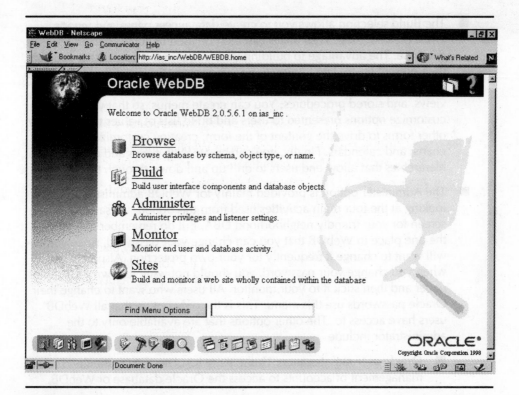

FIGURE 20-2. *The WebDB main menu*

Initially, you are presented with five options in your Web browser; again, the simple son comes to life. Each of these options is rich in its depth. This is the tip of the proverbial iceberg. Each option leads you to another menu to another menu to another menu—you get the idea. The default main menu provides access to the following options:

■ The Browse selection allows you to look at the objects contained in your database schema, or objects to which you have been given Browse In access. *Browse In* access allows users to view objects in other users' schemas. This privilege is set up in the Administration option of WebDB—don't worry, we will get to that in a minute (depending on how fast you read). You may also be saying to yourself, "Why do we keep saying *objects* and not *tables*?" Well, that's because you can view more than tables. You can look at tables and views, packages, procedures and functions, sequences, indexes, and triggers. No matter what types of objects you would like to investigate, if you have access, you can look at them.

■ The Build selection allows you to create data access pages and reports. Once created, these Web pages can then be used to access data in the database. The advantage to building Web pages in this way is that you can then present up-to-date information to your users. From the Build menu you can create simple and master-detail forms to provide access to tables, views, and stored procedures. You can create menus, so that you can customize options presented to users and build lists of values to be used by other forms to drive the content of the form, creating customized reports, charts, and calendars. Finally, you can create Web pages and data hierarchies that allow end users to drill up and down through their data.

■ The Administer option is provided mainly for WebDB administrators. After looking at the four main activities used from this option, we saw this as a screen for your friendly neighborhood DBA. But do remember that this is the one place in WebDB that you can change your password, since you will want to change it frequently for your own protection. Also note that when you change your password, you should not write it down on a slip of paper and then stick it to your monitor. All users who want to change their Oracle passwords use this menu. This is the only option that all WebDB users have access to. The other options that are available only to the administrator include

■ **Oracle user maintenance:** This activity involves the creation and management of accounts to access the Oracle database or WebDB.

■ **Object grant administration:** This function provides access to database objects to users who would like access to an object that they have not created.

■ **Role administration:** This activity assigns roles to users. Roles define a group of grants and are used to simplify grant administration.

■ **Internal WebDB administration:** This activity involves the maintenance of WebDB user accounts, including granting WebDB roles, managing the WebDB listener, and according Browse and Build privileges.

■ The Monitor option is another one of the features that DBAs love. This option is monitoring with a twist. Here you are monitoring WebDB and the performance and usage of the product. Although this page is aimed at DBAs and Web Administrators, we would recommend that everyone look at these options, since they can provide you with insight and help you tune your Web applications and your database. Although you may not be a DBA, you should nonetheless understand how performance tuning is done. The monitoring menu opens up with a number of powerful options, including:

■ Response times

■ Database requests by component, day, user, browser, network, and Web pages

■ The Sites menu option allows DBAs to create Web sites for specific uses. It is with this option that you create, enhance, and manage Web sites that you create.

These may seem like a relatively small selection of choices; but, again, the depth of the product will appear in these options as well. You will find that you may look at a usage report by user, but you can then drill down and look at the details for the user. Such drill-down capabilities can be found throughout WebDB, enabling you to better understand summarized values while also looking more closely at the details that constitute the value.

As you can see, WebDB has many features and functions that enable you to empower users, so let's look at these features in more detail so you can see just how simple it is to use, yet how much potential it has to offer.

Database and WebDB

By now you must have a feeling of how much WebDB has to offer, but you need the details. As always when it comes to any product that you use with Oracle, you want to know how you can use it to see your data and create objects. It's for those reasons that we include chapters in this book discussing SQL*Plus and the task of creating tables, views, and so on. In the context of WebDB, life is a little simpler than with the SQL*Plus tool, since WebDB guides you through the steps to create and retrieve data from database objects. SQL*Plus is a blank sheet, and you must know how to write SQL (and we are sure you do if you've been reading this book); this makes it more difficult when you do not use the product every day. WebDB has wizards and forms to aid you in doing the little things that you do with a database. Not only does it make life easier, it also makes database access simpler, mainly because you do all your work through your Web browser and you do not have to be concerned with the configuration of your local PC, only with where to find WebDB on your network. Let's look at how WebDB approaches accessing data and then how you can use it to create and manage objects in the database.

Browsing Database Objects

Browsing, viewing, querying, interrogating, retrieving—what do all these verbs have in common? It is these verbs that describe the extraction of data from the database. This is a basic requirement for any of us who have data in a database; after all, what's a database without an access tool? Without access to your database, you may as well have a sheet of ice without skates, a puck, and a stick. It's cool to have, but it's not of much use. WebDB is the kit that can provide your users access to their data. The browse module allows you to simply access the objects in your database. Whether you want to see the structure of a table, the data contained in a table, the table triggers, stored procedures, or any other database object, you can do this from within the tool.

VIP
To use the Browse option, you minimally require the WEBDB_DEVELOPER role.

After selecting the Browse link from the WebDB main menu, you will be presented with the option of selecting the object that you would like to browse. You may enter any of these:

■ The schema name

■ The object type

■ The name of the object you would like to browse

These three criteria then tell the database to provide you with a list of eligible objects that met your criteria. You will also notice a small box beside the schema criteria box, which is a button to create a List of Values window that will give you a list of the schemas to which you have access. Figure 20-3 illustrates the results that WebDB will return to you after you enter your criteria for object selection.

In our case, Figure 20-3 has returned only the tables and views that we have been granted access to in the schema that we requested. For you to browse objects in other users' schemas, you must be granted the Browse In privilege by the DBA from within the WebDB administration. As you should notice, you also have the option to browse other schema object types by simply selecting one of the more appropriate links. By selecting the All Objects link, you will be presented with a list of all the object types that you have access to for the schema that you selected.

Now that we have access to a list of tables from the IAS schema displayed in our browser, as illustrated in Figure 20-3, we will move on to select data from one of these tables and present it to you in a simple, easy-to-read format. Not only is the data output easy to read, but selecting the data itself is an exercise in simplicity. After selecting the table that you wish to view by clicking the table name link, you are then presented with a form that allows you to perform any of the following functions:

■ Query data

■ Update data

■ Insert a single row of data

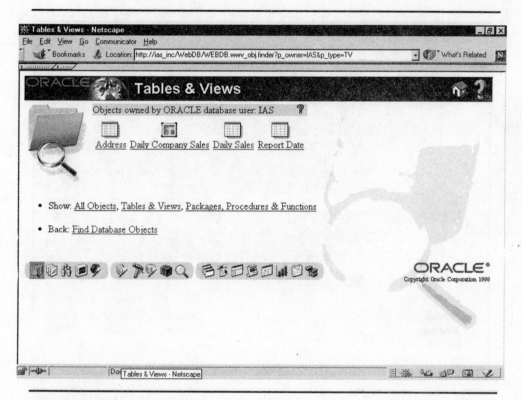

FIGURE 20-3. *Tables that you can browse*

These functions really provide you with a very powerful array of functions to view and manage your data. You may decide that you do not want to maintain your data using these functions, but that you may want some user-friendly form. WebDB allows you to create these as well. This functionality is powerful and (should we say it?) simple to use, so it may be an option in certain cases. We entered a simple query, using data from our DAILY_SALES tables, and in a matter of a few seconds, ordered by data; grouped the data; but did not enter a **where** clause, although we could have, and we present the results in Figure 20-4.

Figure 20-4 illustrates a simple example of extracting data from the database using WebDB. As you see, we have ordered the data by TRANSACTION DATE, COMPANY, and FRANCHISE. We have also grouped the data and computed the sum of the data based on the date of the transactions. When you create your query

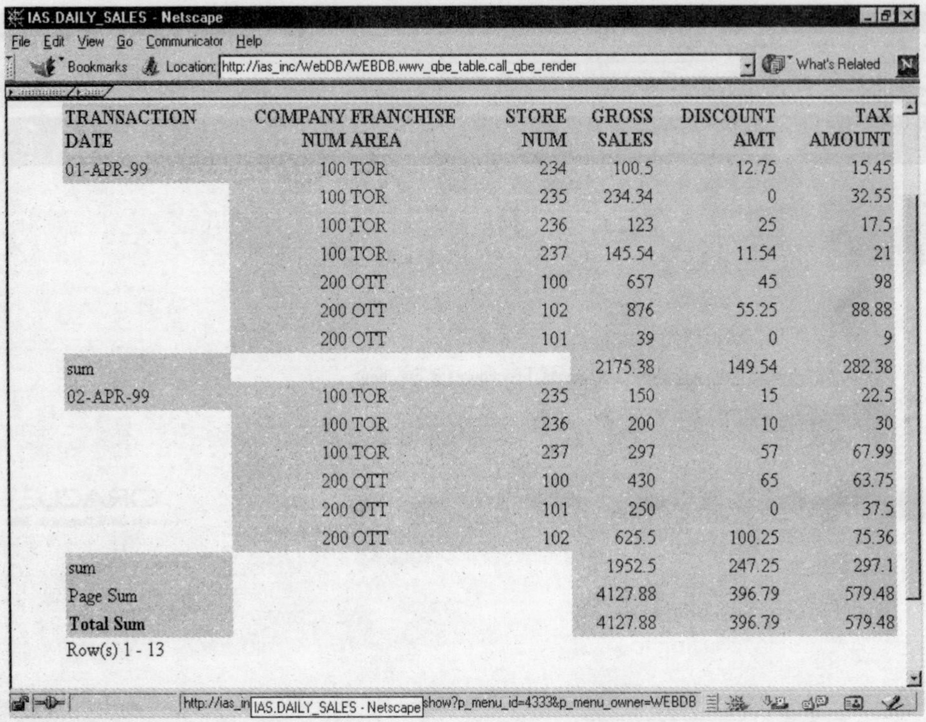

TRANSACTION DATE	COMPANY NUM	FRANCHISE AREA	STORE NUM	GROSS SALES	DISCOUNT AMT	TAX AMOUNT
01-APR-99	100	TOR	234	100.5	12.75	15.45
	100	TOR	235	234.34	0	32.55
	100	TOR	236	123	25	17.5
	100	TOR	237	145.54	11.54	21
	200	OTT	100	657	45	98
	200	OTT	102	876	55.25	88.88
	200	OTT	101	39	0	9
sum				2175.38	149.54	282.38
02-APR-99	100	TOR	235	150	15	22.5
	100	TOR	236	200	10	30
	100	TOR	237	297	57	67.99
	200	OTT	100	430	65	63.75
	200	OTT	101	250	0	37.5
	200	OTT	102	625.5	100.25	75.36
sum				1952.5	247.25	297.1
Page Sum				4127.88	396.79	579.48
Total Sum				4127.88	396.79	579.48

Row(s) 1 - 13

FIGURE 20-4. *Query Results using the WebDB browse option*

in the Query and Update Table page, you have many different options to customize your query. You can enter data into any of the following options:

- **Where clause:** This clause allows you to specify conditions that must be satisfied so that you can view only information that you are interest in viewing or updating.
- **Order By:** This clause allows your output to be returned in an ordered manner.
- **Break on Columns:** This clause provides you with the ability to group similar information and compute totals on columns at the break level.
- **Sum Columns**: These are columns that WebDB will compute totals on. For example, you may wish to see the sales column added to provide a total sales value.

As you see, you have almost the same flexibility as you have when using SQL*Plus. You can customize the output format of your query, just as in SQL*Plus. You can even specify the output format of your page, so you can output the information in HTML, ASCII, or Excel format, depending on how you want your users to view their information.

VIP
When you save your query as an Excel spreadsheet, you will be prompted to save the file on your local machine, so you can then open it using Excel.

You have a number of options for the information that is to be output. Besides viewing or updating data, you can also choose to output any of the following details:

- **The SQL statement:** This is the text of the query that was executed to return the data from the database.

- **A formatted table of results:** When your information is returned from the database, WebDB will format the data—fonts, colors, and so on—according to your organization's standard.

- **The total row count, for all rows retrieved including summaries**: This provides you with a total number of rows of data that was retrieved by the SQL statement. This is valuable when you are returning potentially large data sets.

- **Increased formatting of displayed data**: Within WebDB you can increase the formatting included on a report.

Although these are simple, you can select one or more of these options to display the data in the best possible format for your requirements. When you choose to update data in the table you are viewing, you click Query&Update, on the table page. By selecting this option, you will be presented with a Web page that has an additional link on each record. This link is displayed as Update on the page. By pressing the Update link on the record you choose to modify, you will be presented with the window shown in Figure 20-5.

As shown in Figure 20-5, you now can change values in each of the individual columns; when you click Update, WebDB will save the changed information in the database. You also have the ability to delete the record, or to insert a record, all from this one Web page.

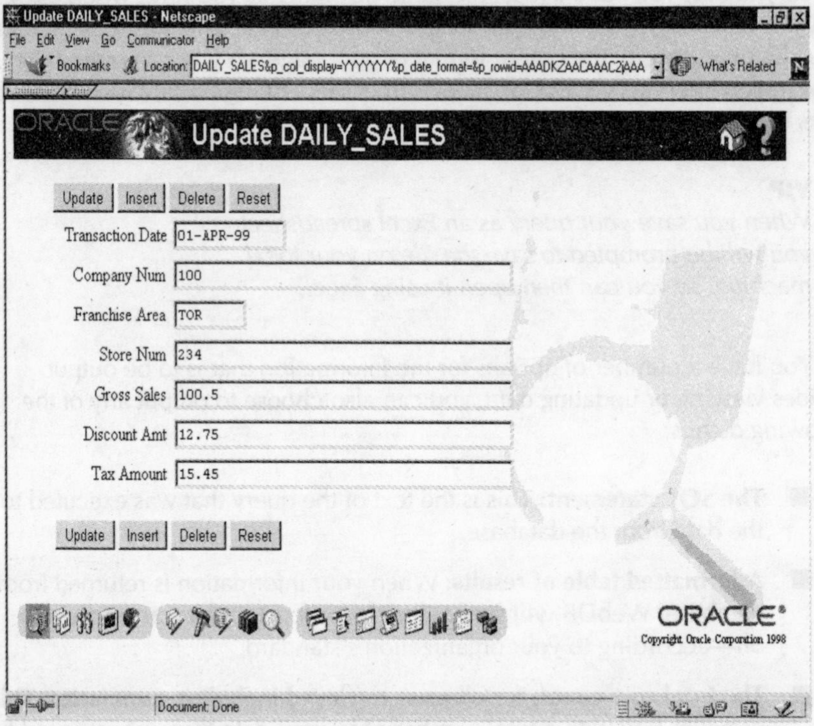

FIGURE 20-5. *The Update Record page*

VIP

*If you are deleting a record using the **update** option, take care. WebDB does not require confirmation or a commit statement. Once you press Update, the transaction is committed immediately.*

Okay, now that you have looked at the Browse function of WebDB, it's time to move on to creating and maintaining your database. You can now start by building your tables and views, but you can also offer your users some more utility after you look at the Build function of WebDB.

Building WeDB Objects

Big deal, I can view data in the database with WebDB—that and a dollar can buy me a small latte. There are so many tools to access my data anyway; but WebDB provides you with an interface that is efficient and powerful. WebDB is a great tool to provide browser access to your data, but it is also an environment to create and maintain the objects in your database. When it comes to database objects, they come in many shapes and sizes. As so often occurs, new product, new objects; WebDB has its own new lists, which include forms, calendars, Web pages, and Java scripts. WebDB allows you to build, to be an iDeveloper, and to deliver applications to users via the Internet. The main menu of the Build function is just the tip of the next iceberg. As you can see in Figure 20-6, the Build function provides you with the tools to create and maintain your database and create and provide data to your users.

As shown in Figure 20-6, you have the access to the tools to start creating the objects that your users need to get to their data. From tables to Web pages, this is the place that can do the job. Let's move on and look under the hood, and explore deeper into some of these options.

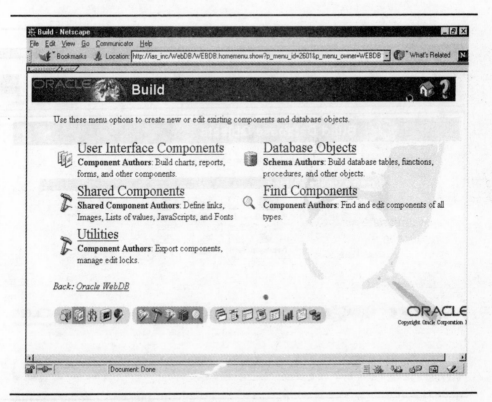

FIGURE 20-6. *The Build Function main menu*

Creating Database Objects

WebDB provides you with a number of wizards that walk you through the object creation process, be it tables, views, procedures, or sequences. We discussed how to perform this job using SQL, but with WebDB you can also do it through your Web browser, while knowing little SQL. As you can see in Figure 20-7, WebDB will guide you through the creation of numerous database objects. Whether you choose to create a table, an index, or any other type of object, you can be guided through the creation process.

You may find that you prefer to do this work in SQL*Plus or some other access tool, but most of these other products require that you have a fat client machine. WebDB does not have this need. Let's now walk through the process of creating a table using WebDB.

By clicking the Table icon on the Build Database Objects pages, you will enter into the Table Creation Wizard. The wizard will then ask you to select a schema in which you want to create the table, or object. You will also supply the name of the

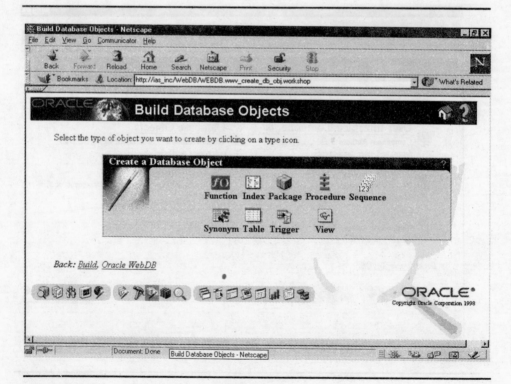

FIGURE 20-7. *Constructable database objects*

table to the wizard. Figure 20-8 illustrates the next step, in which you specify the columns that will be contained in the table.

Although the table we are creating has only six columns, you are not limited to this number; you can add more columns by clicking Add More; WebDB will reformat the page and add additional fields that can be used for these extra columns. Finally, you will be asked to specify the storage parameters for the table. You will need to define the tablespace in which to store the table, along with the amount of space required when the object is created and for subsequent requests. We advise you to carefully consider the values that you define here. A table that starts out with the wrong storage parameters can become a nightmare in short order, so define the storage for your table. Finally, WebDB will ask you if you are really sure that you wish to create the object, with one final confirmation. If you have everything that you want in the objects, you simply click Yes.

At any point that you encounter an error in this wizard or any other creation wizard in WebDB, you simply can step back in your browser, fix the error, and then

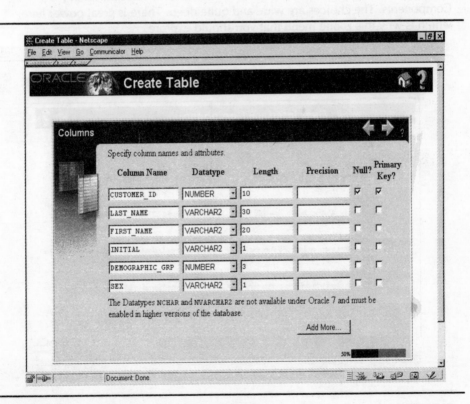

FIGURE 20-8. *The Column Specification page*

move on to your next task again. Now that you see how easy it is to create a table, let's put our database to work and provide some powerful access tools to the data.

Building WebDB Components

Now you know that WebDB allows you to access your data and create the objects that you want to view, but, of course, you want more. As we continue in this chapter, you will start to see the great depth of this product. We want you to get a feel for the product and how it can make your job easier and much more fun. In that light, consider another example of how you can construct objects, but this time, we mean Web objects. We can start by looking at creating simple forms to allow you to provide controlled access to your data.

Forms, reports, charts, calendars, Web pages, and menus are the access paths that your users are looking for to access and understand their data. The old adage that a picture is worth a thousand words is recalled by these components that can graphically depict your information.

Figure 20-9 illustrates the default main menu for these User Interface Components. The choices are wide and quite deep. There is great power here, which is why this is one menu that you should explore.

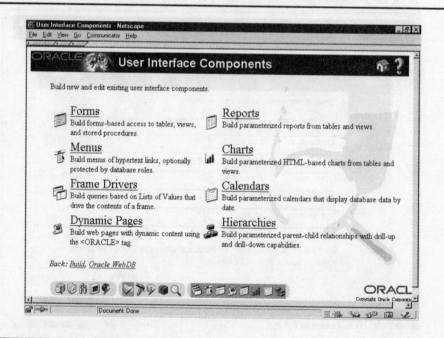

FIGURE 20-9. *The User Interface Components main menu*

Let's look at each of the choices one by one and then work our way through some of the objects that we can create in WebDB.

- **Forms**: Recall that Oracle Developer (described in Chapter 9) is the wise son. Well, when he was just a baby, Oracle Developer was known as Forms. Now that Developer has grown and the other son has started playing the same games as his brother, it creates new ways to look at old things. WebDB provides you with forms that can be used to view, update, delete, and create the data that sits in your database. With that we can now create forms that we can view through a Web browser to achieve this goal. Well, guess what—WebDB shoots and scores! WebDB does a solid job, allowing you to deploy simple forms to your users. The WebDB forms will not replace Oracle Developer but will allow you to quickly get simple forms to the general public. You can create forms based on a single table, a view, or a stored procedure, or in a master-detail–type form. While the level of validation and the inherent power of the product are quite complete, it is not Oracle Forms, a fact that may limit the tasks that you perform using WebDB forms.

- **Menus**: It's always nice to give your users a suggested access path. At other times, you want to provide added security. Depending on the desired results, it's always better to control security as close to your data as possible. By providing some menu security, you can add another layer to your total security solution. WebDB allows you to create menus restricting access to the links that you want your users to see and base that all on roles you grant the users in your database.

- **WebDB Reports**: Create customized reports that your users can use to get data, without asking you. We always create applications with some sort of reporting, so we need reports; at least our users say they do. We have now created reports, let users run them, and allowed the users to enter report parameters to limit the reports to only the data they want to see. WebDB allows you to create those reports, but now we can have our users see them wherever they are in the world through their browsers. Instead of relying on e-mail with data that could be stale, users can now have instantaneous access to current information.

- **WebDB Charts**: Drawing on data in your database, you can deploy graphical data representations to your users. WebDB Reports allows you to create HTML-based reports to users.

- **WebDB Calendars**: You can display your data in a clear date-driven calendar format.

■ **Frames Drivers**: You can build Web frames that provide lists of values to help users put the right data into the database, or get the right data from the database. The frames drivers provide this functionality that is so imperative in our heterogeneous user community.

■ **Dynamic Web Pages**: These pages are driven by your own HTML. This all starts to form a complete circle to allow you to create custom applications to your users' requirements and store it all in the database, but allow access for your users.

The creation of forms allows you to create an object in which you can query, insert, update, and delete your table-based data. It seems like a great place to start, and that's where we will start. WebDB provides you with the ability to create forms in a number of ways. You can create forms based on any of the following methods:

■ Forms based on a table or view

■ Forms based on a stored procedure

■ Master-detail–type forms

■ Query-by-example forms

The first three methods are straightforward, allowing you to manage your data. Each form is a data entry form that has its origins based in a table or multiple tables of the database. These forms allow you to insert data, update existing data, delete data, and query the contents of the table. The forms provide you with an easy entry method into the database for users who have little knowledge of the power behind the page.

The final choice, query by example, is a bit different. This is more of a report format in which you can use parameters to drive your result set. For our example, we will guide you through the creation of a form based on a table. Figure 20-10 illustrates the page that you will see when you choose to build a form.

As Figure 20-10 shows, the first section at the top of the page is used to create a new form, by selecting the type of form you wish to create and then clicking Create; you then enter into the Form Builder Wizard. Next you can use this page to find an existing form that has been created in a schema to which you have access. Finally, WebDB presents you with a short list of the most recently created and edited forms. The information presented here shows you the name of the form, its type, the time of the last update, and the owner of the form. We will use the wizard now to create a form based on a table.

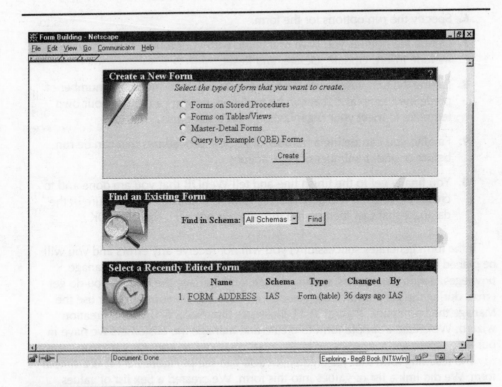

FIGURE 20-10. *The Form Building page*

The following steps will guide you through the creation process:

1. Select the Forms on Tables/Views option and then click Create.

2. Choose the schema that will own the form.

3. Name the form, remembering to make it meaningful. WebDB will not help you here; it gives you one of those meaningless names that developers should learn to dislike.

4. From the list of tables and views, select the table upon which the form will be based.

5. You define the nature of each column that you wish to include at this point. These characteristics include the text for the header, font, default value, or a list of values.

6. Specify the run options for the form.

7. Define the buttons you wish to include with your forms. Your choices include Insert, Update, Delete, and Reset.

8. Define the template to use with your form. WebDB includes a number of predefined templates that can be modified, or you can create your own template to meet your organization's Web standards.

9. Finally, you can define a number of PL/SQL procedures that can be run before or after a number of page actions.

10. You finally get to the finish line and tell WebDB that you are done and to create the form. It will generate the form as a packaged procedure in the database that can then be run through our browser. Just click OK.

If the form generates successfully, you will not receive any errors and you will be placed in the Manage Forms page. In this form, you can run, edit, manage privileges, define parameters, monitor usage, and manage the form. If you do get errors during the generation step, you can go back and fix your error, or use the Manage the Form page. Figure 20-11 illustrates the results of the form creation wizard. We create a simple form to create and manage the customers we have in our little database.

The resulting form that we created, as you can see in Figure 20-11, is a simple form. We did link a list of values into this form. We created a Sex list of values, which allow us to create the two radio buttons on this form. The list of values can now be shared among all the users and developers of our application, to provide it with a common look and feel.

NOTE
You can access this form directly, by using the URL for the form. The form that we created can be accessed by a link defined as http://ias_inc/WebDB/ias_customer.show. You may find at times that the page name is preceded by the name of the schema owner. Users who do not own the schema may need to use the link: http://ias_inc/WebDB/ias.ias_customer.show.

As we discussed, you can also define menus that help guide your users through the access path that works for your organization. Within menus you have the ability to link to pages that you have created in WebDB. From a menu you can use the appropriate URL to link to forms, reports, or any other object you choose. Also, you can include links to any Web pages that you choose. The Create Wizard for menus

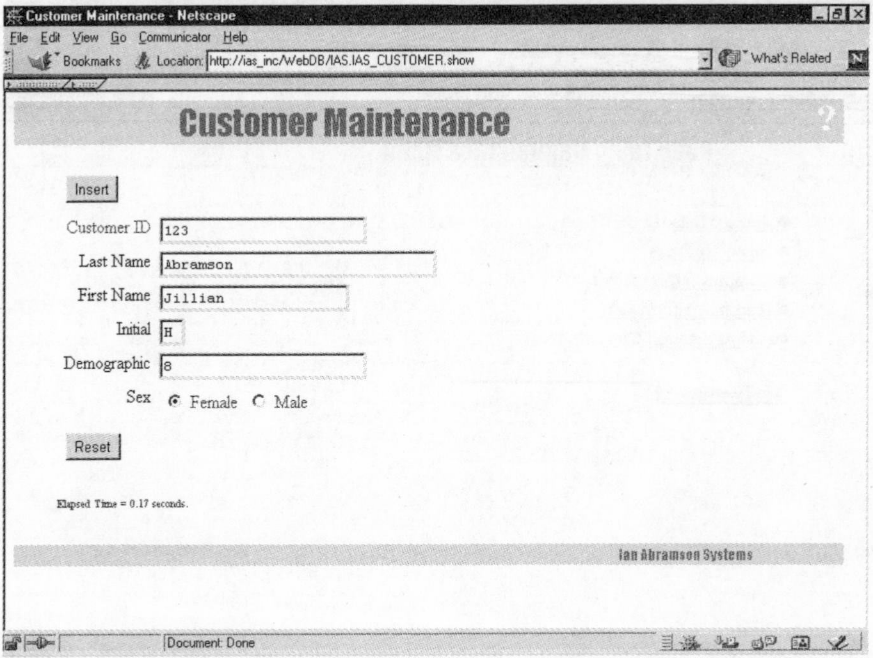

FIGURE 20-11. *A WebDB-generated form*

is the standard interface within WebDB. You are required to name the menu and define the look and feel. What is special is the creation of menu options. You are asked to name the option and then provide a URL that will be used to link to the appropriate WebDB page. Figure 20-12 illustrates a menu that we created.

You will notice that in Figure 20-12, we have created a number of menu options. For example we have included an option to access the Customer Data form. This is the form that we previously created in this chapter. When we created the menu selection, we entered *http://ias_inc/WebDB/ias_customer.show* as the URL name. When your users run this menu, they will then link to the Customer page by simply clicking the menu option. As you can see, menus do have their place in our businesses, and using the WebDB menus can further your WebDB application deployment and development. Again, WebDB allows you to create new functionality within your application; and, when it's complete, you simply change or add the menu options to access the new object. This allows you to deploy quickly and meet your organization's changing needs. Now that you've created

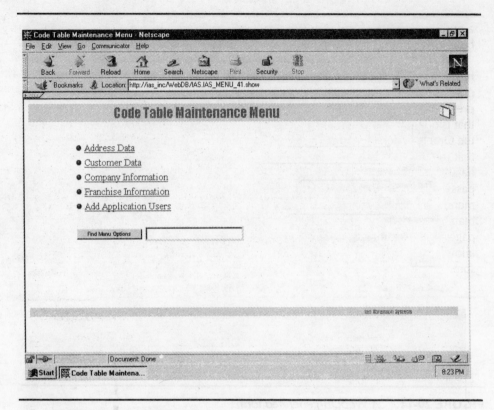

FIGURE 20-12. *WebDB menu*

some tables and some forms, it's starting to look as if you can do anything, so let's look at managing our WebDB applications.

Administration of WebDB and the Database

WebDB and the database are administered through simple-to-navigate Web pages. Through the administration pages you are able to manage database users. With the interface you can create and modify users and control the access to the database that these users have. The administration option also allows you to manage settings that are specific to WebDB and the WebDB environment. This facility provides you with the ability to control the world around you, not including the weather, and the database in which you work. Let's look into some of the options provided to you within WebDB. The Administration menu shown in Figure 20-13 provides you with a number of different options. Whether you are the administrator or a user, you will be using this menu for a number of important tasks.

As Figure 20-13 illustrates, from within the WebDB Administration menu, you have the ability to create and manage users, to grant database users access to objects such as tables and procedures, to include users in a role that existed previously, or to create a new database role. You can change your password here; that is one job that you must remember to do. It's incredible how often we find that the Oracle system account password has been left "manager." This is a practice that is dangerous, so pause for a second and reset the system password in your databases. Remember, if you're not the DBA, you should tell the DBA to change the password before someone does something they shouldn't. You can do this from a menu option here, so get used to doing it, before it's too late. Finally, WebDB management settings are made from this menu, ranging from the privilege to build pages to the settings that the Web Listener uses. The Web Listener is provided to allow access to the database from the Web browser. Let's now look more closely at some of the tasks that you might perform from the WebDB Administration menu.

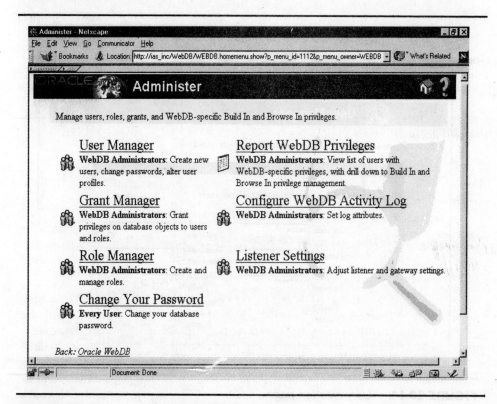

FIGURE 20-13.   *The WebDB Administration menu*

Administering Users

Users are the most underrated factor in the database. Everyone who talks about databases talks about tables, views, and stored procedures. We are the first to admit that database objects are important, and we work very hard to build top-quality objects and programs that then turn into an application, but users are critical. Then again sometimes we talk about users in not very favorable terms, but realize that designers and DBAs only mean it in a loving way. Users give us the reason to continue to program, they make us complete developers. Just as hockey players who love to play the game prefer to play in front of people who appreciate the game, so it is with programmers vis à vis users. WebDB provides a number of pages in which the DBA can manage those users. The first task that we will look at is the creation of new users, so be our guest in our database.

By selecting the User Manager link on the page, you will enter into a page that allows you to create a new user or find an existing user's profile to modify. Figure 20-14 illustrates the Create User option on this page.

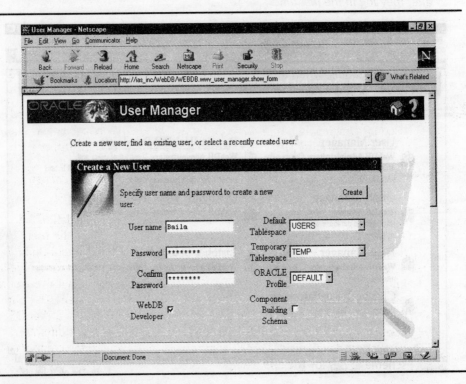

FIGURE 20-14. *User creation page*

As you can see in Figure 20-14, the task to create a new user is not rocket science, but it is important if you want an audience for your database. As the first step in creating a user, this facility allows you to define a new user and a number of environmental defaults. This is what has to be done.

■ Define the user name. This name should be meaningful and follow standards that you define in your organization. We often create user names that are the same as those that our users use to log in to the network in our organizations. You will also need to define the default password that the user will use the first time that he or she logs in to the database. Enter the user name, and the password (twice, just in case).

VIP
It is advisable to create users with an organizational default password and then require your users to change their passwords after they log in the first time.

■ Define the default tablespace for the user. The *default tablespace* is the place in the database that users will create their database objects, such as tables, when they do not specify a tablespace in their object creation scripts.

■ Define the temporary tablespace for the user. The *temporary tablespace* is used by Oracle when it performs a number of internal tasks, such as groupings and summaries. You will notice that both of these options are drop-down boxes that provide you with a simple list to select the tablespace that you would like to use, thus ensuring that you choose a tablespace that actually exists in the database.

■ Define the Oracle User Profile for the user. The *User Profile* define the amount of system and database resources that is available to the user. Then there are two check boxes—WebDB Developer and Component Building Schema. WebDB Developer allows users to build components and objects under their own user accounts. The Component Schema allows the user to own the components or objects built by other Web Developers. This allows you to have an account that will become the owner or user of a WebDB application. The advantage is that you may have a number of different developers developing WebDB components and then use the component schema to deploy the application.

When you have finished with all this, click Create, and your new user will be created. By default, when you create a user through WebDB, the user that you have just created will only have the connect role. This role allows a user to connect to the database and access objects to which that user has been granted access. The user cannot yet create database objects. To perform this function, the user will require the RESOURCE role.

NOTE
Actually, the CONNECT role allows the user to create tables, views, synonyms, sequences, clusters, and database links, as well as connect to the database. However, since the user has no quotas on tablespaces yet, the CREATE TABLE statements will fail. The ability to create packages (and hence PL/SQL WebDB forms and reports) comes with the RESOURCE role, as does the unlimited tablespace system privilege.

Now, if you defined this user as a WebDB developer, the user will be granted the WEBDB_DEVELOPER role; this role will allow the user to create Web objects within WebDB. At least that's a step in the right direction, but you know your users want more. After you click Create, you are then faced with the User Maintenance page. From this page you can define and update the following user characteristics:

- **Grants:** These are to allow access to specific objects in the database.

- **Roles:** These are groups of grants that have been organized into a single job function.

- **Build Privileges:** This privilege allows you to build objects in other users' schemas.

- **Browse Privileges:** This privilege allows you to look at objects in other users' schemas.

By selecting either the tab or the link, you can modify the user's characteristics. You also can change the default values for the user, such as the user's tablespaces or password. The roles and grants previously described in this book are what provide users access to the database and its objects. However, the Build and Browse privileges are specific to WebDB. The Build privilege allows users to create Web objects in other users' schemas. This is important if you want your users to have a central development and deployment accounts. The Browse privilege allows your user to browse the objects in other schemas. Figure 20-15 illustrates the Browse privilege for our user named susan. This user already had access to browse the IAS schema, but we also want them to look at objects in the BAILA schema.

As you see in Figure 20-15, we defined the schemas you want your user to be able to browse in. You can also revoke access by unchecking the check box beside the current privileges. Notice that the screen is organized with a number of tabs that let you quickly move from one task to another, without returning to another page. Click Apply, and the changes are made to the user's account.

Changing Your Password

We told you that we think it important for users to change their own passwords. There are two basic methods; the first uses tools like SQL*Plus in which you change

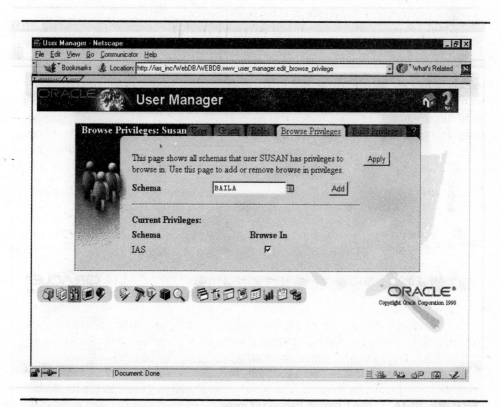

FIGURE 20-15. *Granting browse privileges*

your password on the command line. The following is an example of a SQL*Plus command that changes your password.

```
SQL> grant connect to LUCY identified by DREIDLE;
Grant succeeded.
```

We changed the password for the **lucy** account to **dreidle**. The **lucy** user, or another user with change password privileges, such as a DBA, can perform this command. Since this chapter is about WebDB, we want to show you how it's done with this product. Figure 20-16 illustrates this task.

By selecting the Change Password option, you make your task quite simple. Enter the same password twice, click Apply, and voilà, your password is set to the new value. The administration of users and WebDB are tasks that are necessary for

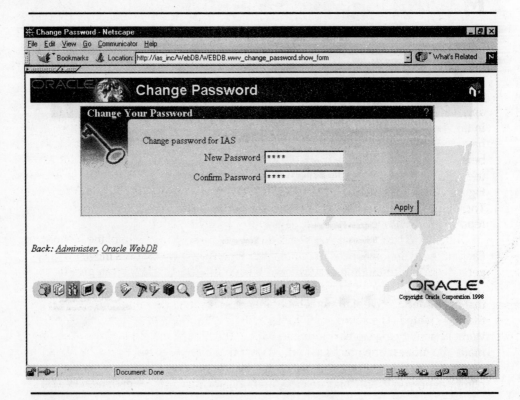

FIGURE 20-16. *The Change Password page*

your database to run smoothly, and here is a product that we can use remotely through a Web browser to manage our database. Just think of it, your DBA is away at an Oracle conference and you need a new user added to your database for the new employee that started when the DBA left. You send a page for your DBA at 1-800-CALL-DBA. The DBA calls you back in a matter of minutes; let that lucky person (the DBA who just stepped out of a conference session) know the details for the new user, the user's name, and the access that the user needs. Unfortunately, the DBA does not have a PC close at hand, so the user cannot be added at once. The DBA then remembers that your organization had installed WebDB and so walks over to the Internet Café at the conference and through a Web browser performs the task. The paradigm of the Internet is one that creates great autonomy and flexibility for administering our databases, and it is here that products like WebDB excel. Let's now move on and look at the monitoring facilities available in WebDB.

Monitoring with WebDB

When we use the database and applications that we create, we are always interested in how our users are using the objects that we have created for them. We need this information to make sure that we are creating objects that users need and that they are not being overburdened or putting a heavy load on our resources. As we discussed earlier in the book, it's important to tune your database and applications so that they run as efficiently as possible. With information we gather in the Monitor options, we can discover how our users are accessing the objects we have built for them. This is especially important in the database: When a table is being used extensively, we may choose to place it on its own disk drive to provide users with more efficient disk usage, since the only object on a disk is this one table. Figure 20-17 illustrates the monitoring options that you have available in WebDB. The data that WebDB uses to build these reports is held within the database, so the reports are dynamic, providing up-to-the-minute information.

Again, the options that you see in Figure 20-17 are just the tip of the iceberg. Each of these options opens to much more extensive choices. Let's move on and get a better understanding of what details each monitoring choice can give us.

The User Interface Components options allow you to see the number of requests that are issued for WebDB objects, including forms, reports, and any other objects that we created. The source of the information is the WebDB activity log. The WebDB activity log stores information about the time of the request, the user who made the request, the machine and browser that was used, and when the object was last updated by a developer. This logging is defined when you create a component; you simply choose to capture logging during the creation process.

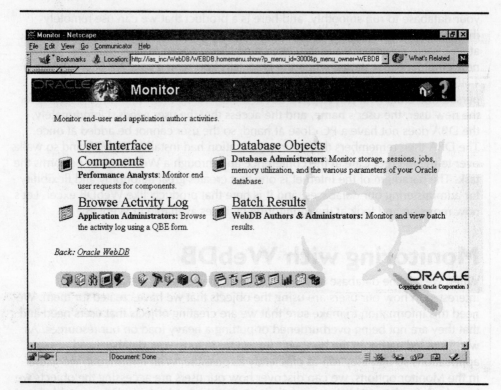

FIGURE 20-17. *The WebDB Monitor menu*

VIP
When you create or edit a component, you specify that it log activity in the run options page of the creation or editing page of the Component Wizard.

As you can imagine, this information can be very useful in providing you with some important metrics, and you can figure out who's been working and who's been out for coffee. Then there's component activity. Component activity provides you a view on the volume of requests for a particular WebDB component. This allows you to see which are the most used, and the response time the system takes to process the requests for information. Figure 20-18 illustrates the type of information that you can view about your components.

As illustrated in Figure 20-18, you can view response time of the components. Based upon information in the database about the various Web objects for which you record activity, you can see the response time for all objects. This figure shows

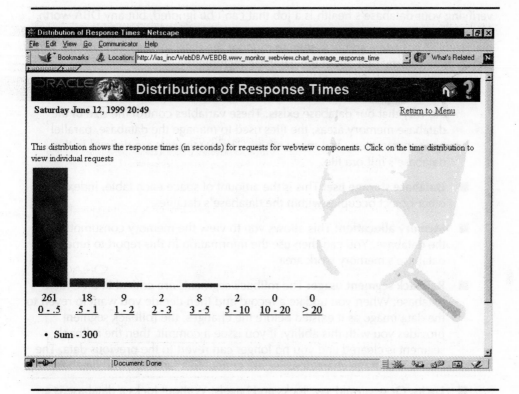

FIGURE 20-18. *Component response time*

you a histogram, which measures the time it takes for WebDB and the database to return the information requested. This time is represented in seconds, so you can see that 261 of 300 requests are satisfied in under one-half second. That's 87 percent, so this sounds like an application that is keeping the users really happy. From what we can see, it also sounds as if the person who programmed our application should get a raise for keeping the users so happy. Now most of the monitoring reports allow you to drill down deeper into the data. A *drill-down* provides the user the details of a summarized value. Notice in Figure 20-18 that the time ranges are underlined. The underline on the time range indicates that you can click the range, and it will link to a another report that provides you with a list of the requests that had been satisfied in that time range. This is very valuable, especially when you want to know which components are performing poorly.

Besides monitoring component activity, WebDB also provides some useful tools to monitor the database. As DBAs, we are always looking for tools to monitor the health of our database. Whether you use Enterprise Manager or a third-party tool, verifying your database's health is a job that can't be ignored, but any DBA worth his or her salt is using some mechanism to check the database. It only makes sense that WebDB has some sort of system to monitor the database using the product. You can monitor information about the database including:

- **Database parameters:** These are the environmental variables that control the way that our database exists. These variables control the size of the database memory areas, the files used to manage the database, parallel query parameters, and many others. The parameters are defined in the database's init.ora file.

- **Database storage use:** This is the amount of space each table, index, or other object occupies within the database's datafiles.

- **Memory allocation:** This allows you to view the memory consumption of the database. You can then use the information in this report to tune your database's memory work area.

- **Rollback segment usage:** The rollback segments are critical to an Oracle database. When you update a record and then decide you want to revert to the data image as it existed before the changes, the rollback segment provides you with this ability. If you issue a commit, then the rollback segment is cleared and you no longer can revert to the previous data. The health and usage characteristics are critical to a smoothly run database.

- **Locks:** Or we could say, locks and bagels. Without locks a database is a plain bagel. It's good (especially if it's a Montreal, Canada bagel), but it's better with locks; I mean lox. Data query and update requests request locks on a particular object, so you can take steps to avoid it from happening, you need to monitor the locks on your database. You will often find that locks that meet tend not to get along. You need to discover what has caused the contention and remove the source of the lock.

- **Session monitoring:** This is user activity. With this facility you are able to see system use by users and monitor how your system is acting. You can kill users, now we mean very peacefully: From the comfort of your browser, you can tell the database to terminate a session. This is done for many reasons, such as a process that has gone awry. You also can view details of your System Global Area, known to its friends as the SGA. The SGA is the area in memory that is allocated specifically to the database. You can see how memory is being used by the database, which is helpful when sometimes you have to fix the SGA to optimize your database's performance caused by memory usage.

You can see the monitoring facility is needed for many different reasons. Whether you want to monitor how many people are accessing your WebDB objects, or view the objects in your database, or check the health of the database, monitoring is an important weapon in the DBA's toolkit. Up to now, we've created database objects, Web objects, and Web pages; given our database a physical exam; and tuned our machine until it hums—sound like enough? Well, WebDB has a little more. It has Web sites. Let's move on to look at creating Web sites that will turn into the windows for our organization on the Web.

WebDB Sites

You know about Web sites; you visit them on a very regular basis. Whether you want to buy a book or bid for a Mickey Mantle rookie card or check on why your hair has fallen out, you find a Web site that delivers the information you need. The Web site that you visit is probably a guided tour through the information that you want to discover; it's a combination of information that may or may not be stored in a database. Whether you realize it or not, all of the major e-commerce vendors have a database behind the information that you are looking for. Let's say you want to find all the books written by Ian Abramson; you would search the vendor's database using the name as your search criterion. The database would then return the list of books he has written. Now you can buy them all, because he really knows his stuff.

You can see the advantage of having a database behind the scenes supporting your organization. With WebDB you create specific sites so that you can create unique applications with each residing under its own unique URL and separate the responsibilities for the development, administration, and use of a Web site. In Figure 20-19, you can see the final check for a Web site that we have created. This Web site will be completely autonomous from WebDB; well, it will be more independent. You will access the site through its own URL, but it will still reside in the Oracle database, and more exactly the WebDB tables.

Let's look more closely at the pieces of information that we have entered to create the site and that are summarized in the final step of the site creation wizard, which you see in Figure 20-19. As you can see, we have named our site customer_knowledge, as this site is planned for a Marketing department that provides marketing strategies based on information and trends identified by data supplied in the Customer Knowledge data warehouse. We guess that makes the site name meaningful to our intranet. The schema that will own the information and the site components is the MARKETING user. WebDB will create a new user for this site, along with a number of special users. It is these users that will administer and provide access to your newly created site. The site will be completely contained within the marketing Oracle user account. This is important, since when you back up the site and its components, you will simply back up the schema owner.

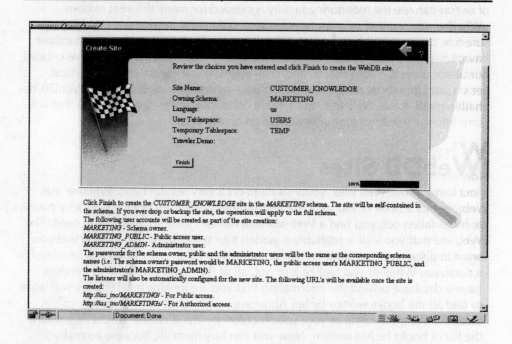

FIGURE 20-19. *The WebDB site creation wizard*

The other advantage to creating a Web site as WebDB does is that it allows you to simply deploy a site to your Web server. Often, in our development shops, we have a number of different servers: one server for development, another for testing, and our production server. This multitude of servers requires you to move programs and applications to various platforms so that, eventually, they can be released to our users. By simply performing a backup using a facility such as export, you can move a site between platforms. Finally, the summary shows you the URLs that are created to provide access to the new site. In our case, the URL to access the site will be *http://ias_inc/MARKETING*. The name indicates the Web server (ias_inc) and the name of the site marketing, this will be the address for the site that provides public access. The other URL, *http://ias_inc/MARKETINGs/*, is provided for authorized access. This allows for user verification when users access your site. As you can see, WebDB sites are quite powerful in their own right. By creating Web sites, you can now control and manage the information that you deploy to the Web.

WebDB may at first appear to be a simple son, but it is far more complex than it appears to be on the surface. This is a tool that provides facilities to satisfy a number of user requirements. Whether you think of those users as DBAs, developers, or end users, there's something for everyone. WebDB is an evolving product, and we are sure that Oracle will continue to add functionality to this rich product. Here we have a new product that allows us to deliver solutions through a Web browser to our users, while utilizing the power of the database to store the application within it. Let's move on now to some more details on how Oracle and Oracle8*i* meet the challenges of the Web.

What's Next

Now that was a mouthful! Oracle WebDB seems to be a dream come true. The jury is out—yes, no, no, no, yes, yes, no, yes, yes! The verdict is *yes*. We believe WebDB is more than a dream come true. It is the fastest and most complete solution we have encountered in our travels when you want to work on the Web, the whole Web, and nothing but the Web. The next chapter is dedicated to that pesky contrary son—Dan. Remember him from a way back at the top of the chapter? Onward...

CHAPTER
21

JDeveloper

n this chapter, we will expose you to another tool Oracle has for development of Web applications. Using JDeveloper, programmers can build Java-based applications that provide users access, over a company intranet or the Internet, to information stored in a database.

Java has been widely accepted as the choice flavor for object-oriented programming for the Web. Oracle's JDeveloper allows you to create Java applications and applets quickly and easily, with little manual writing of code. The key to how JDeveloper simplifies the process of writing and compiling Java programs is its integrated development environment or IDE.

NOTE
The Java programming language will be briefly introduced, but this chapter will be focusing primarily on JDeveloper. It is assumed that you have a basic familiarity with Java.

When you are done reading this chapter, you will know about the following topics:

- Overview of Java language

- Types of Java applications

- JDeveloper's integrated development environment for development of Java applications

- How Java applications interact with an Oracle database using JDBC

- Developing Java applications using JDeveloper's wizards

Terminology

The following definitions will arm you with the technical jargon you need to make it through this chapter:

- *Exception handling* is a technique that allows control to be transferred to an alternative block of code when an exception has been detected.

- *HTML* stands for Hypertext Markup Language. HTML is a format for encoding hypertext documents that may contain text, graphics, and references to programs and other hypertext documents commonly used for the Internet and identified as Web pages.

■ *Multithreading* is a method of easily separating component processes (or parts) of a request for computer resources and allowing each component process to execute simultaneously.

■ A *multitier application* is an application that has a user interface code layer, one or more computation code (or business logic) layers, and a database access layer.

■ *Object-oriented programming (OOP)* is a method of programming that organizes a program around its data (defined as objects) and a set of well-defined interfaces to that data.

■ A *Web server* is a program that delivers pages to a client browser.

Overview of Java

By now the programming world has had a good taste of Java. (Sorry, but you had to expect some play on the word, didn't you?) Java is a true object-oriented language that hides much of the complexity that is visible in other languages from the programmer. Java includes native support for multithreading development. It makes use of modern exception handling and has sophisticated memory management, or what is termed garbage collection.

The cool thing about Java is that though it is a compiled language, the object code is not machine specific. To run a Java program you must have a JVM, or *Java virtual machine*. The Java virtual machine is responsible for the memory safety, platform independence, and security features of the Java programming language. Although virtual machines have been around for a long time, prior to Java they hadn't quite entered the mainstream. Given today's emerging hardware realities using various operating systems (UNIX or Windows), software developers welcome the idea of only having to write their code once. Manufacturers are trying to oblige by standardizing with Java.

Types of Java Applications

Just like the coffees at your corner café, Java applications come in various types and tastes, depending on the requirements as explained in the text that follows.

Applets

The first and still most common use for the Java language is the *applet*. An applet is Java code that is automatically downloaded from the Web and runs within a Web browser, like Netscape Navigator, on the user's desktop. The program code is typically small. Applets follow a very secure programming model, so users do not have to worry about having their desktop or network hacked into by a malignant applet. It is for this reason that applets have become very useful for the collection of data—users sign on and give passwords to their bank accounts or enter other personal information to be collected such as address and phone numbers.

Applets also are used for those wizzy-wig-type graphics you see on many Web pages displaying advertising or providing interactive entertainment over the Web. The Achilles heel for applets is that they can become slow to download and run if the code is too large. There are two reasons for this: The first issue is more of a bandwidth issue than a Java issue. If the user has a low bandwidth connection to the Internet, downloading the applet code will take some time. The second issue is the code has to be completely downloaded to the user's workstation before it can be verified and interpreted.

NOTE
A Just In Time (JIT) compiler helps speed up the execution of the code by compiling it while it is being downloaded. This increases performance by almost a thousand percent. Currently the JIT compiler is included with Netscape Navigator.

Applications (Client/server or multitier)

Java *applications* are similar to the usual programs that you would create with other comparable programming languages. Java applications have fewer security restrictions than do their applet counterparts. These applications are installed on individual desktops or networks as part of client/server or multitier implementations. Java has outstanding multithreading and network connectivity, with applications written entirely in Java running on a variety of systems without recompilation. The trend with Java applications is toward distributed applications for a company intranet.

Servlet

Servlets are server-side Java programs that are run via a Java-based Web server. A servlet would be commonly used to request a database search or update. The Java-based Web server would then format the results into an HTML page and send it to the user. For example, you might use a servlet when you register your name in a database to place an order. Servlets are traditionally slower than Java programs or applets that receive the raw data at the client for local processing. Servlets have the added burden of taking the results from the database request and building the HTML page, creating more load on the server.

While Java is still maturing, it has become widely accepted as a technology for solving many of today's problems and beyond. Now that we have briefly discussed the Java language, let's look at Oracle's Java application development tool—JDeveloper.

What Is JDeveloper?

JDeveloper has become part of Oracle's new generation of tools for application development on the World Wide Web. JDeveloper is a visual programming environment that is rich with predeveloped Java classes. These classes include buttons, pull-down menus, labels, frames, and database objects—to name a few. JDeveloper is a fully mouse-driven interface, giving the ability to do most of the development without a great deal of coding. The programmer can simply select a class off a palette by using the mouse and place it in a program to create objects. The actual code that defines these objects is created by JDeveloper, relieving the programmer from the task of programming and instead allowing him or her to focus on the actions these objects may take, for instance, to identify what happens after a menu item is selected by a user. Let's get ready to look a little closer at JDeveloper, but first you must prepare your workstation to be able to use JDeveloper to develop Java applications against an Oracle database.

Preparing Your Workstation to Run JDeveloper Against Oracle

The following must be done before JDeveloper can be used to develop Java applications against an Oracle database:

■ You must have access to a local or remote Oracle database. To access a remote database, you or your database administrator must have installed Net8 and been able to successfully connect to the database.

NOTE
The work involved in setting this up may have to be done by a more senior resource or with help from Oracle Worldwide Customer Support.

■ You must have already loaded your network software if you are accessing a remote database. If you are using a local Personal Oracle8*i* database, this is not necessary.

Your workstation is now ready to build Java applications against an Oracle database. Before getting started actually using the product, take a look at its main components, or the integrated development environment as it is referred to, with which you will become familiar.

JDeveloper—A Quick Tour

The primary tools that you will work with in JDeveloper, the integrated development environment, consist of a number of windows and dialogs. Let's delve into the part each plays in the interface to JDeveloper.

The Main Window

When you load JDeveloper, the main window of the integrated development environment is displayed with the last project that you had opened. If this is the first time you have loaded JDeveloper, a sample project named Welcome.jpr is displayed, as shown in Figure 21-1. The window in which the project is displayed is

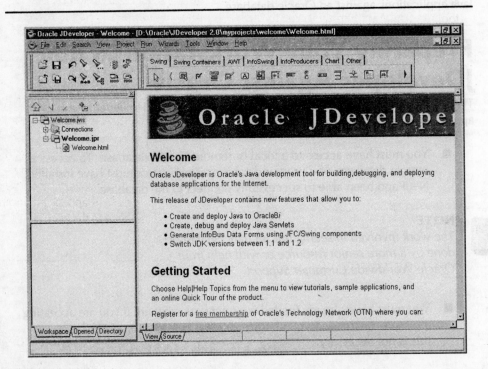

FIGURE 21-1. *The JDeveloper main window*

called the AppBrowser, and like the Navigator in the Form Builder (see Chapter 9), it to is used primarily to move quickly between the other interfaces.

There are three parts to the main window—the main menu, the toolbar, and the component palette—each of which we will discuss as we go on.

The Main Menu

The main menu contains menu items that provide you with access to most of JDeveloper's features. The actions of some of the items available from JDeveloper's main menu are also available through other parts of JDeveloper's interface, such as the toolbar.

The Toolbar

The toolbar, consisting of a collection of buttons at the upper left-hand side of the main window, provides you with instant access to the features of JDeveloper that you are likely to use most often. These buttons permit you to open and close projects, run and debug applications and applets, make or build your code, and search your projects and source files, among other things. Each button on the toolbar displays a bitmap that indicates its purpose. In addition, if you rest the mouse pointer over one of the toolbar buttons momentarily, the name of the tool button will appear, describing what that button does.

The Component Palette

The Component palette appears in the upper right-hand side of the JDeveloper main window. You use the Component palette in order to manually place components into your project. These components are predefined Java classes. The Component palette consists of multiple pages, each identified by a tab as shown in Figure 21-2.

Each page of the Component palette contains a number of component buttons that you use to place components. If you pause the mouse pointer over one of the component buttons momentarily, the name of the component will appear, including the package name for the class in parentheses. A package name is the relative

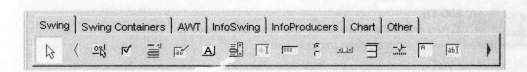

FIGURE 21-2. *The JDeveloper Component palette*

directory in which the class that defines the component can be found. For example, JButton (on the Swing component tab that looks like an OK button) is the class name, and Javax.swing the package (directory) in which this class is stored. When you want to place a component from the Component palette, you begin by selecting the tab associated with the page on which the component appears. You then click the component button to select it. Once the component is selected, you can place it into your project using the AppBrowser. We have mentioned the AppBrowser as the major component of JDeveloper, so take a look at why we regard it as the nerve center of the integrated development environment.

The AppBrowser

A JDeveloper application is made up of a set of files that together are placed in a container, or project. To manage these application projects, JDeveloper includes the AppBrowser in its integrated development environment. This powerful tool helps build, maintain, run, debug, and document your Java application projects. The AppBrowser has three modes:

■ **Workspace:** The primary mode used to track components in the project and environment settings while developing your Java program. When you open JDeveloper, the last workspace is opened by default, enabling you to pick up where you left off.

■ **Opened:** Displays a list of your currently active or open files.

■ **Directory:** This mode is used to browse through directories to locate files.

The AppBrowser is divided into three parts, called *panes,* which we will examine in closer detail:

■ Navigation

■ Structure

■ Content

NOTE
When one pane is selected, you can easily move to the next pane by pressing ALT-N.

The Navigation Pane

The upper-left pane of the AppBrowser initially displays the files of the project. Depending on the mode of the AppBrowser, however, it may display classes, selected reference files, a file browser, or object hierarchies. You use the Navigation pane to navigate to the objects that appear within it.

Structure Pane

The Structure pane shows the structural analysis of the currently selected file. For example, if a .Java file is selected as shown in Figure 21-3, the Structure pane will show structural information about the Java code in that file, such as:

- Imported packages
- The classes and/or interfaces in the file
- Any ancestor classes and/or interfaces
- Variables and methods

This structural analysis is displayed in the form of a hierarchical tree, much like a table of contents for the file.

The Content Pane

The Content pane is affected by what you select in the Navigation pane. Initially, when the project file is selected, the HTML file associated with the project (this is the HTML file that has the same name as the project) is displayed in the Content pane. When you click Frame1.Java, the Java source file for Frame1 is displayed. The Content pane has four modes: source, design, bean, and doc. These modes are accessed by clicking the tabs that appear at the bottom of the Content pane. Which mode it defaults to depends on the type of file selected in the Navigation pane. For example, when an HTML file is selected in the Navigation pane, the view mode is the default. By comparison, when a Java file is selected, the source mode is the default. In addition, the number of modes available also depends on the type of field you have selected in the Navigation pane. When you select a Java file in the Navigation pane, the tabs you will see at the bottom of the Content pane are the Source, Design, Bean, and Doc tabs. When you select an HTML file in the

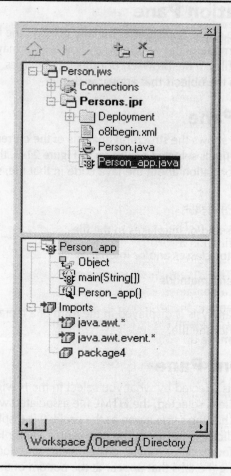

FIGURE 21-3. *The JDeveloper Structure pane*

Navigation pane, the tabs you will see at the bottom of the Content pane are the View and Source tabs.

- View mode is used for displaying formatted HTML or graphics files. When an HTML file is selected, the view mode acts as a limited browser, displaying the formatted HTML. It is limited in that it does not recognize all HTML that the most current browsers recognize, nor is it capable of running applets (that task is left up to the AppletViewer that ships with JDeveloper). When a graphics file is selected in the Navigation pane, the image contained in the graphics file is displayed. For all other file types, the View tab is not available on the Content pane, and consequently, this mode is not available. When a project is selected in the Navigation pane, the HTML file associated with that file is displayed in the Content pane.

■ Doc mode is used to display documentation for classes that you select in the Navigation pane. This documentation exists for all classes installed by JDeveloper. The classes you create will not have this documentation unless you actually create it.

■ Source mode is used to display the contents of the selected Java file or text file. When a Java file is selected, the source mode serves as a powerful code editor.

■ Design mode is where all the fun happens as you design the interface with your application. This mode allows you to visually create and manipulate objects defined in a Java file. There are actually two Designers in this version of JDeveloper. The most obvious is the UI or User Interface Designer. The UI Designer is where you visually place and configure the objects on a container, such as a frame, dialog, or applet. Figure 21-4 shows a frame in the UI Designer. The second Designer is the Menu Designer. The Menu Designer permits you to visually define the menu items that make up your menu bars.

■ Bean mode allows you to create or modify your own Java classes or what is commonly known as JavaBeans. This mode brings up a very powerful development tool that gives you the ability to develop your own JavaBean without doing too much coding. It has multiple modes where you can define the properties and actions taken according to events.

The topic of developing your own JavaBean requires a good understanding of the Java language, and so we will continue with our quick tour of JDeveloper with a look at the Inspector.

The Inspector

The Inspector is a special dialog box in which you set component properties and define event handlers. *Properties* are values whose settings influence the appearance and/or the behavior of objects. In this capacity the inspector is used like the Property palette in Form Builder (see Chapter 9). Event handlers are methods to which you to add custom Java code that will be executed in response to some event. The Inspector contains two tabbed pages, one labeled Properties and the other labeled Events. The Inspector is usually visible when the Design tab of the Content pane is selected. Figure 21-5 shows the properties of a frame.

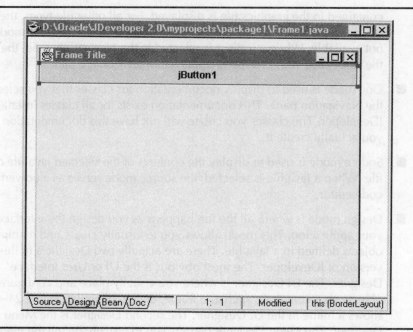

FIGURE 21-4. *A Java frame in the UI designer*

JDeveloper Projects

Java programs are structured as *projects*. A project consists of a collection of files that can be in any directory and settings that are compiled Java classes making up an applet or application. The project ties them all together. Information about each JDeveloper project is stored in a project file that has a .jpr file extension. This project file contains a list of all the project's files, settings, and properties. JDeveloper uses the information in the project file when you load, save, or build a project. The project file is modified whenever you use the JDeveloper development environment to add or remove files, or to set project options. In the Navigation pane, the project file appears as a node at the top of a project tree.

While you can include any type of file in a JDeveloper project, Table 21-1 lists the types of files that JDeveloper automatically recognizes and displays in an appropriate viewer.

NOTE
JDeveloper's Navigation pane is organized by workspace. A workspace keeps track of the projects you use and environment settings while developing your Java application. A workspace can contain many projects. It is advised that you keep one workspace per project to avoid confusion.

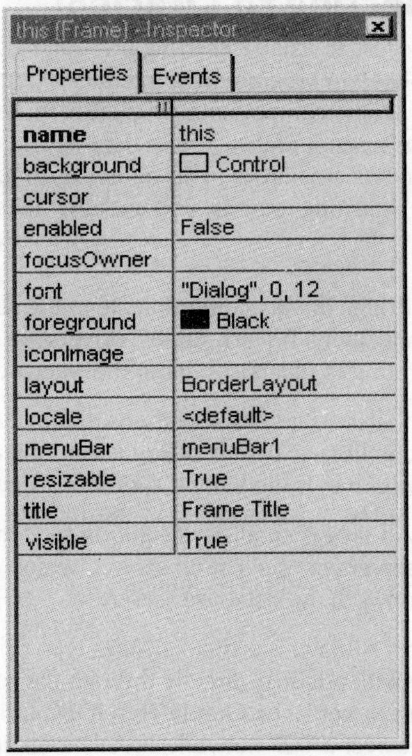

FIGURE 21-5.   *Frame1 properties in the Inspector*

File Types	Description
.jpr	Jdeveloper project file.
.java	Java source file.
.class	Compiled class file. There is one for each class in a .Java source file.
.gif	Graphics file.
.jpg	Graphics file.
.bmp	Graphics file.
.au	Sound file.
.wav	Sound file.
.html	HTML document.

TABLE 21-1.   *JDeveloper Project File Types*

JDBC—Connecting to Oracle8*i*

JDeveloper provides access to databases using JavaSoft's JDBC (*JavaSoft database connectivity*) API (*application programming interface*). Oracle has done us a great favor by creating data-access components, or JavaBeans, that encapsulate the calls to the JDBC API, and as a result of using these data-access components, most of the complexities of data access are hidden. This allows us to focus on tasks such as creating database files, inserting records, and updating data. Four types of JDBC drivers are defined:

- JDBC-ODBC Bridge drivers communicate to the server via ODBC (Open Database Connectivity) drivers. ODBC drivers are an SQL-based standard for communicating to databases under the Microsoft Windows platform.

- The JDBC to Native API defines methods that include calls to a proprietary, platform-specific library, which in turn communicates to the server. An example of this driver is the JDBC-OCI8 driver that ships with JDeveloper.

- Net-Protocol All-Java is an all-Java solution for communicating across a network to a server (an application server), which in turn is responsible for communication with the database server.

- Native-Protocol All-Java is a small all-Java type driver, designed to communicate with a DBMS directly through the server's native protocol. An example of this driver is the Oracle Thin JDBC Driver. This driver communicates over a TCP network directly with an Oracle8*i* database.

When choosing a JDBC driver, you should keep three considerations in mind.

- If you are developing an applet, use the JDBC thin driver. OCI-based driver classes cannot be downloaded to a Web browser, because they are written in C.

- If you want maximum performance, choose the OCI drivers. Bear in mind that the client-side files must match the version of OCI driver you are using with the Oracle8*i* database server.

- If you want platform independence, choose the All-Java driver.

Next you will learn about the two-stage method of data access employed by the JDBC—providing and resolving.

The Provide-Resolve Model of Data Access

Given the limitations of Internet bandwidth, performance of Java applications is a major concern. JDBC helps increase performance by using a provide-resolve model of data access. This model reduces database overhead. It consists of two distinct steps.

- **Providing:** Data is requested from and provided by a database. It is the responsibility of the application requesting the information to provide for the storage of the data. While stored in the application, this data can then be viewed, edited, navigated, sorted, and so forth.

- **Resolving:** Changes made to the table by the user or Java code are resolved back to the database that provided the data.

Building Your First Application

As with Form Builder, Oracle has included many wizards and code snippets that you can use to speed your development of applications and applets. The wizards are small programs that perform some specialized task and add the result to the project in your active AppBrowser. As in Form Builder, the resulting Java code (or HTML, as in the case of the HTML Wizard) that is generated from these wizards is very comprehensive and easy to modify. Most wizards display a dialog or dialogs, providing you with the chance to define options that customize the task they perform.

Enough talk, let's start building an application. JDeveloper has two versions, JDK 1.1.7 and JDK 1.2, with the difference being the version of the JDK (Java Development Kit). You will choose the JDK 1.2 version by clicking the JDeveloper (JDK 1.2) icon in the JDeveloper 2.0 program menu. JDeveloper's integrated development environment will appear. You must first have a project to keep your files consolidated, so it only makes sense to start with a Project Wizard.

1. Clear a new workspace by selecting New Workspace on the main menu.

2. The workspace name will default to Untitled1.jws. While the workspace is highlighted in the navigation pane, rename it by selecting Rename in the File menu. Figure 21-6 shows you where the workspace will be saved. Rename your workspace **o8ibegin** and click Save.

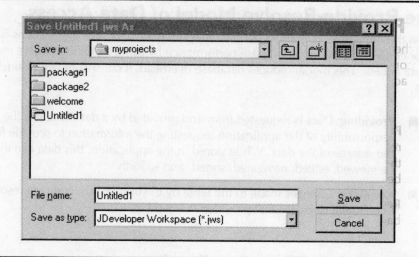

FIGURE 21-6. *Saving your workspace*

3. You will now create your project by selecting New project on the main menu, bringing up the Project Wizard as shown in Figure 21-7. Click Next to continue.

4. There are multiple types of projects for you to choose, as shown in Figure 21-8. You will want to build an application that accesses an Oracle8i database—so ensure Create a Project for a New Application is selected and click Next to go on.

5. You are asked to give your project a name, along with identifying the package it will be associated with and the directory in which you will be storing your project files, as shown in Figure 21-9. Enter **Person** as your Project Name and use the default package name and project path given to you by JDeveloper. Click Next to continue.

6. A Project Information dialog box is displayed to allow you to describe your project. You will be using the defaults, so click Next to continue.

7. JDeveloper now has enough information to build your project. Click Finish, and JDeveloper will now start the Application Wizard as shown in Figure 21-10.

8. Enter **Person_app** as the Class Name and, because you want to connect to an Oracle8i database, ensure that InfoBus-based Data Form is selected. Click OK to continue.

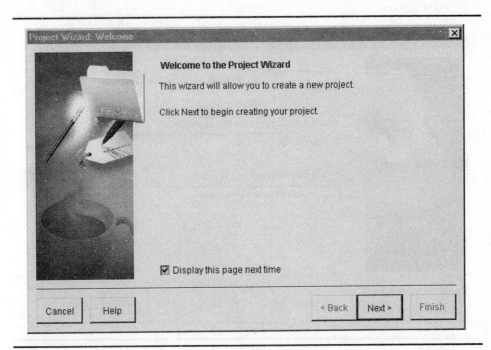

FIGURE 21-7.   *The first dialog box in the Project Wizard*

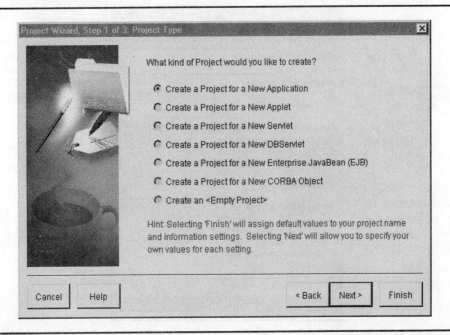

FIGURE 21-8.   *Project types*

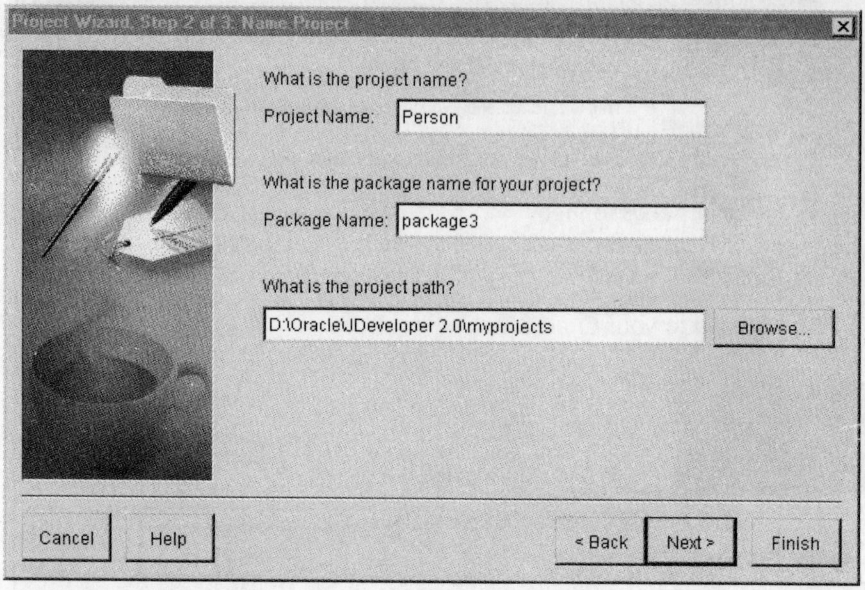

FIGURE 21-9. *Choosing a project name*

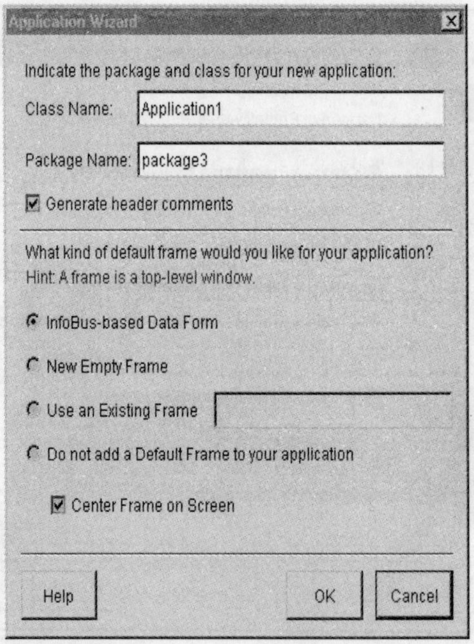

FIGURE 21-10. *The first dialog box in the Application Wizard*

9. The InfoBus Data Form welcome screen is displayed, Click Next to continue.

10. You have two kinds of forms to choose from as displayed in Figure 21-11. Ensure Single Table (a total of 6 steps) is selected and click Next.

11. A form is made up of a frame class that must be identified. Enter **Person_frame** as the class name and **Persons** as the title.

12. JDeveloper needs to identify the database the application will be connected to. Click New to create a connection to an Oracle8*i* database.

13. The Connection dialog box shown in Figure 21-12 is where you define the connection to your Oracle8*i* database.

VIP
*Before creating a new connection for JDeveloper to an Oracle8i database, you must set up a Net8 connection and have a user and password defined on your database. We set up a connect string of **o8ibegin** to our Oracle8i database along with a username of **sean** and a password of **speedo**; these values may differ from yours.*

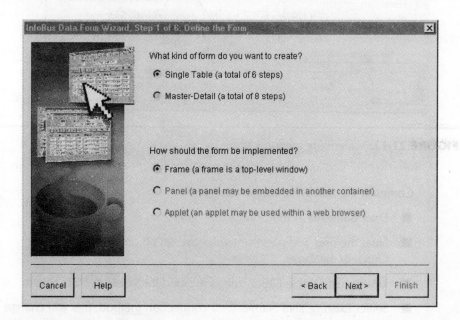

FIGURE 21-11. *Defining the form*

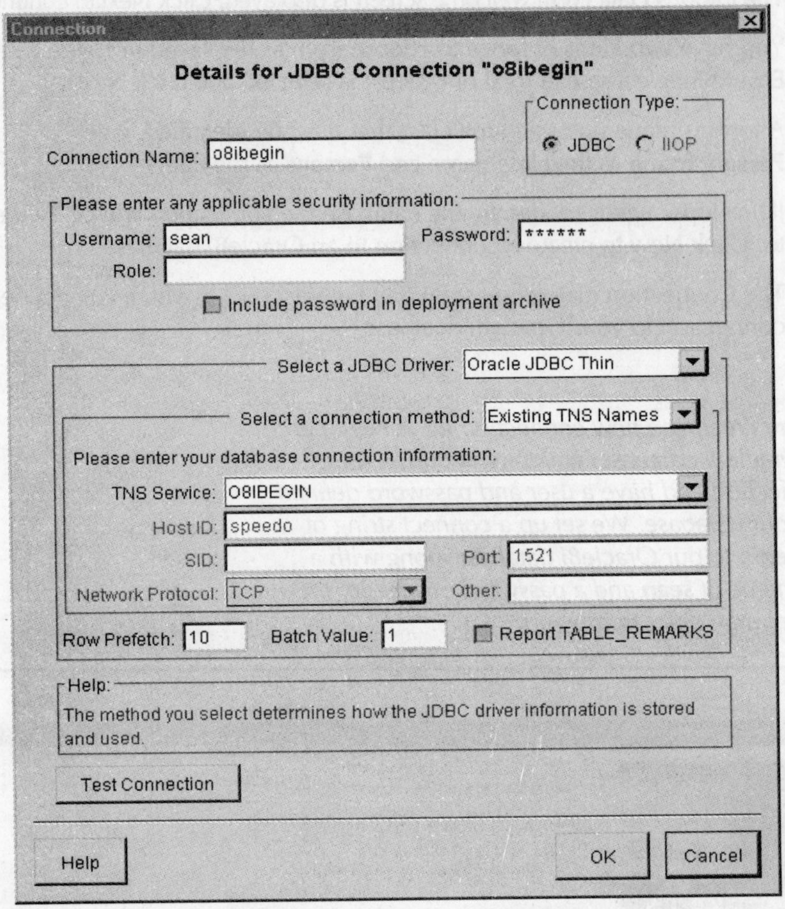

FIGURE 21-12. *Defining a connection*

Complete the following on this dialog box:

- Enter **o8ibegin** as the Connection name.

- Enter the user and password you have set up on your Oracle8*i* database.

- Ensure that Oracle JDBC Thin is selected for Select a JDBC Driver.

- Select Existing TNS Names for a connection method; this will change the screen to reflect the method of connection JDeveloper will use to connect to the Oracle8*i* database.

- Chose the O8IBEGIN TNS Service from the list.

- Test to see if the connection works by clicking Test. (Hurray, the connection is successful!)

14. Click OK to save the connection and continue creating your form. Click Next to go to Step 3 of the InfoBus Data Form Wizard.

15. Figure 21-13 shows Step 3 of the InfoBus Data Form Wizard. Listed are the entities under sean's schema. Select the person table and click Next to continue.

16. Step 4 of the InfoBus Data Form Wizard shows the columns you can choose to be included in the form, as in Figure 21-14. Select them all by clicking >>. This will place the list under Available Columns over to the Selected Columns list. Click Next to continue.

17. Step 5 of the InfoBus Data Form Wizard asks how you would like to lay out your columns you selected from step 16 onto your form. Select the default and continue on by clicking Next.

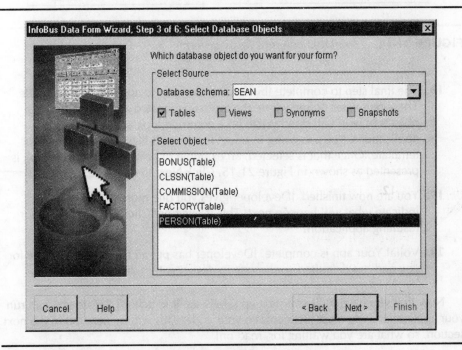

FIGURE 21-13. *Selecting the PERSON table*

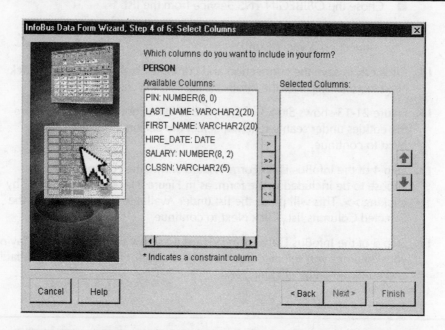

FIGURE 21-14. *Available columns for your form*

18. The final step to complete this form allows you to apply a form template. These templates define where the toolbar is located and may add other objects to help you standardize on a common look and feel for your applications. You are going to select Frame with Navigation Bar as your template. Once that is selected, an example of how your form will look is presented as shown in Figure 21-15. Click Next to continue.

19. You are now finished. JDeveloper gives you one more dialog to indicate what will happen next. This is exciting! Click Finish to see your resulting application!

20. Voilà! Your app is complete. JDeveloper has put all the pieces in place for you and has defaulted your mode in design within the Content pane.

Now that you have built your first app, let's see it in action! Before you can run your application, you must first compile your code. This will be detailed in the next section, so what are you waiting for, read on!

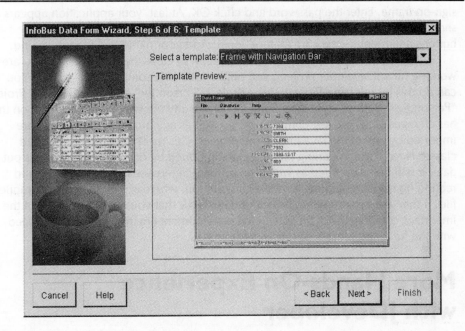

FIGURE 21-15. *Selecting a form template*

Compiling and Running the Project

In order to run the application you have just created in JDeveloper, you must compile it. The result of the compilation is the generation of class files, one for each class declaration that appears within the Java source files in your project. By default, these class files are written to the corresponding myclasses subdirectory under the JDeveloper 2.0 directory.

Compile and run your application by first selecting Run|Run "person_app" from JDeveloper's main menu.

NOTE
Alternatively, you can either press SHIFT-F9 or click the Run button on the JDeveloper toolbar.

After you tell JDeveloper to run the project, it will first compile all of the Java files in your application, creating the necessary class file(s) from each. It will then run the file named Person_app.class, which starts the application, resulting in the sign-on frame. Enter the password and click OK. At last, your application appears as shown in Figure 21-16. This is sooooo cooool! Take a break and play with the buttons and menus—they are all functional! Add your name and then do a Find.

Select File|Exit from the running application to close the frame. While you are working on a JDeveloper project, you might need to recompile your project. You can do this by selecting Project|Make Project "Person.jpr" or Project|Rebuild Project "Person.jpr." Both of these selections recompile any file within your application that has changed since the last compilation, as well as any outdated classes that are imported by one of the Java files in the project. This recompilation of imported classes is recursive, meaning that if a class imported by one that you import is out of date, it will be recompiled as well. The primary difference between making and rebuilding is that rebuilding forces recompilation, whereas making only recompiles files if they are determined to be out of date. Now that you have seen some of the important components of the integrated development environment, let's proceed with the fun of building a couple more applications!

More Hands-On Experience with JDeveloper

In your first application you built a single table application. As you did with Form Builder in Chapter 9, let's build an application with a master-detail relationship, and then to add something different let's create a servlet. For these applications, you will be using tables from your sample database you loaded in Chapter 9. We entered a

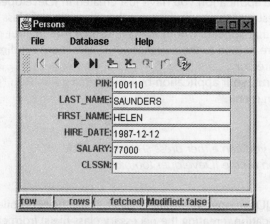

FIGURE 21-16. *Person_app*

username of **sean**, a password of **speedo**, and a connect string of **o8ibegin**, which may differ from yours.

Exercise #1

In this exercise, you will be using the same InfoBus Wizard you used in your first application, only this time to build a master-detail relationship. If you remember from Chapter 9, we defined a master-detail relationship as an association between two base tables; the parent is called a master table, and there is a detail table whose records are associated with the parent's. The master-detail relationship in JDeveloper ensures that the detail table displays only those records that are associated with the current record in the master table and coordinates querying between the two. Now we will create this type of relationship with JDeveloper:

1. Click the JDeveloper (JDK 1.2) icon in the JDeveloper 2.0 group of the Windows Program Manager. When the JDeveloper integrated development environment is done loading, follow steps 1 through 9 that you took to create the first application you built in this chapter for a singular table. Once you are into the first step of the InfoBus Data Form Wizard, select Master-Detail as the form type as displayed in Figure 21-17.

NOTE
To keep the first application you built in this chapter, use different names for workspace and project for this exercise.

2. You will again need to identify a connection the application will have to your Oracle8*i* database. In Step 2 of InfoBus Data Form Wizard you can select the connection you created when you built your first application, o8ibegin. Select o8ibegin and click Next to continue.

3. You are now ready to select the tables you will use as the master and the detail. Using the SEAN Database Schema, select the table CLSSN in the list box at the bottom left (this is your master table) and select the PERSON table in the list box at the bottom right (the detail table) as shown in Figure 21-18. Once these tables are selected, click Next to go on.

4. Step 4 of the InfoBus Data Form Wizard shows where you will define the join condition, or association, between your master and detail tables. Click Add to bring up the Association editor. As shown in Figure 21-19, a default association of CLSSN_TOPERSON_ASSOC is given for the association name. Select CLSSN.CLSSN as the master table join located in the Master:Table:CLSSN column list box. Select PERSON.CLSSN as the detail join located in the Detail:Table:PERSON column list box. Click Add and the association is added. Click OK to return to the join condition screen and then click Next to continue on to your next step.

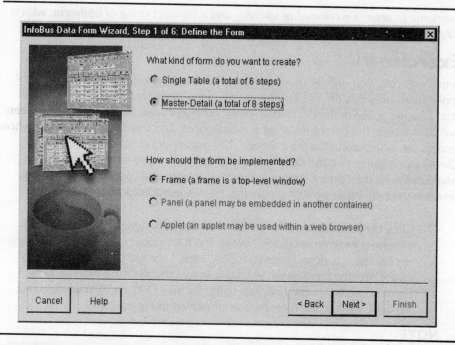

FIGURE 21-17. *Selecting the Master-Detail form type*

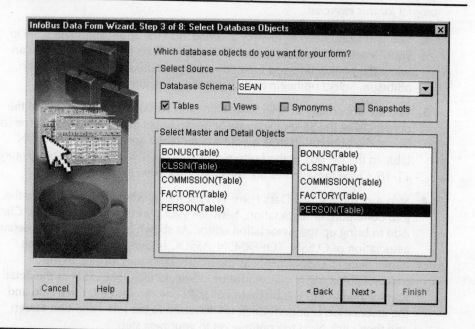

FIGURE 21-18. *Selecting master and detail tables*

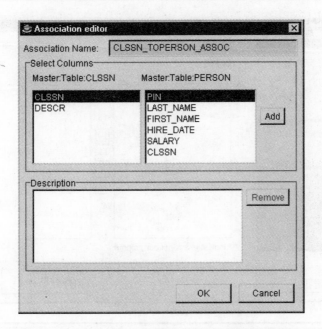

FIGURE 21-19. *Joining the master and the detail tables*

5. Step 5 in the InfoBus Data Form Wizard allows you to identify which columns from the master table you want displayed on your form. Select CLSSN.DESCR by highlighting the CLSSN.DESCR column in the Available Columns list box and click the > button to place the column in the Selected Columns list box as displayed in Figure 21-20. Once it is selected, click Next to continue.

6. Step 6 in the InfoBus Data Form Wizard allows you to identify the columns from your detail table that you will want displayed. As displayed in Figure 21-21, select all columns from the Available Columns list box to copy over to the Selected Columns list box as you did in your previous step with the master column. Click Next to continue.

7. There are various ways your form can be laid out as seen in Figure 21-22. Take the default given to you by clicking Next to continue.

8. Again take the default for your template and click Finish.

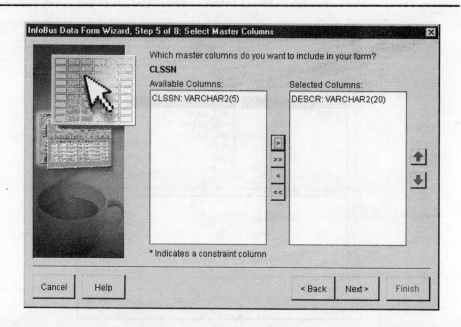

FIGURE 21-20. *CLSSN.DESCR selected for display*

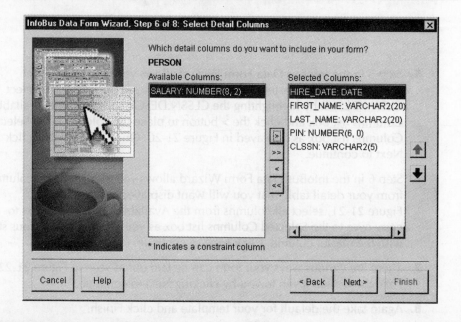

FIGURE 21-21. *Selecting detail columns for display*

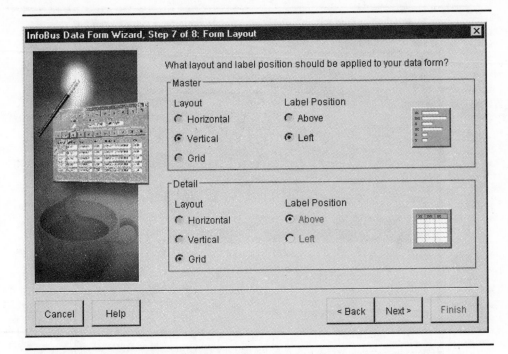

FIGURE 21-22. *Form layout*

9. Run your application as you did with your first in this chapter. Wow, you did this?! Amazing. Let's see how this works. Select Next under the Database menu. This will get the next record in the master table and bring up the records for the detail table that relates to it. Figure 21-23 shows that we have two people identified as Leaders in our database.

Okay, this completes your second application, but let's not stop here. You have one more to go.

Exercise #2

In this exercise you will build a servlet. What is cool about building a servlet with JDeveloper is that you do not need a Web server to test it. JDeveloper has the capability to mimic a Web server for exactly this purpose. The application you will be building will be the same singular table form as with the first application you

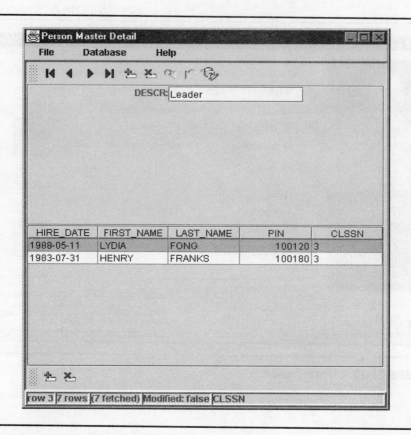

FIGURE 21-23. *Leaders shown in master-detail form*

built in this chapter, only it's implementation will be as a Dbservlet. As you have done before, create a new workspace.

1. Create a new Project as you have done before, only select Create a Project for a New DBServlet as shown in Figure 21-24. Follow to the completion of the Project Wizard as done in your previous applications. Once the project is completed, the DBServlet Wizard will be displayed as shown in Figure 21-25. Click Next to continue.

2. Step 1 of the DBServlet Wizard allows you to choose your form type. As with the first application that you built in this chapter, select a singular table form. Click Next to continue.

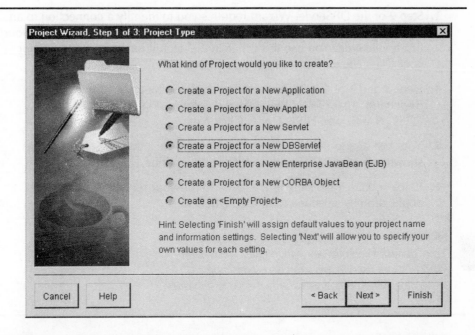

FIGURE 21-24.   *DBServlet*

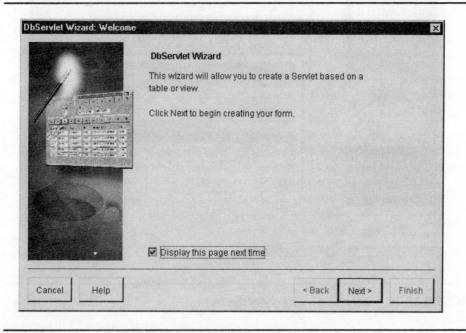

FIGURE 21-25.   *Welcome to the DBServlet Wizard*

3. Step 2 of the DBServlet Wizard requires you to identify a connection to an Oracle8*i* database. Again use the o8ibegin connection you created for your first application. You can then change the default names given to you for your Class Name, Package Name, and Title. Click Next to continue.

4. Steps 3 and 4 of the DBServlet Wizard ask for the table you will be displaying. Again select PERSON and columns PIN, LAST_NAME, FIRST_NAME, and HIRE_DATE. Click Next.

5. Your last step to define your servlet is to choose a theme. Select Gold as shown in Figure 21-26 and click Next to continue.

6. Once you click Finish, you are ready to run your servlet. Run your application by selecting Run|Run "DBServlet1."

NOTE
Your default Web browser will initiate. The default Web browser used in this exercise is Netscape Navigator, which is not necessarily the same as yours.

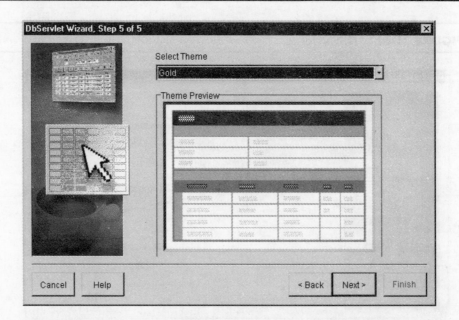

FIGURE 21-26.   *Selecting a DBServlet theme*

7. Figure 21-27 shows the HTML page that will launch the application. Follow the instructions given on this page to run the servlet.

8. Figure 21-28 displays a Web page that will allow you to execute queries against the Oracle8*i* database. Let's find all persons whose first name starts with *F*. Select First Name as the Column Name, Starts With as the Condition, and capital F as the Value. Click Execute Query to continue.

9. Voilà, the results of your query are displayed as in Figure 21-29. Play with this and you will find full functionality. Servlets are a little more difficult to code visually because they are written in HTML and JDeveloper does not have a design interface for HTML.

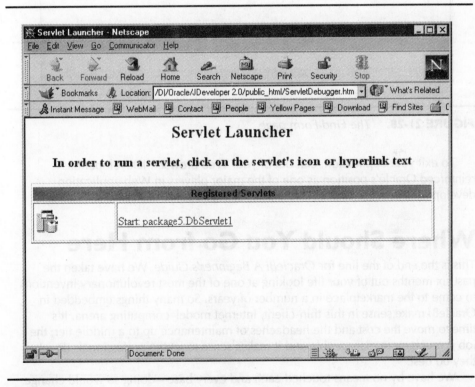

FIGURE 21-27. *The Servlet Launcher*

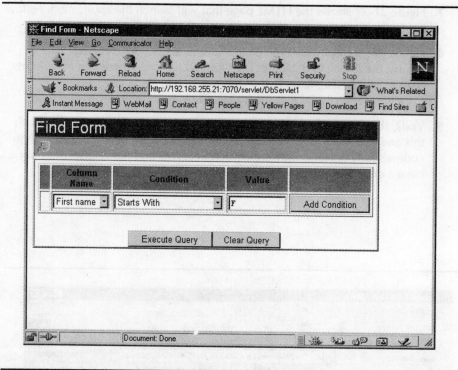

FIGURE 21-28. *The Find Form page*

To exit your application, exit out of your Web browser. JDeveloper has reinforced Oracle's position as one of the major players in Web application development using Java. We have only shown you some basics.

Where Should You Go from Here

This is the end of the line for *Oracle8i A Beginner's Guide.* We have taken the past six months out of your life looking at one of the most revolutionary inventions to come to the marketplace in a number of years. So many things embedded in Oracle8*i* make sense in this thin-client, Internet model–computing arena. It's time to move the cost and the headaches of maintenance up to a middle tier; the job is much more manageable and it makes sense to let the professionals do what they do best.

We have by no means touched each and every base—doing so would change the name of this book to *Oracle8i: The Encyclopedia* in 43 Volumes. What we have done is scratch enough off the surface to give you a good grounding in the marvel

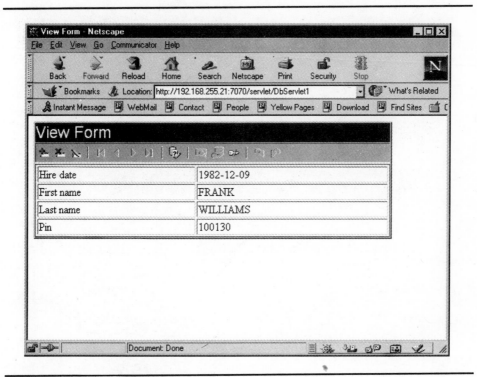

FIGURE 21-29. *Results of your query*

we refer to as Oracle8*i*. You are familiar with Oracle the company as well as Oracle the software. Regard this book as a starting point on the Oracle highway—where do you want to go next? This is entirely up to you. *Oracle8i A Beginner's Guide* is a primer. It is designed to whet your appetite and allow you to dive head first into this technology solution. A word of warning—the Oracle technology is very addictive. It starts as an interest but spreads like a disease into the technological abyss also called your mind and your skill set. If you are not already a dedicated, enthusiastic, well informed, and addicted Oracle professional, think of *Oracle8i A Beginner's Guide* as the start of the next chapter in your career path and/or interest area. If you are a seasoned professional or master of parts of Oracle's solution, think of *Oracle8i A Beginner's Guide* as a refresher course. When Neil Armstrong walked on the moon, he said "Here's to you Mr. Gorsky." When Jimmy Durante signed off, he said "Good night Mrs. Kalabash, wherever you are." When Lloyd Robertson closes the 11 o'clock news, he says "That's the kind of day it's been." When we close this book, we say "We'll be baaaaack...."

Index